CU01459341

Asset Pricing

Asset Pricing

John H. Cochrane

Princeton University Press
Princeton and Oxford

Library of Congress Cataloging-in-Publication Data

Cochrane, John H. (John Howland)
  Asset Pricing / John H. Cochrane.
    p. cm.
  Includes bibliographical references and index.
  ISBN 0-691-07498-4
    1. Capital assets pricing model. 2. Securities. I. Title.

  HG4636 .C56 2001
  332.6—dc21
                                   00-053748

Acknowledgments

This book owes an enormous intellectual debt to Lars Hansen and Gene Fama. Most of the ideas in the book developed from long discussions with each of them, and from trying to make sense of what each was saying in the language of the other. I am also grateful to all my colleagues in Finance and Economics at the University of Chicago, and to George Constantinides especially, for many discussions about the ideas in this book. I thank all of the many people who have taken the time to give me comments, and especially George Constantinides, Andrea Eisfeldt, Gene Fama, Wayne Ferson, Michael Johannes, Owen Lamont, Anthony Lynch, Dan Nelson, Monika Piazzesi, Alberto Pozzolo, Michael Roberts, Juha Seppala, Mike Stutzer, Pierto Veronesi, an anonymous reviewer, and several generations of Ph.D. students at the University of Chicago. Peter Dougherty was instrumental in shepherding this book to publication. I thank the National Science Foundation and the Graduate School of Business for research support.

You will find typos, corrections, and additional materials, as they develop, on my website http://gsbwww.uchicago.edu/fac/john.cochrane/ research/Papers

To Sally, Eric, Gene and Lydia

Contents

Preface

Asset pricing theory tries to understand the prices or values of claims to uncertain payments. A low price implies a high rate of return, so one can also think of the theory as explaining why some assets pay higher average returns than others.

To value an asset, we have to account for the *delay* and for the *risk* of its payments. The effects of time are not too difficult to work out. However, corrections for risk are much more important determinants of many assets' values. For example, over the last 50 years U.S. stocks have given a real return of about 9% on average. Of this, only about 1% is due to interest rates; the remaining 8% is a premium earned for holding risk. *Uncertainty*, or *corrections for risk* make asset pricing interesting and challenging.

Asset pricing theory shares the positive versus normative tension present in the rest of economics. Does it describe the way the world *does* work, or the way the world *should* work? We observe the prices or returns of many assets. We can use the theory positively, to try to understand why prices or returns are what they are. If the world does not obey a model's predictions, we can decide that the model needs improvement. However, we can also decide that the *world* is wrong, that some assets are "mispriced" and present trading opportunities for the shrewd investor. This latter use of asset pricing theory accounts for much of its popularity and practical application. Also, and perhaps most importantly, the prices of many assets or claims to uncertain cash flows are not observed, such as potential public or private investment projects, new financial securities, buyout prospects, and complex derivatives. We can apply the theory to establish what the prices of these claims *should* be as well; the answers are important guides to public and private decisions.

Asset pricing theory all stems from one simple concept, presented in the first page of the first chapter of this book: price equals expected discounted payoff. The rest is elaboration, special cases, and a closet full of tricks that make the central equation useful for one or another application.

There are two polar approaches to this elaboration. I call them *absolute pricing* and *relative pricing*. In *absolute pricing*, we price each asset by reference to its exposure to fundamental sources of macroeconomic risk. The consumption-based and general equilibrium models are the purest examples of this approach. The absolute approach is most common in academic settings, in which we use asset pricing theory positively to give an economic explanation for why prices are what they are, or in order to predict how prices might change if policy or economic structure changed.

In *relative pricing*, we ask a less ambitious question. We ask what we can learn about an asset's value *given* the prices of some other assets. We do not ask where the prices of the other assets came from, and we use as little information about fundamental risk factors as possible. Black–Scholes option pricing is the classic example of this approach. While limited in scope, this approach offers precision in many applications.

Asset pricing problems are solved by judiciously choosing how much absolute and how much relative pricing one will do, depending on the assets in question and the purpose of the calculation. Almost no problems are solved by the pure extremes. For example, the CAPM and its successor factor models are paradigms of the absolute approach. Yet in applications, they price assets "relative" to the market or other risk factors, without answering what determines the market or factor risk premia and betas. The latter are treated as free parameters. On the other end of the spectrum, even the most practical financial engineering questions usually involve assumptions beyond pure lack of arbitrage, assumptions about equilibrium "market prices of risk."

The central and unfinished task of absolute asset pricing is to understand and measure the sources of aggregate or macroeconomic risk that drive asset prices. Of course, this is also the central question of macroeconomics, and this is a particularly exciting time for researchers who want to answer these fundamental questions in macroeconomics and finance. A lot of empirical work has documented tantalizing stylized facts and links between macroeconomics and finance. For example, expected returns vary across time and across assets in ways that are linked to macroeconomic variables, or variables that also forecast macroeconomic events; a wide class of models suggests that a "recession" or "financial distress" factor lies behind many asset prices. Yet theory lags behind; we do not yet have a well-described model that explains these interesting correlations.

In turn, I think that what we are learning about finance must feed back on macroeconomics. To take a simple example, we have learned that the risk premium on stocks—the expected stock return less interest rates—is much larger than the interest rate, and varies a good deal

means that attempts to line investment up
opeless—most variation in the cost of capi-
k premium. Similarly, we have learned that
n must be quite high, or people would all
s. Most macroeconomics pursues small devi-
at equilibria, but the large equity premium
t-order effect, not a second-order effect. Stan-
ls predict that people really do not care much
as [1987]). Asset prices reveal that they do—
l return premia to avoid assets that fall in reces-
ell us something about recessions!
s a discount factor/generalized method of
cing theory and associated empirical procedures.
g by two equations:

$$p_t = E(m_{t+1}x_{t+1}),$$

$$n_{t+1} = f(\text{data, parameters}),$$

e, x_{t+1} = asset payoff, m_{t+1} = stochastic discount

ntages of the discount factor/moment condition
licity and universality. Where once there were three
apparently dinc. theories for stocks, bonds, and options, now we see
each as special cases of the same theory. The common language also allows
us to use insights from each field of application in other fields.

This approach allows us to conveniently separate the step of specifying economic assumptions of the model (second equation) from the step
of deciding which kind of empirical representation to pursue or understand. For a given model—choice of $f(\cdot)$—we will see how the first equation can lead to predictions stated in terms of returns, price-dividend
ratios, expected return-beta representations, moment conditions, continuous versus discrete-time implications, and so forth. The ability to translate
between such representations is also very helpful in digesting the results
of empirical work, which uses a number of apparently distinct but fundamentally connected representations.

Thinking in terms of discount factors often turns out to be much
simpler than thinking in terms of portfolios. For example, it is easier
to insist that there is a positive discount factor than to check that every
possible portfolio that dominates every other portfolio has a larger price,
and the long arguments over the APT stated in terms of portfolios are
easy to digest when stated in terms of discount factors.

The discount factor approach is also associated with a state-space
geometry in place of the usual mean-variance geometry, and this book
emphasizes the state-space intuition behind many classic results.

For these reasons, the discount factor language and the associated state-space geometry are common in academic research and high-tech practice. They are not yet common in textbooks, and that is the niche that this book tries to fill.

I also diverge from the usual order of presentation. Most books are structured following the history of thought: portfolio theory, mean-variance frontiers, spanning theorems, CAPM, ICAPM, APT, option pricing, and finally consumption-based model. Contingent claims are an esoteric extension of option pricing theory. I go the other way around: contingent claims and the consumption-based model are the basic and simplest models around; the others are specializations. Just because they were discovered in the opposite order is no reason to present them that way.

I also try to unify the treatment of empirical methods. A wide variety of methods are popular, including time-series and cross-sectional regressions, and methods based on generalized method of moments (GMM) and maximum likelihood. However, in the end all of these apparently different approaches do the same thing: they pick free parameters of the model to make it fit best, which usually means to minimize pricing errors; and they evaluate the model by examining how big those pricing errors are.

As with the theory, I do not attempt an encyclopedic compilation of empirical procedures. The literature on econometric methods contains lots of methods and special cases (likelihood ratio analogues of common Wald tests; cases with and without risk-free assets and when factors do and do not span the mean-variance frontier, etc.) that are seldom used in practice. I try to focus on the basic ideas and on methods that are actually used in practice.

The accent in this book is on understanding statements of theory, and working with that theory to applications, rather than rigorous or general proofs. Also, I skip very lightly over many parts of asset pricing theory that have faded from current applications, although they occupied large amounts of the attention in the past. Some examples are portfolio separation theorems, properties of various distributions, or asymptotic APT. While portfolio theory is still interesting and useful, it is no longer a cornerstone of pricing. Rather than use portfolio theory to find a demand curve for assets, which intersected with a supply curve gives prices, we now go to prices directly. One can then find optimal portfolios, but it is a side issue for the asset pricing question.

My presentation is consciously informal. I like to see an idea in its simplest form and learn to use it before going back and understanding all the foundations of the ideas. I have organized the book for similarly minded readers. If you are hungry for more formal definitions and background, keep going, they usually show up later on.

Again, my organizing principle is that everything can be traced back to specializations of the basic pricing equation $p = E(mx)$. Therefore, after reading the first chapter, one can pretty much skip around and read topics in as much depth or order as one likes. Each major subject always starts back at the same pricing equation.

The target audience for this book is economics and finance Ph.D. students, advanced MBA students, or professionals with similar background. I hope the book will also be useful to fellow researchers and finance professionals, by clarifying, relating, and simplifying the set of tools we have all learned in a hodgepodge manner. I presume some exposure to undergraduate economics and statistics. A reader should have seen a utility function, a random variable, a standard error, and a time series, should have some basic linear algebra and calculus, and should have solved a maximum problem by setting derivatives to zero. The hurdles in asset pricing are really conceptual rather than mathematical.

Asset Pricing

PART I
Asset Pricing Theory

1
Consumption-Based Model and Overview

An investor must decide how much to save and how much to consume, and what portfolio of assets to hold. The most basic pricing equation comes from the first-order condition for that decision. The marginal utility loss of consuming a little less today and buying a little more of the asset should equal the marginal utility gain of consuming a little more of the asset's payoff in the future. If the price and payoff do not satisfy this relation, the investor should buy more or less of the asset. It follows that the asset's price should equal the expected discounted value of the asset's payoff, using the investor's marginal utility to discount the payoff. With this simple idea, I present many classic issues in finance.

Interest rates are related to expected marginal utility growth, and hence to the expected path of consumption. In a time of high real interest rates, it makes sense to save, buy bonds, and then consume more tomorrow. Therefore, high real interest rates should be associated with an expectation of growing consumption.

Most importantly, risk corrections to asset prices should be driven by the covariance of asset payoffs with marginal utility and hence by the covariance of asset payoffs with consumption. Other things equal, an asset that does badly in states of nature like a recession, in which the investor feels poor and is consuming little, is less desirable than an asset that does badly in states of nature like a boom in which the investor feels wealthy and is consuming a great deal. The former asset will sell for a lower price; its price will reflect a discount for its "riskiness," and this riskiness depends on a *co*-variance, not a variance.

Marginal utility, not consumption, is the fundamental measure of how you feel. Most of the theory of asset pricing is about how to go from marginal utility to observable indicators. Consumption is low when marginal utility is high, of course, so consumption may be a useful indicator. Consumption is also low and marginal utility is high when the investor's other assets have done poorly; thus we may expect that prices are low for assets that covary positively with a large index such as the market portfolio. This is a Capital Asset Pricing Model. We will see a wide variety of additional indicators for marginal utility, things against which to compute a convariance in order to predict the risk-adjustment for prices.

1.1 Basic Pricing Equation

An investor's first-order conditions give the basic consumption-based model,

$$p_t = E_t\left[\beta \frac{u'(c_{t+1})}{u'(c_t)} x_{t+1}\right].$$

Our basic objective is to figure out the value of any stream of uncertain cash flows. I start with an apparently simple case, which turns out to capture very general situations.

Let us find the value at time t of a *payoff* x_{t+1}. If you buy a stock today, the payoff next period is the stock price plus dividend, $x_{t+1} = p_{t+1} + d_{t+1}$. x_{t+1} is a random variable: an investor does not know exactly how much he will get from his investment, but he can assess the probability of various possible outcomes. Do not confuse the *payoff* x_{t+1} with the *profit* or *return*; x_{t+1} is the value of the investment at time $t+1$, without subtracting or dividing by the cost of the investment.

We find the value of this payoff by asking what it is worth to a typical investor. To do this, we need a convenient mathematical formalism to capture what an investor wants. We model investors by a *utility function* defined over current and future values of consumption,

$$U(c_t, c_{t+1}) = u(c_t) + \beta E_t\left[u(c_{t+1})\right],$$

where c_t denotes consumption at date t. We often use a convenient power utility form,

$$u(c_t) = \frac{1}{1-\gamma} c_t^{1-\gamma}.$$

The limit as $\gamma \to 1$ is

$$u(c) = \ln(c).$$

The utility function captures the fundamental desire for more *consumption,* rather than posit a desire for intermediate objectives such as mean and variance of portfolio returns. Consumption c_{t+1} is also random; the investor does not know his wealth tomorrow, and hence how much he will decide to consume tomorrow. The period utility function $u(\cdot)$ is increasing, reflecting a desire for more consumption, and concave, reflecting the declining marginal value of additional consumption. The last bite is never as satisfying as the first.

This formalism captures investors' impatience and their aversion to risk, so we can quantitatively correct for the risk and delay of cash flows. Discounting the future by β captures impatience, and β is called the *subjective discount factor.* The curvature of the utility function generates aversion to risk and to intertemporal substitution: The investor prefers a consumption stream that is steady over time and across states of nature.

Now, assume that the investor can freely buy or sell as much of the payoff x_{t+1} as he wishes, at a price p_t. How much will he buy or sell? To find the answer, denote by e the original consumption level (if the investor bought none of the asset), and denote by ξ the amount of the asset he chooses to buy. Then, his problem is

$$\max_{\{\xi\}} u(c_t) + E_t\left[\beta u(c_{t+1})\right] \quad s.t.$$

$$c_t = e_t - p_t\xi,$$

$$c_{t+1} = e_{t+1} + x_{t+1}\xi.$$

Substituting the constraints into the objective, and setting the derivative with respect to ξ equal to zero, we obtain the first-order condition for an optimal consumption and portfolio choice,

$$p_t u'(c_t) = E_t\left[\beta u'(c_{t+1})x_{t+1}\right], \tag{1.1}$$

or

$$p_t = E_t\left[\beta \frac{u'(c_{t+1})}{u'(c_t)} x_{t+1}\right]. \tag{1.2}$$

The investor buys more or less of the asset until this first-order condition holds.

Equation (1.1) expresses the standard marginal condition for an optimum: $p_t u'(c_t)$ is the loss in utility if the investor buys another unit of the asset; $E_t\left[\beta u'(c_{t+1})x_{t+1}\right]$ is the increase in (discounted, expected) utility he obtains from the extra payoff at $t+1$. The investor continues to buy or sell the asset until the marginal loss equals the marginal gain.

Equation (1.2) is *the* central asset pricing formula. Given the payoff x_{t+1} and given the investor's consumption choice c_t, c_{t+1}, it tells you what market price p_t to expect. Its economic content is simply the first-order conditions for optimal consumption and portfolio formation. Most of the theory of asset pricing just consists of specializations and manipulations of this formula.

We have stopped short of a complete solution to the model, i.e., an expression with exogenous items on the right-hand side. We relate one endogenous variable, price, to two other endogenous variables, consumption and payoffs. One can continue to solve this model and derive the optimal consumption choice c_t, c_{t+1} in terms of more fundamental givens of the model. In the model I have sketched so far, those givens are the income sequence e_t, e_{t+1} and a specification of the full set of assets that the investor may buy and sell. We will in fact study such fuller solutions below. However, for many purposes one can stop short of specifying (possibly wrongly) all this extra structure, and obtain very useful predictions about asset prices from (1.2), even though consumption is an endogenous variable.

1.2 Marginal Rate of Substitution/Stochastic Discount Factor

> We break up the basic consumption-based pricing equation into
>
> $$p = E(mx),$$
>
> $$m = \beta \frac{u'(c_{t+1})}{u'(c_t)},$$
>
> where m_{t+1} is the *stochastic discount factor.*

A convenient way to break up the basic pricing equation (1.2) is to define the *stochastic discount factor* m_{t+1}

$$m_{t+1} \equiv \beta \frac{u'(c_{t+1})}{u'(c_t)}. \tag{1.3}$$

Then, the basic pricing formula (1.2) can simply be expressed as

$$p_t = E_t(m_{t+1}x_{t+1}). \tag{1.4}$$

When it is not necessary to be explicit about time subscripts or the difference between conditional and unconditional expectation, I will suppress the subscripts and just write $p = E(mx)$. The price always comes at t, the payoff at $t + 1$, and the expectation is conditional on time-t information.

The term *stochastic discount factor* refers to the way m generalizes standard discount factor ideas. If there is no uncertainty, we can express prices via the standard present value formula

$$p_t = \frac{1}{R^f} x_{t+1}, \tag{1.5}$$

where R^f is the gross risk-free rate. $1/R^f$ is the *discount factor*. Since gross interest rates are typically greater than one, the payoff x_{t+1} sells "at a discount." Riskier assets have lower prices than equivalent risk-free assets, so they are often valued by using risk-adjusted discount factors,

$$p_t^i = \frac{1}{R^i} E_t(x_{t+1}^i).$$

Here, I have added the i superscript to emphasize that each risky asset i must be discounted by an asset-specific risk-adjusted discount factor $1/R^i$.

In this context, equation (1.4) is obviously a generalization, and it says something deep: one can incorporate all risk corrections by defining a *single* stochastic discount factor—the same one for each asset—and putting it inside the expectation. m_{t+1} is *stochastic* or *random* because it is not known with certainty at time t. The correlation between the random components of the common discount factor m and the asset-specific payoff x^i generate asset-specific risk corrections.

m_{t+1} is also often called the *marginal rate of substitution* after (1.3). In that equation, m_{t+1} is the rate at which the investor is willing to substitute consumption at time $t + 1$ for consumption at time t. m_{t+1} is sometimes also called the *pricing kernel*. If you know what a kernel is and you express the expectation as an integral, you can see where the name comes from. It is sometimes called a *change of measure* or a *state-price density*.

For the moment, introducing the discount factor m and breaking the basic pricing equation (1.2) into (1.3) and (1.4) is just a notational convenience. However, it represents a much deeper and more useful separation. For example, notice that $p = E(mx)$ would still be valid if we changed the utility function, but we would have a different function connecting m to data. *All* asset pricing models amount to alternative ways of connecting the stochastic discount factor to data. At the same time, we will study lots of alternative expressions of $p = E(mx)$, and we can summarize many empirical approaches by applying them to $p = E(mx)$. By separating our models into these two components, we do not have to redo all that elaboration for each asset pricing model.

1.3 Prices, Payoffs, and Notation

The *price* p_t gives rights to a *payoff* x_{t+1}. In practice, this notation covers a variety of cases, including the following:

	Price p_t	Payoff x_{t+1}
Stock	p_t	$p_{t+1} + d_{t+1}$
Return	1	R_{t+1}
Price-dividend ratio	$\dfrac{p_t}{d_t}$	$\left(\dfrac{p_{t+1}}{d_{t+1}} + 1\right)\dfrac{d_{t+1}}{d_t}$
Excess return	0	$R_{t+1}^e = R_{t+1}^a - R_{t+1}^b$
Managed portfolio	z_t	$z_t R_{t+1}$
Moment condition	$E(p_t z_t)$	$x_{t+1} z_t$
One-period bond	p_t	1
Risk-free rate	1	R^f
Option	C	$\max(S_T - K, 0)$

The price p_t and payoff x_{t+1} seem like a very restrictive kind of security. In fact, this notation is quite general and allows us easily to accommodate many different asset pricing questions. In particular, we can cover stocks, bonds, and options and make clear that there is one theory for all asset pricing.

For stocks, the one-period payoff is of course the next price plus dividend, $x_{t+1} = p_{t+1} + d_{t+1}$. We frequently divide the payoff x_{t+1} by the price p_t to obtain a *gross return*

$$R_{t+1} \equiv \frac{x_{t+1}}{p_t}.$$

We can think of a return as a payoff with price one. If you pay one dollar today, the return is how many dollars or units of consumption you get tomorrow. Thus, returns obey

$$1 = E(mR),$$

which is by far the most important special case of the basic formula $p = E(mx)$. I use capital letters to denote *gross* returns R, which have a numerical value like 1.05. I use lowercase letters to denote *net* returns $r = R - 1$ or log (continuously compounded) returns $r = \ln(R)$, both of which have numerical values like 0.05. One may also quote *percent* returns $100 \times r$.

Returns are often used in empirical work because they are typically stationary over time. (Stationary in the statistical sense; they do not have trends and you can meaningfully take an average. "Stationary" does not mean constant.) However, thinking in terms of returns takes us away from the central task of finding asset *prices*. Dividing by dividends and creating a payoff of the form

$$x_{t+1} = \left(1 + \frac{p_{t+1}}{d_{t+1}}\right)\frac{d_{t+1}}{d_t}$$

corresponding to a price p_t/d_t is a way to look at prices but still to examine stationary variables.

Not everything can be reduced to a return. If you borrow a dollar at the interest rate R^f and invest it in an asset with return R, you pay no money out-of-pocket today, and get the payoff $R - R^f$. This is a payoff with a *zero* price, so you obviously cannot divide payoff by price to get a return. Zero price does not imply zero payoff. It is a bet in which the value of the chance of losing exactly balances the value of the chance of winning, so that no money changes hands when the bet is made. It is common to study equity strategies in which one short-sells one stock or portfolio and invests the proceeds in another stock or portfolio, generating an excess return. I denote any such difference between returns as an *excess return*, R^e. It is also called a *zero-cost portfolio*.

In fact, much asset pricing focuses on excess returns. Our economic understanding of interest rate variation turns out to have little to do with our understanding of risk premia, so it is convenient to separate the two phenomena by looking at interest rates and excess returns separately.

We also want to think about the *managed portfolios*, in which one invests more or less in an asset according to some signal. The "price" of such a strategy is the amount invested at time t, say z_t, and the payoff is $z_t R_{t+1}$. For example, a market timing strategy might make an investment in stocks proportional to the price-dividend ratio, investing less when prices are higher. We could represent such a strategy as a payoff using $z_t = a - b(p_t/d_t)$.

When we think about conditioning information below, we will think of objects like z_t as *instruments*. Then we take an unconditional expectation of $p_t z_t = E_t(m_{t+1}x_{t+1})z_t$, yielding $E(p_t z_t) = E(m_{t+1}x_{t+1}z_t)$. We can think of this operation as creating a "security" with payoff $x_{t+1}z_{t+1}$, and "price" $E(p_t z_t)$ represented with unconditional expectations.

A one-period bond is of course a claim to a unit payoff. Bonds, options, investment projects are all examples in which it is often more useful to think of prices and payoffs rather than returns.

Prices and returns can be real (denominated in goods) or nominal (denominated in dollars); $p = E(mx)$ can refer to either case. The only difference is whether we use a real or nominal discount factor. If prices, returns, and payoffs are nominal, we should use a nominal discount factor. For example, if p and x denote nominal values, then we can create real prices and payoffs to write

$$\frac{p_t}{\Pi_t} = E_t\left[\left(\beta\frac{u'(c_{t+1})}{u'(c_t)}\right)\frac{x_{t+1}}{\Pi_{t+1}}\right],$$

where Π denotes the price level (cpi). Obviously, this is the same as defining a nominal discount factor by

$$p_t = E_t\left[\left(\beta\frac{u'(c_{t+1})}{u'(c_t)}\frac{\Pi_t}{\Pi_{t+1}}\right)x_{t+1}\right].$$

To accommodate all these cases, I will simply use the notation price p_t and payoff x_{t+1}. These symbols can denote $0, 1$, or z_t and R_t^e, r_{t+1}, or $z_t R_{t+1}$, respectively, according to the case. Lots of other definitions of p and x are useful as well.

1.4 Classic Issues in Finance

> I use simple manipulations of the basic pricing equation to introduce classic issues in finance: the economics of interest rates, risk adjustments, systematic versus idiosyncratic risk, expected return-beta representations, the mean-variance frontier, the slope of the mean-variance frontier, time-varying expected returns, and present-value relations.

A few simple rearrangements and manipulations of the basic pricing equation $p = E(mx)$ give a lot of intuition and introduce some classic issues in finance, including determinants of the interest rate, risk corrections, idiosyncratic versus systematic risk, beta pricing models, and mean-variance frontiers.

Risk-Free Rate

The risk-free rate is related to the discount factor by

$$R^f = 1/E(m).$$

With lognormal consumption growth,

$$r_t^f = \delta + \gamma E_t(\Delta \ln c_{t+1}) - \frac{\gamma^2}{2}\sigma_t^2(\Delta \ln c_{t+1}).$$

Real interest rates are high when people are impatient (δ), when expected consumption growth is high (intertemporal substitution), or when risk is low (precautionary saving). A more curved utility function (γ) or a lower elasticity of intertemporal substitution ($1/\gamma$) means that interest rates are more sensitive to changes in expected consumption growth.

The risk-free rate is given by

$$R^f = 1/E(m). \tag{1.6}$$

The risk-free rate is known ahead of time, so $p = E(mx)$ becomes $1 = E(mR^f) = E(m)R^f$.

If a risk-free security is not traded, we can define $R^f = 1/E(m)$ as the "shadow" risk-free rate. In some models it is called the "zero-beta" rate. If one introduced a risk-free security with return $R^f = 1/E(m)$, investors would be just indifferent to buying or selling it. I use R^f to simplify formulas below with this understanding.

To think about the economics behind real interest rates in a simple setup, use power utility $u'(c) = c^{-\gamma}$. Start by turning off uncertainty, in which case

$$R^f = \frac{1}{\beta}\left(\frac{c_{t+1}}{c_t}\right)^{\gamma}.$$

We can see three effects right away:

1. Real interest rates are high when people are impatient, i.e. when β is low. If everyone wants to consume now, it takes a high interest rate to convince them to save.

2. Real interest rates are high when consumption growth is high. In times of high interest rates, it pays investors to consume less now, invest more, and consume more in the future. Thus, high interest rates lower the level of consumption today, while raising its growth rate from today to tomorrow.

3. Real interest rates are more sensitive to consumption growth if the power parameter γ is large. If utility is highly curved, the investor cares more about maintaining a consumption profile that is smooth over time, and is less willing to rearrange consumption over time in response to interest rate incentives. Thus it takes a larger interest rate change to induce him to a given consumption growth.

To understand how interest rates behave when there is some uncertainty, I specify that consumption growth is lognormally distributed. In this case, the real risk-free rate equation becomes

$$r_t^f = \delta + \gamma E_t(\Delta \ln c_{t+1}) - \frac{\gamma^2}{2}\sigma_t^2(\Delta \ln c_{t+1}), \qquad (1.7)$$

where I have defined the log risk-free rate r_t^f and subjective discount rate δ by

$$r_t^f = \ln R_t^f; \qquad \beta = e^{-\delta},$$

and Δ denotes the first difference operator,

$$\Delta \ln c_{t+1} = \ln c_{t+1} - \ln c_t.$$

To derive expression (1.7) for the risk-free rate, start with

$$R_t^f = 1/E_t\left[\beta\left(\frac{c_{t+1}}{c_t}\right)^{-\gamma}\right].$$

Using the fact that normal z means

$$E\left(e^z\right) = e^{E(z)+(1/2)\sigma^2(z)}$$

(you can check this by writing out the integral that defines the expectation), we have

$$R_t^f = \left[e^{-\delta}e^{-\gamma E_t(\Delta \ln c_{t+1})+(\gamma^2/2)\sigma_t^2(\Delta \ln c_{t+1})}\right]^{-1}.$$

Then take logarithms. The combination of lognormal distributions and power utility is one of the basic tricks to getting analytical solutions in this kind of model. Section 1.5 shows how to get the same result in continuous time.

Looking at (1.7), we see the same results as we had with the deterministic case. Real interest rates are high when impatience δ is high and when consumption growth is high; higher γ makes interest rates more sensitive to consumption growth. The new σ^2 term captures *precautionary savings.* When consumption is more volatile, people with this utility function are more worried about the low consumption states than they are pleased by the high consumption states. Therefore, people want to save more, driving down interest rates.

We can also read the same terms backwards: consumption growth is high when real interest rates are high, since people save more now and spend it in the future, and consumption is less sensitive to interest rates as the desire for a smooth consumption stream, captured by γ, rises. Section 2.2 takes up the question of which way we should read this equation—as consumption determining interest rates, or as interest rates determining consumption.

For the power utility function, the curvature parameter γ simultaneously controls intertemporal substitution—aversion to a consumption stream that varies over time, risk aversion—aversion to a consumption stream that varies across states of nature, and precautionary savings, which turns out to depend on the third derivative of the utility function. This link is particular to the power utility function. More general utility functions loosen the links between these three quantities.

Risk Corrections

> Payoffs that are positively correlated with consumption growth have lower prices, to compensate investors for risk.
>
> $$p = \frac{E(x)}{R^f} + \text{cov}(m, x),$$
>
> $$E(R^i) - R^f = -R^f \, \text{cov}(m, R^i).$$
>
> Expected returns are proportional to the covariance of returns with discount factors.

Using the definition of covariance $\text{cov}(m, x) = E(mx) - E(m)E(x)$, we can write $p = E(mx)$ as

$$p = E(m)E(x) + \text{cov}(m, x). \tag{1.8}$$

Substituting the risk-free rate equation (1.6), we obtain

$$p = \frac{E(x)}{R^f} + \text{cov}(m, x). \tag{1.9}$$

The first term in (1.9) is the standard discounted present-value formula. This is the asset's price in a risk-neutral world—if consumption is constant or if utility is linear. The second term is a *risk adjustment*. An

asset whose payoff covaries positively with the discount factor has its price
raised and vice versa.

To understand the risk adjustment, substitute back for m in terms of
consumption, to obtain

$$p = \frac{E(x)}{R^f} + \frac{\text{cov}\left[\beta u'(c_{t+1}), x_{t+1}\right]}{u'(c_t)}. \tag{1.10}$$

Marginal utility $u'(c)$ declines as c rises. Thus, an asset's price is lowered if
its payoff covaries positively with consumption. Conversely, an asset's price
is raised if it covaries negatively with consumption.

Why? Investors do not like uncertainty about consumption. If you
buy an asset whose payoff covaries positively with consumption, one that
pays off well when you are already feeling wealthy, and pays off badly
when you are already feeling poor, that asset will make your consumption
stream more volatile. You will require a low price to induce you to buy
such an asset. If you buy an asset whose payoff covaries negatively with
consumption, it helps to smooth consumption and so is more valuable
than its expected payoff might indicate. Insurance is an extreme example.
Insurance pays off exactly when wealth and consumption would otherwise
be low—you get a check when your house burns down. For this reason,
you are happy to hold insurance, even though you expect to lose money—
even though the price of insurance is greater than its expected payoff
discounted at the risk-free rate.

To emphasize why the *covariance* of a payoff with the discount factor
rather than its *variance* determines its riskiness, keep in mind that the
investor cares about the volatility of consumption. He does *not* care about
the volatility of his individual assets or of his portfolio, if he can keep
a steady consumption. Consider then what happens to the volatility of
consumption if the investor buys a little more ξ of payoff x. $\sigma^2(c)$ becomes

$$\sigma^2(c + \xi x) = \sigma^2(c) + 2\xi \, \text{cov}(c, x) + \xi^2 \sigma^2(x).$$

For small (marginal) portfolio changes, the *covariance* between consumption and payoff determines the effect of adding a bit more of each payoff
on the volatility of consumption.

We use returns so often that it is worth restating the same intuition
for the special case that the price is 1 and the payoff is a return. Start with
the basic pricing equation for returns,

$$1 = E(mR^i).$$

I denote the return R^i to emphasize that the point of the theory is to
distinguish the behavior of one asset R^i from another R^j.

The asset pricing model says that, although expected *returns* can vary across time and assets, expected *discounted* returns should always be the same, 1. Applying the covariance decomposition,

$$1 = E(m)E(R^i) + \text{cov}(m, R^i) \tag{1.11}$$

and, using $R^f = 1/E(m)$,

$$E(R^i) - R^f = -R^f \; \text{cov}(m, R^i) \tag{1.12}$$

or

$$E(R^i) - R^f = -\frac{\text{cov}\left[u'(c_{t+1}), R^i_{t+1}\right]}{E\left[u'(c_{t+1})\right]}. \tag{1.13}$$

All assets have an expected return equal to the risk-free rate, plus a risk adjustment. Assets whose returns covary positively with consumption make consumption more volatile, and so must promise higher expected returns to induce investors to hold them. Conversely, assets that covary negatively with consumption, such as insurance, can offer expected rates of return that are lower than the risk-free rate, or even negative (net) expected returns.

Much of finance focuses on expected returns. We think of expected returns increasing or decreasing to clear markets; we offer intuition that "riskier" securities must offer higher expected returns to get investors to hold them, rather than saying "riskier" securities trade for lower prices so that investors will hold them. Of course, a low initial price for a given payoff corresponds to a high expected return, so this is no more than a different language for the same phenomenon.

Idiosyncratic Risk Does Not Affect Prices

Only the component of a payoff perfectly correlated with the discount factor generates an extra return. *Idiosyncratic* risk, uncorrelated with the discount factor, generates no premium.

You might think that an asset with a volatile payoff is "risky" and thus should have a large risk correction. However, if the payoff is uncorrelated with the discount factor m, the asset receives *no* risk correction to its price, and pays an expected return equal to the risk-free rate! In equations, if

$$\text{cov}(m, x) = 0,$$

then

$$p = \frac{E(x)}{R^f},$$

no matter how large $\sigma^2(x)$. This prediction holds even if the payoff x is highly volatile and investors are highly risk averse. The reason is simple: if you buy a little bit more of such an asset, it has no first-order effect on the variance of your consumption stream.

More generally, one gets no compensation or risk adjustment for holding *idiosyncratic* risk. Only *systematic* risk generates a risk correction. To give meaning to these words, we can decompose any payoff x into a part correlated with the discount factor and an idiosyncratic part uncorrelated with the discount factor by running a regression,

$$x = \text{proj}(x|m) + \varepsilon.$$

Then, the price of the residual or idiosyncratic risk ε is zero, and the price of x is the same as the price of its projection on m. The projection of x on m is of course that part of x which is perfectly correlated with m. The *idiosyncratic* component of any payoff is that part uncorrelated with m. Thus only the systematic *part* of a payoff accounts for its price.

Projection means linear regression without a constant,

$$\text{proj}(x|m) = \frac{E(mx)}{E(m^2)}m.$$

You can verify that regression residuals are orthogonal to right-hand variables $E(m\varepsilon) = 0$ from this definition. $E(m\varepsilon) = 0$ of course means that the price of ε is zero,

$$p(\text{proj}(x|m)) = p\left(\frac{E(mx)}{E(m^2)}m\right) = E\left(m^2\frac{E(mx)}{E(m^2)}\right) = E(mx) = p(x).$$

The words "systematic" and "idiosyncratic" are defined differently in different contexts, which can lead to some confusion. In this decomposition, the residuals ε can be correlated with each other, though they are not correlated with the discount factor. The APT starts with a factor-analytic decomposition of the covariance of payoffs, and the word "idiosyncratic" there is reserved for the component of payoffs uncorrelated with all of the other payoffs.

Expected Return-Beta Representation

We can write $p = E(mx)$ as

$$E(R^i) = R^f + \beta_{i,m}\lambda_m.$$

We can express the expected return equation (1.12), for a return R^i, as

$$E(R^i) = R^f + \left(\frac{\text{cov}(R^i, m)}{\text{var}(m)}\right)\left(-\frac{\text{var}(m)}{E(m)}\right) \quad (1.14)$$

or

$$E(R^i) = R^f + \beta_{i,m}\lambda_m, \quad (1.15)$$

where β_{im} is the regression coefficient of the return R^i on m. This is a *beta pricing model*. It says that each expected return should be proportional to the regression coefficient, or beta, in a regression of that return on the discount factor m. Notice that the coefficient λ_m is the same for all assets i, while the $\beta_{i,m}$ varies from asset to asset. The λ_m is often interpreted as the *price of risk* and the β as the *quantity* of risk in each asset. As you can see, the price of risk λ_m depends on the volatility of the discount factor.

Obviously, there is nothing deep about saying that expected returns are proportional to betas rather than to covariances. There is a long historical tradition and some minor convenience in favor of betas. The betas refer to the projection of R on m that we studied above, so you see again a sense in which only the systematic component of risk matters.

With $m = \beta(c_{t+1}/c_t)^{-\gamma}$, we can take a Taylor approximation of equation (1.14) to express betas in terms of a more concrete variable, consumption growth, rather than marginal utility. The result, which I derive more explicitly and conveniently in the continuous-time limit below, is

$$E(R^i) = R^f + \beta_{i,\Delta c}\lambda_{\Delta c}, \quad (1.16)$$

$$\lambda_{\Delta c} = \gamma \text{ var}(\Delta c).$$

Expected returns should increase linearly with their betas on consumption growth itself. In addition, though it is treated as a free parameter in many applications, the factor risk premium $\lambda_{\Delta c}$ is determined by risk aversion and the volatility of consumption. The more risk averse people are, or the riskier their environment, the larger an expected return premium one must pay to get investors to hold risky (high beta) assets.

Mean-Variance Frontier

> All asset returns lie inside a mean-variance frontier. Assets on the frontier are perfectly correlated with each other and with the discount factor. Returns on the frontier can be generated as portfolios of any two frontier returns. We can construct a discount factor from any frontier return (except R^f), and an expected return-beta representation holds using any frontier return (except R^f) as the factor.

Asset pricing theory has focused a lot on the means and variances of asset returns. Interestingly, the set of means and variances of returns is limited. All assets priced by the discount factor m must obey

$$\left|E(R^i) - R^f\right| \le \frac{\sigma(m)}{E(m)}\sigma(R^i). \tag{1.17}$$

To derive (1.17) write for a given asset return R^i

$$1 = E(mR^i) = E(m)E(R^i) + \rho_{m,\,R^i}\sigma(R^i)\sigma(m)$$

and hence

$$E(R^i) = R^f - \rho_{m,\,R^i}\frac{\sigma(m)}{E(m)}\sigma(R^i). \tag{1.18}$$

Correlation coefficients cannot be greater than 1 in magnitude, leading to (1.17).

This simple calculation has many interesting and classic implications.

1. Means and variances of asset returns must lie in the wedge-shaped region illustrated in Figure 1.1. The boundary of the mean-variance region in which assets can lie is called the *mean-variance frontier*. It answers a naturally interesting question, "how much mean return can you get for a given level of variance?"
2. All returns on the frontier are perfectly correlated with the discount factor: the frontier is generated by $|\rho_{m,\,R^i}| = 1$. Returns on the upper part of the frontier are perfectly negatively correlated with the discount factor and hence positively correlated with consumption. They are "maximally risky" and thus get the highest expected returns. Returns on the lower part of the frontier are perfectly positively correlated with the discount factor and hence negatively correlated with consumption. They thus provide the best insurance against consumption fluctuations.

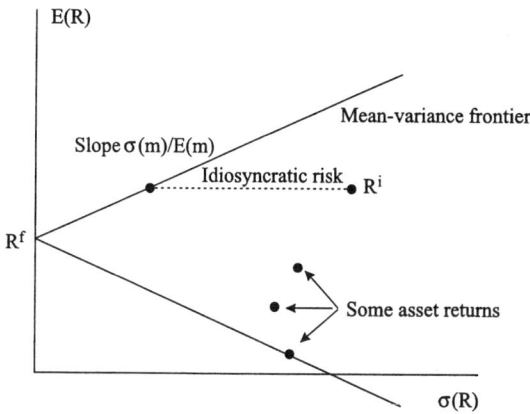

Figure 1.1. *Mean-variance frontier. The mean and standard deviation of all assets priced by a discount factor m must lie in the wedge-shaped region.*

3. All frontier returns are also perfectly correlated with each other, since they are all perfectly correlated with the discount factor. This fact implies that we can *span* or *synthesize* any frontier return from two such returns. For example, if you pick any single frontier return R^m, then all frontier returns R^{mv} must be expressible as

$$R^{mv} = R^f + a(R^m - R^f)$$

for some number a.

4. Since each point on the mean-variance frontier is perfectly correlated with the discount factor, we must be able to pick constants a, b, d, e such that

$$m = a + bR^{mv},$$
$$R^{mv} = d + em.$$

Thus, *any mean-variance efficient return carries all pricing information.* Given a mean-variance efficient return and the risk-free rate, we can find a discount factor that prices all assets and vice versa.

5. Given a discount factor, we can also construct a single-beta representation, so *expected returns can be described in a single-beta representation using any mean-variance efficient return* (except the risk-free rate),

$$E(R^i) = R^f + \beta_{i,mv}[E(R^{mv}) - R^f].$$

The essence of the beta pricing model is that, even though the means and standard deviations of returns fill out the space inside the mean-variance frontier, a graph of mean returns versus *betas* should yield a straight line. Since the beta model applies to every return including R^{mv} itself, and R^{mv} has a beta of 1 on itself, we can identify the factor risk premium as $\lambda = E(R^{mv} - R^f)$.

The last two points suggest an intimate relationship between discount factors, beta models, and mean-variance frontiers. I explore this relation in detail in Chapter 6. A problem at the end of this chapter guides you through the algebra to demonstrate points 4 and 5 explicitly.

6. We can plot the decomposition of a return into a "priced" or "systematic" component and a "residual," or "idiosyncratic" component as shown in Figure 1.1. The priced part is perfectly correlated with the discount factor, and hence perfectly correlated with any frontier return. The residual or idiosyncratic part generates no expected return, so it lies flat as shown in the figure, and it is uncorrelated with the discount factor or any frontier return. Assets inside the frontier or even on the lower portion of the frontier are not "worse" than assets on the frontier. The frontier and its internal region characterize equilibrium asset returns, with rational investors happy to hold all assets. You would not want to put your whole portfolio in one "inefficient" asset, but you are happy to put some wealth in such assets.

Slope of the Mean-Standard Deviation Frontier and Equity Premium Puzzle

The Sharpe ratio is limited by the volatility of the discount factor. The maximal risk-return trade-off is steeper if there is more risk or more risk aversion,

$$\left| \frac{E(R) - R^f}{\sigma(R)} \right| \leq \frac{\sigma(m)}{E(m)} \approx \gamma\sigma(\Delta \ln c).$$

This formula captures the equity premium puzzle, which suggests that either people are very risk averse, or the stock returns of the last 50 years were good luck which will not continue.

The ratio of mean excess return to standard deviation

$$\frac{E(R^i) - R^f}{\sigma(R^i)}$$

is known as the *Sharpe ratio*. It is a more interesting characterization of a security than the mean return alone. If you borrow and put more money into a security, you can increase the mean return of your position, but you do not increase the Sharpe ratio, since the standard deviation increases at the same rate as the mean.

The slope of the mean-standard deviation frontier is the largest available Sharpe ratio, and thus is naturally interesting. It answers "how much more mean return can I get by shouldering a bit more volatility in my portfolio?"

Let R^{mv} denote the return of a portfolio on the frontier. From equation (1.17), the slope of the frontier is

$$\left| \frac{E(R^{mv}) - R^f}{\sigma(R^{mv})} \right| = \frac{\sigma(m)}{E(m)} = \sigma(m)R^f.$$

Thus, the slope of the frontier is governed by the volatility of the discount factor.

For an economic interpretation, again consider the power utility function, $u'(c) = c^{-\gamma}$,

$$\left| \frac{E(R^{mv}) - R^f}{\sigma(R^{mv})} \right| = \frac{\sigma\left[(c_{t+1}/c_t)^{-\gamma}\right]}{E\left[(c_{t+1}/c_t)^{-\gamma}\right]}. \qquad (1.19)$$

The standard deviation on the right hand side is large if consumption is volatile or if γ is large. We can state this approximation precisely using the lognormal assumption. If consumption growth is lognormal,

$$\left| \frac{E(R^{mv}) - R^f}{\sigma(R^{mv})} \right| = \sqrt{e^{\gamma^2\sigma^2(\Delta \ln c_{t+1})} - 1} \approx \gamma\sigma(\Delta \ln c). \qquad (1.20)$$

(A problem at the end of the chapter guides you through the algebra of the first equality. The relation is exact in continuous time, and thus the approximation is easiest to derive by reference to the continuous-time result; see Section 1.5.)

Reading the equation, *the slope of the mean-standard deviation frontier is higher if the economy is riskier—if consumption is more volatile—or if investors are more risk averse.* Both situations naturally make investors more reluctant to take on the extra risk of holding risky assets. Both situations also raise the slope of the expected return-beta line of the consumption beta model, (1.16). (Or, conversely, in an economy with a high Sharpe ratio, low risk-aversion investors should take on so much risk that their consumption becomes volatile.)

In postwar U.S. data, the slope of the historical mean-standard deviation frontier, or of average return-beta lines, is much higher than reasonable risk aversion and consumption volatility estimates suggest. This is the "equity premium puzzle." Over the last 50 years in the United States, real stock returns have averaged 9% with a standard deviation of about 16%, while the real return on treasury bills has been about 1%. Thus, the historical annual market Sharpe ratio has been about 0.5. Aggregate nondurable and services consumption growth had a mean and standard deviation of about 1%. We can only reconcile these facts with (1.20) if investors have a risk-aversion coefficient of 50!

Obvious ways of generalizing the calculation just make matters worse. Equation (1.20) relates consumption growth to the mean-variance frontier of all contingent claims. Market indices with 0.5 Sharpe ratios are if anything inside that frontier, so recognizing market incompleteness makes matters worse. Aggregate consumption has about 0.2 correlation with the market return, while the equality (1.20) takes the worst possible case that consumption growth and asset returns are perfectly correlated. If you add this fact, you need risk aversion of 250 to explain the market Sharpe ratio! Individuals have riskier consumption streams than aggregate, but as their risk goes up their correlation with any aggregate must decrease proportionally, so to first order recognizing individual risk will not help either.

Clearly, either (1) people are a *lot* more risk averse than we might have thought, (2) the stock returns of the last 50 years were largely good luck rather than an equilibrium compensation for risk, or (3) something is deeply wrong with the model, including the utility function and use of aggregate consumption data. This "equity premium puzzle" has attracted the attention of a lot of research in finance, especially on the last item. I return to the equity premium in more detail in Chapter 21.

Random Walks and Time-Varying Expected Returns

> If investors are risk neutral, returns are unpredictable, and prices follow martingales. In general, prices scaled by marginal utility are martingales, and returns can be predictable if investors are risk averse and if the conditional second moments of returns and discount factors vary over time. This is more plausible at long horizons.

So far, we have concentrated on the behavior of prices or expected returns across assets. We should also consider the behavior of the price or return of a given asset over time. Going back to the basic first-order condition,

$$p_t u'(c_t) = E_t[\beta u'(c_{t+1})(p_{t+1} + d_{t+1})].$$ (1.21)

If investors are risk neutral, i.e., if $u(c)$ is linear or there is no variation in consumption, if the security pays no dividends between t and $t+1$, and for short time horizons where β is close to 1, this equation reduces to

$$p_t = E_t(p_{t+1}).$$

Equivalently, prices follow a time-series process of the form

$$p_{t+1} = p_t + \varepsilon_{t+1}.$$

If the variance $\sigma_t^2(\varepsilon_{t+1})$ is constant, prices follow a *random walk*. More generally, prices follow a *martingale*. Intuitively, if the price today is a lot lower than investors' expectations of the price tomorrow, then investors will try to buy the security. But this action will drive up the price of the security until the price today does equal the expected price tomorrow. Another way of saying the same thing is that returns should not be predictable; dividing by p_t, expected returns $E_t(p_{t+1}/p_t) = 1$ should be constant; returns should be like coin flips.

The more general equation (1.21) says that prices should follow a martingale after adjusting for dividends and scaling by marginal utility. Since martingales have useful mathematical properties, and since risk neutrality is such a simple economic environment, many asset pricing results are easily derived by scaling prices and dividends by discounted marginal utility first, and then using "risk-neutral" formulas and risk-neutral economic arguments.

Since consumption and risk aversion do not change much day to day, we might expect the random walk view to hold pretty well on a day-to-day basis. This idea contradicts the still popular notion that there are "systems" or "technical analysis" by which one can predict where stock prices are going on any given day. The random walk view has been remarkably successful. Despite decades of dredging the data, and the popularity of media reports that purport to explain where markets are going, trading rules that reliably survive transactions costs and do not implicitly expose the investor to risk have not yet been reliably demonstrated.

However, more recently, evidence has accumulated that long-horizon excess returns are quite predictable, and to some this evidence indicates that the whole enterprise of economic explanation of asset returns is flawed. To think about this issue, write our basic equation for expected returns as

$$
\begin{aligned}
E_t(R_{t+1}) - R_t^f &= -\frac{\text{cov}_t(m_{t+1}, R_{t+1})}{E_t(m_{t+1})} \\
&= \frac{\sigma_t(m_{t+1})}{E_t(m_{t+1})} \sigma_t(R_{t+1}) \rho_t(m_{t+1}, R_{t+1}) \qquad (1.22) \\
&\approx \gamma_t \sigma_t(\Delta c_{t+1}) \sigma_t(R_{t+1}) \rho_t(m_{t+1}, R_{t+1}).
\end{aligned}
$$

I include the t subscripts to emphasize that the relation applies to *conditional* moments. Sometimes, the *conditional* mean or other moment of a random variable is different from its *unconditional* moment. Conditional on tonight's weather forecast, you can better predict rain tomorrow than just knowing the average rain for that date. In the special case that random variables are i.i.d. (independent and identically distributed), like coin flips, the conditional and unconditional moments are the same, but that is a special case and not likely to be true of asset prices, returns, and macroeconomic variables. In the theory so far, we have thought of an investor, today, forming expectations of payoffs, consumption, and other variables tomorrow. Thus, the moments are really all *conditional*, and if we want to be precise we should include some notation to express this fact. I use subscripts $E_t(x_{t+1})$ to denote conditional expectation; the notation $E(x_{t+1}|I_t)$ where I_t is the information set at time t is more precise but a little more cumbersome.

Examining equation (1.22), we see that returns can be somewhat predictable—the expected return can vary over time. First, if the conditional variance of returns changes over time, we might expect the conditional mean return to vary as well—the return can just move in and out along a line of constant Sharpe ratio. This explanation does not seem to help much in the data; variables that forecast means do not seem to forecast variances and vice versa. Unless we want to probe the conditional correlation, predictable excess returns have to be explained by changing risk—$\sigma_t(\Delta c_{t+1})$—or changing risk aversion γ. It is not plausible that risk or risk aversion change at daily frequencies, but fortunately returns are not predictable at daily frequencies. It is much more plausible that risk and risk aversion change over the business cycle, and this is exactly the horizon at which we see predictable excess returns. Models that make this connection precise are a very active area of current research.

Present-Value Statement

$$p_t = E_t \sum_{j=0}^{\infty} m_{t,t+j} d_{t+j}.$$

It is convenient to use only the two-period valuation, thinking of a price p_t and a payoff x_{t+1}. But there are times when we want to relate a price to the entire cash flow stream, rather than just to one dividend and next period's price.

The most straightforward way to do this is to write out a longer-term objective,

$$E_t \sum_{j=0}^{\infty} \beta^j u(c_{t+j}).$$

Now suppose an investor can purchase a stream $\{d_{t+j}\}$ at price p_t. As with the two-period model, his first-order condition gives us the pricing formula directly,

$$p_t = E_t \sum_{j=0}^{\infty} \beta^j \frac{u'(c_{t+j})}{u'(c_t)} d_{t+j} = E_t \sum_{j=0}^{\infty} m_{t,t+j} d_{t+j}. \tag{1.23}$$

You can see that if this equation holds at time t and time $t+1$, then we can derive the two-period version

$$p_t = E_t[m_{t+1}(p_{t+1} + d_{t+1})]. \tag{1.24}$$

Thus, the infinite-period and two-period models are equivalent.

(Going in the other direction is a little tougher. If you chain together (1.24), you get (1.23) plus an extra term. To get (1.23) you also need the "transversality condition" $\lim_{t\to\infty} E_t[m_{t,t+j}p_{t+j}] = 0$. This is an extra first-order condition of the infinite-period investor, which is not present with overlapping generations of two-period investors. It rules out "bubbles" in which prices grow so fast that people will buy now just to resell at higher prices later, even if there are no dividends.)

From (1.23) we can write a risk adjustment to prices, as we did with one-period payoffs,

$$p_t = \sum_{j=1}^{\infty} \frac{E_t d_{t+j}}{R_{t,t+j}^f} + \sum_{j=1}^{\infty} \mathrm{cov}_t(d_{t+j}, m_{t,t+j}),$$

where $R_{t,t+j}^f \equiv E_t(m_{t,t+j})^{-1}$ is the j period interest rate. Again, assets whose dividend streams covary negatively with marginal utility, and positively with consumption, have lower prices, since holding those assets gives the investor a more volatile consumption stream. (It is common instead to write prices as a discounted value using a risk-adjusted discount factor, e.g., $p_t^i = \sum_{j=1}^{\infty} E_t d_{t+j}^i / (R^i)^j$, but this approach is difficult to use correctly for multiperiod problems, especially when expected returns can vary over time.)

At a deeper level, the expectation in the two-period formula $p = E(mx)$ sums over states of nature. Equation (1.23) just sums over time as well and is mathematically identical.

———————

1.5 Discount Factors in Continuous Time

Continuous-time versions of the basic pricing equations.

Discrete	Continuous

$$p_t = E_t \sum_{j=1}^{\infty} \beta^j \frac{u'(c_{t+j})}{u'(c_t)} D_{t+j} \qquad p_t u'(c_t) = E_t \int_{s=0}^{\infty} e^{-\delta s} u'(c_{t+s}) D_{t+s} \, ds$$

$$m_{t+1} = \beta \frac{u'(c_{t+1})}{u'(c_t)} \qquad\qquad \Lambda_t = e^{-\delta t} u'(c_t)$$

$$p = E(mx) \qquad\qquad 0 = \Lambda D \, dt + E_t[d(\Lambda p)]$$

$$E(R) = R^f - R^f \operatorname{cov}(m, R) \qquad E_t\left(\frac{dp}{p}\right) + \frac{D}{p} \, dt = r_t^f \, dt - E_t\left[\frac{d\Lambda}{\Lambda} \frac{dp}{p}\right]$$

It is often convenient to express asset pricing ideas in the language of continuous-time stochastic differential equations rather than discrete-time stochastic difference equations as I have done so far. The appendix contains a brief introduction to continuous-time processes that covers what you need to know for this book. Even if you want to end up with a discrete-time representation, manipulations are often easier in continuous time. For example, relating interest rates and Sharpe ratios to consumption growth in the last section required a clumsy lognormal approximation; you will see the same sort of thing done much more cleanly in this section.

The choice of discrete versus continuous time is one of modeling convenience. The richness of the theory of continuous-time processes often allows you to obtain analytical results that would be unavailable in discrete time. On the other hand, in the complexity of most practical situations, you often end up resorting to numerical simulation of a discretized model anyway. In those cases, it might be clearer to start with a discrete model. But this is all a choice of language. One should become familiar enough with discrete- as well as continuous-time representations of the same ideas to pick the representation that is most convenient for a particular application.

First, we need to think about how to model securities, in place of price p_t and one-period payoff x_{t+1}. Let a generic security have price p_t at any moment in time, and let it pay dividends at the rate $D_t \, dt$. (I will continue to denote functions of time as p_t rather than $p(t)$ to maintain continuity with the discrete-time treatment, and I will drop the time subscripts where they are obvious, e.g., dp in place of dp_t. In an interval dt, the security pays dividends $D_t\ dt$. I use capital D for dividends to distinguish them from the differential operator d.)

The instantaneous total return is

$$\frac{dp_t}{p_t} + \frac{D_t}{p_t}\ dt.$$

We model the price of risky assets as diffusions, for example,

$$\frac{dp_t}{p_t} = \mu(\cdot)\ dt + \sigma(\cdot)\ dz.$$

(I use the notation dz for increments to a standard Brownian motion, e.g., $z_{t+\Delta} - z_t \sim \mathcal{N}(0, \Delta)$. I use the notation $(\cdot)$ to indicate that the drift and diffusions μ and σ can be functions of state variables. I limit the discussion to diffusion processes—no jumps.) What is nice about this diffusion model is that the increments dz are normal. However, the dependence of μ and σ on state variables means that the finite-time distribution of prices $f(p_{t+\Delta}|I_t)$ need not be normal.

We can think of a risk-free security as one that has a constant price equal to 1 and pays the risk-free rate as a dividend,

$$p = 1 \qquad D_t = r_t^f, \tag{1.25}$$

or as a security that pays no dividend but whose price climbs deterministically at a rate

$$\frac{dp_t}{p_t} = r_t^f\ dt. \tag{1.26}$$

Next, we need to express the first-order conditions in continuous time. The utility function is

$$U(\{c_t\}) = E\int_{t=0}^{\infty} e^{-\delta t}u(c_t)\ dt.$$

Suppose the investor can buy a security whose price is p_t and that pays a dividend stream D_t. As we did in deriving the present-value price relation in discrete time, the first-order condition for this problem gives us the infinite-period version of the basic pricing equation right away,[1]

$$p_t u'(c_t) = E_t\int_{s=0}^{\infty} e^{-\delta s} u'(c_{t+s})D_{t+s}\ ds. \tag{1.27}$$

---

[1] One unit of the security pays the dividend stream D_t, i.e., $D_t\ dt$ units of the numeraire consumption good in a time interval dt. The security costs p_t units of the consumption good. The investor can finance the purchase of ξ units of the security by reducing consumption from e_t to $c_t = e_t - \xi p_t/dt$ during time interval dt. The loss in utility from doing so is $u'(c_t)(e_t - c_t)\ dt = u'(c_t)\xi p_t$. The gain is the right-hand side of (1.27) multiplied by ξ.

This equation is an obvious continuous-time analogue to

$$p_t = E_t \sum_{j=0}^{\infty} \beta^t \frac{u'(c_{t+j})}{u'(c_t)} D_{t+j}.$$

It turns out that dividing by $u'(c_t)$ is not a good idea in continuous time, since the ratio $u'(c_{t+\Delta})/u'(c_t)$ is not well behaved for small time intervals. Instead, we can keep track of the *level* of marginal utility. Therefore, define the "discount factor" in continuous time as

$$\Lambda_t \equiv e^{-\delta t} u'(c_t).$$

Then we can write the pricing equation as

$$p_t \Lambda_t = E_t \int_{s=0}^{\infty} \Lambda_{t+s} D_{t+s} \, ds. \tag{1.28}$$

(Some people like to define $\Lambda_t = u'(c_t)$, in which case you keep the $e^{-\delta t}$ in the equation. Others like to scale Λ_t by the risk-free rate, in which case you get an extra $e^{-\int_{\tau=0}^{s} r_{t+\tau}^f \, d\tau}$ in the equation. The latter procedure makes it look like a risk-neutral or present-value formula valuation.)

The analogue to the one-period pricing equation $p = E(mx)$ is

$$0 = \Lambda D \, dt + E_t \big[d(\Lambda p) \big]. \tag{1.29}$$

To derive this fundamental equation, take the difference of equation (1.28) at t and $t + \Delta$ (or, start directly with the first-order condition for buying the security at t and selling it at $t + \Delta$),

$$p_t \Lambda_t = E_t \int_{s=0}^{\Delta} \Lambda_{t+s} D_{t+s} \, ds + E_t \big[\Lambda_{t+\Delta} p_{t+\Delta} \big].$$

For Δ small the term in the integral can be approximated as

$$p_t \Lambda_t \approx \Lambda_t D_t \Delta + E_t \big[\Lambda_{t+\Delta} p_{t+\Delta} \big]. \tag{1.30}$$

We want to get to d something, so introduce differences by writing

$$p_t \Lambda_t \approx \Lambda_t D_t \Delta + E_t \big[\Lambda_t p_t + (\Lambda_{t+\Delta} p_{t+\Delta} - \Lambda_t p_t) \big]. \tag{1.31}$$

Canceling $p_t \Lambda_t$,

$$0 \approx \Lambda_t D_t \Delta + E_t (\Lambda_{t+\Delta} p_{t+\Delta} - \Lambda_t p_t).$$

Taking the limit as $\Delta \to 0$,

$$0 = \Lambda_t D_t \, dt + E_t \big[d(\Lambda_t p_t) \big]$$

or, dropping time subscripts, equation (1.29).

Equation (1.29) looks different than $p = E(mx)$ because there is no price on the left-hand side; we are used to thinking of the one-period pricing equation as determining price at t given other things, including price at $t + 1$. But price at t is really here, of course, as you can see from equation (1.30) or (1.31). It is just easier to express the *difference* in price over time rather than price today on the left and payoff (including price tomorrow) on the right.

With no dividends and constant Λ, $0 = E_t(dp_t) = E_t(p_{t+\Delta} - p_t)$ says that price should follow a martingale. Thus, $E_t[d(\Lambda p)] = 0$ means that marginal utility-weighted price should follow a martingale, and (1.29) adjusts for dividends. Thus, it is the same as the equation (1.21), $p_t u'(c_t) = E_t(m_{t+1}(p_{t+1} + d_{t+1}))$ that we derived in discrete time.

Since we will write down price processes for dp and discount factor processes for $d\Lambda$, and to interpret (1.29) in terms of expected returns, it is often convenient to break up the $d(\Lambda_t p_t)$ term using Ito's lemma:

$$d(\Lambda p) = p \, d\Lambda + \Lambda \, dp + dp \, d\Lambda. \tag{1.32}$$

Using the expanded version (1.32) in the basic equation (1.29), and dividing by $p\Lambda$ to make it pretty, we obtain an equivalent, slightly less compact but slightly more intuitive version,

$$0 = \frac{D}{p} \, dt + E_t \left[\frac{d\Lambda}{\Lambda} + \frac{dp}{p} + \frac{d\Lambda}{\Lambda} \frac{dp}{p} \right]. \tag{1.33}$$

(This formula only works when both Λ and p can never be zero. It is often enough the case that this formula is useful. If not, multiply through by Λ and p and keep them in numerators.)

Applying the basic pricing equations (1.29) or (1.33) to a risk-free rate, defined as (1.25) or (1.26), we obtain

$$r_t^f \, dt = -E_t \left(\frac{d\Lambda_t}{\Lambda_t} \right). \tag{1.34}$$

This equation is the obvious continuous-time equivalent to

$$R_t^f = \frac{1}{E_t(m_{t+1})}.$$

If a risk-free rate is not traded, we can use (1.34) to define a shadow risk-free rate or zero-beta rate.

With this interpretation, we can rearrange equation (1.33) as

$$E_t \left(\frac{dp_t}{p_t} \right) + \frac{D_t}{p_t} \, dt = r_t^f \, dt - E_t \left[\frac{d\Lambda_t}{\Lambda_t} \frac{dp_t}{p_t} \right]. \tag{1.35}$$

This is the obvious continuous-time analogue to

$$E(R) = R^f - R^f \operatorname{cov}(m, R). \tag{1.36}$$

The last term in (1.35) is the covariance of the return with the discount factor or marginal utility. Since means are order dt, there is no difference between covariance and second moment in the last term of (1.35). The interest rate component of the last term of (1.36) naturally vanishes as the time interval gets short.

Ito's lemma makes many transformations simple in continuous time. For example, the nonlinear transformation between consumption and the discount factor led us to some tricky approximations in discrete time. This transformation is easy in continuous time (diffusions are locally normal, so it is really the same trick). With $\Lambda_t = e^{-\delta t} u'(c_t)$ we have

$$d\Lambda_t = -\delta e^{-\delta t} u'(c_t)\, dt + e^{-\delta t} u''(c_t)\, dc_t + \frac{1}{2} e^{-\delta t} u'''(c_t)\, dc_t^2,$$

$$\frac{d\Lambda_t}{\Lambda_t} = -\delta\, dt + \frac{c_t u''(c_t)}{u'(c_t)} \frac{dc_t}{c_t} + \frac{1}{2} \frac{c_t^2 u'''(c_t)}{u'(c_t)} \frac{dc_t^2}{c_t^2}. \tag{1.37}$$

Denote the local curvature and third derivative of the utility function as

$$\gamma_t = -\frac{c_t u''(c_t)}{u'(c_t)},$$

$$\eta_t = \frac{c_t^2 u'''(c_t)}{u'(c_t)}.$$

(For power utility, the former is the power coefficient γ and the latter is $\eta_t = \gamma(\gamma + 1)$.)

Using this formula we can quickly redo the relationship between interest rates and consumption growth, equation (1.7),

$$r_t^f = -\frac{1}{dt} E_t\left(\frac{d\Lambda_t}{\Lambda_t}\right) = \delta + \gamma_t \frac{1}{dt} E_t\left(\frac{dc_t}{c_t}\right) - \frac{1}{2} \eta_t \frac{1}{dt} E_t\left(\frac{dc_t^2}{c_t^2}\right).$$

We can also easily express asset prices in terms of consumption risk rather than discount factor risk, as in equation (1.16). Using (1.37) in (1.35),

$$E_t\left(\frac{dp_t}{p_t}\right) + \frac{D_t}{p_t}\, dt - r_t^f\, dt = \gamma E_t\left(\frac{dc_t}{c_t} \frac{dp_t}{p_t}\right). \tag{1.38}$$

Thus, assets whose returns covary more strongly with consumption get higher mean excess returns, and the constant relating covariance to mean return is the utility curvature coefficient γ.

Since correlations are less than 1, equation (1.38) implies that Sharpe ratios are related to utility curvature and consumption volatility directly; we do not need the ugly lognormal facts and an approximation that we needed in (1.20). Using $\mu_p \equiv E_t(dp_t/p_t)$; $\sigma_p^2 = E_t[(dp_t/p_t)^2]$; $\sigma_c^2 = E_t[(dc_t/c_t)^2]$,

$$\frac{\mu_p + \frac{D_t}{p_t}\, dt - r_t^f\, dt}{\sigma_p} \le \gamma \sigma_c.$$

Problems—Chapter 1

1.

(a)   The absolute risk-aversion coefficient is

$$\frac{u''(c)}{u'(c)}.$$

We scale by $u'(c)$ because expected utility is only defined up to linear transformations—$a + bu(c)$ gives the same predictions as $u(c)$—and this measure of the second derivative is invariant to linear transformations. Show that the utility function with constant absolute risk aversion is

$$u(c) = -e^{-\alpha c}.$$

(b)   The coefficient of relative risk aversion in a one-period model (i.e., when consumption equals wealth) is defined as

$$rra = \frac{cu''(c)}{u'(c)}.$$

For power utility $u'(c) = c^{-\gamma}$, show that the risk-aversion coefficient equals the power.

(c)   The elasticity of intertemporal substitution is defined in a non-stochastic model with interest rate R as

$$\xi^I \equiv -\frac{c_2/c_1 d(c_1/c_2)}{dR/R}.$$

Show that with power utility $u'(c) = c^{-\gamma}$, the intertemporal substitution elasticity is equal to $1/\gamma$. (Hint: differentiate the first-order conditions)

2.   Show that the "idiosyncratic risk" line in Figure 1.1 is horizontal.

3.

(a)   Suppose you have a mean–variance efficient return R^{mv} and the risk-free rate. Using the fact that R^{mv} is perfectly correlated with the discount factor, construct a discount factor m in terms of R^f and R^{mv}, with no free parameters. (You have to find the constants a and b in $m = a + bR^{mv}$. They will depend on things like $E(R^{mv})$.)

(b) Using this result, and the beta model in terms of m, show that expected returns can be described in a single-beta representation using any mean-variance efficient return (except the risk-free rate).

$$E(R^i) = R^f + \beta_{i,mv}\left[E(R^{mv}) - R^f\right].$$

4. Can the "Sharpe ratio" between two risky assets exceed the slope of the mean-variance frontier? That is, if R^{mv} is on the frontier, is it possible that

$$\frac{E(R^i) - E(R^j)}{\sigma(R^i - R^j)} > \frac{E(R^{mv}) - R^f}{\sigma(R^{mv})}?$$

5. Show that if consumption growth is lognormal, then

$$\left|\frac{E(R^{mv}) - R^f}{\sigma(R^{mv})}\right| = \frac{\sigma\left[(c_{t+1}/c_t)^{-\gamma}\right]}{E\left[(c_{t+1}/c_t)^{-\gamma}\right]} = \sqrt{e^{\gamma^2\sigma^2(\Delta \ln c_{t+1})} - 1} \approx \gamma\sigma(\Delta \ln c).$$

(Start with $\sigma^2(x) = E(x^2) - E(x)^2$ and the lognormal property $E(e^z) = e^{Ez+(1/2)\sigma^2(z)}$.)

6. There are assets with mean return equal to the risk-free rate, but substantial standard deviation of returns. Long-term bonds are pretty close examples. Why would anyone hold such an asset? Wouldn't it be better to put your money in a mean-variance frontier asset?

7. The first-order conditions for an infinitely lived investor who can buy an asset with dividend stream $\{d_t\}$ are

$$p_t = E_t \sum_{j=1}^{\infty} \beta^j \frac{u'(c_{t+j})}{u'(c_t)} d_{t+j}. \tag{1.39}$$

The first-order conditions for buying a security with price p_t and payoff $x_{t+1} = d_{t+1} + p_{t+1}$ are

$$p_t = E_t\left[\beta\frac{u'(c_{t+1})}{u'(c_t)}(p_{t+1} + d_{t+1})\right]. \tag{1.40}$$

(a) Derive (1.40) from (1.39)

(b) Derive (1.39) from (1.40). You need an extra condition. Show that this extra condition is a first-order condition for maximization. To do this, think about what strategy the consumer could follow to improve utility if the condition did not hold, both if this is if the only security available and if the investor can trade all state- and date-contingent claims.

8. Suppose a consumer has a utility function that includes leisure. (This could also be a second good, or a good produced in another country.) Using the continuous-time setup, show that expected returns will now depend on *two* covariances, the covariance of returns with leisure and the covariance of returns with consumption, so long as leisure enters non-separably, i.e., $u(c, l)$ cannot be written $v(c) + w(l)$. (This is a three line problem, but you need to apply Ito's lemma to Λ.)

9. From

$$1 = E(mR)$$

show that the negative of the mean log discount factor must be larger than *any* mean return,

$$-E(\ln m) > E(\ln R).$$

How is it possible that $E(\ln R)$ is bounded—what about returns of the form $R = (1 - \alpha)R^f + \alpha R^m$ for arbitrarily large α? (Hint: start by assuming m and R are lognormal. Then see if you can generalize the results using Jensen's inequality, $E(f(x)) > f(E(x))$ for f convex. The return that solves $\max_R E(\ln R)$ is known as the *growth optimal portfolio*.)

2

Applying the Basic Model

2.1 Assumptions and Applicability

Writing $p = E(mx)$, we do *not* assume

1. Markets are complete, or there is a representative investor
2. Asset returns or payoffs are normally distributed (no options), or independent over time
3. Two-period investors, quadratic utility, or separable utility
4. Investors have no human capital or labor income
5. The market has reached equilibrium, or individuals have bought all the securities they want to

All of these assumptions come later, in various special cases, but we *have not* made them yet. We *do* assume that the investor can consider a small marginal investment or disinvestment.

The theory of asset pricing contains lots of assumptions used to derive analytically convenient special cases and empirically useful representations. In writing $p = E(mx)$ or $pu'(c_t) = E_t[\beta u'(c_{t+1})x_{t+1}]$, we have *not* made most of these assumptions.

We have *not* assumed complete markets or a representative investor. These equations apply to each individual investor, for each asset to which he has access, independently of the presence or absence of other investors or other assets. Complete markets/representative agent assumptions are used if one wants to use aggregate consumption data in $u'(c_t)$, or other specializations and simplifications of the model.

We have *not* said anything about payoff or return distributions. In particular, we have not assumed that returns are normally distributed or that utility is quadratic. The basic pricing equation should hold for *any* asset, stock, bond, option, real investment opportunity, etc., and any monotone and concave utility function. In particular, it is often thought that mean-variance analysis and beta pricing models require these kinds of limiting assumptions or quadratic utility, but that is not the case. A mean-variance efficient return carries all pricing information no matter what the distribution of payoffs, utility function, etc.

This is *not* a "two-period model." The fundamental pricing equation holds for any two periods of a multiperiod model, as we have seen. Really, everything involves *conditional* moments, so we have not assumed i.i.d. returns over time.

I have written things down in terms of a time- and state-separable utility function and I have focused on the convenient power utility example. Nothing important lies in either choice. Just interpret $u'(c_t)$ as the partial derivative of a general utility function with respect to consumption at time t. State- or time-nonseparable utility (habit persistence, durability) complicates the relation between the discount factor and real variables, but does not change $p = E(mx)$ or any of the basic structure.

We do *not* assume that investors have no nonmarketable human capital, or no outside sources of income. The first-order conditions for purchase of an asset relative to consumption hold no matter what else is in the budget constraint. By contrast, the portfolio approach to asset pricing as in the CAPM and ICAPM relies heavily on the assumption that the investor has no nonasset income, and we will study these special cases below. For example, leisure in the utility function just means that marginal utility $u'(c, l)$ may depend on l as well as c.

We do not even really need the assumption (yet) that the market is "in equilibrium," that the investor has bought all of the asset that he wants to, or even that he can buy the asset at all. We can interpret $p = E(mx)$ as giving us the value, or willingness to pay for, a small amount of a payoff x_{t+1} that the investor does not yet have. Here is why: If the investor had a little ξ more of the payoff x_{t+1} at time $t + 1$, his utility $u(c_t) + \beta E_t u(c_{t+1})$ would increase by

$$\beta E_t \big[u(c_{t+1} + \xi x_{t+1}) - u(c_{t+1}) \big]$$
$$= \beta E_t \Big[u'(c_{t+1}) x_{t+1} \xi + \frac{1}{2} u''(c_{t+1})(x_{t+1}\xi)^2 + \cdots \Big].$$

If ξ is small, only the first term on the right matters. If the investor has to give up a small amount of money $v_t \xi$ at time t, that loss lowers his utility by

$$u(c_t - v_t \xi) = u'(c_t) v_t \xi + \frac{1}{2} u''(c_t)(v_t \xi)^2 + \cdots .$$

Again, for small ξ, only the first term matters. Therefore, in order to receive the small extra payoff ξx_{t+1}, the investor is willing to pay the small amount $v_t \xi$, where

$$v_t = E_t \left[\beta \frac{u'(c_{t+1})}{u'(c_t)} x_{t+1} \right].$$

If this private valuation is higher than the market value p_t, and if the investor can buy some more of the asset, he will. As he buys more, his consumption will change; it will be higher in states where x_{t+1} is higher, driving down $u'(c_{t+1})$ in those states, until the value to the investor has declined to equal the market value. Thus, *after* an investor has reached his optimal portfolio, the *market value* should obey the basic pricing equation as well, using post-trade or equilibrium consumption. But the formula can also be applied to generate the marginal *private* valuation, using pre-trade consumption, or to value a *potential*, not yet traded security.

We *have* calculated the value of a "small" or marginal portfolio change for the investor. For some investment projects, an investor cannot take a small ("diversified") position. For example, a venture capitalist or entrepreneur must usually take all or nothing of a project with payoff stream $\{x_t\}$. Then the value of a project not already taken, $E \sum_j \beta^j u(c_{t+j} + x_{t+j})$, might be substantially different from its marginal counterpart, $E \sum \beta^j u'(c_{t+j}) x_{t+j}$. Once the project is taken, of course, $c_{t+j} + x_{t+j}$ becomes c_{t+j}, so the marginal valuation still applies to the ex post consumption stream. Analysts often forget this point and apply marginal (diversified) valuation models such as the CAPM to projects that must be bought in discrete chunks. Also, we have abstracted from short sales and bid/ask spreads; this modification changes $p = E(mx)$ from an equality to a set of inequalities.

2.2 General Equilibrium

> Asset returns and consumption: which is the chicken and which is the egg? I present the exogenous return model, the endowment economy model, and the argument that it does not matter for studying $p = E(mx)$.

So far, we have not said where the joint statistical properties of the payoff x_{t+1} and marginal utility m_{t+1} or consumption c_{t+1} come from. We have also not said anything about the fundamental exogenous shocks that drive the economy. The basic pricing equation $p = E(mx)$ tells us only what the price should be, *given* the joint distribution of consumption (marginal utility, discount factor) and the asset payoff.

There is nothing that stops us from writing the basic pricing equation as

$$u'(c_t) = E_t[\beta u'(c_{t+1})x_{t+1}/p_t].$$

We can think of this equation as determining today's *consumption* given asset prices and payoffs, rather than determining today's *asset price* in terms of consumption and payoffs. Thinking about the basic first-order condition in this way gives the permanent income model of consumption.

Which is the chicken and which is the egg? Which variable is exogenous and which is endogenous? The answer is, neither, and for many purposes, it does not matter. The first-order conditions characterize any equilibrium; if you happen to know $E(mx)$, you can use them to determine p; if you happen to know p, you can use them to determine consumption and savings decisions.

For most asset pricing applications we are interested in understanding a wide cross section of assets. Thus, it is interesting to contrast the cross-sectional variation in asset prices (expected returns) with cross-sectional variation in their second moments (betas) with a single discount factor. In most applications, the discount factor is a function of aggregate variables (market return, aggregate consumption), so it is plausible to hold the properties of the discount factor constant as we compare one individual asset to another. Permanent income studies typically dramatically restrict the number of assets under consideration, often to just an interest rate, and study the time-series evolution of aggregate or individual consumption.

Nonetheless, it is an obvious next step to complete the solution of our model economy; to find c and p in terms of truly exogenous forces. The results will of course depend on what the rest of the economy looks like, in particular the production or intertemporal transformation technology and the set of markets.

Figure 2.1 shows one possibility for a general equilibrium. Suppose that the production technologies are linear: the real, physical rate of return (the rate of intertemporal *transformation*) is not affected by how much is invested. Now consumption must adjust to these technologically given rates of return. If the rates of return on the intertemporal technologies were to change, the consumption process would have to change as well. This is, implicitly, how the permanent income model works. This is how many finance theories such as the CAPM and ICAPM and the Cox, Ingersoll, and Ross (1986) model of the term structure work as well. These models specify the return process, and then solve the consumer's portfolio and consumption rules.

Figure 2.2 shows another extreme possibility for the production technology. This is an "endowment economy." Nondurable consumption

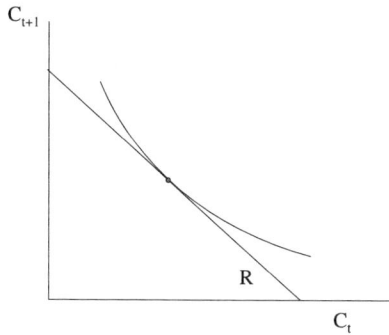

Figure 2.1. *Consumption adjusts when the rate of return is determined by a linear technology.*

appears (or is produced by labor) every period. There is nothing anyone can do to save, store, invest, or otherwise transform consumption goods this period to consumption goods next period. Hence, asset prices must adjust until people are just happy consuming the endowment process. In this case consumption is exogenous and asset prices adjust. Lucas (1978) and Mehra and Prescott (1985) are two very famous applications of this sort of "endowment economy."

Which of these possibilities is correct? Well, neither, of course. The real economy and all serious general equilibrium models look something like Figure 2.3: one can save or transform consumption from one date to the next, but at a decreasing rate. As investment increases, rates of return decline.

Does this observation invalidate the modeling we do with the linear technology (CAPM, CIR, permanent income) model, or the endowment

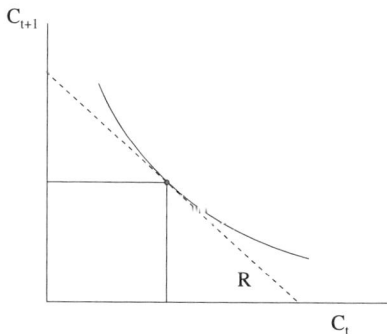

Figure 2.2. *Asset prices adjust to consumption in an endowment economy.*

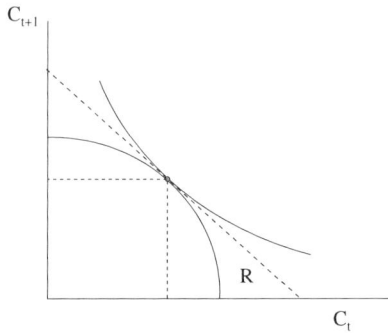

Figure 2.3. *General equilibrium. The solid lines represent the indifference curve and production possibility set. The dashed straight line represents the equilibrium rate of return. The dashed box represents an endowment economy that predicts the same consumption and asset return process.*

economy model? No. Start at the equilibrium in Figure 2.3. Suppose we model this economy as a linear technology, but we happen to choose for the rate of return on the linear technologies exactly the same stochastic process for returns that emerges from the general equilibrium. The resulting joint consumption-asset return process is exactly the same as in the original general equilibrium! Similarly, suppose we model this economy as an endowment economy, but we happen to choose for the endowment process exactly the stochastic process for consumption that emerges from the equilibrium with a concave technology. Again, the joint consumption-asset return process is exactly the same.

Therefore, there is nothing wrong in adopting one of the following strategies for empirical work:

1. Form a statistical model of bond and stock returns, solve the optimal consumption-portfolio decision. Use the equilibrium consumption values in $p = E(mx)$.
2. Form a statistical model of the consumption process, calculate asset prices and returns directly from the basic pricing equation $p = E(mx)$.
3. Form a completely correct general equilibrium model, including the production technology, utility function, and specification of the market structure. Derive the equilibrium consumption and asset price process, including $p = E(mx)$ as one of the equilibrium conditions.

If the statistical models for consumption and/or asset returns are right, i.e., if they coincide with the equilibrium consumption or return process generated by the true economy, either of the first two approaches will give correct predictions for the joint consumption-asset return process.

Most finance models, developed from the 1950s through the early 1970s, take the return process as given, implicitly assuming linear technologies. The endowment economy approach, introduced by Lucas (1978), is a breakthrough because it turns out to be much easier. It is much easier to evaluate $p = E(mx)$ for fixed m than it is to solve joint consumption-portfolio problems for given asset returns, all to derive the equilibrium consumption process. To solve a consumption-portfolio problem we have to model the investor's entire environment: we have to specify *all* the assets to which he has access, what his labor income process looks like (or wage rate process, and include a labor supply decision). Once we model the consumption stream directly, we can look at each asset in isolation, and the actual computation is almost trivial. This breakthrough accounts for the unusual structure of the presentation in this book. It is traditional to start with an extensive study of consumption-portfolio problems. But by modeling consumption directly, we have been able to study pricing directly, and portfolio problems are an interesting side trip which we can defer.

Most uses of $p = E(mx)$ do not require us to take any stand on exogeneity or endogeneity, or general equilibrium. This is a condition that must hold for any asset, for any production technology. Having a taste of the extra assumptions required for a general equilibrium model, you can now appreciate why people stop short of full solutions when they can address an application using only the first-order conditions, using knowledge of $E(mx)$ to make a prediction about p.

It is enormously tempting to slide into an interpretation that $E(mx)$ *determines* p. We routinely think of betas and factor risk prices—components of $E(mx)$—as *determining* expected returns. For example, we routinely say things like "the expected return of a stock increased *because* the firm took on riskier projects, thereby increasing its beta." But the whole consumption process, discount factor, and factor risk premia change when the production technology changes. Similarly, we are on thin ice if we say anything about the effects of policy interventions, new markets and so on. The equilibrium consumption or asset return process one has modeled statistically may change in response to such changes in structure. For such questions one really needs to start thinking in general equilibrium terms. It may help to remember that there is an army of permanent-income macroeconomists who make precisely the opposite assumption, taking our asset return processes as exogenous and studying (endogenous) consumption and savings decisions.

2.3 Consumption-Based Model in Practice

> The consumption-based model is, in principle, a complete answer to all asset pricing questions, but works poorly in practice. This observation motivates other asset pricing models.

The model I have sketched so far can, in principle, give a compete answer to all the questions of the theory of valuation. It can be applied to *any* security—bonds, stocks, options, futures, etc.—or to any uncertain cash flow. All we need is a functional form for utility, numerical values for the parameters, and a statistical model for the conditional distribution of consumption and payoffs.

To be specific, consider the standard power utility function

$$u'(c) = c^{-\gamma}. \tag{2.1}$$

Then, excess returns should obey

$$0 = E_t \left[\beta \left(\frac{c_{t+1}}{c_t} \right)^{-\gamma} R^e_{t+1} \right]. \tag{2.2}$$

Taking unconditional expectations and applying the covariance decomposition, expected excess returns should follow

$$E(R^e_{t+1}) = -R^f \operatorname{cov} \left[\left(\frac{c_{t+1}}{c_t} \right)^{-\gamma}, R^e_{t+1} \right]. \tag{2.3}$$

Given a value for γ, and data on consumption and returns, you can easily estimate the mean and covariance on the right-hand side, and check whether actual expected returns are, in fact, in accordance with the formula.

Similarly, the present-value formula is

$$p_t = E_t \sum_{j=1}^{\infty} \beta^j \left(\frac{c_{t+j}}{c_t} \right)^{-\gamma} d_{t+j}. \tag{2.4}$$

Given data on consumption and dividends or another stream of payoffs, you can estimate the right-hand side and check it against prices on the left.

Bonds and options do not require separate valuation theories. For example, an N-period default-free nominal discount bond (a U.S. Treasury strip) is a claim to one dollar at time $t + N$. Its price should be

$$p_t = E_t \left(\beta^N \left(\frac{c_{t+N}}{c_t} \right)^{-\gamma} \frac{\Pi_t}{\Pi_{t+N}} 1 \right),$$

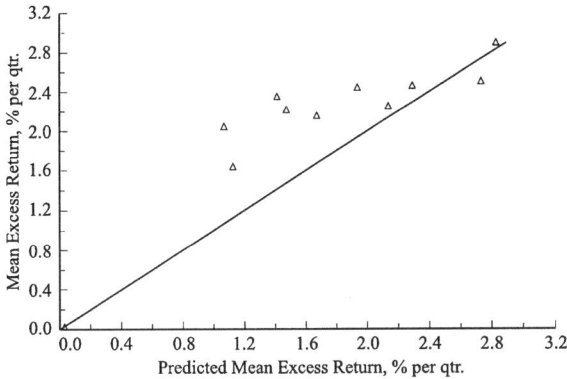

Figure 2.4. *Mean excess returns of 10 CRSP size portfolios versus predictions of the power utility consumption-based model. The predictions are generated by $-R^f \operatorname{cov}(m, R^i)$ with $m = \beta(c_{t+1}/c_t)^{-\gamma}$. $\beta = 0.98$ and $\gamma = 241$ are picked by first-stage GMM to minimize the sum of squared pricing errors (deviation from 45° line). Source: Cochrane (1996).*

where Π = price level ($/good). A European option is a claim to the payoff $\max(S_{t+T} - K, 0)$, where S_{t+T} = stock price at time $t + T$, K = strike price. The option price should be

$$p_t = E_t \left[\beta^T \left(\frac{c_{t+T}}{c_t} \right)^{-\gamma} \max(S_{t+T} - K, 0) \right].$$

Again, we can use data on consumption, prices, and payoffs to check these predictions.

Unfortunately, this specification of the consumption-based model does not work very well. To give a flavor of some of the problems, Figure 2.4 presents the mean excess returns on the ten size-ranked portfolios of NYSE stocks versus the predictions—the right-hand side of (2.3)—of the consumption-based model. I picked the utility curvature parameter $\gamma = 241$ to make the picture look as good as possible. (The section on GMM estimation below goes into detail on how to do this. The figure presents the first-stage GMM estimate.) As you can see, the model is not hopeless—there is some correlation between sample average returns and the consumption-based model predictions. But the model does not do very well. The pricing error (actual expected return − predicted expected return) for each portfolio is of the same order of magnitude as the spread in expected returns across the portfolios.

2.4 Alternative Asset Pricing Models: Overview

> I motivate exploration of different utility functions, general equilibrium models, and linear factor models such as the CAPM, APT, and ICAPM as ways to circumvent the empirical difficulties of the consumption-based model.

The poor empirical performance of the consumption-based model motivates a search for alternative asset pricing models—alternative functions $m = f(\text{data})$. *All* asset pricing models amount to different functions for m. I give here a bare sketch of some of the different approaches; we study each in detail in later chapters.

1) *Different utility functions.* Perhaps the problem with the consumption-based model is simply the functional form we chose for utility. The natural response is to try different utility functions. Which variables determine marginal utility is a far more important question than the functional form. Perhaps the stock of durable goods influences the marginal utility of nondurable goods; perhaps leisure or yesterday's consumption affect today's marginal utility. These possibilities are all instances of *nonseparabilities.* One can also try to use micro data on individual consumption of stockholders rather than aggregate consumption. Aggregation of heterogeneous investors can make variables such as the cross-sectional variance of income appear in aggregate marginal utility.

2) *General equilibrium models.* Perhaps the problem is simply with the consumption *data.* General equilibrium models deliver equilibrium decision rules linking consumption to other variables, such as income, investment, etc. Substituting the decision rules $c_t = f(y_t, i_t, \dots)$ in the consumption-based model, we can link asset prices to other, hopefully better-measured macroeconomic aggregates.

   In addition, true general equilibrium models completely describe the economy, including the stochastic process followed by all variables. They can answer questions such as *why* is the covariance (beta) of an asset payoff x with the discount factor m the value that it is, rather than take this covariance as a primitive. They can in principle answer structural questions, such as how asset prices might be affected by different government policies or the introduction of new securities. Neither kind of question can be answered by just manipulating investor first-order conditions.

3) *Factor pricing models.* Another sensible response to bad consumption data is to model marginal utility in terms of other variables directly. *Factor pricing* models follow this approach. They just specify that the

discount factor is a linear function of a set of proxies,

$$m_{t+1} = a + b_A f_{t+1}^A + b_B f_{t+1}^B + \cdots , \qquad (2.5)$$

where f^i are *factors* and a, b_i are parameters. (This is a different sense of the use of the word "factor" than "discount factor" or "factor analysis." I did not invent the confusing terminology.) By and large, the factors are just selected as plausible proxies for marginal utility: events that describe whether typical investors are happy or unhappy. Among others, the Capital Asset Pricing Model (CAPM) is the model

$$m_{t+1} = a + b R_{t+1}^W ,$$

where R^W is the rate of return on a claim to total wealth, often proxied by a broad-based portfolio such as the value-weighted NYSE portfolio. The Arbitrage Pricing Theory (APT) uses returns on broad-based portfolios derived from a factor analysis of the return covariance matrix. The Intertemporal Capital Asset Pricing Model (ICAPM) suggests macroeconomic variables such as GNP and inflation and variables that forecast macroeconomic variables or asset returns as factors. Term structure models such as the Cox–Ingersoll–Ross model specify that the discount factor is a function of a few term structure variables, for example the short rate of interest and a few interest rate spreads.

Many factor pricing models are derived as general equilibrium models with linear technologies and no labor income; thus they also fall into the general idea of using general equilibrium relations (from, admittedly, very stylized general equilibrium models) to substitute out for consumption.

4) *Arbitrage or near-arbitrage pricing.* The mere existence of a representation $p = E(mx)$ and the fact that marginal utility is positive $m \geq 0$ (these facts are discussed in the next chapter) can often be used to deduce prices of one payoff in terms of the prices of other payoffs. The Black–Scholes option pricing model is the paradigm of this approach: Since the option payoff can be replicated by a portfolio of stock and bond, any discount factor m that prices the stock and bond gives the price for the option. Recently, there have been several suggestions on how to use this idea in more general circumstances by using very weak further restrictions on m, and we will study these suggestions in Chapter 17.

We return to a more detailed derivation and discussion of these alternative models of the discount factor m below. First, and with this brief overview in mind, we look at $p = E(mx)$ and what the discount factor m represents in a little more detail.

Problems—Chapter 2

1. The representative consumer maximizes a CRRA utility function,

$$E_t \sum \beta^j c_{t+j}^{1-\gamma}.$$

Consumption is given by an endowment stream.

(a) Show that with log utility, the price/consumption ratio of the consumption stream is constant, no matter what the distribution of consumption growth.

(b) Suppose there is news at time t that future consumption will be higher. For $\gamma < 1$, $\gamma = 1$, and $\gamma > 1$, evaluate the effect of this news on the price. Make sense of your results. (There is a real-world interpretation here. It is often regarded as a puzzle that the market declines on good economic news. This is attributed to an expectation by the market that the Fed will respond to such news by raising interest rates. Note that $\gamma > 0$ in this problem gives a completely real and frictionless interpretation to this phenomenon! I thank Pete Hecht for this nice problem.)

2. The linear quadratic permanent income model is a very useful general equilibrium model that we can solve in closed form. It specifies a production technology rather than fixed endowments, and it easily allows aggregation of disparate consumers. (Hansen [1987] is a wonderful exposition of what one can do with this setup.)

The consumer maximizes

$$E \sum_{t=0}^{\infty} \beta^t \left(-\frac{1}{2}\right)(c_t - c^*)^2$$

subject to a linear technology

$$k_{t+1} = (1+r)k_t + i_t,$$

$$i_t = e_t - c_t.$$

e_t is an exogenous endowment or labor income stream. Assume $\beta = 1/(1+r)$; the discount rate equals the interest rate or marginal productivity of capital.

(a) Show that optimal consumption follows

$$c_t = rk_t + r\beta \sum_{j=0}^{\infty} \beta^j E_t e_{t+j}, \tag{2.6}$$

$$c_t = c_{t-1} + (E_t - E_{t-1})r\beta \sum_{j-0}^{\infty} \beta^j e_{t+j}, \tag{2.7}$$

i.e., consumption equals permanent income, precisely defined, and consumption follows a random walk whose innovations are equal to innovations in permanent income.

(b) Assume that the endowment e_t follows an AR(1)

$$e_t = \rho e_{t-1} + \varepsilon_t$$

and specialize (2.6) and (2.7). Calculate and interpret the result for $\rho = 1$ and $\rho = 0$. (The result looks like a "consumption function" relating consumption to capital and current income, except that the slope of that function depends on the persistence of income shocks. Transitory shocks will have little effect on consumption, and permanent shocks a larger effect.)

(c) Calculate the one-period interest rate (it should come out to r, of course) and the price of a claim to the consumption stream. e and k are the only state variables, so the price should be a function of e and k. Interpret the time variation in the price of the consumption stream. (This consumer gets more risk averse as consumption rises to c^*. c^* is the bliss point, so at the bliss point there is no average return that can compensate the consumer for greater risk.)

3. Consider again CRRA utility,

$$E_t \sum \beta^j c_{t+j}^{1-\gamma}.$$

Consumption growth follows a two-state Markov process. The states are $\Delta c_t = c_t/c_{t-1} = h, l$, and a 2×2 matrix π governs the set of transition probabilities, i.e., $pr(\Delta c_{t+1} = h | \Delta c_t = l) = \pi_{l \to h}$. (This is the Mehra–Prescott [1986] model, but it will be faster to do it than to look it up. It is a useful and simple endowment economy.)

(a) Find the risk-free rate (price of a certain real payoff of 1) in this economy. This price is generated by

$$p_t^b = E_t(m_{t, t+1}1).$$

You are looking for two values, the price in the l state and the price in the h state.

(b) Find the price of the consumption stream (the price at t of $\{c_{t+1}, c_{t+2}, \dots\}$). To do this, guess that the price/consumption ratio must be a function of state (h, l), and find that function. From

$$p_t^c = E_t(m_{t, t+1}(p_{t+1}^c + c_{t+1}))$$

find a recursive relation for p_t^c/c_t, and hence find the two values of p_t^c/c_t, one for the h state and one for the l state.

(c) Pick $\beta = 0.99$ and try $\gamma = 0.5, 5$. (Try more values if you feel like it.) Calibrate the consumption process to have a 1% mean and 1% standard deviation, and consumption growth uncorrelated over time. Calculate prices and returns in each state.

(d) Now introduce serial correlation in consumption growth with $\gamma = 5$. (You can do this by adding weight to the diagonal entries of the transition matrix π.) What effect does this change have on the model?

3

Contingent Claims Markets

Our first task is to understand the $p = E(mx)$ representation a little more deeply. In this chapter I introduce a very simple market structure, contingent claims. This leads us to an inner product interpretation of $p = E(mx)$ which allows an intuitive visual representation of most of the theorems. We see that discount factors exist, are positive, and the pricing function is linear, just starting from prices and payoffs in a complete market. We don't read any utility functions. The next chapter shows that these properties can be built up in incomplete markets as well.

3.1 Contingent Claims

I describe contingent claims. I interpret the stochastic discount factor m as contingent claims prices divided by probabilities, and $p = E(mx)$ as a bundling of contingent claims.

Suppose that one of S possible *states of nature* can occur tomorrow, i.e., specialize to a finite-dimensional state space. Denote the individual states by s. For example, we might have $S = 2$ and $s = $ rain or $s = $ shine.

A *contingent claim* is a security that pays one dollar (or one unit of the consumption good) in one state s only tomorrow. $pc(s)$ is the price today of the contingent claim. I write pc to specify that it is the price of a contingent claim and (s) to denote in which state s the claim pays off.

In a *complete market* investors can buy any contingent claim. They do not necessarily have to trade explicit contingent claims; they just need enough other securities to *span* or *synthesize* all contingent claims. For example, if the possible states of nature are (rain, shine), one can span or synthesize any contingent claim, or any portfolio that can be achieved by combining contingent claims, by forming portfolios of a security that pays 2 dollars if it rains and one if it shines, or $x_1 = (2, 1)$, and a risk-free security whose payoff pattern is $x_2 = (1, 1)$.

Now, we are on a hunt for discount factors, and the central point is:

If there are complete contingent claims, a discount factor exists, and it is equal to the contingent claim price divided by probabilities.

Let $x(s)$ denote an asset's payoff in state of nature s. We can think of the asset as a bundle of contingent claims—$x(1)$ contingent claims to state 1, $x(2)$ claims to state 2, etc. The asset's price must then equal the value of the contingent claims of which it is a bundle,

$$p(x) = \sum_s pc(s)x(s). \tag{3.1}$$

I denote the price $p(x)$ to emphasize that it is the price of the payoff x. Where the payoff in question is clear, I suppress the (x). I like to think of equation (3.1) as a happy-meal theorem: the price of a happy meal (in a frictionless market) should be the same as the price of one hamburger, one small fries, one small drink, and the toy.

It is easier to take expectations rather than sum over states. To this end, multiply and divide the bundling equation (3.1) by probabilities,

$$p(x) = \sum_s \pi(s) \left(\frac{pc(s)}{\pi(s)} \right) x(s),$$

where $\pi(s)$ is the probability that state s occurs. Then define m as the ratio of contingent claim price to probability,

$$m(s) = \frac{pc(s)}{\pi(s)}.$$

Now we can write the bundling equation as an expectation,

$$p = \sum_s \pi(s)m(s)x(s) = E(mx).$$

Thus, in a complete market, the stochastic discount factor m in $p = E(mx)$ exists, and it is just a set of contingent claims prices, scaled by probabilities. As a result of this interpretation, the combination of discount factor and probability is sometimes called a *state-price density*.

The multiplication and division by probabilities seems very artificial in this finite-state context. In general, we posit states of nature ω that can take continuous (uncountably infinite) values in a space Ω. In this case, the sums become integrals, and we have to use *some* measure to integrate over Ω. Thus, scaling contingent claims prices by some probability-like object is unavoidable.

3.2 Risk-Neutral Probabilities

> I interpret the discount factor m as a transformation to risk-neutral probabilities such that $p = E^*(x)/R^f$.

Another common transformation of $p = E(mx)$ results in "risk-neutral" probabilities. Define

$$\pi^*(s) \equiv R^f m(s)\pi(s) = R^f pc(s),$$

where

$$R^f \equiv 1/\sum pc(s) = 1/E(m).$$

The $\pi^*(s)$ are positive, less than or equal to one and sum to one, so they are a legitimate set of probabilities. Now we can rewrite the asset pricing formula as

$$p(x) = \sum_s pc(s)x(s) = \frac{1}{R^f}\sum \pi^*(s)x(s) = \frac{E^*(x)}{R^f}.$$

I use the notation E^* to remind us that the expectation uses the *risk-neutral probabilities* π^* instead of the real probabilities π.

Thus, we can think of asset pricing as if agents are all risk neutral, but with probabilities π^* in the place of the true probabilities π. The probabilities π^* give greater weight to states with higher than average marginal utility m.

There is something very deep in this idea: risk aversion is equivalent to paying more attention to unpleasant states, relative to their actual probability of occurrence. People who report high subjective probabilities of unpleasant events like plane crashes may not have irrational expectations; they may simply be reporting the risk-neutral probabilities or the product $m \times \pi$. This product is after all the most important piece of information for many decisions: pay a lot of attention to contingencies that are either highly probable or that are improbable but have disastrous consequences.

The transformation from actual to risk-neutral probabilities is given by

$$\pi^*(s) = \frac{m(s)}{E(m)}\pi(s)$$

We can also think of the discount factor m as the *derivative* or *change of measure* from the real probabilities π to the subjective probabilities π^*. The risk-neutral probability representation of asset pricing is quite common, especially in derivative pricing where the results are often independent of risk adjustments.

The risk-neutral representation is particularly popular in continuous-time diffusion processes, because we can adjust only the means, leaving the covariances alone. In discrete time, changing the probabilities typically changes both first and second moments. Suppose we start with a process for prices and discount factor

$$\frac{dp}{p} = \mu^p \, dt + \sigma^p \, dz,$$

$$\frac{d\Lambda}{\Lambda} = \mu^\Lambda \, dt + \sigma^\Lambda \, dz.$$

The discount factor prices the assets,

$$E_t\left(\frac{dp}{p}\right) + \frac{D}{p} \, dt - r^f \, dt = -E_t\left(\frac{d\Lambda}{\Lambda}\frac{dp}{p}\right) = -\sigma^p \sigma^\Lambda \, dt.$$

In the "risk-neutral measure" we just increase the drift of each price process by its covariance with the discount factor, and write a risk-neutral discount factor,

$$\frac{dp}{p} = (\mu^p + \sigma^p \sigma^\Lambda)dt + \sigma^p \, dz = \mu^{p*} \, dt + \sigma^p \, dz,$$

$$\frac{d\Lambda}{\Lambda} = \mu^\Lambda \, dt.$$

Under this new set of probabilities, we can just write

$$E_t^*\left(\frac{dp}{p}\right) + \frac{D}{p} \, dt - r^f \, dt = 0$$

with $E_t^*(dp/p) = \mu^{p*} \, dt$.

3.3 Investors Again

> We look at an investor's first-order conditions in a contingent claims market. The marginal rate of substitution equals the discount factor and the contingent claim price ratio.

Though the focus of this chapter is on how to do without utility functions, it is worth looking at the investor's first-order conditions again in the contingent claim context. The investor starts with a pile of initial wealth y

and a state-contingent income $y(s)$. He may purchase contingent claims to each possible state in the second period. His problem is then

$$\max_{\{c,\, c(s)\}} u(c) + \sum_s \beta\pi(s)u[c(s)] \text{ s.t. } c + \sum_s pc(s)c(s) = y + \sum_s pc(s)y(s).$$

Introducing a Lagrange multiplier λ on the budget constraint, the first-order conditions are

$$u'(c) = \lambda,$$

$$\beta\pi(s)u'[c(s)] = \lambda pc(s).$$

Eliminating the Lagrange multiplier λ,

$$pc(s) = \beta\pi(s)\frac{u'[c(s)]}{u'(c)}$$

or

$$m(s) = \frac{pc(s)}{\pi(s)} = \beta\frac{u'[c(s)]}{u'(c)}.$$

Coupled with $p = E(mx)$, we obtain the consumption-based model again.

The investor's first-order conditions say that the marginal rate of substitution between *states* tomorrow equals the relevant price ratio,

$$\frac{m(s_1)}{m(s_2)} = \frac{u'[c(s_1)]}{u'[c(s_2)]}.$$

$m(s_1)/m(s_2)$ gives the rate at which the investor can give up consumption in state 2 in return for consumption in state 1 through purchase and sales of contingent claims. $u'[c(s_1)]/u'[c(s_2)]$ gives the rate at which the investor is willing to make this substitution. At an optimum, the marginal rate of substitution should equal the price ratio, as usual in economics.

We learn that the discount factor m is the marginal rate of substitution between date- *and* state-contingent commodities. That is why it, like $c(s)$, is a random variable. Also, scaling contingent claims prices by probabilities gives marginal utility, and so is not so artificial as it may have seemed above.

Figure 3.1 gives the economics behind this approach to asset pricing. We observe the investor's choice of date or state contingent consumption. Once we know his utility function, we can calculate the contingent claim prices that must have led to the observed consumption choice, from the derivatives of the utility function.

The relevant probabilities are the investors' *subjective* probabilities over the various states. Asset prices are set, after all, by investors' demands for assets, and those demands are set by investors' subjective evaluations of

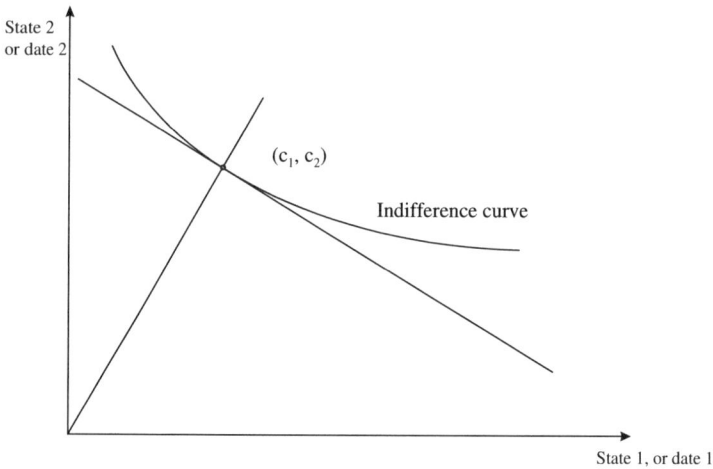

Figure 3.1. *Indifference curve and contingent claim prices.*

the probabilities of various events. We often assume *rational expectations,* namely that subjective probabilities are equal to objective frequencies. But this is an additional assumption that we may not always want to make.

3.4 Risk Sharing

Risk sharing: In complete markets, individuals' consumption moves together. Only aggregate risk matters for security markets.

We deduced that the marginal rate of substitution for any individual investor equals the contingent claim price ratio. But the prices are the same for all investors. Therefore, *marginal utility growth should be the same for all investors,*

$$\beta^i \frac{u'(c_{t+1}^i)}{u'(c_t^i)} = \beta^j \frac{u'(c_{t+1}^j)}{u'(c_t^j)},   \tag{3.2}$$

where i and j refer to different investors. If investors have the same homothetic utility function (for example, power utility), then consumption itself moves in lockstep,

$$\frac{c_{t+1}^i}{c_t^i} = \frac{c_{t+1}^j}{c_t^j}.$$

More generally, shocks to consumption are perfectly correlated across individuals.

This prediction is so radical, it is easy to misread it at first glance. It does not say that *expected* consumption growth is equal; it says that *ex post* consumption growth is equal. If my consumption goes up 10%, yours goes up exactly 10% as well, and so does everyone else's. In a complete contingent claims market, all investors share all risks, so when any shock hits, it hits us all equally (after insurance payments). It does not say the consumption *level* is the same—this is risk sharing, not socialism. The rich have higher levels of consumption, but rich and poor share the *shocks* equally.

This risk sharing is *Pareto optimal.* Suppose a social planner wished to maximize everyone's utility given the available resources. For example, with two investors i and j, he would maximize

$$\max \lambda_i E \sum_t \beta^t u(c_t^i) + \lambda_j E \sum_t \beta^t u(c_t^j) \text{ s.t. } c_t^i + c_t^j = c_t^a,$$

where c^a is the total amount available and λ_i and λ_j are i and j's relative weights in the planner's objective. The first-order condition to this problem is

$$\lambda_i u'(c_t^i) = \lambda_j u'(c_t^j)$$

and hence the same risk sharing that we see in a complete market, equation (3.2).

This simple fact has profound implications. First, it shows you why *only aggregate shocks should matter for risk prices.* Any idiosyncratic income risk will be equally shared, and so $1/N$ of it becomes an aggregate shock. Then the stochastic discount factors m that determine asset prices are no longer affected by truly idiosyncratic risks. Much of this sense that only aggregate shocks matter stays with us in incomplete markets as well.

Obviously, the real economy does not yet have complete markets or full risk sharing—individual consumptions do not move in lockstep. However, this observation tells us much about the function of securities markets. Security markets—state-contingent claims—bring individual consumptions closer together by allowing people to share some risks. In addition, better risk sharing is much of the force behind financial innovation. Many successful new securities can be understood as devices to share risks more widely.

3.5 State Diagram and Price Function

I introduce the state-space diagram and inner product representation
for prices, $p(x) = E(mx) = m \cdot x$.

$p(x) = E(mx)$ implies that $p(x)$ is a linear function.

Think of the contingent claims price pc and asset payoffs x as vectors
in $\mathcal{R}^S$, where each element gives the price or payoff to the corresponding
state,

$$pc = [\, pc(1)\ pc(2)\ \cdots\ pc(S)\,]',$$

$$x = [\, x(1)\ x(2)\ \cdots\ x(S)\,]'.$$

Figure 3.2 is a graph of these vectors in $\mathcal{R}^S$. Next, I deduce the geometry
of Figure 3.2.

The contingent claims price vector pc points in to the positive orthant.
We saw in Section 3.3 that $m(s) = u'[c(s)]/u'(c)$. Now, marginal utility should always be positive (people always want more), so the marginal
rate of substitution and discount factor are always nonnegative, $m > 0$
and $pc > 0$. Do not forget, m and pc are vectors, or random variables.

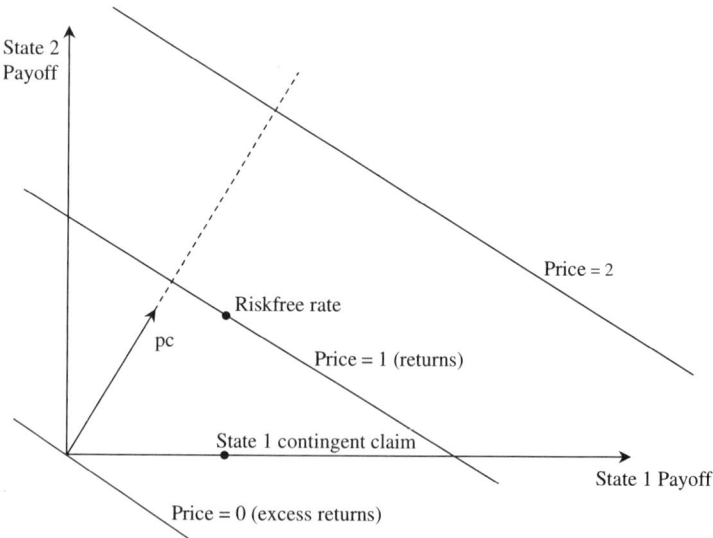

Figure 3.2. *Contingent claims prices (pc) and payoffs.*

Thus, $m > 0$ means the realization of m is positive in every state of nature, or, equivalently every element of the vector m is positive.

The set of payoffs with any given price lie on a (hyper)plane perpendicular to the contingent claim price vector. We reasoned above that the price of the payoff x must be given by its contingent claim value (3.1),

$$p(x) = \sum_s pc(s)x(s). \tag{3.3}$$

Interpreting pc and x as vectors, this means that the price is given by the *inner product* of the contingent claim price and the payoff.

If two vectors are orthogonal—if they point out from the origin at right angles to each other—then their inner product is zero. Therefore, the set of all zero-price payoffs must lie on a plane orthogonal to the contingent claims price vector, as shown in Figure 3.2.

More generally, the inner product of two vectors x and pc equals the product of the magnitude of the projection of x onto pc times the magnitude of pc. Using a dot to denote inner product,

$$p(x) = \sum_s pc(s)x(s) = pc \cdot x = |pc| \times |\operatorname{proj}(x|pc)| = |pc| \times |x| \times \cos(\theta),$$

where $|x|$ means the length of the vector x and θ is the angle between the vectors pc and x. Since all payoffs on planes (such as the price planes in Figure 3.2) that are perpendicular to pc have the same projection onto pc, they must have the inner product with pc and hence the same price. (Only the price $= 0$ plane is, strictly speaking, *orthogonal* to pc. Lacking a better term, I have called the nonzero price planes "perpendicular" to pc.) When vectors are finite dimensional, the prime notation is commonly used for inner products, $pc'x$. This notation does not extend well to infinite-dimensional spaces. The notation $\langle pc|x \rangle$ is also often used for inner products.

Planes of constant price move out linearly, and the origin $x = 0$ must have a price of zero. If payoff $y = 2x$, then its price is twice the price of x,

$$p(y) = \sum_s pc(s)y(s) = \sum_s pc(s)2x(s) = 2\,p(x).$$

Similarly, a payoff of zero must have a price of zero.

We can think of $p(x)$ as a pricing *function*, a map from the state space or payoff space in which x lies ($\mathcal{R}^3$ in this case) to the real line. We have just deduced from the definition (3.3) that $p(x)$ is a *linear function*, i.e., that

$$p(ax + by) = ap(x) + bp(y).$$

The constant price lines in Figure 3.2 are of course exactly what one expects from a linear function from $\mathcal{R}^S$ to $\mathcal{R}$. (One might draw the price on the z axis coming out of the page. Then the price function would be a plane going through the origin and sloping up with iso-price lines as given in Figure 3.2.)

Figure 3.2 also includes the payoffs to a contingent claim to the first state. This payoff is one in the first state and zero in other states and thus located on the axis. The plane of price = 1 payoffs is the plane of asset *returns*; the plane of price = 0 payoffs is the plane of *excess returns*. A risk free unit payoff (the payoff to a risk-free pure discount bond) lies on the $(1, 1)$ point in Figure 3.2; the risk-free return lies on the intersection of the 45° line (same payoff in both states) and the price = 1 plane (the set of all returns).

Geometry with m in Place of pc
The geometric interpretation of Figure 3.2 goes through with the discount factor m in the place of pc. We can define an inner product between the random variables x and y by

$$x \cdot y \equiv E(xy),$$

and retain all the mathematical properties of an inner product. For this reason, random variables for which $E(xy) = 0$ are often called "orthogonal."

This language may be familiar from linear regressions. When we run a regression of y on x,

$$y = b'x + \varepsilon,$$

we find the linear combination of x that is "closest" to y, by minimizing the variance or "size" of the residual ε. We do this by forcing the residual to be "orthogonal" to the right-hand variable $E(x\varepsilon) = 0$. The projection of y on x is defined as the fitted value, $\text{proj}(y|x) = b'x = E(xx')^{-1}E(yx')x$. This idea is often illustrated by a residual vector ε that is perpendicular to a plane defined by the right-hand variables x. Thus, when the inner product is defined by a second moment, the operation "project y onto x" is a *regression*. (If x does not include a constant, you do not add one in this regression.)

The geometric interpretation of Figure 3.2 also is valid if we generalize the setup to an infinite-dimensional state space, i.e., if we think of continuously valued random variables. Instead of vectors, which are functions from $\mathcal{R}^S$ to $\mathcal{R}$, random variables are (measurable) functions from Ω to $\mathcal{R}$. Nonetheless, we can still think of them as vectors. The equivalent of $\mathcal{R}^S$ is now a *Hilbert space* L^2, which denotes spaces generated by linear combinations of square integrable *functions* from Ω to the real line, or the space of random variables with finite second moments. We can still define an "inner product" between two such elements by $x \cdot y = E(xy)$, and $p(x) = E(mx)$ can still be interpreted as "m is perpendicular to (hyper)planes of constant price." *Proving* theorems in this context is a bit harder. You cannot just say things like "we can take a line perpendicular to any plane"; such things have to be proved. Sometimes, finite-dimensional thinking can lead you to errors, so it is important to prove things the right way, keeping the finite-dimensional pictures in mind for interpretation. Hansen and Richard (1987) is a very good reference for the Hilbert space machinery.

4

The Discount Factor

Now WE LOOK more closely at the discount factor. Rather than derive a specific discount factor as with the consumption-based model in the first chapter, I work backwards. A discount factor is just some random variable that generates prices from payoffs, $p = E(mx)$. What does this expression mean? Can one always find such a discount factor? Can we use this convenient representation without implicitly assuming all the structure of the investors, utility functions, complete markets, and so forth?

The chapter focuses on two famous theorems. The *law of one price* states that if two portfolios have the same payoffs (in every state of nature), then they must have the same price. A violation of this law would give rise to an immediate kind of arbitrage profit, as you could sell the expensive version and buy the cheap version of the same portfolio. The first theorem states that there is a discount factor that prices all the payoffs by $p = E(mx)$ if and only if this law of one price holds.

In finance, we reserve the term *absence of arbitrage* for a stronger idea, that if payoff A is always at least as good as payoff B, and sometimes A is better, then the price of A must be greater than the price of B. The second theorem is that there is a *positive* discount factor that prices all the payoffs by $p = E(mx)$ if and only if there are no arbitrage opportunities, so defined.

These theorems are useful to show that we can use stochastic discount factors without implicitly assuming anything about utility functions, aggregation, complete markets, and so on. All we need to know about investors in order to represent prices and payoffs via a discount factor is that they will not leave law of one price violations or arbitrage opportunities on the table. These theorems can be used to describe aspects of a *payoff space* (such as law of one price, absence of arbitrage) by restrictions on the *discount factor* (such as it exists and it is positive). Chapter 18 shows how it can be more convenient to impose and check restrictions on a single discount factor than it is to check the corresponding restrictions on all possible portfolios. Chapter 7 discusses these and other implications of the existence theorems.

The theorems are credited to Ross (1978), Rubinstein (1976) and Harrison and Kreps (1979). My presentation is a simplified version of Hansen and Richard (1987) which contains rigorous proofs and some important technical assumptions.

4.1 Law of One Price and Existence of a Discount Factor

> The definition of the law of one price; price is a linear function.
> $p = E(mx)$ implies the law of one price.
> The law of one price implies that a discount factor exists: There exists a unique x^* in $\underline{X}$ such that $p = E(x^*x)$ for all $x \in \underline{X}$ = space of all available payoffs. Furthermore, for any valid discount factor m,
>
> $$x^* = \text{proj}(m \mid \underline{X}).$$

So far we have derived the basic pricing relation $p = E(mx)$ from environments with a lot of structure: either the consumption-based model or complete markets.

Suppose we observe a set of prices p and payoffs x, and that markets—either the markets faced by investors or the markets under study in a particular application—are *incomplete*, meaning they do not span the entire set of contingencies. In what minimal set of circumstances does some discount factor exist which represents the observed prices by $p = E(mx)$? This section and the following answer this important question.

Payoff Space
The *payoff space* $\underline{X}$ is the set of all the payoffs that investors can purchase, or it is a subset of the tradeable payoffs that is used in a particular study. For example, if there are complete contingent claims to S states of nature, then $\underline{X} = \mathcal{R}^S$. But the whole point is that markets are (as in real life) *incomplete*, so we will generally think of $\underline{X}$ as a proper subset of complete markets $\mathcal{R}^S$.

The payoff space includes some set of primitive assets, but investors can also form new payoffs by forming portfolios of the primitive assets. I assume that investors can form any portfolio of traded assets:

(A1) *(Portfolio formation)* $x_1, x_2 \in \underline{X} \Rightarrow ax_1 + bx_2 \in \underline{X}$ *for any real a, b.*

Of course, $\underline{X} = \mathcal{R}^S$ for complete markets satisfies the portfolio formation assumption. If there is a single underlying, or basis payoff x, then the payoff space must be at least the ray from the origin through x. If there are two basis payoffs in $\mathcal{R}^3$, then the payoff space $\underline{X}$ must include the plane defined by these two payoffs and the origin. Figure 4.1 illustrates these possibilities.

The payoff space is *not* the space of returns. The return space is a subset of the payoff space; if a return R is in the payoff space, then you can pay a price \$2 to get a payoff $2R$, so the payoff $2R$ with price 2 is also in the payoff space. Also, $-R$ is in the payoff space.

Free portfolio formation is in fact an important and restrictive simplifying assumption. It rules out short sales constraints, bid/ask spreads, leverage limitations, and so on. The theory can be modified to incorporate these frictions, but it is a substantial modification.

If investors can form portfolios of a vector of basic payoffs x (say, the returns on the NYSE stocks), then the payoff space consists of all portfolios or linear combinations of these original payoffs $\underline{X} = \{c'x\}$ where c is a vector of portfolio weights. We also can allow truly infinite-dimensional payoff spaces. For example, investors might be able to trade *nonlinear* functions of a basis payoff x, such as call options on x with strike price K, which have payoff $\max\{x(s) - K, 0\}$.

The Law of One Price

(A2) *(Law of one price, linearity)* $p(ax_1 + bx_2) = ap(x_1) + bp(x_2)$.

It does not matter how one forms the payoff x. The price of a burger, shake, and fries must be the same as the price of a Happy Meal. Graphically, if the iso-price curves were not planes, then one could buy two payoffs on the same iso-price curve, form a portfolio whose payoff is on the straight line connecting the two original payoffs, and sell the portfolio for a higher price than it cost to assemble it.

The law of one price basically says that investors cannot make instantaneous profits by repackaging portfolios. If investors can sell securities, this is a very weak characterization of preferences. It says there is at least one investor for whom marketing does not matter, who values a package by its contents.

The law is meant to describe a market that has already reached equilibrium. If there are any violations of the law of one price, traders will quickly eliminate them so they cannot survive in equilibrium.

A1 and A2 also mean that the 0 payoff must be available, and must have price 0.

The Theorem
The existence of a discount factor implies the law of one price. This is obvious to the point of triviality: if $x = y + z$, then $E(mx) = E[m(y + z)]$. The hard,

and interesting part of the theorem reverses this logic. We show that the *law of one price* implies the *existence of a discount factor.*

Theorem: *Given free portfolio formation A1, and the law of one price A2, there exists a unique payoff $x^* \in \underline{X}$ such that $p(x) = E(x^*x)$ for all $x \in \underline{X}$.*

x^* is a discount factor. A1 and A2 imply that the price *function* on $\underline{X}$ looks like Figure 3.2: parallel hyperplanes marching out from the origin. The only difference is that $\underline{X}$ may be a subspace of the original state space, as shown in Figure 4.1. The essence of the proof, then, is that any linear function on a space $\underline{X}$ can be represented by inner products with a vector that lies in $\underline{X}$.

Proof 1: (Geometric) We have established that the price is a linear function as shown in Figure 4.2. (Figure 4.2 can be interpreted as the

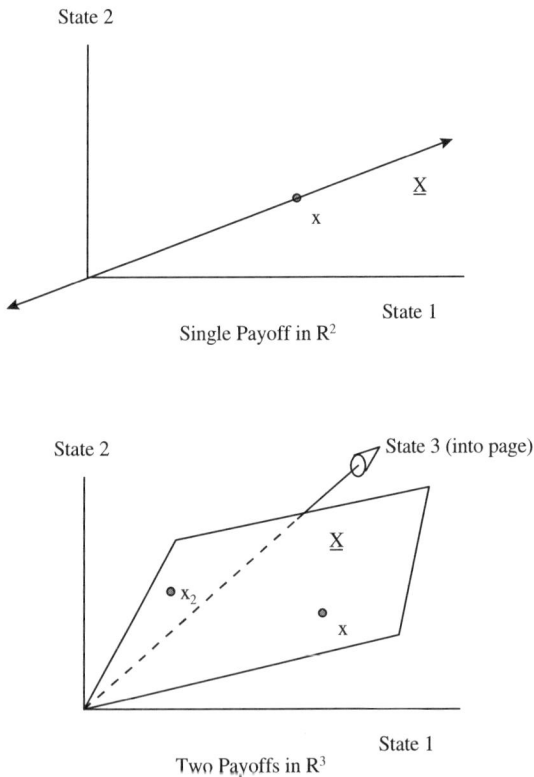

Figure 4.1. *Payoff spaces X generated by one (top) and two (bottom) basis payoffs.*

plane $\underline{X}$ of a larger-dimensional space as in the bottom panel of Figure 4.1, laid flat on the page for clarity). Now we can draw a line from the origin perpendicular to the price planes. Choose a vector x^* on this line. Since the line is orthogonal to the price-zero plane we have $0 = p(x) = E(x^*x)$ for price-zero payoffs x immediately. The inner product between any payoff x on the price $= 1$ plane and x^* is $| \operatorname{proj}(x|x^*)| \times |x^*|$ Thus, every payoff on the price $= 1$ plane has the *same* inner product with x^*. All we have to do is pick x^* to have the right length, and we obtain $p(x) = 1 = E(x^*x)$ for every x on the price $= 1$ plane. Then, of course we have $p(x) = E(x^*x)$ for payoffs x on the other planes as well. Thus, the *linear* pricing function implied by the law of one price can be *represented* by inner products with x^*. □

The basic mathematical point is just that any linear function can be represented by an inner product. The *Riesz representation theorem* extends the proof to infinite-dimensional payoff spaces. See Hansen and Richard (1987).

Proof 2: (Algebraic) We can prove the theorem by construction when the payoff space $\underline{X}$ is generated by portfolios of N basis payoffs (for example, N stocks). This is a common situation, so the formulas are also useful in practice. Organize the basis payoffs into a vector $x = [\, x_1\, x_2\, \cdots\, x_N\,]'$ and similarly their prices p. The payoff space is then $\underline{X} = \{c'x\}$. We want a

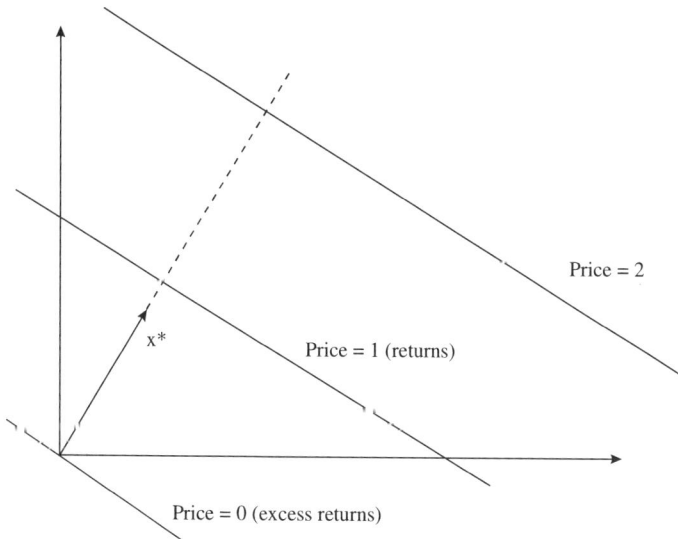

Figure 4.2. *Existence of a discount factor x^*.*

discount factor that is in the payoff space, as the theorem requires. Thus, it must be of the form $x^* = c'x$. Construct c so that x^* prices the basis assets. We want $p = E(x^*x) = E(xx'c)$. Thus we need $c = E(xx')^{-1}p$. If $E(xx')$ is nonsingular, this c exists and is unique. A2 implies that $E(xx')$ is nonsingular (after pruning redundant rows of x). Thus,

$$x^* = p'E(xx')^{-1}x \tag{4.1}$$

is our discount factor. It is a linear combination of x so it is in $\underline{X}$. It prices the basis assets x by construction. It prices every $x \in \underline{X}$: $E[x^*(x'c)] = E[p'E(xx')^{-1}xx'c] = p'c$. By linearity, $p(c'x) = c'p$.   □

What the Theorem Does and Does Not Say
The theorem says there is a unique x^* in $\underline{X}$. There may be many other discount factors m *not* in $\underline{X}$. In fact, unless markets are complete, there are an *infinite* number of random variables that satisfy $p = E(mx)$. If $p = E(mx)$, then $p = E[(m + \varepsilon)x]$ for any ε orthogonal to x, $E(\varepsilon x) = 0$.

Not only does this construction generate some additional discount factors, it generates all of them: *Any discount factor m* (any random variable that satisfies $p = E(mx)$) *can be represented as* $m = x^* + \varepsilon$ with $E(\varepsilon x) = 0$. Figure 4.3 gives an example of a one-dimensional $\underline{X}$ in a two-dimensional state-space, in which case there is a whole line of possible discount factors m. If markets are complete, there is nowhere to go orthogonal to the payoff space $\underline{X}$, so x^* is the only possible discount factor.

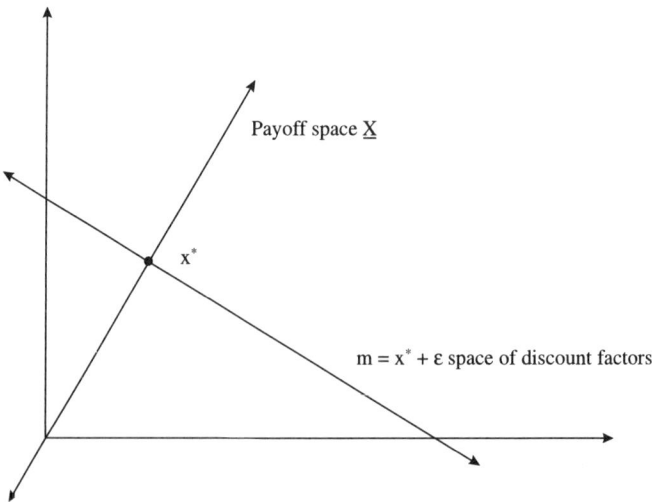

Figure 4.3.   *Many discount factors m can price a given set of assets in incomplete markets.*

Reversing the argument, x^* *is the projection of any stochastic discount factor m on the space $\underline{X}$ of payoffs.* This is a very important fact: *the pricing implications of any discount factor m for a set of payoffs $\underline{X}$ are the same as those of the projection of m on $\underline{X}$.* This discount factor is known as the *mimicking portfolio* for m. Algebraically,

$$p = E(mx) = E[(\text{proj}(m|\underline{X}) + \varepsilon)x] = E[\text{proj}(m|\underline{X})x].$$

Let me repeat and emphasize the logic. Above, we started with investors or a contingent-claim market, and derived a discount factor. $p = E(mx)$ *implies* the linearity of the pricing function and hence the law of one price, a pretty obvious statement in those contexts. Here we work backwards. Markets are *in*complete in that contingent claims to lots of states of nature are not available. We found that the law of one price implies a linear pricing function, and a linear pricing function implies that there exists at least one and usually many discount factors even in an incomplete market.

We *do* allow arbitrary portfolio formation, and that sort of "completeness" is important to the result. If investors cannot form a portfolio $ax + by$, they cannot force the price of this portfolio to equal the price of its constituents. The law of one price is not innocuous; it is an assumption about preferences, albeit a weak one. The point of the theorem is that this is *just* enough information about preferences to deduce the existence of a discount factor.

4.2 No Arbitrage and Positive Discount Factors

> The definition of arbitrage: positive payoff implies positive price.
> There is a *strictly positive* discount factor m such that $p = E(mx)$ if and only if there are *no arbitrage opportunities.*

No arbitrage is another, slightly stronger, *implication* of marginal utility, that can be reversed to show that there is a *positive* discount factor. We need to start with the definition of arbitrage:

Definition (Absence of arbitrage): A payoff space $\underline{X}$ and pricing function $p(x)$ leave no *arbitrage opportunities* if every payoff x that is always non-negative, $x \geq 0$ (almost surely), and positive, $x > 0$, with some positive probability, has positive price, $p(x) > 0$.

No arbitrage says that you cannot get for free a portfolio that *might* pay off positively, but will certainly never cost you anything. This definition is different from the colloquial use of the word "arbitrage." Most people use "arbitrage" to mean a violation of the law of one price—a riskless way of buying something cheap and selling it for a higher price. "Arbitrages" here might pay off, but then again they might not. The word "arbitrage" is also widely abused. "Risk arbitrage" is a Wall Street oxymoron that means making specific kinds of bets.

An equivalent statement is that if one payoff *dominates* another, then its price must be higher—if $x \geq y$, then $p(x) \geq p(y)$. (Or, a bit more carefully but more long-windedly, if $x \geq y$ almost surely and $x > y$ with positive probability, then $p(x) > p(y)$. You cannot forget that x and y are random variables.)

m > 0 Implies No Arbitrage
The absence of arbitrage opportunities is clearly a *consequence* of a positive discount factor, and a positive discount factor naturally results from any sort of utility maximization. Recall,

$$m(s) = \beta \frac{u'[c(s)]}{u'(c)} > 0.$$

It is a sensible characterization of preferences that marginal utility is always positive. Few people are so satiated that they will throw away money. Therefore, *the marginal rate of substitution is positive.* The marginal rate of substitution is a random variable, so "positive" means "positive in every state of nature" or "in every possible realization."

Now, if contingent-claims prices are all positive, a bundle of positive amounts of contingent claims must also have a positive price, even in incomplete markets. A little more formally,

Theorem: $p = E(mx)$ *and* $m(s) > 0$ *imply no arbitrage.*

Proof: We have $m > 0$; $x \geq 0$ and there are some states where $x > 0$. Thus, in some states with positive probability $mx > 0$ and in other states $mx = 0$. Therefore, $E(mx) > 0$.   □

No Arbitrage Implies m > 0
Now we turn the observation around, which is again the hard and interesting part. As the law of one price property guaranteed the existence of a discount factor m, no arbitrage guarantees the existence of a positive m.

The basic idea is pretty simple. No arbitrage means that the prices of any payoff in the positive orthant (except zero, but including the axes) must be strictly positive. The price $= 0$ plane divides the region of positive prices from the region of negative prices. Thus, if the region of negative prices is not to intersect the positive orthant, the iso-price lines must march up and to the right, and the discount factor m must point up and

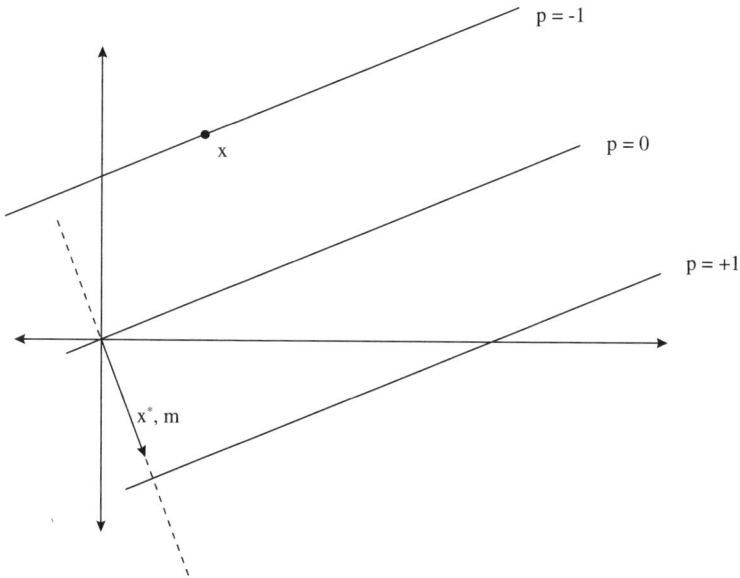

Figure 4.4. *Counterexample for no arbitrage ⇒ m > 0 theorem. The payoff x is positive, but has negative price. The discount factor is not strictly positive.*

to the right. This is how we have graphed it all along, most recently in Figure 4.2. Figure 4.4 illustrates the case that is ruled out: a whole region of negative price payoffs lies in the positive orthant. For example, the payoff x is strictly positive, but has a negative price. As a result, the (unique, since this market is complete) discount factor m is negative in the y-axis state.

The theorem is easy to prove in complete markets. There is only one m, x^*. If it is not positive in some state, then the contingent claim in that state has a positive payoff and a negative price, which violates no arbitrage. More formally,

Theorem: *In complete markets, no arbitrage implies that there exists a unique $m > 0$ such that $p = E(mx)$.*

Proof: No arbitrage implies the law of one price, so there is an x^* such that $p = E(x^*x)$, and in a complete market this is the unique discount factor. Suppose that $x^* \leq 0$ for some states. Then, form a payoff x that is 1 in those states, and zero elsewhere. This payoff is strictly positive, but its price, $\sum_{s:x^*(s)<0} \pi(s)x^*(s)$ is negative, negating the assumption of no arbitrage.   □

The tough part comes if markets are incomplete. There are now many discount factors that price assets. Any m of the form $m = x^* + \varepsilon$, with $E(\varepsilon x) = 0$, will do. We want to show that at least *one* of these is positive. But that one may not be x^*. Since the discount factors other than x^* are not in the payoff space $\underline{X}$, we cannot use the construction of the last argument, since that construction may yield a payoff that is not in $\underline{X}$, and hence to which we do not know how to assign a price. To handle this case, I adopt a different strategy of proof. (This strategy is due to Ross [1978]. Duffie [1992] has a more formal textbook treatment.) The basic idea is another "to every plane there is a perpendicular line" argument, but applied to a space that includes prices and payoffs together. As you can see in Figure 4.4, the price $= 0$ plane is a separating hyperplane between the positive orthant and the negative payoffs, and the proof builds on this idea.

Theorem: *No arbitrage implies the existence of a strictly positive discount factor,* $m > 0$, $p = E(mx) \forall x \in \underline{X}$.

Proof: Join $(-p(x), x)$ together to form vectors in $\mathcal{R}^{S+1}$. Call M the set of all $(-p(x), x)$ pairs,

$$M = \{(-p(x), x); x \in \underline{X}\}.$$

M is still a linear space: $m_1 \in M$, $m_2 \in M \Rightarrow am_1 + bm_2 \in M$. No arbitrage means that elements of M cannot consist entirely of positive elements. If x is positive, $-p(x)$ must be negative. Thus, M is a hyperplane that only intersects the positive orthant $\mathcal{R}_+^{S+1}$ at the point 0. We can then create a linear function $F: \mathcal{R}^{S+1} \Rightarrow \mathcal{R}$ such that $F(-p, x) = 0$ for $(-p, x) \in M$, and $F(-p, x) > 0$ for $(-p, x) \in \mathcal{R}_+^{S+1}$ except the origin. Since we can represent any linear function by a perpendicular vector, there is a vector $(1, m)$ such that $F(-p, x) = (1, m) \cdot (-p, x) = -p + m \cdot x$ or $-p + E(mx)$ using the second moment inner product. Finally, since $F(-p, x)$ is positive for $(-p, x) > 0$, m must be positive. $\square$

In a larger space than $\mathcal{R}_+^{S+1}$, as generated by continuously valued random variables, the *separating hyperplane* theorem assures us that there is a linear function that separates the two convex sets M and the equivalent of $\mathcal{R}_+^{S+1}$, and the *Riesz representation theorem* tells us that we can represent F as an inner product with some vector by $F(-p, x) = -p + m \cdot x$.

What the Theorem Does and Does Not Say
The theorem says that a discount factor $m > 0$ exists, but it does *not* say that $m > 0$ is *unique*. The left-hand panel of Figure 4.5 illustrates the situation. Any m on the line through x^* perpendicular to $\underline{X}$ also prices assets. Again, $p = E[(m + \varepsilon)x]$ if $E(\varepsilon x) = 0$. All of these discount factors that lie

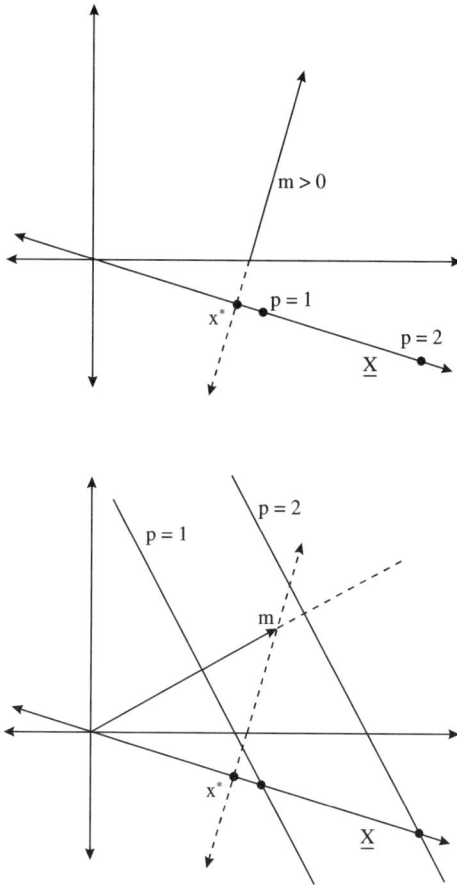

Figure 4.5. *Existence of a discount factor and extensions. The top graph shows that the positive discount factor is not unique, and that discount factors may also exist that are not strictly positive. In particular, x^* need not be positive. The bottom graph shows that each particular choice of $m > 0$ induces an arbitrage-free extension of the prices on $\underline{X}$ to all contingent claims.*

in the positive orthant are positive, and thus satisfy the theorem. There are lots of them! In a complete market, m is unique, but not otherwise.

The theorem says that a positive m exists, but it also does *not* say that *every* discount factor m must be positive. The discount factors in the top panel of Figure 4.5 *outside* the positive orthant are perfectly valid—they satisfy $p = E(mx)$, and the prices they generate on $\underline{X}$ are arbitrage free, but they are not positive in every state of nature. In particular, the discount factor x^* in the payoff space is still perfectly valid—$p(x) = E(x^*x)$—but it need not be positive.

This theorem shows that we can *extend* the pricing function defined on $\underline{X}$ to all possible payoffs $\mathcal{R}^S$, and not imply any arbitrage opportunities on that larger space of payoffs. It says that there is a pricing function $p(x)$ defined over *all* of $\mathcal{R}^S$, that assigns the same (correct, or observed) prices on $\underline{X}$ and that displays no arbitrage on all of $\mathcal{R}^S$. Graphically, it says that we can draw parallel planes to represent prices on all of $\mathcal{R}^S$ in such a way that the planes intersect $\underline{X}$ in the right places, and the price planes march up and to the right so the positive orthant always has positive prices. Any positive discount factor m generates such a no-arbitrage extension, as illustrated in the bottom panel of Figure 4.5. In fact, there are many ways to do this. Each different choice of $m > 0$ generates a different extension of the pricing function.

We can think of strictly positive discount factors as possible contingent-claims prices. We can think of the theorem as answering the question: is it possible that an observed and incomplete set of prices and payoffs is generated by some complete-markets, contingent-claim economy? The answer is, yes, if there is no arbitrage on the observed prices and payoffs. In fact, since there are typically many positive discount factors consistent with a $\{\underline{X}, p(x)\}$, there exist many contingent-claims economies consistent with our observations.

Finally, the absence of arbitrage is another very weak characterization of preferences and market equilibrium. The theorem tells us that this is enough to allow us to use the $p = E(mx)$ formalism with $m > 0$.

As usual, this theorem and proof do not require that the state-space is $\mathcal{R}^S$. State-spaces generated by continuous random variables work just as well.

4.3 An Alternative Formula, and x^* in Continuous Time

In terms of the covariance matrix of payoffs,

$$x^* = E(x^*) + [p - E(x^*)E(x)]'\Sigma^{-1}(x - E(x)).$$

Analogously,

$$\frac{d\Lambda^*}{\Lambda^*} = -r^f \, dt - \left(\mu + \frac{D}{p} - r\right)'\Sigma^{-1} dz$$

prices assets by construction in continuous time.

Being able to compute x^* is useful in many circumstances. This section gives an alternative formula in discrete time, and the continuous-time counterpart.

A Formula that Uses Covariance Matrices

$E(xx')$ in our previous formula (4.1) is a second moment matrix. We typically summarize data in terms of covariance matrices instead. Therefore, a convenient alternative formula is

$$x^* = E(x^*) + [p - E(x^*)E(x)]'\Sigma^{-1}(x - E(x)), \qquad (4.2)$$

where

$$\Sigma \equiv E([x - E(x)][x - E(x)]')$$

denotes the covariance matrix of the x payoffs. (We could just substitute $E(xx') = \Sigma + E(x)E(x')$, but the inverse of this sum is not very useful.)

We can derive this formula by this postulating a discount factor that is a linear function of the shocks to the payoffs,

$$x^* = E(x^*) + (x - E(x))'b,$$

and then finding b to ensure that x^* prices the assets x:

$$p = E(x^*)E(x) + E\big[(x - Ex)x'\big]b$$

so

$$b = \Sigma^{-1}\big[p - E(x^*)E(x)\big].$$

If a risk-free rate is traded, then we know $E(x^*) = 1/R^f$. If a risk-free rate is not traded—if 1 is not in $\underline{X}$—then this formula does not necessarily produce a discount factor x^* that is in $\underline{X}$. In many applications, however, all that matters is producing some discount factor, and the arbitrariness of the risk-free or zero-beta rate is not a problem.

This formula is particularly useful when the payoff space consists solely of excess returns or price-zero payoffs. In that case, $x^* = p'E(xx')^{-1}x$ gives $x^* = 0$. $x^* = 0$ is in fact the only discount factor in $\underline{X}$ that prices all the assets, but in this case it is more interesting (and avoids 1/0 difficulties when we want to transform to expected return-beta or other representations) to pick a discount factor not in $\underline{X}$ by picking a zero-beta rate or price of the risk-free payoff. In the case of excess returns, for arbitrarily chosen R^f, then, (4.2) gives us

$$x^* = \frac{1}{R^f} - \frac{1}{R^f}E(R^e)'\Sigma^{-1}(R^e - E(R^e)); \qquad \Sigma \equiv \mathrm{cov}(R^e).$$

This approach is due to Hansen and Jagannathan (1991).

Continuous Time

The law of one price implies the existence of a discount factor process, and absence of arbitrage implies a positive discount factor process in continuous time as well as discrete time. At one level, this statement requires no new mathematics. If we reinvest dividends for simplicity, then a discount factor must satisfy

$$p_t \Lambda_t = E_t\left(\Lambda_{t+s} p_{t+s}\right).$$

Calling $p_{t+s} = x_{t+s}$, this *is* precisely the discrete time $p = E(mx)$ that we have studied all along. Thus, the law of one price or absence of arbitrage are equivalent to the existence of a positive Λ_{t+s}. The same conditions at all horizons s are thus equivalent to the existence of a discount factor process, or a positive discount factor process Λ_t for all time t.

For calculations it is useful to find explicit formulas for a discount factors. Suppose a set of securities pays dividends

$$D_t dt$$

and their prices follow

$$\frac{dp_t}{p_t} = \mu_t dt + \sigma_t dz_t,$$

where p and z are $N \times 1$ vectors, μ_t and σ_t may vary over time, $\mu(p_t, t,$ other variables), $E(dz_t dz_t') = I$, and the division on the left-hand side is element by element. (As usual, I will drop the t subscripts when not necessary for clarity, but everything can vary over time.)

We can form a discount factor that prices these assets from a linear combination of the shocks that drive the original assets,

$$\frac{d\Lambda^*}{\Lambda^*} = -r^f dt - \left(\mu + \frac{D}{p} - r^f\right)' \Sigma^{-1} \sigma dz, \tag{4.3}$$

where $\Sigma \equiv \sigma\sigma'$ again is the covariance matrix of returns. You can easily check that this equation solves

$$E_t\left(\frac{dp}{p}\right) + \frac{D}{p} dt - r^f dt = -E_t\left(\frac{d\Lambda^*}{\Lambda^*} \frac{dp}{p}\right) \tag{4.4}$$

and

$$E_t\left(\frac{d\Lambda^*}{\Lambda^*}\right) = -r^f dt,$$

or you can show that this is the only diffusion driven by dz, dt with these properties. If there is a risk-free rate r_t^f (also potentially time-varying), then that rate determines r_t^f. If there is no risk-free rate, (4.3) will price the risky assets for any arbitrary (or convenient) choice of r_t^f. As usual, this discount factor is not unique; Λ^* plus orthogonal noise will also act as a discount factor:

$$\frac{d\Lambda}{\Lambda} = \frac{d\Lambda^*}{\Lambda^*} + dw; \qquad E(dw) = 0; \qquad E(dzdw) = 0.$$

You can see that (4.3) is exactly analogous to the discrete-time formula (4.2). (If you do not like answers that pop out of hats, guess a solution of the form

$$\frac{d\Lambda}{\Lambda} = \mu_\Lambda dt + \sigma_\Lambda dz.$$

Then find μ_Λ and σ_Λ to satisfy (4.4) for the risk-free and risky assets.)

Problems—Chapter 4

1. Does the absence of arbitrage imply the law of one price? Does the law of one price imply the absence of arbitrage? Answer directly using portfolio arguments, and indirectly using the corresponding discount factors.

2. If the law of one price or absence of arbitrage hold in population, must they hold in a sample drawn from that population?

3. This problem shows that the *growth optimal* portfolio introduced in problem 9, Chapter 1 can also serve as a discount factor.

(a) Suppose you have a single return R. $x^* = R/E(R^2)$ is one discount factor. What about R^{-1}? Certainly $E(R^{-1}R) = 1$, so what about the theorem that x^* is unique? Is R^{-1} always positive?

(b) Let R denote a $N \times 1$ vector of asset returns. Show that the portfolio that solves

$$\max E[\ln(\alpha' R)] \text{ s.t. } \alpha'1 = 1$$

is also a discount factor. Is this discount factor always positive? Is it in the payoff space? Can you find a formula for α?

(c) Find the continuous-time counterpart to the discount factor of part b.

5

Mean-Variance Frontier and Beta Representations

Much empirical work in asset pricing is written in terms of expected return-beta representations and mean-variance frontiers. This chapter introduces expected return-beta representations and mean-variance frontiers.

I discuss here the beta *representation* of factor pricing models. Chapters 6 and 9 discuss where the factor models came from. Chapter 6 shows how an expected return-beta model is equivalent to a linear model for the discount factor, i.e., $m = b'f$. Chapter 9 discusses the *derivation* of popular factor models such as the CAPM, ICAPM, and APT, i.e., under what assumptions the discount factor *is* a linear function of other variables f such as the market return.

I summarize the classic Lagrangian approach to the mean-variance frontier. I then introduce a powerful and useful representation of the mean-variance frontier due to Hansen and Richard (1987). This representation uses the state-space geometry familiar from the existence theorems. It is also useful because it is valid in infinite-dimensional payoff spaces, which we shall soon encounter when we add conditioning information, dynamic trading, or options.

5.1 Expected Return-Beta Representations

The expected return-beta expression of a factor pricing model is

$$E(R^i) = \gamma + \beta_{i,a}\lambda_a + \beta_{i,b}\lambda_b + \cdots .$$

The model is equivalent to a restriction that the intercept is the same for all assets in time-series regressions.

When the factors are excess returns, then $\lambda_a = E(f^a)$. If the test assets are also excess returns, then the intercept should be zero, $\alpha = 0$.

Much empirical work in finance is cast in terms of expected return-beta representations of linear factor pricing models, of the form

$$E(R^i) = \gamma + \beta_{i,a}\lambda_a + \beta_{i,b}\lambda_b + \cdots , \qquad i = 1, 2, \ldots, N. \qquad (5.1)$$

The β terms are defined as the coefficients in a multiple regression of returns on factors,

$$R^i_t = a_i + \beta_{i,a}f^a_t + \beta_{i,b}f^b_t + \cdots + \varepsilon^i_t, \qquad t = 1, 2, \ldots, T. \qquad (5.2)$$

This is often called a *time-series regression*, since one runs a regression over time for each security i. The "factors" f are proxies for marginal utility growth. I discuss the stories used to select factors at some length in Chapter 9. For the moment keep in mind the canonical examples, $f = $ consumption growth, or $f = $ the return on the market portfolio (CAPM). Notice that we run returns R^i_t on contemporaneous factors f^j_t. This regression is not about predicting returns from variables seen ahead of time. Its objective is to measure contemporaneous relations or risk exposure: whether returns are typically high in "good times" or "bad times" as measured by the factors.

The point of the beta model (5.1) is to explain the variation in average returns across assets. I write $i = 1, 2, \ldots, N$ in (5.1) to emphasize this fact. The model says that assets with higher betas should get higher average returns. Thus the betas in (5.1) are the explanatory (x) variables, which vary asset by asset. The γ and λ—common for all assets—are the intercept and slope in this cross-sectional relation. For example, equation (5.1) says that if we plot expected returns versus betas in a one-factor model, we should expect all $(E(R^i), \beta_i)$ pairs to line up on a straight line with slope λ and intercept γ.

$\beta_{i,a}$ is interpreted as the amount of exposure of asset i to factor a risks, and λ_a is interpreted as the price of such risk exposure. Read the beta pricing model to say: "for each unit of exposure β to risk factor a, you must provide investors with an expected return premium λ_a." Assets must give investors higher average returns (low prices) if they pay off well in times that are already good, and pay off poorly in times that are already bad, as measured by the factors.

One way to estimate the free parameters (γ, λ) and to test the model (5.1) is to run a *cross-sectional regression* of average returns on betas,

$$E(R^i) = \gamma + \beta_{i,a}\lambda_a + \beta_{i,b}\lambda_b + \cdots + \alpha_i, \qquad i = 1, 2, \ldots, N. \qquad (5.3)$$

Again, the β_i are the right-hand variables, and the γ and λ are the intercept and slope coefficients that we estimate in this cross-sectional regression. The errors α_i are *pricing errors*. The model predicts $\alpha_i = 0$, and they should be statistically insignificant and economically small in a test. In the chapters on empirical technique, we will see test statistics based on the sum of squared pricing errors.

The fact that the betas are regression coefficients is crucially important. If the betas are also free parameters, then there is no content to the model. More importantly (and this is an easier mistake to make), the betas cannot be asset-specific or firm-specific characteristics, such as the size of the firm, book to market ratio, or (to take an extreme example) the first letter of its ticker symbol. It is true that expected returns are *associated with* or *correlated with* many such characteristics. Stocks of small companies or of companies with high book/market ratios do have higher average returns. But this correlation must be *explained* by some beta regression coefficient. The proper betas should drive out any characteristics in cross-sectional regressions. If, for example, expected returns were truly related to size, one could buy many small companies to form a large holding company. It would be a "large" company, and hence pay low average returns to the shareholders, while earning a large average return on its holdings. The managers could enjoy the difference. What ruins this promising idea? The "large" holding company will still *behave* like a portfolio of small stocks—it will have their high betas. Thus, only if asset returns depend on *how you behave*, not *who you are*—on betas rather than characteristics—can a market equilibrium survive such simple repackaging schemes.

Some Common Special Cases

If there is a risk-free rate, its betas in (5.1) are all zero,[1] so the intercept is equal to the risk-free rate,

$$R^f = \gamma.$$

We can impose this condition rather than estimate γ in the cross-sectional regression (5.3). If there is no risk-free rate, then γ must be estimated in the cross-sectional regression. Since it is the expected return of a portfolio with zero betas on all factors, γ is called the (expected) *zero-beta rate* in this circumstance.

We often examine factor pricing models using excess returns directly. (There is an implicit, though not necessarily justified, division of labor between models of interest rates and models of equity risk premia.) Differencing (5.1) between any two returns $R^{ei} = R^i - R^j$ (R^j does not have to be risk free), we obtain

$$E(R^{ei}) = \beta_{i,a}\lambda_a + \beta_{i,b}\lambda_b + \cdots, \qquad i = 1, 2, \ldots, N. \qquad (5.4)$$

Here, β_{ia} represents the regression coefficient of the excess return R^{ei} on the factors. This formulation removes the intercept γ.

It is often the case that the factors are also returns or excess returns. For example, the CAPM uses the return on the market portfolio as the single factor. In this case, the model should apply to the factors as well, and this fact allows us to measure the λ coefficients directly rather than via a cross-sectional regression. Each factor has beta of one on itself and zero on all the other factors, of course. Therefore, if the factors are excess returns, we have $E(f^a) = \lambda_a$, and so forth. We can then write the factor model as

$$E(R^{ei}) = \beta_{i,a}E(f^a) + \beta_{i,b}E(f^b) + \cdots, \qquad i = 1, 2, \ldots, N. \qquad (5.5)$$

The cross-sectional beta pricing model (5.1)–(5.5) and the time-series regression definition of the betas in (5.2) look very similar. It seems that one can take expectations of the time-series regression (5.2) and arrive at the beta model (5.1), in which case the latter would be vacuous since one can always run a regression of anything on anything. The difference is subtle but crucial: the time-series regressions (5.2) will in general have

---

[1]The betas are zero because the risk-free rate is known ahead of time. When we consider the effects of conditioning information, i.e., that the interest rate could vary over time, we have to interpret the means and betas as *conditional* moments. Thus, if you are worried about time-varying risk free rates, betas, and so forth, either assume all variables are i.i.d. (and thus that the risk-free rate is constant), or interpret all moments as conditional on time-t information.

a different intercept a_i for each return i, while the intercept γ is the same for all assets in the beta pricing equation (5.1). The beta pricing equation is a restriction on expected returns, and thus imposes a restriction on intercepts in the time-series regression.

In the special case that the factors are themselves excess returns, the restriction is particularly simple: the time-series regression intercepts should all be zero. In this case, we can avoid the cross-sectional regression entirely, since there are no free parameters left.

5.2 Mean-Variance Frontier: Intuition and Lagrangian Characterization

The *mean-variance frontier* of a given set of assets is the boundary of the set of means and variances of the returns on all portfolios of the given assets. One can find or define this boundary by minimizing return variance for a given mean return. Many asset pricing propositions and test statistics have interpretations in terms of the mean-variance frontier.

Figure 5.1 displays a typical mean-variance frontier. As displayed in Figure 5.1, it is common to distinguish the mean-variance frontier of all risky assets, graphed as the hyperbolic region, and the mean-variance frontier of all assets, i.e., including a risk-free rate if there is one, which is the larger wedge-shaped region. Some authors reserve the terminology "mean-variance frontier" for the upper portion, calling the whole thing the *minimum variance frontier*. The risky asset frontier lies between two asymptotes,

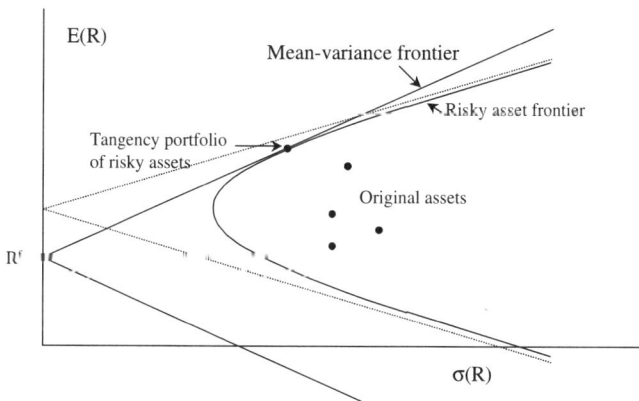

Figure 5.1.   *Mean-variance frontier.*

shown as dotted lines. The risk-free rate is typically drawn below the intersection of the asymptotes and the vertical axis, or the point of minimum variance on the risky frontier. If it were above this point, investors with a mean-variance objective would try to short the risky assets, which cannot represent an equilibrium.

In general, portfolios of two assets fill out a hyperbolic curve through the two assets. The curve is sharper the less correlated are the two assets, because the portfolio variance benefits from increasing diversification. Portfolios of a risky asset and risk-free rate give rise to straight lines in mean-standard deviation space.

In Chapter 1, we derived a similar wedge-shaped region as the set of means and variances of all assets that are priced by a given discount factor. This chapter is about incomplete markets, so we think of a mean-variance frontier generated by a given set of assets, typically less than complete.

When does the mean-variance frontier exist? That is, when is the set of portfolio means and variances less than the whole $\{E, \sigma\}$ space? We basically have to rule out a special case: two returns are perfectly correlated but yield different means. In that case one could short one, long the other, and achieve infinite expected returns with no risk. More formally, eliminate purely redundant securities from consideration, then

Theorem: *So long as the variance-covariance matrix of returns is nonsingular, there is a mean-variance frontier.*

To prove this theorem, just follow the construction below. This theorem should sound very familiar: Two perfectly correlated returns with different mean are a violation of the law of one price. Thus, the law of one price implies that there is a mean-variance frontier as well as a discount factor.

Lagrangian Approach to Mean-Variance Frontier

The standard definition and the computation of the mean-variance frontier follow a brute-force approach.

Problem: Start with a vector of asset returns R. Denote by E the vector of mean returns, $E \equiv E(R)$, and denote by Σ the variance-covariance matrix $\Sigma = E[(R - E)(R - E)']$. A portfolio is defined by its weights w on the initial securities. The portfolio return is $w'R$ where the weights sum to one, $w'1 = 1$. The problem "choose a portfolio to minimize variance for a given mean" is then

$$\min_{\{w\}} w'\Sigma w \qquad \text{s.t.} \quad w'E = \mu; \quad w'1 = 1. \tag{5.6}$$

Solution: Let

$$A = E'\Sigma^{-1}E; \qquad B = E'\Sigma^{-1}1; \qquad C = 1'\Sigma^{-1}1.$$

Then, for a given mean portfolio return μ, the minimum variance portfolio has variance

$$\text{var}(R^p) = \frac{C\mu^2 - 2B\mu + A}{AC - B^2} \tag{5.7}$$

and is formed by portfolio weights

$$w = \Sigma^{-1} \frac{E(C\mu - B) + 1(A - B\mu)}{(AC - B^2)}.$$

Equation (5.7) shows that the variance is a quadratic function of the mean. The square root of a parabola is a hyperbola, which is why we draw hyperbolic regions in mean-standard deviation space.

The *minimum-variance portfolio* is interesting in its own right. It appears as a special case in many theorems and it appears in several test statistics. We can find it by minimizing (5.7) over μ, giving $\mu^{\text{min var}} = B/C$. The weights of the minimum variance portfolio are thus $1/C$, or

$$w = \Sigma^{-1}1/(1'\Sigma^{-1}1).$$

We can get to any point on the mean-variance frontier by starting with two returns on the frontier and forming portfolios. The frontier is *spanned* by any two frontier returns. To see this fact, notice that w is a linear function of μ. Thus, if you take the portfolios corresponding to any two distinct mean returns μ_1 and μ_2, the weights on a third portfolio with mean $\mu_3 = \lambda\mu_1 + (1 - \lambda)\mu_2$ are given by $w_3 = \lambda w_1 + (1 - \lambda)w_2$.

Derivation: To derive the solution, introduce Lagrange multipliers 2λ and 2δ on the constraints. The first-order conditions to (5.6) are then

$$\Sigma w - \lambda E - \delta 1 = 0,$$
$$w = \Sigma^{-1}(\lambda E + \delta 1). \tag{5.8}$$

We find the Lagrange multipliers from the constraints,

$$E'w = E'\Sigma^{-1}(\lambda E + \delta 1) = \mu,$$
$$1'w = 1'\Sigma^{-1}(\lambda E + \delta 1) = 1,$$

or

$$\begin{bmatrix} E'\Sigma^{-1}E & E'\Sigma^{-1}1 \\ 1'\Sigma^{-1}E & 1'\Sigma^{-1}1 \end{bmatrix} \begin{bmatrix} \lambda \\ \delta \end{bmatrix} = \begin{bmatrix} \mu \\ 1 \end{bmatrix},$$

$$\begin{bmatrix} A & B \\ B & C \end{bmatrix} \begin{bmatrix} \lambda \\ \delta \end{bmatrix} = \begin{bmatrix} \mu \\ 1 \end{bmatrix}.$$

Hence,

$$\lambda = \frac{C\mu - B}{AC - B^2},$$

$$\delta = \frac{A - B\mu}{AC - B^2}.$$

Plugging in to (5.8), we get the portfolio weights and variance.

5.3 An Orthogonal Characterization of the Mean-Variance Frontier

> Every return can be expressed as $R^i = R^* + w^i R^{e*} + n^i$.
> The mean-variance frontier is $R^{mv} = R^* + wR^{e*}$.
> R^* is defined as $x^*/p(x^*)$. It is a return that represents prices.
> R^{e*} is defined as $R^{e*} = \text{proj}(1|\underline{R^e})$. It represents mean excess returns,
> $E(R^e) = E(R^{e*}R^e) \, \forall R^e \in \underline{R^e}$.

The Lagrangian approach to the mean-variance frontier is straightforward but cumbersome. Our further manipulations will be easier if we follow an alternative approach due to Hansen and Richard (1987). Technically, Hansen and Richard's approach is also valid when we cannot generate the payoff space by portfolios of a finite set of basis payoffs $c'x$. This happens, for example, when we think about conditioning information in Chapter 8. Also, it is the natural geometric way to think about the mean-variance frontier given that we have started to think of payoffs, discount factors, and other random variables as vectors in the space of payoffs. Rather than write portfolios as combinations of basis assets, and pose and solve a minimization problem, we first describe any return by a three-way orthogonal decomposition. The mean-variance frontier then pops out easily without any algebra.

Definitions of R^*, R^{e*}

I start by defining two special returns. R^* is the return corresponding to the payoff x^* that can act as the discount factor. The price of x^* is, like any other price, $p(x^*) = E(x^*x^*)$. Thus,

The definition of R^* is

$$R^* \equiv \frac{x^*}{p(x^*)} = \frac{x^*}{E(x^{*2})}. \tag{5.9}$$

The definition of R^{e*} is

$$R^{e*} \equiv \mathrm{proj}(1 \mid \underline{R}^e),$$
$$\underline{R}^e \equiv \text{space of excess returns} = \{x \in \underline{X} \, s.t. \, p(x) = 0\}. \tag{5.10}$$

Why R^{e*}? We are heading towards a mean-variance frontier, so it is natural to seek a special return that changes means. R^{e*} is an excess return that represents means on $\underline{R}^e$ with an inner product in the same way that x^* is a payoff in $\underline{X}$ that represents prices with an inner product. As

$$p(x) = E(mx) = E[\mathrm{proj}(m|\underline{X})x] = E(x^*x),$$

so

$$E(R^e) = E(1 \times R^e) = E[\mathrm{proj}(1 \mid R^e) \times R^e] = E(R^{e*}R^e).$$

If R^* and R^{e*} are still a bit mysterious at this point, they will make more sense as we use them, and discover their many interesting properties.

Now we can state a beautiful orthogonal decomposition.

Theorem: *Every return R^i can be expressed as*

$$R^i = R^* + w^i R^{e*} + n^i,$$

where w^i is a number, and n^i is an excess return with the property

$$E(n^i) = 0.$$

The three components are orthogonal,

$$E(R^*R^{e*}) = E(R^*n^i) = E(R^{e*}n^i) = 0.$$

This theorem quickly implies the characterization of the mean-variance frontier which we are after:

Theorem: R^{mv} *is on the mean-variance frontier if and only if*

$$R^{mv} = R^* + wR^{e*} \tag{5.11}$$

for some real number w.

As you vary the number w, you sweep out the mean-variance frontier. $E(R^{e*}) \neq 0$, so adding more w changes the mean and variance of R^{mv}. You can interpret (5.11) as a "two-fund" theorem for the mean-variance frontier. It expresses every frontier return as a portfolio of R^* and R^{e*}, with varying weights on the latter.

As usual, first I will argue why the theorems are sensible, then I will offer a simple algebraic proof. Hansen and Richard (1987) give a much more careful algebraic proof.

Graphical Construction

Figure 5.2 illustrates the decomposition. Start at the origin (0). Recall that the x^* vector is perpendicular to planes of constant price; thus the R^* vector lies perpendicular to the plane of returns as shown. Go to R^*.

R^{e*} is the excess return that is closest to the vector 1; it lies at right angles to planes (in $\underline{R}^e$) of constant *mean* return, shown in the $E = 1, E = 2$ lines, just as the return R^* lies at right angles to planes of constant price. Since R^{e*} is an excess return, it is orthogonal to R^*. Proceed an amount w^i in the direction of R^{e*}, getting as close to R^i as possible.

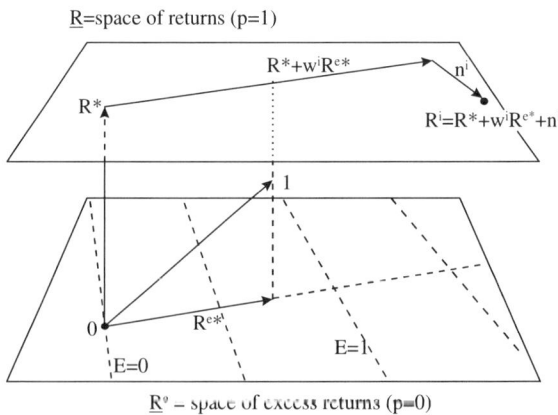

$\underline{R}$=space of returns (p=1)

$R^*+w^i R^{e*}$

n^i

R^*

$R^i=R^*+w^i R^{e*}+n^i$

1

R^{e*}

0

$E=0$

$E=1$

$\underline{R}^e$ – space of excess returns (p=0)

Figure 5.2. *Orthogonal decomposition and mean-variance frontier.*

Now move, again in an orthogonal direction, by an amount n^i to get to the return R^i. We have thus expressed $R^i = R^* + w^i R^{e*} + n^i$ in a way that all three components are orthogonal.

Returns with $n = 0$, $R^* + wR^{e*}$, are the mean-variance frontier. Since $E(R^2) = \sigma^2(R) + E(R)^2$, we can define the mean-variance frontier by minimizing second moment for a given mean. The length of each vector in Figure 5.2 is its second moment, so we want the shortest vector that is on the return plane for a given mean. The shortest vectors in the return plane with given mean are on the $R^* + wR^{e*}$ line.

The graph also shows how R^{e*} represents means in the space of excess returns. Expectation is the inner product with 1. Planes of constant expected value in Figure 5.2 are perpendicular to the 1 vector, just as planes of constant price are perpendicular to the x^* or R^* vectors. I do not show the full extent of the constant expected payoff planes for clarity; I do show lines of constant expected excess return in $\underline{R}^e$, which are the intersection of constant expected payoff planes with the $\underline{R}^e$ plane. Therefore, just as we found an x^* in $\underline{X}$ to represent prices in $\underline{X}$ by projecting m onto $\underline{X}$, we find R^{e*} in $\underline{R}^e$ by projecting of 1 onto $\underline{R}^e$. Yes, this is a regression with one on the left-hand side and no constant. Planes perpendicular to R^{e*} in $\underline{R}^e$ are payoffs with constant *mean*, just as planes perpendicular to x^* in $\underline{X}$ are payoffs with the same *price*.

Algebraic Argument

Now, I present an algebraic proof of the decomposition and characterization of mean-variance frontier. The algebra just represents statements about what is at right angles to what with second moments.

Proof: Straight from their definitions, (5.9) and (5.10), we know that R^{e*} is an excess return (price zero), and hence that R^* and R^{e*} are orthogonal,

$$E(R^*R^{e*}) = \frac{E(x^*R^{e*})}{E(x^{*2})} = 0.$$

We define n^i so that the decomposition adds up to R^i as claimed, and we define w^i to make sure that n^i is orthogonal to the other two components. Then we prove that $E(n^i) = 0$. Pick any w^i and then define

$$n^i \equiv R^i - R^* - w^i R^{e*}.$$

n^i is an excess return so already orthogonal to R^*,

$$E(R^*n^i) = 0.$$

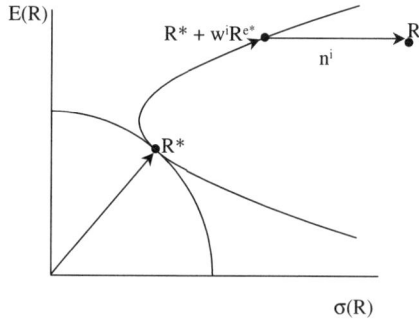

Figure 5.3.   *Orthogonal decomposition of a return R^i in mean-standard deviation space.*

To show $E(n^i) = 0$ and n^i orthogonal to R^{e*}, we exploit the fact that since n^i is an excess return,

$$E(n^i) = E(R^{e*}n^i).$$

Therefore, R^{e*} is orthogonal to n^i if and only if we pick w^i so that $E(n^i) = 0$. We do not have to explicitly calculate w^i for the proof.[2]

Once we have constructed the decomposition, the frontier drops out. Since $E(n^i) = 0$ and the three components are orthogonal,

$$E(R^i) = E(R^*) + w^i E(R^{e*}),$$

$$\sigma^2(R^i) = \sigma^2(R^* + w^i R^{e*}) + \sigma^2(n^i).$$

Thus, for each desired value of the mean return, there is a unique w^i. Returns with $n^i = 0$ minimize variance for each mean.   □

Decomposition in Mean-Variance Space

Figure 5.3 illustrates the decomposition in mean-variance space rather than in state-space.

First, let us locate R^*. R^* is the minimum second moment return. One can see this fact from the geometry of Figure 5.2: R^* is the return closest to the origin, and thus the return with the smallest "length" which is second moment. As with OLS regression, minimizing the length of R^* and creating an R^* orthogonal to all excess returns are the same thing.

---

[2]Its value

$$w^i = \frac{E(R^i) - E(R^*)}{E(R^{e*})}$$

is not particularly enlightening.

One can also verify this property algebraically. Since any return can be expressed as $R = R^* + wR^{e*} + n$, $E(R^2) = E(R^{*2}) + w^2 E(R^{e*2}) + E(n^2)$. $n = 0$ and $w = 0$ thus give the minimum second moment return.

In mean-standard deviation space, lines of constant second moment are circles. Thus, the minimum second moment return R^* is on the smallest circle that intersects the set of all assets, which lie in the hyperbolic mean-variance frontier. Notice that R^* is on the lower, or "inefficient" segment of the mean-variance frontier. It is initially surprising that this is the location of the most interesting return on the frontier! R^* is *not* the "market portfolio" or "wealth portfolio," which typically lie on the upper portion of the frontier.

Adding more R^{e*} moves one along the frontier. Adding n does not change mean but does change variance, so it is an *idiosyncratic* return that just moves an asset off the frontier as graphed.

5.4 Spanning the Mean-Variance Frontier

The characterization of the mean-variance frontier in terms of R^* and R^{e*} is most natural in our setup. However, you can equivalently span the mean-variance frontier with any two portfolios that are on the frontier— any two distinct linear combinations of R^* and R^{e*}. In particular, take any return

$$R^{\alpha} = R^* + \gamma R^{e*}, \qquad \gamma \neq 0. \tag{5.12}$$

Using this return in place of R^{e*},

$$R^{e*} = \frac{R^{\alpha} - R^*}{\gamma},$$

you can express the mean-variance frontier in terms of R^* and R^{α}:

$$\begin{aligned} R^* + wR^{e*} &= R^* + y(R^{\alpha} - R^*) \\ &= (1 - y)R^* + yR^{\alpha}, \end{aligned} \tag{5.13}$$

where I have defined a new weight $y = w/\gamma$.

The most common alternative approach is to use a risk-free rate or a risky rate that somehow behaves like the risk-free rate in place of R^{e*} to span the frontier. When there is a risk-free rate, it is on the frontier with representation

$$R^f = R^* + R^f R^{e*}.$$

I derive this expression in equation (5.20) below. Therefore, we can use (5.13) with $R^a = R^f$. When there is no risk-free rate, several risky returns that retain some properties of the risk-free rate are often used. In Section 6.5 I present a "zero-beta" return, which is uncorrelated with R^*, a "constant-mimicking portfolio" return, which is the return on the traded payoff closest to unity, $\hat{R} = \text{proj}(1|\underline{X})/p[\text{proj}(1|\underline{X})]$, and the minimum variance return. Each of these returns is on the mean-variance frontier, with form (5.12), though different values of γ. Therefore, we can span the mean-variance frontier with R^* and any of these risk-free rate proxies.

5.5 A Compilation of Properties of R^*, R^{e*}, and x^*

The special returns R^*, R^{e*} that generate the mean-variance frontier have lots of interesting and useful properties. Some I derived above, some I will derive and discuss below in more detail, and some will be useful tricks later on. Most properties and derivations are extremely obscure if you do not look at the pictures!

(1)

$$E(R^{*2}) = \frac{1}{E(x^{*2})}. \tag{5.14}$$

To derive this fact, multiply both sides of the definition $R^* = x^*/E(x^{*2})$ by R^*, take expectations, and remember R^* is a return so $1 = E(x^*R^*)$.

(2) We can reverse the definition and recover x^* from R^* via

$$x^* = \frac{R^*}{E(R^{*2})}. \tag{5.15}$$

To derive this formula, start with the definition $R^* = x^*/E(x^{*2})$ and substitute from (5.14) for $E(x^{*2})$.

(3) R^* can be used to represent prices just like x^*. This is not surprising, since they both point in the same direction, orthogonal to planes of constant price. Most obviously, from (5.15),

$$p(x) = E(x^*x) = \frac{E(R^*x)}{E(R^{*2})} \qquad \forall x \in \underline{X}.$$

For returns, we can nicely express this result as

$$E(R^{*2}) = E(R^*R) \qquad \forall R \in \underline{R}. \tag{5.16}$$

This fact can also serve as an alternative defining property of R^*.

(4) R^{e*} represents means on $\underline{R}^e$ via an inner product in the same way that x^* represents prices on $\underline{X}$ via an inner product. R^{e*} is orthogonal to planes of constant mean in $\underline{R}^e$ as x^* is orthogonal to planes of constant price. Algebraically, in analogy to $p(x) = E(x^*x)$, we have

$$E(R^e) = E(R^{e*}R^e) \qquad \forall R^e \in \underline{R}^e. \tag{5.17}$$

This fact can serve as an alternative defining property of R^{e*}.

(5) If a risk-free rate is traded, we can construct R^f from R^* via

$$R^f = \frac{1}{E(x^*)} = \frac{E(R^{*2})}{E(R^*)}. \tag{5.18}$$

If not, this gives a "zero-beta rate" interpretation of the right-hand expression. You can also derive this formula by applying (5.16) to R^f.

(6) R^{e*} and R^* are orthogonal,

$$E(R^*R^{e*}) = 0.$$

More generally, R^* is orthogonal to any excess return.

(7) The mean-variance frontier is given by

$$R^{mv} = R^* + wR^{e*}.$$

We proved this in Section 5.3; $E(R^2) = E[(R^* + wR^{e*} + n)^2] = E(R^{*2}) + w^2 E(R^{e2}) + E(n^2)$, and $E(n) = 0$, so set n to zero. The conditional mean-variance frontier allows w in the conditioning information set. The unconditional mean-variance frontier requires w to equal a constant (Chapter 8).

(8) R^* is the minimum second moment return. Graphically, R^* is the return closest to the origin. To see this, use the decomposition in (7), and set w^2 and n to zero to minimize second moment (Figure 5.3).

(9) R^{e*} has the same first and second moment,

$$E(R^{e*}) = E(R^{e*2}).$$

Just apply fact (5.17) to R^{e*} itself. Therefore,

$$\text{var}(R^{e*}) = E(R^{e*2}) - E(R^{e*})^2 = E(R^{e*})[1 - E(R^{e*})].$$

(10) If there is a risk-free rate, then R^{e*} can also be defined as the residual in the projection of 1 on R^*:

$$R^{e*} = 1 - \text{proj}(1|R^*) = 1 - \frac{E(R^*)}{E(R^{*2})}R^* = 1 - \frac{1}{R^f}R^*. \tag{5.19}$$

Figure 5.2 makes the first equality obvious. To prove it analytically, note that since R^* and $\underline{R^e}$ are orthogonal and together span $\underline{X}$, $1 = \text{proj}(1|\underline{R^e}) + \text{proj}(1|R^*) = R^{e*} + \text{proj}(1|R^*)$. The last equality comes from equation (5.18).

You can also verify (5.19) analytically. Check that R^{e*} so defined is an excess return in $\underline{X}$—its price is zero—and $E(R^{e*}R^e) = E(R^e)$; $E(R^*R^{e*}) = 0$.

(11) As a result of (5.19), R^f has the decomposition

$$R^f = R^* + R^f R^{e*}. \tag{5.20}$$

Since $R^f > 1$ typically, this means that $R^* + R^{e*}$ is located on the lower portion of the mean-variance frontier in mean-variance space, just a bit to the right of R^f. If the risk-free rate were one, then the unit vector would lie in the return space, and we would have $R^f = R^* + R^{e*}$. Typically, the space of returns is a little bit above the unit vector. As you stretch the unit vector by the amount R^f to arrive at the return R^f, so you stretch the amount R^{e*} that you add to R^* to get to R^f.

(12) If there is no risk-free rate, then we can use

$$\text{proj}(1|\underline{X}) = \text{proj}(\text{proj}(1|\underline{X})|\underline{R^e}) + \text{proj}(\text{proj}(1|\underline{X})|R^*)$$

$$= \text{proj}(1|\underline{R^e}) + \text{proj}(1|\underline{R^*})$$

to deduce an analogue to equation (5.19),

$$R^{e*} = \text{proj}(1|\underline{X}) - \text{proj}(1|R^*) = \text{proj}(1|\underline{X}) - \frac{E(R^*)}{E(R^{*2})}R^*. \tag{5.21}$$

(13) Since we have a formula $x^* = p'E(xx')^{-1}x$ for constructing x^* from basis assets (see Section 4.1), we can construct R^* in this case from

$$R^* = \frac{x^*}{p(x^*)} = \frac{p'E(xx')^{-1}x}{p'E(xx')^{-1}p}.$$

($p(x^*) = E(x^*x^*)$ leading to the denominator.)

(14) We can construct R^{e*} from a set of basis assets as well. Following the definition to project one on the space of excess returns,

$$R^{e*} = E(R^e)'E(R^eR^{e'})^{-1}R^e,$$

where R^e is the vector of basis excess returns. (You can always use $R^e = R - R^*$ to form excess returns.) This construction obviously mirrors the way we constructed x^* in Section 4.1 as $x^* = p'E(xx')^{-1}x$, and you can see the similarity in the result, with E in place of p, since R^{e*} represents means rather than prices.

If there is a risk-free rate, we can also use (5.19) to construct R^{e*}:

$$R^{e*} = 1 - \frac{1}{R^f}R^* = 1 - \frac{1}{R^f}\frac{p'E(xx')^{-1}x}{p'E(xx')^{-1}p}. \tag{5.22}$$

If there is no risk-free rate, we can use (5.21) to construct R^{e*}. The central ingredient is

$$\text{proj}(1|\underline{X}) = E(x)'E(xx')^{-1}x.$$

5.6 Mean-Variance Frontiers for Discount Factors: The Hansen–Jagannathan Bounds

The mean-variance frontier of all discount factors that price a given set of assets is related to the mean-variance frontier of asset returns by

$$\frac{\sigma(m)}{E(m)} \geq \frac{|E(R^e)|}{\sigma(R^e)},$$

and hence

$$\min_{\{\text{all } m \text{ that price } x \in \underline{X}\}} \frac{\sigma(m)}{E(m)} = \max_{\{\text{all excess returns } R^e \text{ in } \underline{X}\}} \frac{E(R^e)}{\sigma(R^e)}.$$

The discount factors on the frontier can be characterized analogously to the mean-variance frontier of asset returns,

$$m - x^* + we^*,$$

$$e^* \equiv 1 - \text{proj}(1|\underline{X}) = \text{proj}(1|\underline{E}) = 1 - E(x)'E(xx')^{-1}x,$$

$$\underline{E} = \{m - x^*\}.$$

We derived in Chapter 1 a relation between the Sharpe ratio of an excess return and the volatility of discount factors necessary to price that return,

$$\frac{\sigma(m)}{E(m)} \geq \frac{|E(R^e)|}{\sigma(R^e)}. \tag{5.23}$$

Quickly,

$$0 = E(mR^e) = E(m)E(R^e) + \rho_{m,\,R^e}\sigma(m)\sigma(R^e),$$

and $|\rho| \leq 1$. If we had a risk-free rate, then we know in addition

$$E(m) = 1/R^f.$$

Hansen and Jagannathan (1991) had the brilliant insight to read this equation as a restriction on the set of *discount factors* that can price a given set of returns, as well as a restriction on the set of *returns* we will see given a specific discount factor. This calculation teaches us that we need very volatile discount factors with a mean near one to understand stock returns. This and more general related calculations turn out to be a central tool in understanding and surmounting the equity premium puzzle, surveyed in Chapter 21.

We would like to derive a bound that uses a large number of assets, and that is valid if there is no risk-free rate. What is the set of $\{E(m), \sigma(m)\}$ consistent with a given set of asset prices and payoffs? What is the mean-variance frontier for discount factors?

Obviously from (5.23) the higher the Sharpe ratio, the tighter the bound on $\sigma(m)$. This suggests a way to construct the frontier we are after. For any hypothetical risk-free rate, find the highest Sharpe ratio. That is, of course, the tangency portfolio. Then the slope to the tangency portfolio gives the ratio $\sigma(m)/E(m)$. Figure 5.4 illustrates.

As we increase $E(m)$, the slope to the tangency becomes lower, and the Hansen–Jagannathan bound declines. At the mean return corresponding to the minimum variance point, the HJ bound attains its minimum. Continuing, the Sharpe ratio rises again and so does the bound. If there were a risk-free rate, then we know $E(m)$, the return frontier is a V shape, and the HJ bound is purely a bound on variance.

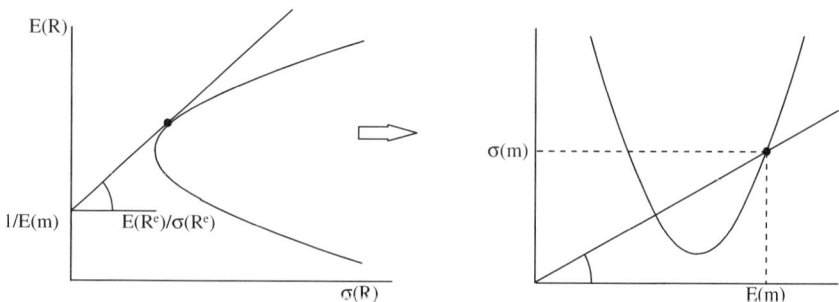

Figure 5.4. *Graphical construction of the Hansen–Jagannathan bound.*

This discussion implies a beautiful duality between discount factor volatility and Sharpe ratios:

$$\min_{\{\text{all } m \text{ that price } x\in \underline{X}\}} \frac{\sigma(m)}{E(m)} = \max_{\{\text{all excess returns } R^e \text{ in } \underline{X}\}} \frac{E(R^e)}{\sigma(R^e)}. \tag{5.24}$$

We need formulas for an explicit calculation. Following the same logic we used to derive equation (4.2), we can find a representation for the set of discount factors that price a given set of asset returns—that satisfy $p = E(mx)$:

$$m = E(m) + [p - E(m)E(x)]\Sigma^{-1}[x - E(x)] + \varepsilon, \tag{5.25}$$

where $\Sigma \equiv \text{cov}(x, x')$ and $E(\varepsilon) = 0$, $E(\varepsilon x) = 0$. You can think of this as a regression or projection of any discount factor on the space of payoffs, plus an error. Since $\sigma^2(\varepsilon) > 0$, this representation leads immediately to an explicit expression for the Hansen–Jagannathan bound,

$$\sigma^2(m) \geq (p - E(m)E(x))'\Sigma^{-1}(p - E(m)E(x)). \tag{5.26}$$

As all asset returns must lie in a cup-shaped region in $\{E(R), \sigma(R)\}$ space, all discount factors must lie in a parabolic region in $\{E(m), \sigma(m)\}$ space, as illustrated in the right-hand panel of Figure 5.4.

We would like an expression for the discount factors on the bound, as we wanted an expression for the returns on the mean-variance frontier instead of just a formula for the means and variances. As we found a three-way decomposition of all returns, in which two elements generated the mean-variance frontier of returns, so we can find a three-way decomposition of discount factors, in which two elements generate the mean-variance frontier of discount factors (5.26). I illustrate the construction in Figure 5.5.

Any discount factor m must lie in the plane marked $\underline{M}$, perpendicular to $\underline{X}$ through x^*. Any m must be of the form

$$m = x^* + we^* + n.$$

Here, I have just broken up the residual ε in the familiar representation $m = x^* + \varepsilon$ into two components. e^* is defined as the residual from the projection of 1 onto $\underline{X}$ or, equivalently the projection of 1 on the space $\underline{E}$ of "excess m's," random variables of the form $m - x^*$.

$$e^* \equiv 1 - \text{proj}(1|\underline{X}) = \text{proj}(1|\underline{E}).$$

e^* generates means of m just as R^{e*} did for returns:

$$E(m - x^*) = E[1 \times (m - x^*)] = E[\text{proj}(1|\underline{E})(m - x^*)].$$

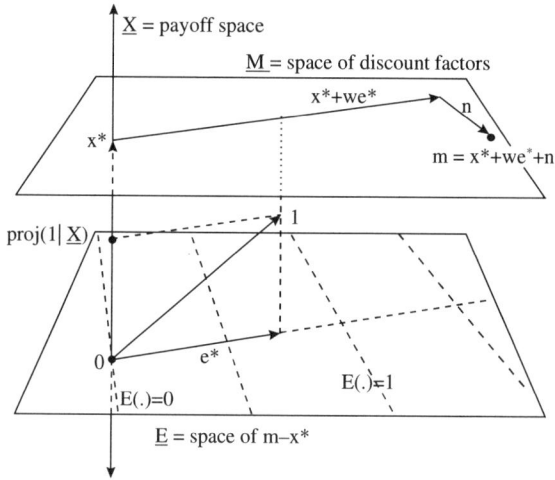

Figure 5.5. *Decomposition of any discount factor $m = x^* + we + n$.*

Finally n, defined as the leftovers, has mean zero since it is orthogonal to 1 and is orthogonal to $\underline{X}$.

As with returns, then, the mean-variance frontier of discount factors is given by

$$m = x^* + we^*. \tag{5.27}$$

If the unit payoff is in the payoff space, then we know $E(m)$, and the frontier and bound are just $m = x^*$, $\sigma^2(m) \geq \sigma^2(x^*)$. This is exactly like the case of risk neutrality for return mean-variance frontiers, in which the frontier reduces to the single point R^*.

The construction (5.27) can be used to derive the formula (5.26) for the Hansen–Jagannathan bound for the finite-dimensional cases discussed above. It is more general, since it can be used in infinite-dimensional payoff spaces as well. Along with the corresponding return formula $R^{mv} = R^* + wR^{e^*}$, we see in Chapter 8 that it extends more easily to the calculation of conditional versus unconditional mean-variance frontiers (Gallant, Hansen, and Tauchen [1995]).

It will make construction (5.27) come alive if we find equations for its components. We find x^* as before; it is the portfolio $c'x$ in $\underline{X}$ that prices x:

$$x^* = p'E(xx')^{-1}x.$$

Similarly, let us find e^*. The projection of 1 on $\underline{X}$ is

$$\text{proj}(1|\underline{X}) = E(x)'E(xx')^{-1}x.$$

(After a while you get used to the idea of running regressions with 1 on the left-hand side and random variables on the right-hand side!) Thus,

$$e^* = 1 - E(x)'E(xx')^{-1}x.$$

Again, you can construct time series of x^* and e^* from these definitions.

Finally, we now can construct the variance-minimizing discount factors

$$m^* = x^* + we^* = p'E(xx')^{-1}x + w[1 - E(x)'E(xx')^{-1}x]$$

or

$$m^* = w + [p - wE(x)]'E(xx')^{-1}x. \tag{5.28}$$

As w varies, we trace out discount factors m^* on the frontier with varying means and variances. It is easiest to find mean and second moment:

$$E(m^*) = w + [p - wE(x)]'E(xx')^{-1}E(x),$$

$$E(m^{*2}) = [p - wE(x)]'E(xx')^{-1}[p - wE(x)].$$

Variance follows from $\sigma^2(m) = E(m^2) - E(m)^2$. With a little algebra one can also show that these formulas are equivalent to equation (5.26).

As you can see, Hansen–Jagannathan frontiers are equivalent to mean-variance frontiers. For example, an obvious exercise is to see how much the addition of assets raises the Hansen–Jagannathan bound. This is *exactly* the same as asking how much those assets expand the mean-variance frontier. Knez and Chen (1996) and DeSantis (1994) test for mean-variance efficiency using Hansen–Jagannathan bounds.

Hansen–Jagannathan bounds have the potential to do more than mean-variance frontiers. Hansen and Jagannathan show how to solve the problem

$$\min \sigma^2(m) \text{ s.t. } p = E(mx), \ m > 0, \ E(m) \text{ fixed}$$

This is the "Hansen–Jagannathan bound with positivity." It is strictly tighter than the Hansen–Jagannathan bound since there is an extra restriction. It allows you to impose no-arbitrage conditions. In stock applications, this extra bound ended up not being that informative. However, in the option application of this idea of Chapter 18, positivity is really important. That chapter shows how to solve for a bound with positivity.

Hansen, Heaton, and Luttmer (1995) develop a distribution theory for the bounds. Luttmer (1996) develops bounds with market frictions such as short-sales constraints and bid/ask spreads, to account for ludicrously high apparent Sharpe ratios and bounds in short-term bond data. Cochrane and Hansen (1992) survey a variety of bounds, including bounds that incorporate information that discount factors are poorly correlated with stock returns (the HJ bounds use the extreme $|\rho| = 1$), bounds on conditional moments that illustrate how many models imply excessive interest rate variation, bounds with short-sales constraints and market frictions, etc.

Chapter 21 discusses the results of Hansen–Jagannathan bound calculations and what they mean for discount factors that can price stock and bond return data.

Problems—Chapter 5

1. Prove that R^{e*} lies at right angles to planes (in $\underline{R}^e$) of constant *mean* return, as shown in Figure 5.2.

2. Should we draw x^* above, below, or on the plane of returns? Consider (a) a risk-free economy (b) a risky, but risk-neutral economy (c) our economy with market Sharpe ratio $E(R - R^f)/\sigma(R - R^f) \simeq 0.5$ and $R^f = .01$ on an annual basis.

  Hint: Show that $|R^*||x^*| = 1$ and $R^f E(\text{proj}(x^*|1)) = 1$.

3. Show that if there is a risk-free rate—if the unit payoff is in the payoff space $\underline{X}$—then $R^{e*} = (R^f - R^*)/R^f$.

4. If no risk-free rate is traded, can you construct R^{e*} from knowledge of m, x^*, or R^*?

5. What happens to R^*, R^{e*}, and the mean-variance frontier if investors are risk neutral?

  (a) If a risk-free rate is traded?

  (b) If no risk-free rate is traded?

(Hint: make a drawing or think about the case that payoffs are generated by an N-dimensional vector of basis assets x.)

6. $x^* = \text{proj}(m|\underline{X})$. Is $R^* = \text{proj}(m|\underline{R})$?

6

Relation between Discount Factors, Betas, and Mean-Variance Frontiers

IN THIS CHAPTER, I draw the connection between discount factors, mean-variance frontiers, and beta representations. In the first chapter, I showed how mean-variance and a beta representation follow from $p = E(mx)$ in a complete markets setting. Here, I discuss the connections in both directions and in incomplete markets, drawing on the representations studied in the last chapter.

The central theme of the chapter is that *all three representations are equivalent*. Figure 6.1 summarizes the ways one can go from one representation to another. A discount factor, a reference variable for betas—the thing you put on the right-hand side in the regressions that give betas—and a return on the mean-variance frontier all carry the same information, and given any one of them, you can find the others. More specifically,

1. $p = E(mx) \Rightarrow \beta$. Given m such that $p = E(mx)$, then m, x^*, R^*, or $R^* + wR^{e*}$ all can serve as reference variables for betas.
2. $p = E(mx) \Rightarrow$ mean-variance frontier. You can construct R^* from $x^* = \text{proj}(m|\underline{X})$, $R^* = x^*/E(x^{*2})$. Then R^*, $R^* + wR^{e*}$ are on the mean-variance frontier.
3. Mean-variance frontier $\Rightarrow p = E(mx)$. If R^{mv} is on the mean-variance frontier, then $m = a + bR^{mv}$ linear in that return is a discount factor; it satisfies $p = E(mx)$.
4. $\beta \Rightarrow p = E(mx)$. If we have an expected return-beta model with factors f, then $m = b'f$ linear in the factors satisfies $p = E(mx)$.
5. If a return is on the mean-variance frontier, then there is an expected return-beta model with that return as reference variable.

The following subsections discuss the mechanics of going from one representation to the other in detail. The last section of the chapter collects some special cases when there is no risk-free rate. The next chapter

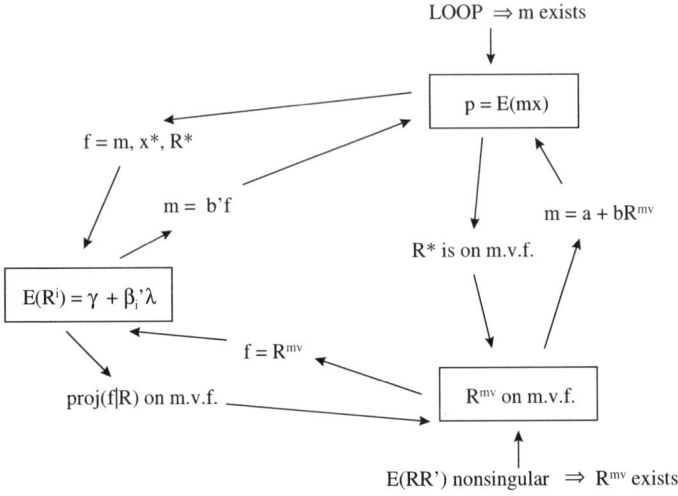

Figure 6.1. *Relation between three views of asset pricing.*

discusses some of the implications of these equivalence theorems, and why they are important.

Roll (1976) pointed out the connection between mean-variance frontiers and beta pricing. Ross (1978) and Dybvig and Ingersoll (1982) pointed out the connection between linear discount factors and beta pricing. Hansen and Richard (1987) pointed out the connection between a discount factor and the mean-variance frontier.

―――――

6.1 From Discount Factors to Beta Representations

> m, x^*, and R^* can all be the single factor in a single-beta representation.

Beta Representation Using m

$p = E(mx)$ implies $E(R^i) = \gamma + \beta_{i,m}\lambda_m$. Start with

$$1 = E(mR^i) = E(m)E(R^i) + \text{cov}(m, R^i).$$

Thus,

$$E(R^i) = \frac{1}{E(m)} - \frac{\text{cov}(m, R^i)}{E(m)}.$$

Multiply and divide by var(m), define $\gamma \equiv 1/E(m)$ to get

$$E(R^i) = \gamma + \left(\frac{\text{cov}(m, R^i)}{\text{var}(m)}\right)\left(-\frac{\text{var}(m)}{E(m)}\right) = \gamma + \beta_{i,m} \lambda_m.$$

As advertised, we have a single-beta representation.

For example, we can equivalently state the consumption-based model as: mean asset returns should be linear in the regression betas of asset returns on $(c_{t+1}/c_t)^{-\gamma}$. Furthermore, the slope of this cross-sectional relationship λ_m is not a free parameter, though it is usually treated as such in empirical evaluation of factor pricing models. λ_m should equal the ratio of variance to mean of $(c_{t+1}/c_t)^{-\gamma}$.

The factor risk premium λ_m for marginal utility growth is negative. Positive expected returns are associated with positive correlation with consumption growth, and hence negative correlation with marginal utility growth and m. Thus, we expect $\lambda_m < 0$.

β *Representation Using x^* and R^**

It is often useful to express a pricing model in a way that the factor is a payoff rather than a real variable such as consumption growth. In applications, we can then avoid measurement difficulties of real data. We have already seen the idea of "factor-mimicking portfolios" formed by projection: project m on to $\underline{X}$, and the resulting payoff x^* also serves as a discount factor. Unsurprisingly, x^* can also serve as the factor in an expected return-beta representation. It is even more useful if the reference payoff is a return. Unsurprisingly, the return $R^* = x^*/E(x^{*2})$ can also serve as the factor in a beta pricing model. When the factor is also a return, the model is particularly simple, since the factor risk premium is also the expected excess return.

Theorem: $1 = E(mR^i)$ *implies an expected return-beta model with $x^* =$ proj$(m|\underline{X})$ or $R^* \equiv x^*/E(x^{*2})$ as factors, e.g., $E(R^i) = \gamma + \beta_{i,x^*}\lambda_{x^*}$ and $E(R^i) = \gamma + \beta_{i,R^*}[E(R^*) - \gamma]$.*

Proof: Recall that $p = E(mx)$ implies $p = E[\text{proj}(m \mid \underline{X})\, x]$, or $p = E(x^*x)$. Then

$$1 = E(mR^i) = E(x^*R^i) = E(x^*)E(R^i) + \text{cov}(x^*, R^i).$$

Solving for the expected return,

$$E(R^i) = \frac{1}{E(x^*)} - \frac{\text{cov}(x^*, R^i)}{E(x^*)} = \frac{1}{E(x^*)} - \frac{\text{cov}(x^*, R^i)}{\text{var}(x^*)}\frac{\text{var}(x^*)}{E(x^*)}, \tag{6.1}$$

which we can write as the desired single-beta model,

$$E(R^i) = \gamma + \beta_{i,x^*}\lambda_{x^*}.$$

Notice that the zero-beta rate $1/E(x^*)$ appears when there is no risk-free rate.

To derive a single-beta representation with R^*, recall the definition,

$$R^* = \frac{x^*}{E(x^{*2})}.$$

Substituting R^* for x^*, equation (6.1) implies that we can in fact construct a return R^* from m that acts as the single factor in a beta model,

$$E(R^i) = \frac{E(R^{*2})}{E(R^*)} - \frac{\text{cov}(R^*, R^i)}{E(R^*)} = \frac{E(R^{*2})}{E(R^*)} + \left(\frac{\text{cov}(R^*, R^i)}{\text{var}(R^*)}\right)\left(-\frac{\text{var}(R^*)}{E(R^*)}\right)$$

or, defining Greek letters in the obvious way,

$$E(R^i) = \gamma + \beta_{R^i, R^*}\lambda_{R^*}. \tag{6.2}$$

Since the factor R^* is also a return, its expected excess return over the zero-beta rate gives the factor risk premium λ_{R^*}. Applying equation (6.2) to R^* itself,

$$E(R^*) = \gamma - \frac{\text{var}(R^*)}{E(R^*)}. \tag{6.3}$$

So we can write the beta model in an even more traditional form

$$E(R^i) = \gamma + \beta_{R^i, R^*}[E(R^*) - \gamma]. \tag{6.4}$$

$\square$

Recall that R^* is the minimum second moment frontier, on the lower portion of the mean-variance frontier. This is why R^* has an unusual negative expected excess return or factor risk premium, $\lambda_{R^*} = -\text{var}(R^*)/E(R^*) < 0$. γ is the zero-beta rate on R^*.

Special Cases
A footnote to these constructions is that $E(m)$, $E(x^*)$, or $E(R^*)$ cannot be zero, or you could not divide by them. This is a pathological case: $E(m) = 0$ implies a zero price for the risk-free asset, and an infinite risk-free rate. If a risk-free rate is traded, we can simply observe that it is not infinite and verify the fact. Also, in a complete market, $E(m)$ cannot be zero since, by absence of arbitrage, $m > 0$. We will see similar special cases in

the remaining theorems: the manipulations only work for discount factor choices that do not imply zero or infinite risk-free rates. I discuss the issue in Section 6.6.

The manipulation from expected return-covariance to expected return-beta breaks down if $\text{var}(m)$, $\text{var}(x^*)$, or $\text{var}(R^*)$ is zero. This is the case of pure risk neutrality. In this case, all expected returns become the same as the risk-free rate.

6.2 From Mean-Variance Frontier to a Discount Factor and Beta Representation

> R^{mv} is on mean-variance frontier $\Rightarrow m = a + bR^{mv}$; $E(R^i) - \gamma = \beta_i[E(R^{mv}) - \gamma]$.

We have seen that $p = E(mx)$ implies a single-beta model with a mean-variance efficient reference return, namely R^*. The converse is also true: for (almost) *any* return on the mean-variance frontier, we can derive a discount factor m that is a linear function of the mean-variance efficient return. Also, expected returns mechanically follow a single-beta representation using the mean-variance efficient return as reference.

I start with the discount factor.

Theorem: *There is a discount factor of the form $m = a + bR^{mv}$ if and only if R^{mv} is on the mean-variance frontier, and R^{mv} is not the risk-free rate. (When there is no risk-free rate, if R^{mv} is not the constant-mimicking portfolio return.)*

Graphical Argument

The basic idea is very simple, and Figure 6.2 shows the geometry for the complete-markets case. The discount factor $m = x^*$ is proportional to R^*. The mean-variance frontier is $R^* + wR^{e*}$. Pick a vector R^{mv} on the mean-variance frontier as shown in Figure 6.2. Then stretch it (bR^{mv}) and then subtract some of the 1 vector (a). Since R^{e*} is generated by the unit vector, we can get rid of the R^{e1} component and get back to the discount factor x^* if we pick the right a and b.

If the original return vector were not on the mean-variance frontier, then any linear combination $a + bR^{mv}$ with $b \neq 0$ would point in some of the n direction, which R^* and x^* do not. If $b = 0$, though, just stretching up and down the 1 vector will not get us to x^*. Thus, we can *only* get a discount factor of the form $a + bR^{mv}$ if R^{mv} is on the frontier.

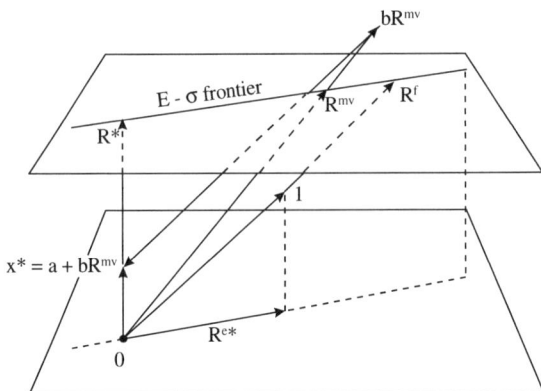

Figure 6.2. *There is a discount factor $m = a + bR^{mv}$ if and only if R^{mv} is on the mean-variance frontier and not the risk-free rate.*

You may remember that x^* is not the only discount factor—all discount factors are of the form $m = x^* + \varepsilon$ with $E(\varepsilon x) = 0$. Perhaps $a + bR$ gives one of these discount factors, when R is not on the mean-variance frontier? This does not work, however; n is still in the payoff space $\underline{X}$ while, by definition, ε is orthogonal to this space.

If the mean-variance efficient return R^{mv} that we start with happens to lie right on the intersection of the stretched unit vector and the frontier, then stretching the R^{mv} vector and adding some unit vector are the same thing, so we again cannot get back to x^* by stretching and adding some unit vector. The stretched unit payoff is the risk-free rate, so the theorem rules out the risk-free rate. When there is no risk-free rate, we have to rule out the "constant-mimicking portfolio return." I treat this case in Section 6.6.

Algebraic Proof
Now, an algebraic proof that captures the same ideas.

Proof. For an arbitrary R, try the discount factor model

$$m = a + bR = a + b(R^* + wR^{e*} + n). \qquad (6.5)$$

We show that this discount factor prices an arbitrary payoff if and only if $n = 0$, and except for the w choice that makes R the risk-free rate (or the constant-mimicking portfolio return if there is no risk-free rate).

We can determine a and b by forcing m to price any two assets. I find a and b to make the model price R^* and R^{e*}:

$$1 = E(mR^*) = aE(R^*) + bE(R^{*2}),$$

$$0 = E(mR^{e*}) = aE(R^{e*}) + bwE(R^{e*2}) = (a + bw)E(R^{e*}).$$

Solving for a and b,

$$a = \frac{w}{wE(R^*) - E(R^{*2})},$$

$$b = -\frac{1}{wE(R^*) - E(R^{*2})}.$$

Thus, if it is to price R^* and R^{e*}, the discount factor must be

$$m = \frac{w - (R^* + wR^{e*} + n)}{wE(R^*) - E(R^{*2})}. \tag{6.6}$$

Now, let us see if m prices an arbitrary payoff x^i. Any $x^i \in \underline{X}$ can also be decomposed as

$$x^i = y^i R^* + w^i R^{e*} + n^i.$$

(See Figure 5.2 if this is not obvious.) The price of x^i is y^i, since both R^{e*} and n^i are zero-price (excess return) payoffs. Therefore, we want $E(mx^i) = y^i$. Does it?

$$E(mx^i) = E\left(\frac{(w - R^* - wR^{e*} - n)(y^i R^* + w^i R^{e*} + n^i)}{wE(R^*) - E(R^{*2})}\right).$$

Using the orthogonality of R^*, R^{e*}, n; $E(n) = 0$ and $E(R^{e*2}) = E(R^{e*})$ to simplify the product,

$$E(mx^i) = \frac{wy^i E(R^*)}{wE(R^*) - E(R^{*2})} \quad \frac{y^i E(R^{*2}) - E(nn^i)}{wE(R^*) - E(R^{*2})} = y^i - \frac{E(nn^i)}{wE(R^*) - E(R^{*2})}.$$

To get $p(x^i) = y^i = E(mx^i)$, we need $E(nn^i) = 0$. The only way to guarantee this condition for *every* payoff $x^i \in \underline{X}$ is to insist that $n = 0$.

Obviously, this construction cannot work if the denominator of (6.6) is zero, i.e., if $w = E(R^{*2})/E(R^*) = 1/E(x^*)$. If there is a risk-free rate, then $R^f = 1/E(x^*)$, so we are ruling out the case $R^{mv} = R^* + R^f R^{e*}$, which is the risk-free rate. If there is no risk-free rate, I interpret $\widehat{R} = R^* + E(R^{*2})/E(R^*)R^{e*}$ as a "constant-mimicking portfolio return" in Section 6.6. □

We can generalize the theorem somewhat. Nothing is special about returns; any payoff of the form $yR^* + wR^{e*}$ or $yx^* + wR^{e*}$ can be used to price assets; such payoffs have minimum variance among all payoffs with given mean and price. Of course, we proved existence, not uniqueness: $m = a + bR^{mv} + \epsilon$, $E(\epsilon x) = 0$ also price assets as always.

To get from the mean-variance frontier to a beta pricing model, we can just chain this theorem and the theorem of the last section together. There is a slight subtlety about special cases when there is no risk-free rate, but since it is not important for the basic points I relegate the direct connection and the special cases to Section 6.6.

6.3 Factor Models and Discount Factors

> Beta pricing models are equivalent to linear models for the discount factor m,
> $$E(R^i) = \alpha + \lambda'\beta_i \Leftrightarrow m = a + b'f.$$

We have shown that $p = E(mx)$ implies a single-beta representation using m, x^*, or R^* as factors. Let us ask the converse question: suppose we have an expected return-beta model such as CAPM, APT, ICAPM, etc. What discount factor does this model imply? I show that an expected return-beta model is equivalent to a discount factor that is a linear function of the factors in the beta model. This is an important and central result. It gives the connection between the discount factor formulation emphasized in this book and the expected return-beta, factor model formulation common in empirical work.

You can write a linear factor model most compactly as $m = b'f$, letting one of the factors be a constant. However, since we want a connection to the beta representation based on covariances rather than second moments, it is easiest to fold means of the factors in to the constant, and write $m = a + b'f$ with $E(f) = 0$ and hence $E(m) = a$.

The connection is easiest to see in the special case that all the test assets are excess returns. Then $0 = E(mR^e)$ does not identify the mean of m, and we can normalize a arbitrarily. I find it convenient to normalize to $E(m) = 1$, or $m = 1 + b'[f - E(f)]$. Then,

Theorem: *Given the model*

$$m = 1 + b'[f - E(f)], \qquad 0 = E(mR^e), \tag{6.7}$$

one can find λ such that

$$E(R^e) = \beta'\lambda, \tag{6.8}$$

where β are the multiple regression coefficients of excess returns R^e on the factors. Conversely, given λ in (6.8), we can find b such that (6.7) holds.

Proof: From (6.7),

$$0 = E(mR^e) = E(R^e) + b'\operatorname{cov}(f, R^e),$$

$$E(R^e) = -b'\operatorname{cov}(f, R^e).$$

From covariance to beta is quick,

$$E(R^e) = -b'\operatorname{var}(f)\operatorname{var}(f)^{-1}\operatorname{cov}(f, R^e) = \lambda'\beta.$$

Thus, λ and b are related by

$$\lambda = -\operatorname{var}(f)b. \qquad \square$$

When the test assets are returns, the same idea works just as well, but gets a little more drowned in algebra since we have to keep track of the constant in m and the zero-beta rate in the beta model.

Theorem: *Given the model*

$$m = a + b'f, \qquad 1 = E(mR^i), \tag{6.9}$$

one can find γ and λ such that

$$E(R^i) = \gamma + \lambda'\beta_i, \tag{6.10}$$

where β_i are the multiple regression coefficients of R^i on f with a constant. Conversely, given γ and λ in a factor model of the form (6.10), one can find a, b such that (6.9) holds.

Proof: We just have to construct the relation between (γ, λ) and (a, b) and show that it works. Start with $m = a + b'f$, $1 = E(mR)$, and hence, still folding the mean of the factors in a so $E(f) = 0$,

$$E(R) = \frac{1}{E(m)} - \frac{\operatorname{cov}(m, R)}{E(m)} = \frac{1}{a} - \frac{E(Rf')b}{a}. \tag{6.11}$$

β_i is the vector of the appropriate regression coefficients,

$$\beta_i \equiv E(ff')^{-1}E(fR^i),$$

so to get β in the formula, continue with

$$E(R) = \frac{1}{a} - \frac{E(Rf')E(ff')^{-1}E(ff')b}{a} = \frac{1}{a} - \beta'\frac{E(ff')b}{a}.$$

Now, define γ and λ to make it work,

$$\gamma \equiv \frac{1}{E(m)} = \frac{1}{a},$$

$$\lambda \equiv -\frac{1}{a}\text{cov}(ff')b = -\gamma E[mf]. \qquad (6.12)$$

Using (6.12), we can just as easily go backwards from the expected return-beta representation to $m = a + b'f$.

As always, we have to worry about a special case of zero or infinite risk-free rates. We rule out $E(m) = E(a + b'f) = 0$ to keep (6.11) from exploding, and we rule out $\gamma = 0$ and $\text{cov}(ff')$ singular to go from γ, β, λ in (6.12) back to m. □

Given either model, *there is* a model of the other form. They are not *unique*. We can add to m any random variable orthogonal to returns, and we can add spurious risk factors with zero β and/or λ, leaving pricing implications unchanged. We can also express the multiple-beta model as a single-beta model with $m = a + b'f$ as the single factor, or use its corresponding R^*.

Equation (6.12) shows that the factor risk premium λ can be interpreted as the price of the factor; a test of $\lambda \neq 0$ is often called a test of whether the "factor is priced." More precisely, λ captures the price $E(mf)$ of the (de-meaned) factors brought forward at the risk-free rate. If we start with underlying factors $\tilde{f}$ such that the de-meaned factors are $f = \tilde{f} - E(\tilde{f})$,

$$\lambda \equiv -\gamma p[\tilde{f} - E(\tilde{f})] = -\gamma\left[p(\tilde{f}) - \frac{E(\tilde{f})}{\gamma}\right].$$

λ represents the price of the factors less their risk-neutral valuation, i.e., the *factor risk premium*. If the factors are not traded, λ is the model's predicted price rather than a market price. Low prices are high risk premia, resulting in the negative sign. If the factors are returns with price one, then the factor risk premium is the expected return of the factor, less γ, $\lambda = E(f) - \gamma$.

Note that the "factors" need not be returns (though they may be); they need not be orthogonal, and they need not be serially uncorrelated or conditionally or unconditionally mean-zero. Such properties may occur as natural special cases, or as part of the economic derivation of specific factor models, but they are not required for the existence of a factor pricing representation. For example, if the risk-free rate is constant, then $E_t(m_{t+1})$ is constant and at least the sum $b'f_{t+1}$ should be uncorrelated over time. But if the risk-free rate is not constant, then $E_t(m_{t+1}) = E_t(b'f_{t+1})$ *should* vary over time.

Factor-Mimicking Portfolios

It is often convenient to use factor-mimicking payoffs

$$f^* = \text{proj}(f|\underline{X}),$$

factor-mimicking returns

$$f^* = \frac{\text{proj}(f|\underline{X})}{p[\text{proj}(f|\underline{X})]},$$

or factor-mimicking excess returns

$$f^* = \text{proj}(f|\underline{R}^e)$$

in place of true factors. These payoffs carry the same pricing information as the original factors, and can serve as reference variables in expected return-beta representations.

When the factors are not already returns or excess returns, it is convenient to express a beta pricing model in terms of its *factor-mimicking portfolios* rather than the factors themselves. Recall that $x^* = \text{proj}(m|\underline{X})$ carries all of m's pricing implications on $\underline{X}$; $p(x) = E(mx) = E(x^*x)$. The factor-mimicking portfolios are just the same idea using the individual factors.

Define the payoffs f^* by

$$f^* = \text{proj}(f|\underline{X}).$$

Then, $m = b'f^*$ carries the same pricing implications on $\underline{X}$ as does $m = b'f$:

$$p = E(mx) = E(b'f\,x) = E[b'(\text{proj}f|\underline{X})x] = E[b'f^*x]. \tag{0.13}$$

(I include the constant as one of the factors.)

The factor-mimicking portfolios also form a beta representation. Just go from (6.13) back to an expected return-beta representation

$$E(R^i) = \gamma^* + \beta^{*\prime}\lambda^*, \tag{6.14}$$

and find λ^*, γ^* using (6.12). The β^* are the regression coefficients of the returns R^i on the factor-mimicking portfolios, not on the factors, as they should be.

It is more traditional to use the *returns* or *excess returns* on the factor-mimicking portfolios rather than payoffs as I have done so far. To generate returns, divide each payoff by its price,

$$f_i^* = \frac{\text{proj}(f_i|\underline{X})}{p[\text{proj}(f_i|\underline{X})]}.$$

The resulting b_i will be scaled down by the price of the factor-mimicking payoff, and the model is the same. Note that you project on the space of payoffs, not of returns. Returns $\underline{R}$ are not a space, since they do not contain zero.

If the test assets are all excess returns, you can even more easily project the factors on the set of excess returns, which are a space since they do include zero. If we define

$$f^* = \text{proj}(f|\underline{R}^e),$$

then of course the excess returns f^* carry the same pricing implications as the factors f for a set of excess returns; $m = b'f^*$ satisfies $0 = E(mR^{ei})$ and

$$E(R^{ei}) = \beta_{i,f^*} \lambda = \beta_{i,f^*} E(f^*).$$

6.4 Discount Factors and Beta Models to Mean-Variance Frontier

> From m, we can construct R^* which is on the mean-variance frontier
>
> If a beta pricing model holds, then a linear combination of the factor-mimicking portfolio returns is on the mean-variance frontier.
>
> Any frontier return is a combination of R^* and one other return, a risk-free rate or a risk-free rate proxy. Thus, any frontier return is a linear function of the factor-mimicking returns plus a risk-free rate proxy.

It is easy to show that, given m, we can find *a* return on the mean-variance frontier. Given m, construct $x^* = \text{proj}(m|\underline{X})$ and $R^* = x^*/E(x^{*2})$. R^* is the minimum second moment return, and hence on the mean-variance frontier.

Similarly, if you have a set of factors f for a beta model, then a linear combination of the factor-mimicking portfolios is on the mean-variance frontier. A beta model is the same as $m = b'f$. Since m is linear in f, x^* is linear in $f^* = \mathrm{proj}(f|\underline{X})$, so R^* is linear in the factor-mimicking payoffs f^* or their returns $f^*/p(f^*)$.

Section 5.4 showed how we can span the mean-variance frontier with R^* and a risk-free rate, if there is one, or the zero-beta, minimum-variance, or constant-mimicking portfolio return $\widehat{R} = \mathrm{proj}(1|\underline{X})/p[\mathrm{proj}(1|\underline{X})]$ if there is no risk-free rate. The latter is particularly nice in the case of a linear factor model, since we may consider the constant as a factor, so the frontier is entirely generated by factor-mimicking portfolio returns.

6.5 Three Risk-Free Rate Analogues

> I introduce three counterparts to the risk-free rate that show up in asset pricing formulas when there is no risk-free rate. The three returns are the *zero-beta* return, the *minimum-variance return*, and the *constant-mimicking portfolio* return.

Three different generalizations of the risk-free rate are useful when a risk-free rate or unit payoff is not in the set of payoffs. These are the *zero-beta* return, the *minimum-variance* return, and the *constant-mimicking portfolio* return. I introduce the returns in this section, and I use them in the next section to state some special cases involving the mean-variance frontier. Each of these returns maintains one property of the risk-free rate in a market in which there is no risk-free rate. The zero-beta return is a mean-variance efficient return that is uncorrelated with another given mean-variance efficient return. The minimum-variance return is just that. The constant-mimicking portfolio return is the return on the payoff "closest" to the unit payoff. Each of these returns has a representation in the standard form R^*+wR^{e*} with slightly different w. In addition, the expected returns of these risky assets are used in some asset pricing representations. For example, the zero-beta *rate* is often used to refer to the expected value of the zero-beta return.

Each of these risk-free rate analogues is mean-variance efficient. Thus, I characterize each one by finding its weight w in a representation of the form $R^* + wR^{e*}$. We derived such a representation above for the risk-free rate as equation (5.20),

$$R^f = R^* + R^f R^{e*}. \tag{6.15}$$

In the last subsection, I show how each risk-free rate analogue reduces to the risk-free rate when there is one.

Zero-Beta Return for R^*

The zero-beta return for R^*, denoted R^γ, is the mean-variance efficient return uncorrelated with R^*. Its expected return is the zero-beta rate $\gamma = E(R^a)$. This zero-beta return has representation

$$R^\gamma = R^* + \frac{\text{var}(R^*)}{E(R^*)E(R^{e*})} R^{e*},$$

and the corresponding zero-beta rate is

$$\gamma = E(R^\gamma) = \frac{E(R^{*2})}{E(R^*)} = \frac{1}{E(x^*)}.$$

The zero-beta rate is found graphically in mean-standard deviation space by extending the tangency at R^* to the vertical axis. It is also the inverse of the price that x^* and R^* assign to the unit payoff.

The risk-free rate R^f is of course uncorrelated with R^*. Risky returns uncorrelated with R^* earn the same average return as the risk-free rate if there is one, so such returns might take the place of R^f when R^f does not exist. For any return R^γ that is uncorrelated with R^* we have $E(R^* R^\gamma) = E(R^*)E(R^\gamma)$, so

$$\gamma = E(R^\gamma) = \frac{E(R^* R^\gamma)}{E(R^*)} = \frac{E(R^{*2})}{E(R^*)} = \frac{1}{E(x^*)}.$$

I call γ the zero-beta *rate*, and R^γ the zero-beta *return*. There is no risk-free rate, so there is no security that just pays γ.

As you can see from the formula, the zero-beta rate is the inverse of the price that R^* and x^* assign to the unit payoff, which is another natural generalization of the risk-free rate. It is called the zero-*beta* rate because $\text{cov}(R^*, R^\gamma) = 0$ implies that the regression beta of R^γ on R^* is zero. More precisely, one might call it the zero-beta rate *on* R^*, since one can calculate zero-beta rates for returns other than R^* and they are not the same as the zero-beta rate for R^*. In particular, the zero-beta rate on the "market portfolio" will generally be different from the zero-beta rate on R^*.

I draw γ in Figure 6.3 as the intersection of the tangency and the vertical axis. This is a property of any return on the mean-variance frontier: The expected return on an asset uncorrelated with the mean-variance efficient asset (a *zero-beta* asset) lies at the point so constructed. To check this geometry, use similar triangles: The length of R^* in Figure 6.3

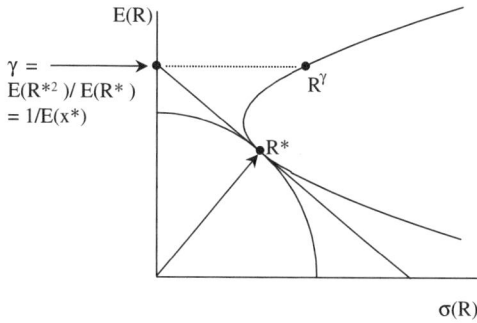

Figure 6.3. *Zero-beta rate γ and zero-beta return R^γ for R^*.*

is $\sqrt{E(R^{*2})}$, and its vertical extent is $E(R^*)$. Therefore, $\gamma/\sqrt{E(R^{*2})} = \sqrt{E(R^{*2})}/E(R^*)$, or $\gamma = E(R^{*2})/E(R^*)$. Since R^* is on the lower portion of the mean-variance frontier, this zero-beta rate γ is above the minimum-variance return.

Note that in general $\gamma \neq 1/E(m)$. Projecting m on $\underline{X}$ preserves asset pricing implications on $\underline{X}$ but not for payoffs not in $\underline{X}$. Thus if a risk-free rate is not traded, x^* and m may differ in their predictions for the risk-free rate as they do for other nontraded assets.

The zero-beta *return* is the rate of return on the mean-variance frontier with mean equal to the zero-beta rate, shown as R^γ in Figure 6.3. We want to characterize this return in $R^* + wR^{e*}$ form. To do this, we want to find w such that

$$E(R^\gamma) = \frac{E(R^{*2})}{E(R^*)} = E(R^*) + wE(R^{e*}).$$

Solving, the answer is

$$w = \frac{E(R^{*2}) - E(R^*)^2}{E(R^*)E(R^{e*})} = \frac{\text{var}(R^*)}{E(R^*)E(R^{e*})}.$$

Thus, the zero-beta *return* is

$$R^\gamma = R^* + \frac{\text{var}(R^*)}{E(R^*)E(R^{e*})} R^{e*}.$$

Note that the weight is not $E(R^\gamma) = E(R^{*2})/E(R^*)$, as $R^f = R^* + R^f R^{e*}$. When there is no risk-free rate, the weight and the mean return are different.

Minimum-Variance Return

The minimum-variance return has the representation

$$R^{\text{min. var.}} = R^* + \frac{E(R^*)}{1 - E(R^{e*})} R^{e*}.$$

The risk-free rate obviously is the minimum-variance return when it exists. When there is no risk-free rate, the minimum-variance return is

$$R^{\text{min. var.}} = R^* + \frac{E(R^*)}{1 - E(R^{e*})} R^{e*}. \tag{6.16}$$

Taking expectations,

$$E(R^{\text{min. var.}}) = E(R^*) + \frac{E(R^*)}{1 - E(R^{e*})} E(R^{e*}) = \frac{E(R^*)}{1 - E(R^{e*})}.$$

Thus, the minimum-variance return retains the nice property of the risk-free rate, that its weight on R^{e*} is the same as its mean,

$$R^{\text{min. var.}} = R^* + E(R^{\text{min. var.}})R^{e*},$$

just as $R^f = R^* + R^f R^{e*}$. When there is no risk-free rate, the zero-beta and minimum-variance returns are not the same. You can see this fact clearly in Figure 6.3.

We can derive expression (6.16) for the minimum-variance return by brute force: choose w in $R^* + wR^{e*}$ to minimize variance:

$$\min_{w} \text{var}(R^* + wR^{e*}) = E[(R^* + wR^{e*})^2] - E(R^* + wR^{e*})^2$$

$$= E(R^{*2}) + w^2 E(R^{e*}) - E(R^*)^2$$

$$- 2wE(R^*)E(R^{e*}) - w^2 E(R^{e*})^2.$$

The first-order condition is

$$0 = wE(R^{e*})[1 - E(R^{e*})] - E(R^*)E(R^{e*}),$$

$$w = \frac{E(R^*)}{1 - E(R^{e*})}.$$

Constant-Mimicking Portfolio Return

The constant-mimicking portfolio return is defined as the return on the projection of the unit vector on the payoff space,

$$\widehat{R} = \frac{\text{proj}(1|\underline{X})}{p[\text{proj}(1|\underline{X})]}.$$

It has the representation

$$\widehat{R} = R^* + \frac{E(R^{*2})}{E(R^*)} R^{e*}.$$

When there is a risk-free rate, it is the rate of return on a unit payoff, $R^f = 1/p(1)$. When there is no risk-free rate, we might define the rate of return on the mimicking portfolio for a unit payoff,

$$\widehat{R} = \frac{\text{proj}(1|\underline{X})}{p[\text{proj}(1|\underline{X})]}.$$

I call this object the *constant-mimicking portfolio return.*

The mean-variance representation of the constant-mimicking portfolio return is

$$\widehat{R} = R^* + \gamma R^{e*} = R^* + \frac{E(R^{*2})}{E(R^*)} R^{e*}. \tag{6.17}$$

Note that the weight γ equal to the zero-beta rate creates the constant-mimicking return, not the zero-beta return. To show (6.17), start with property (5.21),

$$R^{e*} = \text{proj}(1|\underline{X}) - \frac{E(R^*)}{E(R^{*2})} R^*. \tag{6.18}$$

Take the price of both sides. Since the price of R^{e*} is zero and the price of R^* is one, we establish

$$p[\text{proj}(1|\underline{X})] = \frac{E(R^*)}{E(R^{*2})}. \tag{6.19}$$

Solving (6.18) for $\text{proj}(1|\underline{X})$, dividing by (6.19), we obtain the right-hand side of (6.17).

Risk-Free Rate

> The risk-free rate has the mean-variance representation
> $$R^f = R^* + R^f R^{e*}.$$
> The zero-beta, minimum-variance, and constant-mimicking portfolio returns reduce to this formula when there is a risk-free rate.

Again, we derived in equation (5.20) that the risk-free rate has the representation,

$$R^f = R^* + R^f R^{e*}. \tag{6.20}$$

Obviously, we should expect that the zero-beta return, minimum-variance return, and constant-mimicking portfolio return reduce to the risk-free rate when there is one. These other rates are

constant-mimicking: $$\widehat{R} = R^* + \frac{E(R^{*2})}{E(R^*)} R^{e*}, \tag{6.21}$$

minimum-variance: $$R^{\text{min. var.}} = R^* + \frac{E(R^*)}{1 - E(R^{e*})} R^{e*}, \tag{6.22}$$

zero-beta: $$R^{\alpha} = R^* + \frac{\text{var}(R^*)}{E(R^*)E(R^{e*})} R^{e*}. \tag{6.23}$$

To establish that these are all the same when there is a risk-free rate, we need to show that

$$R^f = \frac{E(R^{*2})}{E(R^*)} = \frac{E(R^*)}{1 - E(R^{e*})} = \frac{\text{var}(R^*)}{E(R^*)E(R^{e*})}. \tag{6.24}$$

We derived the first equality above as equation (5.18). To derive the second equality, take expectations of (6.15),

$$R^f = E(R^*) + R^f E(R^{e*}) \tag{6.25}$$

and solve for R^f. To derive the third equality, use the first equality from (6.24) in (6.25),

$$\frac{E(R^{*2})}{E(R^*)} = E(R^*) + R^f E(R^{e*}).$$

Solving for R^f,

$$R^f = \frac{E(R^{*2}) - E(R^*)^2}{E(R^*)E(R^{e*})} = \frac{\text{var}(R^*)}{E(R^*)E(R^{e*})}.$$

6.6 Mean-Variance Special Cases with No Risk-Free Rate

> We can find a discount factor from any mean-variance efficient return except the constant-mimicking return.
>
> We can find a beta representation from any mean-variance efficient return except the minimum-variance return.

I collect in this section the special cases for the equivalence theorems of this chapter. The special cases all revolve around the problem that the expected discount factor, price of a unit payoff, or risk-free rate must not be zero or infinity. This is typically an issue of theoretical rather than practical importance. In a complete, arbitrage-free market, $m > 0$ so we know $E(m) > 0$. If a risk-free rate is traded, you can observe $\infty > E(m) = 1/R^f > 0$. However, in an incomplete market in which no risk-free rate is traded, there are many discount factors with the same asset pricing implications, and you might have happened to choose one with $E(m) = 0$ in your manipulations. By and large, this is easy to avoid: choose another of the many discount factors with the same pricing implications that does not have $E(m) = 0$. More generally, when you choose a particular discount factor you are choosing an extension of the current set of prices and payoffs; you are viewing the current prices and payoffs as a subset of a particular contingent-claim economy. Make sure you pick a sensible one. Therefore, we could simply state the special cases as "when a risk-free rate is not traded, make sure you use discount factors with $0 < E(m) < \infty$." However, it is potentially useful and it certainly is traditional to specify the special *return* on the mean-variance frontier that leads to the infinite or zero implied risk-free rate, and to rule it out directly. This section works out what those returns are and shows why they must be avoided.

———————

The Special Case for Mean-Variance Frontier to Discount Factor

> When there is no risk-free rate, we can find a discount factor that is a linear function of any mean-variance efficient return except the constant-mimicking portfolio return.

In Section 6.2, we saw that we can form a discount factor $a + bR^{mv}$ from any mean-variance efficient return R^{mv} except one particular return, of the form $R^* + [E(R^{*2})/E(R^*)]R^{e*}$. This return led to an infinite m. We now recognize this return as the risk-free rate, when there is one, or the constant-mimicking portfolio return, if there is no risk-free rate.

Figure 6.4 shows the geometry of this case. To use no more than three dimensions I had to reduce the return and excess return sets to lines. The payoff space $\underline{X}$ is the plane joining the return and excess return sets as shown. The set of all discount factors is $m = x^* + \varepsilon$, $E(\varepsilon x) = 0$, the line through x^* orthogonal to the payoff space $\underline{X}$ in the figure. I draw the unit payoff (the dot marked "1" in Figure 6.4) closer to the viewer than the plane $\underline{X}$, and I draw a vector through the unit payoff coming out of the page.

Take any return on the mean-variance frontier, R^{mv}. (Since the return space only has two dimensions, all returns are on the frontier.) For a given R^{mv}, the space $a + bR^{mv}$ is the plane spanned by R^{mv} and the unit payoff. This plane lies sideways in the figure. As the figure shows, there is a vector $a + bR^{mv}$ in this plane that lies on the line of discount factors.

Next, the special case. This construction would go awry if the plane spanning the unit payoff and the return R^{mv} were parallel to the plane containing the discount factor. Thus, the construction would not work for the return marked $\widehat{R}$ in the figure. This is a return corresponding to a payoff that is the projection of the unit payoff on to $\underline{X}$, so that the residual will be orthogonal to $\underline{X}$, as is the line of discount factors.

With Figure 6.4 in front of us, we can also see why the constant-mimicking portfolio return is not the same thing as the minimum-variance return. Variance is the size or second moment of the residual in a projection (regression) on 1:

$$\mathrm{var}(x) = E[(x - E(x))^2] = E[(x - \mathrm{proj}(x|1))^2] = \|x - \mathrm{proj}(x|1)\|^2.$$

Thus, the minimum-variance return is the return closest to extensions of the unit vector. It is formed by projecting *returns* on the *unit vector*. The constant-mimicking portfolio return is the return on the payoff closest to 1. It is formed by projecting the *unit vector* on the set of *payoffs*.

The Special Case for Mean-Variance Frontier to a Beta Model

> We can use any return on the mean-variance frontier as the reference return for a single-beta representation, except the minimum-variance return.

We already know mean-variance frontiers $\Leftrightarrow$ discount factor and discount factor $\Leftrightarrow$ single-beta representation, so at a superficial level we can string the two theorems together to go from a mean-variance efficient return to a beta representation. However, it is more elegant to go directly, and the special cases are also a bit simpler this way.

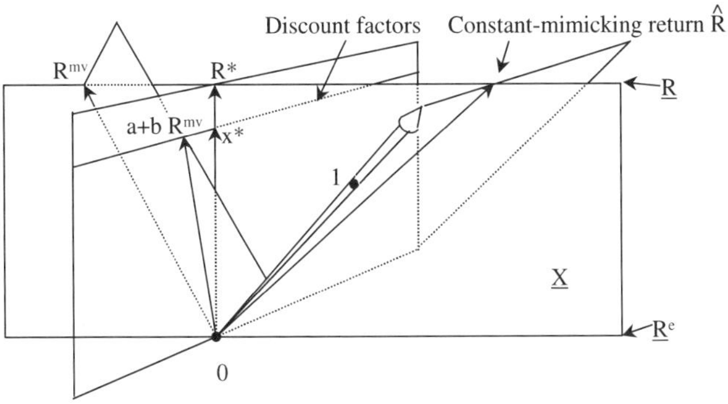

Figure 6.4. *One can construct a discount factor $m = a + bR^{mv}$ from any mean-variance efficient return except the constant-mimicking return $\widehat{R}$.*

Theorem: *There is a single-beta representation with a return R^{mv} as factor,*

$$E(R^i) = \gamma_{R^{mv}} + \beta_{i,R^{mv}}[E(R^{mv}) - \gamma_{R^{mv}}],$$

if and only if R^{mv} is mean-variance efficient and not the minimum-variance return.

This famous theorem is given by Roll (1976) and Hansen and Richard (1987). We rule out minimum variance to rule out the special case $E(m) = 0$. Graphically, the zero-beta rate is formed from the tangency to the mean-variance frontier as in Figure 6.3. I use the notation $\gamma_{R^{mv}}$ to emphasize that we use the zero-beta rate corresponding to the particular mean-variance return R^{mv} that we use as the reference return. If we used the minimum-variance return, that would lead to an infinite zero-beta rate.

Proof: The mean-variance frontier is $R^{mv} = R^* + wR^{e*}$. Any return is $R^i = R^* + w^i R^{e*} + n^i$. Thus,

$$E(R^i) = E(R^*) + w^i E(R^{e*}). \tag{6.26}$$

Now,

$$\begin{aligned}
\text{cov}(R^i, R^{mv}) &= \text{cov}[(R^* + wR^{e*}), (R^* + w^i R^{e*})] \\
&= \text{var}(R^*) + ww^i \text{var}(R^{e*}) - (w + w^i)E(R^*)E(R^{e*}) \\
&= \text{var}(R^*) - wE(R^*)E(R^{e*}) + w^i[w\,\text{var}(R^{e*}) \\
&\quad - E(R^*)E(R^{e*})].
\end{aligned}$$

Thus, $\text{cov}(R^i, R^{mv})$ and $E(R^i)$ are both linear functions of w^i. We can solve $\text{cov}(R^i, R^{mv})$ for w^i, plug into the expression for $E(R^i)$ and we are done.

To do this, of course, we must be able to solve $\text{cov}(R^i, R^{mv})$ for w^i. This requires

$$w \neq \frac{E(R^*)E(R^{e*})}{\text{var}(R^{e*})} = \frac{E(R^*)E(R^{e*})}{E(R^{e*2}) - E(R^{e*})^2} = \frac{E(R^*)}{1 - E(R^{e*})}, \qquad (6.27)$$

which is the condition for the minimum-variance return.   □

Problems—Chapter 6

1. In the argument that R^{mv} on the mean-variance frontier, $R^{mv} = R^* + wR^{e*}$, implies a discount factor $m = a + bR^{mv}$, do we have to rule out the case of risk neutrality? (Hint: what is R^{e*} when the economy is risk neutral?)

2. If you use factor-mimicking portfolios as in (6.13), you know that the predictions for expected returns are the same as they are if you use the factors themselves. Are the γ^*, λ^*, and β^* for the factor-mimicking portfolio representation the same as the original γ, λ, and β of the factor pricing model?

3. Suppose the CAPM is true, $m = a - bR^m$ prices a set of assets, and there is a risk-free rate R^f. Find R^* in terms of the moments of R^m, R^f.

4. If you express the mean-variance frontier as a linear combination of factor-mimicking portfolios from a factor model, do the relative weights of the various factor portfolios in the mean-variance efficient return change as you sweep out the frontier, or do they stay the same? (Start with the risk-free rate case.)

5. For an arbitrary mean-variance efficient return of the form $R^* + wR^{e*}$, find its zero-beta return and zero-beta rate. Show that your rate reduces to the risk-free rate when there is one.

6. When the economy is risk neutral, and if there is no risk-free rate, show that the zero-beta, minimum-variance, and constant-mimicking portfolio returns are again all equivalent, though not equal to the risk-free rate. What is R^* in this economy? ($R^* \neq 1/R^f$ since there is no risk-free rate.)

7

Implications of Existence and
Equivalence Theorems

> The existence of a discount factor means that $p = E(mx)$ is innocuous, and all content flows from the discount factor model.
>
> The theorems apply to sample moments too; the dangers of fishing up ex post or sample mean-variance efficient portfolios.
>
> Sources of discipline in factor fishing expeditions.
>
> The joint hypothesis problem. How efficiency tests are the same as tests of economic discount factor models.
>
> Factors vs. their mimicking portfolios.
>
> Testing the number of factors.
>
> Plotting contingent claims on the axis vs. mean and variance.

THE THEOREMS on the existence of a discount factor, and the equivalence between the $p = E(mx)$, expected return-beta, and mean-variance views of asset pricing have important implications for how we approach and evaluate empirical work.

The equivalence theorems are obviously important to the theme of this book. They show that the choice of discount factor language versus expected return-beta language or mean-variance frontier is entirely one of convenience. Nothing in the more traditional statements is lost.

$p = E(mx)$ is Innocuous

Before Roll (1976), expected return-beta representations had been derived in the context of special and explicit economic models, especially the CAPM. In empirical work, the success of any expected return-beta model seemed like a vindication of the whole structure. The fact that, for example, one might use the NYSE value-weighted index portfolio in place of the return on total wealth predicted by the CAPM seemed like a minor issue of empirical implementation.

When Roll showed that mean-variance efficiency implies a single-beta representation, all that changed. *Some* single-beta representation always exists, since there is some mean-variance efficient return. The asset pricing model only serves to predict that a particular return (say, the "market return") will be mean-variance efficient. Thus, if one wants to "test the CAPM" it becomes much more important to be choosy about the reference portfolio, to guard against stumbling on something that happens to be mean-variance efficient and hence prices assets by construction.

This insight led naturally to the use of broader wealth indices (Stambaugh [1982]) in the reference portfolio, to provide a more grounded test of the CAPM. However, this approach has not caught on. Stocks are priced with stock factors, bonds with bond factors, and so on. More recently, stocks sorted on size, book/market, and past performance characteristics are priced by portfolios sorted on those characteristics (Fama and French [1993], [1996]). Part of the reason for this result is that the betas are small; asset classes are not highly correlated so risk premia from one source of betas have small impacts on another set of average returns. Also, more comprehensive wealth measures that include human capital and real estate do not come with high-frequency price data, so adding them to a wealth portfolio has little effect on betas. However, one is left with the nagging (and exciting, to a researcher) suspicion that markets may be somewhat segmented, especially at high frequency.

The good news in Roll's existence theorem is that you can always start by writing an expected return-beta model, knowing that you have imposed almost no structure in doing so. The bad news is that you have not gotten very far. All the economic, statistical, and predictive content comes in picking the factors.

The theorem that, from the law of one price, there exists some discount factor m such that $p = E(mx)$ is just an updated restatement of Roll's theorem. The content is all in $m = f(\text{data})$, not in $p = E(mx)$. Again, an asset pricing framework that initially seemed to require a lot of completely unbelievable structure—the representative consumer consumption-based model in complete frictionless markets—turns out to require (almost) no structure at all. Again, the good news is that you can always start by writing $p = E(mx)$, and need not suffer criticism about hidden contingent-claim or representative consumer assumptions in so doing. The bad news is that you have not gotten very far by writing $p = E(mx)$ as all the economic, statistical, and predictive content comes in picking the discount factor model $m = f(\text{data})$.

Ex Ante and Ex Post

I have been deliberately vague about the probabilities underlying expectations and other moments in the theorems. The fact is, the theorems hold for *any* set of probabilities. Thus, the existence and equivalence theorems work equally well *ex ante* as *ex post*: $E(mx)$, β, $E(R)$, and so forth can refer to agents' subjective probability distributions, objective population probabilities, or to the moments realized in a given sample.

Thus, if the law of one price holds in a sample, one may form an x^* from *sample* moments that satisfies $p(x) = E(x^*x)$, *exactly*, in that sample, where $p(x)$ refers to observed prices and $E(x^*x)$ refers to the sample average. Equivalently, if the *sample* covariance matrix of a set of returns is nonsingular, there exists an *ex post* mean-variance efficient portfolio for which sample average returns line up exactly with sample regression betas.

This observation points to a great danger in the widespread exercise of searching for and statistically evaluating ad hoc asset pricing models. Such models are *guaranteed* empirical success in a sample if one places little enough structure on what is included in the discount factor or reference portfolios. The only reason the model does not work *perfectly* is the restrictions the researcher has imposed on the number or identity of the factors included in m, or the parameters of the function relating the factors to m. Since these restrictions are the *entire* content of the model, they had better be interesting, carefully described, and well motivated!

Obviously, this is typically not the case or I would not be making such a fuss about it. Most empirical asset pricing research posits an ad hoc pond of factors, fishes around a bit in that pond, and reports statistical measures that show "success," in that the model is not statistically rejected in pricing a set of portfolios. The discount factor pond is usually not large enough to give the zero pricing errors we know are possible, yet the boundaries are not clearly defined.

Discipline

What is wrong, you might ask, with finding an ex post efficient portfolio or x^* that prices assets by construction? Perhaps the lesson we should learn from the existence theorems is to forget about economics, the CAPM, marginal utility, and all that, and simply price assets with ex post mean-variance efficient portfolios that we know set pricing errors to zero!

The mistake is that a portfolio that is ex post efficient in one sample, and hence prices all assets in that sample, is unlikely to be mean-variance efficient, ex ante or ex post, in the next sample, and hence is likely to do a poor job of pricing assets in the future. Similarly, the portfolio $x^* = p'E(xx')^{-1}x$ (using the sample second moment matrix) that is a discount factor by construction in one sample is unlikely to be a discount factor in the next sample; the required portfolio weights $p'E(xx')^{-1}$ change, often drastically, from sample to sample.

For example, suppose the CAPM is true, the market portfolio is ex ante mean-variance efficient, and sets pricing errors to zero if you use true or subjective probabilities. Nonetheless, the market portfolio is unlikely to be *ex post* mean-variance efficient in any given sample. In any sample, there will be lucky winners and unlucky losers. An *ex post* mean-variance efficient portfolio will be a Monday-morning quarterback; it will tell you to put large weights on assets that happened to be lucky in a given sample, but are no more likely than indicated by their betas to generate high returns in the future. "Oh, if I had only bought Microsoft in 1982. . . " is not a useful guide to forming a mean-variance efficient portfolio today. (In fact, mean-reversion and book/market effects suggest that assets with unusually good returns in the past are likely to do poorly in the future!)

The only solution is to impose some kind of discipline in order to avoid dredging up spuriously good in-sample pricing.

The situation is the same as in traditional regression analysis. Regressions are used to forecast or to explain a variable y by other variables x in a regression $y = x'\beta + \varepsilon$. By blindly including right-hand variables, one can produce models with arbitrarily good statistical measures of fit. But this kind of model is typically unstable out of sample or otherwise useless for explanation or forecasting. One has to carefully and thoughtfully limit the search for right-hand variables x in order to produce good models.

What makes for an interesting set of restrictions? Econometricians wrestling with $y = x'\beta + \varepsilon$ have been thinking about this question for about 50 years, and the best answers are 1) use economic theory to carefully specify the right-hand side and 2) use a battery of cross-sample and out-of-sample stability checks.

Alas, this advice is hard to follow. Economic theory is usually either silent on what variables to put on the right-hand side of a regression, or allows a huge range of variables. The same is true in finance. "What are the fundamental risk factors?" is still an unanswered question. At the same time one can appeal to the APT and ICAPM to justify the inclusion of just about any desirable factor. (Fama [1991] calls these theories a "fishing license.") Thus, you will grow old waiting for theorists to provide sharp restrictions.

Following the purely statistical advice, the battery of cross-sample and out-of-sample tests often reveals the model is unstable, and needs to be changed. Once it is changed, there is no more out-of-sample left to check it. Furthermore, even if one researcher is pure enough to follow the methodology of classical statistics, and wait 50 years for another fresh sample to be available before contemplating another model, his competitors and journal editors are unlikely to be so patient. In practice, then, out-of-sample validation is not as strong a guard against fishing as one might hope.

Nonetheless, these are the only tools we have to guard against fishing. In my opinion, the best hope for finding pricing factors that are robust out of sample and across different markets, is to try to understand the fundamental macroeconomic sources of risk. By this I mean, tying asset prices to macroeconomic events, in the way the ill-fated consumption-based model does via $m_{t+1} = \beta u'(c_{t+1})/u'(c_t)$. The difficulties of the consumption-based model have made this approach lose favor in recent years. However, the alternative approach is also running into trouble in that the number and identity of empirically determined risk factors do not seem stable. In the quarter century since Merton (1973) and Ross (1976a) inaugurated multiple-factor models, the standard set of risk factors has changed about every two years. Efforts such as Lettau and Ludvigson (1999), to find macroeconomic explanations for empirically determined risk factors may prove a useful compromise.

In any case, one should always ask of a factor model, "what is the compelling economic story that restricts the range of factors used?" and/or what *statistical* restraints are used to keep from discovering ex post mean-variance efficient portfolios, or to ensure that the results will be robust across samples. The existence theorems tell us that the answers to these questions are the *only* content of the exercise. If the purpose of the model is not just to *predict* asset prices but also to *explain* them, this puts an additional burden on economic motivation of the risk factors.

There is a natural resistance to such discipline built in to our current statistical methodology for evaluating models and papers. When the last author fished around and produced an ad hoc factor pricing model that generates 1% average pricing errors, it is awfully hard to persuade readers, referees, journal editors, and clients that your economically motivated factor pricing model is interesting despite 2% average pricing errors. Your model may really be better and will therefore continue to do well out of sample when the fished model falls by the wayside of financial fashion, but it is hard to get past statistical measures of in-sample fit. One hungers for a formal measurement of the number of hurdles imposed on a factor fishing expedition, like the degrees-of-freedom correction in $\overline{R}^2$. Absent a numerical correction, we have to use judgment to scale back apparent statistical successes by the amount of economic and statistical fishing that produced them.

Mimicking Portfolios

The theorem $x^* = \text{proj}(m|\underline{X})$ also has interesting implications for empirical work. The pricing implications of any model can be equivalently represented by its factor-mimicking portfolio. If there is any measurement error in a set of economic variables driving m, the factor-mimicking portfolios for the true m will price assets better than an estimate of m that uses the measured macroeconomic variables.

Thus, it is probably not a good idea to evaluate economically interesting models with statistical horse races against models that use portfolio returns as factors. Economically interesting models, even if true and perfectly measured, will just equal the performance of their own factor-mimicking portfolios, even in large samples. Add any measurement error, and the economic model will underperform its own factor-mimicking portfolios. And both models will always lose in sample against ad hoc factor models that find nearly ex post efficient portfolios.

This said, there is an important place for models that use returns as factors. *After* we have found the underlying macro factors, practitioners will be well advised to look at the factor-mimicking portfolio on a day-by-day basis. Good data on the factor-mimicking portfolios will be available on a minute-by-minute basis. For many purposes, one does not have to understand the *economic* content of a model.

But this fact does not tell us to circumvent the process of understanding the true macroeconomic factors by simply fishing for factor-mimicking portfolios. The experience of practitioners who use factor models seems to bear out this advice. Large commercial factor models resulting from extensive statistical analysis (otherwise known as fishing) perform poorly out of sample, as revealed by the fact that the factors and loadings (β) change all the time.

Irrationality and Joint Hypothesis
Finance contains a long history of fighting about "rationality" versus "irrationality" and "efficiency" versus "inefficiency" of asset markets. The results of many empirical asset pricing papers are sold as evidence that markets are "inefficient" or that investors are "irrational." For example, the crash of October 1987, and various puzzles such as the small-firm, book/market, seasonal effects, or long-term predictability have all been sold this way.

However, none of these puzzles documents an exploitable arbitrage opportunity. Therefore, we know that there is *a* "rational model"—*a* stochastic discount factor, *an* efficient portfolio to use in a single-beta representation—that rationalizes them all. And we can confidently predict this situation to continue; real arbitrage opportunities do not last long! Fama (1970) contains a famous statement of the same point. Fama emphasized that any test of "efficiency" is a *joint* test of efficiency and a "model of market equilibrium." Translated, an asset pricing model, or a model of m. No test based only on asset market data can conclusively show that markets are "rational" or not. Small wonder that 30 years and thousands of papers have not moved the debate an inch closer to resolution.

But surely markets can be "irrational" or "inefficient" without requiring *arbitrage* opportunities? Yes, they can, *if (and only if) the discount factors that generate asset prices are disconnected from marginal rates of substitution or transformation in the real economy.* But now we are right back to specifying and testing economic models of the discount factor! At best, an asset pricing puzzle might be so severe that the required discount factors are completely "unreasonable" (by some standard) measures of real marginal rates of substitution and/or transformation, but we still have to say *something* about what a reasonable marginal rate looks like.

    In sum, the existence theorems mean that there are no quick proofs of "rationality" or "irrationality." The only game in town for the purpose of *explaining* asset prices is thinking about economic models of the discount factor.

The Number of Factors

Many asset pricing tests focus on the *number* of factors required to price a cross section of assets. The equivalence theorems imply that this is a silly question. A linear factor model $m = b'f$ or its equivalent expected return-beta model $E(R^i) = \alpha + \beta'_{if}\lambda_f$ are not unique representations. In particular, given any multiple-factor or multiple-beta representation, we can easily find a single-beta representation. The single factor $m = b'f$ will price assets just as well as the original factors f, as will $x^* = \text{proj}(b'f|\underline{X})$ or the corresponding R^*. All three options give rise to single-beta models with exactly the same pricing ability as the multiple-factor model. We can also easily find equivalent representations with different numbers (greater than one) of factors. For example, write

$$m = a + b_1 f_1 + b_2 f_2 + b_3 f_3 = a + b_1 f_1 + b_2\left(f_2 + \frac{b_3}{b_2}f_3\right) = a + b_1 f_1 + b_2 \hat{f}_2$$

to reduce a "three-factor" model to a "two-factor" model. In the ICAPM language, consumption itself could serve as a single state variable, in place of the S state variables presumed to drive it.

    There are times when one is interested in a multiple-factor representation. Sometimes the factors have an economic interpretation that is lost on taking a linear combination. But the pure *number* of pricing factors is not a meaningful question.

Discount Factors vs. Mean, Variance, and Beta

Chapter 7 showed how the discount factor, mean-variance, and expected return-beta models are all equivalent representations of asset pricing. It seems a good moment to contrast them as well; to understand why the mean-variance and beta language developed first, and to think about why the discount factor language seems to be taking over.

    Asset pricing started by putting mean and variance of returns on the axes, rather than payoff in state 1, payoff in state 2, etc. as we do now. The early asset pricing theorists, in particular Markowitz (1952), posed the question just right: they wanted to treat assets in the apples and oranges, indifference curve and budget set framework of microeconomics.

The problem was, what labels to put on the axes? Clearly, "IBM stock" and "GM stock" is not a good idea; investors do not value securities per se, but value some aspects of the stream of random cash flows that those securities give rise to.

Their brilliant insight was to put the mean and variance of the portfolio return on the axes: to treat these as "hedonics" by which investors valued their portfolios. Investors plausibly want more mean and less variance. They gave investors "utility functions" defined over this mean and variance, just as standard utility functions are defined over apples and oranges. The mean-variance frontier is the "budget set."

With this focus on portfolio mean and variance, the next step was to realize that each security's mean return measures its contribution to the portfolio mean, and that regression betas on the overall portfolio give each security's contribution to the portfolio variance. The mean-return versus beta description for each security followed naturally (Sharpe 1964).

In a deep sense, the transition from mean-variance frontiers and beta models to discount factors represents the realization that putting consumption in state 1 and consumption in state 2 on the axes—specifying preferences and budget constraints over state-contingent consumption—is a much more natural mapping of standard microeconomics into finance than putting mean, variance, etc. on the axes. If for no other reason, the contingent-claim budget constraints are linear, while the mean-variance frontier is not. Thus, I think, the focus on means and variance, the mean-variance frontier, and expected return-beta models is all due to an accident of history, that the early asset pricing theorists happened to put mean and variance on the axes rather than state-contingent consumption. Of course, contingent claims go back just as far, to Debreu (1959). However, Debreu seemed to think of them as an unrealistic mathematical formalism. It has taken us a long time to realize that a contingent claim framework can be applied to real-world phenomena.

Well, here we are, why prefer one language over another? The discount factor language has an advantage for its simplicity, generality, mathematical convenience, and elegance. These virtues are to some extent in the eye of the beholder, but to this beholder, it is inspiring to be able to start *every* asset pricing calculation with one equation, $p = E(mx)$. This equation covers all assets, including bonds, options, and real investment opportunities, while the expected return-beta formulation is not useful or very cumbersome in the latter applications. Thus, it has seemed that there are several different asset pricing theories: expected return-beta for stocks, yield-curve models for bonds, arbitrage models for options. In fact all three are just cases of $p = E(mx)$. As a particular example, *arbitrage*, in the precise sense of positive payoffs with negative prices, has not entered the equivalence discussion at all. I do not know of any way to cleanly graft absence of arbitrage on to expected return-beta models. You have to tack it on after the fact—"by the way, make sure that every portfolio with positive payoffs has a positive price." It is trivially easy to graft it on to a discount factor model: just add $m > 0$.

The discount factor and state-space language also makes it easier to think about different horizons and the present-value statement of models. $p = E(mx)$ generalizes quickly to $p_t = E_t \sum_j m_{t,t+j} x_{t+j}$, while returns have to be chained together to think about multiperiod models.

The choice of language is *not* about normality or return distributions. There is a lot of confusion about where return distribution assumptions show up in finance. I have made *no* distributional assumptions in any of the discussion so far. Second moments as in betas and the variance of the mean-variance frontier show up because $p = E(mx)$ involves a second moment. One does not need to assume normality to talk about the mean-variance frontier. Returns on the mean-variance frontier price other assets even when returns are not normally distributed.

8

Conditioning Information

ASSET PRICING THEORY really describes prices in terms of *conditional* moments. The investor's first-order conditions are

$$p_t u'(c_t) = \beta E_t[u'(c_{t+1})x_{t+1}],$$

where E_t means expectation *conditional* on the investor's time-t information. Sensibly, the price at time t should be higher if there is information at time t that the discounted payoff is likely to be higher than usual at time $t+1$. The basic asset pricing equation should be

$$p_t = E_t(m_{t+1}x_{t+1}).$$

(Conditional expectation can also be written

$$p_t = E[m_{t+1}x_{t+1}|I_t]$$

when it is important to specify the *information set I_t*.)

If payoffs and discount factors were independent and identically distributed (i.i.d.) over time, then conditional expectations would be the same as unconditional expectations and we would not have to worry about the distinction between the two concepts. But stock price/dividend ratios, and bond and option prices all change over time, which must reflect changing conditional moments of something on the right-hand side.

One approach is to specify and estimate explicit statistical models of conditional distributions of asset payoffs and discount factor variables (e.g., consumption growth, market return). This approach is useful in some applications, but it is usually cumbersome. As we make the conditional mean, variance, covariance, and other parameters of the distribution of (say) N returns depend flexibly on M information variables, the number of required parameters can quickly exceed the number of observations.

More importantly, this explicit approach typically requires us to assume that investors use the same model of conditioning information that we do.

We obviously do not even observe all the conditioning information used by economic agents, and we cannot include even a fraction of observed conditioning information in our models. The basic feature and beauty of asset prices (like all prices) is that they summarize an enormous amount of information that only individuals see. The events that make the price of IBM stock change by a dollar, like the events that make the price of tomatoes change by 10 cents, are inherently unobservable to economists or would-be social planners (Hayek [1945]). Whenever possible, our treatment of conditioning information should allow agents to see more than we do.

If we do not want to model conditional distributions explicitly, and if we want to avoid assuming that investors only see the variables that we include in an empirical investigation, we eventually have to think about unconditional moments, or at least moments conditioned on less information than agents see. Unconditional implications are also interesting in and of themselves. For example, we may be interested in finding out why the unconditional mean returns on some stock portfolios are higher than others, even if every agent fundamentally seeks high conditional mean returns. Most statistical estimation essentially amounts to characterizing unconditional means, as we will see in the chapter on GMM. Thus, rather than *model conditional distributions*, this chapter focuses on what implications for *unconditional* moments we can derive from the *conditional* theory.

8.1 Scaled Payoffs

> One can incorporate conditioning information by adding *scaled payoffs* and doing everything unconditionally. I interpret scaled returns as payoffs to *managed portfolios*.
>
> $$p_t = E_t(m_{t+1}x_{t+1}) \Rightarrow E(p_t z_t) = E(m_{t+1}x_{t+1}z_t).$$

Conditioning Down

The unconditional implications of any pricing model are pretty easy to state. From

$$p_t = E_t(m_{t+1}x_{t+1})$$

we can take unconditional expectations to obtain[1]

$$E(p_t) = E(m_{t+1}x_{t+1}). \tag{8.1}$$

---

[1]We need a small technical assumption that the unconditional moment or moment conditioned on a coarser information set *exists*. For example, if X and Y are normal $(0, 1)$, then $E\left(\frac{X}{Y}|Y\right) = 0$ but $E\left(\frac{X}{Y}\right)$ is infinite.

Thus, if we just interpret p to stand for $E(p_t)$, everything we have done above applies to unconditional moments. In the same way, we can also condition down from agents' fine information sets to coarser sets that we observe,

$$p_t = E(m_{t+1}x_{t+1} \mid \Omega) \Rightarrow E(p_t \mid I \subset \Omega) = E(m_{t+1}x_{t+1} \mid I \subset \Omega)$$
$$\Rightarrow p_t = E(m_{t+1}x_{t+1} \mid I_t \subset \Omega_t) \quad \text{if } p_t \in I_t.$$

In making the above statements I used the *law of iterated expectations*, which is important enough to highlight it. This law states that your best forecast today of your best forecast tomorrow is the same as your best forecast today. In various useful guises,

$$E(E_t(x)) = E(x),$$
$$E_{t-1}(E_t(x_{t+1})) = E_{t-1}(x_{t+1}),$$
$$E[E(x|\Omega)|I \subset \Omega] = E[x|I].$$

Instruments and Managed Portfolios

We can do more than just condition down. Suppose we multiply the payoff and price by any variable or instrument z_t observed at time t. Then,

$$z_t p_t = E_t(m_{t+1}x_{t+1}z_t)$$

and, taking unconditional expectations,

$$E(p_t z_t) = E(m_{t+1}x_{t+1}z_t). \tag{8.2}$$

This is an *additional* implication of the conditional model, not captured by just conditioning down as in (8.1). This trick originates from the GMM method of estimating asset pricing models, discussed below. The word *instruments* for the z variables comes from the *instrumental variables estimation* heritage of GMM.

To think about equation (8.2), group $(x_{t+1}z_t)$. Call this product a *payoff* $x = x_{t+1}z_t$, with *price* $p = E(p_t z_t)$. Then (8.2) reads

$$p = E(mx)$$

once again. Rather than thinking about (8.2) as a instrumental variables estimate of a conditional model, we can think of it as a price and a payoff, and apply all the asset pricing theory directly.

This interpretation is not as artificial as it sounds. $z_t x_{t+1}$ are the payoffs to *managed portfolios*. An investor who observes z_t can, rather than "buy and hold," invest in an asset according to the value of z_t. For example, if a high value of z_t forecasts that asset returns are likely to be high the next period, the investor might buy more of the asset when z_t is high and vice versa. If the investor follows a linear rule, he puts $z_t p_t$ dollars into the asset each period and receives $z_t x_{t+1}$ dollars the next period.

This all sounds new and different, but practically every test uses managed portfolios. For example, the size, beta, industry, book/market, and so forth portfolios of stocks are all managed portfolios, since their composition changes every year in response to conditioning information—the size, beta, etc., of the individual stocks. This idea is also closely related to the idea of *dynamic spanning*. Markets that are apparently very incomplete can in reality provide many more state contingencies through dynamic (conditioned on information) trading strategies.

Equation (8.2) offers a very simple view of how to incorporate the extra information in conditioning information: *Add managed portfolio payoffs, and proceed with unconditional moments as if conditioning information did not exist!*

The linearity of xz is not an important restriction. If the investor wanted to place, say, $2 + 3z^2$ dollars in the asset, we could capture this desire with an instrument $z_2 = 2 + 3z^2$. Nonlinear (measurable) transformations of time-t random variables are again random variables.

We can thus incorporate conditioning information while still looking at unconditional moments instead of conditional moments, without any of the statistical machinery of explicit models with time-varying moments. The only subtleties are: 1) The set of asset payoffs expands dramatically, since we can consider all managed portfolios as well as basic assets, potentially multiplying every asset return by every information variable. 2) Expected prices of managed portfolios show up for p instead of just $p = 0$ and $p = 1$ if we started with basic asset returns and excess returns.

8.2 Sufficiency of Adding Scaled Returns

Checking the expected price of all managed portfolios is, in principle, sufficient to check *all* the implications of conditioning information.

$$E(z_t p_t) = E(m_{t+1} x_{t+1} z_t) \, \forall z_t \in I_t \quad \Rightarrow \quad p_t = E(m_{t+1} x_{t+1} | I_t)$$

We have shown that we can derive *some* extra implications from the presence of conditioning information by adding scaled returns. But does this exhaust the implications of conditioning information? Are we missing something important by relying on this trick? The answer is, in principle, *no*.

I rely on the following mathematical fact: The conditional expectation of a variable y_{t+1} given an information set I_t, $E(y_{t+1} \mid I_t)$ is equal to a regression forecast of y_{t+1} using every variable $z_t \in I_t$. Now, "every random variable" means every variable and every nonlinear (measurable) transformation of every variable, so there are a lot of variables in this regression! (The word *projection* and $\text{proj}(y_{t+1}|z_t)$ are used to distinguish the best forecast of y_{t+1} using only *linear* combinations of z_t.) Applying this fact to our case, let $y_{t+1} = m_{t+1}x_{t+1} - p_t$. Then $E[(m_{t+1}x_{t+1} - p_t)z_t] = 0$ for every $z_t \in I_t$ implies $0 = E(m_{t+1}x_{t+1} - p_t \mid I_t)$. Thus, no implications are lost in principle by looking at scaled returns.

We really don't have to write the z_t explicitly. $x_{t+1}z_{t+1}$ *is* a payoff available at time $t + 1$ and $p_t z_t$ is its price. Thus, the space of all payoffs $\underline{X}_{t+1}$ already includes the time-$(t + 1)$ payoffs you can generate with a basis set of assets x_{t+1} and all dynamic strategies that use information in the set I_t. With that definition of the space $\underline{X}_{t+1}$ we can write the sufficiency of scaled returns, simply recognizing that $z_t p_t$ *is* a price and $z_t x_{t+1}$ *is* a payoff, as

$$E(p_t) = E(m_{t+1}x_{t+1}) \forall x_t \in \underline{X}_{t+1} \quad \Rightarrow \quad p_t = E(m_{t+1}x_{t+1} \mid I_t)$$

"All linear and nonlinear transformations of all variables observed at time t" sounds like a lot of instruments, and it is. But there is a practical limit to the number of instruments z_t one needs to scale by, since only variables that forecast returns or m (or their higher moments and co-moments) add any information.

Since adding instruments is the same thing as including potential managed portfolios, the thoughtful choice of a few instruments is the same thing as the thoughtful choice of a few assets or portfolios that one makes in any test of an asset pricing model. Even when evaluating completely unconditional asset pricing models, one always forms portfolios and omits many possible assets from analysis. Few studies, in fact, go beyond checking whether a model correctly prices 10–25 stock portfolios and a few bond portfolios. Implicitly, one feels that the chosen payoffs do a pretty good job of spanning the set of available risk loadings or mean returns, and hence that adding additional assets will not affect the results. Nonetheless, since data are easily available on thousands of NYSE, AMEX and NASDAQ stocks, to say nothing of government and corporate bonds, mutual funds, foreign exchange, foreign equities, real investment opportunities, etc., the use of a few portfolios means that a tremendous number of potential asset payoffs are left out in an ad hoc manner.

Similarly, if one had a small set of instruments that capture all the predictability of discounted returns $m_{t+1}R_{t+1}$, then there would be no need to add more instruments. Thus, we carefully but arbitrarily select a few instruments that we think do a good job of characterizing the conditional distribution of returns. Exclusion of potential instruments is exactly the same thing as exclusion of assets. It is no better founded, but the fact that it is a common sin may lead one to worry less about it.

There is nothing really special about unscaled returns, and no fundamental economic reason to place them above scaled returns. A mutual fund might come into being that follows the managed portfolio strategy and then its *unscaled* returns would be the same as an original scaled return. Models that cannot price scaled returns are no more interesting than models that can only price (say) stocks with first letter A through L. There are some econometric reasons to trust results for non-scaled returns a bit more, since the correlation of a slow moving instrument with a discounted payoff may be poorly measured in short samples. Transactions costs raise doubts about instruments that move quickly, implying highly dynamic trading strategies. But transactions costs also raise doubts about the unconditional pricing errors of small illiquid and thinly traded stocks.

Of course, the other way to incorporate conditioning information is by constructing explicit parametric models of conditional distributions. With this procedure one can in practice test *all* of a model's implications about conditional moments. However, the parametric model may be incorrect, or may not reflect some variable used by investors. Including instruments may not be as efficient if the statistical model is literally and completely true, but it is still consistent if the parametric model is incorrect.

8.3 Conditional and Unconditional Models

A conditional factor model does not imply a fixed-weight or unconditional factor model:

1) $m_{t+1} = b'_t f_{t+1}$, $p_t = E_t(m_{t+1} x_{t+1})$ does not imply that $\exists b$ s.t. $m_{t+1} = b' f_{t+1}$, $E(p_t) = E(m_{t+1} x_{t+1})$.

2) $E_t(R_{t+1}) = \beta'_t \lambda_t$ does not imply $E(R_{t+1}) = \beta' \lambda$.

3) Conditional mean-variance efficiency does not imply unconditional mean-variance efficiency.

The converse statements are true, if managed portfolios are included.

For explicit discount factor models—models whose parameters are constant over time—the fact that one looks at conditional versus unconditional implications makes no difference to the statement of the model:

$$p_t = E_t(m_{t+1} x_{t+1}) \Rightarrow E(p_t) = E(m_{t+1} x_{t+1})$$

and that's it. Examples include the consumption-based model with power utility, $m_{t+1} = \beta(c_{t+1}/c_t)^{-\gamma}$, and the log utility CAPM, $m_{t+1} = 1/R_{t+1}^W$.

However, linear factor models include parameters that may vary over time and as functions of conditioning information. In these cases the transition from conditional to unconditional moments is much more subtle. We cannot easily condition down the *model* at the same time as we condition down the prices and payoffs.

Conditional vs. Unconditional Factor Models in Discount Factor Language

As an example, consider the CAPM

$$m = a - b R^W,$$

where R^W is the return on the market or wealth portfolio. We can find a and b from the condition that this model correctly price any two returns, for example R^W itself and a risk-free rate:

$$
\begin{cases} 1 = E_t\left(m_{t+1} R_{t+1}^W\right) \\ 1 = E_t(m_{t+1}) R_t^f \end{cases}
\Rightarrow
\begin{cases} a = \dfrac{1}{R_t^f} + b E_t\left(R_{t+1}^W\right), \\ b = \dfrac{E_t\left(R_{t+1}^W\right) - R_t^f}{R_t^f \sigma_t^2\left(R_{t+1}^W\right)}. \end{cases} \tag{8.3}
$$

As you can see, $a > 0$ and $b > 0$. To make a payoff proportional to the minimum second moment return (on the lower part of the mean-variance frontier), we need a portfolio long the risk-free rate and short the market R^W.

Equation (8.3) shows explicitly that *a and b must vary over time, as* $E_t(R_{t+1}^W)$, $\sigma_t^2(R_{t+1}^W)$, *and* R_t^f *vary over time.* If it is to price assets conditionally, the CAPM must be a linear factor model with time-varying weights, of the form

$$m_{t+1} = a_t - b_t R_{t+1}^W.$$

This fact means that we can no longer transparently condition down. The statement that

$$1 = E_t\left[(a_t + b_t R_{t+1}^W) R_{t+1}\right]$$

does not imply that we can find constants a and b so that

$$1 = E\left[(a + bR_{t+1}^W)R_{t+1}\right].$$

Just try it. Taking unconditional expectations,

$$
\begin{aligned}
1 &= E\left[(a_t + b_t R_{t+1}^W)R_{t+1}\right]\\
&= E\left[a_t R_{t+1} + b_t R_{t+1}^W R_{t+1}\right]\\
&= E(a_t)E(R_{t+1}) + E(b_t)E(R_{t+1}^W R_{t+1})\\
&\quad + \mathrm{cov}(a_t, R_{t+1}) + \mathrm{cov}(b_t, R_{t+1}^W R_{t+1}).
\end{aligned}
$$

Thus, the unconditional model

$$1 = E\left[\left(E(a_t) + E(b_t)R_{t+1}^W\right)R_{t+1}\right]$$

Only holds if the covariance terms above happen to be zero. Since a_t and b_t are formed from conditional moments of returns, the covariances will not, in general, be zero.

On the other hand, suppose it *is* true that a_t and b_t are constant over time. Even if R_t^f and R_t^W are not i.i.d., the combinations given by (8.3) may be constant over time. Then

$$1 = E_t\left[(a + bR_{t+1}^W)R_{t+1}\right]$$

does imply

$$1 = E\left[(a + bR_{t+1}^W)R_{t+1}\right].$$

Furthermore, the latter unconditional model implies the former conditional model, if the latter holds for all managed portfolios.

Conditional vs. Unconditional in an Expected Return-Beta Model

To put the same observation in beta pricing language,

$$E_t(R_{t+1}^i) = R_t^f + \beta_t^i \lambda_t \tag{8.4}$$

does *not* imply that

$$E(R_{t+1}^i) = \gamma + \beta^i \lambda. \tag{8.5}$$

Obviously, conditioning down (8.4) to (8.5) leads to a covariance term between β_t^i and λ_t. Furthermore, the β^i in (8.5) must be the unconditional regression coefficient of the return on the factor, and this fact means that we often cannot condition down, even if the covariance term is absent.

For example, if $\lambda_t = \lambda$, a constant, but the betas vary over time, then you might think you can derive (8.5) with $\beta^i = E(\beta^i_t)$. But the average of a conditional regression coefficient is not the same thing as the unconditional regression coefficient, so this derivation is not valid. Even constant conditional betas are not enough to derive (8.5). For example, some models specify that $\mathrm{cov}_t(R^i_{t+1}, f_{t+1})$ and $\mathrm{var}_t(f_{t+1})$ both vary through time, but their ratio $\beta^i_t = \mathrm{cov}_t(R^i_{t+1}, f_{t+1})/\mathrm{var}_t(f_{t+1})$ is constant. However, the unconditional regression coefficient is the ratio of unconditional covariance to unconditional variance, $\beta^i = \mathrm{cov}(R^i_{t+1}, f_{t+1})/\mathrm{var}(f_{t+1})$. Even if the conditional β^i_t is constant, it is not necessarily equal to that ratio. We can only ensure this equality if the conditional covariance and variance are separately constant over time. Finally, if the betas are constant and the conditional covariance and variance that form them are constant, you might hope for an unconditional model with $\lambda = E(\lambda_t)$. However, most factor pricing models relate the factor risk premium to the variance of the factor, so it is unlikely that a model with constant $\mathrm{var}_t(f_{t+1})$ really does predict a time-varying risk premium.

A Precise Statement

Let us formalize these observations somewhat. Let $\underline{X}$ denote the space of all portfolios of the primitive assets, *including* managed portfolios in which the weights may depend on conditioning information, i.e., scaled returns.

A *conditional factor pricing model* is a model $m_{t+1} = a_t + b'_t f_{t+1}$ that satisfies $p_t = E_{t+1}(m_{t+1} x_{t+1})$ for all $x_{t+1} \in \underline{X}$.

An *unconditional factor pricing model* is model $m_{t+1} = a + b' f_{t+1}$ that satisfies $E(p_t) = E(m_{t+1} x_{t+1})$ for all $x_{t+1} \in \underline{X}$. It might be more appropriately called a *fixed-weight factor pricing model*.

Given these definitions it is almost trivial that the unconditional model is just a special case of the conditional model, one that happens to have fixed weights. Thus, *a conditional factor model does not imply an unconditional factor model* (because the weights may vary) but *an unconditional factor model does imply a conditional factor model*.

There is one important subtlety. The payoff space $\underline{X}$ is common, and contains all managed portfolios in both cases. The payoff space for the unconditional factor pricing model is *not* just fixed combinations of a set of basis assets. For example, we might check that the static (constant a, b) CAPM captures the unconditional mean returns of a set of assets. If this model does not also price those assets *scaled* by instruments, then it is not a conditional model, or, as I argued above, really a valid factor pricing model at all.

Of course, everything applies for the relation between a conditional factor pricing model using a fine information set (like investors' information sets) and conditional factor pricing models using coarser information sets (like ours). If a set of factors prices assets with respect to investors' information, that does not mean the same set of factors prices assets with respect to our, coarser, information sets.

Mean-Variance Frontiers

Define the *conditional mean-variance frontier* as the set of returns that minimize $\text{var}_t(R_{t+1})$ given $E_t(R_{t+1})$. (This definition includes the lower segment as usual.) Define the *unconditional mean-variance frontier* as the set of returns *including managed portfolio returns* that minimize $\text{var}(R_{t+1})$ given $E(R_{t+1})$. These two frontiers are related by:

> *If a return is on the unconditional mean-variance frontier, it is on the conditional mean-variance frontier.*

However,

> *If a return is on the conditional mean-variance frontier, it need not be on the unconditional mean-variance frontier.*

These statements are exactly the opposite of what you first expect from the language. The law of iterated expectations $E(E_t(x)) = E(x)$ leads you to expect that "conditional" should imply "unconditional." But we are studying the conditional versus unconditional mean-variance *frontier*, not raw conditional and unconditional expectations, and it turns out that exactly the opposite words apply. Of course, "unconditional" can also mean "conditional on a coarser information set."

Again, keep in mind that the unconditional mean-variance frontier *includes* returns on managed portfolios. This definition is eminently reasonable. If you are trying to minimize variance for given mean, why tie your hands to fixed-weight portfolios? Equivalently, why not allow yourself to include in your portfolio the returns of mutual funds whose advisers promise the ability to adjust portfolios based on conditioning information?

You could form a mean-variance frontier of fixed-weight portfolios of a basis set of assets, and this is what many people often mean by "unconditional mean-variance frontier." The return on the true unconditional mean-variance frontier will, in general, include some managed portfolio returns, and so will lie outside this *mean-variance frontier of fixed-weight portfolios*. Conversely, a return on the fixed-weight portfolio MVF is, in general, *not* on the unconditional or conditional mean-variance frontier. All we know is that the fixed-weight frontier lies inside the other two. It may touch, but it need not. This is not to say the fixed-weight unconditional frontier is uninteresting. For example, returns on this frontier will price fixed-weight portfolios of the basis assets. The point is that this frontier has no connection to the other two frontiers. In particular, a conditionally mean-variance efficient return (conditional CAPM) need not unconditionally price the fixed-weight portfolios.

I offer several ways to see this relation between conditional and unconditional mean-variance frontiers.

Using the Connection to Factor Models

We have seen that the conditional CAPM $m_{t+1} = a_t - b_t R_{t+1}^W$ does not imply an unconditional CAPM $m_{t+1} = a - b R_{t+1}^W$. We have seen that the existence of such a conditional factor model is equivalent to the statement that the return R_{t+1}^W lies on the conditional mean-variance frontier, and the existence of an unconditional factor model $m_{t+1} = a - b R_{t+1}^W$ is equivalent to the statement that R^W is on the unconditional mean-variance frontier. Then, from the "trivial" fact that an unconditional factor model is a special case of a conditional one, we know that R^W on the unconditional frontier implies R^W on the conditional frontier but not vice versa.

Using the Orthogonal Decomposition

We can see the relation between conditional and unconditional mean-variance frontiers using the orthogonal decomposition characterization of the mean-variance frontier, $R^{mv} = R^* + w R^{e*}$ (see chapter 5). This beautiful argument is the main point of Hansen and Richard (1987).

By the law of iterated expectations, x^* and R^* generate expected prices and R^{e*} generates unconditional means as well as conditional means:

$$E\big[p = E_t(x^*x)\big] \Rightarrow E(p) = E(x^*x),$$

$$E\big[E_t(R^{*2}) = E_t(R^*R)\big] \Rightarrow E(R^{*2}) = E(R^*R),$$

$$E\big[E_t(R^{e*}R^e) = E_t(R^e)\big] \Rightarrow E(R^{e*}R^e) = E(R^e).$$

This fact is subtle and important. For example, starting with $x^* = p_t' E_t(x_{t+1}x_{t+1}')^{-1}x_{t+1}$, you might think we need a different x^*, R^*, R^{e*} to represent expected prices and unconditional means, using unconditional probabilities to define inner products. The three lines above show that this is not the case. The same old x^*, R^*, R^{e*} represent conditional as well as unconditional prices and means.

Recall that a return is mean variance efficient if and only if it is of the form

$$R^{mv} = R^* + w R^{e*}.$$

Thus, R^{mv} is conditionally mean-variance efficient if w is any number in the time-t information set:

conditional frontier: $\quad R_{t+1}^{mv} = R_{t+1}^* + w_t R_{t+1}^{e*},$

and R^{mv} is unconditionally mean-variance efficient if w is any constant:

$$\text{unconditional frontier:} \quad R^{mv}_{t+1} = R^*_{t+1} + w R^{e*}_{t+1}.$$

Constants are in the t information set; time-t random variables are not necessarily constant. Thus unconditional efficiency (including managed portfolios) implies conditional efficiency but not vice versa. As with the factor models, once you see the decomposition, it is a trivial argument about whether a weight is constant or time varying.

Brute Force and Examples
If you are still puzzled, an additional argument by brute force may be helpful.

If a return is on the unconditional mean-variance frontier it must be on the conditional mean-variance frontier at each date. If not, you could improve the unconditional mean-variance trade-off by moving to the conditional mean-variance frontier at each date. The unconditional mean-variance frontier solves

$$\min E(R^2) \ s.t. \ E(R) = \mu.$$

Writing the unconditional moment in terms of conditional moments, the problem is

$$\min E\big[E_t(R^2)\big] \ s.t. \ E\big[E_t(R)\big] = \mu.$$

Now, suppose you could lower $E_t(R^2)$ at one date t without affecting $E_t(R)$ at that date. This change would lower the objective, without changing the constraint. Thus, you should have done it: you should have picked returns on the *conditional* mean-variance frontiers.

It almost seems that, reversing the argument, we can show that conditional efficiency implies unconditional efficiency, but it does not. Just because you have minimized $E_t(R^2)$ for given value of $E_t(R)$ at each date t *does not* imply that you have minimized $E(R^2)$ for a given value of $E(R)$. In showing that unconditional efficiency implies conditional efficiency we held fixed $E_t(R)$ at each date at μ, and showed it is a good idea to minimize $\sigma_t(R)$. In trying to go backwards, the problem is that a given value of $E(R)$ does not specify what $E_t(R)$ should be at each date. We can increase $E_t(R)$ in one conditioning information set and decrease it in another, leaving the return on the conditional mean-variance frontier.

Figure 8.1 presents an example. Return B is conditionally mean-variance efficient. It also has zero unconditional variance, so it is the unconditionally mean-variance efficient return at the expected return shown. Return A is on the conditional mean-variance frontiers, and has the same unconditional expected return as B. But return A *has* some

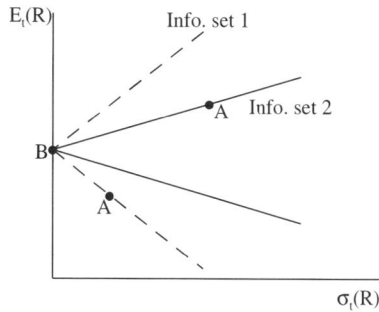

Figure 8.1. *Return A is on the conditional mean-variance frontiers but not the unconditional mean-variance frontier. Return B is on the conditional and unconditional frontier.*

unconditional variance, and so is inside the unconditional mean-variance frontier.

As a second example, the risk-free rate is only on the unconditional mean-variance frontier if it is a constant. Remember the expression (6.15) for the risk-free rate,

$$R^f = R^* + R^f R^{e*}.$$

The unconditional mean-variance frontier is $R^* + wR^{e*}$ with w a constant. Thus, the risk-free rate is only unconditionally mean-variance efficient if it is a constant. Of course, the risk-free rate is always on the conditional frontier.

Implications: Hansen–Richard Critique

Many models, such as the CAPM, imply a *conditional* linear factor model $m_{t+1} = a_t + b_t' f_{t+1}$. These theorems show that such a model *does not* imply an unconditional model. Equivalently, if the model predicts that the market portfolio is conditionally mean-variance efficient, this does *not* imply that the market portfolio is unconditionally mean-variance efficient. We often test the CAPM by seeing if it explains the average returns of some portfolios or (equivalently) if the market is on the unconditional mean-variance frontier. The CAPM may quite well be true (conditionally) and fail these tests; assets may do better in terms of *unconditional* mean versus *unconditional* variance, while obeying the CAPM *conditionally*.

The situation is not repaired by simple inclusion of some conditioning information. Models such as the CAPM imply a conditional linear factor model with respect to *investors'* information sets. However, the best we can hope to do is to test implications conditioned down on variables that we can observe and include in a test. Thus, a conditional linear factor model *is not testable!*

I like to call this observation the "Hansen–Richard critique" by analogy to the "Roll Critique." Roll pointed out, among other things, that the wealth portfolio might not be observable, making tests of the CAPM impossible. Hansen and Richard point out that the conditioning information of agents might not be observable, and that one cannot omit it in testing a conditional model. Thus, even if the wealth portfolio *were* observable, the fact that we cannot observe agents' *information sets* dooms tests of the CAPM.

8.4 Scaled Factors: A Partial Solution

> You can expand the set of factors to test conditional factor pricing models
>
> $$\text{factors} = f_{t+1} \otimes z_t.$$

The problem is that the parameters of the factor pricing model $m_{t+1} = a_t + b_t f_{t+1}$ may vary over time. A partial solution is to *model* the dependence of parameters a_t and b_t on variables in the time-t information set; let $a_t = a(z_t)$, $b_t = b(z_t)$, where z_t is a vector of variables observed at time t (including a constant). In particular, why not try *linear* models

$$a_t = a'z_t, \qquad b_t = b'z_t.$$

Linearity is not restrictive: z_t^2 is just another instrument. The only criticism one can make is that some instrument z_{jt} might be important for capturing the variation in a_t and b_t, and was omitted. For instruments on which we have data, we can meet this objection by trying z_{jt} and seeing whether it does, in fact, enter significantly. However, for instruments z_t that are observed by agents but not by us, this criticism remains valid.

Linear discount factor models lead to a nice interpretation as *scaled factors*, in the same way that linearly managed portfolios are scaled returns. With a single factor and instrument, write

$$m_t = a(z_t) + b(z_t) f_{t+1} \tag{8.6}$$

$$= a_0 + a_1 z_t + (b_0 + b_1 z_t) f_{t+1}$$

$$= a_0 + a_1 z_t + b_0 f_{t+1} + b_1 (z_t f_{t+1}). \tag{8.7}$$

Thus, in place of the one-factor model with time-varying coefficients (8.6), we have a three-factor model $(z_t, f_{t+1}, z_t f_{t+1})$ with fixed coefficients, (8.7).

Since the coefficients are now fixed, we *can* use the scaled-factor model with unconditional moments:

$$p_t = E_t\big[\big(a_0 + a_1 z_t + b_0 f_{t+1} + b_1(z_t f_{t+1})\big)x_{t+1}\big] \Rightarrow$$

$$E(p_t) = E\big[\big(a_0 + a_1 z_t + b_0 f_{t+1} + b_1(z_t f_{t+1})\big)x_{t+1}\big].$$

For example, in standard derivations of CAPM, the market (wealth portfolio) return is *conditionally* mean-variance efficient; investors want to hold portfolios on the *conditional* mean-variance frontier; *conditionally* expected returns follow a *conditional* single-beta representation, or the discount factor *m* follows a *conditional* linear factor model

$$m_{t+1} = a_t - b_t R^W_{t+1}$$

as we saw above.

But none of these statements mean that we can use the CAPM *unconditionally*. Rather than throw up our hands, we can add some scaled factors. Thus, if, say, the dividend/price ratio and term premium do a pretty good job of summarizing variation in conditional moments, the *conditional* CAPM implies an *unconditional, five-factor (plus constant) model*. The factors are a constant, the market return, the dividend/price ratio, the term premium, and the market return *times* the dividend/price ratio and the term premium. Jagannathan and Wang (1996) test whether similar factors can explain CAPM anomalies.

The unconditional pricing implications of such a five-factor model could, of course, be summarized by a single-beta representation. The reference portfolio would not be the market portfolio, of course, but a mimicking portfolio of the five factors. However, the single mimicking portfolio would not be easily interpretable in terms of a single-factor conditional model and two instruments. In this case, it might be more interesting to look at a multiple-beta or multiple-factor representation.

If we have many factors f and many instruments z, we should in principle multiply every factor by every instrument,

$$m = b_1 f_1 + b_2 f_1 z_1 + b_3 f_1 z_2 + \cdots + b_{N+1} f_2 + b_{N+2} f_2 z_1 + b_{N+3} f_2 z_2 + \cdots.$$

This operation can be compactly summarized with the *Kronecker product* notation, $a \otimes b$, which means "multiply every element in vector a by every element in vector b, or

$$m_{t+1} = b'(f_{t+1} \otimes z_t).$$

8.5 Summary

When you first think about it, conditioning information sounds scary—how do we account for time-varying expected returns, betas, factor risk premia, variances, covariances, etc. However, the methods outlined in this chapter allow a very simple and beautiful solution to the problems raised by conditioning information. To express the conditional implications of a given model, all you have to do is include some well-chosen scaled or managed portfolio returns, and then pretend you never heard about conditioning information.

Some factor models are conditional models, and have coefficients that are functions of investors' information sets. In general, there is no way to test such models, but if you are willing to assume that the relevant conditioning information is well summarized by a few variables, then you can just add new factors, equal to the old factors scaled by the conditioning variables, and again forget that you ever heard about conditioning information.

You may want to remember conditioning information as a diagnostic, or when giving an economic interpretation of the results. It may be interesting to take estimates of a many-factor model, $m_t = a_0 + a_1 z_t + b_0 f_{t+1} + b_1 z_t f_{t+1}$, and see what they say about the implied conditional model, $m_t = (a_0 + a_1 z_t) + (b_0 + b_1 z_t) f_{t+1}$. You may want to make plots of conditional b's, betas, factor risk premia, expected returns, etc. But you do not have to worry a lot about *conditioning* information in estimation and testing.

Problems—Chapter 8

1. If there is a risk-free asset, is it on the (a) conditional, or (b) unconditional mean-variance frontier, or (c) on both?

2. If there is a conditionally risk-free asset—a claim to 1 is traded at each date, does this mean that there is an unconditionally risk-free asset? (Define the latter first!) How about vice versa?

3. Suppose you took the unconditional population moments $E(R)$, $E(RR')$ of assets returns and constructed the mean-variance frontier. Does this frontier correspond to the conditional or the unconditional mean-variance frontier, or neither?

9

Factor Pricing Models

IN CHAPTER 2, I noted that the consumption-based model, while a complete answer to most asset pricing questions in principle, does not (yet) work well in practice. This observation motivates efforts to tie the discount factor m to other data. Linear factor pricing models are the most popular models of this sort in finance. They dominate discrete-time empirical work.

Factor pricing models replace the consumption-based expression for marginal utility growth with a linear model of the form

$$m_{t+1} = a + b'f_{t+1}.$$

a and b are free parameters. As we saw in Chapter 6, this specification is equivalent to a multiple-beta model

$$E(R_{t+1}) = \gamma + \beta'\lambda,$$

where β are multiple regression coefficients of returns R on the factors f, and γ and λ are free parameters.

The big question is, what should one use for factors f_{t+1}? Factor pricing models look for variables that are good proxies for aggregate marginal utility growth, i.e., variables for which

$$\beta\frac{u'(c_{t+1})}{u'(c_t)} \approx a + b'f_{t+1} \tag{9.1}$$

is a sensible and economically interpretable approximation.

More directly, the essence of asset pricing is that there are special states of the world in which investors are especially concerned that their portfolios not do badly. They are willing to trade off some overall performance—average return—to make sure that portfolios do not do badly in these particular states of nature. The factors are variables that indicate that these "bad states" have occurred.

In any sensible economic model, as well as in the data, consumption is related to returns on broad-based portfolios, to interest rates, to growth in GDP, investment, or other macroeconomic variables, and to returns on real production processes. All of these variables can measure the state of the economy.

Furthermore, consumption and marginal utility respond to *news*: if a change in some variable today signals high income in the future, then consumption rises *now*, by permanent income logic. This fact opens the door to *forecasting* variables: any variable that forecasts asset returns ("changes in the investment opportunity set") or that forecasts macroeconomic variables is a candidate factor. Variables such as the term premium, dividend/price ratio, stock returns, etc., can be defended as pricing factors on this logic. Though they are not direct measures of aggregate good or bad times, they *forecast* such times.

Should factors be unpredictable over time? The answer is, sort of. If there is a constant real interest rate, then marginal utility growth should be unpredictable. ("Consumption is a random walk" in the quadratic utility permanent income model.) To see this, look at the first-order condition with a constant interest rate,

$$u'(c_t) = \beta R^f E_t\big[u'(c_{t+1})\big],$$

or in a more time-series notation,

$$\frac{u'(c_{t+1})}{u'(c_t)} = \frac{1}{\beta R^f} + \varepsilon_{t+1}, \qquad E_t(\varepsilon_{t+1}) = 0.$$

The real risk-free rate is not constant, but it does not vary a lot, especially compared to asset returns. Measured consumption growth is not exactly unpredictable but it is the least predictable macroeconomic time series, especially if one accounts properly for temporal aggregation (consumption data are quarterly averages). Thus, factors that proxy for marginal utility growth, though they do not have to be totally unpredictable, should not be highly predictable. If one chooses highly predictable factors, the model will counterfactually predict large interest rate variation.

In practice, this consideration means that you should choose the right units: Use GNP *growth* rather than level, portfolio *returns* rather than prices or price/dividend ratios, etc. However, unless you want to impose an exactly constant risk-free rate, you do not have to filter or prewhiten factors to make them exactly unpredictable. Furthermore, we often apply factor pricing models to excess returns in a way that the conditional mean of the discount factor is not identified, and hence has no effect on the results.

This view of factors as intuitively motivated proxies for marginal utility growth is sufficient to carry the reader through current empirical tests of factor models. The extra constraints that result from formal derivations in this chapter have not much constrained empirical specifications.

The derivations all proceed in the way I have motivated factor models: One writes down a general equilibrium model, in particular a specification of the production technology by which real investment today results in real output tomorrow. This general equilibrium produces relations that express the determinants of consumption from exogenous variables, and relations linking consumption to other endogenous variables; equations of the form $c_t = g(f_t)$. One then uses this kind of equation to substitute out for consumption in the basic first-order conditions. The CAPM and ICAPM are general equilibrium models with linear technologies, rates of return R that do not depend on the quantity invested.

The derivations accomplish two things: they determine one particular *list of factors* that can proxy for marginal utility growth, and they prove that the relation should be *linear*. Some assumptions can often be substituted for others in the quest for these two features of a factor pricing model.

This is a point worth remembering: *all factor models are derived as specializations of the consumption-based model.* Many authors of factor model papers disparage the consumption-based model, forgetting that their factor model *is* the consumption-based model plus extra assumptions that allow one to proxy for marginal utility growth from some other variables. (Constantinides [1989] is a good statement of this point.)

In Chapter 7, I argued that clear economic foundation was important for factor models, since it helps us to guard against fishing. Alas, the current state of factor pricing models is not a particularly good guard. One can call for better theories or derivations, more carefully aimed at limiting the list of potential factors and describing the fundamental macroeconomic sources of risk, and thus providing more discipline for empirical work. But the best minds in finance have been working on this problem for 40 years, so a ready solution is not immediately in sight. Furthermore, even current theory can provide more discipline than is commonly imposed in empirical work. So it's not clear that tighter theories will change practice. For example, the derivations of the CAPM and ICAPM make predictions for the risk-free rate and for factor risk premia that are often ignored; these quantities are typically estimated as free parameters. The ICAPM gives tighter restrictions on state variables than are commonly checked: "State variables" should forecast something.

The derivations also show how special and unrealistic are the general equilibrium setups necessary to derive popular specifications such as CAPM and ICAPM. This observation motivates a more serious look at real general equilibrium models.

9.1 Capital Asset Pricing Model (CAPM)

> The CAPM is the model $m = a + bR^w$; R^w = wealth portfolio return.
> I derive it from the consumption-based model by (1) two-period quadratic
> utility; (2) two periods, exponential utility, and normal returns; (3) infinite
> horizon, quadratic utility, and i.i.d. returns; (4) log utility.

The CAPM, credited to Sharpe (1964) and Lintner (1965), is the first,
most famous, and (so far) most widely used model in asset pricing. It ties
the discount factor m to the return on the "wealth portfolio." The function
is linear,

$$m_{t+1} = a + bR_{t+1}^{W}.$$

a and b are free parameters. One can find theoretical values for the parameters a and b by requiring the discount factor m to price any two assets,
such as the wealth portfolio return and risk-free rate, $1 = E(mR^{W})$ and
$1 = E(m)R^{f}$. [For example, see equation (8.3).] In empirical applications, we can also pick a and b to best price larger cross sections of assets.
We do not have good data on, or even a good empirical definition for, the
return on total wealth. It is conventional to proxy R^{W} by the return on a
broad-based stock portfolio such as the value- or equally-weighted NYSE,
S&P500, etc.

The CAPM is, of course, most frequently stated in equivalent expected
return-beta language,

$$E(R^{i}) = \gamma + \beta_{i, R^{W}}\left[E(R^{W}) - \gamma\right].$$

This section briefly describes some classic derivations of the CAPM.
Again, we need to find assumptions that defend *which* factors proxy
for marginal utility (R^{W} here), and assumptions to defend the *linearity*
between m and the factor.

I present several derivations of the same model. Many of these derivations use classic and widely applicable modeling assumptions. You can also
see that various sets of assumptions can often be used to get to the same
place. By seeing several derivations, you can see how one assumption can
be traded for another. For example, the CAPM does not require normal
distributions, if one is willing to swallow quadratic utility instead.

Two-Period Quadratic Utility

> Two-period investors with no labor income and quadratic utility imply the CAPM.

Investors have quadratic preferences and only live two periods,

$$U(c_t, c_{t+1}) = -\frac{1}{2}(c_t - c^*)^2 - \frac{1}{2}\beta E\left[(c_{t+1} - c^*)^2\right]. \tag{9.2}$$

Their marginal rate of substitution is thus

$$m_{t+1} = \beta \frac{u'(c_{t+1})}{u'(c_t)} = \beta \frac{(c_{t+1} - c^*)}{(c_t - c^*)}.$$

The quadratic utility assumption means marginal utility is *linear* in consumption. Thus, we have achieved one target of the derivation, linearity.

Investors are born with wealth W_t in the first period and earn no labor income. They can invest in N assets with prices p_t^i and payoffs x_{t+1}^i, or, to keep the notation simple, returns R_{t+1}^i. They choose how much to consume at the two dates, c_t and c_{t+1}, and *portfolio weights* w_i. Thus, the budget constraint is

$$
\begin{aligned}
c_{t+1} &= W_{t+1}, \\
W_{t+1} &= R_{t+1}^W(W_t - c_t), \\
R_{t+1}^W &= \sum_{i=1}^N w_i R_{t+1}^i, \qquad \sum_{i=1}^N w_i = 1.
\end{aligned}
\tag{9.3}
$$

R^W is the rate of return on total wealth.

The two-period assumption means that investors consume everything in the second period, by constraint (9.3). This fact allows us to substitute wealth and the return on wealth for consumption, achieving the second goal of the derivation, naming the factor that proxies for consumption or marginal utility:

$$m_{t+1} = \beta \frac{R_{t+1}^W(W_t - c_t) - c^*}{c_t - c^*} = \frac{-\beta c^*}{c_t - c^*} + \frac{\beta(W_t - c_t)}{c_t - c^*} R_{t+1}^W, \tag{9.4}$$

i.e.,

$$m_{t+1} = a_t + b_t R_{t+1}^W.$$

Exponential Utility, Normal Distributions

> $u(c) = -e^{-\alpha c}$ and a normally distributed set of returns also produces the CAPM.

The combination of exponential utility and normal distributions is another set of assumptions that deliver the CAPM in a one- or two-period model. This structure has a particularly convenient analytical form. Since it gives rise to linear demand curves, it is very widely used in models that complicate the trading structure, by introducing incomplete markets or asymmetric information. Grossman and Stiglitz (1980) is a very famous example.

I present a model with consumption only in the last period. (You can do the quadratic utility model of the last section this way as well.) Utility is

$$E[u(c)] = E[-e^{-\alpha c}].$$

α is known as the *coefficient of absolute risk aversion.* If consumption is normally distributed, we have

$$Eu(c) = -e^{-\alpha E(c) + (\alpha^2/2)\sigma^2(c)}.$$

Suppose this investor has initial wealth W which can be split between a risk-free asset paying R^f and a set of risky assets paying return R. Let y denote the amount of this wealth W (amount, not fraction) invested in each security. Then, the budget constraint is

$$c = y^f R^f + y' R,$$

$$W = y^f + y' 1.$$

Plugging the first constraint into the utility function, we obtain

$$Eu(c) = -e^{-\alpha[y^f R^f + y' E(R)] + (\alpha^2/2) y' \Sigma y}. \tag{9.5}$$

As with quadratic utility, the two-period model is what allows us to set consumption to wealth and then substitute the return on the wealth portfolio for consumption growth in the discount factor.

Maximizing (9.5) with respect to y, y^f, we obtain the first-order condition describing the optimal amount to be invested in the risky asset,

$$y = \Sigma^{-1} \frac{E(R) - R^f}{\alpha}.$$

Sensibly, the investor invests more in risky assets if their expected return is higher, less if his risk aversion coefficient is higher, and less if the assets are riskier. Notice that total wealth does not appear in this expression. With this setup, the amount invested in risky assets is independent of the level of wealth. This is why we say that this investor has *absolute* rather than *relative* (to wealth) risk aversion. Note also that these "demands" for the risky assets are linear in expected returns.

Inverting the first-order conditions, we obtain

$$E(R) - R^f = \alpha \Sigma y = \alpha \operatorname{cov}(R, R^W). \tag{9.6}$$

The investor's total risky portfolio is $y'R$. Hence, Σy gives the covariance of each return with $y'R$, and also with the investor's overall portfolio $y^f R^f + y'R$. If all investors are identical, then the market portfolio is the same as the individual's portfolio so Σy also gives the correlation of each return with $R^m = y^f R^f + y'R$. (If investors differ in risk aversion α, the same thing goes through but with an aggregate risk aversion coefficient.)

Thus, we have the CAPM. This version is especially interesting because it ties the market price of risk to the risk aversion coefficient. Applying (9.6) to the market return itself, we have

$$E(R^W) - R^f = \alpha \sigma^2(R^W).$$

Quadratic Value Function, Dynamic Programming

We can let investors live forever in the quadratic utility CAPM so long as we assume that the environment is independent over time. Then the *value function* is quadratic, taking the place of the quadratic second-period utility function. This case is a nice introduction to *dynamic programming*.

The two-period structure is unpalatable, since most investors live longer than two periods. It is natural to try to make the same basic ideas work with less restrictive assumptions.

We can derive the CAPM in a multiperiod context by replacing the second-period quadratic utility function with a quadratic *value* function. However, the quadratic value function requires the additional assumption that returns are i.i.d. (no "shifts in the investment opportunity set"). This observation, due to Fama (1970), is also a nice introduction to *dynamic programming*, which is a powerful way to handle multiperiod problems by expressing them as two-period problems. Finally, I think this derivation makes the CAPM more realistic, transparent, and intuitively compelling. Buying stocks amounts to taking bets over *wealth*; really the fundamental assumption driving the CAPM is that marginal utility of *wealth* is linear in wealth and does not depend on other state variables.

Let us start in a simple ad hoc manner by just writing down a "utility function" defined over this period's consumption and next period's *wealth*,

$$U = u(c_t) + \beta E_t V(W_{t+1}).$$

This is a reasonable objective for an investor, and does not require us to make the very artificial assumption that he will die tomorrow. If an investor with this "utility function" can buy an asset at price p_t with payoff x_{t+1}, his first-order condition (buy a little more, then x contributes to wealth next period) is

$$p_t u'(c_t) = \beta E_t \big[V'(W_{t+1}) x_{t+1} \big].$$

Thus, the discount factor uses next period's marginal value of wealth in place of the more familiar marginal utility of consumption

$$m_{t+1} = \beta \frac{V'(W_{t+1})}{u'(c_t)}.$$

(The *envelope condition* states that, at the optimum, a penny saved has the same value as a penny consumed, $u'(c_t) = V'(W_t)$. We could also use this condition to express the denominator in terms of wealth.)

Now, suppose the value function were quadratic,

$$V(W_{t+1}) = -\frac{\eta}{2}(W_{t+1} - W^*)^2.$$

Then, we would have

$$m_{t+1} = -\beta\eta \frac{W_{t+1} - W^*}{u'(c_t)} = -\beta\eta \frac{R^W_{t+1}(W_t - c_t) - W^*}{u'(c_t)}$$

$$= \left[\frac{\beta\eta W^*}{u'(c_t)} \right] + \left[-\frac{\beta\eta(W_t - c_t)}{u'(c_t)} \right] R^W_{t+1},$$

or, once again,

$$m_{t+1} = a_t + b_t R^W_{t+1},$$

the CAPM!

Let us be clear about the assumptions and what they do.

(1) *The value function only depends on wealth.* If other variables entered the value function, then $\partial V/\partial W$ would depend on those other variables, and so would m. This assumption bought us the first objective of any derivation: the identity of the factors. The ICAPM, below, allows other variables in the value function, and obtains more factors. (Actually, other variables could enter the value function so long as they do not affect the *marginal* value of wealth. The weather is an example: You, like I, might be happier on sunny days, but you do not value *additional* wealth more on sunny than on rainy days. Hence, covariance with weather does not affect how you value stocks.)

(2) *The value function is quadratic.* We wanted the *marginal* value function $V'(W)$ to be linear, to buy us the second objective, showing m is *linear* in the factor. Quadratic utility and value functions deliver a globally linear marginal value function $V'(W)$.

Why is the Value Function Quadratic?

You might think we are done. But good economists are unhappy about a utility function that has *wealth* in it. Few of us are like Disney's Uncle Scrooge, who got pure enjoyment out of a daily swim in the coins in his vault. Wealth is only valuable because it gives us access to more consumption. Utility functions should always be written over *consumption*. One of the few real rules in economics to keep our theories from being vacuous is that ad hoc "utility functions" over other objects like wealth (or means and variances of portfolio returns) should eventually be defended as arising from a more fundamental desire for consumption or leisure.

More practically, being careful about the derivation makes clear that the superficially plausible assumption that the value function is only a function of wealth derives from the much less plausible, in fact certainly false, assumption that interest rates are constant, the distribution of returns is i.i.d., and that the investor has no risky labor income. So, let us see what it takes to defend the quadratic *value* function in terms of some *utility* function.

Suppose investors last forever, and have the standard sort of utility function

$$U = -\frac{1}{2}E_t \sum_{j=0}^{\infty} \beta^j u(c_{t+j}).$$

Again, investors start with wealth W_0 which earns a random return R^W and they have no other source of income. In addition, suppose that interest rates are constant, and stock returns are i.i.d. over time.

Define the *value function* as the *maximized value* of the utility function in this environment. Thus, define $V(W)$ as[1]

$$V(W_t) \equiv \max_{\{c_t, c_{t+1}, c_{t+2}, \ldots, w_t, w_{t+1}, \ldots\}} E_t \sum_{j=0}^{\infty} \beta^j u(c_{t+j})$$ (9.7)

$$\text{s.t.} \quad W_{t+1} = R_{t+1}^W (W_t - c_t); \qquad R_t^W = w_t' R_t; \qquad w_t' 1 = 1.$$

(I use vector notation to simplify the statement of the portfolio problem; $R \equiv [R^1 \ R^2 \ \cdots \ R^N]'$, etc.) The value function is the total level of utility the investor can achieve, given how much wealth he has, and any other variables constraining him. This is where the assumptions of no labor income, a constant interest rate, and i.i.d. returns come in. Without these assumptions, the value function as defined above might depend on these other characteristics of the investor's environment. For example, if there were some variable, say, "D/P" that indicated returns would be high or low for a while, then the investor might be happier, and have a high value, when D/P is high, for a given level of wealth. Thus, we would have to write $V(W_t, D/P_t)$.

Value functions allow you to express an infinite-period problem as a two-period problem. Break up the maximization into the first period and all the remaining periods, as follows:

$$V(W_t) = \max_{\{c_t, w_t\}} \left\{ u(c_t) + \beta E_t \left[\max_{\{c_{t+1}, c_{t+2}, \ldots, w_{t+1}, w_{t+2}, \ldots\}} E_{t+1} \sum_{j=0}^{\infty} \beta^j u(c_{t+1+j}) \right] \right\}$$

or

$$V(W_t) = \max_{\{c_t, w_t\}} \left\{ u(c_t) + \beta E_t V(W_{t+1}) \right\}$$ (9.8)

Thus, we have defended the *existence* of a value function. Writing down a two-period "utility function" over this period's consumption and next period's *wealth* is not as crazy as it might seem.

The value function is also an attractive view of how people actually make decisions. People do not think "If I buy an expensive lunch today, I will not be able to go out to dinner one night 20 years from now"—trading off goods directly as expressed by the utility function. They think "I cannot 'afford' an expensive lunch" meaning that the decline in the value of wealth is not worth the increase in the marginal utility of consumption. Thus, the maximization in (9.8) describes people's psychological approach to utility maximization.

---

[1] There is also a transversality condition or a lower limit on wealth $W_t > \underline{W}$ in the budget constraints. This keeps the consumer from consuming a bit more and rolling over more and more debt, and it means we can write the budget constraint in present-value form.

The remaining question is, can the value function be quadratic? What utility function assumption leads to a quadratic value function? Here is the fun fact: *A quadratic utility function leads to a quadratic value function in this environment.* This fact is not a law of nature; it is not true that for any $u(c)$, $V(W)$ has the same functional form. But it is true here and a few other special cases. The "in this environment" clause is not innocuous. The value function—the achieved level of expected utility—is a result of the utility function *and* the constraints.

How could we show this fact? One way would be to try to calculate the value function by brute force from its definition, equation (9.7). This approach is not fun, and it does not exploit the beauty of dynamic programming, which is the reduction of an infinite-period problem to a two-period problem.

Instead solve (9.8) as a functional equation. *Guess* that the value function $V(W_{t+1})$ is quadratic, with some unknown parameters. Then use the *recursive* definition of $V(W_t)$ in (9.8), and solve a *two*-period problem— find the optimal consumption choice, plug it into (9.8), and calculate the value function $V(W_t)$. If the guess was right, you obtain a quadratic function for $V(W_t)$, and determine any free parameters.

Let us do it. Specify

$$u(c_t) = -\frac{1}{2}(c_t - c^*)^2.$$

Guess

$$V(W_{t+1}) = -\frac{\eta}{2}(W_{t+1} - W^*)^2$$

with η and W^* parameters to be determined later. Then the problem (9.8) is (I do not write the portfolio choice w part for simplicity; it does not change anything)

$$V(W_t) = \max_{\{c_t\}} \left[-\frac{1}{2}(c_t - c^*)^2 - \beta\frac{\eta}{2}E(W_{t+1} - W^*)^2 \right]$$

$$s.t.\ W_{t+1} = R^W_{t+1}(W_t - c_t).$$

(E_t is now E since I assumed i.i.d.) Substituting the constraint into the objective,

$$V(W_t) = \max_{\{c_t\}} \left[-\frac{1}{2}(c_t - c^*)^2 - \beta\frac{\eta}{2}E\left[R^W_{t+1}(W_t - c_t) - W^*\right]^2 \right]. \quad (9.9)$$

The first-order condition with respect to c_t, using $\hat{c}$ to denote the optimal value, is

$$\hat{c}_t - c^* = \beta\eta E\left\{\left[R^W_{t+1}(W_t - \hat{c}_t) - W^*\right]R^W_{t+1}\right\}.$$

Solving for $\hat{c}_t$,

$$\hat{c}_t = c^* + \beta\eta E\{[R_{t+1}^{W2}W_t - \hat{c}_t R_{t+1}^{W2} - W^* R_{t+1}^W]\},$$

$$\hat{c}_t[1 + \beta\eta E(R_{t+1}^{W2})] = c^* + \beta\eta E(R_{t+1}^{W2})W_t - \beta\eta W^* E(R_{t+1}^W),$$

$$\hat{c}_t = \frac{c^* - \beta\eta E(R_{t+1}^W)W^* + \beta\eta E(R_{t+1}^{W2})W_t}{1 + \beta\eta E(R_{t+1}^{W2})}. \tag{9.10}$$

This is a *linear* function of W_t. Writing (9.9) in terms of the optimal value of c, we get

$$V(W_t) = -\frac{1}{2}(\hat{c}_t - c^*)^2 - \beta\frac{\eta}{2}E[R_{t+1}^W(W_t - \hat{c}_t) - W^*]^2. \tag{9.11}$$

This is a *quadratic* function of W_t and $\hat{c}_t$. A quadratic function of a linear function is a quadratic function, so *the value function is a quadratic function of W_t.* If you want to spend a pleasant few hours doing algebra, plug (9.10) into (9.11), check that the result really is quadratic in W_t, and determine the coefficients η, W^* in terms of fundamental parameters β, c^*, $E(R^W)$, $E(R^{W2})$ (or $\sigma^2(R^W)$). The expressions for η, W^* do not give much insight, so I do not do the algebra here.

Log Utility

> Log utility rather than quadratic utility also implies a CAPM. Log utility implies that consumption is proportional to wealth, allowing us to substitute the wealth return for consumption data.

The point of the CAPM is to avoid the use of consumption data, and to use wealth or the rate of return on wealth instead. Log utility is another special case that allows this substitution. Log utility is much more plausible than quadratic utility. Rubinstein (1976) introduced the log utility CAPM.

Suppose that the investor has log utility

$$u(c) = \ln(c).$$

Define the wealth portfolio as a claim to all future consumption. Then, *with log utility, the price of the wealth portfolio is proportional to consumption itself,*

$$p_t^W = E_t \sum_{j=1}^{\infty} \beta^j \frac{u'(c_{t+j})}{u'(c_t)} c_{t+j} = E_t \sum_{j=1}^{\infty} \beta^j \frac{c_t}{c_{t+j}} c_{t+j} = \frac{\beta}{1-\beta}c_t.$$

The return on the wealth portfolio is proportional to consumption growth,

$$R_{t+1}^W = \frac{p_{t+1}^W + c_{t+1}}{p_t^W} = \frac{(\beta/(1-\beta) + 1)}{\beta/(1-\beta)} \frac{c_{t+1}}{c_t} = \frac{1}{\beta} \frac{c_{t+1}}{c_t} = \frac{1}{\beta} \frac{u'(c_t)}{u'(c_{t+1})}.$$

Thus, the log utility discount factor equals the *inverse* of the wealth portfolio return,

$$m_{t+1} = \frac{1}{R_{t+1}^W}. \tag{9.12}$$

Equation (9.12) could be used by itself: it attains the goal of replacing consumption data by some other variable. (Brown and Gibbons [1982] test a CAPM in this form.) Note that log utility is the *only* assumption so far. We do *not* assume constant interest rates, i.i.d. returns, or the absence of labor income.

Log utility has a special property that "income effects offset substitution effects," or in an asset pricing context, that "discount rate effects offset cashflow effects." News of higher consumption = dividend should make the claim to consumption more valuable. However, through $u'(c)$ it also raises the discount rate, lowering the value of the claim to consumption. For log utility, these two effects exactly offset.

Linearizing Any Model

Taylor expansions, the continuous time limit, and normal distributions can all turn a nonlinear linear model $m = g(f)$ into a linear model $m = a + bf$.

The twin goals of a linear factor model derivation are to derive what variables drive the discount factor, wealth in the case of the CAPM, and to derive a linear relation between the discount factor and these variables. The first goal is often easier than the second. For example, the log utility CAPM got us the right variable, the return on the market potfolio, but a nonlinear functional form. This section covers three standard tricks that are used to obtain a linear functional form. Section 9.3 considers whether linearity is still an important goal.

Taylor Expansion
The most obvious way to linearize the model is by a Taylor expansion,

$$m_{t+1} = g(f_{t+1}) \approx a_t + b_t f_{t+1}.$$

I write the coefficients as a_t and b_t because the chosen expansion point may well change over time, so that f_{t+1} does not stray too far from the expansion point. For example, a natural expansion point is the conditional mean of the factor. Then,

$$m_{t+1} \approx g(E_t(f_{t+1})) + g'(E_t(f_{t+1}))(f_{t+1} - E_t(f_{t+1})).$$

Continuous Time
We can often derive an exact linearization in continuous time. Then, if the discrete time interval is short enough, we can apply the continuous time result as an approximation.

Write the nonlinear discount factor as

$$\Lambda_t = g(f_t, t)$$

so

$$d\Lambda_t = \frac{\partial g}{\partial t} + \frac{\partial g(f_t, t)}{\partial f} \frac{df_t}{f_t} + \frac{1}{2} \frac{\partial^2 g}{\partial f^2} df_t^2.$$

Then, the basic pricing equation in continuous time for asset i reads

$$E_t\left(\frac{dp_t^i}{p_t^i}\right) + \frac{D_t^i}{p_t^i} dt - r_t^f dt = -E_t\left(\frac{dp_t^i}{p_t^i} \frac{d\Lambda_t}{\Lambda_t}\right)$$

$$= -\frac{1}{g(f, t)} \frac{\partial g(f_t, t)}{\partial f} E_t\left(\frac{dp_t^i}{p_t^i} df_t\right),$$

or, for a short discrete time interval,

$$E_t(R_{t+1}^i) - R_t^f \approx \text{cov}_t(R_{t+1}^i, f_{t+1})\left(-\frac{1}{g(f, t)} \frac{\partial g(f_t, t)}{\partial f}\right)$$

$$\approx \beta_{i, f; t} \lambda_t^f.$$

Working backward, we have a discrete-time discount factor that is linear in f.

Consumption-based model. We used this trick in Chapter 1 to derive a linearized version of the consumption-based model. With

$$\Lambda_t = e^{-\delta t} c_t^{-\gamma},$$

we have

$$\frac{d\Lambda_t}{\Lambda_t} = -\delta dt - \gamma \frac{dc_t}{c_t} + \gamma(\gamma + 1)\frac{dc_t^2}{c_t^2}$$

and hence

$$E_t\left(\frac{dp_t^i}{p_t^i}\right) + \frac{D_t^i}{p_t^i}dt - r_t^f dt = -E_t\left(\frac{dp_t^i}{p_t^i}\frac{d\Lambda_t}{\Lambda_t}\right)$$

$$= \gamma E_t\left(\frac{dp_t^i}{p_t^i}\frac{dc_t}{c_t}\right)$$

or, for a short discrete time interval,

$$E_t(R_{t+1}^i) - R_t^f \approx \gamma \operatorname{cov}_t\left(R_{t+1}^i, \frac{c_{t+1}}{c_t}\right)$$

$$\approx \beta_{i,\Delta c;t}\lambda_t^{\Delta c}.$$

Log utility CAPM. The price of the consumption stream or wealth portfolio is, in continuous time,

$$u'(c_t)p_t^W = E_t\int_0^\infty e^{-\delta s}u'(c_{t+s})c_{t+s}ds.$$

With log utility, we have $u'(c_t) = 1/c_t$, so again the value of the market portfolio is exactly proportional to consumption,

$$\frac{p_t^W}{c_t} = \int_0^\infty e^{-\delta s}ds = \frac{1}{\delta}.$$

The discount factor is proportional to the inverse of the value of the market portfolio,

$$\Lambda_t = e^{-\delta t}u'(c_t) = \frac{e^{-\delta t}}{c_t} = \frac{e^{-\delta t}}{\delta p_t^W}$$

so

$$\frac{d\Lambda_t}{\Lambda_t} = -\delta dt - \frac{dp_t^W}{p_t^W} + \frac{1}{2}\frac{dp_t^{W2}}{p_t^{W2}}.$$

Now, the basic pricing equation in continuous time for asset i reads

$$E_t\left(\frac{dp_t^i}{p_t^i}\right) + \frac{D_t^i}{p_t^i}dt - r_t^f dt = E_t\left(\frac{dp_t^i}{p_t^{it}}\frac{dp_t^W}{p_t^{Wt}}\right)$$

or, for a short discrete time interval,

$$E_t(R_{t+1}^i) - R_t^f \approx \operatorname{cov}_t(R_{t+1}^i, R_{t+1}^W)$$

$$\approx \beta_{i,W;t}\operatorname{var}_t(R_t^W)$$

$$\approx \beta_{i,W;t}\lambda_t^W \tag{9.13}$$

Working backwards, equation (9.13) corresponds to a discrete-time discount factor that is a linear function of the market return.

Normal distributions in discrete time: Stein's lemma
The essence of the continuous time approximation is that diffusion processes are locally normally distributed. If we assume that returns are normally distributed in discrete time, we can make the linearization exact in discrete time.

Again, the point of the linearization is to give us an expected return-beta model with betas calculated against the factors themselves rather than nonlinear functions of the factors. We need a way to transform from $\mathrm{cov}(g(f), R)$ to $\mathrm{cov}(f, R)$. The central mathematical trick is *Stein's lemma*:

Lemma: *If f, R are bivariate normal, $g(f)$ is differentiable and $E|g'(f)| < \infty$, then*

$$\mathrm{cov}[g(f), R] = E[g'(f)] \, \mathrm{cov}(f, R).$$

At this point, we're really done. We can substitute covariances and betas with the nonlinear function $g(f)$ with covariances and betas with f itself.

Though it may belabor the point, this lemma allows us to derive a linear discount factor:

$$
\begin{aligned}
p = E(mx) &= E(g(f)x) \\
&= E[g(f)]E(x) + \mathrm{cov}[g(f), x] \\
&= E[g(f)]E(x) + E[g'(f)] \, \mathrm{cov}[f, x] \\
&= E(\{E[g(f)] + E[g'(f)](f - Ef)\}x) \\
&= E(\{E[g(f)] - E[g'(f)]E(f) + E[g'(f)]f\}x)
\end{aligned}
$$

or

$$
\begin{aligned}
m_{t+1} &= \{E_t[g(f_{t+1})] - E_t[g'(f_{t+1})]E_t(f_{t+1})\} + E_t[g'(f_{t+1})]f_{t+1} \\
&= a_t + b_t f_{t+1}.
\end{aligned}
$$

Similarly, it allow us to derive an expected return-beta model using the factors

$$
\begin{aligned}
E_t(R^i_{t+1}) &= R^f_t - \mathrm{cov}_t(R^i_{t+1}, m_{t+1}) \\
&= R^f_t - E_t[g'(f_{t+1})] \, \mathrm{cov}_t(R^i_{t+1}, f_{t+1}) \qquad (9.14) \\
&= R^f_t + \beta_{i, f; t} \lambda^f_t. \qquad (9.15)
\end{aligned}
$$

Two period CAPM. The classic use of Stein's lemma allows us to sub-stitute a normal distribution assumption for the quadratic utility assumption in the two period CAPM. Repeating the analysis starting with equation (9.2), using an arbitrary utility function, we have

$$m_{t+1} = \beta \frac{u'(c_{t+1})}{u'(c_t)} = \beta \frac{u'[R_{t+1}^W(W_t - c_t)]}{u'(c_t)}.$$

Assuming that R^W and R^i are normally distributed, using Stein's lemma, we have

$$\text{cov}_t(R_{t+1}^i, m_{t+1}) = E\left[\beta \frac{(W_t - c_t)u''[R_{t+1}^W(W_t - c_t)]}{u'(c_t)}\right] \text{cov}_t(R_{t+1}^i, R_{t+1}^W).$$

Up to the technical assumption that the expectation exists, the trick is done.

Log utility CAPM. Interestingly, Stein's lemma cannot be applied to the log utility CAPM because the market return *cannot* be normally dis-tributed. It's easy to miss this fact, since in empirical applications we usually take the factor risk premium λ in equation (9.15) as a free parameter. However, the term in equation (9.14), applied to the log utility CAPM $g(f) = 1/R^W$ is

$$E(R_{t+1}^i) = R_t^f + E_t\left(\frac{1}{R_{t+1}^{W2}}\right)\text{cov}_t(R_{t+1}^i, R_{t+1}^W).$$

If R_{t+1}^W is normally distributed, $E(1/R_{t+1}^{W2})$ *does not exist.* The Stein's lemma condition $E|g'(f)| < \infty$ is violated.

This is not a little technical problem to be swept under the rug. If R^W is normally distributed, it can range from $-\infty$ to ∞, including negative values. To get a non-positive return on the wealth portfolio, price and con-sumption must be non-positive. Log utility and $1/c$ marginal utility blow up as consumption nears zero. A log utility consumer will never choose a consumption path with zero or negative consumption. The return on the wealth portfolio *cannot* be normally distributed in a log utility economy.

This fact warns us not to apply the approximation derived from the continuous time model, (9.15), to a long time horizon. We can derive a CAPM-like relation for *log* returns, by assuming that the market and each asset return are jointly *log* normally distributed. The horizon should be short enough that the distinction between log and actual returns is small.

Similarly, even though we can approximate a nonlinear discount fac-tor model—$(c_{t+1}/c_t)^{-\gamma}$ or $1/R_{t+1}^W$—by a linear discount factor model for short time horizons, it would be a mistake to do so for longer time hori-zons, or to discount a stream of dividends. $a - bR^W$ becomes a worse and worse approximation to $1/R^W$. In particular, the former can become negative while the latter does not. The point of Rubinstein (1976), in fact, was not to derive a log utility CAPM, but to advocate the nonlinear model $m = 1/R^W$ as a good way to use the CAPM for arbitrage-free multiperiod discounting.

9.2 Intertemporal Capital Asset Pricing Model (ICAPM)

> Any "state variable" z_t can be a factor. The ICAPM is a linear factor model with wealth and state variables that forecast changes in the distribution of future returns or income.

The ICAPM generates linear discount factor models

$$m_{t+1} = a + b'f_{t+1}$$

in which the factors are "state variables" for the investor's consumption-portfolio decision.

The "state variables" are the variables that determine how well the investor can do in his maximization. Current wealth is obviously a state variable. Additional state variables describe the conditional distribution of asset returns the agent will face in the future or "shifts in the investment opportunity set." In multiple-good or international models, relative price changes are also state variables.

Optimal consumption is a function of the state variables, $c_t = g(z_t)$. We can use this fact once again to substitute out consumption, and write

$$m_{t+1} = \beta \frac{u'\big[g(z_{t+1})\big]}{u'\big[g(z_t)\big]}.$$

From here, it is a simple linearization to deduce that the state variables z_{t+1} will be factors.

Alternatively, the *value* function depends on the state variables

$$V(W_{t+1}, z_{t+1}),$$

so we can write

$$m_{t+1} = \beta \frac{V_W(W_{t+1}, z_{t+1})}{V_W(W_t, z_t)}.$$

(The marginal value of a dollar must be the same in any use, so $u'(c_t) = V_W(W_t, z_t)$.)

This completes the first step, naming the proxies. To obtain a linear relation, we can take a Taylor approximation, assume normality and use Stein's lemma, or, most conveniently, move to continuous time. Starting from

$$\Lambda_t = e^{-\delta t} V_W(W_t, z_t)$$

we have

$$\frac{d\Lambda_t}{\Lambda_t} = -\delta dt + \frac{W_t V_{WW}(W_t, z_t)}{V_W(W_t, z_t)} \frac{dW}{W}$$
$$+ \frac{V_{Wz}(W_t, z_t)}{V_W(W_t, z_t)} dz_t$$
$$+ (\text{second derivative terms}).$$

The elasticity of marginal value with respect to wealth is often called the *coefficient of relative risk aversion*,

$$rra_t \equiv -\frac{WV_{WW}(W_t, z_t)}{V_W(W_t, z_t)}.$$

It captures the investor's reluctance to take monetary or wealth bets.

Substituting into the basic pricing equation, we obtain the ICAPM, which relates expected returns to the covariance of returns with wealth, and also with the other state variables,

$$E\frac{dp_t^i}{p_t^i} + \frac{D_t^i}{p_t^i} dt - r_t^f dt = rra_t \, E\left(\frac{dW_t}{W_t} \frac{dp_t^i}{p_t^i}\right) - \frac{V_{Wz,t}}{V_{W,t}} E\left(dz_t \frac{dp_t^i}{p_t^i}\right).$$

From here, it is fairly straightforward to express the ICAPM in terms of betas rather than covariances, or as a linear discount factor model. Most empirical work occurs in discrete time; we often simply approximate the continuous-time result as

$$E_t\left(R_{t+1}^i\right) - R_t^f \approx rra_t \, \text{cov}_t\left(R_{t+1}^i, \Delta W_{t+1}\right) + \lambda_{zt} \, \text{cov}_t\left(R_{t+1}^i, \Delta z_{t+1}\right).$$

We can substitute covariance with the wealth portfolio in place of covariance with wealth—shocks to the two are the same—and we can use factor-mimicking portfolios for the other factors dz as well. The factor-mimicking portfolios are interesting for portfolio advice as well, as they give the purest way of hedging against or profiting from state variable risk exposure.

This short presentation does not do justice to the beauty of Merton's portfolio theory and ICAPM. What remains is to actually state the consumer's problem and prove that the value function depends on W and

z, the state variables for future investment opportunities, and that the optimal portfolio holds the market and hedge portfolios for the investment opportunity variables. Working this out is not vacuous. For example, we saw that the log utility CAPM holds even with time-varying investment opportunities. Thus the ICAPM will only work if the utility curvature parameter is not equal to one.

9.3 Comments on the CAPM and ICAPM

Conditional vs. unconditional models.
Do they price options?
Why bother linearizing?
The wealth portfolio.
The implicit consumption-based model, and ignored predictions.
Portfolio intuition and recession state variables.

A look at the formal derivations of the models should allow us to understand their empirical application and to understand, if not settle, common controversies.

Is the CAPM Conditional or Unconditional?
Is the CAPM a conditional or an unconditional factor model? That is, are the parameters a and b in $m = a - bR^W$ constants, or do they change at each time period, as conditioning information changes? We saw in Chapter 8 that a conditional CAPM does not imply an unconditional CAPM. If conditional, additional steps must be taken to say anything about observed average returns and empirical failures might just come from conditioning information.

The two-period quadratic utility-based derivation results in a *conditional* CAPM, since the parameters a_t and b_t in equation (9.4), change over time. Also we know from equation (8.3) that a_t and b_t must vary over time if the conditional moments of R^W, R^f vary over time. This two-period investor chooses a portfolio on the *conditional* mean-variance frontier, which is not on the *unconditional* frontier. The multiperiod quadratic utility CAPM only holds if returns are i.i.d. so it only holds if there is no difference between conditional and unconditional models.

On the other hand, the log utility CAPM expressed with the inverse market return holds both conditionally and unconditionally. There are no free parameters that can change with conditioning information:

$$1 = E_t\left(\frac{1}{R_{t+1}^W}R_{t+1}\right) \Leftrightarrow 1 = E\left(\frac{1}{R_{t+1}^W}R_{t+1}\right).$$

However, it makes additional predictions that can be quickly rejected, which I will detail below. Furthermore, when we linearize the log utility CAPM, all the coefficients are again time-varying.

In sum, alternative assumptions give different answers. Whether the CAPM can be rescued by more careful treatment of conditioning information remains an empirical question.

Should the CAPM Price Options?
You may hear the statement "the CAPM is not designed to price derivative securities." This statement also depends on which derivation one has in mind. The quadratic utility CAPM and the log utility CAPM should apply to *all* payoffs: stocks, bonds, options, contingent claims, etc. Rubinstein (1976) shows that the log utility CAPM delivers the Black-Scholes optimum pricing formula. However, if we assume normal return distributions to obtain a linear CAPM in discrete time, we can no longer hope to price options, since option returns are nonnormally distributed. Even the normal distribution for regular returns is a questionable assumption. Again, having looked at the derivations, we see that theory is not decisive on this point.

Why Linearize?
Why bother linearizing a model? Why take the log utility model $m = 1/R^W$ which should price *any* asset, and turn it into $m_{t+1} = a_t + b_t R_{t+1}^W$ that loses the clean conditioning-down property, cannot price nonnormally distributed payoffs and must be applied at short horizons? The tricks were developed when it was hard to estimate nonlinear models. It is clear how to estimate a β and a λ by regressions, but estimating nonlinear models used to be a big headache. Now, GMM has made it easy to estimate and evaluate nonlinear models. Thus, in my opinion, linearization is not that important anymore. If the nonlinear model makes important predictions or simplifications that are lost on linearizing, there is no reason to lose those features.

What About the Wealth Portfolio?
The log utility derivation makes clear just how expansive is the concept of the wealth portfolio. To own a (share of the) *consumption* stream, you have to own not only all stocks, but all bonds, real estate, privately held capital, publicly held capital (roads, parks, etc.), and human capital—a nice word for "people." Clearly, the CAPM is a poor defense of common proxies such as the value-weighted NYSE portfolio. And keep in mind that since it is easy to find ex post mean-variance efficient portfolios of any subset of assets (like stocks) out there, taking the theory seriously is our only guard against fishing.

Implicit Consumption-Based Models

Many users of alternative models clearly are motivated by a belief that the consumption-based model does not work, no matter how well measured consumption might be. This view is not totally unreasonable; perhaps transactions costs de-link consumption and asset returns at high frequencies, and the perfect risk-sharing behind the use of aggregate consumption has always seemed extreme.

However, the derivations make clear that the CAPM and ICAPM are not *alternatives* to the consumption-based model; they are *special cases* of that model. In each case $m_{t+1} = \beta u'(c_{t+1})/u'(c_t)$ still operates. We just added assumptions that allowed us to substitute other variables in place of c_t. You cannot adopt the CAPM on the belief that the consumption-based model is *wrong*. If you think the consumption-based model is fundamentally wrong, the economic justification for the alternative factor models evaporates as well.

Now that we have seen the derivations, the only consistent motivation for factor models is a belief that consumption *data* are unsatisfactory. However, while asset return data are well measured, it is not obvious that the S&P500 or other portfolio returns are terrific measures of the return to total wealth. "Macro factors" used by Chen, Roll, and Ross (1986) and others are distant proxies for the quantities they want to measure, and macro factors based on other NIPA aggregates (investment, output, etc.) suffer from the same measurement problems as aggregate consumption.

In large part, the "better performance" of the CAPM and ICAPM relative to consumption-based models comes from throwing away content. Again, $m_{t+1} = \delta u'(c_{t+1})/u'(c_t)$ is there in any CAPM or ICAPM. The CAPM and ICAPM do make predictions concerning consumption data, and these predictions are often wildly implausible, not only of admittedly poorly measured aggregate consumption data but of any imaginable perfectly measured individual consumption data as well.

For example, the log utility CAPM predicts

$$R_{t+1}^W = \frac{1}{\beta} \frac{c_{t+1}}{c_t}. \tag{9.16}$$

Equation (9.16) implies that the standard deviation of the wealth portfolio return equals the standard deviation of consumption growth. The standard deviation of stock returns is about 16%, that of measured consumption growth is only 1%, and it is inconceivable that perfectly measured consumption varies 16 times more.

Worse, equation (9.16) links consumption with returns *ex post* as well as ex ante. The wealth portfolio return is high, *ex post*, when consumption is high. This holds at every frequency: If stocks go up between 12:00 and

1:00, it must be because (on average) we all decided to have a big lunch. This seems silly. Aggregate consumption and asset returns are likely to be de-linked at high frequencies, but *how* high (quarterly?) and by what mechanism are important questions to be answered. In any case, this is another implication of the log utility CAPM that is just thrown out.

All of the models make further predictions, including the size of the factor risk premia λ, the magnitude of the risk-free rate, or predictions about prices ($p/c =$ constant for the log utility CAPM) that are conventionally ignored when "testing" them.

In sum, the poor performance of the consumption-based model is an important nut to chew on, not just a blind alley or failed attempt that we can safely disregard and go on about our business.

Identity of State Variables
The ICAPM does not tell us the *identity* of the state variables z_t, and many authors use the ICAPM as an obligatory citation to theory on the way to using factors composed of ad hoc portfolios, leading Fama (1991) to characterize the ICAPM as a "fishing license." The ICAPM really is not quite such an expansive license. One could do a lot to insist that the factor-mimicking portfolios actually are the projections of some identifiable state variables on the space of returns, and one could do a lot to make sure the candidate state variables really are plausible state variables for an explicitly stated optimization problem. For example, one could check that investment–opportunity-set state variables actually do forecast something. The fishing license comes as much from habits of applying the theory as from the theory itself.

On the other hand, the conventions of empirical work may be healthy. The CAPM and multiple factor models are obviously very artificial. Their central place really comes from a long string of empirical successes rather than theoretical purity. Perhaps researchers are wise to pick and choose implications of what are, after all, stylized quantitative parables.

Portfolio Intuition and Recession State Variables
I have derived the factor models as instances of the consumption-based model, tricks for substituting consumption out of the discount factor. The more traditional portfolio approach to multifactor models gives a lot of useful intuition, which helps to explain why the CAPM and successor factor models have been so compelling for so long despite the artificiality of these formal derivations. The traditional intuition looks past consumption to think directly about its determinants in sources of income or news.

Start at a portfolio R^W. Now, think about changing the portfolio— adding ε more R^i and ε less R^f. This modification raises the mean portfolio return by $\varepsilon E(R^i - R^f)$. This change also raises the variance of the portfolio return to

$$\sigma^2(R^W + \varepsilon(R^i - R^f)) = \sigma^2(R^W) + 2\varepsilon \operatorname{cov}(R^W, R^i) + \varepsilon^2 \operatorname{var}(R^i).$$

Thus, for small ε (we're really taking a derivative here), this modification raises the portfolio variance by $2\varepsilon \operatorname{cov}(R^W, R^i)$.

This is the central insight. The *covariance (or beta) of R^i with R^W measures how much a marginal increase in R^i affects the **portfolio** variance.* I highlight *portfolio* variance. Modern asset pricing starts when we realize that investors care about *portfolio* returns, not about the behavior of specific assets.

The benefit of the portfolio change is the increased portfolio mean return, $\varepsilon E(R^i - R^f)$. The cost of the change is the increased portfolio variance, $2\varepsilon \operatorname{cov}(R^W, R^i)$. At an optimum, the cost-benefit tradeoff must be the same for each asset. Thus, at an optimum, mean excess returns must be proportional to the covariance of returns with the investor's portfolio, or beta.

The ICAPM adds long investment horizons and time-varying investment opportunities to this picture. An investor with a long horizon (and utility more curved than log) is unhappy when news comes that future returns are lower, because his long-term wealth or consumption will be lower. He will thus prefer stocks that do well on such news, hedging the reinvestment risk. Demanding more of such stocks, investors raise their prices and depress their expected returns for a given market beta. Thus, equilibrium expected returns depend on covariation with news of future returns, as well as covariation with the current market return. The ICAPM remained on the theoretical shelf for 20 years mostly because it took that long to accumulate empirical evidence that returns are, in fact, predictable.

Most current theorizing and empirical work, while citing the ICAPM, really considers another source of additional risk factors: *Investors have jobs.* Or they own houses and shares of small businesses. The CAPM and ICAPM simplify matters by assuming pure (retired) investors who sit on a pile of wealth, all invested in stocks or bonds. Alternatively, these models assume leisure and consumption are separable and that all sources of income including labor income correspond to traded securities. For this reason, the only risk in the CAPM is the market return, and the only state variables in the ICAPM are those that forecast future market returns.

People with jobs will prefer stocks that don't fall in recessions. Demanding such stocks, they drive up prices and drive down expected returns. Thus, expected returns may depend on additional betas that capture labor market conditions, house values, fortunes of small businesses, or other non-marketed assets. Yet these state variables need not forecast returns on any traded assets—this is not the ICAPM. Much current empirical work seems to be headed towards additional state variables of this type for "distress" "recession" etc. However, I know of no famous paper or name to cite for this idea, perhaps because at this point its theoretical content is so obvious.

It is crucial that the extra factors affect the *average* investor. If an event makes investor A worse off and investor B better off, then investor A buys assets that do well when the event happens, and investor B sells them. They transfer the risk of the event, but the price or expected return of the asset is unaffected. For a factor to affect prices or expected returns, the average investor must be affected by it. We should expect many factors, common movements in returns, that do not carry risk prices. Industry portfolios seem to be an example; industries move together but average returns do not vary by industry once you control for other betas.

As you can see, this traditional intuition is encompassed by consumption, or marginal utility more generally. Bad labor market outcomes or bad news about future returns are bad news that raise the marginal utility of wealth, which equals the marginal utility of consumption. The promise of the consumption-based model was that it would give us a single indicator that captures all of these general-equilibrium determinants. It still does, theoretically, but not (yet) in empirical practice.

9.4 Arbitrage Pricing Theory (APT)

> The APT: If a set of asset returns are generated by a linear factor model,
>
> $$R^i = E(R^i) + \sum_{j=1}^{N} \beta_{ij} \tilde{f}_j + \varepsilon^i,$$
>
> $$E(\varepsilon^i) = E(\varepsilon^i \tilde{f}_j) = 0.$$
>
> Then (with additional assumptions) there is a discount factor m linear in the factors $m = a + b'f$ that prices the returns.

The APT, developed by Ross (1976), starts from a statistical characterization. There is a big common component to stock returns: when the market goes up, most individual stocks also go up. Beyond the market, groups of stocks move together, such as computer stocks, utilities, small stocks, value stocks, and so forth. Finally, each stock's return has some completely idiosyncratic movement. This is a characterization of *realized* returns, *outcomes*, or *payoffs*. The point of the APT is to start with this statistical characterization of *outcomes*, and derive something about *expected* returns or *prices*.

The intuition behind the APT is that the completely idiosyncratic movements in asset returns should not carry any risk prices, since investors can diversify idiosyncratic returns away by holding portfolios. Therefore, risk prices or expected returns on a security should be related to the security's covariance with the common components or "factors" only.

The job of this section is then (1) to describe a mathematical model of the tendency for stocks to move together, and thus to define the "factors" and residual idiosyncratic components, and (2) to think carefully about what it takes for the idiosyncratic components to have zero (or small) risk prices, so that only the common components matter to asset pricing.

There are two lines of attack for the second item. (1) If there were no residual, then we could price securities from the factors by *arbitrage* (really, by the law of one price). Perhaps we can extend this logic and show that if the residuals are *small*, they must have small risk prices. (2) If investors all hold well-diversified portfolios, then only variations in the factors drive consumption and hence marginal utility.

Much of the original appeal of the APT came from the first line of attack, the idea that we could derive pricing implications *without* the economic structure required of the CAPM, ICAPM, or any other model derived as a specialization of the consumption-based model. In this section, I will first try to see how far we can in fact get with purely law of one price arguments. I will conclude that the answer is, "not very far," and that the most satisfactory argument for the APT must rely on some economic restrictions.

Factor Structure in Covariance Matrices

I define and examine the factor decomposition

$$x^i = a_i + \beta'_i f + \varepsilon^i, \qquad E(\varepsilon^i) = 0, \quad E(f\varepsilon^i) = 0.$$

The factor decomposition is equivalent to a restriction on the payoff covariance matrix.

The APT models the tendency of asset payoffs (returns) to move together via a statistical *factor decomposition*

$$x^i = a_i + \sum_{j=1}^{M} \beta_{ij} f_j + \varepsilon^i = a_i + \beta'_i f + \varepsilon^i. \tag{9.17}$$

The f_j are the *factors*, the β_{ij} are the *betas* or *factor loadings*, and the ε^i are *residuals*. As usual, I use the same letter without subscripts to denote a vector, for example $f = [f_1\, f_2\, \dots\, f_K]'$. A discount *factor m*, pricing *factors f* in $m = b'f$, and this *factor decomposition* (or *factor structure*) for returns are totally unrelated uses of the word "factor." The APT is conventionally written with x^i = returns, but it ends up being much less confusing to use prices and payoffs.

It is a convenient and conventional simplification to fold the factor means into the first, constant, factor and write the factor decomposition with zero-mean factors $\tilde{f} \equiv f - E(f)$,

$$x^i = E(x^i) + \sum_{j=1}^{M} \beta_{ij}\tilde{f}_j + \varepsilon^i. \tag{9.18}$$

Remember that $E(x^i)$ is still just a statistical characterization, not a prediction of a model.

We can construct the factor decomposition as a regression equation. Define the β_{ij} as regression coefficients, and then the ε_i are uncorrelated with the factors by construction,

$$E(\varepsilon^i) = 0;\; E(\varepsilon_i\tilde{f}_j) = 0.$$

The content—the assumption that keeps (9.18) from describing any arbitrary set of payoffs—is an assumption that the ε_i are *uncorrelated with each other*,

$$E(\varepsilon^i\varepsilon^j) = 0.$$

(More general versions of the model allow some limited correlation across the residuals but the basic story is the same.)

The factor structure is thus a restriction on the covariance matrix of payoffs. For example, if there is only one factor, then

$$\mathrm{cov}(x^i, x^i) - E[(\beta_i\tilde{f} + \varepsilon^i)(\beta_j f + \varepsilon^i)] = \beta_i\beta_j\sigma^2(f) + \begin{cases} \sigma_{\varepsilon^i}^2 & \text{if } i = j, \\ 0 & \text{if } i \neq j. \end{cases}$$

Thus, with N = number of securities, the $N(N-1)/2$ elements of a variance-covariance matrix are described by N betas and $N+1$ variances.

A vector version of the same thing is

$$
\text{cov}(x, x') = \beta\beta'\sigma^2(f) + \begin{bmatrix} \sigma_1^2 & 0 & 0 \\ 0 & \sigma_2^2 & 0 \\ 0 & 0 & \ddots \end{bmatrix}.
$$

With multiple (orthogonalized) factors, we obtain

$$
\text{cov}(x, x') = \beta_1\beta_1'\sigma^2(f_1) + \beta_2\beta_2'\sigma^2(f_2) + \cdots + \text{(diagonal matrix)}.
$$

In all these cases, we describe the covariance matrix as a singular matrix $\beta\beta'$ (or a sum of a few such singular matrices) plus a diagonal matrix.

If we know the factors we want to use ahead of time, say the market (value-weighted portfolio) and industry portfolios, or size and book/market portfolios, we can estimate a factor structure by running regressions. Often, however, we do not know the identities of the factor portfolios ahead of time. In this case we have to use one of several statistical techniques under the broad heading of *factor analysis* (that is where the word "factor" came from in this context) to estimate the factor model. One can estimate a factor structure quickly by simply taking an eigenvalue decomposition of the covariance matrix, and then setting small eigenvalues to zero.

Exact Factor Pricing

> With no error term,
> $$
> x^i = E(x^i)1 + \beta_i'\tilde{f}
> $$
> implies
> $$
> p(x^i) = E(x^i)p(1) + \beta_i'p(\tilde{f})
> $$
> and thus
> $$
> m = a + b'f, \qquad p(x^i) = E(mx^i), \qquad E(R^i) = R^f + \beta_i'\lambda,
> $$
> using only the law of one price.

Suppose that there are no idiosyncratic terms ε^i. This is called an *exact factor model*. Now look again at the factor decomposition,

$$
x^i = E(x^i)1 + \beta_i'\tilde{f}. \tag{9.19}
$$

It started as a statistical decomposition. But it also says that the payoff x^i can be synthesized as a *portfolio* of the factors and a constant (risk-free payoff). Thus, the price of x^i can only depend on the prices of the factors f,

$$p(x^i) = E(x^i)p(1) + \beta'_i p(\tilde{f}). \tag{9.20}$$

The *law of one price* assumption lets you take prices of right and left sides.

If the factors are returns, their prices are 1. If the factors are not returns, their prices are free parameters which can be picked to make the model fit as well as possible. Since there are fewer factors than payoffs, this procedure is not vacuous.

We are really done, but the APT is usually stated as "there is a *discount factor* linear in f that prices returns R^i," or "there is an expected return-beta representation with f as factors." Therefore, we should take a minute to show that the rather obvious relationship (9.20) between prices is equivalent to discount factor and expected return statements.

Assuming only the law of one price, we know there is a discount factor m linear in factors that prices the factors. We usually call it x^*, but call it f^* here to remind us that it prices the factors. If the discount factor prices the factors, it must price any portfolio of the factors; hence f^* prices all payoffs x^i that follow the factor structure (9.19). To see the point explicitly, denote $\hat{f} = \begin{bmatrix} 1 & \tilde{f} \end{bmatrix}'$ the factors including the constant. As with x^*, $f^* = p(\hat{f})'E(\hat{f}\hat{f}')^{-1}\hat{f} = a + b'f$ satisfies $p(\hat{f}) = E(f^*\hat{f})$ and $p(1) = E(f^*)$.

We could now go from m linear in the factors to an expected return-beta model using the connections between the two representations outlined in Chapter 6. But there is a more direct and elegant connection. Start with (9.20), specialized to returns $x^i = R^i$ and of course $p(R^i) = 1$. Use $p(1) = 1/R^f$ and solve for expected return as

$$E(R^i) = R^f + \beta'_i \left[-R^f p(\tilde{f}) \right] = R^f + \beta'_i \lambda$$

The last equality defines λ. Expected returns are linear in the betas, and the constants (λ) are related to the prices of the factors. This is the same definition of λ that we arrived at in Chapter 6 connecting $m = b'f$ to expected return-beta models.

Approximate APT Using the Law of One Price

> Attempts to extend the exact factor pricing model to an approximate factor pricing model when errors are "small," or markets are "large," still only using law of one price.
>
> For fixed m, the APT gets better and better as R^2 or the number of assets increases.
>
> However, for any fixed R^2 or size of market, the APT can be arbitrarily bad.
>
> These observations mean that we must go beyond the law of one price to derive factor pricing models.

Actual returns do not display an exact factor structure. There is some idiosyncratic or residual risk; we cannot exactly replicate the return of a given stock with a portfolio of a few large factor portfolios. However, the idiosyncratic risks are often small. For example, factor model regressions of the form (9.17) often have very high R^2, especially when portfolios rather than individual securities are on the left-hand side. And the residual risks are still idiosyncratic: Even if they are a large part of an individual security's variance, they should be a small contribution to the variance of well-diversified portfolios. Thus, there is reason to hope that the APT holds approximately, especially for reasonably large portfolios. Surely, if the residuals are "small" and/or "idiosyncratic," the price of an asset cannot be "too different" from the price predicted from its factor content?

To think about these issues, start again from a factor structure, but this time put in a residual,

$$x^i = E(x^i)1 + \beta_i'\tilde{f} + \varepsilon^i.$$

Again take prices of both sides,

$$p(x^i) = E(x^i)p(1) + \beta_i'p(\tilde{f}) + E(m\varepsilon^i).$$

Now, what can we say about the price of the residual $p(\varepsilon^i) = E(m\varepsilon^i)$?

Figure 9.1 illustrates the situation. Portfolios of the factors span a payoff space, the line from the origin through $\beta_i'f$ in the figure. The payoff we want to price, x^i, is not in that space, since the residual ε^i is not zero. A discount factor f^* that is in the f payoff space prices the factors. The set of all discount factors that price the factors is the line m perpendicular to f^*. The residual ε^i is orthogonal to the factor space, since it is a regression residual, and to f^* in particular, $E(f^*\varepsilon^i) = 0$. This means that f^* assigns zero price to the residual. But the other discount factors

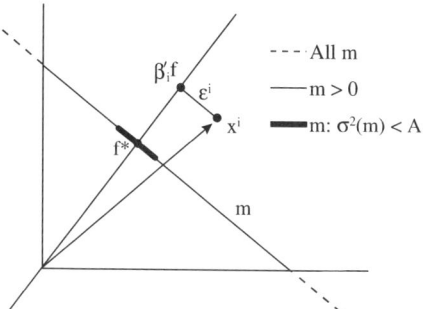

Figure 9.1. *Approximate arbitrage pricing.*

on the m line are *not* orthogonal to ε^i, so generate nonzero price for the residual ε^i. As we sweep along the line of discount factors m that price the f, in fact, we generate every price from $-\infty$ to ∞ for the residual. Thus, the law of one price does not nail down the price of the residual ε^i and hence does not determine the price or expected return of x^i.

Limiting Arguments

We would like to show that the price of x^i has to be "close to" the price of $\beta'_i f$. One notion of "close to" is that in some appropriate limit the price of x^i converges to the price of $\beta'_i f$. "Limit" means, of course, that you can get arbitrarily good accuracy by going far enough in the direction of the limit (for every $\varepsilon > 0$ there is a $\delta \dots$). Thus, establishing a limit result is a way to argue for an approximation.

Here is one theorem that seems to imply that the APT should be a good approximation for portfolios that have high R^2 on the factors. I state the argument for the case that there is a constant factor, so the constant is in the f space and $E(\varepsilon^i) = 0$. The same ideas work in the less usual case that there is no constant factor, using second moments in place of variance.

Thoerem: *Fix a discount factor m that prices the factors. Then, as* $\mathrm{var}(\varepsilon^i) \to 0$, $p(x^i) \to p(\beta'_i f)$.

This is easiest to see by just looking at the graph. $E(\varepsilon^i) = 0$ so $\mathrm{var}(\varepsilon^i) = E(\varepsilon^{i2}) = \|\varepsilon^i\|^2$. Thus, as the size of the ε^i vector in Figure 9.1 gets smaller, x^i gets closer and closer to $\beta'_i f$. For any fixed m, the induced pricing function (lines perpendicular to the chosen m) is continuous. Thus, as x^i gets closer and closer to $\beta'_i f$, its price gets closer and closer to $p(\beta'_i f)$.

The factor model is defined as a regression, so

$$\mathrm{var}(x^i) = \mathrm{var}(\beta'_i f) + \mathrm{var}(\varepsilon^i).$$

Thus, the variance of the residual is related to the regression R^2,

$$\frac{\text{var}(\varepsilon^i)}{\text{var}(x^i)} = 1 - R^2.$$

The theorem says that as $R^2 \to 1$, the price of the residual goes to zero.

We were hoping for some connection between the fact that the risks are *idiosyncratic* and factor pricing. Even if the idiosyncratic risks are a large part of the payoff at hand, they are a small part of a well-diversified portfolio. The next theorem shows that portfolios with high R^2 do not have to happen by chance; well-diversified portfolios will always have this characteristic.

Thoerem: *As the number of primitive assets increases, the R^2 of well-diversified portfolios increases to 1.*

Proof: Start with an equally weighted portfolio

$$x^p = \frac{1}{N} \sum_{i=1}^{N} x^i.$$

Going back to the factor decomposition (9.17) for each individual asset x^i, the factor decomposition of x^p is

$$x^p = \frac{1}{N} \sum_{i=1}^{N} \left(a_i + \beta_i' f + \varepsilon^i \right) = \frac{1}{N} \sum_{i=1}^{N} a_i + \frac{1}{N} \sum_{i=1}^{N} \beta_i' f + \frac{1}{N} \sum_{i=1}^{N} \varepsilon^i$$

$$= a^p + \beta_p' f + \varepsilon^p.$$

The last equality defines notation $\alpha^p, \beta_p, \varepsilon^p$. But

$$\text{var}(\varepsilon^p) = \text{var}\left(\frac{1}{N} \sum_{i=1}^{N} \varepsilon^i \right).$$

So long as the variance of ε^i is bounded, and given the factor assumption $E(\varepsilon^i \varepsilon^j) = 0$,

$$\lim_{N \to \infty} \text{var}(\varepsilon^p) = 0.$$

Obviously, the same idea goes through so long as the portfolio spreads some weight on all the new assets, i.e., so long as it is "well diversified." □

These two theorems can be interpreted to say that the APT holds approximately (in the usual limiting sense) for either portfolios that naturally have high R^2, or well-diversified portfolios in large enough markets. (Chamberlain and Rothschild (1983) is a classic treatment.) We have only used the law of one price.

Law of One Price Arguments Fail

Now, let me pour some cold water on these results. I *fixed m* and then let other things take limits. The flip side is that for any nonzero residual ε^i, no matter how small, we can pick a discount factor *m* that prices the factors and assigns *any* price to x^i! As often in mathematics, the order of "for all" and "there exists" matters a lot.

Thoerem: *For any nonzero residual ε^i, there is a discount factor that prices the factors f (consistent with the law of one price) and that assigns any desired price in $(-\infty, \infty)$ to the payoff x^i.*

So long as $\|\varepsilon^i\| > 0$, as we sweep the choice of *m* along the dashed line of figure 9.1, the inner product of *m* with ε^i and hence x^i varies from $-\infty$ to ∞. Thus, for a given size $R^2 < 1$, or a given finite market, the law of one price says absolutely nothing about the prices of payoffs that do not exactly follow the factor structure. The law of one price says that two ways of constructing the same portfolio must give the same price. If the residual is not exactly zero, there is no way of replicating the payoff x^i from the factors and no way to infer anything about the price of x^i from the price of the factors.

I think the contrast between this theorem and those of the last subsection accounts for most of the huge theoretical controversy over the APT. (For example, Shanken [1985], Dybvig and Ross [1985].) If you fix *m* and take limits of N or ε, the APT gets arbitrarily good. But if you fix N or ε, as one does in any application, the APT can get arbitrarily bad as you search over possible *m*.

The lesson I learn is that the effort to *extend* prices from an original set of securities (*f* in this case) to new payoffs that are not exactly spanned by the original set of securities, using only the law of one price, is fundamentally doomed. To extend a pricing function, you need to add some restrictions beyond the law of one price.

Beyond the Law of One Price: Arbitrage and Sharpe Ratios

We can find a well-behaved approximate APT if we impose the law of one price *and* a restriction on the volatility of discount factors, or, equivalently, a bound on the Sharpe ratio achievable by portfolios of the factors and test assets.

The approximate APT based on the law of one price fell apart because we could always choose a discount factor sufficiently "far out" to generate an arbitrarily large price for an arbitrarily small residual. But those discount factors are surely "unreasonable." Surely, we can rule them out, reestablishing an approximate APT, without jumping all the way to fully specified discount factor models such as the CAPM or consumption-based model.

A natural first idea is to impose the no-arbitrage restriction that m must be positive. Graphically, we are now restricted to the solid m line in Figure 9.1. Since that line only extends a finite amount, restricting us to strictly positive $m's$ gives rise to finite upper and lower *arbitrage bounds* on the price of ε^i and hence x^i. (The phrase *arbitrage bounds* comes from option pricing, and we will see these ideas again in that context. If this idea worked, it would restore the APT to "arbitrage pricing" rather than "law of one pricing.")

Alas, in applications of the APT (as often in option pricing), the arbitrage bounds are too wide to be of much use. The positive discount factor restriction is equivalent to saying "if portfolio A gives a higher payoff than portfolio B in *every state of nature*, then the price of A must be higher than the price of B." Since stock returns and factors are continuously distributed, not two-state distributions as I have graphed for Figure 9.1, there typically are no strictly dominating portfolios, so adding $m > 0$ does not help.

A second restriction does let us derive an approximate APT that is useful in finite markets with $R^2 < 1$. We can restrict the *variance* and hence the size ($\|m\| = E(m^2)$) of the discount factor. Figure 9.1 includes a plot of the discount factors with limited variance, size, or length in the geometry of that figure. The restricted range of discount factors produces a restricted range of prices for x^i. The restricted range of discount factors gives us upper and lower price *bounds* for the price of x^i in terms of the factor prices. Precisely, the upper and lower bounds solve the problem

$$\min_{\{m\}} \text{ (or } \max_{\{m\}}) \ p(x^i) = E(mx^i) \quad \text{s.t.} \ E(mf) = p(f), \ m \geq 0, \ \sigma^2(m) \leq A.$$

Limiting the variance of the discount factor is of course the same as limiting the maximum *Sharpe ratio* (mean/standard deviation of excess return) available from portfolios of the factors and x^i. Recall from Chapter 1 that

$$\frac{E(R^e)}{\sigma(R^e)} \leq \frac{\sigma(m)}{E(m)}.$$

Though a bound on Sharpe ratios or discount factor volatility is not a totally preference-free concept, it clearly imposes a great deal less structure than the CAPM or ICAPM which are essentially full general-equilibrium models. Ross (1976) included this suggestion in his original APT paper, though it seems to have disappeared from the literature since then in the failed effort to derive an APT from the law of one price alone. Ross pointed out that deviations from factor pricing could provide very high Sharpe ratio opportunities, which seem implausible though not violations of the law of one price. Saá-Requejo and I (2000) dub this idea "good-deal" pricing, as an extension of "arbitrage pricing." Limiting $\sigma(m)$ rules out "good deals" as well as pure arbitrage opportunities.

Having imposed a limit on discount factor volatility or Sharpe ratio A, then the APT limit does work, and does not depend on the order of "for all" and "there exists."

Thoerem: As $\varepsilon^i \to 0$ and $R^2 \to 1$, the price $p(x^i)$ assigned by any discount factor m that satisfies $E(mf) = p(f)$, $m \geq 0$, $\sigma^2(m) \leq A$ approaches $p(\beta_i' f)$.

9.5 APT vs. ICAPM

A factor structure in the covariance of returns or high R^2 in regressions of returns on factors can imply factor pricing (APT) but factors can price returns without describing their covariance matrix (ICAPM).

Differing inspiration for factors.

The disappearance of absolute pricing.

The APT and ICAPM stories are often confused. Factor structure can imply factor pricing (APT), but factor pricing does not require a factor structure. In the ICAPM there is no presumption that factors f in a pricing model $m = b'f$ describe the covariance matrix of returns. The factors do not have to be orthogonal or i.i.d. either. High R^2 in time-series regressions of the returns on the factors may imply factor pricing (APT), but again are not necessary (ICAPM). The regressions of returns on factors can have low R^2 in the ICAPM. Factors such as industry may describe large parts of returns' variances but not contribute to the explanation of average returns.

The biggest difference between APT and ICAPM for empirical work is in the inspiration for factors. The APT suggests that one start with a statistical analysis of the covariance matrix of returns and find portfolios that characterize common movement. The ICAPM suggests that one start by thinking about state variables that describe the conditional distribution of future asset returns. More generally, the idea of proxying for marginal utility growth suggests macroeconomic indicators, and indicators of shocks to nonasset income in particular.

The difference between the derivations of factor pricing models, and in particular an approximate law of one price basis versus a proxy for marginal utility basis seems not to have had much impact on practice. In practice, we just test models $m = b'f$ and rarely worry about derivations.

The best evidence for this view lies in the introductions of famous papers. Chen, Roll, and Ross (1986) describe one of the earliest popular multifactor models, using industrial production and inflation as some of the main factors. They do not even present a factor decomposition of test asset returns, or the time-series regressions. A reader might well categorize the paper as a macroeconomic factor model or perhaps an ICAPM, but their introduction calls it an APT. Fama and French (1993) describe the currently most popular multifactor model, and their introduction describes it as an ICAPM in which the factors proxy for state variables. But the factors are portfolios of assets sorted on size and book/market just like the test assets, the time-series R^2 are all above 90%, and much of the explanation involves "common movement" in test assets captured by the factors. A reader might well categorize the model as much closer to an APT.

In the preface, I made a distinction between *relative* pricing and *absolute* pricing. In the former, we price one security given the prices of others, while in the latter, we price each security by reference to fundamental sources of risk. The factor pricing stories are interesting in that they start with a nice absolute pricing model, the consumption-based model, and throw out enough information to end up with relative models. The CAPM prices R^i *given* the market, but throws out the consumption-based model's description of where the market return came from. Though the derivation says the CAPM should price any asset as an absolute model, everyone knows better than to test it, say, on options data. The APT is a true relative pricing model. It pretends to do no more than extend the prices of factor portfolios to "nearby" securities.

Problems—Chapter 9

1. Suppose the investor only has a one-period horizon. He invests wealth W at date zero, and only consumes with expected utility $Eu(c) = Eu(W)$ in period 1. Derive the quadratic utility CAPM in this case. (This is an even simpler derivation. The Lagrange multiplier on initial wealth W now becomes the denominator of m in place of $u'(c_0)$.)

2. Figure 9.1 suggests that $m > 0$ is enough to establish a well-behaved approximate APT. The text claims this is not true. Which is right?

3. Can you use any excess return for the market factor in the CAPM, or must it be the market less the risk-free rate?

PART II
Estimating and Evaluating Asset Pricing Models

Our first task in bringing an asset pricing model to data is to *estimate* the free parameters: the β and γ in $m = \beta(c_{t+1}/c_t)^{-\gamma}$, or the b in $m = b'f$. Then we want to *evaluate* the model. Is it a good model or not? Is another model better?

Statistical analysis helps us to evaluate a model by providing a *distribution theory* for numbers such as parameter estimates that we create from the data. A distribution theory pursues the following idea: Suppose that we generate artificial data over and over again from a statistical model. For example, we could specify that the market return is an i.i.d. normal random variable, and a set of stock returns is generated by $R_t^{ei} = \alpha_i + \beta_i R_t^{em} + \varepsilon_t^i$. After picking values for the mean and variance of the market return and the $\alpha_i, \beta_i, \sigma^2(\varepsilon^i)$, we could ask a computer to simulate many artificial data sets. We can repeat our statistical procedure in each of these artificial data sets, and graph the *distribution* of any statistic which we have estimated from the real data, i.e., the frequency that it takes on any particular value in our artificial data sets.

In particular, we are interested in a distribution theory for the estimated parameters, to give us some sense of how much the data really has to say about their values; and for the pricing errors, which helps us to judge whether pricing errors we observe are just bad luck of one particular historical accident or if they indicate a failure of the model. We also will want to generate distributions for statistics that compare one model to another, or that provide other interesting evidence, to judge how much sample luck affects those calculations.

The statistical methods I discuss in this part achieve these ends. They give methods for estimating free parameters, they provide a distribution theory for those parameters, and they provide distributions for statistics that we can use to evaluate models, most often a quadratic form of pricing errors in the form $\hat{\alpha}' V^{-1} \hat{\alpha}$.

I start by focusing on the GMM approach. The GMM approach is a natural fit for a discount factor formulation of asset pricing theories, since we just use sample moments in the place of population moments. As you will see, there is no singular "GMM estimate and test." GMM is a large canvas and a big set of paints and brushes; a flexible tool for doing all kinds of sensible (and, unless you are careful, not-so-sensible) things to the data. Then I consider traditional regression tests, naturally paired with expected return-beta statements of factor models, and their maximum likelihood formalization. I emphasize the fundamental similarities between these three methods, as I emphasized the similarity between $p = E(mx)$, expected return-beta models, and mean-variance frontiers. A concluding chapter highlights some of the differences between the methods, as I contrasted $p = E(mx)$ and beta or mean-variance representations of the models.

10
GMM in Explicit Discount Factor Models

THE BASIC IDEA in the GMM approach is very straightforward. The asset pricing model predicts

$$E(p_t) = E\big[m(\text{data}_{t+1},\ \text{parameters})\ x_{t+1}\big]. \tag{10.1}$$

The most natural way to check this prediction is to examine sample averages, i.e., to calculate

$$\frac{1}{T}\sum_{t=1}^{T} p_t \quad \text{and} \quad \frac{1}{T}\sum_{t=1}^{T}\big[m(\text{data}_{t+1},\ \text{parameters})\ x_{t+1}\big]. \tag{10.2}$$

GMM *estimates* the parameters by making the sample averages in (10.2) as close to each other as possible. It seems natural, before evaluating a model, to pick parameters that give it its best chance. GMM then works out a distribution theory for the estimates. This distribution theory is a generalization of the simplest exercise in statistics: the distribution of the sample mean. Then, it suggests that we *evaluate* the model by looking at how close the sample averages of price and discounted payoff *are* to each other, or equivalently by looking at the pricing errors. GMM gives a statistical *test* of the hypothesis that the underlying population means are in fact zero.

10.1 The Recipe

Definitions:

$$u_{t+1}(b) \equiv m_{t+1}(b)x_{t+1} - p_t,$$

$$g_T(b) \equiv E_T[u_t(b)],$$

$$S \equiv \sum_{j=-\infty}^{\infty} E[u_t(b)\, u_{t-j}(b)'].$$

GMM estimate:

$$\hat{b}_2 = \operatorname{argmin}_b g_T(b)'\widehat{S}^{-1}g_T(b).$$

Standard errors:

$$\operatorname{var}(\hat{b}_2) = \frac{1}{T}(d'S^{-1}d)^{-1}; \qquad d \equiv \frac{\partial g_T(b)}{\partial b}.$$

Test of the model ("overidentifying restrictions"):

$$TJ_T = T\,\min[g_T(b)'S^{-1}g_T(b)] \sim \chi^2\ (\#\text{moments} - \#\text{parameters}).$$

It is easiest to start our discussion of GMM in the context of an explicit discount factor model, such as the consumption-based model. I treat the special structure of linear factor models later. I start with the basic classic recipe as given by Hansen and Singleton (1982).

Discount factor models involve some unknown parameters as well as data, so I write $m_{t+1}(b)$ when it is important to remind ourselves of this dependence. For example, if $m_{t+1} = \beta(c_{t+1}/c_t)^{-\gamma}$, then $b \equiv [\beta\ \gamma]'$. I write $\hat{b}$ to denote an estimate when it is important to distinguish estimated from other values.

Any asset pricing model implies

$$E(p_t) = E[m_{t+1}(b)x_{t+1}]. \tag{10.3}$$

It is easiest to write this equation in the form $E(\cdot) = 0$,

$$E[m_{t+1}(b)x_{t+1} - p_t] = 0. \tag{10.4}$$

x and p are typically vectors; we typically check whether a model for m can price a number of assets simultaneously. Equations (10.4) are often called the *moment conditions*.

It is convenient to define the *errors* $u_t(b)$ as the object whose mean should be zero,

$$u_{t+1}(b) = m_{t+1}(b)x_{t+1} - p_t.$$

Given values for the parameters b, we could construct a time series on u_t and look at its mean.

Define $g_T(b)$ as the sample mean of the u_t errors, when the parameter vector is b in a sample of size T:

$$g_T(b) \equiv \frac{1}{T} \sum_{t=1}^{T} u_t(b) = E_T\big[u_t(b)\big] = E_T\big[m_{t+1}(b)x_{t+1} - p_t\big].$$

The second equality introduces the handy notation E_T for sample means,

$$E_T(\cdot) = \frac{1}{T} \sum_{t=1}^{T}(\cdot).$$

(It might make more sense to denote these estimates $\widehat{E}$ and $\hat{g}$. However, Hansen's T subscript notation is so widespread that doing so would cause more confusion than it solves.)

The *first-stage estimate* of b minimizes a quadratic form of the sample mean of the errors,

$$\hat{b}_1 = \mathrm{argmin}_{\{b\}} \; g_T(\hat{b})'Wg_T(\hat{b})$$

for some arbitrary matrix W (often, $W = I$). This estimate is consistent and asymptotically normal. You can and often should stop here, as I explain below.

Using $\hat{b}_1$, form an estimate $\widehat{S}$ of

$$S \equiv \sum_{j=-\infty}^{\infty} E\big[u_t(b)\, u_{t-j}(b)'\big]. \tag{10.5}$$

(Below I discuss various interpretations of and ways to construct this estimate.) Form a *second-stage* estimate $\hat{b}_2$ using the matrix $\widehat{S}$ in the quadratic form,

$$\hat{b}_2 = \mathrm{argmin}_{b} \; g_T(b)'\widehat{S}^{-1}g_T(b).$$

$\hat{b}_2$ is a consistent, asymptotically normal, and asymptotically efficient estimate of the parameter vector b. "Efficient" means that it has the smallest variance-covariance matrix among all estimators that set different linear combinations of $g_T(b)$ to zero or all choices of weighting matrix W. The variance-covariance matrix of $\hat{b}_2$ is

$$\mathrm{var}(\hat{b}_2) = \frac{1}{T}(d'S^{-1}d)^{-1},$$

where

$$d \equiv \frac{\partial g_T(b)}{\partial b}$$

or, more explicitly,

$$d = E_T\left(\frac{\partial}{\partial b}\left[(m_{t+1}(b)x_{t+1} - p_t)\right]\right)\Bigg|_{b=\hat{b}}.$$

(More precisely, d should be written as the object to which $\partial g_T/\partial b$ converges, and $\partial g_T/\partial b$ is an estimate of that object used to form a consistent estimate of the asymptotic variance-covariance matrix.)

This variance-covariance matrix can be used to test whether a parameter or group of parameters is equal to zero, via

$$\frac{\hat{b}_i}{\sqrt{\text{var}(\hat{b})_{ii}}} \sim N(0, 1)$$

and

$$\hat{b}_j\left[\text{var}(\hat{b})_{jj}\right]^{-1}\hat{b}_j \sim \chi^2(\#\text{included } b)$$

where b_j = subvector, $\text{var}(b)_{jj}$ = submatrix.

Finally, the *test of overidentifying restrictions* is a test of the overall fit of the model. It states that T times the minimized value of the second-stage objective is distributed χ^2 with degrees of freedom equal to the number of moments less the number of estimated parameters:

$$TJ_T = T\min_{\{b\}}\left[g_T(b)'S^{-1}g_T(b)\right] \sim \chi^2(\#\text{moments} - \#\text{parameters}).$$

10.2 Interpreting the GMM Procedure

$g_T(b)$ is a pricing error. It is proportional to α.

GMM picks parameters to minimize a weighted sum of squared pricing errors.

The second stage picks the linear combination of pricing errors that are best measured, by having smallest sampling variation. First and second stage are like OLS and GLS regressions.

The standard error formula can be understood as an application of the delta method.

The J_T test evaluates the model by looking at the sum of squared pricing errors.

Pricing Errors
The moment conditions are

$$g_T(b) = E_T\left[m_{t+1}(b)x_{t+1}\right] - E_T\left[p_t\right].$$

Thus, each moment is the difference between actual $(E_T(p))$ and predicted $(E_T(mx))$ price, or *pricing error*. What could be more natural than to pick parameters so that the model's predicted prices are as close as possible to the actual prices, and then to evaluate the model by how large these pricing errors are?

In the language of expected returns, the moments $g_T(b)$ are proportional to the difference between actual and predicted returns: Jensen's alphas, or the vertical distance between the points and the line in a graph of actual vs. predicted average returns such as Figure 2.4. To see this fact, recall that $0 = E(mR^e)$ can be translated to a predicted expected return,

$$E(R^e) = -\frac{\text{cov}(m, R^e)}{E(m)}.$$

Therefore, we can write the pricing error as

$$g(b) = E(mR^e) = E(m)\left(E(R^e) - \left(-\frac{\text{cov}(m, R^e)}{E(m)}\right)\right)$$

$$= \frac{1}{R^f}(\text{actual mean return} - \text{predicted mean return}).$$

If we express the model in expected return-beta language,

$$E(R^{ei}) = \alpha_i + \beta_i'\lambda,$$

then the GMM objective is proportional to the Jensen's alpha measure of mis-pricing,

$$g(b) = \frac{1}{R^f}\alpha_i.$$

First-Stage Estimates

If we could, we would pick b to make every element of $g_T(b) = 0$—to have the model price assets perfectly in sample. However, there are usually more moment conditions (returns times instruments) than there are parameters. There should be, because theories with as many free parameters as facts (moments) are vacuous. Thus, we choose b to make the pricing errors $g_T(b)$ as small as possible, by minimizing a quadratic form,

$$\min_{\{b\}} g_T(b)'Wg_T(b). \tag{10.6}$$

W is a *weighting matrix* that tells us how much attention to pay to each moment, or how to trade off doing well in pricing one asset or linear combination of assets versus doing well in pricing another. In the common case $W = I$, GMM treats all assets symmetrically, and the objective is to minimize the sum of squared pricing errors.

The sample pricing error $g_T(b)$ may be a nonlinear function of b. Thus, you may have to use a numerical search to find the value of b that minimizes the objective in (10.6). However, since the objective is locally quadratic, the search is usually straightforward.

Second-Stage Estimates: Why S^{-1}?
What weighting matrix should you use? The weighting matrix directs GMM to emphasize some moments or linear combinations of moments at the expense of others. You might start with $W = I$, i.e., try to price all assets equally well. A W that is not the identity matrix can be used to offset differences in units between the moments. You might also start with different elements on the diagonal of W if you think some assets are more interesting, more informative, or better measured than others.

The second-stage estimate picks a weighting matrix based on *statistical* considerations. Some asset returns may have much more variance than others. For those assets, the sample mean $g_T = E_T(m_t R_t - 1)$ will be a much less accurate measurement of the population mean $E(mR - 1)$, since the sample mean will vary more from sample to sample. Hence, it seems like a good idea to pay less attention to pricing errors from assets with high variance of $m_t R_t - 1$. One could implement this idea by using a W matrix composed of inverse variances of $E_T(m_t R_t - 1)$ on the diagonal. More generally, since asset returns are correlated, one might think of using the covariance matrix of $E_T(m_t R_t - 1)$. This weighting matrix pays most attention to *linear combinations* of moments about which the data set at hand has the most information. This idea is exactly the same as heteroskedasticity and cross-correlation corrections that lead you from OLS to GLS in linear regressions.

The covariance matrix of $g_T = E_T(u_{t+1})$ is the variance of a sample mean. Exploiting the assumption that $E(u_t) = 0$, and that u_t is stationary so $E(u_1 u_2) = E(u_t u_{t+1})$ depends only on the time interval between the two u's, we have

$$\text{var}(g_T) = \text{var}\left(\frac{1}{T}\sum_{t=1}^{T} u_{t+1}\right)$$

$$= \frac{1}{T^2}\left[TE(u_t u_t') + (T-1)\left(E(u_t u_{t-1}') + E(u_t u_{t+1}')\right) + \cdots\right].$$

As $T \to \infty$, $(T-j)/T \to 1$, so

$$\text{var}(g_T) \to \frac{1}{T}\sum_{j=-\infty}^{\infty} E(u_t u_{t-j}') = \frac{1}{T}S.$$

The last equality denotes S, known for other reasons as the *spectral density matrix at frequency zero* of u_t. (Precisely, S so defined is the variance-covariance matrix of the g_T for fixed b. The actual variance-covariance matrix of g_T must take into account the fact that we chose b to set a linear combination of the g_T to zero in each sample. I give that formula below. The point here is heuristic.)

This fact suggests that a good weighting matrix might be the inverse of S. In fact, Hansen (1982) shows formally that the choice

$$W = S^{-1}, \qquad S \equiv \sum_{j=-\infty}^{\infty} E(u_t u'_{t-j}),$$

is the statistically optimal weighting matrix, meaning that it produces estimates with lowest asymptotic variance.

You may be familiar with the formula $\sigma(u)/\sqrt{T}$ for the standard deviation of a sample mean. This formula is a special case that holds when the u_ts are uncorrelated over time. If $E_t(u_t u'_{t-j}) = 0$, $j \neq 0$, then the previous equation reduces to

$$\mathrm{var}\left(\frac{1}{T}\sum_{t=1}^{T} u_{t+1}\right) = \frac{1}{T}E(uu') = \frac{\mathrm{var}(u)}{T}.$$

This is probably the first statistical formula you ever saw—the variance of the sample mean. In GMM, it is the last statistical formula you will ever see as well. GMM amounts to just generalizing the simple ideas behind the distribution of the sample mean to parameter estimation and general statistical contexts.

The first- and second-stage estimates should remind you of standard linear regression models. You start with an OLS regression. If the errors are not i.i.d., the OLS estimates are consistent, but not efficient. If you want efficient estimates, you can use the OLS estimates to obtain a series of residuals, estimate a variance-covariance matrix of residuals, and then do GLS. GLS is also consistent and more efficient, meaning that the sampling variation in the estimated parameters is lower.

Standard Errors

The formula for the standard error of the estimate,

$$\mathrm{var}(\hat{b}_2) = \frac{1}{T}(d'S^{-1}d)^{-1}, \tag{10.7}$$

can be understood most simply as an instance of the "delta method" that the asymptotic variance of $f(x)$ is $f'(x)^2\mathrm{var}(x)$. Suppose there is only one parameter and one moment. S/T is the variance matrix of the moment g_T. d^{-1} is $[\partial g_T/\partial b]^{-1} = \partial b/\partial g_T$. Then the delta method formula gives

$$\text{var}(\hat{b}_2) = \frac{1}{T}\frac{\partial b}{\partial g_T}\ \text{var}(g_T)\frac{\partial b}{\partial g_T}.$$

The actual formula (10.7) just generalizes this idea to vectors.

J_T Test

Once you have estimated the parameters that make a model "fit best," the natural question is, how well does it fit? It is natural to look at the pricing errors and see if they are "big." The J_T test asks whether they are "big" by statistical standards—if the model is true, how often should we see a (weighted) sum of squared pricing errors this big? If not often, the model is "rejected." The test is

$$TJ_T = T[g_T(\hat{b})'S^{-1}g_T(\hat{b})] \sim \chi^2(\#\text{moments} - \#\text{parameters}).$$

Since S is the variance-covariance matrix of g_T, this statistic is the minimized pricing errors divided by their variance-covariance matrix. Sample means converge to a normal distribution, so sample means squared divided by variance converges to the square of a standard normal, or χ^2.

The reduction in degrees of freedom corrects for the fact that S is really the covariance matrix of g_T for fixed b. We set a linear combination of the g_T to zero in each sample, so the actual covariance matrix of g_T is singular, with rank $\#\text{moments} - \#\text{parameters}$.

10.3 Applying GMM

> Notation.
> Forecast errors and instruments.
> Stationarity and choice of units.

Notation; Instruments and Returns

Most of the effort involved with GMM is simply mapping a given problem into the very general notation. The equation

$$E[m_{t+1}(b)x_{t+1} - p_t] = 0$$

can capture a lot. We often test asset pricing models using returns, in which case the moment conditions are

$$E[m_{t+1}(b)R_{t+1} - 1] = 0.$$

It is common to add *instruments* as well. Mechanically, you can multiply both sides of

$$1 = E_t[m_{t+1}(b)R_{t+1}]$$

by any variable z_t observed at time t before taking unconditional expectations, resulting in

$$E(z_t) = E[m_{t+1}(b)R_{t+1}z_t].$$

Expressing the result in $E(\cdot) = 0$ form,

$$0 = E\left\{[m_{t+1}(b)R_{t+1} - 1]z_t\right\}. \tag{10.8}$$

We can do this for a whole vector of returns and instruments, multiplying each return by each instrument. For example, if we start with two returns $R = [R^a \, R^b]'$ and one instrument z, equation (10.8) looks like

$$E\left\{\begin{bmatrix} m_{t+1}(b) \, R_{t+1}^a \\ m_{t+1}(b) \, R_{t+1}^b \\ m_{t+1}(b) \, R_{t+1}^a z_t \\ m_{t+1}(b) \, R_{t+1}^b z_t \end{bmatrix} - \begin{bmatrix} 1 \\ 1 \\ z_t \\ z_t \end{bmatrix}\right\} = \begin{bmatrix} 0 \\ 0 \\ 0 \\ 0 \end{bmatrix}.$$

Using the Kronecker product $\otimes$ meaning "multiply every element by every other element" and including the constant 1 as the first element of the instrument vector z_t, we can denote the same relation compactly by

$$E\left\{[m_{t+1}(b) \, R_{t+1} - 1] \otimes z_t\right\} = 0, \tag{10.9}$$

or, emphasizing the managed-portfolio interpretation and $p = E(mx)$ notation,

$$E[m_{t+1}(b)(R_{t+1} \otimes z_t) - (1 \otimes z_t)] = 0.$$

Forecast Errors and Instruments

The asset pricing model says that, although expected *returns* can vary across time and assets, expected *discounted* returns should always be the same, 1. The error $u_{t+1} = m_{t+1}R_{t+1} - 1$ is the ex-post discounted return. $u_{t+1} = m_{t+1}R_{t+1} - 1$ represents a *forecast error*. Like any forecast error, u_{t+1} should be conditionally and unconditionally mean zero.

In an econometric context, z is an *instrument* because it should be uncorrelated with the error u_{t+1}. $E(z_t u_{t+1})$ is the numerator of a regression coefficient of u_{t+1} on z_t; thus adding instruments basically checks that the ex-post discounted return is unforecastable by linear regressions.

If an asset's return is higher than predicted when z_t is unusually high, but not on average, scaling by z_t will pick up this feature of the data. Then, the moment condition checks that the discount rate is unusually low at such times, or that the conditional covariance of the discount rate and asset return moves sufficiently to justify the high conditionally expected return. As in Section 8.1, the addition of instruments is equivalent to adding the returns of managed portfolios to the analysis, and is in principle able to capture *all* of the model's predictions.

Stationarity and Distributions

The GMM distribution theory does require some statistical assumptions. Hansen (1982) and Ogaki (1993) cover them in depth. The most important assumption is that m, p, and x must be *stationary* random variables. ("Stationary" is often misused to mean constant, or i.i.d. The statistical definition of stationarity is that the joint distribution of x_t, x_{t-j} depends only on j and not on t.) Sample averages must converge to population means as the sample size grows, and stationarity is necessary for this result.

Assuring stationarity usually amounts to a choice of sensible units. For example, though we could express the pricing of a stock as

$$p_t = E_t \left[m_{t+1} (d_{t+1} + p_{t+1}) \right],$$

it would not be wise to do so. For stocks, p and d rise over time and so are typically not stationary; their unconditional means are not defined. It is better to divide by p_t and express the model as

$$1 = E_t \left[m_{t+1} \frac{d_{t+1} + p_{t+1}}{p_t} \right] = E_t \left(m_{t+1} R_{t+1} \right).$$

The stock *return* is plausibly stationary.

Dividing by dividends is an alternative and, I think, underutilized way to achieve stationarity (at least for portfolios, since many individual stocks do not pay regular dividends):

$$\frac{p_t}{d_t} = E_t \left[m_{t+1} \left(1 + \frac{p_{t+1}}{d_{t+1}} \right) \frac{d_{t+1}}{d_t} \right].$$

Now we map $\left(1 + (p_{t+1}/d_{t+1}) \right)(d_{t+1}/d_t)$ into x_{t+1} and p_t/d_t into p_t. This formulation allows us to focus on *prices* rather than one-period returns.

Bonds are a claim to a dollar, so bond prices and yields do not grow over time. Hence, it might be all right to examine

$$p_t^b = E(m_{t+1} 1)$$

with no transformations.

Stationarity is not always a clear-cut question in practice. As variables become "less stationary," as they experience longer swings in a sample, the asymptotic distribution can become a less reliable guide to a finite-sample distribution. For example, the level of nominal interest rates is surely a stationary variable in a fundamental sense: we have observations near 6% as far back as ancient Babylon, and it is about 6% again today. Yet it takes very long swings away from this unconditional mean, moving slowly up or down for even 20 years at a time. Therefore, in an estimate and test that uses the level of interest rates, the asymptotic distribution theory might be a bad approximation to the correct finite-sample distribution theory. This is true even if the number of data points is large. Ten thousand data points measured every minute are a "smaller" data set than 100 data points measured every year. In such a case, it is particularly important to develop a finite-sample distribution by simulation or bootstrap, which is easy to do given today's computing power.

It is also important to choose *test assets* in a way that is stationary. For example, individual stocks change character over time, increasing or decreasing size, exposure to risk factors, leverage, and even nature of the business. For this reason, it is common to sort stocks into portfolios based on characteristics such as betas, size, book/market ratios, industry, and so forth. The statistical characteristics of the *portfolio* returns may be much more constant than the characteristics of individual securities, which float in and out of the various portfolios. (One can alternatively include the characteristics as instruments.)

Many econometric techniques require assumptions about distributions. As you can see, the variance formulas used in GMM *do not* include the usual assumptions that variables are i.i.d., normally distributed, homoskedastic, etc. You can put such assumptions in if you want to—we will see how below, and adding such assumptions simplifies the formulas and can improve the small-sample performance when the assumptions are justified—but you do not *have* to add these assumptions.

11

GMM: General Formulas and Applications

LOTS OF CALCULATIONS beyond parameter estimation and model testing are useful in the process of evaluating a model and comparing it to other models. You still want to understand sampling variation in such calculations, and mapping the questions into the GMM framework allows you to do this easily. In addition, alternative estimation and evaluation procedures may be more intuitive or robust to model misspecification than the two- (or multi-) stage procedure described in the last chapter.

In this chapter I lay out the general GMM framework, and I discuss five applications and variations on the basic GMM method. (1) I show how to derive standard errors of nonlinear functions of sample moments, such as correlation coefficients. (2) I apply GMM to OLS regressions, easily deriving standard error formulas that correct for autocorrelation and conditional heteroskedasticity. (3) I show how to use prespecified weighting matrices W in asset pricing tests in order to overcome the tendency of efficient GMM to focus on spuriously low-variance portfolios. (4) As a good parable for prespecified linear combination of moments a, I show how to mimic "calibration" and "evaluation" phases of real business cycle models. (5) I show how to use the distribution theory for the g_T beyond just forming the J_t test in order to evaluate the importance of individual pricing errors. The next chapter continues, and collects GMM variations useful for evaluating linear factor models and related mean-variance frontier questions.

Many of these calculations amount to creative choices of the a_T matrix that selects which linear combination of moments are set to zero, and reading off the resulting formulas for variance-covariance matrix of the estimated coefficients, equation (11.4) and variance-covariance matrix of the moments g_T, equation (11.5).

11.1 General GMM Formulas

> The general GMM estimate:
> $$a_T g_T(\hat{b}) = 0.$$
> Distribution of $\hat{b}$:
> $$T\operatorname{cov}(\hat{b}) = (ad)^{-1} aSa'(ad)^{-1'}.$$
> Distribution of $g_T(\hat{b})$:
> $$T\operatorname{cov}\left[g_T(\hat{b})\right] = (I - d(ad)^{-1}a)S(I - d(ad)^{-1}a)'.$$
> The "optimal" estimate uses $a = d'S^{-1}$. In this case,
> $$T\operatorname{cov}(\hat{b}) = (d'S^{-1}d)^{-1},$$
> $$T\operatorname{cov}\left[g_T(\hat{b})\right] = S - d(d'S^{-1}d)^{-1}d',$$
> and
> $$TJ_T = Tg_T(\hat{b})'S^{-1}g_T(\hat{b}) \to \chi^2(\#\text{moments} - \#\text{parameters}).$$
> An analogue to the likelihood ratio test,
> $$TJ_T(\text{restricted}) - TJ_T(\text{unrestricted}) \sim \chi^2_{\text{Number of restrictions}}.$$

GMM procedures can be used to implement a host of estimation and testing exercises. Just about anything you might want to estimate can be written as a special case of GMM. To do so, you just have to remember (or look up) a few very general formulas, and then map them into your case.

Express a model as

$$E\left[f(x_t, b)\right] = 0.$$

Everything is a vector: f can represent a vector of L sample moments, x_t can be M data series, b can be N parameters. $f(x_t, b)$ generalizes the errors $u_t(b)$ in the last chapter.

Definition of the GMM Estimate
We estimate parameters $\hat{b}$ to set some linear combination of sample means of f to zero,

$$\hat{b}: \text{ set } a_T g_T(\hat{b}) = 0, \tag{11.1}$$

where

$$g_T(b) \equiv \frac{1}{T}\sum_{t=1}^{T} f(x_t, b),$$

and a_T is a matrix that defines which linear combination of $g_T(b)$ will be set to zero. This defines the GMM estimate.

If there are as many moments as parameters, you will set each moment to zero; when there are fewer parameters than moments, (11.1) captures the natural idea that you will set some moments, or some linear combination of moments, to zero in order to estimate the parameters.

The minimization of the last chapter is a special case. If you estimate b by $\min g_T'(b)' W g_T(b)$, the first-order conditions are

$$\frac{\partial g_T'}{\partial b} W g_T(b) = 0,$$

which is of the form (11.1) with $a_T = \partial g_T' / \partial b W$. The general GMM procedure allows you to pick arbitrary linear combinations of the moments to set to zero in parameter estimation.

Standard Errors of the Estimate
Hansen (1982, Theorem 3.1) tells us that the asymptotic distribution of the GMM estimate is

$$\sqrt{T}(\hat{b} - b) \to \mathcal{N}\left[0, \ (ad)^{-1} a S a' (ad)^{-1'}\right], \tag{11.2}$$

where

$$d \equiv E\left[\frac{\partial f}{\partial b'}(x_t, \ b)\right] = \frac{\partial g_T(b)}{\partial b'}$$

(precisely, d is defined as the population moment in the first equality, which we estimate in sample by the second equality), where

$$a \equiv \text{plim} \ a_T,$$

and where

$$S \equiv \sum_{j=-\infty}^{\infty} E\left[f(x_t, b), \ f(x_{t-j}, b)'\right]. \tag{11.3}$$

In practical terms, this means to use

$$\text{var}(\hat{b}) = \frac{1}{T}(ad)^{-1} a S a' (ad)^{-1'} \tag{11.4}$$

as the covariance matrix for standard errors and tests. As in the last chapter, you can understand this formula as an application of the delta method.

Distribution of the Moments
Hansen's Lemma 4.1 gives the sampling distribution of the moments $g_T(b)$:

$$\sqrt{T}g_T(\hat{b}) \rightarrow \mathcal{N}\left[0, (I - d(ad)^{-1}a)S(I - d(ad)^{-1}a)'\right]. \qquad (11.5)$$

As we have seen, S would be the asymptotic variance-covariance matrix of sample means, if we did not estimate any parameters. The $I - d(ad)^{-1}a$ terms account for the fact that in each sample some linear combinations of g_T are set to zero in order to estimate parameters. Thus, this variance-covariance matrix is singular.

χ^2 Tests
It is natural to use the distribution theory for g_T to see if the g_T are jointly "too big." Equation (11.5) suggests that we form the statistic

$$Tg_T(\hat{b})'\left[(I - d(ad)^{-1}a)S(I - d(ad)^{-1}a)'\right]^{-1}g_T(\hat{b}) \qquad (11.6)$$

A sum of squared standard normals is distributed χ^2. So this statistic should have a χ^2 distribution. It does, but with a hitch: The variance-covariance matrix is singular, so you have to pseudo-invert it. For example, you can perform an eigenvalue decomposition $\Sigma = Q\Lambda Q'$ and then invert only the nonzero eigenvalues. Also, the χ^2 distribution has degrees of freedom given by the number of nonzero linear combinations of g_T, the number of moments less the number of estimated parameters.

Efficient Estimates
The theory so far allows us to estimate parameters by setting any linear combination of moments to zero. Hansen shows that one particular choice is statistically optimal,

$$a = d'S^{-1}. \qquad (11.7)$$

This choice is the first-order condition to $\min_{\{b\}} g_T(b)'S^{-1}g_T(b)$ that we studied in the last chapter. With this weighting matrix, the standard error formula (11.4) reduces to

$$\sqrt{T}(\hat{b} - b) \rightarrow \mathcal{N}\left[0, (d'S^{-1}d)^{-1}\right]. \qquad (11.8)$$

This is Hansen's Theorem 3.2. The sense in which (11.7) is "efficient" is that the sampling variation of the parameters for arbitrary a matrix,

(11.4), equals the sampling variation of the "efficient" estimate in (11.8) plus a positive semidefinite matrix. Thus, it is "efficient" in the class of estimates that set different linear combinations of the moments g_T to zero. Estimators based on other moments may be move efficient still.

With the optimal weights (11.7), the variance of the moments (11.5) simplifies to

$$\text{cov}(g_T) = \frac{1}{T}(S - d(d'S^{-1}d)^{-1}d').\tag{11.9}$$

We can use this matrix in a test of the form (11.6). However, Hansen's Lemma 4.2 tells us that there is an equivalent and simpler way to construct this test,

$$Tg_T(\hat{b})'S^{-1}g_T(\hat{b}) \to \chi^2(\#\text{moments} - \#\text{parameters}).\tag{11.10}$$

This result is nice since we get to use the already-calculated and nonsingular S^{-1}.

To derive (11.10) from (11.5), factor $S = CC'$ and then find the asymptotic covariance matrix of $C^{-1}g_T(\hat{b})$ using (11.5). The result is

$$\text{var}\left[\sqrt{T}C^{-1}g_T(\hat{b})\right] = I - C^{-1}d(d'S^{-1}d)^{-1}d'C^{-1'}.$$

This is an idempotent matrix of rank $\#\text{moments} - \#\text{parameters}$, so (11.10) follows.

Alternatively, note that S^{-1} is a pseudo-inverse of the second stage $\text{cov}(g_T)$ (a pseudo-inverse times $\text{cov}(g_T)$ should result in an idempotent matrix of the same rank as $\text{cov}(g_T)$),

$$S^{-1}\text{cov}(g_T) = S^{-1}(S - d(d'S^{-1}d)^{-1}d') = I - S^{-1}d(d'S^{-1}d)^{-1}d'.$$

Then, check that the result is idempotent,

$$(I - S^{-1}d(d'S^{-1}d)^{-1}d')(I - S^{-1}d(d'S^{-1}d)^{-1}d') = I - S^{-1}d(d'S^{-1}d)^{-1}d',$$

This derivation not only verifies that J_T has the same distribution as $g_T'\text{cov}(g_T)^{-1}g_T$, but that they are numerically the same in every sample.

I emphasize that (11.8) and (11.10) only apply to the "optimal" choice of weights, (11.7). If you use another set of weights, as in a first-stage estimate, you must use the general formulas (11.4) and (11.5).

Model Comparisons

You often want to compare one model to another. If one model can be expressed as a special or "restricted" case of the other or "unrestricted" model, we can perform a statistical comparison that looks very much like a likelihood ratio test. If we use the same S matrix—usually that of the unrestricted model—the restricted J_T must rise. But if the restricted model is really true, it should not rise "much." How much?

$$TJ_T(\text{restricted}) - TJ_T(\text{unrestricted}) \sim \chi^2(\text{\# of restrictions}).$$

This is a "χ^2 difference" test, due to Newey and West (1987a), who call it the "D-test."

11.2 Testing Moments

> How to test one or a group of pricing errors. (1) Use the formula for $\text{var}(g_T)$. (2) A χ^2 difference test.

You may want to see how well a model does on particular moments or particular pricing errors. For example, the celebrated "small firm effect" states that an unconditional CAPM ($m = a + bR^W$, no scaled factors) does badly in pricing the returns on a portfolio that always holds the smallest 1/10th or 1/20th of firms in the NYSE. You might want to see whether a new model prices the small firm returns well. The standard error of pricing errors also allows you to add error bars to a plot of predicted versus actual mean returns such as Figure 2.4, or to compute standard errors for other diagnostics based on pricing errors.

We have already seen that individual elements of g_T measure the pricing errors. Thus, the sampling variation of g_T given by (11.5) provides exactly the standard error we are looking for. You can use the sampling distribution of g_T to evaluate the significance of individual pricing errors, to construct a t-test (for a single g_T, such as small firms) or a χ^2 test (for groups of g_T, such as small firms $\otimes$ instruments).

Alternatively, you can use the χ^2 difference approach. Start with a general model that includes all the moments, and form an estimate of the spectral density matrix S. Now *set* to zero the moments you want to test, and denote $g_{sT}(b)$ the vector of moments, including the zeros (s for "smaller"). Choose b_s to minimize $g_{sT}(b_s)'S^{-1}g_{sT}(b_s)$ using the same weighting matrix S. The criterion will be lower than the original criterion $g_T(b)'S^{-1}g_T(b)$, since there are the same number of parameters and fewer moments. But, if the moments we want to test truly are zero, the criterion should not be that much lower. The χ^2 difference test applies,

$$Tg_T(\hat{b})'S^{-1}g_T(\hat{b}) - Tg_{sT}(\hat{b}_s)S^{-1}g_{sT}(\hat{b}_s) \sim \chi^2(\#\text{eliminated moments}).$$

Of course, do not fall into the obvious trap of picking the largest of 10 pricing errors and noting it is more than two standard deviations from zero. The distribution of the *largest* of 10 pricing errors is much wider than the distribution of a single one. To use this distribution, you have to pick which pricing error you are going to test *before* you look at the data.

———————

11.3 Standard Errors of Anything by Delta Method

One quick application illustrates the usefulness of the GMM formulas. Often, we want to estimate a quantity that is a nonlinear function of sample means,

$$b = \phi[E(x_t)] = \phi(\mu).$$

In this case, the formula (11.2) reduces to

$$\text{var}(b_T) = \frac{1}{T}\left[\frac{d\phi}{d\mu}\right]' \sum_{j=-\infty}^{\infty} \text{cov}(x_t, x'_{t-j})\left[\frac{d\phi}{d\mu}\right]. \tag{11.11}$$

The formula is very intuitive. The variance of the sample mean is the covariance term inside. The derivatives just linearize the function ϕ near the true b.

For example, a correlation coefficient can be written as a function of sample means as

$$\text{corr}(x_t, y_t) = \frac{E(x_t y_t) - E(x_t)E(y_t)}{\sqrt{E(x_t^2) - E(x_t)^2}\sqrt{E(y_t^2) - E(y_t)^2}}.$$

Thus, take

$$\mu = \left[\, E(x_t)\ \ E(x_t^2)\ \ E(y_t)\ \ E(y_t^2)\ \ E(x_t y_t)\,\right]'.$$

A problem at the end of the chapter asks you to take derivatives and derive the standard error of the correlation coefficient. One can derive standard errors for impulse-response functions, variance decompositions, and many other statistics in this way.

———————

11.4 Using GMM for Regressions

By mapping OLS regressions in to the GMM framework, we derive formulas for OLS standard errors that correct for autocorrelation and conditional heteroskedasticity of the errors. The general formula is

$$\text{var}(\hat{\beta}) = \frac{1}{T} E(x_t x_t')^{-1} \left[\sum_{j=-\infty}^{\infty} E(\varepsilon_t x_t x_{t-j}' \varepsilon_{t-j}) \right] E(x_t x_t')^{-1},$$

and it simplifies in special cases.

Mapping any statistical procedure into GMM makes it easy to develop an asymptotic distribution that corrects for statistical problems such as serial correlation, and conditional heteroskedasticity. To illustrate, as well as to develop the very useful formulas, I map OLS regressions into GMM.

Correcting OLS standard errors for econometric problems is *not* the same thing as GLS. When errors do not obey the OLS assumptions, OLS is consistent, and often more robust than GLS, but its standard errors need to be corrected.

OLS picks parameters β to minimize the variance of the residual:

$$\min_{\{\beta\}} E_T\left[(y_t - \beta' x_t)^2\right].$$

We find $\hat{\beta}$ from the first-order condition, which states that the residual is orthogonal to the right-hand variable:

$$g_T(\hat{\beta}) = E_T\left[x_t(y_t - x_t'\hat{\beta})\right] = 0. \tag{11.12}$$

This condition is exactly identified—the number of moments equals the number of parameters. Thus, we set the sample moments exactly to zero and there is no weighting matrix ($a = I$). We can solve for the estimate analytically,

$$\hat{\beta} = \left[E_T(x_t x_t')\right]^{-1} E_T(x_t y_t).$$

This is the familiar OLS formula. The rest of the ingredients to equation (11.2) are

$$d = E(x_t x_t'),$$

$$f(x_t, \beta) = x_t(y_t - x_t'\beta) = x_t e_t,$$

where e_t is the regression residual. Equation (11.2) gives a formula for OLS standard errors,

$$\text{var}(\hat{\beta}) = \frac{1}{T} E(x_t x_t')^{-1} \left[\sum_{j=-\infty}^{\infty} E(\varepsilon_t x_t x_{t-j}' \varepsilon_{t-j}) \right] E(x_t x_t')^{-1}. \qquad (11.13)$$

(As we estimate σ_ε^2 by the sample variance of the residuals, we can estimate the quantity in brackets in (11.13) by its sample counterpart.) This formula reduces to some interesting special cases.

Serially Uncorrelated, Homoskedastic Errors

These are the usual OLS assumptions, and it is good the usual formulas emerge. Formally, the OLS assumptions are

$$E(\varepsilon_t \mid x_t, x_{t-1} \ldots \varepsilon_{t-1}, \varepsilon_{t-2} \ldots) = 0, \qquad (11.14)$$

$$E(\varepsilon_t^2 \mid x_t, x_{t-1} \ldots \varepsilon_{t-1} \ldots) = \text{constant} = \sigma_\varepsilon^2. \qquad (11.15)$$

To use these assumptions, I use the fact that

$$E(ab) = E(E(a|b)b).$$

The first assumption means that only the $j = 0$ term enters the sum

$$\sum_{j=-\infty}^{\infty} E(\varepsilon_t x_t x_{t-j}' \varepsilon_{t-j}) = E(\varepsilon_t^2 x_t x_t').$$

The second assumption means that

$$E(\varepsilon_t^2 x_t x_t') = E(\varepsilon_t^2) E(x_t x_t') = \sigma_\varepsilon^2 E(x_t x_t').$$

Hence equation (11.13) reduces to our old friend,

$$\text{var}(\hat{\beta}) = \frac{1}{T} \sigma_\varepsilon^2 E(x_t x_t')^{-1} = \sigma_\varepsilon^2 (X'X)^{-1}.$$

The last notation is typical of econometrics texts, in which $X = [x_1 \ x_2 \ \ldots \ x_T]'$ represents the data matrix.

Heteroskedastic Errors

If we delete the conditional homoskedasticity assumption (11.15), we cannot pull the ε out of the expectation, so the standard errors are

$$\text{var}(\hat{\beta}) = \frac{1}{T} E(x_t x_t')^{-1} E(\varepsilon_t^2 x_t x_t') E(x_t x_t')^{-1}.$$

These are known as "heteroskedasticity consistent standard errors" or "White standard errors" after White (1980).

Hansen–Hodrick Errors

Hansen and Hodrick (1982) run forecasting regressions of (say) six-month returns, using monthly data. We can write this situation in regression notation as

$$y_{t+k} = \beta'_k x_t + \varepsilon_{t+k}, \qquad t = 1, 2, \ldots, T.$$

Fama and French (1988) also use regressions of overlapping long-horizon returns on variables such as dividend/price ratio and term premium. Such regressions are an important part of the evidence for predictability in asset returns.

Under the null that one-period returns are unforecastable, we will still see correlation in the ε_t due to overlapping data. Unforecastable returns imply

$$E(\varepsilon_t \varepsilon_{t-j}) = 0 \qquad \text{for } |j| \geq k$$

but not for $|j| < k$. Therefore, we can only rule out terms in S lower than k. Since we might as well correct for potential heteroskedasticity while we are at it, the standard errors are

$$\text{var}(\beta_k) = \frac{1}{T} E(x_t x'_t)^{-1} \left[\sum_{j=-k}^{k} E(\varepsilon_t x_t x'_{t-j} \varepsilon_{t-j}) \right] E(x_t x'_t)^{-1}.$$

11.5 Prespecified Weighting Matrices and Moment Conditions

> Prespecified rather than "optimal" weighting matrices can emphasize economically interesting results, they can avoid the trap of blowing up standard errors rather than improving pricing errors, they can lead to estimates that are more robust to small model misspecifications. This is analogous to the fact that OLS is often preferable to GLS in a regression context. The GMM formulas for a fixed weighting matrix W are
>
> $$\text{var}(\hat{b}) = \frac{1}{T}(d'Wd)^{-1}d'WSWd(d'Wd)^{-1},$$
>
> $$\text{var}(g_T) = \frac{1}{T}(I - d(d'Wd)^{-1}d'W)S(I - Wd(d'Wd)^{-1}d').$$

In the basic approach outlined in Chapter 10, our final estimates were based on the "efficient" S^{-1} weighting matrix. This objective maximizes the asymptotic statistical information in the sample about a model, given the choice of moments g_T. However, you may want to use a pre-specified weighting matrix $W \neq S^{-1}$ instead, or at least as a diagnostic accompanying more formal statistical tests. A prespecified weighting matrix lets you, rather than the S matrix, specify which moments or linear combination of moments GMM will value in the minimization $\min_{\{b\}} g_T(b)' W g_T(b)$. A higher value of W_{ii} forces GMM to pay more attention to getting the ith moment right in the parameter estimation. For example, you might feel that some assets suffer from measurement error, are small and illiquid, and hence should be deemphasized, or you may want to keep GMM from looking at portfolios with strong long and short position. I give some additional motivations below.

You can also go one step further and impose which linear combinations a_T of moment conditions will be set to zero in estimation rather than use the choice resulting from a minimization, $a_T = d' S^{-1}$ or $a_T = d' W$. The fixed W estimate still trades off the accuracy of individual moments according to the sensitivity of each moment with respect to the parameter. For example, if $g_T = \begin{bmatrix} g_T^1 & g_T^2 \end{bmatrix}'$, $W = I$, but $\partial g_T / \partial b = [1 \; 10]$, so that the second moment is 10 times more sensitive to the parameter value than the first moment, then GMM with fixed weighting matrix sets

$$1 \times g_T^1 + 10 \times g_T^2 = 0.$$

The second moment condition will be 10 times closer to zero than the first. If you *really* want GMM to pay equal attention to the two moments, then you can fix the a_T matrix directly, for example $a_T = [1 \; 1]$ or $a_T = [1 \; -1]$.

Using a prespecified weighting matrix or using a prespecified set of moments is *not* the same thing as ignoring correlation of the errors u_t in the distribution theory. The S matrix will still show up in all the standard errors and test statistics.

How to Use Prespecified Weighting Matrices

Once you have decided to use a prespecified weighting matrix W or a prespecified set of moments $a_T g_T(b) = 0$, the general distribution theory outlined in Section 11.1 quickly gives standard errors of the estimates and moments, and therefore a χ^2 statistic that can be used to test whether all the moments are jointly zero. Section 11.1 gives the formulas for the case that a_T is prespecified. If we use weighting matrix W, the first-order conditions to $\min_{\{b\}} g_T'(b) W g_T(b)$ are

$$\frac{\partial g_T(b)'}{\partial b} W g_T(b) = d' W g_T(b) = 0,$$

so we map into the general case with $a_T = d'W$. Plugging this value into (11.4), the variance-covariance matrix of the estimated coefficients is

$$\text{var}(\hat{b}) = \frac{1}{T}(d'Wd)^{-1}d'WSWd(d'Wd)^{-1}. \tag{11.16}$$

(You can check that this formula reduces to $1/T \ (d'S^{-1}d)^{-1}$ with $W = S^{-1}$.)

Plugging $a = d'W$ into equation (11.5), we find the variance-covariance matrix of the moments g_T,

$$\text{var}(g_T) = \frac{1}{T}(I - d(d'Wd)^{-1}d'W)S(I - Wd(d'Wd)^{-1}d'). \tag{11.17}$$

As in the general formula, the terms to the left and right of S account for the fact that some linear combinations of moments are set to zero in each sample.

Equation (11.17) can be the basis of χ^2 tests for the overidentifying restrictions. If we interpret $(\ )^{-1}$ to be a generalized inverse, then

$$g_T' \, \text{var}(g_T)^{-1} g_T \sim \chi^2(\#\text{moments} - \#\text{parameters}).$$

As in the general case, you have to pseudo-invert the singular $\text{var}(g_T)$, for example by inverting only the nonzero eigenvalues.

The major danger in using prespecified weighting matrices or moments a_T is that the choice of moments, units, and (of course) the prespecified a_T or W must be made carefully. For example, if you multiply the second moment by 10 times its original value, the optimal S^{-1} weighting matrix will undo this transformation and weight them in their original proportions. The identity weighting matrix will not undo such transformations, so the units should be picked right initially.

Motivations for Prespecified Weighting Matrices

Robustness, as with OLS vs. GLS

When errors are autocorrelated or heteroskedastic, every econometrics textbook shows you how to "improve" on OLS by making appropriate GLS corrections. If you correctly model the error covariance matrix and if the regression is perfectly specified, the GLS procedure can improve efficiency, i.e., give estimates with lower asymptotic standard errors. However, GLS is less robust. If you model the error covariance matrix incorrectly, the GLS estimates can be much worse than OLS. Also, the GLS transformations can zero in on slightly misspecified areas of the model. This may be good to show that the glass is half-empty, but keeps you from seeing that it is half-full, or tasting what's inside. GLS is "best," but OLS is "pretty darn good." You often have enough data that wringing every last ounce of statistical precision (low standard errors) from the data is less important than producing estimates that do not depend on questionable statistical assumptions, and that transparently focus on the interesting features of the data. In these cases, it is often a good idea to use OLS estimates. The OLS standard error formulas are wrong, though, so you must correct the *standard errors* of the OLS estimates for these features of the error covariance matrices, using the formulas we developed in Section 11.4.

GMM works the same way. First-stage or otherwise fixed weighting matrix estimates may give up something in asymptotic efficiency, but they are still consistent, and they can be more robust to statistical and economic problems. You still want to use the S matrix in computing standard errors, though, as you want to correct OLS standard errors, and the GMM formulas show you how to do this.

Even if in the end you want to produce "efficient" estimates and tests, it is a good idea to calculate first-stage estimates, standard errors and model fit tests. Ideally, the parameter estimates should not change by much, and the second-stage standard errors should be tighter. If the "efficient" parameter estimates do change a great deal, it is a good idea to diagnose why this is so. It must come down to the "efficient" parameter estimates strongly weighting moments or linear combinations of moments that were not important in the first stage, and that the former linear combination of moments disagrees strongly with the latter about which parameters fit well. Then, you can decide whether the difference in results is truly due to efficiency gain, or whether it signals a model misspecification.

Near-Singular S
The spectral density matrix is often nearly singular, since asset returns are highly correlated with each other, and since we often include many assets relative to the number of data points. As a result, second-stage GMM (and, as we will see below, maximum likelihood or any other efficient technique) tries to minimize differences and differences of differences of moments in order to extract statistically orthogonal components with lowest variance. One may feel that this feature leads GMM to place a lot of weight on poorly estimated, economically uninteresting, or otherwise nonrobust aspects of the data. In particular, portfolios of the form $100R_1 - 99R_2$ assume that investors can in fact purchase such heavily leveraged portfolios. Short-sale costs often rule out such portfolios or significantly alter their returns, so one may not want to emphasize pricing them correctly in the estimation and evaluation.

For example, suppose that S is given by

$$S = \begin{bmatrix} 1 & \rho \\ \rho & 1 \end{bmatrix},$$

so

$$S^{-1} = \frac{1}{1 - \rho^2} \begin{bmatrix} 1 & -\rho \\ -\rho & 1 \end{bmatrix}.$$

We can factor S^{-1} into a "square root" by the Choleski decomposition. This produces a triangular matrix C such that $C'C = S^{-1}$. You can check that the matrix

$$C = \begin{bmatrix} \frac{1}{\sqrt{1-\rho^2}} & \frac{-\rho}{\sqrt{1-\rho^2}} \\ 0 & 1 \end{bmatrix} \qquad (11.18)$$

works. Then, the GMM criterion

$$\min g_T' S^{-1} g_T$$

is equivalent to

$$\min(g_T' C')(C g_T).$$

$C g_T$ gives the linear combination of moments that efficient GMM is trying to minimize. Looking at (11.18), as $\rho \to 1$, the $(2, 2)$ element stays at 1, but the $(1, 1)$ and $(1, 2)$ elements get very large and of opposite signs. For example, if $\rho = 0.95$, then

$$C = \begin{bmatrix} 3.20 & -3.04 \\ 0 & 1 \end{bmatrix}.$$

In this example, GMM pays a little attention to the second moment, but places *three* times as much weight on the *difference* between the first and second moments. Larger matrices produce even more extreme weights. At a minimum, it is a good idea to look at S^{-1} and its Choleski decomposition to see what moments GMM is prizing.

The same point has a classic interpretation, and is a well-known danger with classic regression-based tests. Efficient GMM wants to focus on well-measured moments. In asset pricing applications, the errors are typically close to uncorrelated over time, so GMM is looking for portfolios with small values of $\mathrm{var}(m_{t+1} R_{t+1}^e)$. Roughly speaking, those will be assets with small *return* variance. Thus, *GMM will pay most attention to correctly pricing the sample minimum-variance portfolio*, and GMM's evaluation of the model by the J_T test will focus on its ability to price this portfolio.

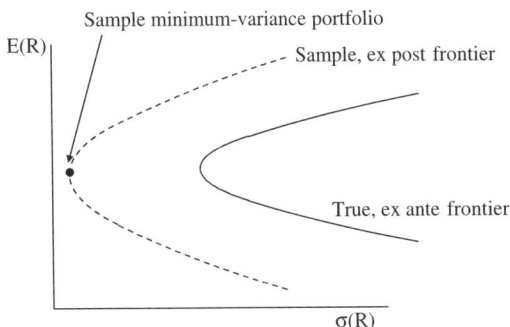

Figure 11.1. *True or ex ante and sample or ex post mean-variance frontier. The sample often shows a spurious minimum-variance portfolio.*

Now, consider what happens in a sample, as illustrated in Figure 11.1. The sample mean-variance frontier is typically a good deal wider than the true, or ex ante mean-variance frontier. In particular, the sample minimum-variance portfolio may have little to do with the true minimum-variance portfolio. Like any portfolio on the sample frontier, its composition largely reflects luck—that is why we have asset pricing models in the first place rather than just price assets with portfolios on the sample frontier. The sample minimum variance return is also likely to be composed of strong long-short positions.

In sum, you may want to force GMM not to pay quite so much attention to correctly pricing the sample minimum-variance portfolio, and you may want to give less importance to a statistical measure of model evaluation that focuses on the model's ability to price that portfolio.

Economically Interesting Moments
The optimal weighting matrix makes GMM pay close attention to linear combinations of moments with small sampling error in both estimation and evaluation. You may want to force the estimation and evaluation to pay attention to *economically* interesting moments instead. The initial portfolios are usually formed on an economically interesting characteristic such as size, beta, book/market, or industry. You typically want in the end to see how well the model prices these initial portfolios, not how well the model prices potentially strange portfolios of those portfolios. If a model fails, you may want to characterize that failure as "the model does not price small stocks," not "the model does not price a portfolio of $900 \times$ small firm returns $-600 \times$ large firm returns $-299 \times$ medium firm returns."

Level Playing Field

The S matrix changes as the model and as its parameters change. (See the definition, (10.5) or (11.3).) As the S matrix changes, which assets the GMM estimate tries hard to price well changes as well. For example, the S matrix from one model may put a lot of weight on the T bill return, while that of another model may put a lot of weight on a stock excess return. Comparing the results of such estimations is like comparing apples and oranges. By fixing the weighting matrix, you can force GMM to pay attention to the various assets in the same proportion while you vary the model.

The fact that S matrices change with the model leads to another subtle trap. One model may "improve" a $J_T = g_T' S^{-1} g_T$ statistic because it blows up the estimates of S, rather than by making any progress on lowering the pricing errors g_T. No one would formally use a comparison of J_T tests across models to compare them, of course. But it has proved nearly irresistible for authors to claim success for a new model over previous ones by noting improved J_T statistics, despite different weighting matrices, different moments, and sometimes much larger pricing errors. For example, if you take a model m_t and create a new model by simply adding noise, unrelated to asset returns (in sample), $m_t' = m_t + \varepsilon_t$, then the moment condition $g_T = E_T(m_t' R_t^e) = E_T((m_t + \varepsilon_t) R_t^e)$ is unchanged. However, the spectral density matrix $S = E[(m_t + \varepsilon_t)^2 R_t^e R_t^{e'}]$ can rise dramatically. This can reduce the J_T, leading to a false sense of "improvement."

Conversely, if the sample contains a nearly risk-free portfolio of the test assets, or a portfolio with apparently small variance of $m_{t+1} R_{t+1}^e$, then the J_T test essentially evaluates the model by how well it can price this one portfolio. This can lead to a statistical rejection of a much-improved model—even a very small g_T will produce a large $g_T' S^{-1} g_T$ if there is a small eigenvalue of S.

If you use a common weighting matrix W for all models, and evaluate the models by $g_T' W g_T$, then you can avoid this trap. The question "are the pricing errors small?" is as interesting as the question "if we drew artificial data over and over again from a null statistical model, how often would we estimate a ratio of pricing errors to their estimated variance $g_T' S^{-1} g_T$ this big or larger?"

Some Prespecified Weighting Matrices

Two examples of economically interesting weighting matrices are the second-moment matrix of returns, advocated by Hansen and Jagannathan (1997), and the simple identity matrix, which is used implicitly in much empirical asset pricing.

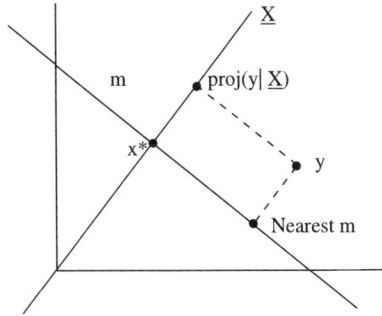

Figure 11.2. *Distance between* y *and nearest* m = *distance between* $\text{proj}(y|X)$ *and* x^*.

Second-Moment Matrix

Hansen and Jagannathan (1997) advocate the use of the second-moment matrix of payoffs $W = E(xx')^{-1}$ in place of S. They motivate this weighting matrix as an interesting distance measure between a model for m, say y, and the space of true m's. Precisely, the minimum distance (second moment) between a candidate discount factor y and the space of true discount factors is the same as the minimum value of the GMM criterion with $W = E(xx')^{-1}$ as weighting matrix.

To see why this is true, refer to Figure 11.2. The distance between y and the nearest valid m is the same as the distance between $\text{proj}(y \mid \underline{X})$ and x^*. As usual, consider the case that $\underline{X}$ is generated from a vector of payoffs x with price p. From the OLS formula,

$$\text{proj}(y \mid \underline{X}) = E(yx')E(xx')^{-1}x.$$

x^* is the portfolio of x that prices x by construction,

$$x^* = p'E(xx')^{-1}x.$$

Then, the distance between y and the nearest valid m is

$$
\begin{aligned}
\left\| y - \text{nearest } m \right\| &= \left\| \text{proj}(y|\underline{X}) - x^* \right\| \\
&= \left\| E(yx')E(xx')^{-1}x - p'E(xx')^{-1}x \right\| \\
&= \left\| (E(yx') - p')E(xx')^{-1}x \right\| \\
&= [E(yx) - p]'E(xx')^{-1}[E(yx) - p] \\
&= g_T'E(xx')^{-1}g_T.
\end{aligned}
$$

You might want to choose parameters of the model to minimize this "economic" measure of model fit, or this economically motivated linear combination of pricing errors, rather than the statistical measure of fit S^{-1}. You might also use the minimized value of this criterion to compare two models. In that way, you are sure the better model is better because it improves on the pricing errors rather than just blowing up the weighting matrix.

Identity Matrix
Using the identity matrix weights the initial choice of assets or portfolios equally in estimation and evaluation. This choice has a particular advantage with large systems in which S is nearly singular, as it avoids most of the problems associated with inverting a near-singular S matrix. Many empirical asset pricing studies use OLS cross-sectional regressions, which are the same thing as a first-stage GMM estimate with an identity weighting matrix.

Comparing the Second-Moment and Identity Matrices
The second-moment matrix gives an objective that is invariant to the initial choice of assets or portfolios. If we form a portfolio Ax of the initial payoffs x, with nonsingular A (i.e., a transformation that does not throw away information), then

$$\big[E(yAx) - Ap\big]'E(Axx'A')^{-1}\big[E(yAx) - Ap\big]$$
$$= \big[E(yx) - p\big]'E(xx')^{-1}\big[E(yx) - p\big].$$

The optimal weighting matrix S shares this property. It is not true of the identity or other fixed matrices. In those cases, the results will depend on the initial choice of portfolios.

Kandel and Stambaugh (1995) have suggested that the results of several important asset pricing model tests are highly sensitive to the choice of portfolio, i.e., that authors inadvertently selected a set of portfolios on which the CAPM does unusually badly in a particular sample. Insisting that weighting matrices have this kind of invariance to portfolio selection might be a good device to guard against this problem.

On the other hand, if you want to focus on the model's predictions for economically interesting portfolios, then it would not make much sense for the weighting matrix to undo the specification of economically interesting portfolios! For example, many studies want to focus on the ability of a model to describe expected returns that seem to depend on a characteristic such as size, book/market, industry, momentum, etc. Also, the second-moment matrix is often even more nearly singular than the spectral density matrix, since $E(xx') = \text{cov}(x) + E(x)E(x)'$. Therefore, it often emphasizes portfolios with even more extreme short and long positions, and is no help on overcoming the near singularity of the S matrix.

11.6 Estimating on One Group of Moments, Testing on Another

You may want to force the system to use one set of moments for *estimation* and another for *testing*. The real business cycle literature in macroeconomics does this extensively, typically using "first moments" for estimation ("calibration") and "second moments" (i.e., first moments of squares) for evaluation. A statistically minded macroeconomist might like to know whether the departures of model from data "second moments" are large compared to sampling variation, and would like to include sampling uncertainty about the parameter estimates in this evaluation.

You might want to choose parameters using one set of asset returns (stocks, domestic assets, size portfolios, first nine size deciles, well-measured assets) and then see how the model does "out of sample" on another set of assets (bonds, foreign assets, book/market portfolios, small firm portfolio, questionably measured assets, mutual funds). However, you want the distribution theory for evaluation on the second set of moments to incorporate sampling uncertainty about the parameters from their estimation on the first set of moments, and correlation between the "estimation" moments and the "evaluation" moments.

You can do all this very simply by using an appropriate weighting matrix or a prespecified moment matrix a_T. For example, if the first N moments will be used to estimate N parameters, and the remaining M moments will be used to test the model "out of sample," use $a_T = \begin{bmatrix} I_N & 0_{N+M} \end{bmatrix}$. If there are more moments N than parameters in the "estimation" block, you can construct a weighting matrix W which is an identity matrix in the $N \times N$ estimation block and zero elsewhere. Then $a_T = \partial g'_T / \partial b W$ will simply contain the first N columns of $\partial g'_T / \partial b$ followed by zeros. The test moments will not be used in estimation. You could even use the inverse of the upper $N \times N$ block of S (not the upper block of the inverse of S!) to make the estimation a bit more efficient.

11.7 Estimating the Spectral Density Matrix

> Hints on estimating the spectral density or long-run covariance matrix. (1) Use a sensible first-stage estimate. (2) Remove means. (3) Downweight higher-order correlations. (4) Consider parametric structures for autocorrelation and heteroskedasticity. (5) Use the null to limit the number of correlations or to impose other structure on S. (6) Size problems; consider a factor or other parametric cross-sectional structure for S. (7) Iteration and simultaneous b, S estimation.

The optimal weighting matrix S depends on *population* moments, and depends on the parameters b. Work back through the definitions,

$$S = \sum_{j=-\infty}^{\infty} E(u_t u'_{t-j}),$$

$$u_t \equiv \left(m_t(b) x_t - p_{t-1} \right).$$

How do we estimate this matrix? The big picture is simple: following the usual philosophy, estimate population moments by their sample counterparts. Thus, use the first-stage b estimates and the data to construct sample versions of the definition of S. This produces a consistent estimate of the true spectral density matrix, which is all the asymptotic distribution theory requires.

The details are important, however, and this section gives some hints. Also, you may want a different, and less restrictive, estimate of S for use in standard errors than you do when you are estimating S for use in a weighting matrix.

1) Use a sensible first-stage W, or transform the data.

In the asymptotic theory, you can use consistent first-stage b estimates formed by *any* nontrivial weighting matrix. In practice, of course, you should use a sensible weighting matrix so that the first-stage estimates are not ridiculously inefficient. $W = I$ is often a good choice.

Sometimes, some moments will have different units than other moments. For example, the dividend/price ratio is a number like 0.04. Therefore, the moment formed by $R_{t+1} \times d/p_t$ will be about 0.04 as large as the moment formed by $R_{t+1} \times 1$. If you use $W = I$, GMM will pay much less attention to the $R_{t+1} \times d/p_t$ moment. It is wise, then, to either use an initial weighting matrix that overweights the $R_{t+1} \times d/p_t$ moment, or to transform the data so the two moments are about the same mean and variance. For example, you could use $R_{t+1} \times (1 + d/p_t)$. It is also useful to start with moments that are not horrendously correlated with each other, or to remove such correlation with a clever W.

For example, you might consider R^a and $R^b - R^a$ rather than R^a and R^b. You can accomplish this directly, or by starting with

$$W = \begin{bmatrix} 1 & -1 \\ 0 & 1 \end{bmatrix} \begin{bmatrix} 1 & 0 \\ -1 & 1 \end{bmatrix} = \begin{bmatrix} 2 & -1 \\ -1 & 1 \end{bmatrix}.$$

2) Remove means.

Under the null, $E(u_t) = 0$, so it does not matter to the asymptotic distribution theory whether you estimate the covariance matrix by removing means, using

$$\frac{1}{T} \sum_{t=1}^{T} \left[(u_t - \bar{u})(u_t - \bar{u})' \right], \qquad \bar{u} \equiv \frac{1}{T} \sum_{t=1}^{T} u_t,$$

or whether you estimate the second-moment matrix by not removing means. However, Hansen and Singleton (1982) advocate removing the means in sample, and this is generally a good idea.

It is already an obstacle to second-stage estimation that estimated S matrices (and even simple variance-covariance matrices) are often nearly singular, providing an unreliable weighting matrix when inverted. Since second-moment matrices $E(uu') = \text{cov}(u, u') + E(u)E(u')$ add a singular matrix $E(u)E(u')$, they are often even worse.

3) Downweight higher-order correlations.

You obviously cannot use a direct sample counterpart to the spectral density matrix. In a sample of size 100, there is no way to estimate $E(u_t u'_{t+101})$. Your estimate of $E(u_t u'_{t+99})$ is based on *one* data point, $u_1 u'_{100}$. Hence, it will be a pretty unreliable estimate. For this reason, the estimator using all possible autocorrelations in a given sample is *inconsistent*. (Consistency means that as the sample grows, the probability distribution of the estimator converges to the true value. Inconsistent estimates typically have very large sample variation.)

Furthermore, even S estimates that use few autocorrelations are not always positive definite in sample. This is embarrassing when one tries to invert the estimated spectral density matrix, which you have to do if you use it as a weighting matrix. Therefore, it is a good idea to construct consistent estimates that are automatically positive definite in every sample. One such estimate is the Bartlett estimate, used in this application by Newey and West (1987b). It is

$$\widehat{S} = \sum_{j=-k}^{k} \left(\frac{k - |j|}{k} \right) \frac{1}{T} \sum_{t=1}^{T} (u_t u'_{t-j}). \qquad (11.19)$$

As you can see, only autocorrelations up to kth ($k < T$) order are included, and higher-order autocorrelations are downweighted. (It is important to use $1/T$, not $1/(T-k)$; this is a further downweighting.) The Newey–West estimator is basically the variance of kth sums, which is why it is positive definite in sample:

$$
\begin{aligned}
\mathrm{Var}\left(\sum_{j=1}^{k} u_{t-j}\right) &= kE(u_t u_t') + (k-1)\left[E(u_t u_{t-1}') + E(u_{t-1} u_t')\right] \\
&\quad + \cdots + \left[E(u_t u_{t-k}') + E(u_{t-k} u_t')\right] \\
&= k \sum_{j=-k}^{k} \frac{k - |j|}{k} E(u_t u_{t-k}').
\end{aligned}
$$

Andrews (1991) gives some additional weighting schemes for spectral density estimates.

This calculation also gives some intuition for the S matrix. We are looking for the variance *across samples* of the sample mean $\mathrm{var}\left(\frac{1}{T}\sum_{t=1}^{T} u_t\right)$. We only have one sample mean to look at, so we estimate the variance of the sample mean by looking at the variance *in a single sample* of shorter sums, $\mathrm{var}\left(\frac{1}{k}\sum_{j=1}^{k} u_j\right)$. The S matrix is sometimes called the *long-run covariance* matrix for this reason. In fact, one could estimate S directly as a variance of kth sums and obtain almost the same estimator, that would also be positive definite in any sample,

$$
v_t = \sum_{j=1}^{k} u_{t-j}, \qquad \bar{v} = \frac{1}{T-k} \sum_{t=k+1}^{T} v_t,
$$

$$
\widehat{S} = \frac{1}{k} \frac{1}{T-k} \sum_{t=k+1}^{T} (v_t - \bar{v})(v_t - \bar{v})'.
$$

This estimator has been used when measurement of S is directly interesting (Cochrane [1998], Lo and MacKinlay [1988]). A variety of other weighting schemes have been advocated.

What value of k, or how wide a window if of another shape, should you use? Here again, you have to use some judgment. Too short values of k, together with a u_t that is significantly autocorrelated, and you do not correct for correlation that might be there in the errors. Too long a value of k, together with a series that does not have much autocorrelation, and the performance of the estimate and test deteriorates. If $k = T/2$, for example, you are really using only two data points to estimate the variance of the mean. The optimum value then depends on

how much persistence or low-frequency movement there is in a particular application, versus accuracy of the estimate.

There is an extensive statistical literature about optimal window
width, or size of k. Alas, this literature mostly characterizes the *rate*
at which k should increase with sample size. You must promise to
increase k as sample size increases, but not as quickly as the sample
size increases—$\lim_{T \to \infty} k = \infty$, $\lim_{T \to \infty} k/T = 0$—in order to obtain
consistent estimates. In practice, promises about what you would do
with more data are pretty meaningless, and usually broken once more
data arrives.

4) Consider parametric structures for autocorrelation and heteroskedasticity.

"Nonparametric" corrections such as (11.19) often do not perform
very well in typical samples. The problem is that "nonparametric" techniques are really very highly parametric; you have to estimate many
correlations in the data. Therefore, the nonparametric estimate varies
a good deal from sample to sample. This variation may make S^{-1}
weighted estimates much less efficient, and sometimes worse than
estimates formed on a fixed weighting matrix. Also, the asymptotic
distribution theory ignores sampling variation in covariance matrix
estimates. The asymptotic distribution can therefore be a poor approximation to the finite-sample distribution of statistics like the J_T.

You can get more accurate standard errors with a Monte Carlo or
bootstrap rather than relying on asymptotic theory. Alternatively, you
can impose a parametric structure on the S matrix which can address
both problems. Just because the formulas are expressed in terms of a
sum of covariances does not mean you have to estimate them that way;
GMM is not inherently tied to "nonparametric" covariance matrix estimates. For example, if you model a scalar u as an AR(1) with parameter ρ, then you can estimate two numbers ρ and σ_u^2 rather than a
whole list of autocorrelations, and calculate

$$S = \sum_{j=-\infty}^{\infty} E(u_t u_{t-j}) = \sigma_u^2 \sum_{j=-\infty}^{\infty} \rho^{|j|} = \sigma_u^2 \frac{1+\rho}{1-\rho}.$$

If this structure is not a bad approximation, imposing it can result in
more reliable estimates and test statistics since you have to estimate
many fewer coefficients. You could transform the data in such a way
that there is less correlation to correct for in the first place.

(This is a very useful formula, by the way. You are probably used to
calculating the standard error of the mean as

$$\sigma(\bar{x}) = \frac{\sigma(x)}{\sqrt{T}}.$$

This formula assumes that the x are uncorrelated over time. If an AR(1) is not a bad model for their correlation, you can quickly adjust for correlation by using

$$\sigma(\bar{x}) = \frac{\sigma(x)}{\sqrt{T}} \sqrt{\frac{1+\rho}{1-\rho}}$$

instead.)

This sort of parametric correction is very familiar from OLS regression analysis. The textbooks commonly advocate the AR(1) model for serial correlation as well as parametric models for heteroskedasticity corrections. There is no reason not to follow a similar approach for GMM statistics.

5) *Use the null to limit correlations?*

In the typical asset pricing setup, the null hypothesis specifies that $E_t(u_{t+1}) = E_t(m_{t+1}R_{t+1} - 1) = 0$, as well as $E(u_{t+1}) = 0$. This implies that all the autocorrelation terms of S drop out; $E(u_t u'_{t-j}) = 0$ for $j \neq 0$. The lagged u could be an instrument z; the discounted return should be unforecastable, using past discounted returns as well as any other variable. In this situation, you could exploit the null to only include *one* term, and estimate

$$\widehat{S} = \frac{1}{T} \sum_{t=1}^{T} u_t u'_t.$$

Similarly, if you run a regression forecasting returns from some variable z_t,

$$R_{t+1} = a + bz_t + \varepsilon_{t+1},$$

the null hypothesis that returns are not forecastable by any variable at time t means that the errors should not be autocorrelated. You can then simplify the standard errors in the OLS regression formulas given in Section 11.4, eliminating all the leads and lags.

In other situations, the null hypothesis can suggest a functional form for $E(u_t u'_{t-j})$ or that some but not all are zero. For example, as we saw in Section 11.4, regressions of long-horizon returns on overlapping data lead to a correlated error term, even under the null hypothesis of no return forecastability. We can impose this null, ruling out terms past the overlap, as suggested by Hansen and Hodrick,

$$\text{var}(b_T) = \frac{1}{T} E(x_t x'_t)^{-1} \left[\sum_{j=-k}^{k} E(\varepsilon_t x_t x'_{t-j} \varepsilon_{t-j}) \right] E(x_t x'_t)^{-1}. \qquad (11.20)$$

However, the null might not be correct, and the errors might be correlated. If so, you might make a mistake by leaving them out. If the null is correct, the extra terms will converge to zero and you will only have lost a few (finite-sample) degrees of freedom needlessly estimating them. If the null is not correct, you have an inconsistent estimate. With this in mind, you might want to include at least a few extra autocorrelations, even when the null says they do not belong.

Furthermore, there is no guarantee that the unweighted sum in (11.20) is positive definite in sample. If the sum in the middle is not positive definite, you could add a weighting to the sum, possibly increasing the number of lags so that the lags near k are not unusually underweighted. Again, estimating extra lags that should be zero under the null only loses a little bit of power.

Monte Carlo evidence (Hodrick [1992]) suggests that imposing the null hypothesis to simplify the spectral density matrix helps to get the finite-sample *size* of test statistics right—the probability of rejection given the null is true. One should not be surprised that if the null is true, imposing as much of it as possible makes estimates and tests work better. On the other hand, adding extra correlations can help with the *power* of test statistics—the probability of rejection given that an alternative is true—since they converge to the correct spectral density matrix.

This trade-off requires some thought. For *measurement* rather than pure *testing*, using a spectral density matrix that can accommodate alternatives may be the right choice. For example, in the return-forecasting regressions, one is really focused on measuring return forecastability rather than just formally testing the hypothesis that it is zero.

If you are testing an asset pricing model that predicts u should not be autocorrelated, and there is a lot of correlation—if this issue makes a big difference—then this is an indication that something is wrong with the model: that including u as one of your instruments z would result in a rejection or at least substantially change the results. If the u are close to uncorrelated, then it really does not matter if you add a few extra terms or not.

6) *Size problems; consider a factor or other parametric cross-sectional structure.*

If you try to estimate a covariance matrix that is larger than the number of data points (say 2000 NYSE stocks and 800 monthly observations), the estimate of S, like any other covariance matrix, is singular by construction. This fact leads to obvious problems when you try to invert S! More generally, when the number of moments is more than around $1/10$ the number of data points, S estimates tend to become unstable and near singular. Used as a weighting matrix, such an S matrix tells you to pay lots of attention to strange and probably spurious linear combinations of the moments, as I emphasized in Section 11.5. For this reason, most second-stage GMM estimations are limited to a few assets and a few instruments.

A good, but as yet untried alternative might be to impose a factor structure or other well-behaved structure on the covariance matrix. The near-universal practice of grouping assets into portfolios before analysis already implies an assumption that the true S of the underlying assets has a factor structure. Grouping in portfolios means that the individual assets have no information not contained in the portfolio, so that a weighting matrix S^{-1} would treat all assets in the portfolio identically. It might be better to estimate an S imposing a factor structure on all the primitive assets.

Another response to the difficulty of estimating S is to stop at first-stage estimates, and only use S for standard errors. One might also use a highly structured estimate of S as weighting matrix, while using a less constrained estimate for the standard errors.

This problem is of course not unique to GMM. Any estimation technique requires us to calculate a covariance matrix. Many traditional estimates simply assume that u_t errors are cross-sectionally independent. This false assumption leads to understatements of the standard errors far worse than the small-sample performance of any GMM estimate.

Our econometric techniques all are designed for large time series and small cross sections. Our data has a large cross section and short time series. A large unsolved problem in finance is the development of appropriate large-N small-T tools for evaluating asset pricing models.

7) *Alternatives to the two-stage procedure: iteration and one-step.*

Hansen and Singleton (1982) describe the above two-step procedure, and it has become popular for that reason. Two alternative procedures may perform better in practice, i.e., may result in asymptotically equivalent estimates with better small-sample properties. They can also be simpler to implement, and require less manual adjustment or care in specifying the setup (moments, weighting matrices) which is often just as important.

(a) *Iterate.* The second-stage estimate $\hat{b}_2$ will not imply the same spectral density as the first stage. It might seem appropriate that the estimate of b and of the spectral density should be consistent, i.e., to find a fixed point of $\hat{b} = \min_{\{b\}} \left[g_T(b)' S(\hat{b})^{-1} g_T(b) \right]$. One way to search for such a fixed point is to iterate: find b_2 from

$$\hat{b}_2 = \min_{\{b\}} g_T(b)' S^{-1}(b_1) g_T(b), \qquad (11.21)$$

where b_1 is a first-stage estimate, held fixed in the minimization over b_2. Then use $\hat{b}_2$ to find $S(\hat{b}_2)$, find

$$\hat{b}_3 = \min_{\{b\}} \left[g_T(b)' S(\hat{b}_2)^{-1} g_T(b) \right],$$

and so on. There is no fixed-point theorem that such iterations will converge, but they often do, especially with a little massaging. (I once used $S[(b_j + b_{j-1})/2]$ in the beginning part of an iteration to keep it from oscillating between two values of b.) Ferson and Foerster (1994) find that iteration gives better small-sample performance than two-stage GMM in Monte Carlo experiments. This procedure is also likely to produce estimates that do not depend on the initial weighting matrix.

(b) *Pick b and S simultaneously.* It is *not* true that S must be held fixed as one searches for b. Instead, one can use a new $S(b)$ for each value of b. Explicitly, one can estimate b by

$$\min_{\{b\}} \left[g_T(b)' S^{-1}(b) g_T(b) \right]. \tag{11.22}$$

The estimates produced by this simultaneous search will not be numerically the same in a finite sample as the two-step or iterated estimates. The first-order conditions to (11.21) are

$$\left(\frac{\partial g_T(b)}{\partial b} \right)' S^{-1}(b_1) g_T(b) = 0, \tag{11.23}$$

while the first-order conditions in (11.22) add a term involving the derivatives of $S(b)$ with respect to b. However, the latter terms vanish asymptotically, so the asymptotic distribution theory is not affected. Hansen, Heaton, and Yaron (1996) conduct some Monte Carlo experiments and find that this estimate may have small-sample advantages in certain problems. However, one-step minimization may find regions of the parameter space that blow up the spectral density matrix $S(b)$ rather than lower the pricing errors g_T.

Often, one choice will be much more convenient than another. For linear models, you can find the minimizing value of b from the first-order conditions (11.23) analytically. This fact eliminates the need to search so an iterated estimate is much faster than a one-step estimator. For nonlinear models, each step involves a numerical search over $g_T(b)' S g_T(b)$. Rather than perform this search many times, it may be much quicker to minimize once over $g_T(b)' S(b) g_T(b)$. On the other hand, the latter is not a locally quadratic form, so the search may run into greater numerical difficulties.

Problems—Chapter 11

1. Use the delta method version of the GMM formulas to derive the sampling variance of an autocorrelation coefficient.

2. Write a formula for the standard error of OLS regression coefficients that corrects for autocorrelation but not heteroskedasticity.

3. Write a formula for the standard error of OLS regression coefficients if $E(\varepsilon_t \varepsilon_{t-j}) = \rho^j \sigma^2$.

4. If the GMM errors come from an asset pricing model, $u_t = m_t R_t - 1$, can you ignore lags in the spectral density matrix? What if you know that returns are predictable? What if the error is formed from an instrument/managed portfolio $u_t z_{t-1}$?

12

Regression-Based Tests of
Linear Factor Models

THE NEXT FOUR chapters study the question, how should we estimate and evaluate linear factor models: models of the form $p = E(mx)$, $m = b'f$ or equivalently $E(R^e) = \beta'\lambda$? These models are by far the most common in empirical asset pricing, and there is a large literature on econometric techniques to estimate and evaluate them. Each technique focuses on the same questions: how to estimate parameters, how to calculate standard errors of the estimated parameters, how to calculate standard errors of the pricing errors, and how to test the model, usually with a test statistic of the form $\hat{\alpha}'V^{-1}\hat{\alpha}$.

I start in this chapter with simple and long-standing time-series and cross-sectional regression tests. In Chapter 13, I pursue the GMM approach to the model expressed in $p = E(mx)$, $m = b'f$ form. Chapter 14 summarizes the principle of maximum likelihood estimation and derives maximum likelihood estimates and tests. Finally, Chapter 15 compares the different approaches.

As always, the theme is the underlying unity. All of the techniques come down to one of two basic ideas: time-series regression or cross-sectional regression. Time-series regression turns out to be a limiting case of cross-sectional regression. The GMM, $p = E(mx)$ approach turns out to be almost identical to cross-sectional regressions. Maximum likelihood (with appropriate statistical assumptions) justifies the time-series and cross-sectional regression approaches. The formulas for parameter estimates, standard errors, and test statistics are all strikingly similar.

229

12.1 Time-Series Regressions

When the factor is also a return, we can evaluate the model

$$E(R^{ei}) = \beta_i E(f)$$

by running OLS *time-series regressions*

$$R_t^{ei} = \alpha_i + \beta_i f_t + \varepsilon_t^i, \qquad t = 1, 2, \ldots, T,$$

for each asset. The OLS distribution formulas (with corrected standard errors) provide standard errors of α and β.

With errors that are i.i.d. over time, homoskedastic, and independent of the factors, the asymptotic joint distribution of the intercepts gives the model test statistic,

$$T\left[1 + \left(\frac{E_T(f)}{\hat{\sigma}(f)}\right)^2\right]^{-1} \hat{\alpha}' \widehat{\Sigma}^{-1} \hat{\alpha} \sim \chi_N^2.$$

The Gibbons–Ross–Shanken test is a multivariate, finite-sample counterpart to this statistic, when the errors are also normally distributed,

$$\frac{T - N - K}{N}\left(1 + E_T(f)'\widehat{\Omega}^{-1} E_T(f)\right)^{-1} \hat{\alpha}' \widehat{\Sigma}^{-1} \hat{\alpha} \sim F_{N, T-N-K}.$$

I show how to construct the same test statistics with heteroskedastic and autocorrelated errors via GMM.

I start with the simplest case. We have a factor pricing model with a single factor. The factor is an excess return (for example, the CAPM, with $R^{em} = R^m - R^f$), and the test assets are all excess returns. We express the model in expected return-beta form. The betas are defined by regression coefficients

$$R_t^{ei} = \alpha_i + \beta_i f_t + \varepsilon_t^i \tag{12.1}$$

and the model states that expected returns are linear in the betas:

$$E(R^{ei}) = \beta_i E(f). \tag{12.2}$$

Since the factor is also an excess return, the model applies to the factor as well, so $E(f) = 1 \times \lambda$.

Comparing the model (12.2) and the expectation of the time-series regression (12.1), we see that the model has one and only one implication for the data: *all the regression intercepts α_i should be zero.* The regression intercepts are equal to the pricing errors.

Given this fact, Black, Jensen and Scholes (1972) suggested a natural strategy for estimation and evaluation: Run time-series regressions (12.1) for each test asset. The estimate of the factor risk premium is just the sample mean of the factor,

$$\hat{\lambda} = E_T(f).$$

Then, use standard OLS formulas for a distribution theory of the parameters. In particular, you can use t-tests to check whether the pricing errors α are in fact zero. These distributions are usually presented for the case that the regression errors in (12.1) are uncorrelated and homoskedastic, but the formulas in Section 11.4 show easily how to calculate standard errors for arbitrary error covariance structures.

We also want to know whether all the pricing errors are *jointly* equal to zero. This requires us to go beyond standard formulas for the regression (12.1) taken alone, as we want to know the joint distribution of α estimates from separate regressions running side by side but with errors correlated across assets ($E(\varepsilon_t^i \varepsilon_t^j) \neq 0$). (We can think of (12.1) as a panel regression, and then it is a test whether the firm dummies are jointly zero.) The classic form of these tests assume no autocorrelation or heteroskedasticity. Dividing the $\hat{\alpha}$ regression coefficients by their variance-covariance matrix leads to a χ^2 test,

$$T\left[1 + \left(\frac{E_T(f)}{\hat{\sigma}(f)}\right)^2\right]^{-1} \hat{\alpha}'\widehat{\Sigma}^{-1}\hat{\alpha} \sim \chi_N^2, \qquad (12.3)$$

where $E_T(f)$ denotes sample mean, $\hat{\sigma}^2(f)$ denotes sample variance, $\hat{\alpha}$ is a vector of the estimated intercepts,

$$\hat{\alpha} = \begin{bmatrix} \hat{\alpha}_1 & \hat{\alpha}_2 & \cdots & \hat{\alpha}_N \end{bmatrix}'.$$

$\widehat{\Sigma}$ is the residual covariance matrix, i.e., the sample estimate of $E(\varepsilon_t \varepsilon_t') = \Sigma$, where

$$\varepsilon_t = \begin{bmatrix} \varepsilon_t^1 & \varepsilon_t^2 & \cdots & \varepsilon_t^N \end{bmatrix}'.$$

As usual when testing hypotheses about regression coefficients, this test is valid asymptotically. The asymptotic distribution theory assumes that $\sigma^2(f)$ (i.e., $X'X$) and Σ have converged to their probability limits; therefore, it is asymptotically valid even though the factor is stochastic and Σ is estimated, but it ignores those sources of variation in a finite sample. It does not require that the errors are normal, relying on the central limit theorem so that $\hat{\alpha}$ is normal. I derive (12.3) below.

Also as usual in a regression context, we can derive a finite-sample F distribution for the hypothesis that a set of parameters are jointly zero,

$$\frac{T - N - 1}{N}\left[1 + \left(\frac{E_T(f)}{\hat{\sigma}(f)}\right)^2\right]^{-1} \hat{\alpha}'\widehat{\Sigma}^{-1}\hat{\alpha} \sim F_{N, T-N-1}. \qquad (12.4)$$

This is the Gibbons, Ross and Shanken (1989) or "GRS" test statistic. The F distribution recognizes sampling variation in $\widehat{\Sigma}$, which is not included in (12.3). This distribution requires that the errors ε are normal as well as uncorrelated and homoskedastic. With normal errors, the $\hat{\alpha}$ are normal and $\widehat{\Sigma}$ is an independent Wishart (the multivariate version of a χ^2), so the ratio is F. This distribution is exact in a finite sample.

Tests (12.3) and (12.4) have a very intuitive form. The basic part of the test is a quadratic form in the pricing errors, $\hat{\alpha}'\widehat{\Sigma}^{-1}\hat{\alpha}$. If there were no βf in the model, then the $\hat{\alpha}$ would simply be the sample mean of the regression errors ε_t. Assuming i.i.d. ε_t, the variance of their sample mean is just $1/T\Sigma$. Thus, if we knew Σ, then $T\hat{\alpha}'\Sigma^{-1}\hat{\alpha}$ would be a sum of squared sample means divided by their variance-covariance matrix, which would have an asymptotic χ^2_N distribution, or a finite-sample χ^2_N distribution if the ε_t are normal. But we have to estimate Σ, which is why the finite-sample distribution is F rather than χ^2. We also estimate the β, and the second term in (12.3) and (12.4) accounts for that fact.

Recall that a single-beta representation exists if and only if the reference return is on the mean-variance frontier. Thus, the test can also be interpreted as a test whether f is ex ante mean-variance efficient—whether it is on the mean-variance frontier using *population* moments—after accounting for sampling error. Even if f is on the true or ex ante mean-variance frontier, other returns will outperform it in sample due to luck, so the return f will usually be inside the ex post mean-variance frontier—i.e., the frontier drawn using *sample* moments. Still, it should not be too far inside the sample frontier. Gibbons, Ross and Shanken show that the test statistic can be expressed in terms of how far inside the ex post frontier the return f is,

$$\frac{T-N-1}{N} \frac{\left(\mu_q/\sigma_q\right)^2 - \left(E_T(f)/\hat{\sigma}(f)\right)^2}{1 + \left(E_T(f)/\hat{\sigma}(f)\right)^2}. \tag{12.5}$$

$\left(\mu_q/\sigma_q\right)^2$ is the Sharpe ratio of the ex post tangency portfolio (maximum ex post Sharpe ratio) formed from the test assets plus the factor f. The last term in the numerator is the Sharpe ratio of the factor, so the numerator expresses how for the factor is inside the ex-post frontier.

If there are many factors that are excess returns, the same ideas work, with some cost of algebraic complexity. The regression equation is

$$R^{ei} = \alpha_i + \beta_i' f_t + \varepsilon_t^i.$$

The asset pricing model

$$E(R^{ei}) = \beta_i' E(f)$$

again predicts that the intercepts should be zero. We can estimate α and β with OLS time-series regressions. Assuming normal i.i.d. errors, the quadratic form $\hat{\alpha}'\hat{\Sigma}^{-1}\hat{\alpha}$ has the distribution

$$\frac{T-N-K}{N}\left(1+E_T(f)'\widehat{\Omega}^{-1}E_T(f)\right)^{-1}\hat{\alpha}'\hat{\Sigma}^{-1}\hat{\alpha} \sim F_{N,\,T-N-K}, \qquad (12.6)$$

where

$$N = \text{number of assets},$$

$$K = \text{number of factors},$$

$$\widehat{\Omega} = \frac{1}{T}\sum_{t=1}^{T}[f_t - E_T(f)][f_t - E_T(f)]'.$$

The main difference is that the Sharpe ratio of the single factor is replaced by the natural generalization $E_T(f)'\widehat{\Omega}^{-1}E_T(f)$.

Derivation of The χ^2 Statistic, and Distributions with General Errors

I derive (12.3) as an instance of GMM. This approach allows us to generate straightforwardly the required corrections for autocorrelated and heteroskedastic disturbances. (MacKinlay and Richardson [1991] advocate GMM approaches to regression tests in this way.) It also serves to remind us that GMM and $p = E(mx)$ are not necessarily paired; one can do a GMM estimate of an expected return-beta model, too. The mechanics are only slightly different than what we did to generate distributions for OLS regression coefficients in Section 11.4, since we keep track of N OLS regressions simultaneously.

Write the equations for all N assets together in vector form,

$$R_t^e = \alpha + \beta f_t + \varepsilon_t.$$

We use the usual OLS moments to estimate the coefficients,

$$g_T(b) = \begin{bmatrix} E_T(R_t^e - \alpha - \beta f_t) \\ E_T[(R_t^e - \alpha - \beta f_t)f_t] \end{bmatrix} = E_T\left(\begin{bmatrix} \varepsilon_t \\ f_t\varepsilon_t \end{bmatrix}\right) = 0.$$

These moments exactly identify the parameters α, β, so the a matrix in $ag_T(\hat{b}) = 0$ is the identity matrix. Solving, the GMM estimates are of course the OLS estimates,

$$\hat{\alpha} = E_T(R_t^e) - \hat{\beta}E_T(f_t),$$

$$\hat{\beta} = \frac{E_T[(R_t^e - E_T(R_t^e))f_t]}{E_T[(f_t - E_T(f_t))f_t]} = \frac{\text{cov}_T(R_t^e, f_t)}{\text{var}_T(f_t)}.$$

The d matrix in the general GMM formula is

$$d \equiv \frac{\partial g_T(b)}{\partial b'} = -\begin{bmatrix} I_N & I_N E(f_t) \\ I_N E(f_t) & I_N E(f_t^2) \end{bmatrix} = -\begin{bmatrix} 1 & E(f_t) \\ E(f_t) & E(f_t^2) \end{bmatrix} \otimes I_N,$$

where I_N is an $N \times N$ identity matrix. The S matrix is

$$S = \sum_{j=-\infty}^{\infty} \begin{bmatrix} E(\varepsilon_t \varepsilon'_{t-j}) & E(\varepsilon_t \varepsilon'_{t-j} f_{t-j}) \\ E(f_t \varepsilon_t \varepsilon'_{t-j}) & E(f_t \varepsilon_t \varepsilon'_{t-j} f_{t-j}) \end{bmatrix}.$$

Using the GMM variance formula (11.4) with $a = I$, we have

$$\mathrm{var}\left(\begin{bmatrix} \hat{\alpha} \\ \hat{\beta} \end{bmatrix}\right) = \frac{1}{T} d^{-1} S d^{-1'}. \tag{12.7}$$

At this point, we are done. The upper left-hand corner of $\mathrm{var}(\hat{\alpha}\hat{\beta})$ gives us $\mathrm{var}(\hat{\alpha})$ and the test we are looking for is $\hat{\alpha}' \mathrm{var}(\hat{\alpha})^{-1} \hat{\alpha} \sim \chi_N^2$.

The standard formulas make this expression prettier by assuming that the errors are uncorrelated over time and not heteroskedastic. These assumptions simplify the S matrix, as for the standard OLS formulas in Section 11.4. If we assume that f and ε are independent as well as orthogonal, $E(f \varepsilon \varepsilon') = E(f) E(\varepsilon \varepsilon')$ and $E(f^2 \varepsilon \varepsilon') = E(f^2) E(\varepsilon \varepsilon')$. If we assume that the errors are independent over time as well, we lose all the lead and lag terms. Then, the S matrix simplifies to

$$S = \begin{bmatrix} E(\varepsilon_t \varepsilon'_t) & E(\varepsilon_t \varepsilon'_t) E(f_t) \\ E(f_t) E(\varepsilon_t \varepsilon'_t) & E(\varepsilon_t \varepsilon'_t) E(f_t^2) \end{bmatrix} = \begin{bmatrix} 1 & E(f_t) \\ E(f_t) & E(f_t^2) \end{bmatrix} \otimes \Sigma. \tag{12.8}$$

Now we can plug into (12.7). Using $(A \otimes B)^{-1} = A^{-1} \otimes B^{-1}$ and $(A \otimes B)(C \otimes D) = AC \otimes BD$, we obtain

$$\mathrm{var}\left(\begin{bmatrix} \hat{\alpha} \\ \hat{\beta} \end{bmatrix}\right) = \frac{1}{T}\left(\begin{bmatrix} 1 & E(f_t) \\ E(f_t) & E(f_t^2) \end{bmatrix}^{-1} \otimes \Sigma\right).$$

Evaluating the inverse,

$$\mathrm{var}\left(\begin{bmatrix} \hat{\alpha} \\ \hat{\beta} \end{bmatrix}\right) = \frac{1}{T} \frac{1}{\mathrm{var}(f)} \begin{bmatrix} E(f_t^2) & -E(f_t) \\ -E(f_t) & 1 \end{bmatrix} \otimes \Sigma.$$

We are interested in the top left corner. Using $E(f^2) = E(f)^2 + \mathrm{var}(f)$,

$$\mathrm{var}(\hat{\alpha}) = \frac{1}{T}\left(1 + \frac{E(f)^2}{\mathrm{var}(f)}\right)\Sigma.$$

This is the traditional formula (12.3). Though this formula is pretty, there is now no real reason to assume that the errors are i.i.d. or independent of the factors. By simply calculating (12.7), we can easily construct standard errors and test statistics that do not require these assumptions.

12.2 Cross-Sectional Regressions

> We can fit
> $$E(R^{ei}) = \beta_i'\lambda + \alpha_i$$
> by running a *cross-sectional* regression of average returns on the betas. This technique can be used whether the factor is a return or not.
>
> I discuss OLS and GLS cross-sectional regressions, I find formulas for the standard errors of λ, and a χ^2 test whether the α are jointly zero. I derive the distributions as an instance of GMM, and I show how to implement the same approach for autocorrelated and heteroskedastic errors. I show that the GLS cross-sectional regression is the same as the time-series regression when the factor is also an excess return, and is included in the set of test assets.

Start again with the K factor model, written as

$$E(R^{ei}) = \beta_i'\lambda, \qquad i = 1, 2, \ldots, N.$$

The central economic question is why average returns vary *across* assets; expected returns of an asset should be high if that asset has high betas or a large risk exposure to factors that carry high risk premia.

Figure 12.1 graphs the case of a single factor such as the CAPM. Each dot represents one asset i. The model says that average returns should be proportional to betas, so plot the sample average returns against the betas. Even if the model is true, this plot will not work out perfectly in each sample, so there will be some spread as shown.

Given these facts, a natural idea is to run a *cross-sectional regression* to fit a line through the scatterplot of Figure 12.1. First find estimates of the betas from time-series regressions,

$$R_t^{ei} = a_i + \beta_i'f_t + \varepsilon_t^i, \qquad t = 1, 2, \ldots, T \quad \text{for each } i. \tag{12.9}$$

Then estimate the factor risk premia λ from a regression across assets of average returns on the betas,

$$E_T(R^{ei}) = \beta_i'\lambda + \alpha_i, \qquad i = 1, 2, \ldots, N. \tag{12.10}$$

As in the figure, β are the right-hand variables, λ are the regression coefficients, and the cross-sectional regression residuals α_i are the pricing

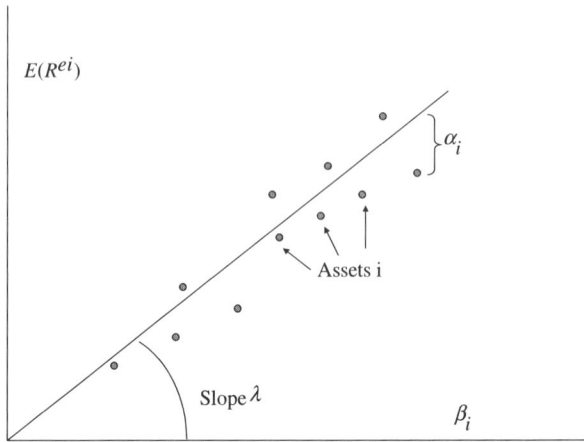

Figure 12.1.   *Cross-sectional regression.*

errors. This is also known as a *two-pass* regression estimate, because one estimates first time-series and then cross-sectional regressions.

You can run the cross-sectional regression with or without a constant. The theory says that the constant or zero-beta excess return should be zero. You can impose this restriction or estimate a constant and see if it turns out to be small. The usual trade-off between efficiency (impose the null as much as possible to get efficient estimates) and robustness applies.

OLS Cross-Sectional Regression

It will simplify notation to consider a single factor; the case of multiple factors looks the same with vectors in place of scalars. I denote vectors from 1 to N with missing sub or superscripts, i.e., $\varepsilon_t = \begin{bmatrix} \varepsilon_t^1 \ \varepsilon_t^2 \cdots \varepsilon_t^N \end{bmatrix}'$, $\beta = \begin{bmatrix} \beta_1 \ \beta_2 \cdots \beta_N \end{bmatrix}'$, and similarly for R_t^e and α. For simplicity take the case of no intercept in the cross-sectional regression. With this notation OLS cross-sectional estimates are

$$\hat{\lambda} = (\beta'\beta)^{-1}\beta' E_T(R^e),$$
$$\hat{\alpha} = E_T(R^e) - \hat{\lambda}\beta. \tag{12.11}$$

Next, we need a distribution theory for the estimated parameters. The most natural place to start is with the standard OLS distribution formulas. I start with the traditional assumption that the true errors are i.i.d. over time, and independent of the factors. This will give us some easily interpretable formulas, and we will see most of these terms remain when we do the distribution theory right later on.

In an OLS regression $Y = X\beta + u$ and $E(uu') = \Omega$, the standard error of the β estimate is $(X'X)^{-1}X'\Omega X(X'X)^{-1}$. The residual covariance matrix is $(I - X(X'X)^{-1}X')\Omega(I - X(X'X)^{-1}X')'$.

Denote $\Sigma = E(\varepsilon_t\varepsilon_t')$. Since the α_i are just time-series averages of the true ε_t^i shocks (the average of the sample residuals is always zero), the errors in the cross-sectional regression have covariance matrix[1] $E(\alpha\alpha') = \frac{1}{T}\Sigma$. Thus the conventional OLS formulas for the covariance matrix of OLS estimates and residual with correlated errors give

$$\sigma^2(\hat{\lambda}) = \frac{1}{T}(\beta'\beta)^{-1}\beta'\Sigma\beta(\beta'\beta)^{-1}, \tag{12.12}$$

$$\text{cov}(\hat{\alpha}) = \frac{1}{T}(I - \beta(\beta'\beta)^{-1}\beta')\Sigma(I - \beta(\beta'\beta)^{-1}\beta'). \tag{12.13}$$

The correct formulas, (12.19) and (12.20) are straightforward generalizations.

We could test whether all pricing errors are zero with the statistic

$$\hat{\alpha}'\,\text{cov}(\hat{\alpha})^{-1}\hat{\alpha} \sim \chi_{N-1}^2. \tag{12.14}$$

The distribution is χ_{N-1}^2, not χ_N^2, because the covariance matrix is singular. The singularity and the extra terms in (12.13) result from the fact that the λ coefficient was estimated along the way, and means that we have to use a generalized inverse. (If there are K factors, we obviously end up with χ_{N-K}^2.)

A test of the residuals is unusual in OLS regressions. We do not usually test whether the residuals are "too large," since we have no information other than the residuals themselves about how large they should be. In this case, however, the first-stage time-series regression gives us some independent information about the size of $\text{cov}(\alpha\alpha')$, information that we could not get from looking at the cross-sectional residual α itself.

GLS Cross-Sectional Regression

Since the residuals in the cross-sectional regression (12.10) are correlated with each other, standard textbook advice is to run a GLS cross-sectional regression rather than OLS, using $E(\alpha\alpha') = \frac{1}{T}\Sigma$ as the error covariance matrix:

$$\hat{\lambda} = (\beta'\Sigma^{-1}\beta)^{-1}\beta'\Sigma^{-1}E_T(R^e),$$
$$\hat{\alpha} = E_T(R^e) - \hat{\lambda}\beta. \tag{12.15}$$

[1] You might think from (12.10) that $E(\alpha\alpha')$ is related to the covariance matrix of returns. However, λ is not fixed from sample to sample. For example, if there were only one test asset, the factor itself, we would have zero α and zero residual in each sample, yet variation in the average return.

The standard regression formulas give the variance of these estimates as

$$\sigma^2(\hat{\lambda}) = \frac{1}{T}(\beta'\Sigma^{-1}\beta)^{-1}, \tag{12.16}$$

$$\text{cov}(\hat{\alpha}) = \frac{1}{T}(\Sigma - \beta(\beta'\Sigma^{-1}\beta)^{-1}\beta'). \tag{12.17}$$

The comments of Section 11.5 warning that OLS is sometimes much more robust than GLS apply in this case. The GLS regression should improve efficiency, i.e., give more precise estimates. However, Σ may be hard to estimate and to invert, especially if the cross section N is large. One may well choose the robustness of OLS over the asymptotic statistical advantages of GLS.

A GLS regression can be understood as a transformation of the space of returns, to focus attention on the statistically most informative portfolios. Finding (say, by Choleski decomposition) a matrix C such that $CC' = \Sigma^{-1}$, the GLS regression is the same as an OLS regression of $CE_T(R^e)$ on $C\beta$, i.e., of testing the model on the portfolios CR^e. The statistically most informative portfolios are those with the lowest residual variance Σ. But this asymptotic statistical theory assumes that the covariance matrix has converged to its true value. In most samples, the ex post or sample mean-variance frontier still seems to indicate lots of luck, and this is especially true if the cross section is large, anything more than $1/10$ of the time series. The portfolios CR^e are likely to contain many extreme long-short positions.

Again, we could test the hypothesis that all the α are equal to zero with (12.14). Though the appearance of the statistic is the same, the covariance matrix is smaller, reflecting the greater power of the GLS test. As with the J_T test, (11.10), we can develop an equivalent test that does not require a generalized inverse:

$$T\hat{\alpha}'\Sigma^{-1}\hat{\alpha} \sim \chi^2_{N-1}. \tag{12.18}$$

To derive (12.18), I proceed exactly as in the derivation of the J_T test (11.10). Define, say by Choleski decomposition, a matrix C such that $CC' = \Sigma^{-1}$. Now, find the covariance matrix of $\sqrt{T}C'\hat{\alpha}$:

$$\text{cov}(\sqrt{T}C\alpha) = C'((CC')^{-1} - \beta(\beta'CC'\beta)^{-1}\beta')C = I - \delta(\delta'\delta)^{-1}\delta',$$

where

$$\delta = C'\beta.$$

In sum, $\hat{\alpha}$ is asymptotically normal so $\sqrt{T}C'\hat{\alpha}$ is asymptotically normal, $\text{cov}(\sqrt{T}C'\hat{\alpha})$ is an idempotent matrix with rank $N - 1$; therefore $T\hat{\alpha}'CC'\hat{\alpha} = T\hat{\alpha}'\Sigma^{-1}\hat{\alpha}$ is χ^2_{N-1}.

Correction for the Fact that β Are Estimated, and
GMM Formulas that Do Not Need i.i.d. Errors

In applying standard OLS formulas to a cross-sectional regression, we assume that the right-hand variables β are fixed. The β in the cross-sectional regression are not fixed, of course, but are estimated in the time-series regression. This turns out to matter, even asymptotically.

In this section, I derive the correct asymptotic standard errors. With the simplifying assumption that the errors ε are i.i.d. over time and independent of the factors, the result is

$$
\sigma^2(\hat{\lambda}_{\mathrm{OLS}}) = \frac{1}{T}\left[(\beta'\beta)^{-1}\beta'\Sigma\beta(\beta'\beta)^{-1}\left(1 + \lambda'\Sigma_f^{-1}\lambda\right) + \Sigma_f\right],
$$
$$
\sigma^2(\hat{\lambda}_{\mathrm{GLS}}) = \frac{1}{T}\left[(\beta'\Sigma^{-1}\beta)^{-1}\left(1 + \lambda'\Sigma_f^{-1}\lambda\right) + \Sigma_f\right],
$$
(12.19)

where Σ_f is the variance-covariance matrix of the factors. This correction is due to Shanken (1992). Comparing these standard errors to (12.12) and (12.16), we see that there is a multiplicative correction $\left(1 + \lambda'\Sigma_f^{-1}\lambda\right)$ and an additive correction Σ_f.

The asymptotic variance-covariance matrix of the pricing errors is

$$
\mathrm{cov}(\hat{\alpha}_{\mathrm{OLS}}) = \frac{1}{T}\left(I_N - \beta(\beta'\beta)^{-1}\beta'\right)\Sigma\left(I_N - \beta(\beta'\beta)^{-1}\beta'\right)
$$
$$
\times\left(1 + \lambda'\Sigma_f^{-1}\lambda\right)
$$
(12.20)

$$
\mathrm{cov}(\hat{\alpha}_{\mathrm{GLS}}) = \frac{1}{T}\left(\Sigma - \beta(\beta'\Sigma^{-1}\beta)^{-1}\beta'\right)\left(1 + \lambda'\Sigma_f^{-1}\lambda\right).
$$
(12.21)

Comparing these results to (12.13) and (12.17), we see the same multiplicative correction.

We can form the asymptotic χ^2 test of the pricing errors by dividing pricing errors by their variance-covariance matrix, $\hat{\alpha}\,\mathrm{cov}(\hat{\alpha})^{-1}\hat{\alpha}$. Following (12.18), we can simplify this result for the GLS pricing errors resulting in

$$
T\left(1 + \lambda'\Sigma_f^{-1}\lambda\right)\hat{\alpha}_{\mathrm{GLS}}'\Sigma^{-1}\hat{\alpha}_{\mathrm{GLS}} \sim \chi^2_{N-K}.
$$
(12.22)

Are the corrections important relative to the simple-to-derive regression formulas (12.12), (12.13), (12.16), (12.17)? In the CAPM, $\lambda = E(R^{em})$ so $\lambda^2/\sigma^2(R^{em}) \approx (0.08/0.16)^2 = 0.25$ in annual data. In annual data, then, the multiplicative term is too large to ignore. However, the mean and variance both scale with horizon, so the Sharpe ratio scales with the square root of horizon. Therefore, for a monthly interval $\lambda^2/\sigma^2(R^{em}) \approx 0.25/12 \approx 0.02$, which is quite small and ignoring the multiplicative term makes little difference.

The additive term in the standard error of $\hat{\lambda}$ can be very important. Consider a one-factor model, suppose all the β are 1.0, all the residuals are uncorrelated so Σ is diagonal, suppose all assets have the same residual covariance $\sigma^2(\varepsilon)$, and ignore the multiplicative term. Now we can write either covariance matrix in (12.19) as

$$\sigma^2(\hat{\lambda}) = \frac{1}{T}\left[\frac{1}{N}\sigma^2(\varepsilon) + \sigma^2(f)\right].$$

Even with $N = 1$, most factor models have fairly high R^2, so $\sigma^2(\varepsilon) < \sigma^2(f)$. Typical CAPM values of $R^2 = 1 - \sigma^2(\varepsilon)/\sigma^2(f)$ for large portfolios are 0.6–0.7; and multifactor models such as the Fama French 3 factor model have R^2 often over 0.9. Typical numbers of assets $N = 10$ to 50 make the first term vanish compared to the second term.

More generally, suppose the factor were in fact a return. Then the factor risk premium is $\lambda = E(f)$, and we would use Σ_f/T as the standard error of λ. This is the "correction" term in (12.19), so we expect it to be, in fact, the most important term. Note that Σ_f/T is the standard error of the mean of f. Thus, in the case that the return is a factor, so $E(f) = \lambda$, this is the only term you would use.

This example and intuition suggests that Σ_f is not just an important correction; it is likely to be the dominant consideration in the sampling error of the $\hat{\lambda}$. *Even if the Shanken correction can be ignored for model tests, it should be included in $\sigma(\hat{\lambda})$.*

Comparing (12.22) to the GRS tests for a time-series regression, (12.3), (12.4), (12.6), we see the same statistic. The only difference is that by estimating λ from the cross section rather than imposing $\lambda = E(f)$, the cross-sectional regression loses degrees of freedom equal to the number of factors.

Though these formulas are standard classics, I emphasize that we do not have to make the severe assumptions on the error terms that are used to derive them. As with the time-series case, I derive a general formula for the distribution of $\hat{\lambda}$ and $\hat{\alpha}$, and only at the last moment make classic error term assumptions to make the spectral density matrix pretty.

Derivation and Formulas that Do Not Require i.i.d. Errors

The easy and elegant way to account for the effects of "generated regressors" such as the β in the cross-sectional regression is to map the whole thing into GMM. Then, we treat the moments that generate the regressors β at the same time as the moments that generate the cross-sectional regression coefficient λ, and the covariance matrix S between the two sets of moments captures the effects of generating the regressors on the standard error of the cross-sectional regression coefficients. Comparing this straightforward derivation with the difficulty of Shanken's (1992) paper that originally derived the corrections for $\hat{\lambda}$, and noting that Shanken did not go on to find the formulas (12.20) that allow a test of the pricing errors is a nice argument for the simplicity and power of the GMM framework.

To keep the algebra manageable, I treat the case of a single factor. The moments are

$$
g_T(b) = \begin{bmatrix} E(R_t^e - a - \beta f_t) \\ E[(R_t^e - a - \beta f_t)f_t] \\ E(R^e - \beta\lambda) \end{bmatrix} = \begin{bmatrix} 0 \\ 0 \\ 0 \end{bmatrix}. \tag{12.23}
$$

The top two moment conditions exactly identify a and β as the time-series OLS estimates. (Note a not α. The time-series intercept is not necessarily equal to the pricing error in a cross-sectional regression.) The bottom moment condition is the asset pricing model. It is in general overidentified in a sample, since there is only one extra parameter (λ) and N extra moment conditions. If we use a weighting vector β' on this condition, we obtain the OLS cross-sectional estimate of λ. If we use a weighting vector $\beta'\Sigma^{-1}$, we obtain the GLS cross-sectional estimate of λ. To accommodate both cases, use a weighting vector γ', and then substitute $\gamma' = \beta'$ or $\gamma' = \beta'\Sigma^{-1}$ at the end.

The standard errors for $\hat{\lambda}$ come straight from the general GMM standard error formula (11.4). The $\hat{a}$ are not parameters, but are the last N moments. Their covariance matrix is thus given by the GMM formula (11.5) for the sample variation of the g_T. All we have to do is map the problem into the GMM notation.

The parameter vector is

$$
b' = \begin{bmatrix} a' & \beta' & \lambda \end{bmatrix}.
$$

The a matrix chooses which moment conditions are set to zero in estimation,

$$
a = \begin{bmatrix} I_{2N} & 0 \\ 0 & \gamma' \end{bmatrix}.
$$

The d matrix is the sensitivity of the moment conditions to the parameters,

$$
d = \frac{\partial g_T}{\partial b'} = \begin{bmatrix} -I_N & -I_N E(f) & 0 \\ -I_N E(f) & -I_N E(f^2) & 0 \\ 0 & -\lambda I_N & -\beta \end{bmatrix}.
$$

The S matrix is the long-run covariance matrix of the moments,

$$
S = \sum_{j=-\infty}^{\infty} E\left(\begin{bmatrix} R_t^e - a - \beta f_t \\ (R_t^e - a - \beta f_t) f_t \\ R_t^e - \beta \lambda \end{bmatrix} \begin{bmatrix} R_{t-j}^e - a - \beta f_{t-j} \\ (R_{t-j}^e - a - \beta f_{t-j}) f_{t-j} \\ R_{t-j}^e - \beta \lambda \end{bmatrix}'\right)
$$

$$
= \sum_{j=-\infty}^{\infty} E\left(\begin{bmatrix} \varepsilon_t \\ \varepsilon_t f_t \\ \beta(f_t - Ef) + \varepsilon_t \end{bmatrix} \begin{bmatrix} \varepsilon_{t-j} \\ \varepsilon_{t-j} f_{t-j} \\ \beta(f_{t-j} - Ef) + \varepsilon_{t-j} \end{bmatrix}'\right).
$$

In the second expression, I have used the regression model and the restriction under the null that $E(R_t^e) = \beta \lambda$. In calculations, of course, you could simply estimate the first expression.

We are done. We have the ingredients to calculate the GMM standard error formula (11.4) and formula for the covariance of moments (11.5).

We can recover the classic formulas (12.19), (12.20), (12.21) by adding the assumption that the errors are i.i.d. and independent of the factors, and that the factors are uncorrelated over time as well. The assumption that the errors and factors are uncorrelated over time means we can ignore the lead and lag terms. Thus, the top left corner of S is $E(\varepsilon_t \varepsilon_t') = \Sigma$. The assumption that the errors are independent from the factors f_t simplifies the terms in which ε_t and f_t are multiplied: $E(\varepsilon_t(\varepsilon_t' f_t)) = E(f)\Sigma$ for example. The result is

$$
S = \begin{bmatrix} \Sigma & E(f)\Sigma & \Sigma \\ E(f)\Sigma & E(f^2)\Sigma & E(f)\Sigma \\ \Sigma & E(f)\Sigma & \beta\beta'\sigma^2(f) + \Sigma \end{bmatrix}.
$$

Multiplying a, d, S together as specified by the GMM formula for the covariance matrix of parameters (11.4), we obtain the covariance matrix of all the parameters, and its $(3, 3)$ element gives the variance of $\hat{\lambda}$. Multiplying the terms together as specified by (11.5), we obtain the sampling distribution of the $\hat{a}$, (12.20). The formulas (12.19) reported above are derived the same way with a vector of factors f_t rather than a scalar; the second-moment condition in (12.23) then reads $E\left[(R_t^e - a - \beta f_t) \otimes f_t\right]$. The matrix multiplication is not particularly enlightening.

Once again, there is really no need to make the assumption that the errors are i.i.d. and especially that they are conditionally homoskedastic—that the factor f and errors ε are independent. It is quite easy to estimate an S matrix that does not impose these conditions and calculate standard errors. They will not have the pretty analytic form given above, but they will more closely report the true sampling uncertainty of the estimate. Furthermore, if one is really interested in efficiency, the GLS cross-sectional estimate should use the spectral density matrix as weighting matrix rather than Σ^{-1}.

Time Series vs. Cross Section

How are the time-series and cross-sectional approaches different?

Most importantly, you can run the cross-sectional regression when the factor is not a return. The time-series test requires factors that are also returns, so that you can estimate factor risk premia by $\hat{\lambda} = E_T(f)$. The asset pricing model does predict a restriction on the intercepts in the time-series regression. Why not just test these? If you impose the restriction $E(R^{ei}) = \beta'_i \lambda$, you can write the time-series regression (12.9) as

$$R^{ei}_t = \beta'_i \lambda + \beta'_i \left(f_t - E(f)\right) + \varepsilon^i_t, \qquad t = 1, 2, \ldots, T \quad \text{for each } i.$$

Thus, the intercept restriction is

$$a_i = \beta'_i (\lambda - E(f)).$$

This restriction makes sense. The model says that mean returns should be proportional to betas, and the intercept in the time-series regression controls the mean return. You can also see how $\lambda = E(f)$ results in a zero intercept. Finally, however, you see that without an estimate of λ, you cannot check this intercept restriction. If the factor is not a return, you will be forced to do something like a cross-sectional regression.

When the factor is a return, so that we can compare the two methods, time-series and cross-sectional regressions are not necessarily the same. The time-series regression estimates the factor risk premium as the sample mean of the factor. Hence, the factor receives a zero pricing error in each sample. Also, the predicted zero-beta excess return is also zero. Thus, the time-series regression describes the cross section of expected returns by drawing a line as in Figure 12.1 that runs through the origin and through the factor, ignoring all of the other points. The OLS cross-sectional regression picks the slope and intercept, if you include one, to best fit all the points: to minimize the sum of squares of all the pricing errors.

If the factor is a return, *the GLS cross-sectional regression, including the factor as a test asset, is identical to the time-series regression.* The time-series regression for the factor is, of course,

$$f_t = 0 + 1f_t + 0,$$

so it has a zero intercept, beta equal to one, and zero residual in every sample. The residual variance-covariance matrix of the returns, including the factor, is

$$E\left(\begin{bmatrix} R^e - a - \beta f \\ f - 0 - 1f \end{bmatrix}[\cdot]'\right) = \begin{bmatrix} \Sigma & 0 \\ 0 & 0 \end{bmatrix}.$$

Since the factor has *zero* residual variance, a GLS regression puts all its weight on that asset. Therefore, $\hat{\lambda} = E_T(f)$ just as for the time-series regression. The pricing errors are the same, as is their distribution and the χ^2 test. (You gain a degree of freedom by adding the factor to the cross-sectional regression, so the test is a χ^2_N.)

Why does the "efficient" technique ignore the pricing errors of all of the other assets in estimating the factor risk premium, and focus only on the mean return? The answer is simple, though subtle. In the regression model

$$R^e_t = a + \beta f_t + \varepsilon_t,$$

the average return of each asset in a sample is equal to beta times the average return of the factor in the sample, plus the average residual in the sample. An average return carries *no* information about the mean of the factor that is not already observed in the sample mean of the factor. A signal plus noise carries no additional information beyond that in the *same* signal. Thus, an "efficient" cross-sectional regression wisely ignores all the information in the other asset returns and uses only the information in the factor return to estimate the factor risk premium.

12.3 Fama–MacBeth Procedure

> I introduce the Fama–MacBeth procedure for running cross-sectional regression and calculating standard errors that correct for cross-sectional correlation in a panel. I show that, when the right-hand variables do not vary over time, Fama–MacBeth is numerically equivalent to pooled time-series, cross-section OLS with standard errors corrected for cross-sectional correlation, and also to a single cross-sectional regression on time-series averages with standard errors corrected for cross-sectional correlation. Fama–MacBeth standard errors do not include corrections for the fact that the betas are also estimated.

Fama and MacBeth (1973) suggest an alternative procedure for running cross-sectional regressions, and for producing standard errors and test statistics. This is a historically important procedure, it is computationally simple to implement, and is still widely used, so it is important to understand it and relate it to other procedures.

First, you find beta estimates with a time-series regression. Fama and MacBeth use rolling 5-year regressions, but one can also use the technique with full-sample betas, and I will consider that simpler case. Second, instead of estimating a single cross-sectional regression with the sample averages, we now run a cross-sectional regression *at each time period*, i.e.,

$$R_t^{ei} = \beta_i' \lambda_t + \alpha_{it}, \qquad i = 1, 2, \ldots, N \quad \text{for each } t.$$

I write the case of a single factor for simplicity, but it is easy to extend the model to multiple factors. Then, Fama and MacBeth suggest that we estimate λ and α_i as the average of the cross-sectional regression estimates,

$$\hat{\lambda} = \frac{1}{T} \sum_{t=1}^{T} \hat{\lambda}_t, \qquad \hat{\alpha}_i = \frac{1}{T} \sum_{t=1}^{T} \hat{\alpha}_{it}.$$

Most importantly, they suggest that we use the standard deviations of the cross-sectional regression estimates to generate the sampling errors for these estimates,

$$\sigma^2(\hat{\lambda}) = \frac{1}{T^2} \sum_{t=1}^{T} \left(\hat{\lambda}_t - \hat{\lambda} \right)^2, \qquad \sigma^2(\hat{\alpha}_i) = \frac{1}{T^2} \sum_{t=1}^{T} \left(\hat{\alpha}_{it} - \hat{\alpha}_i \right)^2.$$

It is $1/T^2$ because we are finding standard errors of sample means, σ^2/T.

This is an intuitively appealing procedure once you stop to think about it. Sampling error is, after all, about how a statistic would vary from one sample to the next if we repeated the observations. We cannot do that with only one sample, but why not cut the sample in half, and deduce how a statistic would vary from one full sample to the next from how it varies from the first half of the sample to the next half? Proceeding, why not cut the sample in fourths, eighths, and so on? The Fama–MacBeth procedure carries this idea to its logical conclusion, using the variation in the statistic $\hat{\lambda}_t$ over time to deduce its variation across samples.

We are used to deducing the sampling variance of the sample mean of a series x_t by looking at the variation of x_t through time in the sample, using $\sigma^2(\bar{x}) = \sigma^2(x)/T = \frac{1}{T^2} \sum_t \left(x_t - \bar{x} \right)^2$. The Fama–MacBeth technique just applies this idea to the slope and pricing error estimates. The formula assumes that the time series is not autocorrelated, but one could easily extend the idea to estimates $\hat{\lambda}_t$ that are correlated over time by using a long-run variance matrix, i.e., estimate

$$\sigma^2(\hat{\lambda}) = \frac{1}{T} \sum_{j=-\infty}^{\infty} \text{cov}_T(\hat{\lambda}_t, \hat{\lambda}_{t-j}).$$

One should of course use some sort of weighting matrix or a parametric description of the autocorrelations of $\hat{\lambda}$, as explained in Section 11.7. Asset return data are usually not highly correlated, but accounting for such correlation could have a big effect on the application of the Fama–MacBeth technique to corporate finance data or other regressions in which the cross-sectional estimates are highly correlated over time.

It is natural to use this sampling theory to test whether all the pricing errors are jointly zero as we have before. Denote by α the vector of pricing errors across assets. We could estimate the covariance matrix of the sample pricing errors by

$$\hat{\alpha} = \frac{1}{T} \sum_{t=1}^{T} \hat{\alpha}_t,$$

$$\text{cov}(\hat{\alpha}) = \frac{1}{T^2} \sum_{t=1}^{T} \left(\hat{\alpha}_t - \hat{\alpha} \right) \left(\hat{\alpha}_t - \hat{\alpha} \right)',$$

(or a general version that accounts for correlation over time) and then use the test

$$\hat{\alpha}' \text{cov}(\hat{\alpha})^{-1} \hat{\alpha} \sim \chi_{N-1}^2.$$

Fama–MacBeth in Depth

The GRS procedure and the analysis of a single cross-sectional regression are familiar from any course in regression. We will see them justified by maximum likelihood below. The Fama–MacBeth procedure seems unlike anything you have seen in any econometrics course, and it is obviously a useful and simple technique that can be widely used in panel data in economics and corporate finance as well as asset pricing. Is it truly different? Is there something different about asset pricing data that requires a fundamentally new technique not taught in standard regression courses? Or is it similar to standard techniques? To answer these questions it is worth looking in a little more detail at what it accomplishes and why.

It is easier to do this in a more standard setup, with left-hand variable y and right-hand variable x. Consider a regression

$$y_{it} = \beta' x_{it} + \varepsilon_{it}, \qquad i = 1, 2, \ldots, N, \quad t = 1, 2, \ldots, T.$$

The data in this regression have a cross-sectional element as well as a time-series element. In corporate finance, for example, you might be interested in the relationship between investment and financial variables, and the data set has many firms (N) as well as time-series observations for each firm (T). In an expected return-beta asset pricing model, the x_{it} stands for the β_i and β stands for λ.

An obvious thing to do in this context is simply to stack the i and t observations together and estimate β by OLS. I will call this the *pooled time-series cross-section estimate*. However, the error terms are not likely to be uncorrelated with each other. In particular, the error terms are likely to be cross-sectionally correlated at a given time. If one stock's return is unusually high this month, another stock's return is also likely to be high; if one firm invests an unusually great amount this year, another firm is also likely to do so. When errors are correlated, OLS is still consistent, but the OLS distribution theory is wrong, and typically suggests standard errors that are much too small. In the extreme case that the N errors are perfectly correlated at each time period, there is really only one observation for each time period, so one really has T rather than NT observations. Therefore, a pooled time-series cross-section estimate must include corrected standard errors. People often ignore this fact and report OLS standard errors.

Another thing we could do is first take time-series averages and then run a *pure cross-sectional* regression of

$$E_T(y_{it}) = \beta' E_T(x_{it}) + u_i, \qquad i = 1, 2, \ldots, N.$$

This procedure would lose any information due to variation of the x_{it} over time, but at least it might be easier to figure out a variance-covariance matrix for u_i and correct the standard errors for residual correlation. (You could also average cross-sectionally and then run a single time-series regression. We will get to that option later.) In either case, the standard error corrections are just applications of the standard formula for OLS regressions with correlated error terms.

Finally, we could run the Fama–MacBeth procedure: run a cross-sectional regression at each point in time, average the cross-sectional $\hat{\beta}_t$ estimates to get an estimate $\hat{\beta}$, and use the time-series standard deviation of $\hat{\beta}_t$ to estimate the standard error of $\hat{\beta}$.

It turns out that the Fama–MacBeth procedure is another way of calculating the standard errors, corrected for cross-sectional correlation.

Proposition: *If the x_{it} variables do not vary over time, and if the errors are cross-sectionally correlated but not correlated over time, then the Fama–MacBeth estimate, the pure cross-sectional OLS estimate, and the pooled time-series cross-sectional OLS estimates are identical. Also, the Fama–MacBeth standard errors are identical to the cross-sectional regression or stacked OLS standard errors, corrected for residual correlation. None of these relations hold if the x_{it} vary through time.*

Since they are identical procedures, whether one calculates estimates and standard errors in one way or the other is a matter of taste.

I emphasize one procedure that is incorrect: pooled time-series and cross-section OLS with no correction of the standard errors. The errors are so highly cross-sectionally correlated in most finance applications that the standard errors so computed are often off by a factor of 10.

The assumption that the errors are not correlated over time is probably not so bad for asset pricing applications, since returns are close to independent. However, when pooled time-series cross-section regressions are used in corporate finance applications, errors are likely to be as severely correlated over time as across firms, if not more so. The "other factors" (ε) that cause, say, company i to invest more at time t than predicted by a set of right-hand variables is surely correlated with the other factors that cause company j to invest more. But such factors are especially likely to cause company i to invest more at time $t + 1$ as well. In this case, any standard errors must also correct for serial correlation in the errors; the GMM-based formulas in Section 11.4 can do this easily.

The Fama–MacBeth standard errors also do not correct for the fact that $\hat{\beta}$ are generated regressors. If one is going to use them, it is a good idea to at least calculate the Shanken correction factors outlined above, and check that the corrections are not large.

Proof: We just have to write out the three approaches and compare them. Having assumed that the x variables do not vary over time, the regression is

$$y_{it} = x_i'\beta + \varepsilon_{it}.$$

We can stack up the cross sections $i = 1, \ldots, N$ and write the regression as

$$y_t = x\beta + \varepsilon_t.$$

x is now a matrix with the x_i' as rows. The error assumptions mean $E(\varepsilon_t \varepsilon_t') = \Sigma$.

Pooled OLS: To run pooled OLS, we stack the time series and cross sections by writing

$$Y = \begin{bmatrix} y_1 \\ y_2 \\ \vdots \\ y_T \end{bmatrix}, \qquad X = \begin{bmatrix} x \\ x \\ \vdots \\ x \end{bmatrix}, \qquad \epsilon = \begin{bmatrix} \varepsilon_1 \\ \varepsilon_2 \\ \vdots \\ \varepsilon_T \end{bmatrix}$$

and then

$$Y = X\beta + \epsilon,$$

with

$$E(\epsilon\epsilon') = \Omega = \begin{bmatrix} \Sigma & & \\ & \ddots & \\ & & \Sigma \end{bmatrix}.$$

The estimate and its standard error are then

$$\hat{\beta}_{\text{OLS}} = (X'X)^{-1}X'Y,$$
$$\text{cov}(\hat{\beta}_{\text{OLS}}) = (X'X)^{-1}X'\Omega X(X'X)^{-1}.$$

Writing this out from the definitions of the stacked matrices, with $X'X = Tx'x$,

$$\hat{\beta}_{\text{OLS}} = (x'x)^{-1}x'E_T(y_t),$$
$$\text{cov}(\hat{\beta}_{\text{OLS}}) = \frac{1}{T}(x'x)^{-1}(x'\Sigma x)(x'x)^{-1}.$$

We can estimate this sampling variance with

$$\widehat{\Sigma} = E_T(\hat{\varepsilon}_t\hat{\varepsilon}_t'), \qquad \hat{\varepsilon}_t \equiv y_t - x\hat{\beta}_{\text{OLS}}.$$

Pure cross-section: The pure cross-sectional estimator runs one cross-sectional regression of the time-series averages. So, take those averages,

$$E_T\left(y_t\right) = x\beta + E_T\left(\varepsilon_t\right),$$

where $x = E_T(x)$ since x is constant. Having assumed i.i.d. errors over time, the error covariance matrix is

$$E\left(E_T\left(\varepsilon_t\right)E_T\left(\varepsilon_t'\right)\right) = \frac{1}{T}\Sigma.$$

The cross-sectional estimate and corrected standard errors are then

$$\hat{\beta}_{XS} = (x'x)^{-1}x'E_T(y_t),$$
$$\sigma^2(\hat{\beta}_{XS}) = \frac{1}{T}(x'x)^{-1}x'\Sigma x^{-1}(x'x)^{-1}.$$

Thus, the cross-sectional and pooled OLS estimates and standard errors are exactly the same, in each sample.

Fama–MacBeth: The Fama–MacBeth estimator is formed by first running the cross-sectional regression at each moment in time,

$$\hat{\beta}_t = \left(x'x\right)^{-1}x'y_t.$$

Then the estimate is the average of the cross-sectional regression estimates,

$$\hat{\beta}_{FM} = E_T(\hat{\beta}_t) = \left(x'x\right)^{-1}x'E_T(y_t).$$

Thus, the Fama–MacBeth estimator is also the same as the OLS estimator, in each sample. The Fama–MacBeth standard error is based on the time-series standard deviation of the $\hat{\beta}_t$. Using cov_T to denote sample covariance,

$$\text{cov}(\hat{\beta}_{FM}) = \frac{1}{T}\text{cov}_T(\hat{\beta}_t) = \frac{1}{T}(x'x)^{-1}x'\,\text{cov}_T(y_t)x(x'x)^{-1},$$

with

$$y_t = x\beta_{FM} + \hat{\varepsilon}_t,$$

we have

$$\text{cov}_T(y_t) = E_T(\hat{\varepsilon}_t\hat{\varepsilon}_t') = \widehat{\Sigma},$$

and finally

$$\text{cov}(\hat{\beta}_{FM}) = \frac{1}{T}(x'x)^{-1}x'\widehat{\Sigma}x(x'x)^{-1}.$$

Thus, the FM estimator of the standard error is also numerically equivalent to the OLS corrected standard error.

Varying x. If the x_{it} vary through time, none of the three procedures are equal anymore, since the cross-sectional regressions ignore time-series variation in the x_{it}. As an extreme example, suppose a scalar x_{it} varies over time but not cross-sectionally,

$$y_{it} = \alpha + x_t\beta + \varepsilon_{it}, \qquad i = 1, 2, \ldots, N, \quad t = 1, 2, \ldots, T.$$

The grand OLS regression is

$$\hat{\beta}_{OLS} = \frac{\sum_{it}\tilde{x}_t y_{it}}{\sum_{it}\tilde{x}_t^2} = \frac{\sum_t \tilde{x}_t(1/N)\sum_i y_{it}}{\sum_t \tilde{x}_t^2},$$

where $\tilde{x} = x - E_T(x)$ denotes the de-meaned variables. The estimate is driven by the covariance over time of x_t with the cross-sectional average of the y_{it}, which is sensible because all of the information in the sample lies in time variation. It is identical to a regression over *time* of *cross-sectional* averages. However, you cannot even run a cross-sectional estimate, since the right-hand variable is constant across i.

As a practical example, you might be interested in a CAPM specification in which the betas vary over time (β_t) but not across test assets. This sample still contains information about the CAPM: the time-variation in betas should be matched by time variation in expected returns. But any method based on cross-sectional regressions will completely miss it.   □

In historical context, the Fama–MacBeth procedure was also important because it allowed changing betas, which a single unconditional cross-sectional regression or a time-series regression test cannot easily handle.

Problems—Chapter 12

1. When we express the CAPM in excess return form, can the test assets be differences between risky assets, $R^i - R^j$? Can the market excess return also use a risky asset, or must it be relative to a risk-free rate? (Hint: start with $E(R^i) - R^f = \beta_{i,m}\left(E(R^m) - R^f\right)$ and see if you can get to the other forms. Betas must be regression coefficients.)

2. Can you run the GRS test on a model that uses industrial production growth as a factor, $E(R^{ei}) = \beta_{i,\Delta ip}\lambda_{ip}$?

3. Fama and French (1997b) report that pricing errors are correlated with betas in a test of a factor pricing model on industry portfolios. How is this possible?

4. We saw that a GLS cross-sectional regression of the CAPM passes through the market and risk-free rate by construction, though the OLS regression does not do so. Show that if the market return is an *equally* weighted portfolio of the test assets, then an OLS cross-sectional regression with an estimated intercept passes through the market return by construction. What if you force the intercept to zero? Does either regression also pass through the risk-free rate or origin?

GMM for Linear Factor Models in Discount Factor Form

IN THIS CHAPTER, I study estimation and testing of linear discount factor models expressed as $p = E(mx)$, $m = b'f$. This form naturally suggests a GMM approach using the pricing errors as moments. The resulting estimates look a lot like the regression estimates of Chapter 12.

13.1 GMM on the Pricing Errors Gives a Cross-Sectional Regression

The first-stage GMM estimate is an OLS cross-sectional regression, and the second stage is a GLS regression,

$$\text{First stage} : \hat{b}_1 = (d'd)^{-1}d'E_T(p),$$

$$\text{Second stage} : \hat{b}_2 = (d'S^{-1}d)d'S^{-1}E(p).$$

Standard errors are the corresponding regression formulas, and the variance of the pricing errors are the standard regression formula for variance of a residual.

Treating the constant $a \times 1$ as a constant factor, the model is

$$m = b'f,$$

$$E(p) = E(mx),$$

or simply

$$E(p) = E(xf')b. \tag{13.1}$$

Keep in mind that p and x are $N \times 1$ vectors of asset prices and payoffs respectively; f is a $K \times 1$ vector of factors, and b is a $K \times 1$ vector of parameters. I suppress the time indices $m_{t+1}, f_{t+1}, x_{t+1}, p_t$. The payoffs are typically returns or excess returns, including returns scaled by instruments. The prices are typically one (returns), zero (excess returns), or instruments.

To implement GMM, we need to choose a set of moments. The obvious set of moments to use are the pricing errors,

$$g_T(b) = E_T(xf'b - p).$$

This choice is natural but not necessary. You do not *have* to use $p = E(mx)$ with GMM, and you do not *have* to use GMM with $p = E(mx)$. You can (we will) use GMM on expected return-beta models, and you can use maximum likelihood on $p = E(mx)$. It is a choice, and the results will depend on this choice of moments as well as the specification of the model.

The GMM estimate is formed from

$$\min_b g_T(b)' W g_T(b)$$

with first-order condition

$$d' W g_T(b) = d' W \, E_T(xf'b - p) = 0,$$

where

$$d' = \frac{\partial g_T'(b)}{\partial b} = E_T(fx').$$

This is the second-moment matrix of payoffs and factors. The first stage has $W = I$, the second stage has $W = S^{-1}$. Since this is a linear model, we can solve analytically for the GMM estimate, and it is

$$\text{First stage}: \hat{b}_1 = (d'd)^{-1}d' E_T(p),$$

$$\text{Second stage}: \hat{b}_2 = (d'S^{-1}d)d'S^{-1}E_T(p).$$

The first-stage estimate is an OLS cross-sectional regression of average prices on the second moment of payoff with factors, and the second-stage estimate is a GLS cross-sectional regression. What could be more sensible? The model (13.1) says that average prices should be a linear function of the second moment of payoff with factors, so the estimate runs a linear regression. These are *cross-sectional* regressions since they operate across assets on sample averages. The "data points" in the regression are sample average prices (y) and second moments of payoffs with factors (x) *across* test assets. We are picking the parameter b to make the model fit explain the cross section of asset prices as well as possible.

We find the distribution theory from the usual GMM standard error formulas (11.2) and (11.8). In the first stage, $a = d'$:

$$\text{First stage}: \text{cov}(\hat{b}_1) = \frac{1}{T}(d'd)^{-1}d'Sd(d'd)^{-1},$$

$$\text{Second stage}: \text{cov}(\hat{b}_2) = \frac{1}{T}(d'S^{-1}d)^{-1}. \tag{13.2}$$

Unsurprisingly, these are exactly the formulas for OLS and GLS regression errors with error covariance S. The pricing errors are correlated across assets, since the payoffs are correlated. Therefore the OLS cross-sectional regression standard errors need to be corrected for correlation, as they are in (13.2), and one can pursue an efficient estimate as in GLS. The analogy in GLS is close, since S is the covariance matrix of $E(p) - E(xf')b$; S is the covariance matrix of the "errors" in the cross-sectional regression.

The covariance matrix of the pricing errors is, from (11.5), (11.9), and (11.10),

$$\text{First stage}: T\text{cov}\left[g_T(\hat{b})\right] = \left(I - d(d'd)^{-1}d'\right)S\left(I - d(d'd)^{-1}d'\right),$$

$$\text{Second stage}: T\text{cov}\left[g_T(\hat{b})\right] = S - d\left(d'S^{-1}d\right)^{-1}d'. \tag{13.3}$$

These are obvious analogues to the standard regression formulas for the covariance matrix of regression residuals.

The model test

$$g_T(b)'\text{cov}(g_T)^{-1}g_T(b) \sim \chi^2(\#\text{moments} - \#\text{parameters})$$

which specializes for the second-stage estimate as

$$Tg_T(\hat{b})'S^{-1}g_T(\hat{b}) \sim \chi^2(\#\text{moments} - \#\text{parameters}).$$

There is not much point in writing these out, other than to point out that the test is a quadratic form in the vector of pricing errors. It turns out that the χ^2 test has the same value for first and second stage for this model, even though the parameter estimates, pricing errors, and covariance matrix are not the same.

13.2 The Case of Excess Returns

When $m_{t+1} = a - b' f_{t+1}$ and the test assets are excess returns, the GMM estimate is a GLS cross-sectional regression of average returns on the second moments of returns with factors,

$$\text{First stage}: \hat{b}_1 = (d'd)^{-1} d' E_T(R^e),$$

$$\text{Second stage}: \hat{b}_2 = (d'S^{-1}d)d'S^{-1} E_T(R^e),$$

where d is the covariance matrix between returns and factors. The other formulas are the same.

The analysis of the last section requires that at least one asset has a nonzero price. If all assets are excess returns, then $\hat{b}_1 = (d'd)^{-1} d' E_T(p) = 0$. Linear factor models are most often applied to excess returns, so this case is important. The trouble is that in this case the mean discount factor is not identified. If $E(mR^e) = 0$, then $E((2 \times m)R^e) = 0$. Analogously in expected return-beta models, if all test assets are excess returns, then we have no information on the level of the zero-beta rate.

Writing out the model as $m = a - b'f$, we cannot separately identify a and b so we have to choose some normalization. The choice is entirely one of convenience; lack of identification means precisely that the pricing errors do not depend on the choice of normalization.

The easiest choice is $a = 1$. Then

$$g_T(b) = E_T(mR^e) = E_T(R^e) - E(R^e f')b.$$

We have

$$d' = \frac{\partial g_T(b)}{\partial b'} = E(fR^{e'}),$$

the second-moment matrix of returns and factors. The first-order condition to min $g_T' W g_T$ is

$$d' W[d\, b + E_T(R^e)] = 0.$$

Then, the GMM estimates of b are

$$\text{First stage}: \hat{b}_1 = (d'd)^{-1} d' E_T(R^e),$$

$$\text{Second stage}: \hat{b}_2 = (d'S^{-1}d)d'S^{-1} E_T(R^e).$$

The GMM estimate is a cross-sectional regression of mean excess returns on the second moments of returns with factors. From here on in, the distribution theory is unchanged from the last section.

Mean Returns on Covariances

We can obtain a cross-sectional regression of mean excess returns on *covariances*, which are just a heartbeat away from betas, by choosing the normalization $a = 1 + b'E(f)$ rather than $a = 1$. Then, the model is $m = 1 - b'(f - E(f))$ with mean $E(m) = 1$. The pricing errors are

$$g_T(b) = E_T(mR^e) = E_T(R^e) - E_T(R^e \tilde{f}')b,$$

where I denote $\tilde{f} \equiv f - E(f)$. We have

$$d' = \frac{\partial g_T(b)}{\partial b'} = E_T(\tilde{f}R^{e\prime}),$$

which now denotes the covariance matrix of returns and factors. The first-order condition to min $g_T'Wg_T$ is now

$$d'W[d\,b + E_T(R^e)] = 0.$$

Then, the GMM estimates of b are

$$\text{First stage} : \hat{b}_1 = (d'd)^{-1}d'E_T(R^e),$$
$$\text{Second stage} : \hat{b}_2 = (d'S^{-1}d)d'S^{-1}E_T(R^e).$$

The GMM estimate is a cross-sectional regression of expected excess returns on the covariance between returns and factors. Naturally, the model says that expected excess returns should be proportional to the covariance between returns and factors, and we estimate that relation by a linear regression. The standard errors and variance of the pricing errors are the same as in (13.2) and (13.3), with d now representing the covariance matrix. The formulas are almost exactly identical to those of the cross-sectional regressions in Section 12.2. The $p = E(mx)$ formulation of the model for excess returns is equivalent to $E(R^e) = -\text{cov}(R^e, f')b$; thus covariances enter in place of betas β.

There is one fly in the ointment; the mean of the factor $E(f)$ is estimated, and the distribution theory should recognize sampling variation induced by this fact, as we did for the fact that betas are generated regressors in the cross-sectional regressions of Section 12.2. The distribution theory is straightforward, and a problem at the end of the chapter guides you through it. However, I think it is better to avoid the complication and just use the second-moment approach, or some other non–sample-dependent normalization for a. The pricing errors are identical—the whole point is that the normalization of a does not matter to the pricing errors. Therefore, the χ^2 statistics are also identical. As you change the normalization for a, you change the estimate of b. Therefore, the only effect is to add a term in the sampling variance of the estimated parameter b.

13.3 Horse Races

> How to test whether one set of factors drives out another. Test $b_2 = 0$ in $m = b_1' f_1 + b_2' f_2$ using the standard error of $\hat{b}_2$, or the χ^2 difference test.

It is often interesting to test whether one set of factors drives out another. For example, Chen, Roll and Ross (1986) test whether their five macroeconomic factors price assets so well that one can ignore even the market return. Given the large number of factors that have been proposed, a statistical procedure for testing which factors survive in the presence of the others is desirable.

In this framework, such a test is very easy. Start by estimating a general model

$$m = b_1' f_1 + b_2' f_2. \tag{13.4}$$

We want to know, given factors f_1, do we need the f_2 to price assets—i.e., is $b_2 = 0$? There are two ways to do this.

First and most obviously, we have an asymptotic covariance matrix for $[b_1 b_2]$, so we can form a t test (if b_2 is scalar) or χ^2 test for $b_2 = 0$ by forming the statistic

$$\hat{b}_2' \operatorname{var}(\hat{b}_2)^{-1} \hat{b}_2 \sim \chi^2_{\#b_2},$$

where $\#b_2$ is the number of elements in the b_2 vector. This is a Wald test.

Second, we can estimate a restricted system $m = b_1' f_1$. Since there are fewer free parameters than in (13.4), and the same number of moments, we expect the criterion J_T to rise. If we use the same weighting matrix (usually the one estimated from the unrestricted model (13.4)), then the J_T cannot in fact decline. But if b_2 really is zero, it should not rise "much." How much? The χ^2 difference test answers that question;

$$T J_T(\text{restricted}) - T J_T(\text{unrestricted}) \sim \chi^2(\#\text{of restrictions}).$$

This is very much like a likelihood ratio test.

13.4 Testing for Characteristics

> How to check whether an asset pricing model drives out a characteristic
> such as size, book/market, or volatility. Run cross-sectional regressions of
> pricing errors on characteristics; use the formulas for covariance matrix of
> the pricing errors to create standard errors.

It is often interesting to characterize a model by checking whether the
model drives out a characteristic. For example, portfolios organized by size
or market capitalization show a wide dispersion in average returns (at least
up to 1979). Small stocks gave higher average returns than large stocks.
The size of the portfolio is a characteristic. A good asset pricing model
should account for average returns by betas. It is ok if a characteristic
is associated with average returns, but in the end betas should drive out
the characteristic; the alphas or pricing errors should not be associated
with the characteristic. The original tests of the CAPM similarly checked
whether the variance of the individual portfolio had anything to do with
average returns once betas were included.

Denote the characteristic of portfolio i by y_i. An obvious idea is to
include both betas and the characteristic in a multiple, cross-sectional
regression. In addition, the characteristic is sometimes estimated rather
than being a fixed number such as the size rank of a size portfolio, and
you would like to include the sampling uncertainty of its estimation in the
standard errors of the characteristic's effect. Let y_t^i denote the time series
whose mean $E(y_t^i)$ determines the characteristic. Now, write the moment
condition for the ith asset as

$$g_T^i = E_T(m_{t+1}(b)x_{t+1}^i - p_t^i - \gamma y_t^i),$$

and let y denote the vector of y^i across assets. The estimate of γ tells
you how the characteristic $E(y^i)$ is associated with model pricing errors
$E(m_{t+1}(b)x_{t+1}' - p_t')$. The GMM estimate of γ is

$$\hat{\gamma} = \left(E_T(y)'WE_T(y)\right)^{-1}E_T(y)'Wg_T,$$

an OLS or GLS regression of the pricing errors on the estimated characteristics. The standard GMM formulas for the standard deviation of γ or
the χ^2 difference test for $\gamma = 0$ tell you whether the γ estimate is statistically significant, including the fact that $E(y)$ must be estimated.

13.5 Testing for Priced Factors: Lambdas or *b*'s?

b_j asks whether factor j *helps to price* assets given the other factors. b_j gives the *multiple* regression coefficient of m on f_j given the other factors.

λ_j asks whether factor j *is priced*, or whether its factor-mimicking portfolio carries a positive risk premium. λ_j gives the *single* regression coefficient of m on f_j.

Therefore, when factors are correlated, one should test $b_j = 0$ to see whether to include factor j given the other factors rather than test $\lambda_j = 0$.

In the context of expected return-beta models, it has been more traditional to evaluate the relative strengths of models by testing the factor risk premia λ of additional factors, rather than test whether their b is zero. (The b's are not the same as the β's. b are the regression coefficients of m on f, β are the regression coefficients of R^i on f.)

To keep the equations simple, I will use mean-zero factors, excess returns, and normalize to $E(m) = 1$, since the mean of m is not identified with excess returns.

The parameters b and λ are related by

$$\lambda = E(ff')b.$$

See Section 6.3. Briefly,

$$0 = E(mR^e) = E[R^e(1 - f'b)],$$

$$E(R^e) = \text{cov}(R^e, f')b = \text{cov}(R^e, f')E(ff')^{-1}E(ff')b = \beta'\lambda.$$

When the factors are orthogonal, $E(ff')$ is diagonal, and each $\lambda_j = 0$ if and only if the corresponding $b_j = 0$. The distinction between b and λ only matters when the factors are correlated. Factors are often correlated, however.

λ_j captures whether factor f_j *is priced*. We can write $\lambda = E[f(f'b)] = -E(mf)$ to see that λ is (the negative of) the price that the discount factor m assigns to f. b captures whether factor f_j is marginally useful in pric*ing* assets, given the presence of other factors. If $b_j = 0$, we can price assets just as well without factor f_j as with it.

λ_j is proportional to the *single* regression coefficient of m on f. $\lambda_j = \text{cov}(m, f_j)$. $\lambda_j = 0$ asks the corresponding single regression coefficient question—"is factor j correlated with the true discount factor?"

b_j is the *multiple* regression coefficient of m on f_j given all the other factors. This just follows from $m = b'f$. (Regressions do not have to have error terms!) A multiple regression coefficient β_j in $y = x\beta + \varepsilon$ is the way to answer "does x_j help to explain variation in y given the presence of the other x's?" When you want to ask the question, "should I include factor j given the other factors?" you want to ask the multiple regression question.

For example, suppose the CAPM is true, which is the single-factor model

$$m = a - bR^{em},$$

where R^{em} is the market excess return. Consider any other excess return R^{ex} (x for extra), positively correlated with R^{em}. If we try a factor model with the spurious factor R^{ex}, the answer is

$$m = a - bR^{em} + 0 \times R^{ex}.$$

b_x is obviously zero, indicating that adding this factor does not help to price assets.

However, since the correlation of R^{ex} with R^{em} is positive, the CAPM beta of R^{ex} on R^{em} is positive, R^{ex} earns a positive expected excess return, and $\lambda_x = E(R^{ex}) > 0$. In the expected return-beta model

$$E(R^{ei}) = \beta_{im}\lambda_m + \beta_{ix}\lambda_x$$

$\lambda_m = E(R^{em})$ is unchanged by the addition of the spurious factor. However, since the factors R^{em}, R^{ex} are correlated, the multiple regression *betas* of R^{ei} on the factors change when we add the extra factor R^{ex}. If β_{ix} is positive, β_{im} will decline from its single-regression value, so the new model explains the same expected return $E(R^{ei})$. The expected return-beta model will indicate a risk premium for β_x exposure, and many assets will have β_x exposure (R^x for example!) even though factor R^x is spurious. In particular, R^{ex} will of course have multiple regression coefficients $\beta_{x,m} = 0$ and $\beta_{x,x} = 1$, and its expected return will be entirely explained by the new factor x.

So, as usual, the answer depends on the question. If you want to know whether factor i *is priced*, look at λ (or $E(mf^i)$). If you want to know whether factor i *helps to price other assets*, look at b_i. This is not an issue about sampling error or testing. All moments above are population values.

Of course, testing $b = 0$ is particularly easy in the GMM, $p = E(mx)$ setup. But you can always test the same ideas in any expression of the model. In an expected return-beta model, estimate b by $E(ff')^{-1}\lambda$ and test the elements of that vector rather than λ itself.

You can write an asset pricing model as $ER^e = \beta'\lambda$ and use the λ to test whether each factor can be dropped in the presence of the others, if you use *single* regression betas rather than multiple regression betas. In this case each λ is proportional to the corresponding b. Problem 2 at the end of this chapter helps you to work out this case. You can also make sure that your factors are orthogonal, in which case testing λ is the same thing as testing b.

Mean-Variance Frontier and Performance Evaluation

> A GMM, $p = E(mx)$ approach to testing whether a return expands the mean-variance frontier. Just test whether $m = a + bR$ prices all returns. If there is no risk-free rate, use two values of a.

We often summarize asset return data by mean-variance frontiers. For example, a large literature has examined the desirability of international diversification in a mean-variance context. Stock returns from many countries are not perfectly correlated, so it looks like one can reduce portfolio variance a great deal for the same mean return by holding an internationally diversified portfolio. But is this phenomenon real or just sampling error? Even if the value-weighted portfolio were ex ante mean-variance efficient, an ex post mean-variance frontier constructed from historical returns on the roughly 6000 NYSE stocks would leave the value-weighted portfolio well inside the ex post frontier. So is "I should have bought Japanese stocks in 1960" (and sold them in 1990!) a signal that broad-based international diversification is a good idea now, or is it simply 20/20 hindsight regret like "I should have bought Microsoft in 1982?" Similarly, when evaluating fund managers, we want to know whether the manager is truly able to form a portfolio that beats mean-variance efficient passive portfolios, or whether better performance in sample is just due to luck.

Since a factor model is true if and only if a linear combination of the factors (or factor-mimicking portfolios if the factors are not returns) is mean-variance efficient, one can interpret a test of any factor pricing model as a test whether a given return is on the mean-variance frontier. Section 12.1 showed how the Gibbons, Ross and Shanken pricing error statistic can be interpreted as a test whether a given portfolio is on the mean-variance frontier, when returns and factors are i.i.d., and the GMM distribution theory of that test statistic allows us to extend the test to non-i.i.d. errors. A GMM, $p = E(mx)$, $m = a - bR^p$ test analogously tests whether R^p is on the mean-variance frontier of the test assets.

We may want to go one step further, and not just test whether a combination of a set of assets R^d (say, domestic assets) is *on* the mean-variance frontier, but whether the R^d assets *span* the mean-variance frontier of R^d and R^i (say, foreign or international) assets. The trouble is that if there is no risk-free rate, the frontier generated by R^d might just *intersect* the frontier generated by R^d and R^i together, rather than span or coincide

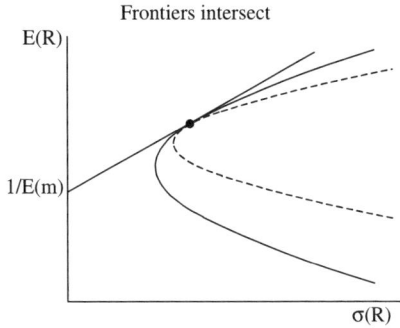

Figure 13.1. *Mean-variance frontiers might intersect rather than coincide.*

with the latter frontier, as shown in Figure 13.1. Testing that $m = a - b'R^d$ prices both R^d and R^i only checks for intersection.

DeSantis (1992) and Chen and Knez (1992, 1993) show how to test for spanning as opposed to intersection. For *intersection*, $m = a - b'_d R^d$ will price both R^d and R^f only for one value of a, or equivalently $E(m)$ or choice of the intercept, as shown. If the frontiers coincide or span, then $m = a + b'_d R^d$ prices both R^d and R^f for any value of a. Thus, we can test for coincident frontiers by testing whether $m = a + b'_d R^d$ prices both R^d and R^f for two prespecified values of a simultaneously.

To see how this works, start by noting that there must be at least two assets in R^d. If not, there is no mean-variance frontier of R^d assets; it is simply a point. If there are two assets in R^d, R^{d1} and R^{d2}, then the mean-variance frontier of domestic assets connects them; they are each on the frontier. If they are both on the frontier, then there must be discount factors

$$m^1 = a^1 - \tilde{b}^1 R^{d1}$$

and

$$m^2 = a^2 - \tilde{b}^2 R^{d2}$$

and, of course, any linear combination,

$$m = \left[\lambda a^1 + (1-\lambda)a^2\right] - \left[\lambda \tilde{b}^1 R^{d1} + (1-\lambda)\tilde{b}^2 R^{d2}\right].$$

Equivalently, for any value of a, there is a discount factor of the form

$$m = a - \left(b^1 R^{d1} + b^2 R^{d2}\right).$$

Thus, you can test for spanning with a J_T test on the moments

$$E\left[(a^1 - b^{1\prime}R^d)R^d\right] = 0,$$
$$E\left[(a^1 - b^{1\prime}R^d)R^i\right] = 0,$$
$$E\left[(a^2 - b^{2\prime}R^d)R^d\right] = 0,$$
$$E\left[(a^2 - b^{2\prime}R^d)R^i\right] = 0,$$

for any two fixed values of a^1, a^2.

Problems—Chapter 13

1. Work out the GMM distribution theory for the model $m = 1 - b'(f - E(f))$ and test assets are excess returns. The distribution should recognize the fact that $E(f)$ is estimated in sample. To do this, set up

$$g_T = \begin{bmatrix} E_T(R^e - R^e(f' - Ef')b) \\ E_T(f - Ef) \end{bmatrix},$$

$$a_T = \begin{bmatrix} E_T(\tilde{f}R^{e\prime}) & 0 \\ 0 & I_K \end{bmatrix}.$$

The estimated parameters are $b, E(f)$. You should end up with a formula for the standard error of b that resembles the Shanken correction (12.19), and an unchanged J_T test.

2. Show that if you use *single* regression betas, then the corresponding λ can be used to test for the marginal importance of factors. However, the λ are no longer the expected return of factor-mimicking portfolios.

14

Maximum Likelihood

MAXIMUM LIKELIHOOD IS, like GMM, a general organizing principle that is a useful place to start when thinking about how to choose parameters and evaluate a model. It comes with an asymptotic distribution theory, which, like GMM, is a good place to start when you are unsure about how to treat various problems such as the fact that betas must be estimated in a cross-sectional regression.

As we will see, maximum likelihood is a special case of GMM. Given a statistical description of the data, it prescribes which moments are statistically most informative. Given those moments, ML and GMM are the same. Thus, ML can be used to defend why one picks a certain set of moments, or for advice on which moments to pick if one is unsure. In this sense, maximum likelihood (paired with carefully chosen statistical models) justifies the regression tests above, as it justifies standard regressions. On the other hand, ML does not easily allow you to use other non-"efficient" moments, if you suspect that ML's choices are not robust to misspecifications of the economic or statistical model. For example, ML will tell you how to do GLS, but it will not tell you how to adjust OLS standard errors for nonstandard error terms.

Hamilton (1994, pp. 142–148) and the appendix in Campbell, Lo, and MacKinlay (1997) give nice summaries of maximum likelihood theory. Campbell, Lo, and MacKinlay's Chapters 5 and 6 treat many more variations of regression-based tests and maximum likelihood.

14.1 Maximum Likelihood

The maximum likelihood principle says to pick the parameters that make the observed data most likely. Maximum likelihood estimates are asymptotically efficient. The information matrix gives the asymptotic standard errors of ML estimates.

The maximum likelihood principle says to pick that set of parameters that makes the observed data most likely. This is not "the set of parameters that are most likely given the data"—in classical (as opposed to Bayesian) statistics, parameters are numbers, not random variables.

To implement this idea, you first have to figure out what the probability of seeing a data set $\{x_t\}$ is, given the free parameters θ of a model. This probability distribution is called the *likelihood function* $f(\{x_t\}; \theta)$. Then, the maximum likelihood principle says to pick

$$\hat{\theta} = \arg\max_{\{\theta\}} f(\{x_t\}; \theta).$$

For reasons that will soon be obvious, it is much easier to work with the log of this probability distribution

$$\mathcal{L}(\{x_t\}; \theta) = \ln f(\{x_t\}; \theta).$$

Maximizing the log likelihood is the same thing as maximizing the likelihood.

Finding the likelihood function is not always easy. In a time-series context, the best way to do it is often to first find the log *conditional likelihood function* $f(x_t|x_{t-1}, x_{t-2}, \ldots, x_0; \theta)$, the chance of seeing x_{t+1} given $x_t, x_{t-1}, \ldots$ and given values for the parameters. Since joint probability is the product of conditional probabilities, the log likelihood function is just the sum of the conditional log likelihood functions,

$$\mathcal{L}(\{x_t\}; \theta) = \sum_{t=1}^{T} \ln f(x_t|x_{t-1}, x_{t-2} \ldots, x_0; \theta). \tag{14.1}$$

More concretely, we usually assume normal errors, so the likelihood function is

$$\mathcal{L} = -\frac{T}{2}\ln(2\pi|\Sigma|) - \frac{1}{2}\sum_{t=1}^{T} \varepsilon_t' \Sigma^{-1} \varepsilon_t, \tag{14.2}$$

where ε_t denotes a vector of shocks; $\varepsilon_t = x_t - E(x_t|x_{t-1}, x_{t-2} \ldots, x_0; \theta)$.

This expression gives a simple recipe for constructing a likelihood function. You usually start with a model that generates x_t from errors, e.g.,

$x_t = \rho x_{t-1} + \varepsilon_t$. Invert that model to express the errors ε_t in terms of the data $\{x_t\}$ and plug in to (14.2).

There is a small issue about how to start off a model such as (14.1). Ideally, the first observation should be the unconditional density, i.e.,

$$\mathcal{L}(\{x_t\}; \theta) = \ln f(x_1; \theta) + \ln f(x_2|x_1; \theta) + \ln f(x_3|x_2, x_1; \theta).\ldots$$

However, it is usually hard to evaluate the unconditional density or the first terms with only a few lagged x's. Therefore, if, as usual, the conditional density can be expressed in terms of a finite number k of lags of x_t, one often maximizes the *conditional* likelihood function (conditional on the first k observations), treating the first k observations as fixed rather than random variables. Alternatively, one can treat k presample values $\{x_0, x_{-1}, \ldots, x_{-k+1}\}$ as additional parameters over which to maximize the likelihood function.

Maximum likelihood estimators come with a useful asymptotic (i.e., approximate) distribution theory. First, the distribution of the estimates is

$$\hat{\theta} \sim \mathcal{N}\left(\theta, \left[-\frac{\partial^2 \mathcal{L}}{\partial \theta\, \partial \theta'}\right]^{-1}\right). \tag{14.3}$$

If the likelihood $\mathcal{L}$ has a sharp peak at $\hat{\theta}$, then we know a lot about the parameters, while if the peak is flat, other parameters are just as plausible. The maximum likelihood estimator is *asymptotically efficient*, meaning that no other estimator can produce a smaller covariance matrix.

The second derivative in (14.3) is known as the *information matrix*,

$$\mathcal{I} = -\frac{1}{T} \frac{\partial^2 \mathcal{L}}{\partial \theta\, \partial \theta'} = -\frac{1}{T} \sum_{t=1}^{T} \frac{\partial^2 \ln f(x_t|x_{t-1}, x_{t-2}, \ldots; \theta)}{\partial \theta\, \partial \theta'}. \tag{14.4}$$

(More precisely, the information matrix is defined as the expected value of the second partial, which is estimated with the sample value.) The information matrix can also be estimated as a product of first derivatives. The expression

$$\mathcal{I} = -\frac{1}{T} \sum_{t-1}^{T} \left(\frac{\partial \ln f(x_t|x_{t-1}, x_{t-2}, \ldots; \theta)}{\partial \theta}\right)$$
$$\times \left(\frac{\partial \ln f(x_t|x_{t-1}, x_{t-2}, \ldots; \theta)}{\partial \theta}\right)'$$

converges to the same value as (14.4). (Hamilton [1994, p. 429] gives a proof.)

If we estimate a model restricting the parameters, the maximum value of the likelihood function will necessarily be lower. However, if the restriction is true, it should not be that much lower. This intuition is captured in the *likelihood ratio test*

$$2\left(\mathcal{L}_{\text{unrestricted}} - \mathcal{L}_{\text{restricted}}\right) \sim \chi^2_{\text{number of restrictions}}. \tag{14.5}$$

The form and idea of this test are much like the χ^2 difference test for GMM objectives that we met in Section 11.1.

14.2 ML is GMM on the Scores

ML is a special case of GMM. ML uses the information in the auxiliary statistical model to derive statistically most informative moment conditions. To see this fact, start with the first-order conditions for maximizing a likelihood function

$$\frac{\partial \mathcal{L}(\{x_t\}; \theta)}{\partial \theta} = \sum_{t=1}^{T} \frac{\partial \ln f(x_t | x_{t-1}, x_{t-2} \ldots; \theta)}{\partial \theta} = 0. \tag{14.6}$$

This is a GMM estimate. It is the sample counterpart to a population moment condition

$$g(\theta) = E\left(\frac{\partial \ln f(x_t | x_{t-1}, x_{t-2} \ldots; \theta)}{\partial \theta}\right) = 0. \tag{14.7}$$

The term $\partial \ln f(x_t | x_{t-1}, x_{t-2} \ldots; \theta)/\partial \theta$ is known as the "score." It is a random variable, formed as a combination of current and past data $(x_t, x_{t-1}, \ldots)$. Thus, maximum likelihood is a special case of GMM, a special choice of which moments to examine.

For example, suppose that x follows an AR(1) with known variance,

$$x_t = \rho x_{t-1} + \varepsilon_t,$$

and suppose the error terms are i.i.d. normal random variables. Then,

$$\ln f(x_t | x_{t-1}, x_{t-2}, \ldots; \rho) = \text{const.} - \frac{\varepsilon_t^2}{2\sigma^2} = \text{const.} - \frac{(x_t - \rho x_{t-1})^2}{2\sigma^2}$$

and the score is

$$\frac{\partial \ln f(x_t | x_{t-1}, x_{t-2} \ldots; \rho)}{\partial \rho} = \frac{(x_t - \rho x_{t-1}) x_{t-1}}{\sigma^2}.$$

The first-order condition for maximizing likelihood is

$$\frac{1}{T}\sum_{t=1}^{T}(x_t - \rho x_{t-1})x_{t-1} = 0.$$

This expression is a moment condition, and you will recognize it as the OLS estimator of ρ, which we have already regarded as a case of GMM.

The example shows another property of scores: *The scores should be unforecastable.* In the example,

$$E_{t-1}\left[\frac{(x_t - \rho x_{t-1})x_{t-1}}{\sigma^2}\right] = E_{t-1}\left[\frac{\varepsilon_t x_{t-1}}{\sigma^2}\right] = 0. \tag{14.8}$$

Intuitively, if we used a combination of the x variables $E(h(x_t, x_{t-1}, \dots)) = 0$ that was predictable, we could form another moment—an instrument—that described the predictability of the h variable and use that moment to get more information about the parameters. To prove this property more generally, start with the fact that $f(x_t|x_{t-1}, x_{t-2}, \dots; \theta)$ is a conditional density and therefore must integrate to one,

$$1 = \int f(x_t|x_{t-1}, x_{t-2}, \dots; \theta)\, dx_t,$$

$$0 = \int \frac{\partial f(x_t|x_{t-1}, x_{t-2}, \dots; \theta)}{\partial \theta}\, dx_t,$$

$$0 = \int \frac{\partial \ln f(x_t|x_{t-1}, x_{t-2}, \dots; \theta)}{\partial \theta} f(x_t|x_{t-1}, x_{t-2}, \dots; \theta)\, dx_t,$$

$$0 = E_{t-1}\left[\frac{\partial \ln f(x_t|x_{t-1}, x_{t-2}, \dots; \theta)}{\partial \theta}\right].$$

Furthermore, as you might expect, *the GMM distribution theory formulas give the same result as the ML distribution,* i.e., the information matrix is the asymptotic variance-covariance matrix. To show this fact, apply the GMM distribution theory (11.2) to (14.6). The derivative matrix is

$$d = \frac{\partial g_T(\theta)}{\partial \theta'} = \frac{1}{T}\sum_{i=1}^{T}\frac{\partial^2 \ln f(x_t|x_{t-1}, x_{t-2}, \dots; \theta)}{\partial \theta\, \partial \theta'} = \mathcal{I}.$$

This is the second derivative expression of the information matrix. The S matrix is

$$E\left[\frac{\partial \ln f(x_t|x_{t-1}, x_{t-2}, \dots; \theta)}{\partial \theta}\frac{\partial \ln f(x_t|x_{t-1}, x_{t-2}, \dots; \theta)'}{\partial \theta}\right] = \mathcal{I}.$$

The lead and lag terms in S are all zero since we showed above that scores should be unforecastable. This is the outer product definition of the information matrix. There is no a matrix, since the moments themselves are set to zero. The GMM asymptotic distribution of $\hat{\theta}$ is therefore

$$\sqrt{T}(\hat{\theta} - \theta) \to \mathcal{N}\left[0, \; d^{-1}Sd^{-1\prime}\right] = \mathcal{N}\left[0, \; \mathcal{I}^{-1}\right].$$

We recover the inverse information matrix, as specified by the ML asymptotic distribution theory.

14.3 When Factors Are Returns, ML Prescribes a Time-Series Regression

> I add to the economic model $E(R^e) = \beta E(f)$ a statistical assumption that the regression errors are independent over time and independent of the factors. ML then prescribes a time-series regression with no constant. To prescribe a time-series regression with a constant, we drop the model prediction $\alpha = 0$. I show how the information matrix gives the same result as the OLS standard errors.

Given a linear factor model whose factors are also returns, as with the CAPM, ML prescribes a time-series regression test. To keep notation simple, I again treat a single factor f. The economic model is

$$E(R^e) = \beta E(f). \tag{14.9}$$

R^e is an $N \times 1$ vector of test assets, and β is an $N \times 1$ vector of regression coefficients of these assets on the factor (the market return R^{em} in the case of the CAPM).

To apply maximum likelihood, we need to add an explicit statistical model that fully describes the joint distribution of the data. I assume that the market return and regression errors are i.i.d. normal, i.e.,

$$R^e_t = \alpha + \beta f_t + \varepsilon_t, \tag{14.10}$$

$$f_t = E(f) + u_t,$$

$$\begin{bmatrix} \varepsilon_t \\ u_t \end{bmatrix} \sim \mathcal{N}\left(\begin{bmatrix} 0 \\ 0 \end{bmatrix}, \begin{bmatrix} \Sigma & 0 \\ 0 & \sigma_u^2 \end{bmatrix} \right).$$

(We can get by with nonnormal factors, but the notation will be messier.) Equation (14.10) has no content other than normality. The zero correlation between u_t and ε_t identifies β as a regression coefficient. You can just write R^e, R^{em} as a general bivariate normal, and you will get the same results.

The economic model (14.9) implies restrictions on this statistical model. Taking expectations of (14.10), the CAPM implies that the intercepts α should all be zero. Again, this is also the only restriction that the CAPM places on the statistical model (14.10).

The most principled way to apply maximum likelihood is to impose the null hypothesis throughout. Thus, we write the likelihood function imposing $\alpha = 0$. To construct the likelihood function, we reduce the statistical model to independent error terms, and then add their log probability densities to get the likelihood function:

$$\mathcal{L} = (\text{const.}) - \frac{1}{2}\sum_{t=1}^{T}(R_t^e - \beta f_t)'\Sigma^{-1}(R_t^e - \beta f_t) - \frac{1}{2}\sum_{t=1}^{T}\frac{(f_t - E(f))^2}{\sigma_u^2}.$$

The estimates follow from the first-order conditions,

$$\frac{\partial\mathcal{L}}{\partial\beta} = \Sigma^{-1}\sum_{t=1}^{T}(R_t^e - \beta f_t)f_t = 0 \;\Rightarrow\; \hat{\beta} = \left(\sum_{t=1}^{T}f_t^2\right)^{-1}\sum_{t=1}^{T}R_t^e f_t,$$

$$\frac{\partial\mathcal{L}}{\partial E(f)} = \frac{1}{\sigma_u^2}\sum_{t=1}^{T}(f_t - E(f)) = 0 \;\Rightarrow\; \widehat{E(f)} = \hat{\lambda} = \frac{1}{T}\sum_{t=1}^{T}f_t.$$

($\partial\mathcal{L}/\partial\Sigma$ and $\partial\mathcal{L}/\partial\sigma^2$ also produce ML estimates of the covariance matrices, which turn out to be the standard averages of squared residuals.)

The ML estimate of β is the OLS regression *without* a constant. The null hypothesis says the constant is zero, and the ML estimator uses that fact to avoid estimating a constant. Since the factor risk premium is equal to the expected value of the factor, it is not too surprising that the λ estimate is equal to the sample average of the factor.

We know that the ML distribution theory must give the same result as the GMM distribution theory which we already derived in Section 12.1, but it is worth seeing it explicitly. The asymptotic standard errors follow from either estimate of the information matrix, for example,

$$\frac{\partial^2\mathcal{L}}{\partial\beta\,\partial\beta'} = -\Sigma^{-1}\sum_{t=1}^{T}f_t^2 = 0.$$

Thus,

$$\text{cov}(\hat{\beta}) = \frac{1}{T}\frac{1}{E(f^2)}\Sigma = \frac{1}{T}\frac{1}{E(f)^2 + \sigma^2(f)}\Sigma. \qquad (14.11)$$

This is the standard OLS formula.

We also want pricing error measurements, standard errors, and tests. We can apply maximum likelihood to estimate an unconstrained model, containing intercepts, and then use Wald tests (estimate/standard error) to test the restriction that the intercepts are zero. We can also use the unconstrained model to run the likelihood ratio test. The unconstrained likelihood function is

$$\mathcal{L} = (\text{const.}) - \frac{1}{2}\sum_{t=1}^{T}(R_t^e - \alpha - \beta f_t)'\Sigma^{-1}(R_t^e - \alpha - \beta f_t) + \cdots.$$

(I ignore the term in the factor, since it will again just tell us to use the sample mean to estimate the factor risk premium.)

The estimates are now

$$\frac{\partial\mathcal{L}}{\partial\alpha} = \Sigma^{-1}\sum_{t=1}^{T}(R_t^e - \alpha - \beta f_t) = 0 \;\Rightarrow\; \hat{\alpha} = E_T(R_t^e) - \hat{\beta}E_T(f_t),$$

$$\frac{\partial\mathcal{L}}{\partial\beta} = \Sigma^{-1}\sum_{t=1}^{T}(R_t^e - \alpha - \beta f_t)f_t = 0 \Rightarrow \hat{\beta} = \frac{\text{cov}_T(R_t^e, f_t)}{\sigma_T^2(f_t)}.$$

Unsurprisingly, the unconstrained maximum likelihood estimates of α and β are the OLS estimates, with a constant.

The inverse of the information matrix gives the asymptotic distribution of these estimates. Since they are just OLS estimates, we are going to get the OLS standard errors, but it is worth seeing it come out of ML:

$$-\left[\frac{\partial^2\mathcal{L}}{\partial\begin{bmatrix}\alpha\\\beta\end{bmatrix}\partial[\alpha\ \beta]}\right]^{-1} = \begin{bmatrix}\Sigma^{-1} & \Sigma^{-1}E(f)\\\Sigma^{-1}E(f) & \Sigma^{-1}E(f^2)\end{bmatrix}^{-1}$$

$$= \frac{1}{\sigma^2(f)}\begin{bmatrix}E(f^2) & E(f)\\E(f) & 1\end{bmatrix}\otimes\Sigma.$$

The covariance matrices of $\hat{\alpha}$ and $\hat{\beta}$ are thus

$$\text{cov}(\hat{\alpha}) = \frac{1}{T}\left[1 + \left(\frac{E(f)}{\sigma(f)}\right)^2\right]\Sigma,$$

$$\text{cov}(\hat{\beta}) = \frac{1}{T}\frac{1}{\sigma^2(f)}\Sigma.$$

(14.12)

These are just the usual OLS standard errors, which we derived in Section 12.1 as a special case of GMM standard errors for the OLS time-series regressions when errors are uncorrelated over time and independent of the factors, or by specializing $\sigma^2(X'X)^{-1}$.

You cannot just invert $\partial^2 \mathcal{L} / \partial \alpha \, \partial \alpha'$ to find the covariance of $\hat{\alpha}$. That attempt would give just Σ as the covariance matrix of $\hat{\alpha}$, which would be wrong. You have to invert the entire information matrix to get the standard error of any parameter. Otherwise, you are ignoring the effect that estimating β has on the distribution of $\hat{\alpha}$. In fact, what I presented is really wrong, since we also must estimate Σ. However, it turns out that $\widehat{\Sigma}$ is independent of $\hat{\alpha}$ and $\hat{\beta}$—the information matrix is block-diagonal—so the top left two elements of the true inverse information matrix are the same as I have written here.

The variance of $\hat{\beta}$ in (14.12) is larger than it was in (14.11) when we imposed the null of no constant. True, constrained ML uses all the information it can to produce efficient estimates—estimates with the smallest possible covariance matrix. The ratio of the two formulas is equal to the familiar term $1 + E(f)^2/\sigma^2(f)$. In annual data for the CAPM, $\sigma(R^{em}) = 16\%$, $E(R^{em}) = 8\%$, means that unrestricted estimate (14.12) has a variance 25% larger than the restricted estimate (14.11), so the gain in efficiency can be important. In monthly data, however, the gain is smaller since variance and mean both scale with the horizon.

We can also view this fact as a warning: ML will ruthlessly exploit the null hypothesis and do things like running regressions without a constant in order to get any small improvement in efficiency.

We can use these covariance matrices to construct a Wald (estimate/standard error) test of the restriction of the model that the alphas are all zero,

$$T\left(1 + \left(\frac{E(f)}{\sigma(f)}\right)^2\right)^{-1} \hat{\alpha}' \Sigma^{-1} \hat{\alpha} \sim \chi_N^2. \tag{14.13}$$

Again, we already derived this χ^2 test in (12.3), and its finite sample F counterpart, the GRS F test (12.4).

The other test of the restrictions is the likelihood ratio test (14.5). Quite generally, likelihood ratio tests are asymptotically equivalent to Wald tests, and so give the same result.

14.4 When Factors Are Not Excess Returns, ML Prescribes a Cross-Sectional Regression

If the factors are not returns, we do not have a choice between time-series and cross-sectional regression, since the intercepts are not zero. As you might suspect, ML prescribes a cross-sectional regression in this case.

The factor model, expressed in expected return-beta form, is

$$E(R^{ei}) = \alpha_i + \beta_i'\lambda, \qquad i = 1, 2, \ldots, N. \qquad (14.14)$$

The betas are defined from time-series regressions

$$R_t^{ei} = a_i + \beta_i' f_t + \varepsilon_t^i. \qquad (14.15)$$

The intercepts a_i in the time-series regressions need not be zero, since the model does not apply to the factors. They are not unrestricted, however. Taking expectations of the time-series regression (14.15) and comparing it to (14.14) (as we did to derive the restriction $\alpha = 0$ for the time-series regression), the restriction $\alpha = 0$ implies

$$a_i = \beta_i'\big(\lambda - E(f_t)\big). \qquad (14.16)$$

Plugging into (14.15), the time-series regressions must be of the restricted form

$$R_t^{ei} = \beta_i'\lambda + \beta_i'[f_t - E(f_t)] + \varepsilon_t^i. \qquad (14.17)$$

In this form, you can see that $\beta_i'\lambda$ determines the mean return. Since there are fewer factors than returns, this is a restriction on the regression (14.17).

Stack assets $i = 1, 2, \ldots, N$ to a vector, and introduce the auxiliary statistical model that the errors and factors are i.i.d. normal and uncorrelated with each other. Then, the restricted model is

$$R_t^e = B\lambda + B[f_t - E(f_t)] + \varepsilon_t,$$
$$f_t = E(f) + u_t,$$
$$\begin{bmatrix} \varepsilon_t \\ u_t \end{bmatrix} \sim \mathcal{N}\left(0, \begin{bmatrix} \Sigma & 0 \\ 0 & V \end{bmatrix}\right),$$

where B denotes a $N \times K$ matrix of regression coefficients of the N assets on the K factors. The likelihood function is

$$\mathcal{L} = (\text{const.}) - \frac{1}{2}\sum_{t=1}^{T} \varepsilon_t'\Sigma^{-1}\varepsilon_t - \frac{1}{2}\sum_{t=1}^{T} u_t'V^{-1}u_t,$$
$$\varepsilon_t = R_t^e - B[\lambda + f_t - E(f)], \qquad u_t = f_t - E(f).$$

Maximizing the likelihood function,

$$\frac{\partial \mathcal{L}}{\partial E(f)} : 0 = \sum_{t=1}^{T} B'\Sigma^{-1}\left(R_t^e - B[\lambda + f_t - E(f)]\right) + \sum_{t=1}^{T} V^{-1}(f_t - E(f)),$$

$$\frac{\partial \mathcal{L}}{\partial \lambda} : 0 = B'\sum_{t=1}^{T} \Sigma^{-1}\left(R_t^e - B[\lambda + f_t - E(f)]\right).$$

The solution to this pair of equations is

$$\widehat{E(f)} = E_T(f_t), \tag{14.18}$$

$$\hat{\lambda} = \left(B'\Sigma^{-1}B\right)^{-1}B'\Sigma^{-1}E_T\left(R_t^e\right). \tag{14.19}$$

The maximum likelihood estimate of the factor risk premium is a GLS cross-sectional regression of average returns on betas.

The maximum likelihood estimates of the regression coefficients B are again not the same as the standard OLS formulas. Again, ML imposes the null to improve efficiency:

$$\frac{\partial \mathcal{L}}{\partial B} : \sum_{t=1}^{T}\Sigma^{-1}\left(R_t^e - B[\lambda + f_t - E(f)]\right)[\lambda + f_t - E(f)]' = 0,$$

$$\widehat{B} = \sum_{t=1}^{T} R_t^e[f_t + \lambda - E(f)]'\left(\sum_{t=1}^{T}[f_t + \lambda - E(f)][f_t + \lambda - E(f)]'\right)^{-1}. \tag{14.20}$$

This is true, even though the B are defined in the theory as population regression coefficients. (The matrix notation hides a lot here! If you want to rederive these formulas, it is helpful to start with scalar parameters, e.g., B_{ij}, and to think of it as $\partial \mathcal{L}/\partial\theta = \sum_{t=1}^{T}(\partial\mathcal{L}/\partial\varepsilon_t)'\partial\varepsilon_t/\partial\theta$.) Therefore, to really implement ML, you have to solve (14.19) and (14.20) simultaneously for $\hat{\lambda}$, $\widehat{B}$, along with $\widehat{\Sigma}$ whose ML estimate is the usual second-moment matrix of the residuals. This can usually be done iteratively: Start with OLS $\widehat{B}$, run an OLS cross-sectional regression for $\hat{\lambda}$, form $\widetilde{\Sigma}$, and iterate.

Problems—Chapter 14

1. Why do we use restricted ML when the factor is a return, but unrestricted ML when the factor is not a return? To see why, try to formulate a ML estimator based on an unrestricted regression when factors are not returns, equation (12.1). Add pricing errors α_i to the regression as we did for the unrestricted regression in the case that factors are returns, and then find ML estimators for B, λ, α, $E(f)$. (Treat V and Σ as known to make the problem easier.)

2. Instead of writing a regression, build up the ML for the CAPM a little more formally. Write the statistical model as just the assumption that individual returns and the market return are jointly normal,

$$
\begin{bmatrix} R^e \\ R^{em} \end{bmatrix} \sim \mathcal{N}\left(\begin{bmatrix} E(R^e) \\ E(R^{em}) \end{bmatrix}, \begin{bmatrix} \Sigma & \text{cov}(R^{em}, R^{e\prime}) \\ \text{cov}(R^{em}, R^e) & \sigma_m^2 \end{bmatrix} \right).
$$

The model's restriction is

$$
E(R^e) = \gamma \, \text{cov}(R^{em}, R^e).
$$

Estimate γ and show that this is the same time-series estimator as we derived by presupposing a regression.

15

Time-Series, Cross-Section, and GMM/DF Tests of Linear Factor Models

THE GMM/discount factor, time-series, and cross-sectional regression procedures and distribution theory are similar, but not identical. Cross-sectional regressions on betas are not the same thing as cross-sectional regressions on second moments. Cross-sectional regressions weighted by the residual covariance matrix are not the same thing as cross-sectional regressions weighted by the spectral density matrix.

GLS cross-sectional regressions and second-stage GMM have a theoretical efficiency advantage over OLS cross-sectional regressions and first-stage GMM, but how important is this advantage, and is it outweighed by worse finite-sample performance?

Finally, and perhaps most importantly, the GMM/discount factor approach is still a "new" procedure. Many authors still do not trust it. It is important to verify that it produces similar results and well-behaved test statistics in the setups of the classic regression tests.

To address these questions, I first apply the various methods to a classic empirical question. How do time-series regression, cross-sectional regression, and GMM/stochastic discount factor compare when applied to a test of the CAPM on CRSP size portfolios? I find that three methods produce almost exactly the same results for this classic exercise. They produce almost exactly the same estimates, standard errors, t-statistics, and χ^2 statistics that the pricing errors are jointly zero.

Then I conduct a Monte Carlo and bootstrap evaluation. Again, I find little difference between the methods. The estimates, standard errors, and size and power of tests are almost identical across methods.

The bootstrap does reveal that the traditional i.i.d. assumption generates χ^2 statistics with about $1/2$ the correct size—they reject half as often as they should under the null. Simple GMM corrections to the distribution theory repair this size defect. Also, you can ruin any estimate and test

277

with a bad spectral density matrix estimate. I try an estimate with 24 lags and no Newey–West weights. It is singular in the data sample and many Monte Carlo replications. Interestingly, this singularity has minor effects on standard errors, but causes disasters when you use the spectral density matrix to weight a second-stage GMM.

I also find that second-stage "efficient" GMM is only very slightly more efficient than first-stage GMM, but is somewhat less robust; it is more sensitive to the poor spectral density matrix and its asymptotic standard errors can be misleading. As OLS is often better than GLS, despite the theoretical efficiency advantage of GLS, first-stage GMM may be better than second-stage GMM in many applications.

This section should give comfort that the apparently "new" GMM/discount factor formulation is almost exactly the same as traditional methods in the traditional setup. There is a widespread impression that GMM has difficulty in small samples. The literature on the small-sample properties of GMM (for example, Ferson and Foerster [1994], Fuhrer, Moore, and Schuh [1995]) naturally tries hard setups, with highly nonlinear models, highly persistent and heteroskedastic errors, important conditioning information, potentially weak instruments, and so forth. Nobody would write a paper trying GMM in a simple situation such as this one, correctly foreseeing that the answer would not be very interesting. Unfortunately, many readers take from this literature a mistaken impression that GMM *always* has difficulty in finite samples, even in very standard setups. This is not the case.

Jagannathan and Wang (2000) also compare the GMM/discount factor approach to classic regression tests. They show analytically that the parameter estimates, standard errors, and χ^2 statistics are asymptotically identical to those of an expected return-beta cross-sectional regression when the factor is not a return.

15.1 Three Approaches to the CAPM in Size Portfolios

The time-series approach sends the expected return-beta line through the market return, ignoring other assets. The OLS cross-sectional regression minimizes the sum of squared pricing errors, so allows some market pricing error to fit other assets better. The GLS cross-sectional regression weights pricing errors by the residual covariance matrix, so reduces to the time-series regression when the factor is a return and is included in the test assets.

The GMM/discount factor estimates, standard errors, and χ^2 statistics are very close to time-series and cross-sectional regression estimates in this classic setup.

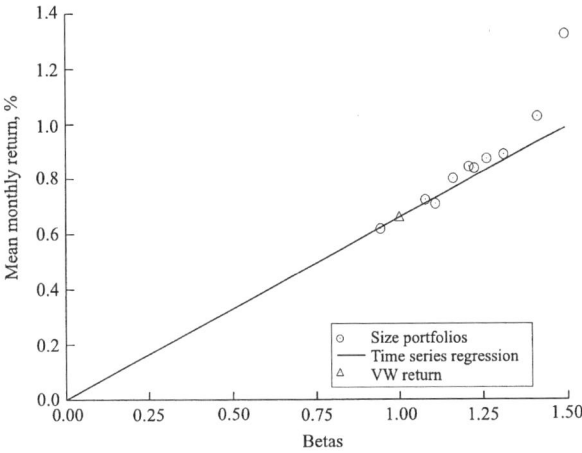

Figure 15.1. *Average excess returns vs. betas on CRSP size portfolios, 1926–1998. The line gives the predicted average return from the time-series regression, $E(R^e) = \beta E(R^{em})$.*

Time Series and Cross Section
Figures 15.1 and 15.2 illustrate the difference between time-series and cross-sectional regressions, in an evaluation of the CAPM on monthly size portfolios.

Figure 15.1 presents the time-series regression. The time-series regression estimates the factor risk premium from the average of the factor,

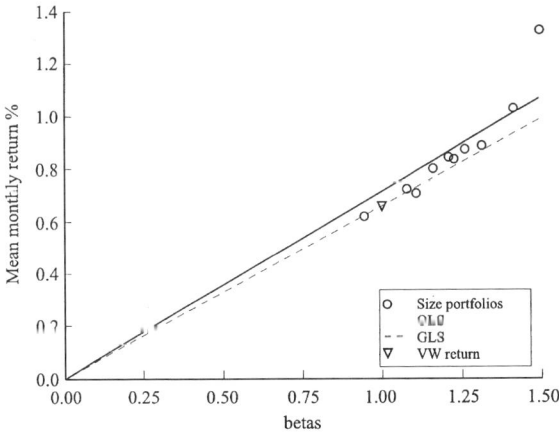

Figure 15.2. *Average excess returns vs. betas of CRSP size portfolios, 1926–1998, and the fit of cross-sectional regressions.*

ignoring any information in the other assets, $\hat{\lambda} = E_T(R^{em})$. Thus, a time-series regression draws the expected return-beta line across assets by making it fit precisely on two points, the market return and the risk-free rate—the market and risk-free rate have zero estimated pricing error in every sample. (The far right portfolios are the smallest firm portfolios, and their positive pricing errors are the small firm anomaly—this data set is the first serious *failure* of the CAPM. I come back to the substantive issue in Chapter 20.)

The time-series regression is the ML estimator in this case, since the factor is a return. As we saw in Section 12.2, when we write $R^e = a + \beta f_t + \varepsilon_t$ and ε independent of f, we tell ML that a sample of returns already includes the same *sample* of the factor, plus extra noise. Thus, the sample of test asset returns cannot possibly tell ML anything more than the sample of the factor alone about the mean of the factor. Second, we tell ML that the factor risk premium equals the mean of the factor, so it may not consider the possibility that the two quantities are different in trying to match the data.

The OLS cross-sectional quantities regression in Figure 15.2 draws the expected return-beta line by minimizing the squared pricing error across all assets. Therefore, it allows some pricing error for the market return, if by doing so the pricing errors on other assets can be reduced. Thus, the OLS cross-sectional regression gives some pricing error to the market return in order to lower the pricing errors of the other portfolios.

When the factor is not also a return, ML prescribes a cross-sectional regression. ML still ignores anything but the factor data in estimating the mean of the factor—$\widehat{E(f)} = E_T(f_t)$. However, ML is now allowed to use a different parameter for the factor risk premium that fits average returns to betas, which it does by cross-sectional regression. However, ML is a GLS cross-sectional regression, not an OLS cross-sectional regression. The GLS cross-sectional regression in Figure 15.2 is almost exactly identical to the time-series regression result—it passes right through the origin and the market return, ignoring all the other pricing errors.

The GLS cross-sectional regression

$$\hat{\lambda} = \left(\beta'\Sigma^{-1}\beta\right)^{-1}\beta'\Sigma^{-1}E_T(R^e)$$

weights the various portfolios by the inverse of the residual covariance matrix Σ. As we saw in Section 12.2, if we include the market return as a test asset, it obviously has no residual variance—$R_t^{em} = 0 + 1 \times R_t^{em} + 0$—so the GLS estimate pays exclusive attention to it in fitting the market line. The same thing happens if the test assets span the factors—if a linear combination of the test assets is equal to the factor and hence has no residual variance. The size portfolios nearly span the market return, so the GLS cross-sectional regression is visually indistinguishable from the time-series regression in this case.

If we allow a free constant in the OLS cross-sectional regression, thus allowing a pricing error for the risk-free rate, you can see from Figure 15.2 that the OLS cross-sectional regression line will fit the size portfolios even better, though allowing a pricing error in the risk-free rate as well as the market return. However, a free intercept in an OLS regression on excess returns puts no weight at all on the intercept pricing error. It is a better idea to include the risk-free rate as a test asset, either directly by doing the whole thing in levels of returns rather than excess returns or by adding $E(R^e) = 0, \beta = 0$ to the cross-sectional regression. The GLS cross-sectional regression will notice that the T-bill rate has no residual variance and so will send the line right through the origin, as it does for the market return.

GMM/Discount Factor First and Second Stage
Figure 15.3 illustrates the GMM/discount factor estimate with the same data. The horizontal axis is the second moment of returns and factors rather than beta, but you would not know it from the placement of the dots. (The estimates are calculated using the formulas from Section 13.2.) The first-stage estimate is an OLS cross-sectional regression of average returns on second moments. It minimizes the sum of squared pricing errors, and so produces pricing errors almost exactly equal to those of the OLS cross-sectional regression of returns on betas. The second-stage

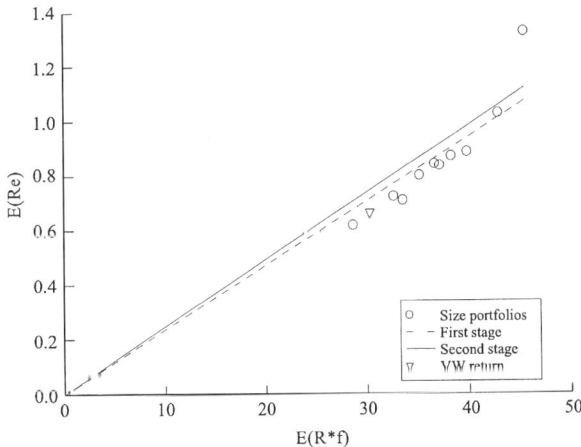

Figure 15.3. *Average excess return vs. predicted value of 10 CRSP size portfolios, 1926–1998, based on GMM/SDF estimate. The model predicts $E(R^e) = bE(R^e R^{em})$. The second-stage estimate of b uses a spectral density estimate with zero lags.*

estimate minimizes pricing errors weighted by the spectral density matrix. The spectral density matrix is not the same as the residual covariance matrix, so the second-stage GMM does not go through the market portfolio as does the GLS cross-sectional regression. In fact, the slope of the line is slightly higher for the second-stage estimate.

(The spectral density matrix of the discount factor formulation does not reduce to the residual covariance matrix even if we assume the regression model, the asset pricing model, is true, and factors and residuals are i.i.d. normal. In particular, when the market is a test asset, the GLS cross-sectional regression focuses all attention on the market portfolio but the second-stage GMM/DF does not do so. The parameter b is related to λ by $b = \lambda / E(R^{em2})$. The other assets still are useful in determining the parameter b, even though, given the market return and the regression model $R_t^{ei} = \beta_i R_t^{em} + \varepsilon_t^i$, seeing the other assets does help to determine the mean of the market return.)

Overall, the figures do not suggest any strong reason to prefer first- and second-stage GMM/discount factor, time-series, OLS, or GLS cross-sectional regression in this standard model and data set. The results are affected by the choice of method. In particular, the size of the small-firm anomaly is substantially affected by how one draws the market line. But the graphs and analysis do not strongly suggest that any method is better than any other for purposes other than fishing for the answer one wants.

Parameter Estimates, Standard Errors, and Tests
Table 15.1 presents the parameter estimates and standard errors from time-series, cross-section, and GMM/discount factor approach in the CAPM size portfolio test illustrated by Figures 15.1 and 15.2. The main

Table 15.1. *Parameter estimates and standard errors*

	Beta model λ			GMM/DF b		
	Time-Series	Cross-section OLS	GLS	1st stage	2nd stage *Estimate*	Standard Error
Estimate	*0.66*	*0.71*	*0.66*	*2.35*		
i.i.d.	0.18 (3.67)	0.20 (3.55)	0.18 (3.67)			
0 lags	0.18 (3.67)	0.19 (3.74)	0.18 (3.67)	0.63 (3.73)	*2.46*	0.61 (4.03)
3 lags, NW	0.20 (3.30)	0.21 (3.38)	0.20 (3.30)	0.69 (3.41)	*2.39*	0.64 (3.73)
24 lags	0.16 (4.13)	0.16 (4.44)	0.16 (4.13)	1.00 (2.35)	*2.15*	0.69 (3.12)

Estimates are shown in italic, standard errors in regular type, and t-statistics in parentheses. The time-series estimate is the mean market return in percent per month. The cross-sectional estimate is the slope coefficient λ in $E(R^e) = \beta\lambda$. The GMM estimate is the parameter b in $E(R^e) = E(R^e f)b$. CRSP monthly data 1926–1998. "Lags" gives the number of lags in the spectral density matrix. "NW" uses Newey–West weighting in the spectral density matrix.

parameter to be estimated is the slope of the lines in the above figures, the market price of risk λ in the expected return-beta model and the relation between mean returns and second moments b in the stochastic discount factor model. The big point of Table 15.1 is that the GMM/discount factor estimate and standard errors behave very similarly to the traditional estimates and standard errors.

The rows compare results with various methods of calculating the spectral density matrix. The row marked "Independent and identical distribution" imposes no serial correlation and regression errors independent of right-hand variables, and is identical to the maximum likelihood based formulas. The 0 lag estimate allows conditional heteroskedasticity, but no times-series correlation of residuals. The 3 lag, Newey–West estimate is a sensible correction for short-order autocorrelation. I include the 24 lag spectral density matrix to show how things can go wrong if you use a ridiculous spectral density matrix.

The OLS cross-sectional estimate of the beta model 0.71 is a little higher than the mean market return 0.66, in order to better fit all of the assets, as seen in Figure 15.2. The GLS cross-sectional estimate is almost exactly the same as the mean market return, and the GLS standard errors are almost exactly the same as the time-series standard errors. The Shanken correction for generated regressors is very important to standard errors of the cross-sectional regressions. Without the Σ_f term in the standard deviation of λ (12.12) and (12.16) (i.e., treating the β as fixed right-hand variables), the standard errors come out to 0.07 for OLS and 0.00 for GLS. These values gave far less than the correct 0.20 and 0.18 shown in the table, and far less than $\sigma/\sqrt{T}$.

The b estimates are not directly comparable to the risk premium estimates, but it is easy to translate their units. Applying the discount factor model with normalization $a = 1$ to the market return itself,

$$b = \frac{E\left(R^{em}\right)}{E\left(R^{em2}\right)}.$$

With $E(R^{em}) = 0.66\%$ and $\sigma(R^{em}) = 5.47\%$, we have $100 \times b = 100(0.66)/(0.66^2 + 5.47^2) = 2.17$. The entries in Table 15.1 are close to this magnitude. Most are slightly larger, as is the OLS cross-sectional regression, in order to better fit the size portfolios. The t-statistics are quite close across methods.

The second-stage GMM/DF estimates (as well as standard errors) depend on which spectral density weighting matrix is used as a weighting matrix. The results are quite similar for all the sensible spectral density estimates. The 24 lag spectral density matrix starts to produce unusual estimates. This spectral density estimate will cause lots of problems below.

Table 15.2. χ^2 *tests that all pricing errors are jointly equal to zero*

	Time series		Cross section		GMM/DF	
	$\chi^2_{(10)}$	% p-value	$\chi^2_{(9)}$	% p-value	$\chi^2_{(9)}$	% p-value
i.i.d.	8.5	58	8.5	49		
GRS F	0.8	59				
0 lags	10.5	40	10.6	31	10.5	31
3 lags NW	11.0	36	11.1	27	11.1	27
24 lags	−432	−100	7.6	57	7.7	57

Table 15.2 presents the χ^2 and F statistics that test whether the pricing errors are jointly significant. The OLS and GLS cross-sectional regression, and the first- and second-stage GMM/discount factor tests give exactly the same χ^2 statistic, though the individual pricing errors and covariance matrix are not the same, so I do not present them separately. The big point of Table 15.2 is that the GMM/discount factor method gives almost exactly the same result as the cross-sectional regression.

For the time-series regression, the GRS F test gives almost exactly the same rejection probability as does the asymptotic χ^2 test. Apparently, the advantages of a statistic that is valid in finite samples is not that important in this data set. The χ^2 tests for the time-series case without the i.i.d. assumption are a bit more conservative, with 30–40% p value rather than almost 60%. However, this difference is not large. The one exception is the χ^2 test using 24 lags and no weights in the spectral density matrix. That matrix turns out not to be positive definite in this sample, with disastrous results for the χ^2 statistic.

(Somewhat surprisingly, the CAPM is not rejected. This is because the small-firm effect vanishes in the latter part of the sample. I discuss this fact further in Chapter 20. See in particular Figure 20.14.)

Looking across the rows, the χ^2 statistic is almost exactly the same for each method. The cross-sectional regression and GMM/DF estimate have one lower degree of freedom (the market premium is estimated from the cross section rather than from the market return), and so show slightly greater rejection probabilities. For a given spectral density estimation technique, the cross-sectional regression and the GMM/DF approach give almost exactly the same χ^2 values and rejection probabilities. The 24 lag spectral density matrix is a disaster as usual. In this case, it is a greater disaster for the time-series test than for the cross section or GMM/discount factor test. It turns out not to be positive definite, so the sample pricing errors produce a nonsensical negative value of $\hat{\alpha}' \text{cov}(\hat{\alpha})^{-1} \hat{\alpha}$.

15.2 Monte Carlo and Bootstrap

The parameter distribution for the time-series regression estimate is quite similar to that from the GMM/discount factor estimate.

The size and power of χ^2 test statistics are nearly identical for the time-series regression test and the GMM/discount factor test.

A bad spectral density matrix can ruin either time-series or GMM/discount factor estimates and tests.

There is enough serial correlation and heteroskedasticity in the data that conventional i.i.d. formulas produce test statistics with about 1/2 the correct size. If you want to do classic regression tests, you should correct the distribution theory rather than use the ML i.i.d. distributions.

Econometrics is not just about sensible point estimates, it is about sampling variability of those estimates, and whether standard error formulas correctly capture that sampling variability. How well do the various standard error and test statistic formulas capture the true sampling distribution of the estimates? To answer this question I conduct two Monte Carlos and two bootstraps. I conduct one each under the null that the CAPM is correct, to study size, and one each under the alternative that the CAPM is false, to study power.

The Monte Carlo experiments follow the standard ML assumption that returns and factors are i.i.d. normally distributed, and the factors and residuals are independent as well as uncorrelated. I generate artificial samples of the market return from an i.i.d. normal, using the sample mean and variance of the value-weighted return. I then generate artificial size decile returns under the null by $R_t^{ei} = 0 + \beta_i R_t^{em} + \varepsilon_{it}$, using the sample residual covariance matrix Σ to draw i.i.d. normal residuals ε_{it} and the sample regression coefficients β_i. To generate data under the alternative, I add the sample α_i. I draw 5000 artificial samples. I try a long sample of 876 months, matching the CRSP sample analyzed above. I also draw a short sample of 240 months or 20 years, which is about as short as one should dare try to test a factor model.

The bootstraps check whether nonnormalities, autocorrelation, heteroskedasticity, and nonindependence of factors and residuals matter to the sampling distribution in this data set. I do a block-bootstrap, resampling the data in groups of three months with replacement, to preserve the short-order autocorrelation and persistent heteroskedasticity in the data. To impose the CAPM, I draw the market return and residuals in the time-series regression, and then compute artificial data on decile portfolio returns by $R_t^{ei} = 0 + \beta_i R_t^{em} + \varepsilon_{it}$. To study the alternative, I simply redraw all the data in groups of three. Of course, the actual data may display conditioning information not displayed by this bootstrap, such as predictability and conditional heteroskedasticity based on additional variables such as the dividend/price ratio, lagged squared returns, or implied volatilities.

The first-stage GMM/discount factor and OLS cross-sectional regression are nearly identical in every artificial sample, as the GLS cross-sectional regression is nearly identical to the time-series regression in every sample. Therefore, the important question is to compare the time-series regression—which is ML with i.i.d. normal returns and factors—to the first- and second-stage GMM/DF procedure. For this reason and to save space, I do not include the cross-sectional regressions in the Monte Carlo and bootstrap.

χ^2 Tests

Table 15.3 presents the χ^2 tests of the hypothesis that all pricing errors are zero under the null that the CAPM is true, and Table 15.4 presents the χ^2 tests under the null that the CAPM is false. Each table presents the percentage of the 5000 artificial data sets in which the χ^2 tests rejected the null at the indicated level. The central point of these tables is that the GMM/discount factor test performs almost exactly the same way as the time-series test. Compare the GMM/DF entry to its corresponding time-series entry; they are all nearly identical. Neither the small efficiency advantage of time series versus cross section, nor the difference between betas and second moments seems to make any difference to the sampling distribution.

Start with the Monte Carlo evaluation of the time-series test in Table 15.3. The i.i.d. and 0 lag distributions produce nearly exact rejection probabilities in the long sample and slightly too many (7.5%) rejections in the short sample. Moving down, GMM distributions here correct for things that are not there. This has a small but noticeable effect on the sensible 3 lag test, which rejects slightly too often under this null. Naturally, this is worse for the short sample, but looking across the rows, the

Table 15.3. *Size. Probability of rejection for χ^2 statistics under the null that all pricing errors are zero*

	Monte Carlo						Block-Bootstrap					
	Time series			GMM/DF			Time series			GMM/DF		
Sample size:	240	876		240	876		240	876		240	876	
level (%):	5	5	1	5	5	1	5	5	1	5	5	1
i.i.d.	7.5	6.0	1.1				6.0	2.8	0.6			
0 lags	7.7	6.1	1.1	7.5	6.3	1.0	7.7	4.3	1.0	6.6	3.7	0.9
3 lags, NW	10.7	6.5	1.4	9.7	6.6	1.3	10.5	5.4	1.3	9.5	5.3	1.3
24 lags	25	39	32	25	41	31	23	38	31	24	41	32

Table 15.4. *Power. Probability of rejection for χ^2 statistics under the null that the CAPM is false, and the true means of the decile portfolio returns are equal to their sample means*

	Monte Carlo					Block-Bootstrap				
	Time-Series			GMM/DF		Time-Series			GMM/DF	
Sample size:	240	876		240	876	240	876		240	876
level (%):		5	1		5	1		5	1		5	1
i.i.d.	17	48	26				11	40	18			
0 lags	17	48	26	17	50	27	15	54	28	14	55	29
3 lags, NW	22	49	27	21	51	29	18	57	31	17	59	33
24 lags	29	60	53	29	66	57	27	63	56	29	68	60

time-series and discount factor tests are nearly identical in every case. The variation *across technique* is almost zero, given the spectral density estimate. The 24 lag unweighted spectral density is the usual disaster, rejecting far too often. It is singular in many samples. In the long sample, the 1% tail of this distribution occurs at a χ^2 value of 440 rather than the 23.2 of the $\chi^2_{(10)}$ distribution!

The long-sample block-bootstrap in the right half of the tables shows even in this simple setup how i.i.d. normal assumptions can be misleading. The traditional i.i.d. χ^2 test has *almost half* the correct size—it rejects a 5% test 2.8% of the time, and a 1% test 0.6% of the time. Removing the assumption that returns and factors are independent, going from i.i.d. to 0 lags, brings about half of the size distortion back, while adding one of the sensible autocorrelation corrections does the rest. In each row, the time-series and GMM/DF methods produce almost exactly the same results again. The 24 lag spectral density matrices are a disaster as usual.

Table 15.4 shows the rejection probabilities under the alternative. The most striking feature of the table is that the GMM/discount factor test gives almost exactly the same rejection probability as the time-series test, for each choice of spectral density estimation technique. When there is a difference, the GMM/discount factor test rejects slightly more often. The 24 lag tests reject most often, but this is not surprising given that they reject almost as often under the null.

Parameter Estimates and Standard Errors

Table 15.5 presents the sampling variation of the λ and b estimates. The rows and columns marked $\sigma(\hat{\lambda})$, $\sigma(\hat{b})$, and in italic font, give the variation of the estimated λ or b across the 5000 artificial samples. The remaining rows and columns give the average across samples of the standard errors. The presence of pricing errors has little effect on the estimated b or λ and their standard errors, so I only present results under the null that

Table 15.5. *Monte Carlo and block-bootstrap evaluation of the sampling variability of parameter estimates b and λ*

	Monte Carlo				Block-Bootstrap			
	Time series	GMM/DF			Time series	GMM/DF		
		1st stage	2nd stage $\sigma(\hat{b})$	E(s.e.)		1st stage	2nd stage $\sigma(\hat{b})$	E(s.e.)
$T = 876$:								
$\sigma(\hat{\lambda})$, $\sigma(\hat{b})$	*0.19*	*0.64*			*0.20*	*0.69*		
i.i.d.	0.18				0.18			
0 lags	0.18	0.65	*0.61*	0.60	0.18	0.63	*0.67*	0.60
3 lags NW	0.18	0.65	*0.62*	0.59	0.19	0.67	*0.67*	0.62
24 lags	0.18	0.62	*130*	0.27	0.19	0.66	*1724*	0.24
$T = 240$:								
$\sigma(\hat{\lambda})$, $\sigma(\hat{b})$	*0.35*	*1.25*			*0.37*	*1.40*		
i.i.d.	0.35				0.35			
0 lags	0.35	1.23	*1.24*	1.14	0.35	1.24	*1.45*	1.15
3 lags NW	0.35	1.22	*1.26*	1.11	0.36	1.31	*1.48*	1.14
24 lags	0.29	1.04	*191*	0.69	0.31	1.15	*893*	0.75

The Monte Carlo redraws 5000 artificial data sets of length $T = 876$ from a random normal assuming that the CAPM is true. The block-bootstrap redraws the data in groups of 3 with replacement. The row and columns marked $\sigma(\hat{\lambda})$ and $\sigma(\hat{b})$ and using italic font give the variation across samples of the estimated λ and b. The remaining entries of "time series" "1st stage" and "E(s.e.)" columns in roman font give the average value of the computed standard error of the parameter estimate, where the average is taken over the 5000 samples.

the CAPM is true. The parameters are not directly comparable—the b parameter includes the variance as well as the mean of the factor, and $E_T(R^{em})$ is the natural GMM estimate of the mean market return as it is the time-series estimate of the factor risk premium. Still, it is interesting to know and to compare how well the two methods do at estimating their central parameter.

The central message of this table is that the GMM/DF estimates behave almost exactly as the time-series beta model estimate, and the asymptotic standard error formulas almost exactly capture the sampling variation of the estimates. The second-stage GMM/DF estimate is a little bit more efficient at the cost of slightly misleading standard errors.

Start with the long sample and the first column. All of the standard error formulas give essentially identical and correct results for the time-series estimate. Estimating the sample mean is not rocket science. The first-stage GMM/DF estimator in the second column behaves the same way, except the usually troublesome 24 lag unweighted estimate.

The second-stage GMM/DF estimate in the third and fourth columns uses the inverse spectral density matrix to weight, and so the estimator depends on the choice of spectral density estimate. The sensible spectral density estimates (not 24 lags) produce second-stage estimates that vary less than the first-stage estimates, 0.61–0.62 rather than 0.64. Second-stage GMM is more efficient, meaning that it produces estimates with smaller sampling variation. However, the table shows that the efficiency gain is quite small, so not much is lost if one prefers first-stage OLS estimates. The sensible spectral density estimates produce second-stage standard errors that again almost exactly capture the sampling variation of the estimated parameters.

The 24 lag unweighted estimate produces hugely variable estimates and artificially small standard errors. Using bad or even singular spectral density estimates seems to have a secondary effect on standard error calculations, but using its inverse as a weighting matrix can have a dramatic effect on estimation.

With the block-bootstrap in the right-hand side of Table 15.5, the time-series estimate is slightly more volatile as a result of the slight autocorrelation in the market return. The i.i.d. and zero-lag formulas do not capture this effect, but the GMM standard errors that allow autocorrelation do pick it up. However, this is a very minor effect as there is very little autocorrelation in the market return. The effect is more pronounced in the first-stage GMM/DF estimate, since the smaller firm portfolios depart more from the normal i.i.d. assumption. The true variation is 0.69, but standard errors that ignore autocorrelation only produce 0.63. The standard errors that correct for autocorrelation are nearly exact. In the second-stage GMM/DF, the sensible spectral density estimates again produce slightly more efficient estimates than the first stage, with variation of 0.67 rather than 0.69. This comes at a cost, though, that the asymptotic standard errors are a bit less reliable.

In the shorter sample, we see that standard errors for the mean market return in the time-series column are all quite accurate, except the usual 24 lag case. In the GMM/DF case, we see that the actual sampling variability of the b estimate is no longer smaller for the second-stage. The second-stage estimate is not more efficient in this "small" sample. Furthermore, while the first-stage standard errors are still decently accurate, the second-stage standard errors substantially understate the true sampling variability of the parameter estimate. They represent a hoped-for efficiency that is not present in the small sample. Even in this simple setup, first-stage GMM is clearly a better choice for estimating the central parameter, and hence for examining individual pricing errors and their pattern across assets.

16

Which Method?

THE POINT of GMM/discount factor methods is not a gain in efficiency or simplicity in a traditional setup—linear factor model, i.i.d. normally distributed returns, etc. It is hard to beat the efficiency or simplicity of regression methods in those setups. The promise of the GMM/discount factor approach is its ability to transparently handle nonlinear or otherwise complex models, especially including conditioning information, and that it allows you to circumvent inevitable model misspecifications or simplifications and data problems by keeping the econometrics focused on interesting issues.

The alternative is usually some form of maximum likelihood. This is much harder in most circumstances, since you have to write down a complete statistical model for the joint distribution of your data. Just evaluating, let alone maximizing, the likelihood function is often challenging. Whole series of papers are written on the econometric issues of particular cases, for example how to maximize the likelihood functions of univariate continuous-time models for the short interest rate.

Empirical asset pricing faces an enduring tension between these two philosophies. The choice essentially involves trade-offs between statistical efficiency, the effects of misspecification of both the economic and statistical models, and the clarity and economic interpretability of the results. There are situations in which it is better to trade some small efficiency gains for the robustness of simpler procedures or more easily interpretable moments; OLS can be better than GLS. The central reason is specification errors: the fact that our statistical and economic models are at best quantitative parables. There are other situations in which you may really need to squeeze every last drop out of the data, intuitive moments are statistically very inefficient, and more intensive maximum likelihood approaches are more appropriate.

Unfortunately, the environments are complex, and differ from case to case. We do not have universal theorems from statistical theory or generally applicable Monte Carlo evidence. Specification errors by their nature resist quantitative modeling—if you knew how to model them, they would not be there. We can only think about the lessons of past experiences.

The rest of this chapter collects some thoughts on the choice between ML and a less formal GMM approach, that focuses on economically interesting rather than statistically informative moments, in the context of empirically evaluating asset pricing models.

"ML" vs. "GMM"

The debate is often stated as a choice between "maximum likelihood" and "GMM." This is a bad way to put the issue. ML is a special case of GMM: it suggests a particular choice of moments that are statistically optimal in a well-defined sense. It is all GMM; the issue is the choice of moments. The choice is between moments selected by an auxiliary statistical model, even if completely economically uninterpretable, and moments selected for their economic or data summary interpretation, even if not statistically efficient.

Also, there is no such thing as "the" GMM estimate. GMM is a flexible tool; you can use any a_T matrix and g_T moments that you want to use. Both ML and GMM are tools that a thoughtful researcher can use in learning what the data says about a given asset pricing model, rather than as stone tablets giving precise directions that lead to truth if followed literally. If followed literally and thoughtlessly, both ML and GMM can lead to horrendous results.

Of course, we do not have to pair GMM with the discount factor expression of a model, and ML with the expected return-beta formulation. Many studies pair discount factor expressions of the model with ML, and many others evaluate expected return-beta model by GMM, as I did in Chapter 12 to adjust regression standard errors for non-i.i.d. residuals.

ML is Often Ignored

As we have seen, ML plus the assumption of normal i.i.d. disturbances leads to easily interpretable time-series or cross-sectional regressions, empirical procedures that are close to the economic content of the model. However, asset returns are *not* normally distributed or i.i.d. They have fatter tails than a normal, they are heteroskedastic (times of high and times of low volatility), they are autocorrelated, and predictable from a variety of variables. If one were to take seriously the ML philosophy and its quest for efficiency, one should model these features of returns. The result would be a different likelihood function, and its scores would prescribe different moment conditions than the familiar and intuitive time-series or cross-sectional regressions.

Interestingly, few empirical workers do this. (The exceptions tend to be papers whose primary point is illustration of econometric technique rather than empirical findings.) ML seems to be fine when it suggests easily interpretable regressions; when it suggests something else, people use the regressions anyway.

For example, ML prescribes that one estimate β's *without* a constant. β's are almost universally estimated with a constant. Researchers often run cross-sectional regressions rather than time-series regressions, even when the factors are returns. ML specifies a GLS cross-sectional regression, but many empirical workers use OLS cross-sectional regressions instead, distrusting the GLS weighting matrix. The true ML formulas require one to iterate between betas, covariance matrix, and the cross-sectional regression. Empirical applications usually use the unconstrained estimates of all these quantities. And of course, any of the regression tests continue to be run at all, with ML justifications, despite the fact that returns are not i.i.d. normal. The regressions came first, and the maximum likelihood formalization came later. If we had to assume that returns had a gamma distribution to justify the regressions, it is a sure bet that we would make that "assumption" behind ML instead of the normal i.i.d. assumption!

Researchers must not really believe that their null hypotheses, statistical and economic, are exactly correct. They want estimates and tests that are robust to reasonable model misspecifications. They also want estimates and tests that are easily interpretable, that capture intuitively clear stylized facts in the data, and that relate directly to the economic concepts of the model. Such estimates are persuasive because the reader can see that they are robust.[1] In pursuit of these goals, researchers seem willing to sacrifice some of the efficiency that would obtain if the null economic and statistical models were exactly correct.

ML does not necessarily produce robust or easily interpretable estimates. It was not designed to do so. The point and advertisement of ML is that it provides *efficient* estimates; it uses every scrap of information in the statistical and economic model in the quest for efficiency. It does the "right" efficient thing if the model is true. It does not necessarily do the "reasonable" thing for "approximate" models.

OLS vs. GLS Cross-Sectional Regressions

One place in which this argument crystallizes is in the choice between OLS and GLS cross-sectional regressions, or equivalently between first- and second-stage GMM.

Chapter 15 can lead to a mistaken impression that the choice does not matter that much. This is true to some extent in that simple environment, but not in more complex environments. For example, Fama and

---

[1] Following this train of thought, one might want to pursue estimation strategies that are even more robust than OLS, since OLS places a lot of weight on outliers. For example, Chen and Ready (1997) claim that size and value effects depend crucially on a few outliers.

French (1997) report important correlations between betas and pricing errors in a time-series test of a three-factor model on industry portfolios. This correlation cannot happen with an OLS cross-sectional estimate, as the cross-sectional estimate sets the cross-sectional correlation between right-hand variables (betas) and error terms (pricing errors) to zero by construction. As another example, first-stage estimates seem to work better in factor pricing models based on macroeconomic data. Figure 2.4 presents the first-stage estimate of the consumption-based model. The second-stage estimate produced much larger individual pricing errors, because by so doing it could lower pricing errors of portfolios with strong long-short positions required by the spectral density matrix. The same thing happened in the investment-based factor pricing model of Cochrane (1996), and the scaled consumption-based model of Lettau and Ludvigson (2000). Authors as far back as Fama and MacBeth (1973) have preferred OLS cross-sectional regressions, distrusting the GLS weights.

GLS and second-stage GMM gain their asymptotic efficiency when the covariance and spectral density matrices have converged to their population values. GLS and second-stage GMM use these matrices to find well-measured portfolios: portfolios with small residual variance for GLS, and small variance of discounted return for GMM. The danger is that these quantities are poorly estimated in a finite sample, that sample minimum-variance portfolios bear little relation to population minimum-variance portfolios. This by itself should not create too much of a problem for a perfect model, one that prices all portfolios. But an imperfect model that does a very good job of pricing a basic set of portfolios may do a poor job of pricing strange linear combinations of those portfolios, especially combinations that involve strong long and short positions, positions that really are outside the payoff space given transactions, margin, and short sales constraints. Thus, the danger is the interaction between spurious sample minimum-variance portfolios and the specification errors of the model.

Interestingly, Kandel and Stambaugh (1995) and Roll and Ross (1995) argue for GLS cross-sectional regressions also as a result of model misspecification. They start by observing that so long as there is any misspecification at all—so long as the pricing errors are not exactly zero; so long as the market proxy is not exactly on the mean-variance frontier—then there are portfolios that produce arbitrarily good and arbitrarily bad fits in plots of expected returns versus betas. Since even a perfect model leaves pricing errors in sample, this is always true in samples.

It is easy to see the basic argument. Take a portfolio long the positive alpha securities and short the negative alpha securities; it will have a really big alpha! More precisely, if the original securities follow

$$E(R^e) = \alpha + \lambda\beta,$$

then consider portfolios of the original securities formed from a nonsingular matrix A. They follow

$$E(AR^e) = A\alpha + \lambda A\beta.$$

You can make all these portfolios have the same β by choosing A so that $A\beta = $ constant, and then they will have a spread in alphas. You will see a plot in which all the portfolios have the same beta but the average returns are spread up and down. Conversely, you can pick A to make the expected return-beta plot look as good as you want.

GLS has an important feature in this situation: the GLS cross-sectional regression is independent of such repackaging of portfolios. If you transform a set of returns R^e to AR^e, then the OLS cross-sectional regression is transformed from

$$\hat{\lambda} = \left(\beta'\beta\right)^{-1}\beta'E(R^e)$$

to

$$\hat{\lambda} = \left(\beta'A'A\beta\right)^{-1}\beta'A'AE(R^e).$$

This does depend on the repackaging A. However, the residual covariance matrix of AR^e is $A\Sigma A'$, so the GLS regression

$$\hat{\lambda} = \left(\beta'\Sigma^{-1}\beta\right)^{-1}\beta'\Sigma^{-1}E(R^e)$$

is not affected so long as A is full rank and therefore does not throw away information

$$\hat{\lambda} = \left(\beta'A'(A\Sigma A')^{-1}A\beta\right)^{-1}\beta'A'(A\Sigma A)^{-1}AE(R^e)$$
$$= \left(\beta'\Sigma^{-1}\beta\right)^{-1}\beta'\Sigma^{-1}E(R^e).$$

(The spectral density matrix and second-stage estimate share this property in GMM estimates. These are not the only weighting matrix choices that are invariant to portfolios. For example, Hansen and Jagannathan's [1997] suggestion of the return second-moment matrix has the same property.)

This is a fact, but it does not show that OLS chooses a particularly good or bad set of portfolios. Perhaps you do not think that GLS' choice of portfolios is particularly informative. In this case, you use OLS precisely to focus attention on a particular set of economically interesting portfolios.

The choice depends subtly on what you want your test to accomplish. If you want to prove the model wrong, then GLS helps you to focus on the most informative portfolios for proving the model wrong. That is exactly what an efficient test is supposed to do. However, many models are wrong, but still pretty darn good. It is a shame to throw out the information that the model does a good job of pricing an interesting set of portfolios. The sensible compromise would seem to be to report the OLS estimate on "interesting" portfolios, and also to report the GLS test statistic that shows the model to be rejected. That is, in fact, the typical collection of facts.

Additional Examples of Trading Off Efficiency for Robustness
Here are some additional examples of situations in which it has turned out to be wise to trade off some apparent efficiency for robustness to model misspecifications.

Low-frequency time-series models. In estimating time-series models such as the AR(1) $y_t = \rho y_{t-1} + \varepsilon_t$, maximum likelihood minimizes one-step-ahead forecast error variance, $E(\varepsilon_t^2)$. But any time-series model is only an approximation, and the researcher's objective may not be one-step-ahead forecasting. For example, in making sense of the yield on long-term bonds, we are interested in the long-run behavior of the short rate of interest. In estimating the magnitude of long-horizon univariate mean reversion in stock returns, we want to know only the sum of autocorrelations or moving average coefficients. Writing $p_t = a(1)\varepsilon_t$, we want to know $a(1)$. (We will study this application in Section 19.1.) The approximate model that generates the smallest one-step-ahead forecast error variance may be quite different from the model that best matches the long-run behavior of the series. (Cochrane [1986] contains a more detailed analysis of this point in the context of long-horizon GDP forecasting.)

Lucas' money demand estimate. Lucas (1988) is a gem of an example. Lucas was interested in estimating the income elasticity of money demand. Money and income trend upwards over time and over business cycles, but also have some high-frequency movement that looks like noise. If you run a regression in log-levels,

$$m_t = a + by_t + \varepsilon_t,$$

you get a sensible coefficient of about $b = 1$, but you find that the error term is strongly serially correlated. Following standard advice, most researchers run GLS, which amounts pretty much to first-differencing the data,

$$m_t - m_{t-1} = b(y_t - y_{t-1}) + \eta_t.$$

This error term passes its Durbin–Watson statistic, but the b estimate is much lower, which does not make much economic sense, and, worse, is unstable, depending a lot on time period and data definitions. Lucas realized that the regression in differences threw out most of the information in the data, which was in the trend, and focused on the high-frequency noise. Therefore, the "inefficient" regression in levels, with standard errors corrected for correlation of the error term, is the right one to look at. Of course, GLS and ML did not know there was any "noise" in the data, which is why they threw out the baby and kept the bathwater. Again, ML ruthlessly exploits the null for efficiency, and has no way of knowing what is "reasonable" or "intuitive."

Stochastic singularities and calibration. Models of the term structure of interest rates (we will study these models in Chapter 18) and real business cycle models in macroeconomics give stark examples. These models are *stochastically singular.* They generate predictions for many time series from a few shocks, so the models predict that there are combinations of the time series that leave no error term. Even though the models have rich and interesting implications, ML will seize on this economically uninteresting singularity, refuse to estimate parameters, and reject any model of this form.

The simplest example of the situation is the linear-quadratic permanent-income model paired with an AR(1) specification for income. The model is

$$y_t = \rho y_{t-1} + \varepsilon_t,$$

$$c_t - c_{t-1} = \left(E_t - E_{t-1}\right) \frac{1}{1-\beta} \sum_{j=0}^{\infty} \beta^j y_{t+j} = \frac{1}{(1-\beta\rho)(1-\beta)} \varepsilon_t.$$

This model generates all sorts of important and economically interesting predictions for the joint process of consumption and income (and asset prices). Consumption should be roughly a random walk, and should respond only to permanent income changes; investment should be more volatile than income and income more volatile than consumption. Since there is only one shock and two series, however, the model taken literally predicts a deterministic relation between consumption and income; it predicts

$$c_t - c_{t-1} = \frac{r\beta}{1-\beta\rho} \left(y_t - \rho y_{t-1}\right).$$

ML will notice that this is the *statistically* most informative prediction of the model. There is no error term! In any real data set there is *no* configuration of the parameters r, β, ρ that makes this restriction hold, data point for data point. The probability of observing a data set $\{c_t, y_t\}$ is exactly zero, and the log likelihood function is $-\infty$ for any set of parameters. ML says to throw the model out.

Popular models of the term structure of interest rates act the same way. They specify that all yields at any moment in time are deterministic functions of a few state variables. Such models can capture much of the important qualitative behavior of the term structure, including rising, falling, and humped shapes, and the information in the term structure for future movements in yields and the volatility of yields. They are very useful for derivative pricing. But it is never the case in actual yield data that yields of all maturities are *exact* functions of K yields. Actual data on N yields always require N shocks. Again, a ML approach reports a $-\infty$ log likelihood function for any set of parameters.

Addressing Model Misspecification
The ML philosophy offers an answer to model misspecification: specify the *right* model, and then do ML. If regression errors are correlated, model and estimate the covariance matrix and do GLS. If you are worried about proxy errors in the pricing factor, short sales costs or other transactions costs so that model predictions for extreme long-short positions should not be relied on, if you are worried about time-aggregation or mismeasurement of consumption data, nonnormal or non-i.i.d. returns, time-varying betas and factor risk premia, additional pricing factors and so on—do not chat about them, write them down, and then do ML.

Following this lead, researchers have added "measurement errors" to real business cycle models (Sargent [1989] is a classic example) and affine yield models in order to break the stochastic singularity (I discuss this case a bit more in Section 19.6). The trouble is, of course, that the assumed structure of the measurement errors now drives what moments ML pays attention to. And seriously modeling and estimating the measurement errors takes us further away from the economically interesting parts of the model. (Measurement error augmented models will often wind up specifying sensible moments, but by assuming ad hoc processes for measurement error, such as i.i.d. errors. Why not just specify the sensible moments in the first place?)

More generally, authors tend not to follow this advice, in part because it is ultimately infeasible. Economics necessarily studies quantitative parables rather than completely specified models. It would be nice if we could write down completely specified models, if we could quantitatively describe all the possible economic and statistical model and specification errors, but we cannot.

The GMM framework, used judiciously, allows us to evaluate misspecified models. It allows us to direct that the statistical effort focus on the "interesting" predictions while ignoring the fact that the world does not match the "uninteresting" simplifications. For example, ML only gives you a choice of OLS, whose standard errors are wrong, or GLS, which you may not trust in small samples or which may focus on uninteresting parts of the data. GMM allows you to keep an OLS estimate, but to correct the standard errors for non-i.i.d. distributions. More generally, GMM allows you to specify an economically interesting set of moments, or a set of moments that you feel will be robust to misspecifications of the economic or statistical model, *without* having to spell out exactly what is the source of model misspecification that makes those moments "optimal" or even "interesting" and "robust." It allows you to accept the lower "efficiency" of the estimates under some sets of statistical assumptions, in return for such robustness.

At the same time, the GMM framework allows you to flexibly incorporate statistical model misspecifications in the distribution theory. For example, knowing that returns are not i.i.d. normal, you may want to use the time-series regression technique anyway. This estimate is not inconsistent, but the *standard errors* that ML formulas pump out under this assumption are inconsistent. GMM gives a flexible way to derive at least an asymptotic set of corrections for statistical model misspecifications of the time-series regression coefficient. Similarly, a pooled time-series cross-sectional OLS regression is not inconsistent, but standard errors that ignore cross correlation of error terms are far too small.

The "calibration" of real business cycle models is often really nothing more than a GMM parameter estimate, using economically sensible moments such as average output growth, consumption/output ratios, etc. to avoid the stochastic singularity that would doom a ML approach. (Kydland and Prescott's [1982] idea that empirical microeconomics would provide accurate parameter estimates for macroeconomic and financial models has pretty much vanished.) Calibration exercises usually do not compute standard errors, nor do they report any distribution theory associated with the "evaluation" stage when one compares the model's predicted second moments with those in the data. Following Burnside, Eichenbaum, and Rebelo (1993), however, it is easy enough to calculate such a distribution theory—to evaluate whether the difference between predicted "second moments" and actual moments is large compared to sampling variation, including the variation induced by parameter estimation in the same sample—by listing the first and second moments together in the g_T vector.

"Used judiciously" is an important qualification. Many GMM estimations and tests suffer from lack of thought in the choice of moments, test assets, and instruments. For example, early GMM papers tended to pick assets and especially instruments pretty much at random. Industry portfolios have almost no variation in average returns to explain. Authors often included many lags of returns and consumption growth as instruments to test a consumption-based model. However, the seventh lag of returns really does not predict much about future returns given lags 1–6, and the first-order serial correlation in seasonally adjusted, ex post revised consumption growth may be economically uninteresting. More recent work tends to emphasize a few well-chosen assets and instruments that capture important and economically interesting features of the data.

Auxiliary Model
ML requires an auxiliary statistical model. For example, in the classic ML formalization of regression tests, we had to stop to assume that returns and factors are jointly i.i.d. normal. As the auxiliary statistical model becomes more and more complex and hence realistic, more and more effort is devoted to estimating the auxiliary statistical model. ML has no way of knowing that some parameters—a, b; β, λ, risk aversion γ—are more "important" than others—Σ, and parameters describing time-varying conditional moments of returns.

A very convenient feature of GMM is that it does not require such an auxiliary statistical model. For example, in studying GMM we went straight from $p = E(mx)$ to moment conditions, estimates, and distribution theory. This is an important saving of the researcher's and the reader's time, effort, and attention.

Finite-Sample Distributions
Many authors say they prefer regression tests and the GRS statistic in particular because it has a finite-sample distribution theory, and they distrust the finite-sample performance of the GMM asymptotic distribution theory.

This argument does not have much force. The finite-sample distribution only holds if returns really are normal and i.i.d., and if the factor is perfectly measured. Since these assumptions do not hold, it is not obvious that a finite-sample distribution that ignores non-i.i.d. returns will be a better approximation than an asymptotic distribution that corrects for them.

All approaches give essentially the same answers in the classic setup of i.i.d. returns. The issue is how the various techniques perform in more complex setups, especially with conditioning information, and here there are no analytic finite-sample distributions.

In addition, once you have picked the estimation method—how you will generate a number from the data; or which moments you will use—finding its finite-sample distribution, given an auxiliary statistical model, is simple. Just run a Monte Carlo or bootstrap. Thus, picking an estimation method because it delivers analytic formulas for a finite-sample distribution (under false assumptions) should be a thing of the past. Analytic formulas for finite-sample distributions are useful for comparing estimation methods and arguing about statistical properties of estimators, but they are not necessary for the empiricists' main task.

Finite-Sample Quality of Asymptotic Distributions, and "Nonparametric" Estimates

Several investigations (Ferson and Foerster [1994], Hansen, Heaton, and Yaron [1996]) have found cases in which the GMM asymptotic distribution theory is a poor approximation to a finite-sample distribution theory. This is especially true when one asks "nonparametric" corrections for autocorrelation or heteroskedasticity to provide large corrections and when the number of moments is large compared to the sample size, or if the moments one uses for GMM turn out to be very inefficient (Fuhrer, Moore, and Schuh [1995]), which can happen if you put in a lot of instruments with low forecast power.

The ML distribution is the same as GMM, conditional on the choice of moments, but typical implementations of ML also use the parametric time-series model to simplify estimates of the terms in the distribution theory as well as to derive the likelihood function.

If this is the case—if the "nonparametric" estimates of the GMM distribution theory perform poorly in a finite sample, while the "parametric" ML distribution works well—there is no reason not to use a parametric time-series model to estimate the terms in the GMM distribution as well. For example, rather than calculate $\sum_{j=-\infty}^{\infty} E(u_t u_{t-j})$ from a large sum of autocorrelations, you can model $u_t = \rho u_{t-1} + \varepsilon_t$, estimate ρ, and then calculate $\sigma^2(u) \sum_{j=-\infty}^{\infty} \rho^j = \sigma^2(u)(1+\rho)/(1-\rho)$. Section 11.7 discussed this idea in more detail.

The Case for ML

In the classic setup, the efficiency gain of ML over GMM on the pricing errors is tiny. However, several studies have found cases in which the statistically motivated choice of moments suggested by ML has important efficiency advantages.

For example, Jacquier, Polson, and Rossi (1994) study the estimation of a time-series model with stochastic volatility. This is a model of the form

$$dS_t/S_t = \mu\, dt + V_t\, dZ_{1t},$$
$$dV_t = \mu_V(V_t)\, dt + \sigma(V_t)\, dZ_{2t}, \tag{16.1}$$

and S is observed but V is not. The obvious and easily interpretable moments include the autocorrelation of squared returns, or the autocorrelation of the absolute value of returns. However, Jacquier, Polson, and Rossi find that the resulting estimates are far less efficient than those resulting from the ML scores.

Of course, this study presumes that the model (16.1) really is exactly true. Whether the uninterpretable scores or the interpretable moments really perform better to give an approximate model of the form (16.1), given some other data-generating mechanism, is open to discussion.

Even in the canonical OLS versus GLS case, a wildly heteroskedastic error covariance matrix can mean that OLS spends all its effort fitting unimportant data points. A "judicious" application of GMM (OLS) in this case would require at least some transformation of units so that OLS is not wildly inefficient.

Statistical Philosophy
The history of empirical work that has been persuasive—that has changed people's understanding of the facts in the data and which economic models understand those facts—looks a lot different than the statistical theory preached in econometrics textbooks.

The CAPM was taught, believed in, and used for years despite formal statistical rejections. It only fell by the wayside when other, coherent views of the world were offered in the multifactor models. And the multifactor models are also rejected! It seems that "it takes a model to beat a model," not a rejection.

Even when evaluating a specific model, most of the interesting calculations come from examining specific alternatives rather than overall pricing error tests. The original CAPM tests focused on whether the intercept in a cross-sectional regression was higher or lower than the risk-free rate, and whether individual variance entered into cross-sectional regressions. The CAPM fell when it was found that characteristics such as size and book/market do enter cross-sectional regressions, not when generic pricing error tests rejected.

Influential empirical work tells a story. The most efficient procedure does not seem to convince people if they cannot transparently see what stylized facts in the data drive the result. A test of a model that focuses on its ability to account for the cross section of average returns of interesting portfolios will in the end be much more persuasive than one that (say) focuses on the model's ability to explain the fifth moment of the second portfolio, even if ML finds the latter moment much more statistically informative.

Most recently, Fama and French (1988b) and (1993) are good examples of empirical work that changed many people's minds, in this case that long-horizon returns really are predictable, and that we need a multifactor model rather than the CAPM to understand the cross section of average returns. These papers are not stunning statistically: long-horizon predictability is on the edge of statistical significance, and the multifactor model is rejected by the GRS test. But these papers made clear what stylized and robust facts in the data drive the results, and why those facts are economically sensible. For example, the 1993 paper focused on tables of average returns and betas. Those tables showed strong variation in average returns that was not matched by variation in market betas, yet was matched by variation in betas on new factors. There is no place in statistical theory for such a table, but it is much more persuasive than a table of χ^2 values for pricing error tests. On the other hand, I can think of no case in which the application of a clever statistical model to wring the last ounce of efficiency out of a data set, changing t statistics from 1.5 to 2.5, substantially changed the way people think about an issue.

Statistical testing is one of many questions we ask in evaluating theories, and usually not the most important one. This is not a philosophical or normative statement; it is a positive or empirical description of the process by which the profession has moved from theory to theory. Think of the kind of questions people ask when presented with a theory and accompanying empirical work. They usually start by thinking hard about the theory itself. What is the central part of the economic model or explanation? Is it internally consistent? Do the assumptions make sense? Then, when we get to the empirical work, how were the numbers produced? Are the data definitions sensible? Are the concepts in the data decent proxies for the concepts in the model? (There is not much room in statistical theory for that question!) Are the model predictions robust to the inevitable simplifications? Does the result hinge on power utility versus another functional form? What happens if you add a little measurement error, or if agents have an information advantage, etc.? What are the identification assumptions, and do they make any sense—why is y on the left and x on the right rather than the other way around? How much fishing around for functional forms, data definitions, proxies, and innumerable other specification issues, did the authors do in order to produce good results? Finally, someone in the back of the room might raise his hand and ask, "if the data were generated by a draw of i.i.d. normal random variables over and over again, how often would you come up with a number this big or bigger?" That is an interesting and important check on the overall believability of the results. But it is not necessarily the first check, and certainly not the last and decisive check. Many models are kept that have economically interesting but statistically rejectable results, and many more models are quickly forgotten that have strong statistics but just do not tell as clean a story.

The classical theory of hypothesis testing, its Bayesian alternative, or the underlying hypothesis-testing view of the philosophy of science are miserable descriptions of the way science in general and economics in particular proceed from theory to theory. And this is probably a good thing too. Given the nonexperimental nature of our data, the inevitable fishing biases of many researchers examining the same data, and the unavoidable fact that our theories are really quantitative parables more than literal descriptions of the way the data are generated, the way the profession settles on new theories makes a good deal of sense. Classical statistics requires that nobody ever looked at the data before specifying the model. Yet more regressions have been run than there are data points in the CRSP database. Bayesian econometrics can in principle incorporate the information of previous researchers, yet it never applied in this way—each study starts anew with an "uninformative" prior. Statistical theory draws a sharp distinction between the *model*—which we know is right; utility is exactly power—and the *parameters* which we estimate. But this distinction is not true; we are just as uncertain about functional forms as we are about parameters. A distribution theory at bottom tries to ask an unknowable question: If we turned the clock back to 1947 and reran the postwar period 1000 times, in how many of those alternative histories would (say) the average S&P500 return be greater than 9%? It is pretty amazing in fact that a statistician can purport to give any answer at all to such a question, having observed only one history.

These paragraphs do not contain original ideas, and they mirror changes in the philosophy of science more broadly. Fifty years ago, the reigning philosophy of science focused on the idea that scientists provide rejectable hypotheses. This idea runs through philosophical writings exemplified by Popper (1959), classical statistical decision theory, and mirrored in economics by Friedman (1953). However, this methodology contains an important inconsistency. Though researchers are supposed to let the data decide, writers on methodology do not look at how actual theories evolved. It was, as in Friedman's title, a "Methodology of positive economics," not a "positive methodology of economics." Why should methodology be normative, a result of philosophical speculation, and not an empirical discipline like everything else? In a very famous book, Kuhn (1970) looked at the history of scientific revolutions, and found that the actual process had very little to do with the formal methodology. McCloskey (1983, 1998) has gone even further, examining the "rhetoric" of economics: the kinds of arguments that persuaded people to change their minds about economic theories. Needless to say, the largest t-statistic did not win!

Kuhn's and especially McCloskey's ideas are not popular in the finance and economics professions. Precisely, they are not popular in how people *talk about* their work, though they describe well how people *actually do* their work. Most people in the fields cling to the normative, rejectable-hypothesis view of methodology. But we need not suppose that they would be popular. The ideas of economics and finance are not popular among the agents in the models. How many stock market investors even know what a random walk or the CAPM is, let alone believe those models have even a grain of truth? Why should the agents in the models of how scientific ideas evolve have an intuitive understanding of the models? "As if" rationality can apply to us as well!

Philosophical debates aside, a researcher who wants his ideas to be convincing, as well as right, would do well to study how ideas have in the past convinced people, rather than just study a statistical decision theorist's ideas about how ideas *should* convince people. Kuhn, and, in economics, McCloskey have done that, and their histories are worth reading. In the end, statistical properties may be a poor way to choose statistical methods.

Summary

The bottom line is simple: *It is ok to do a first-stage or simple GMM estimate rather than an explicit maximum likelihood estimate and test.* Many people (and, unfortunately, many journal referees) seem to think that nothing less than a full maximum likelihood estimate and test is acceptable. This section is long in order to counter that impression; to argue that at least in many cases of practical importance, a simple first-stage GMM approach, focusing on economically interpretable moments, can be adequately efficient, robust to model misspecifications, and ultimately more persuasive.

PART III
Bonds and Options

We value bonds and options with closely related techniques. As you might expect, I present both applications in a discount factor context. Bonds and options are priced with surprisingly simple discount factors.

So far, we have focused on returns, which reduce the pricing problem to a one-period problem. Bonds and options force us to start thinking about chaining together the one-period or instantaneous representations to get a prediction for prices of long-lived securities. Taking this step is very important, and I forecast that we will see much more multiperiod analysis in stocks as well, studying prices and streams of payoffs rather than returns. This step rather than the discount factor accounts for the mathematical complexity of some bond and option pricing models.

There are two standard ways to go from instantaneous or return representations to prices. First, we can chain the discount factors together. Starting with a one-period discount factor $m_{t,t+1}$, we can find a long-term discount factor $m_{t,t+j} = m_{t,t+1}m_{t+1,t+2}\cdots m_{t+j-1,t+j}$ that can price a j-period payoff. Starting with the discount factor increment $d\Lambda$ that satisfies the instantaneous pricing equation $0 = E_t[d(\Lambda P)]$, we can solve its stochastic differential equation to find the level Λ_{t+j} that prices a j-period payoff by $P_t = E_t[\Lambda_{t+j}/\Lambda_t x_{t+j}]$. Second, we can chain the prices together. Starting with $p_{T-1} = E_{T-1}(m_{T-1,T}x_T)$ we can find $p_{T-2} = E_{T-2}(m_{T-2,T-1}p_{T-1})$ and so forth. Conceptually, this is the same as chaining returns $R_{t,t+j} = R_{t,t+1}R_{t+1,t+2}\cdots R_{t+j-1,t+j}$. Starting with $0 = E_t[d(\Lambda P)]$, we can find a differential equation for the prices, and solve that back. We will use both methods to solve interest rate and option pricing models.

17
Option Pricing

OPTIONS ARE A VERY interesting and useful set of instruments. In thinking about their value, we will adopt an extremely *relative* pricing approach. Our objective will be to find out a value for the option, *taking as given* the values of other securities, and in particular the price of the stock on which the option is written and an interest rate.

17.1 Background

Definitions and Payoffs

A call option gives you the right to buy a stock for a specified strike price on a specified expiration date.

The call option payoff is $C_T = \max(S_T - X, 0)$.

Portfolios of options are called strategies. A straddle—a put and a call at the same strike price—is a bet on volatility.

Options allow you to buy and sell pieces of the return distribution.

Before studying option prices, we need to understand option payoffs.

A *call* option gives you the *right*, but not the obligation, to buy a stock (or other "underlying" asset) for a specified *strike price* (X) on (or before) the *expiration date* (T). *European* options can only be *exercised* on the expiration date. *American* options can be exercised anytime before as well as on the expiration date. A *put* option gives the *right* to sell a stock at a specified strike price on (or before) the expiration date. I will use the

311

standard notation,

$$C = C_t = \text{call price today,}$$
$$C_T = \text{call payoff} = \text{value at expiration } (T),$$
$$S = S_t = \text{stock price today,}$$
$$S_T = \text{stock price at expiration,}$$
$$X = \text{strike price.}$$

Our objective is to find the price C. The general framework is (of course) $C = E(mx)$, where x denotes the option's payoff. The option's payoff is the same thing as its value at expiration. If the stock has risen above the strike price, then the option is worth the difference between stock and strike. If the stock has fallen below the strike price, it expires worthless. Thus, the option payoff is

$$\text{Call payoff} = \begin{cases} S_T - X & \text{if } S_T \geq X, \\ 0 & \text{if } S_T \leq X, \end{cases}$$
$$C_T = \max(S_T - X, 0).$$

A put works the opposite way: It gains value as the stock falls below the strike price, since the right to sell it at a high price is more and more valuable,

$$\text{Put payoff} = P_T = \max(X - S_T, 0).$$

It is easiest to keep track of options by a graph of their value as a function of stock price. Figure 17.1 graphs the payoffs from buying calls and puts. Figure 17.1 also graphs the payoffs of the corresponding short positions, which are called *writing* call and put options. One of the easiest mistakes to make is to confuse the *payoff* with the *profit*, which is the value at expiration less the cost of buying the option. I drew in profit lines, payoff – cost, to emphasize this difference.

Some Interesting Features of Options
Right away, you can see some of the interesting features of options. A call option allows you a huge positive beta. Typical at-the-money options (strike price = current stock price) give a beta of about 10, meaning that the option is equivalent to borrowing $10 to invest $11 in the stock. However, your losses are limited to the cost of the option, which is paid up front. Options are obviously very useful for trading. Imagine how difficult it would be to buy stock on such huge margin, and how difficult it would be

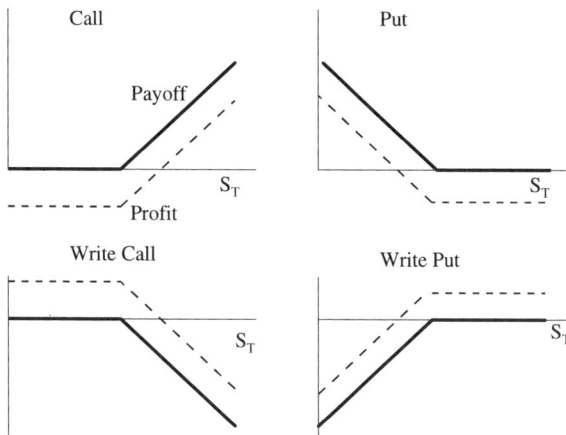

Figure 17.1. *Payoff diagrams for simple option strategies.*

to make sure people paid if the bet went bad. Options solve this problem. No wonder that active options trading started only a year or two after the first stocks started trading.

The huge beta also means that options are very useful for hedging. If you have a large illiquid portfolio, you can offset the risks very cheaply with options.

Finally, options allow you to shape the distribution of returns in interesting and sometimes dangerous ways. For example, if you buy a 40% out-of-the-money put option as well as a stock, you have bought "catastrophe insurance" for your stock portfolio. You cut off the left tail of the return distribution, at a small cost to the mean of the overall distribution.

On the other side, by *writing* out-of-the-money put options, you can earn a small fee year in and year out, only once in a while experiencing a huge loss. You have a large probability of a small gain and a small probability of a large loss. You are providing catastrophe insurance to the market, and it works much like, say, writing earthquake insurance.

The distribution of returns from this strategy is extremely nonnormal, and thus statistical evaluation of its properties will be difficult. This strategy is tempting to a portfolio manager who is being evaluated only by the statistics of his achieved return. If he writes far out-of-the-money options in addition to investing in an index, the chance of beating the index for one or even five years is extremely high. If the catastrophe does happen and he loses a billion dollars or so, the worst you can do is fire him. (His employment contract is a call option.) This is why portfolio management contracts are not purely statistical, but also write down what kind of investments can and cannot be made.

Strategies

Portfolios of put and call options are called *strategies*, and have additional interesting properties. Figure 17.2 graphs the payoff of a *straddle*, which combines a put and call at the same strike price. This strategy pays off if the stock goes up or goes down. It loses money if the stock does not move. Thus the straddle is a bet on *volatility*. Of course, everyone else understands this, and will bid the put and call prices up until the straddle earns only an equilibrium rate of return. Thus, you invest in a straddle if you think that stock volatility is higher than everyone else thinks it will be. Options allow efficient markets and random walks to operate on the second and higher moments of stocks as well as their overall direction! You can also see quickly that volatility will be a central parameter in option prices. The higher the volatility, the higher both put and call prices.

More generally, by combining options of various strikes, you can buy and sell any piece of the return distribution. A complete set of options— call options on every strike price—is equivalent to complete markets, i.e., it allows you to form payoffs that depend on the terminal stock price in any way; you can form any payoff of the form $f(S_T)$.

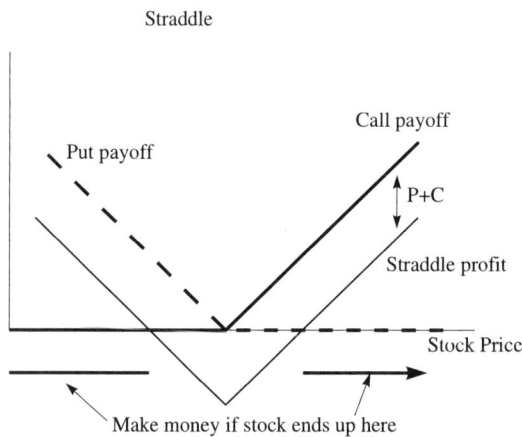

Figure 17.2. *Payoff diagram for a straddle.*

Prices: One-Period Analysis

> I use the law of one price—existence of a discount factor—and no
> arbitrage—existence of a positive discount factor—to characterize option
> prices. The results are: (1) Put-call parity: $P = C - S + X/R^f$. (2) Arbi-
> trage bounds, best summarized by Figure 17.4. (3) The proposition that you
> should never exercise an American call option early on a stock that pays no
> dividends. The arbitrage bounds are a linear program, and this procedure
> can be used to find them in more complex situations where clever identifi-
> cation of arbitrage portfolios may fail.

We have a set of interesting payoffs. Now what can we say about their
prices—their values at dates before expiration? Obviously, $p = E(mx)$ as
always. We have learned about x; now we have to think about m.

We can start by imposing little structure—the law of one price and
the absence of arbitrage, or, equivalently, the existence of some discount
factor or a positive discount factor. In the case of options, these two principles tell you a good deal about the option price.

Put-Call Parity
The law of one price, or the existence of some discount factor that prices
stock, bond, and a call option, allows us to deduce the value of a put in
terms of the price of the stock, bond, and call. Consider the following two
strategies: (1) Hold a call, write a put, same strike price. (2) Hold stock,
promise to pay the strike price X. The *payoffs* of these two strategies are
the same, as shown in Figure 17.3.

Equivalently, the *payoffs* are related by

$$P_T = C_T - S_T + X.$$

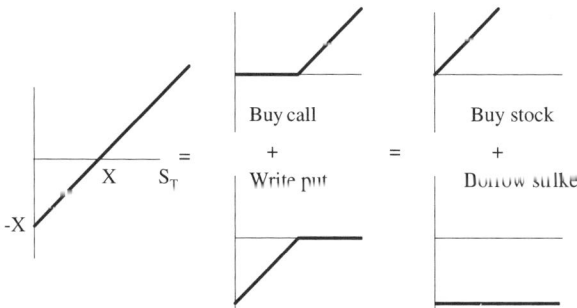

Figure 17.3. Put-call parity.

Thus, so long as the law of one price holds, the *prices* of left- and right-hand sides must be equal. Applying $E(m\cdot)$ to both sides for any m,

$$P = C - S + X/R^f.$$

(The price of S_T is S. The price of the payoff X is X/R^f.)

Arbitrage Bounds

If we add the absence of arbitrage, or equivalently the restriction that the discount factor must be positive, we can deduce bounds on the call option price without needing to know the put price. In this case, it is easiest to cleverly notice arbitrage portfolios—situations in which portfolio A dominates portfolio B. Then, either directly from the definition of no arbitrage or from $A > B$, $m > 0 \Rightarrow E(mA) > E(mB)$, you can deduce that the price of A must be greater than the price of B. The arbitrage portfolios are

1. $C_T > 0 \Rightarrow C > 0$. The call payoff is positive so the call price must be positive.
2. $C_T \geq S_T - X \Rightarrow C \geq S - X/R^f$. The call payoff is better than the stock payoff – the strike price, so the call price is greater than the stock price less the present value of the strike price.
3. $C_T \leq S_T \Rightarrow C \leq S$. The call payoff is worse than stock payoff (because you have to pay the strike price). Thus, the call price is less than stock price.

Figure 17.4 summarizes these arbitrage bounds on the call option value. We have gotten somewhere—we have restricted the range of the option prices. However, the arbitrage bounds are too large to be of much practical use. Obviously, we need to learn more about the discount factor than pure arbitrage or $m > 0$ will allow. We could retreat to economic models, e.g., use the CAPM or other explicit discount factor model.

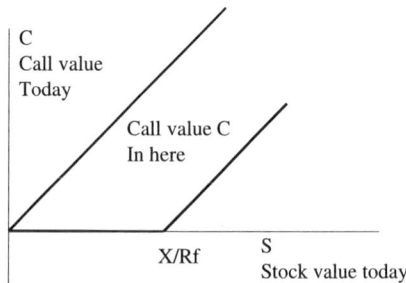

Figure 17.4. *Arbitrage bounds for a call option.*

Option pricing is famous because we do not have to do that. Instead, if we open up dynamic trading—the requirement that the discount factor price the stock and bond *at every date* to expiration—it turns out that we can sometimes determine the discount factor and hence the option value precisely.

Discount Factors and Arbitrage Bounds

This presentation of arbitrage bounds is unsettling for two reasons. First, you may worry that you will not be clever enough to dream up dominating portfolios in more complex circumstances. Second, you may worry that we have not dreamed up all of the arbitrage portfolios in this circumstance. Perhaps there is another one lurking out there, which would reduce the unsettlingly large size of the bounds. This presentation leaves us hungry for a constructive technique for finding arbitrage bounds that would be guaranteed to work in general situations, and to find the tightest arbitrage bound.

We want to know $C_t = E(m_{t,T} x_T^c)$, where $x_T^c = \max(S_T - X, 0)$ denotes the call payoff, we want to use information in the observed stock and bond prices to learn about the option price, and we want to impose the absence of arbitrage. We can capture this search with the following problem:

$$\max_m C_t = E_t\left(m x_T^c\right) \text{ s.t. } m > 0,$$

$$S_t = E_t(m S_T), \tag{17.1}$$

$$1 = E_t(m R^f),$$

and the corresponding minimization. The first constraint implements absence of arbitrage. The second and third use the information in the stock and bond price to learn what we can about the option price.

Write 17.1 out in state notation,

$$\max_{\{m(s)\}} C_t = \sum_s \pi(s)m(s)x_T^c(s) \text{ s.t. } m(s) > 0,$$

$$S_t = \sum_s \pi(s)m(s)S_T(s),$$

$$1 = \sum_s \pi(s)m(s)R^f.$$

This is a linear program—a linear objective and linear constraints. In situations where you do not know the answer, you can calculate arbitrage bounds—and know you have them all—by solving this linear program (Ritchken [1985]). I do not know how you would begin to check that *for every* portfolio A whose payoff dominates B, the price of A is greater than the price of B. The discount factor method lets you construct the arbitrage bounds.

Early Exercise

By applying the absence of arbitrage, we can show quickly that you should never exercise an American call option on a stock that pays no dividends before the expiration date. This is a lovely illustration because such a simple principle leads to a result that is not initially obvious. Follow the table:

Payoffs	$C_T = \max(S_T - X, 0) \geq S_T - X$	
Price	C	$\geq S - X/R^f$
$R^f > 1$	C	$\geq S - X$

$S - X$ is what you get if you exercise now. The value of the call is greater than this value, because you can delay paying the strike, and because exercising early loses the option value. Put-call parity lets us concentrate on call options; this fact lets us concentrate on European call options.

17.2 Black–Scholes Formula

> Write a process for stock and bond, then use Λ^* to price the option. The Black–Scholes formula (17.7) results. You can either solve for the finite-horizon discount factor Λ_T/Λ_0 and find the call option price by taking the expectation $C_0 = E_0(\Lambda_T/\Lambda_0 x_T^C)$, or you can find a differential equation for the call option price and solve it backward.

Our objective, again, is to learn as much as we can about the value of an option, given the value of the underlying stock and bond. The one-period analysis led only to arbitrage bounds, at which point we had to start thinking about discount factor models. Now, we allow intermediate trading, which means we really are thinking about dynamic multiperiod asset pricing.

The standard approach to the Black–Scholes formula rests on explicitly constructing portfolios: at each date we cleverly construct a portfolio of stock and bond that replicates the instantaneous payoff of the option; we reason that the price of the option must equal the price of the replicating portfolio. Instead, I follow the discount factor approach. The law of one price is the same thing as the existence of a discount factor. Thus, rather than construct law-of-one-price replicating portfolios, construct at each date a discount factor that prices the stock and bond, and use that discount factor to price the option. The discount factor approach shows how thinking of the world in terms of a discount factor is equivalent in the result and as easy in the calculation as other approaches.

This case shows some of the interest and engineering complexity of continuous-time models. Though at each instant the analysis is trivial law of one price, chaining that analysis together over time is not trivial.

The call option payoff is

$$C_T = \max(S_T - X, 0),$$

where X denotes the strike price X and S_T denotes the stock price on the expiration date T. The underlying stock follows

$$\frac{dS}{S} = \mu \, dt + \sigma \, dz.$$

There is also a money market security that pays the real interest rate $r \, dt$.

We want a discount factor that prices the stock and bond. All such discount factors are of the form $m = x^* + w$, $E(xw) = 0$. In continuous time, all such discount factors are of the form

$$\frac{d\Lambda}{\Lambda} = -r \, dt - \frac{(\mu - r)}{\sigma} \, dz - \sigma_w \, dw; \qquad E(dw \, dz) = 0.$$

(You can check that this set of discount factors does in fact price the stock and interest rate, or take a quick look back at Section 4.3.)

Now we price the call option with this discount factor, and show that the Black–Scholes equation results. Importantly, the choice of discount factor via choice of $\sigma_w \, dw$ turns out to have no effect on the resulting option price. *Every* discount factor that prices the stock and interest rate gives the same value for the option price. The option is therefore priced using the law of one price alone.

There are two paths to follow. Either we solve the discount factor forward, and then find the call value by $C = E(mx^C)$, or we characterize the price path and solve it backwards from expiration.

Method 1. Price Using Discount Factor

Let us use the discount factor to price the option directly:

$$C_0 = E_t \left\{ \frac{\Lambda_T}{\Lambda_t} \max \left(S_T - X, 0 \right) \right\} = \int \frac{\Lambda_T}{\Lambda_t} \max \left(S_T - X, 0 \right) df \left(\Lambda_T, S_T \right),$$

where Λ_T and S_T are solutions to

$$\frac{dS}{S} = \mu\,dt + \sigma\,dz,$$
$$\frac{d\Lambda}{\Lambda} = -r\,dt - \frac{\mu - r}{\sigma}\,dz - \sigma_w\,dw. \tag{17.2}$$

I simplify the algebra by setting $\sigma_w\,dw$ to zero, anticipating that it does not matter. You can reason that since S does not depend on dw, C_T depends only on S_T, so C will only depend on S, and dw will have no effect on the answer. If this is not good enough, a problem asks you to include the dw, trace through the remaining steps, and verify that the answer does not in fact depend on dw.

"Solving" a stochastic differential equation such as (17.2) means finding the distribution of the random variables S_T and Λ_T, using information as of date 0. This is just what we do with difference equations. For example, if we solve $x_{t+1} = \rho x_t + \varepsilon_{t+1}$ with ε normal forward to $x_T = \rho^T x_0 + \sum_{j=1}^{T} \rho^{T-j}\varepsilon_j$, we have expressed x_T as a normally distributed random variable with mean $\rho^T x_0$ and variance $\sum_{j=1}^{T} \rho^{2(T-j)}$. In the continuous-time case, it turns out that we can solve some nonlinear specifications as well. Integrals of dz give us shocks, as integrals of dt give us deterministic functions of time.

We can find analytical expressions for the solutions of equations of the form (17.2). Start with the stochastic differential equation

$$\frac{dY}{Y} = \mu_Y\,dt + \sigma_Y\,dz. \tag{17.3}$$

Write

$$d\ln Y = \frac{dY}{Y} - \frac{1}{2}\frac{1}{Y^2}\,dY^2 = \left(\mu_Y - \frac{1}{2}\sigma_Y^2\right)dt + \sigma_Y\,dZ.$$

Integrating from 0 to T, (17.3) has solution

$$\int_0^T d\ln Y = \left(\mu_Y - \frac{1}{2}\sigma_Y^2\right)\int_0^T dt + \sigma_Y\int_0^T dZ_t$$
$$\ln Y_T = \ln Y_0 + \left(\mu_Y - \frac{\sigma_Y^2}{2}\right)T + \sigma_Y(z_T - z_0). \tag{17.4}$$

$z_T - z_0$ is a normally distributed random variable with mean zero and variance T. Thus, $\ln Y$ is conditionally normal with mean $\ln Y_0 + \left(\mu_Y - \sigma_Y^2/2\right)T$ and variance $\sigma_Y^2 T$.

Applying the solution (17.4) to (17.2), we have

$$\ln S_T = \ln S_0 + \left(\mu - \frac{\sigma^2}{2}\right)T + \sigma\sqrt{T}\varepsilon,$$

$$\ln \Lambda_T = \ln \Lambda_0 - \left(r + \frac{1}{2}\left(\frac{\mu - r}{\sigma}\right)^2\right)T - \frac{\mu - r}{\sigma}\sqrt{T}\varepsilon,$$

(17.5)

where the random variable ε is a standard normal,

$$\varepsilon = \frac{z_T - z_0}{\sqrt{T}} \sim \mathcal{N}(0, 1).$$

Having found the joint distribution of stock and discount factor, we evaluate the call option value by doing the integral corresponding to the expectation,

$$C_0 = \int_{S_T=X}^{\infty} \frac{\Lambda_T}{\Lambda_t}(S_T - X)\,df(\Lambda_T, S_T)$$

$$= \int_{S_T=X}^{\infty} \frac{\Lambda_T(\varepsilon)}{\Lambda_t}\left(S_T(\varepsilon) - X\right)df(\varepsilon).$$

(17.6)

We know the joint distribution of the terminal stock price S_T and discount factor Λ_T on the right-hand side, so we have all the information we need to calculate this integral. This example has enough structure that we can find an analytical formula. In more general circumstances, you may have to resort to numerical methods. At the most basic level, you can simulate the Λ, S process forward and then take the integral by summing over many such simulations.

Doing the Integral
Start by breaking up the integral (17.6) into two terms,

$$C_0 = \int_{S_T=X}^{\infty} \frac{\Lambda_T(\varepsilon)}{\Lambda_t}S_T(\varepsilon)\,df(\varepsilon) - \int_{S_T=X}^{\infty} \frac{\Lambda_T(\varepsilon)}{\Lambda_t}X\,df(\varepsilon).$$

S_T and Λ_T are both exponential functions of ε. The normal distribution is also an exponential function of ε. Thus, we can approach this integral exactly as we approach the expectation of a lognormal; we can merge the two exponentials in ε into one term, and express the result as integrals against a normal distribution. Here we go. Plug in (17.5) for S_T, Λ_T, and simplify the exponentials in terms of ε,

$$
\begin{aligned}
C_0 &= \int_{S_T=X}^{\infty} e^{-\left(r+\frac{1}{2}\left(\frac{\mu-r}{\sigma}\right)^2\right)T-\frac{\mu-r}{\sigma}\sqrt{T}\varepsilon} S_0 e^{\left(\mu-\frac{1}{2}\sigma^2\right)T+\sigma\sqrt{T}\varepsilon} f(\varepsilon)\,d\varepsilon \\
&\quad -X\int_{S_T=X}^{\infty} e^{-\left(r+\frac{1}{2}\left(\frac{\mu-r}{\sigma}\right)^2\right)T-\frac{\mu-r}{\sigma}\sqrt{T}\varepsilon} f(\varepsilon)\,d\varepsilon \\
&= S_0\int_{S_T=X}^{\infty} e^{\left[\mu-r-\frac{1}{2}\left(\sigma^2+\left(\frac{\mu-r}{\sigma}\right)^2\right)\right]T+\left(\sigma-\frac{\mu-r}{\sigma}\right)\sqrt{T}\varepsilon} f(\varepsilon)\,d\varepsilon \\
&\quad -X\int_{S_T=X}^{\infty} e^{-\left(r+\frac{1}{2}\left(\frac{\mu-r}{\sigma}\right)^2\right)T-\frac{\mu-r}{\sigma}\sqrt{T}\varepsilon} f(\varepsilon).
\end{aligned}
$$

Now add the normal distribution formula for $f(\varepsilon)$,

$$
f(\varepsilon) = \frac{1}{\sqrt{2\pi}} e^{-(1/2)\varepsilon^2}.
$$

The result is

$$
\begin{aligned}
C_0 &= \frac{1}{\sqrt{2\pi}} S_0 \int_{S_T=X}^{\infty} e^{\left[\mu-r-\frac{1}{2}\left(\sigma^2+\left(\frac{\mu-r}{\sigma}\right)^2\right)\right]T+\left(\sigma-\frac{\mu-r}{\sigma}\right)\sqrt{T}\varepsilon-\frac{1}{2}\varepsilon^2}\,d\varepsilon \\
&\quad -\frac{1}{\sqrt{2\pi}} X \int_{S_T=X}^{\infty} e^{-\left[r+\frac{1}{2}\left(\frac{\mu-r}{\sigma}\right)^2\right]T-\frac{\mu-r}{\sigma}\sqrt{T}\varepsilon-\frac{1}{2}\varepsilon^2}\,d\varepsilon \\
&= \frac{1}{\sqrt{2\pi}} S_0 \int_{S_T=X}^{\infty} e^{-\frac{1}{2}\left[\varepsilon-\left(\sigma-\frac{\mu-r}{\sigma}\right)\sqrt{T}\right]^2}\,d\varepsilon \\
&\quad -\frac{1}{\sqrt{2\pi}} X e^{-rT} \int_{S_T=X}^{\infty} e^{-\frac{1}{2}\left(\varepsilon+\frac{\mu-r}{\sigma}\sqrt{T}\right)^2}\,d\varepsilon.
\end{aligned}
$$

Notice that the integrals have the form of a normal distribution with nonzero mean. The lower bound $S_T = X$ is, in terms of ε,

$$
\ln X = \ln S_T = \ln S_0 + \left(\mu - \frac{\sigma^2}{2}\right)T + \sigma\sqrt{T}\varepsilon,
$$

$$
\varepsilon = \frac{\ln X - \ln S_0 - \left(\mu - \sigma^2/2\right)T}{\sigma\sqrt{T}}.
$$

Finally, we can express definite integrals against a normal distribution by the cumulative normal,

$$
\frac{1}{\sqrt{2\pi}} \int_{a}^{\infty} e^{-(1/2)(\varepsilon-\mu)^2}\,d\varepsilon = \Phi(\mu - a),
$$

i.e., $\Phi(\ )$ is the area under the left tail of the normal distribution:

$$C_0 = S_0\Phi\left(-\frac{\ln X - \ln S_0 - (\mu - \sigma^2/2)T}{\sigma\sqrt{T-t}} + \left(\sigma - \frac{\mu - r}{\sigma}\right)\sqrt{T}\right)$$

$$- Xe^{-r(T-t)}\Phi\left(-\frac{\ln X - \ln S_0 - (\mu - \sigma^2/2)T}{\sigma\sqrt{T}} - \frac{\mu - r}{\sigma}\sqrt{T}\right).$$

Simplifying, we get the Black–Scholes formula

$$C_0 = S_0\Phi\left(\frac{\ln S_0/X + [r + \sigma^2/2]T}{\sigma\sqrt{T}}\right)$$

$$- Xe^{-rT}\Phi\left(\frac{\ln S_0/X + [r - \sigma^2/2]T}{\sigma\sqrt{T}}\right). \tag{17.7}$$

Method 2: Derive Black–Scholes Differential Equation

Rather than solve the discount factor *forward* and then integrate, we can solve the price backwards from expiration. The instantaneous or expected return formulation of a pricing model amounts to a differential equation for prices.

Guess that the solution for the call price is a function of stock price and time to expiration, $C_t = C(S, t)$. Use Ito's lemma to find derivatives of $C(S, t)$,

$$dC = C_t\, dt + C_S\, dS + \frac{1}{2}C_{SS}\, dS^2$$

$$= \left[C_t + C_S S\mu + \frac{1}{2}C_{SS}S^2\sigma^2\right]dt + C_S S\sigma\, dz.$$

Plugging into the basic asset pricing equation

$$0 = E_t(d\Lambda C) = CE_t\, d\Lambda + \Lambda E_t\, dC + E_t\, d\Lambda\, dC,$$

using $E_t(d\Lambda/\Lambda) = -r\, dt$ and canceling $\Lambda\, dt$, we get

$$0 = -rC + C_t + C_S S\mu + \frac{1}{2}C_{SS}S^2\sigma^2 - S(\mu - r)C_S$$

or,

$$0 = -rC + C_t + SrC_S + \frac{1}{2}C_{SS}S^2\sigma^2. \tag{17.8}$$

This is the Black–Scholes differential equation for the option price.

We now know a differential equation for the price function $C(S, t)$. We know the value of this function at expiration, $C(S_T, T) = \max(S_T - X, 0)$. The remaining task is to solve this differential equation backwards through time. Conceptually, and numerically, this is easy. Express the differential equation as

$$-\frac{\partial C(S, t)}{\partial t} = -rC(S, t) + Sr\frac{\partial C(S, t)}{\partial S} + \frac{1}{2}\frac{\partial^2 C(S, t)}{\partial S^2}S^2\sigma^2.$$

At any point in time, you know the values of $C(S, t)$ for all S—for example, you can store them on a grid for S. Then, you can take the first and second derivatives with respect to S and form the quantity on the right-hand side at each value of S. Now, you can find the option price at any value of S, one instant earlier in time.

This differential equation, solved with boundary condition

$$C = \max\left\{S_T - X, 0\right\},$$

has an analytic solution—the familiar formula (17.7). One standard way to solve differential equations is to guess and check; and by taking derivatives you can check that (17.7) does satisfy (17.8). Black and Scholes solved the differential equation with a fairly complicated Fourier transform method. The more elegant Feynman–Kac solution amounts to showing that solutions of the partial differential equation (17.8) can be represented as integrals of the form that we already derived independently as in (17.6). (See Duffie [1992, p. 87].)

Problems—Chapter 17

1. We showed that you should never exercise an American call early if there are no dividends. Is the same true for American puts, or are there circumstances in which it is optimal to exercise American puts early?

2. Retrace the steps in the integral derivation of the Black–Scholes formula and show that the dw does not affect the final result.

18
Option Pricing without Perfect Replication

18.1 On The Edges of Arbitrage

THE BEAUTIFUL BLACK–SCHOLES formula launched a thousand techniques for option pricing. The *principle* of no-arbitrage pricing is obvious, but its application leads to many subtle and unanticipated pricing relationships.

However, in many practical situations, the law-of-one-price arguments that we used in the Black–Scholes formula break down. If options really were redundant, it is unlikely that they would be traded as separate assets. It really is easy to synthesize forward rates from zero-coupon bonds, and forward rates are not separately traded or quoted.

We really cannot trade continuously, and trying to do so would drown a strategy in transactions costs. As a practical example, at the time of the 1987 stock market crash, several prominent funds were trying to follow "portfolio insurance" strategies, essentially synthesizing put options by systematically selling stocks as prices declined. During the time of the crash, however, they found that the markets just dried up—they were unable to sell as prices plummeted. We can model this situation mathematically as a Poisson jump, a discontinuous movement in prices. In the face of such jumps the option payoff is *not* perfectly hedged by a portfolio of stock and bond, and cannot be priced as such.

Generalizations of the stochastic setup lead to the same result. If the interest rate or stock volatility are stochastic, we do not have securities that allow us to perfectly hedge the corresponding shocks, so the law of one price again breaks down.

In addition, many options are written on underlying securities that are not traded, or not traded continually and with sufficient liquidity. Real options in particular—the option to build a factory in a particular location—are not based on a tradeable underlying security, so the logic behind Black–Scholes pricing does not apply. Executives are often forbidden to short stock in order to hedge executive options.

Furthermore, trading applications of option pricing formulas seem to suffer a strange inconsistency. We imagine that the stock and bond are perfectly priced and perfectly liquid—available for perfect hedging. Then, we search for options that are priced incorrectly as trading opportunities. If the options can be priced incorrectly, why cannot the stock and bond be priced incorrectly? Trading opportunities involve risk, and a theory that pretends they are arbitrage opportunities does not help to quantify that risk.

In all of these situations, an unavoidable "basis risk" creeps in between the option payoff and the best possible hedge portfolio. Holding the option entails some risk, and the value of the option depends on the "market price" of that risk—the covariance of the risk with an appropriate discount factor.

Nonetheless, we would like not to give up and go back to the consumption-based model, factor models, or other "absolute" methods that try to price all assets. We are still willing to take as given the prices of lots of assets in determining the price of an option, and in particular assets that will be used to hedge the option. We can form an "approximate hedge" or portfolio of basis assets "closest to" the focus payoff, and we can hedge most of the option's risk with that approximate hedge. Then, the uncertainty about the option value is reduced only to figuring out the price of the residual. In addition, since the residuals are small, we might be able to say a lot about option prices with much weaker restrictions on the discount factor than those suggested by absolute models.

Many authors simply add market price of risk assumptions. This leaves the questions, how sensitive are the results to market price of risk assumptions? What are reasonable values for market prices of risk?

In this chapter, I survey "good-deal" option price bounds, a technique that Jesus Saá-Requejo and I (1999) advocated for this situation. The good-deal bounds amount to systematically searching over all possible assignments of the "market price of risk" of the residual, constraining the total market price of risk to a reasonable value, and imposing no arbitrage opportunities, to find upper and lower bounds on the option price. It is *not* equivalent to pricing options with pure Sharpe ratio arguments.

Good deal bonds are just the beginning. Finding ways to merge no-arbitrage and absolute pricing is one of the most exiting new areas of research. The concluding section of this chapter surveys some alternative and additional techniques.

18.2 One-Period Good-Deal Bounds

We want to price the payoff x^c, for example, $x^c = \max(S_T - K, 0)$ for a call option. We have in hand an N-dimensional vector of basis payoffs x, whose prices p we can observe, for example the stock and bond. The good-deal bound finds the minimum and maximum value of x^c by searching over all positive discount factors that price the basis assets and have limited volatility:

$$\overline{C} = \max_{\{m\}} E(mx^c) \ s.t. \ p = E(mx), \quad m \geq 0, \quad \sigma^2(m) \leq h/R^f. \quad (18.1)$$

The corresponding minimization yields the lower bound $\underline{C}$. This is a one-period discrete-time problem. The Black–Scholes formula does not apply because you cannot trade between the price and payoff periods.

The first constraint on the discount factor imposes the price of the basis assets. We want to do as much relative pricing as possible; we want to extend what we know about the prices of x to price x^c, without worrying about where the prices of x come from. The second constraint imposes the absence of arbitrage. This problem without the last constraint yields the arbitrage bounds that we studied in Section 16.1.2. In most situations, the arbitrage bounds are too wide to be of much use.

The last is an additional constraint on discount factors, and the extra content of good-deal versus arbitrage bounds. It is a relatively weak restriction. We could obtain closer bounds on prices with more information about the discount factor. In particular, if we knew the correlation of the discount factor with the payoff x^c we could price the option a lot better!

Discount factor restrictions often have portfolio implications. As $m > 0$ means that no portfolios priced by m may display an arbitrage opportunity, $\sigma^2(m) \leq h/R^f$ means that no portfolio priced by m may have a Sharpe ratio greater than h. Recall $E(mR^e) = 0$ implies $E(m)E(R^e) = -\rho\sigma(m)\sigma(R^e)$ and $|\rho| \leq 1$.

It is a central advantage of a discount factor approach that we can easily impose *both* the discount factor volatility constraint and positivity, merging the lessons of factor models and option pricing models. The prices and payoffs generated by discount factors that satisfy *both* $m \geq 0$ and $\sigma(m) \leq h/R^f$ do more than rule out arbitrage opportunities and high Sharpe ratios.

I will treat the case that there is a risk-free rate, so we can write $E(m) = 1/R^f$. In this case, it is more convenient to express the volatility constraint as a second moment, so the bound (18.1) becomes

$$\underline{C} = \min_{\{m\}} E(m\,x^c) \ s.t. \ p = E(mx), \quad E(m^2) \leq A^2, \quad m \geq 0, \quad (18.2)$$

where $A^2 \equiv (1 + h^2)/R^{f2}$. The problem is a standard minimization with two inequality constraints. Hence we find a solution by trying all the combinations of binding and nonbinding constraints, in order of their ease of calculation. (1) Assume the volatility constraint binds and the positivity constraint is slack. This one is very easy to calculate, since we will find analytic formulas for the solution. If the resulting discount factor $\underline{m}$ is nonnegative, this is the solution. If not, (2) assume that the volatility constraint is slack and the positivity constraint binds. This is the classic arbitrage bound. Find the minimum-variance discount factor that generates the arbitrage bound. If this discount factor satisfies the volatility constraint, this is the solution. If not, (3) solve the problem with both constraints binding.

Volatility Constraint Binds, Positivity Constraint is Slack

If the positivity constraint is slack, the problem reduces to

$$\underline{C} = \min_{\{m\}} \ E(m \, x^c) \ s.t. \ p = E(mx), \qquad E(m^2) \leq A^2. \tag{18.3}$$

We could solve this problem directly, choosing m in each state with Lagrange multipliers on the constraints. But as with the mean-variance frontier, it is much more elegant to set up orthogonal decompositions and then let the solution pop out.

Figure 18.1 describes the idea. $\underline{X}$ denotes the space of payoffs of portfolios of the basis assets x, a stock and a bond in the classic Black–Scholes setup. Though graphed as a line, $\underline{X}$ is typically a larger space. We know all prices in $\underline{X}$, but the payoff x^c that we wish to value does not lie in $\underline{X}$.

Start by decomposing the focus payoff x^c into an approximate hedge $\hat{x}^c$ and a residual w,

$$
\begin{aligned}
x^c &= \hat{x}^c + w, \\
\hat{x}^c &\equiv \text{proj}(x^c|\underline{X}) = E(x^c x') \, E(xx')^{-1}x, \\
w &\equiv x^c - \hat{x}^c.
\end{aligned}
\tag{18.4}
$$

We know the price of $\hat{x}^c$. We want to bound the price of the residual w to learn as much as we can about the price of x^c.

All discount factors that price x—that satisfy $p = E(mx)$—lie in the plane through x^*. As we sweep through these discount factors, we generate any price from $-\infty$ to ∞ for the residual w and hence payoff x^c. All *positive* discount factors $m > 0$ lie in the intersection of the m plane and the positive orthant—the triangular region. Discount factors m in this range generate a limited range of prices for the focus payoff—the arbitrage bounds. Since second moment defines distance in Figure 18.1, the

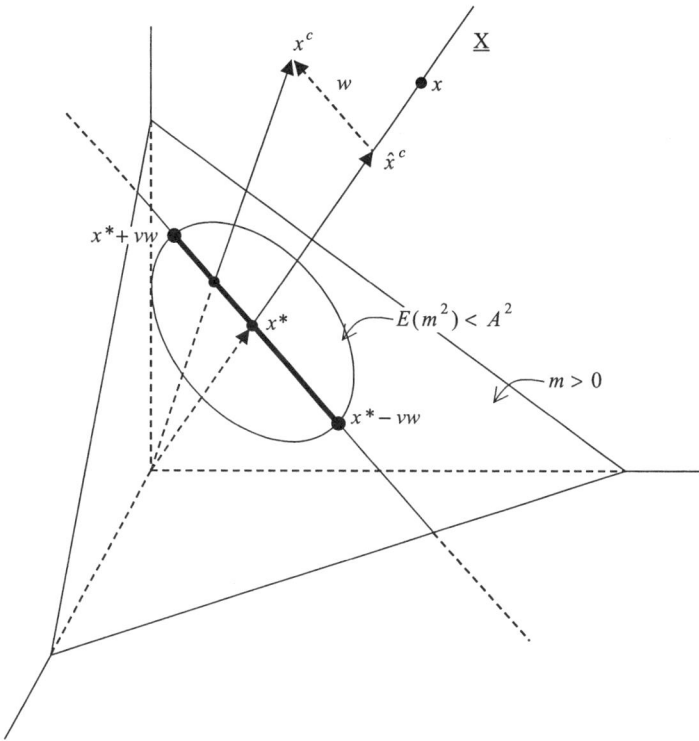

Figure 18.1. *Construction of a discount factor to solve the one-period good-deal bound when the positivity constraint is slack.*

set of discount factors that satisfies the volatility constraint $E(m^2) \leq A^2$ lies inside a sphere around the origin. The circle in Figure 18.1 shows the intersection of this sphere with the set of discount factors. This restricted range of discount factors will produce a restricted range of values for the residual w and hence a restricted range of values for the focus payoff x^c. In the situation I have drawn, the positivity constraint is slack, since the $E(m^2) \leq A^2$ circle lies entirely in the positive orthant.

We want to find the discount factors in the circle that minimize or maximize the price of the residual w. The more a discount factor m points in the w direction, the larger a price $E(mw)$ it assigns to the residual. Obviously, the discount factors that maximize or minimize the price of w point as much as possible towards and away from w. If you add any movement ε orthogonal to w, this increases discount factor volatility without changing the price of w.

Hence, the discount factor that generates the lower bound is

$$\underline{m} = x^* - \underline{v}w, \tag{18.5}$$

where

$$\underline{v} = \sqrt{\frac{A^2 - E(x^{*2})}{E(w^2)}} \tag{18.6}$$

is picked to just satisfy the volatility constraint. The bound is

$$\underline{C} = E(\underline{m}x^c) = E(x^*x^c) - \underline{v}E(w^2). \tag{18.7}$$

The upper bound is given by $\bar{v} = -\underline{v}$.

The first term in equation (18.7) is the value of the approximate hedge portfolio, and can be written several ways, including

$$E(x^*x^c) = E(x^*\hat{x}^c) = E(m\hat{x}^c) \tag{18.8}$$

for any discount factor m that prices basis assets. (To derive (18.8), remember that $E(xy) = E[x \ \text{proj}(y|X)]$.) The second term in equation (18.7) is the lowest possible price of the residual w consistent with the discount factor volatility bound:

$$\underline{v}E(w^2) = E(\underline{v}w \ w) = E[(x^* + \underline{v}w)w] = E(\underline{m}w).$$

For calculations, you can substitute the definitions of x^* and w in equation (18.7) to obtain an explicit, if not very pretty, formula:

$$\underline{C} = p'E(xx')^{-1}E(xx^c)$$
$$- \sqrt{A^2 - p'E(xx')^{-1}p}\sqrt{E(x^{c2}) - E(x^cx')E(xx')^{-1}E(xx^c)}. \tag{18.9}$$

The upper bound $\overline{C}$ is the same formula with a $+$ sign in front of the square root.

Using (18.5), check whether the discount factor is positive in every state of nature. If so, this is the good-deal bound, and the positivity constraint is slack. If not, proceed to the next step.

If you prefer an algebraic and slightly more formal argument, start by noticing that any discount factor that satisfies $p = E(mx)$ can be decomposed as

$$m = x^* + vw + \varepsilon,$$

where $E(x^*w) = E(x^*\varepsilon) = E(w\varepsilon)$. Check these properties from the definition of w and ε; this is just like $R = R^* + wR^{e*} + n$. Our minimization problem is then

$$\min_{\{v, \varepsilon\}} E(mx^c) \text{ s.t. } E(m^2) \leq A^2,$$

$$\min_{\{v, \varepsilon\}} E[(x^* + vw + \varepsilon)(\hat{x}^c + w)] \text{ s.t. } E(x^{*2}) + v^2 E(w^2) + E(\varepsilon^2) \leq A^2,$$

$$\min_{\{v, \varepsilon\}} E(x^*\hat{x}^c) + vE(w^2) \text{ s.t. } E(x^{*2}) + vE(w^2) + E(\varepsilon^2) \leq A^2.$$

The solution is $\varepsilon = 0$ and $v = \pm\sqrt{(A^2 - E(x^{*2}))/E(w^2)}$.

Both Constraints Bind

Next, I find the bounds when both constraints bind. Though this is the third step in the procedure, it is easiest to describe this case next. Introducing Lagrange multipliers, the problem is

$$\underline{C} = \min_{\{m>0\}} \max_{\{\lambda, \delta>0\}} E(m\,x^c) + \lambda'[E(mx) - p] + \frac{\delta}{2}[E(m^2) - A^2].$$

The first-order conditions yield a discount factor that is a truncated linear combination of the payoffs,

$$m = \max\left(-\frac{x^c + \lambda'x}{\delta}, 0\right) = \left[-\frac{x^c + \lambda'x}{\delta}\right]^+. \qquad (18.10)$$

The last equality defines the $[\ ]^+$ notation for truncation. In finance terms, this is a call option with zero strike price.

You can derive (18.10) by introducing a Kuhn–Tucker multiplier $\pi(s)\nu(s)$ on $m(s) > 0$ and taking partial derivatives with respect to m in each state,

$$\underline{C} = \min_{\{m\}} \sum_s \pi(s)m(s)x^c(s) + \lambda'\left[\sum_s \pi(s)m(s)x(s) - p\right]$$

$$+ \frac{\delta}{2}\left[\sum_s \pi(s)m(s)^2 - A^2\right] + \sum_s \pi(s)\nu(s)m(s).$$

$$\frac{1}{\pi(s)}\frac{\partial}{\partial s} : x^c(s) + \lambda'x(s) + \delta m(s) + \nu(s) = 0. \qquad (18.11)$$

If the positivity constraint is slack, the Kuhn–Tucker multiplier $\nu(s)$ is zero,

$$m(s) = -\frac{x^c(s) + \lambda'x(s)}{\delta}.$$

If the positivity constraint binds, then $m(s) = 0$, and $\nu(s)$ is just enough to make (18.11) hold. In sum, we have (18.10).

We could plug expression (18.10) into the constraints, and solve numerically for Lagrange multipliers λ and δ that enforce the constraints. Alas, this procedure requires the solution of a system of nonlinear equations in (λ, δ), which is often a numerically difficult or unstable problem.

Hansen, Heaton, and Luttmer (1995) show how to recast the problem as a maximization, which is numerically much easier. Interchanging min and max,

$$\underline{C} = \max_{\{\lambda, \delta > 0\}} \min_{\{m > 0\}} E(mx^c) + \lambda'[E(mx) - p] + \frac{\delta}{2}[E(m^2) - A^2]. \qquad (18.12)$$

The inner minimization yields the same first-order conditions (18.10). Plugging those first-order conditions into the outer maximization of (18.12) and simplifying, we obtain

$$\underline{C} = \max_{\{\lambda, \delta > 0\}} E\left\{-\frac{\delta}{2}\left[-\frac{x^c + \lambda'x}{\delta}\right]^{+2}\right\} - \lambda'p - \frac{\delta}{2}A^2. \qquad (18.13)$$

You can search numerically over (λ, δ) to find the solution to this problem. The upper bound is found by replacing max with min and replacing $\delta > 0$ with $\delta < 0$.

Positivity Binds, Volatility is Slack

If the volatility constraint is slack and the positivity constraint binds, the problem reduces to

$$\underline{C} = \min_{\{m\}} E(mx^c) \ s.t. \ p = E(mx), \quad m > 0. \qquad (18.14)$$

These are the arbitrage bounds. We found these bounds in Chapter 17 for a call option by being clever. If you cannot be clever, (18.14) is a linear program.

We still have to check that the discount factor volatility constraint can be satisfied at the arbitrage bound. Denote the lower arbitrage bound by C_l. The minimum-variance (second-moment) discount factor that generates the arbitrage bound C_l solves

$$E(m^2)_{\min} = \min_{\{m\}} E(m^2) \ s.t \ \begin{bmatrix} p \\ C_l \end{bmatrix} = E\left(m\begin{bmatrix} x \\ x^c \end{bmatrix}\right), \quad m > 0.$$

Using the same conjugate method, this problem is equivalent to

$$E(m^2)_{\min} = \max_{\{v, \mu\}}\left\{-E\{[-(\mu x^c + v'x)]^{+2}\} - 2v'p - 2\mu C_l\right\}.$$

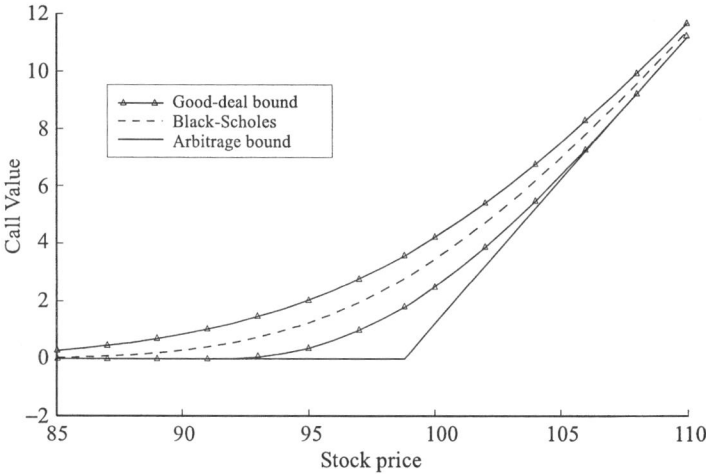

Figure 18.2. *Good-deal option price bounds as a function of stock price. Options have three months to expiration and strike price $K = \$100$. The bounds assume no trading until expiration, and a discount factor volatility bound $h = 1.0$ corresponding to twice the market Sharpe ratio. The stock is lognormally distributed with parameters calibrated to an index option.*

Again, search numerically for (v, μ) to solve this problem. If $E(m^2)_{\min} \leq A$, C_l is the solution to the good-deal bound; if not, we proceed with the case that both constraints are binding described above.

Application to the Black–Scholes Environment with
No Dynamic Hedging

The natural first exercise with this technique is to see how it applies in the Black–Scholes world. Keep in mind, this is the Black–Scholes world with no intermediate trading; compare the results to the arbitrage bounds, not to the Black-Scholes formula. Figure 18.2, taken from Cochrane and Saá-Requejo (1999), presents the upper and lower good-deal bounds for a call option on the S&P500 index with strike price $K = \$100$, and three months to expiration. We used parameter values $E(R) = 13\%$, $\sigma(R) = 16\%$ for the stock index return and a risk-free rate $R^f = 5\%$. The discount factor volatility constraint is twice the historical market Sharpe ratio, $h = 2 \times E(R - R^f)/\sigma(R) = 1.0$. To take the expectations required in the formula, we evaluated integrals against the lognormal stock distribution.

The figure includes the lower arbitrage bounds $C \geq 0, C \geq K/R^f$. The upper arbitrage bound states that $C \leq S$, but this $45°$ line is too far up to fit on the vertical scale and still see anything else. As in many practical situations, the arbitrage bounds are so wide that they are of little use. The upper good-deal bound is much tighter than the upper arbitrage bound. For example, if the stock price is $95, the entire range of option prices between the upper bound of $2 and the upper arbitrage bound of $95 is ruled out.

The lower good-deal bound is the same as the lower arbitrage bound for stock prices less than about $90 and greater than about $110. In this range, the positivity constraint binds and the volatility constraint is slack. This range shows that it is important to impose *both* volatility and positivity constraints. *Good-deal bounds are not just the imposition of low Sharpe ratios on options.* (I emphasize it because this point causes a lot of confusion.) The volatility bound alone admits negative prices. A free out-of-the-money call option is like a lottery ticket: it is an arbitrage opportunity, but its expected return/standard deviation ratio is terrible, because the standard deviation is so high. A Sharpe ratio criterion alone will not rule it out.

In between $90 and $110, the good-deal bound improves on the lower arbitrage bound. It also improves on a bound that imposes only the volatility constraint. In this region, both positivity and volatility constraints bind. This fact has an interesting implication: Not all values outside the good-deal bounds imply high Sharpe ratios or arbitrage opportunities. Such values might be generated by a positive but highly volatile discount factor, and generated by *another* less volatile but sometimes negative discount factor, but no discount factor generates these values that is *simultaneously* nonnegative and respects the volatility constraint.

It makes sense to rule out these values. If we know that an investor will invest in any arbitrage opportunity or take any Sharpe ratio greater than *h*, then we know that his *unique* marginal utility satisfies both restrictions. He would find a utility-improving trade for values outside the good-deal bounds, even though those values may not imply a high Sharpe ratio, an arbitrage opportunity, or any other simple portfolio interpretation.

The right thing to do is to intersect restrictions on the discount factor. Simple portfolio interpretations, while historically important, are likely to fall by the wayside as we add more discount factor restrictions or intersect simple ones.

———

18.3 Multiple Periods and Continuous Time

Now, on to the interesting case. Option pricing is all about dynamic hedging, even if imperfect dynamic hedging. Good-deal bounds would be of little use if we could only apply them to one-period environments.

The Bounds are Recursive

The central fact that makes good-deal bounds tractable in dynamic environments is that the bounds are recursive. Today's bound can be calculated as the minimum price of tomorrow's bound, just as today's option price can be calculated as the value of tomorrow's option price.

To see that the bounds are recursive, consider a two-period version of the problem,

$$\underline{C}_0 = \min_{\{m_1, m_2\}} E_0(m_1 m_2 x_2^c) \ s.t.$$

$$p_t = E_t(m_{t+1} p_{t+1}), \ E_t(m_{t+1}^2) \le A_t^2, \quad m_{t+1} > 0, \quad t = 0, 1. \quad (18.15)$$

This two-period problem is equivalent to a series of one-period problems, in which the C_0 problem finds the lowest price of the C_1 lower bound,

$$\underline{C}_1 = \min_{\{m_2\}} E_1(m_2 x_2^c), \qquad \underline{C}_0 = \min_{\{m_1\}} E_0(m_1 \underline{C}_1),$$

subject to (18.15). Why? The solution to the two-period problem $\min E_0(m_1 E_1(m_2 x^c))$ must minimize $E_1(m_2 x^c)$ in each state of nature at time 1. If not, you could lower $E_1(m_2 x^c)$ without affecting the constraints, and lower the objective. Note that this recursive property only holds if we impose $m > 0$. If $m_1 < 0$ were possible, we might want to maximize $E_1(m_2 x^c)$ in some states of nature.

Basis Risk and Real Options

The general case leads to some dense formulas, so a simple example will let us understand the idea most simply. Let us value a European call option on an event V that is not a traded asset, but is correlated with a traded asset that can be used as an approximate hedge. This situation is common with real options and nonfinancial options and describes some financial options on illiquid assets.

The terminal payoff is

$$x_T^c = \max(V_T - K, 0).$$

Model the joint evolution of the traded asset S and the event V on which the option is written as

$$\frac{dS}{S} = \mu_S \, dt + \sigma_S \, dz,$$

$$\frac{dV}{V} = \mu_V \, dt + \sigma_{V_z} \, dz + \sigma_{Vw} \, dw.$$

The *dw* risk cannot be hedged by the *S* asset, so the market price of *dw* risk—its correlation with the discount factor—will matter to the option price.

We are looking for a discount factor that prices *S* and r^f, has instantaneous volatility *A*, and generates the largest or smallest price for the option. Hence it will have the largest loading on *dw* possible. By analogy with the one-period case (18.5), you can quickly see that the discount factor will have the form

$$\frac{d\underline{\Lambda}}{\underline{\Lambda}} = \frac{d\Lambda^*}{\Lambda^*} \pm \sqrt{A^2 - h_S^2}\, dw,$$

$$\frac{d\Lambda^*}{\Lambda^*} = -r\, dt - h_S\, dz,$$

$$h_S = \frac{\mu_S - r}{\sigma_S}.$$

$d\Lambda^*/\Lambda^*$ is the familiar analogue to x^* that prices stock and bond. We add a loading on the orthogonal shock *dw* just sufficient to satisfy the constraint $E_t(d\Lambda^2/\Lambda^2) = A^2$. One of $\pm$ will generate the upper bound, and one will generate the lower bound.

Now that we have the discount factor, the good-deal bound is given by

$$\underline{C}_t = E_t\left[\frac{\underline{\Lambda}_T}{\underline{\Lambda}_t} \max(V_T - K)\right].$$

S_t, V_t, and Λ_t are all diffusions with constant coefficients. Therefore, S_T, V_T, and Λ_T are jointly lognormally distributed, so the double integral defining the expectation is straightforward to perform, and works very similarly to the integral we evaluated to solve the Black–Scholes formula in Section 16.2.1. (If you get stuck, see Cochrane and Saá-Requejo [1999] for the algebra.)

The result is

$$\underline{C} \text{ or } \overline{C} = V_0 e^{\eta T} \phi\left(d + \frac{1}{2}\sigma_V \sqrt{T}\right) - Ke^{-rT}\phi\left(d - \frac{1}{2}\sigma_V \sqrt{T}\right), \qquad (18.16)$$

where $\phi(\cdot)$ denotes the left tail of the normal distribution and

$$\sigma_V^2 \equiv E_t \frac{dV^2}{V^2} = \sigma_{Vz}^2 + \sigma_{Vw}^2,$$

$$d \equiv \frac{\ln(V_0/K) + (\eta + r)T}{\sigma_V \sqrt{T}},$$

$$\eta \equiv \left[h_V - h_S \left(\rho - a \sqrt{\frac{A^2}{h_S^2} - 1} \sqrt{1 - \rho^2} \right) \right] \sigma_V,$$

$$h_S \equiv \frac{\mu_S - r}{\sigma_S}, \quad h_V \equiv \frac{\mu_V - r}{\sigma_V},$$

$$\rho \equiv \mathrm{corr}\left(\frac{dV}{V}, \frac{dS}{S} \right) = \frac{\sigma_{Vz}}{\sigma_V},$$

$$a = \begin{cases} +1 \text{ upper bound,} \\ -1 \text{ lower bound.} \end{cases}$$

This expression is exactly the Black–Scholes formula with the addition of the η term. μ_V enters the formula because the event V may not grow at the same rate as the asset S. Obviously, the correlation ρ between V shocks and asset shocks enters the formula, and as this correlation declines, the bounds widen. The bounds also widen as the volatility constraint A becomes larger relative to the asset Sharpe ratios h_S.

Market Prices of Risk
Continuous-time pricing problems are often specified in terms of "market prices of risk" rather than discount factors. This is the instantaneous Sharpe ratio that an asset must earn if it loads on a specific shock. If an asset has a price process P that loads on a shock $\sigma\,dw$, then its expected return must be

$$E_t \frac{dP}{P} - r^f dt = -\sigma E_t \left(\frac{d\Lambda}{\Lambda} dw \right)$$

with Sharpe ratio

$$\lambda = \frac{E_t(dP/P) - r^f dt}{\sigma} = -E_t \left(\frac{d\Lambda}{\Lambda} dw \right).$$

I have introduced the common notation λ for the market price of risk. Thus, problems are often attacked by making assumptions about λ directly and then proceeding from

$$E_t \frac{dP}{P} - r^f dt = \lambda \sigma.$$

In this language, the market price of stock risk is h_S and can be measured by observing the stock, and does not matter when you can price by arbitrage (notice it is missing from the Black–Scholes formula). Our problem comes down to choosing the market price of dw risk, which cannot be measured by observing a traded asset, in such a way as to minimize or maximize the option price, subject to a constraint that the total price of risk $\sqrt{h_S^2 + \lambda^2} \leq A$.

Continuous Time

Now, I give a more systematic expression of the same ideas in continuous time. As in the option pricing case in the last chapter and the term structure case in the next chapter, we will obtain a differential characterization. To actually get prices, we have either to solve the discount factor forward, or to find a differential equation for prices which we solve backward.

Basis Assets

In place of $E(x)$, $E(xx')$, etc., model the price processes of an n_S-dimensional vector of basis assets by a diffusion,

$$\frac{dS}{S} = \mu_S(S, V, t)\, dt + \sigma_S(S, V, t)\, dz, \qquad E(dz\, dz') = I. \qquad (18.17)$$

Rather than complicate the notation, understand division to operate element by element on vectors, e.g., $dS/S = [\ dS_1/S_1\ dS_2/S_2 \cdots\ ]$. The basis assets may pay dividends at rate $D(S, V, t)\, dt$.

V represents an n_V-dimensional vector of additional state variables that follow

$$dV = \mu_V(S, V, t)\, dt + \sigma_{Vz}(S, V, t)\, dz + \sigma_{Vw}(S, V, t)\, dw,$$
$$E(dw\, dw') = I, \qquad E(dw\, dz') = 0. \qquad (18.18)$$

This could include a stochastic stock volatility or stochastic interest rate—classic cases in which the Black–Scholes replication breaks down. Again, I keep it simple by assuming there is a risk-free rate.

The Problem

We want to value an asset that pays continuous dividends at rate $x^c(S, V, t)\, dt$ and has a terminal payment $x^c_T(S, V, T)$. Now we must choose a discount factor *process* to minimize the asset's value

$$\underline{C}_t = \min_{\{\Lambda_s,\ t < s \leq T\}} E_t \int_{s=t}^{T} \frac{\Lambda_s}{\Lambda_t} x^c_s\, ds + E_t\left(\frac{\Lambda_T}{\Lambda_t} x^c_T\right) \qquad (18.19)$$

subject to the constraints that (1) the discount factor prices the basis assets S, r at each moment in time, (2) the instantaneous volatility of the discount factor process is less than a prespecified value A^2, and (3) the discount factor is positive $\Lambda_s > 0$, $t \le s \le T$.

One Period at a Time; Differential Statement
Since the problem is recursive, we can study how to move one step back in time,

$$\underline{C}_t \Lambda_t = \min_{\{\Lambda_s\}} E_t \int_{s=t}^{t+\Delta t} \Lambda_s x_s^c \, ds + E_t(\Lambda_{t+\Delta t}\underline{C}_{t+\Delta t})$$

or, for small time intervals,

$$\underline{C}_t \Lambda_t = \min_{\{\Delta\Lambda\}} E_t\{x^c \Delta t + (\underline{C}_t + \Delta\underline{C})(\Lambda_t + \Delta\Lambda)\}.$$

Letting $\Delta t \to 0$, we can write the objective in differential form,

$$0 = \frac{x_t^c}{\underline{C}} \, dt + \min_{\{d\Lambda\}} \frac{E_t[d(\Lambda\underline{C})]}{\Lambda\underline{C}}, \tag{18.20}$$

subject to the constraints. We can also write (18.20) as

$$E_t \frac{d\underline{C}}{\underline{C}} + \frac{x_t^c}{\underline{C}} \, dt - r^f dt = -\min_{\{d\Lambda\}} E_t \left(\frac{d\Lambda}{\Lambda} \frac{d\underline{C}}{\underline{C}} \right). \tag{18.21}$$

This condition sensibly tells us to find the lowest value $\underline{C}$ by maximizing the drift of the bound at each date. You should recognize the form of (18.20) and (18.21) as the basic pricing equations in continuous time, relating expected returns to covariance with discount factors.

Constraints
Now we express the constraints. As in the discrete-time case, we orthogonalize the discount factor in $m = x^* + \varepsilon$ form, and then the solution pops out. Any discount factor that prices the basis assets is of the form

$$\frac{d\Lambda}{\Lambda} = \frac{d\Lambda^*}{\Lambda^*} - v \, dw, \tag{18.22}$$

where

$$\frac{d\Lambda^*}{\Lambda^*} \equiv -r \, dt - \tilde{\mu}_S' \Sigma_S^{-1} \sigma_S \, dz,$$

$$\tilde{\mu}_S \equiv \mu_S + \frac{D}{S} - r, \qquad \Sigma_S = \sigma_S \sigma_S',$$

and v is a $1 \times n_V$ matrix. We can add shocks orthogonal to dw if we like, but they will have no effect on the answer; the minimization will set such loadings to zero.

The volatility constraint is

$$\frac{1}{dt} E_t \frac{d\Lambda^2}{\Lambda^2} \leq A^2,$$

and hence, using (18.22),

$$vv' \leq A^2 - \frac{1}{dt} E_t \frac{d\Lambda^{*2}}{\Lambda^{*2}} = A^2 - \tilde{\mu}'_S \Sigma_S^{-1} \tilde{\mu}_S. \tag{18.23}$$

By expressing the constraints via (18.22) and (18.23), we have again reduced the problem of choosing the stochastic process for Λ to the choice of loadings v on the noises dw with unknown values, subject to a quadratic constraint on vv'. Since we are picking differentials and have ruled out jumps, the positivity constraint is slack so long as $\Lambda > 0$.

Market Prices of Risk
Using equation (18.22), v is the vector of market prices of risks of the dw shocks—the expected return that any asset must offer if its shocks are dw:

$$-\frac{1}{dt} E\left(\frac{d\Lambda}{\Lambda} \, dw\right) = v.$$

Thus, the problem is equivalent to: find at each date the assignment of market prices of risk to the dw shocks that minimizes (maximizes) the focus payoff value, subject to the constraint that the total (sum of squared) market price of risk is bounded by A^2.

Now, we are ready to follow the usual steps. We can characterize a differential equation for the option price bound that must be solved back from expiration, or we can try to solve the discount factor forward and take an expectation.

Solutions: The Discount Factor and Bound Drift at Each Instant
We can start by characterizing the bound's process, just as the basis assets follow (18.17). This step is exactly the instantaneous analogue of the one-period bound without a positivity constraint, so remember that logic if the equations start to get a bit forbidding.

Guess that lower bound $\underline{C}$ follows a diffusion process, and figure out what the coefficients must look like. Write

$$\frac{d\underline{C}}{\underline{C}} = \mu_{\underline{C}}(S, V, t) \, dt + \sigma_{\underline{C}z}(S, V, t) \, dz + \sigma_{\underline{C}w}(S, V, t) \, dw. \tag{18.24}$$

$\sigma_{\underline{C}z}$ and $\sigma_{\underline{C}w}$ capture the stochastic evolution of the bound over the next instant—the analogues to $E(xx^c)$, etc. that were inputs to the one-period problem. Therefore, a differential or moment-to-moment characterization of the bound will tell us $\mu_{\underline{C}}$ and $d\underline{\Lambda}$ in terms of $\sigma_{\underline{C}z}$ and $\sigma_{\underline{C}w}$.

Theorem: *The lower bound discount factor $\underline{\Lambda}_t$ follows*

$$\frac{d\underline{\Lambda}}{\underline{\Lambda}} = \frac{d\Lambda^*}{\Lambda^*} - \underline{v}\,dw \tag{18.25}$$

and $\mu_{\underline{C}}$, $\sigma_{\underline{C}z}$, and $\sigma_{\underline{C}w}$ satisfy the restriction

$$\mu_{\underline{C}} + \frac{x^c}{\underline{C}} - r = -\frac{1}{dt}E_t\left(\frac{d\Lambda^*}{\Lambda^*}\,\sigma_{\underline{C}z}\,dz\right) + \underline{v}\sigma'_{\underline{C}w}, \tag{18.26}$$

where

$$\underline{v} = \sqrt{A^2 - \frac{1}{dt}E_t\frac{d\Lambda^{*2}}{\Lambda^{*2}}}\,\frac{\sigma_{\underline{C}w}}{\sqrt{\sigma_{\underline{C}w}\sigma'_{\underline{C}w}}}. \tag{18.27}$$

The upper bound process $\overline{C}_t$ and discount factor $\overline{\Lambda}_t$ have the same representation with $\overline{v} = -\underline{v}$.

This theorem has the same geometric interpretation as shown in Figure 18.1 $d\Lambda^*/\Lambda^*$ is the combination of basis asset shocks that prices the basis assets by construction, in analogy to x^*. The term $\sigma_{\underline{C}w}\,dw$ corresponds to the error w, and $\sigma_{\underline{C}w}\sigma'_{\underline{C}w}$ corresponds to $E(w^2)$. The proposition looks a little different because now we choose a vector v rather than a number. We could define a residual $\sigma_{\underline{C}w}\,dw$ and then the problem would reduce to choosing a number, the loading of $d\Lambda$ on this residual. It is not convenient to do so in this case since $\sigma_{\underline{C}w}$ potentially changes over time. In the geometry of Figure 18.1, the w direction may change over time. The algebraic proof just follows this logic.

Proof: Substituting equation (18.22) into the problem (18.20) in order to impose the pricing constraint, the problem is

$$0 = \frac{x^c}{\underline{C}}\,dt + E_t\left[\frac{d(\Lambda^*\underline{C})}{\Lambda^*\underline{C}}\right] - \min_{\{v\}} vE_t\left(dw\frac{d\underline{C}}{\underline{C}}\right)$$

$$\text{s.t. } vv' \le A^2 - \frac{1}{dt}E_t\left(\frac{d\Lambda^{*2}}{\Lambda^{*2}}\right).$$

Using equation (18.24) for dC/C in the last term, the problem is

$$0 = \frac{x^c}{\underline{C}} + \frac{1}{dt}E_t\left[\frac{d(\Lambda^*\underline{C})}{\Lambda^*\underline{C}}\right] - \min_{\{v\}} v\sigma'_{\underline{C}w} \quad \text{s.t.}$$

$$vv' \le A^2 - \frac{1}{dt}E_t\left(\frac{d\Lambda^{*2}}{\Lambda^{*2}}\right). \tag{18.28}$$

This is a linear objective in v with a quadratic constraint. Therefore, as long as $\sigma_{\underline{C}w} \neq 0$, the constraint binds and the optimal v is given by (18.27). $\bar{v} = -\underline{v}$ gives the maximum since $\sigma_{\underline{C}w}\sigma'_{\underline{C}w} > 0$. Plugging the optimal value for v in (18.28) gives

$$0 = \frac{x^c}{\underline{C}} + \frac{1}{dt}E_t\left[\frac{d(\Lambda^*\underline{C})}{\Lambda^*\underline{C}}\right] - \underline{v}\sigma'_{\underline{C}w}.$$

For clarity, and exploiting the fact that $d\Lambda^*$ does not load on dw, write the middle term as

$$\frac{1}{dt}E_t\left[\frac{d(\Lambda^*\underline{C})}{\Lambda^*\underline{C}}\right] = \mu_{\underline{C}} - r + \frac{1}{dt}E_t\left(\frac{d\Lambda^*}{\Lambda^*}\sigma_{\underline{C}z}\,dz\right).$$

If $\sigma_{\underline{C}w} = 0$, any v leads to the same price bound. In this case we can most simply take $v = 0$. $\square$

As in the discrete-time case, we can plug in the definition of Λ^* to obtain explicit, if less intuitive, expressions for the optimal discount factor and the resulting lower bound,

$$\frac{d\underline{\Lambda}}{\underline{\Lambda}} = -r\,dt + \tilde{\mu}'_S\Sigma_S^{-1}\sigma_S\,dz - \sqrt{A^2 - \tilde{\mu}'_S\Sigma_S^{-1}\tilde{\mu}_S}\,\frac{\sigma_{\underline{C}w}}{\sqrt{\sigma_{\underline{C}w}\sigma'_{\underline{C}w}}}\,dw, \quad (18.29)$$

$$\mu_{\underline{C}} + \frac{x^c}{\underline{C}} - r = \tilde{\mu}'_S\Sigma_S^{-1}\sigma_S\sigma_{\underline{C}z} + \sqrt{A^2 - \tilde{\mu}'_S\Sigma_S^{-1}\tilde{\mu}_S}\sqrt{\sigma_{\underline{C}w}\sigma'_{\underline{C}w}}. \quad (18.30)$$

A Partial Differential Equation

Now we are ready to apply the standard method; find a partial differential equation and solve it backwards to find the price at any date. The method proceeds exactly as for the Black–Scholes formula: Guess a solution $\underline{C}(S, V, t)$. Use Ito's lemma to derive expressions for $\mu_{\underline{C}}$ and $\sigma_{\underline{C}z}$, $\sigma_{\underline{C}w}$ in terms of the partial derivatives of $\underline{C}(S, V, t)$. Substitute these expressions into restriction (18.30). The result is ugly, but straightforward to evaluate numerically. Just like the Black–Scholes partial differential equation, it expresses the time derivative $\partial \underline{C}/\partial t$ in terms of derivatives with respect to state variables, and thus can be used to work back from a terminal period.

Theorem: *The lower bound $\underline{C}(S, V, t)$ is the solution to the partial differential equation*

$$x^c - r\underline{C} + \frac{\partial \underline{C}}{\partial t} + \frac{1}{2} \sum_{i,j} \frac{\partial^2 \underline{C}}{\partial S_i \partial S_j} S_i S_j \sigma_{S_i} \sigma'_{S_j}$$

$$+ \frac{1}{2} \sum_{i,j} \frac{\partial^2 \underline{C}}{\partial V_i \partial V_j} (\sigma_{Vz_i} \sigma'_{Vz_j} + \sigma_{Vw_i} \sigma'_{Vw_j}) + \sum_{i,j} \frac{\partial^2 \underline{C}}{\partial S_i \partial V_j} S_i \sigma_{S_i} \sigma'_{Vz_j}$$

$$= \left(\frac{D}{S} - r\right)' (S\underline{C}_S) + \left(\tilde{\mu}'_S \Sigma_S^{-1} \sigma_S \sigma'_{Vz} - \mu'_V\right) \underline{C}_V$$

$$+ \sqrt{A^2 - \tilde{\mu}'_S \Sigma_S^{-1} \tilde{\mu}_S} \sqrt{\underline{C}'_V \sigma_{Vw} \sigma'_{Vw} \underline{C}_V},$$

subject to the boundary conditions provided by the focus asset payoff x^c_T. $\underline{C}_V$ denotes the vector with typical element $\partial \underline{C}/\partial V_j$ and $(S\underline{C}_S)$ denotes the vector with typical element $S_i \partial \underline{C}/\partial S_i$. Replacing $+$ with $-$ before the square root gives the partial differential equation satisfied by the upper bound.

The Discount Factor

In general, the $\underline{\Lambda}$ process (18.25) or (18.29) depends on the parameters σ_{Cw}. Hence, without solving the above partial differential equation we do not know how to spread the loading of $d\underline{\Lambda}$ across the multiple sources of risk dw whose risk prices we do not observe. Equivalently, we do not know how to optimally spread the total market price of risk across the elements of dw. Thus, in general we cannot use the integration approach—solve the discount factor forward—to find the bound by

$$\underline{C}_t = E_t \int_{s=t}^{T} \frac{\underline{\Lambda}_s}{\underline{\Lambda}_t} x^c_s \, ds + E_t \left(\frac{\underline{\Lambda}_T}{\underline{\Lambda}_t} x^c_T\right).$$

However, if there is only one shock dw, then we do not have to worry about how the loading of $d\underline{\Lambda}$ spreads across multiple sources of risk. v can be determined simply by the volatility constraint. In this special case, dw and σ_{Cw} are scalars. Hence equation (18.25) simplifies as follows:

Theorem: *In the special case that there is only one extra noise dw driving the V process, we can find the lower bound discount factor $\underline{\Lambda}$ directly from*

$$\frac{d\underline{\Lambda}}{\underline{\Lambda}} = -r \, dt - \tilde{\mu}'_S \Sigma_S^{-1} \sigma_S \, dz - \sqrt{A^2 - \tilde{\mu}'_S \Sigma_S^{-1} \tilde{\mu}_S} \, dw. \qquad (18.31)$$

I used this characterization to solve for the case of a nontraded underlying in the last section. In some applications, the loading of $d\underline{\Lambda}$ on multiple shocks dw may be constant over time. In such cases, one can again construct the discount factor and solve for bounds by (possibly numerical) integration, avoiding the solution of a partial differential equation.

18.4 Extensions, Other Approaches, and Bibliography

The roots of the good-deal idea go a long way back. Ross (1976) bounded APT residuals by assuming that no portfolio can have more than twice the market Sharpe ratio, and I used the corresponding idea that discount factor volatility should be bounded to generate a robust approximate APT in Section 9.4. Good-deal bounds apply the same idea to option payoffs. However, the good-deal bounds also impose positive discount factors, and this constraint is important in an option pricing context. We also study dynamic models that chain discount factors together as in the option pricing literature.

The one-period good-deal bound is the dual to the Hansen–Jagannathan (1991) bound with positivity—Hansen and Jagannathan study the minimum variance of positive discount factors that correctly price a given set of assets. The good-deal bound interchanges the position of the option pricing equation and the variance of the discount factor. The techniques for solving the bound, therefore, are exactly those of the Hansen–Jagannathan bound in this one-period setup.

There is nothing magic about discount factor volatility. This kind of problem needs weak but credible discount factor restrictions that lead to tractable and usefully tight bounds. Several other similar restrictions have been proposed in the literature.

1) Levy (1985) and Constantinides (1998) assume that the discount factor declines monotonically with a state variable; marginal utility should decline with wealth.

2) The good-deal bounds allow the worst case that marginal utility growth is perfectly correlated with a portfolio of basis and focus assets. In many cases one could credibly impose a sharper limit than $-1 \leq \rho \leq 1$ on this correlation to obtain tighter bounds.

3) Bernardo and Ledoit (1999) use the restriction $a \geq m \geq b$ to sharpen the no-arbitrage restriction $\infty \geq m > 0$. They show that this restriction has a beautiful portfolio interpretation—$a < m < b$ corresponds to limited "gain-loss ratios" just as $\sigma(m)/E(m)$ corresponds to limited Sharpe ratios. Define $[R^e]^+ = \max(R^e, 0)$ and $[R^e]^- = -\min(-R^e, 0)$ as the "gains and losses" of an excess return R^e. Then,

$$\max_{\{R^e \in \underline{R}^e\}} \frac{[R^e]^+}{[R^e]^-} = \min_{\{m:\ 0 = E(mR^e)\}} \frac{\sup(m)}{\inf(m)}. \tag{18.32}$$

(The sup and inf ignore measure-zero states.) This is exactly analogous to

$$\max_{\{R^e \in \underline{R}^e\}} \frac{|E(R^e)|}{\sigma(R^e)} = \min_{\{m: \ 0=E(mR^e)\}} \frac{\sigma(m)}{E(m)}$$

and hints at an interesting restatement of asset pricing theory in L^1 with sup norm rather than L^2 with second-moment norm.

Since $m \geq a$, the call option price generated by this restriction in a one-period model is strictly greater than the lower arbitrage bound generated by $m = 0$; as in this case, the gain-loss bound can improve on the good-deal bound.

4) Bernardo and Ledoit also suggest $a \geq m/y \geq b$, where y is an explicit discount factor model such as the consumption-based model or CAPM, as a way of imposing a "weak implication" of that particular model.

These alternatives are really not competitors. Add all the discount factor restrictions that are appropriate and useful for a given problem.

This exercise seems to me a strong case for discount factor methods as opposed to portfolio methods. The combination of positivity and volatility constraints on the discount factor leads to a sharper bound than the intersection of no arbitrage and limited Sharpe ratios. I do not know of a simple portfolio characterization of the set of prices that are ruled out by the good-deal bound when both constraints bind. The same will be true as we add, say, gain-loss restrictions, monotonicity restrictions, etc.

In continuous time, option pricing and term structure problems increasingly feature assumptions about the "market price of risk" of the non traded shocks. The good-deal bounds treat these rather formally; they choose the market prices of risks at each instant to minimize or maximize the option price subject to a constraint that the total market price of risk is less than a reasonable value, compared to the Sharpe ratios of other trading opportunities. One need not be this formal. Many empirical implementations of option pricing and term structure models feature unbelievable sizes and time variation in market prices of risk. Just imposing sensible values for the market prices of risk and trying on a range of sensible values may be good enough for many practical situations.

The continuous-time treatment has not yet been extended to the important case of jumps rather than diffusion processes. With jumps, both the positivity and volatility constraints will bind.

Problems—Chapter 18

1. Prove (18.32),

$$\max_{\{R^e \in \underline{R}^e\}} \frac{[R^e]^+}{[R^e]^-} = \min_{\{m:0=E(mR^e)\}} \frac{\sup(m)}{\inf(m)}.$$

Start with a finite state space.

2. Binomial models are very popular in option pricing. This simple problem illustrates the technique. A stock currently selling at S will either rise to $S_T = uS$ with probability π_u or decline to $S_T = dS$ with probability π_d, paying no dividends in the interim. There is a constant gross interest rate R^f.

  (a) Find a discount factor that prices stock and bond. This means, find its value in each state of nature.

  (b) Use the discount factor to price a call option one step before expiration. Express your results as an expected value using risk-neutral probabilities.

  (c) Do the same thing two steps before expiration.

  (d) Cox, Ross, and Rubinstein (1979) derive these formulas by setting up a hedge portfolio of stocks and bonds, and finding portfolio weights to exactly synthesize the option. Rederive your result with this method.

19

Term Structure of Interest Rates

TERM STRUCTURE MODELS are particularly simple, since bond prices are just the expected value of the discount factor. In equations, the price at time t of a zero-coupon bond that comes due at time $t + j$ is $P_t^{(j)} = E_t(m_{t,t+j})$. Thus, once you specify a time-series process for a one-period discount factor $m_{t,t+1}$, you can in principle find the price of any bond by chaining together the discount factors and finding $P_t^{(j)} = E_t(m_{t,t+1} m_{t+1,t+2} \cdots m_{t+j-1,t+j})$. As with option pricing models, this chaining together can be hard to do, and much of the analytical machinery in term structure models centers on this technical question. As with option pricing models, there are two equivalent ways to do the chaining together: Solve the discount factor forward and take an integral, or find a partial differential equation for prices and solve it backwards from the maturity date.

19.1 Definitions and Notation

A quick introduction to bonds, yields, holding period returns, forward rates, and swaps.

$p_t^{(N)} = $ log price of N period zero-coupon bond at time t.

$y^{(N)} = -\frac{1}{N} p^{(N)} = $ log yield.

$\text{hpr}_{t+1}^{(N)} = p_{t+1}^{(N-1)} - p_t^{(N)} = $ log holding period return.

$\text{hpr} = \frac{dP(N,t)}{P} - \frac{1}{P} \frac{\partial P(N,t)}{\partial N} dt = $ instantaneous return.

$f_t^{(N \to N+1)} = p_t^{(N)} - p_t^{(N+1)} = $ forward rate.

$f(N,t) = -\frac{1}{P} \frac{\partial P(N,t)}{\partial N} = $ instantaneous forward rate.

Bonds

The simplest fixed-income instrument is a *zero-coupon bond*. A zero-coupon bond is a promise to pay one dollar (a nominal bond) or one unit of the consumption good (a real bond) on a specified date. I use a super-script in parentheses to denote maturity: $P_t^{(3)}$ is the price of a three-year zero-coupon bond. I will suppress the t subscript when it is not necessary.

I denote logs by lowercase symbols, $p_t^{(N)} = \ln P_t^{(N)}$. The log price has a nice interpretation. If the price of a one-year zero-coupon bond is 0.95, i.e., 95¢ per dollar face value, the log price is $\ln(0.95) = -0.051$. This means that the bond sells at a 5% discount. Logs also give the continu-ously compounded rate. If we write $e^{rN} = 1/P^{(N)}$, then the continuously compounded rate is $rN = -\ln P^{(N)}$.

Coupon bonds are common in practice. For example, a $100 face value 10-year coupon bond may pay $5 every year for 10 years and $100 at 10 years. (Coupon bonds are often issued with semiannual or more frequent payments, $2.50 every six months for example.) We price coupon bonds by considering them as a portfolio of zeros.

Yield

The yield of a bond is the fictional, constant, known, annual, interest rate that justifies the quoted price of a bond, assuming that the bond does not default. It is not the rate of return of the bond. From this definition, the yield of a zero-coupon bond is the number $Y^{(N)}$ that satisfies

$$P^{(N)} = \frac{1}{\left[Y^{(N)}\right]^N}.$$

Hence

$$Y^{(N)} = \frac{1}{\left[P^{(N)}\right]^{1/N}}, \qquad y^{(N)} = -\frac{1}{N} p^{(N)}.$$

The latter expression nicely connects yields and prices. If the price of a 4-year bond is -0.20 or a 20% discount, that is 5% discount per year, or a yield of 5%. The yield of any stream of cash flows is the number Y that satisfies

$$P = \sum_{j=1}^{N} \frac{CF_j}{Y^j}.$$

In general, you have to search for the value Y that solves this equation, given the cash flows and the price. So long as all cash flows are positive, this is fairly easy to do.

As you can see, *the yield is just a convenient way to quote the price.* In using yields we make *no* assumptions. We do not assume that actual interest rates are known or constant; we do not assume the actual bond is default-free. Bonds that may default trade at lower prices or higher yields than bonds that are less likely to default. This only means a higher return if the bond happens not to default.

Holding Period Returns

If you buy an N-period bond and then sell it—it has now become an $(N-1)$-period bond—you achieve a return of

$$HPR_{t+1}^{(N)} = \frac{\$back}{\$paid} = \frac{P_{t+1}^{(N-1)}}{P_t^{(N)}} \qquad (19.1)$$

or, of course,

$$hpr_{t+1}^{(N)} = p_{t+1}^{(N-1)} - p_t^{(N)}.$$

We date this return (from t to $t+1$) as $t+1$ because that is when you find out its value. If this is confusing, take the time to write returns as $HPR_{t\to t+1}$ and then you will never get lost.

In continuous time, we can easily find the instantaneous holding period return of bonds with fixed maturity *date* $P(T, t)$

$$hpr = \frac{P(T, t+\Delta) - P(T, t)}{P(T, t)},$$

and, taking the limit,

$$hpr = \frac{dP(T, t)}{P}.$$

However, it is nicer to look for a bond pricing function $P(N, t)$ that fixes the *maturity* rather than the *date*. As in (19.1), we then have to account for the fact that you sell bonds that have shorter maturity than you buy:

$$hpr = \frac{P(N - \Delta, t+\Delta) - P(N, t)}{P(N, t)}$$
$$= \frac{P(N - \Delta, t+\Delta) - P(N, t+\Delta) + P(N, t+\Delta) - P(N, t)}{P(N, t)},$$

and, taking the limit

$$hpr - \frac{dP(N, t)}{P} - \frac{1}{P}\frac{\partial P(N, t)}{\partial N}dt. \qquad (19.2)$$

Forward Rate

The forward rate is defined as the rate at which you can contract *today* to borrow or lend money starting at period N, to be paid back at period $N+1$.

You can synthesize a forward contract from a spectrum of zero-coupon bonds, so the forward rate can be derived from the prices of zero-coupon bonds. Here is how. Suppose you buy one N-period zero-coupon bond and simultaneously sell $x(N+1)$-period zero-coupon bonds. Let us track your cash flow at every date:

	Buy N-period zero	Sell x $(N+1)$-period zeros	Net cash flow
Today 0:	$-P^{(N)}$	$+xP^{(N+1)}$	$xP^{(N+1)} - P^{(N)}$
Time N:	1		1
Time $N+1$:		$-x$	$-x$

Now, choose x so that today's cash flow is zero:

$$x = \frac{P^{(N)}}{P^{(N+1)}}.$$

You pay or get nothing today, you get \$1.00 at N, and you pay $P^{(N)}/P^{(N+1)}$ at $N+1$. You have synthesized a contract signed today for a loan from N to $N+1$—a forward rate! Thus,

$$F_t^{(N \to N+1)} = \text{ Forward rate at } t \text{ for } N \to N+1 = \frac{P_t^{(N)}}{P_t^{(N+1)}},$$

and of course

$$f_t^{(N \to N+1)} = p_t^{(N)} - p_t^{(N+1)}. \tag{19.3}$$

People sometimes identify forward rates by the initial date, $f_t^{(N)}$, and sometimes by the ending date, $f_t^{(N+1)}$. I use the arrow notation when I want to be really clear about dating a return.

Forward rates have the lovely property that you can always express a bond price as its discounted present value using forward rates,

$$p_t^{(N)} = p_t^{(N)} - p_t^{(N-1)} + p_t^{(N-1)} - p_t^{(N-2)} - \cdots - p_t^{(2)} - p_t^{(1)} + p_t^{(1)}$$

$$= -f_t^{(N-1 \to N)} - f_t^{(N-2 \to N-1)} - \cdots - f_t^{(1 \to 2)} - y_t^{(1)}$$

$(y_t^{(1)} = f_t^{(0 \to 1)}$ of course), so

$$P_t^{(N)} = -\sum_{j=0}^{N-1} f_t^{(j \to j+1)} = \left(\prod_{j=0}^{N-1} F_t^{(j \to j+1)} \right)^{-1}.$$

Intuitively, the price today must be equal to the present value of the payoff at rates you can lock in today.

In continuous time, we can define the instantaneous forward rate

$$f(N, t) = -\frac{1}{P}\frac{\partial P(N, t)}{\partial N} = -\frac{\partial p(N_t)}{\partial N}. \qquad (19.4)$$

Then, forward rates have the same property that you can express today's price as a discounted value using the forward rate,

$$p(N, t) = -\int_{x=0}^{N} f(x, t)\, dx$$

$$P(N, t) = e^{-\int_{x=0}^{N} f(x, t)\, dx}.$$

Equations (19.3) and (19.4) express forward rates as derivatives of the price versus maturity curve. Since yield is related to price, we can relate forward rates to the yield curve directly. Differentiating the definition of yield $y(N, t) = -p(N, t)/N$,

$$\frac{\partial y(N, t)}{\partial N} = \frac{1}{N^2}p(N, t) - \frac{1}{N}\frac{\partial p(N, t)}{\partial N} = -\frac{1}{N}y(N, t) + \frac{1}{N}f(N, t).$$

Thus,

$$f(N, t) = y(N, t) + N\frac{\partial y(N, t)}{\partial N}.$$

In the discrete case, (19.3) implies

$$f_t^{(N \to N+1)} = -Ny_t^{(N)} + (N+1)y_t^{(N+1)} = y_t^{(N+1)} + N\left(y_t^{(N+1)} - y_t^{(N)}\right).$$

Forward rates are above the yield curve if the yield curve is rising, and vice versa.

Swaps and Options

Swaps are an increasingly popular fixed-income instrument. The simplest example is a fixed-for-floating swap. Party A may have issued a 10-year fixed coupon bond. Party B may have issued a 10-year variable-rate bond— a bond that promises to pay the current one-year rate. (For example, if the current rate is 5%, the variable-rate issuer would pay $5 for every $100 of face value. A long-term variable-rate bond is the same thing as rolling over one-period debt.) They may be unhappy with these choices. For example, the fixed-rate payer may not want to be exposed to interest rate risk that the present value of his promised payments rises if interest rates decline. The variable-rate issuer may want to take on this interest rate risk, betting that rates will rise or to hedge other commitments. If they are unhappy with these choices, they can *swap* the payments. The fixed-rate issuer pays off the variable-rate coupons, and the variable-rate issuer pays off the fixed-rate coupons. Obviously, only the difference between fixed and variable rate actually changes hands.

Swapping the payments is much safer than swapping the bonds. If one party defaults, the other can drop out of the contract, losing the difference in price resulting from intermediate interest rate changes, but not losing the principal. For this reason, and because they match the patterns of cashflows that companies usually want to hedge, swaps have become very popular tools for managing interest rate risk. Foreign exchange swaps are also popular: Party A may swap dollar payments for party B's yen payments. Obviously, you do not need to have issued the underlying bonds to enter into a swap contract—you simply pay or receive the difference between the variable rate and the fixed rate each period.

The value of a pure floating-rate bond is always exactly one. The value of a fixed-rate bond varies. Swaps are set up so no money changes hands initially, and the fixed rate is calibrated so that the present value of the fixed payments is exactly one. Thus, the "swap rate" is the same thing as the yield on a comparable coupon bond.

Many fixed-income securities contain options, and explicit options on fixed-income securities are also popular. The simplest example is a call option. The issuer may have the right to buy the bonds back at a specified price. Typically, he will do this if interest rates fall a great deal, making a bond without this option more valuable. Home mortgages contain an interesting prepayment option: if interest rates decline, the homeowner can pay off the loan at face value, and refinance. Options on swaps also exist; you can buy the right to enter into a swap contract at a future date. Pricing all of these securities is one of the tasks of term structure modeling.

19.2 Yield Curve and Expectations Hypothesis

The *expectations hypothesis* is three equivalent statements about the pattern of yields across maturity:
1. The N-period yield is the average of expected future one-period yields.
2. The forward rate equals the expected future spot rate.
3. The expected holding period returns are equal on bonds of all maturities.
    The expectations hypothesis is not quite the same thing as risk neutrality, since it ignores $1/2\sigma^2$ terms that arise when you move from logs to levels.

The *yield curve* is a plot of yields of zero-coupon bonds as a function of their maturity. Usually, long-term bond yields are higher than short-term bond yields—a *rising* yield curve. Sometimes short yields are higher than long yields—an *inverted* yield curve. The yield curve sometimes has humps or other shapes as well. The *expectations hypothesis* is the classic theory for understanding the shape of the yield curve.

More generally, we want to think about the evolution of yields—the expected value and conditional variance of next period's yields. This is obviously the central ingredient for portfolio theory, hedging, derivative pricing, and economic explanation.

We can state the expectations hypothesis in three mathematically equivalent forms:

1. The *N*-period yield is the average of expected future one-period yields

$$y_t^{(N)} = \frac{1}{N} E_t\left(y_t^{(1)} + y_{t+1}^{(1)} + y_{t+2}^{(1)} + \cdots + y_{t+N-1}^{(1)}\right)(+ \text{ risk premium}). \quad (19.5)$$

2. The forward rate equals the expected future spot rate

$$f_t^{N \to N+1} = E_t\left(y_{t+N}^{(1)}\right)(+ \text{ risk premium}). \quad (19.6)$$

3. The expected holding period returns are equal on bonds of all maturities

$$E_t(\text{hpr}_{t+1}^{(N)}) = y_t^{(1)}(+ \text{ risk premium}). \quad (19.7)$$

You can see how the expectations hypothesis explains the shape of the yield curve. If the yield curve is upward sloping—long-term bond yields are higher than short-term bond yields—the expectations hypothesis says this is because short-term rates are expected to rise in the future.

You can view the expectations hypothesis as a response to a classic misconception. If long-term yields are 10% but short-term yields are 5%, an unsophisticated investor might think that long-term bonds are a better investment. The expectations hypothesis shows how this may not be true. If short rates are expected to rise in the future, this means that you will roll over the short-term bonds at a really high rate, say 20%, giving the same long-term return as the high-yielding long term bond. Contrariwise, when the short-term interest rates rise in the future, long-term bond prices decline. Thus, the long-term bonds will only give a 5% rate of return for the first year.

You can see from the third statement that the expectations hypothesis is roughly the same as risk neutrality. If we had said that the expected *level* of returns was equal across maturities, that would be the same as risk neutrality. The expectations hypothesis specifies that the expected

log return is equal across maturities. This is typically a close approximation to risk neutrality, but not the same thing. If returns are lognormal,
then $E(R) = e^{E(r)+(1/2)\sigma^2(r)}$. If mean returns are about 10% or 0.1 and
the standard deviation of returns is about 0.1, then $\frac{1}{2}\sigma^2$ is about 0.005,
which is very small but not zero. We could easily specify risk neutrality in
the third expression of the expectations hypothesis, but then it would not
imply the other two; $\frac{1}{2}\sigma^2$ terms would crop up.

The intuition of the third form is clear: risk-neutral investors will
adjust positions until the expected one-period returns are equal on all
securities. Any two ways of getting money from t to $t+1$ must offer the
same expected return. The second form adapts the same idea to the
choice of locking in a forward contract versus waiting and borrowing and
lending at the spot rate. Risk-neutral investors will load up on one or the
other contract until the expected returns are the same. Any two ways of
getting money from $t+N$ to $t+N+1$ must give the same expected return.

The first form reflects a choice between two ways of getting money
from t to N. You can buy an N-period bond, or roll over N one-period
bonds. Risk-neutral investors will choose one over the other strategy until
the expected N-period return is the same.

The three forms are mathematically equivalent. If every way of getting
money from t to $t+1$ gives the same expected return, then so must every
way of getting money from $t+1$ to $t+2$, and, chaining these together,
every way of getting money from t to $t+2$.

For example, let us show that forward rate = expected future spot
rate implies the yield curve. Start by writing

$$f_t^{N-1 \to N} = E_t\left(y_{t+N-1}^{(1)}\right).$$

Add these up over N,

$$f_t^{0 \to 1} + f_t^{1 \to 2} + \cdots + f_t^{N-2 \to N-1} + f_t^{N-1 \to N}$$
$$= E_t\left(y_t^{(1)} + y_{t+1}^{(1)} + y_{t+2}^{(1)} + \cdots + y_{t+N-1}^{(1)}\right).$$

The right-hand side is already what we are looking for. Write the left-hand
side in terms of the definition of forward rates, remembering $P^{(0)} = 1$
so $p^{(0)} = 0$,

$$f_t^{0 \to 1} + f_t^{1 \to 2} + \cdots + f_t^{N-2 \to N-1} + f_t^{N-1 \to N}$$
$$= \left(p_t^{(0)} - p_t^{(1)}\right) + \left(p_t^{(1)} - p_t^{(2)}\right) + \cdots + \left(p_t^{(N-1)} - p_t^{(N)}\right)$$
$$= -p_t^{(N)} = N y_t^{(N)}.$$

You can show all three forms (19.5)–(19.7) are equivalent by following similar arguments.

It is common to add a constant *risk premium* and still refer to the resulting model as the expectations hypothesis, and I include a risk premium in parentheses to remind you of this idea. One end of each of the three statements does imply more risk than the other. A forward rate is known while the future spot rate is not. Long-term bond returns are more volatile than short-term bond returns. Rolling over short-term real bonds is a riskier long-term investment than buying a long-term real bond. If real rates are constant, and the bonds are nominal, then the converse can hold: short-term real rates can adapt to inflation, so rolling over short nominal bonds can be a safer long-term real investment than long-term nominal bonds. These risks will generate expected return premia if they covary with the discount factor, and our theory should reflect this fact.

If you allow an arbitrary, time-varying risk premium, the model is a tautology, of course. Thus, the entire content of the "expectations hypothesis" augmented with risk premia is in the restrictions on the risk premium. We will see that the constant risk premium model does not do that well empirically. One of the main points of term structure models is to quantify the size and movement over time in the risk premium.

19.3 Term Structure Models—A Discrete-Time Introduction

> Term structure models specify the evolution of the short rate and potentially other state variables, and the prices of bonds of various maturities at any given time as a function of the short rate and other state variables. I examine a very simple example based on an AR(1) for the short rate and the expectations hypothesis, which gives a geometric pattern for the yield curve. A good way to generate term structure models is to write down a process for the discount factor, and then price bonds as the conditional mean of the discount factor. This procedure guarantees the absence of arbitrage. I give a very simple example of an AR(1) model for the log discount factor, which also results in geometric yield curves.

A natural place to start in modeling the term structure is to model yields statistically. You might run regressions of changes in yields on the levels of lagged yields, and derive a model of the mean and volatility of yield changes. You would likely start with a factor analysis of yield changes and express the covariance matrix of yields in terms of a few large factors that describe their common movement. The trouble with this approach is that you can quite easily reach a statistical representation of yields that implies an arbitrage opportunity, and you would not want to use such a statistical characterization for economic understanding of yields, for portfolio formation, or for derivative pricing. For example, a statistical analysis usually suggests that a first factor should be a "level" factor, in which all yields move up and down together. It turns out that this assumption violates arbitrage: the long-maturity yield must converge to a constant.[1]

How do you model yields without arbitrage? An obvious solution is to use the discount factor existence theorem: Write a statistical model for a positive discount factor, and find bond prices as the expectation of this discount factor. Such a model will be, by construction, arbitrage-free. Conversely, any arbitrage-free distribution of yields can be captured by some positive discount factor, so you do not lose any generality with this approach.

A Term Structure Model Based on the Expectations Hypothesis

We can use the expectations hypothesis to give the easiest example of a term structure model. This one does not start from a discount factor and so may not be arbitrage-free. It does quickly illustrate what we mean by a "term structure model."

Suppose the one-period yield follows an AR(1),

$$y_{t+1}^{(1)} - \delta = \rho(y_t^{(1)} - \delta) + \varepsilon_{t+1}.$$

Now, we can use the expectations hypothesis (19.5) to calculate yields on bonds of all maturities as a function of today's one-period yield,

$$
\begin{aligned}
y_t^{(2)} &= \frac{1}{2} E_t \left[y_t^{(1)} + y_{t+1}^{(1)} \right] \\
&= \frac{1}{2} \left[y_t^{(1)} + \delta + \rho(y_t^{(1)} - \delta) \right] \\
&= \delta + \frac{1+\rho}{2} (y_t^{(1)} - \delta).
\end{aligned}
$$

Continuing in this way,

$$\left(y_t^{(N)} - \delta \right) = \frac{1}{N} \frac{1 - \rho^{N+1}}{1 - \rho} (y_t^{(1)} - \delta). \tag{19.8}$$

---

[1]More precisely, the long-term forward rate, if it exists, must never fall. Problem 7 guides you through a simple calculation. Dybvig, Ingersoll, and Ross (1996) derive the more general statement.

You can see some issues that will recur throughout the term structure models. First, the model (19.8) can describe different yield curve shapes at different times. If the short rate is below its mean, then there is a smoothly upward sloping yield curve. Long-term bond yields are higher, as short rates are expected to increase in the future. If the short rate is above its mean, we get a smoothly inverted yield curve. This particular model cannot produce humps or other interesting shapes that we sometimes see in the term structure. Second, this model predicts no average slope of the term structure: $E(y_t^{(N)}) = E(y_t^{(1)}) = \delta$. In fact, the average term structure seems to slope up slightly and more complex models will reproduce this feature. Third, all bond yields move together in the model. If we were to stack the yields up in a VAR representation, it would be

$$y_{t+1}^{(1)} - \delta = \rho\big(y_t^{(1)} - \delta\big) + \varepsilon_{t+1},$$

$$y_{t+1}^{(2)} - \delta = \rho\big(y_t^{(2)} - \delta\big) + \frac{1+\rho}{2}\varepsilon_{t+1},$$

$$\vdots$$

$$y_{t+1}^{(N)} - \delta = \rho\big(y_t^{(N)} - \delta\big) + \frac{1}{N}\frac{1-\rho^{N+1}}{1-\rho}\varepsilon_{t+1}.$$

(You can write the right-hand variable in terms of $y_t^{(1)}$ if you want—any one yield carries the same information as any other.) The *error terms are all the same.* We can add more factors to the short-rate process, to improve on this prediction, but most tractable term structure models maintain less factors than there are bonds, so some perfect factor structure is a common prediction of term structure models. Fourth, this model has a problem in that the short rate, following an AR(1), can be negative. Since people can always hold cash, nominal short rates are never negative, so we want to start with a short-rate process that does not have this feature. Fifth, this model shows no conditional heteroskedasticity—the conditional variance of yield changes is always the same. The term structure data show times of high and low volatility, and times of high yields and high yield spreads seem to track these changes in volatility. Modeling conditional volatility is crucially important for valuing term structure options.

With this simple model in hand, you can see some obvious directions for generalization. First, we will want more complex driving processes than an AR(1). For example, a hump shape in the conditionally expected short rate will result in a hump-shaped yield curve. If there are multiple state variables driving the short rate, then we will have multiple factors driving the yield curve which will also result in more interesting shapes. We also want processes that keep the short rate positive in all states of nature. Second, we will want to add some "market prices of risk"—some risk premia.

This will allow us to get average yield curves to not be flat, and time-varying risk premia seem to be part of the yield data. We will also want to check that the market prices are reasonable, and in particular that there are no arbitrage opportunities.

The yield curve literature proceeds in exactly this way: specify a short-rate process and the risk premia, and find the prices of long-term bonds. The trick is to specify sufficiently complex assumptions to be interesting, but preserve our ability to solve the models.

The Simplest Discrete-Time Model

The simplest nontrivial model I can think of is to let the log of the discount factor follow an AR(1) with normally distributed shocks. I write the AR(1) for the log rather than the level in order to make sure the discount factor is positive, precluding arbitrage. Log discount factors are typically slightly negative, so I denote the unconditional mean $E(\ln m) = -\delta$

$$(\ln m_{t+1} + \delta) = \rho(\ln m_t + \delta) + \varepsilon_{t+1}.$$

In turn, you can think of this discount factor model as arising from a consumption-based power utility model with normal errors,

$$m_{t+1} = e^{-\delta}\left(\frac{C_{t+1}}{C_t}\right)^{\gamma},$$

$$c_{t+1} - c_t = \rho(c_t - c_{t-1}) + \varepsilon_{t+1}.$$

The term structure literature has only started to explore whether the empirically successful discount factor processes can be connected empirically back to macroeconomic events in this way.

From this discount factor, we can find bond prices and yields. This is easy because the conditional mean and variance of an AR(1) are easy to find. (I am following the strategy of solving the discount factor forward rather than solving the price backward.) We need

$$y_t^{(1)} = -p_t^{(1)} = -\ln E_t(e^{\ln m_{t+1}}),$$

$$y_t^{(2)} = -\frac{1}{2}p_t^{(2)} = -\frac{1}{2}\ln E_t(e^{\ln m_{t+1} + \ln m_{t+2}}),$$

and so on. Iterating the AR(1) forward,

$$(\ln m_{t+2} + \delta) = \rho^2(\ln m_t + \delta) + \rho\varepsilon_{t+1} + \varepsilon_{t+2},$$

$$(\ln m_{t+3} + \delta) = \rho^3(\ln m_t + \delta) + \rho^2\varepsilon_{t+1} + \rho\varepsilon_{t+2} + \varepsilon_{t+3},$$

so

$$(\ln m_{t+1} + \delta) + (\ln m_{t+2} + \delta)$$
$$= (\rho + \rho^2)(\ln m_t + \delta) + (1 + \rho)\varepsilon_{t+1} + \varepsilon_{t+2}.$$

Similarly,

$$(\ln m_{t+1} + \delta) + (\ln m_{t+2} + \delta) + (\ln m_{t+3} + \delta)$$
$$= (\rho + \rho^2 + \rho^3)(\ln m_t + \delta) + (1 + \rho + \rho^2)\varepsilon_{t+1} + (1 + \rho)\varepsilon_{t+2} + \varepsilon_{t+3}.$$

Using the rule for a lognormal $E(e^x) = e^{E(x)+\frac{1}{2}\sigma_x^2}$, we have finally

$$y_t^{(1)} = \delta - \rho(\ln m_t + \delta) - \frac{1}{2}\sigma_\varepsilon^2,$$

$$y_t^{(2)} = \delta - \frac{(\rho + \rho^2)}{2}(\ln m_t + \delta) - \frac{1 + (1 + \rho)^2}{4}\sigma_\varepsilon^2,$$

$$y_t^{(3)} = \delta - \frac{(\rho + \rho^2 + \rho^3)}{3}(\ln m_t + \delta) - \frac{1 + (1 + \rho)^2 + (1 + \rho + \rho^2)^2}{6}\sigma_\varepsilon^2.$$

Notice all yields move as linear functions of a single state variable, $\ln m_t + \delta$. Therefore, we can substitute out the discount factor and express the yields on bonds of any maturity as functions of the yields on bonds of one maturity. Which one we choose is arbitrary, but it is conventional to use the shortest interest rate as the state variable. With $E(y^{(1)}) = \delta - \frac{1}{2}\sigma_\varepsilon^2$, we can write our term structure model as

$$y_t^{(1)} - E(y^{(1)}) = \rho\left[y_{t-1}^{(1)} - E(y^{(1)})\right] + \varepsilon_t,$$

$$y_t^{(2)} = \delta - \frac{(\rho + \rho^2)}{2}\left(y_t^{(1)} - E(y^{(1)})\right) - \frac{1 + (1 + \rho)^2}{4}\sigma_\varepsilon^2,$$

$$y_t^{(3)} = \delta - \frac{(\rho + \rho^9 + \rho^3)}{3}\left(y_t^{(1)} - E(y^{(1)})\right)$$
$$- \frac{1 + (1 + \rho)^2 + (1 + \rho + \rho^2)^2}{6}\sigma_\varepsilon^2, \tag{19.9}$$

$$y_t^{(N)} = \delta - \frac{\rho}{N}\frac{1 - \rho^N}{1 - \rho}\left(y_t^{(1)} - E(y^{(1)})\right) + \sum_{j=1}^{\infty}\sum_{k=1}^{j}\frac{(1 + \rho^k)^2}{2j}\sigma_\varepsilon^2.$$

This is the form in which term structure models are usually written—an evolution equation for the short-rate process (together, in general, with other factors or other yields used to identify those factors), and then longer rates written as functions of the short rate, or the other factors.

This is still not a very realistic term structure model. In the data, the average yield curve—the plot of $\{E[y_t^{(N)}]\}$ versus N—is slightly upward sloping. The average yield curve from this model is slightly downward sloping as the σ_ε^2 terms pile up. The effect is not large; with $\rho = 0.9$ and $\sigma_\varepsilon = 0.02$, I find $E(y_t^{(2)}) = E(y_t^{(1)}) - 0.02\%$ and $E(y_t^{(3)}) = E(y_t^{(1)}) - 0.06\%$. Still, it does not slope up. More importantly, this model only produces smoothly upward sloping or downward sloping term structures. For example, with $\rho = 0.9$, the first three terms multiplying the one-period rate in (19.9) are 0.86, 0.81, 0.78. Two-, three-, and four-period bonds move exactly with one-period bonds using these coefficients.

The solution, of course, is to specify more complex discount rate processes that give rise to more interesting term structures.

19.4 Continuous-Time Term Structure Models

The basic steps:
1. Write a time-series model for the discount factor, typically in the form

$$\frac{d\Lambda}{\Lambda} = -r\,dt - \sigma_\Lambda(\cdot)\,dz,$$

$$dr = \mu_r(\cdot)\,dt + \sigma_r(\cdot)\,dz.$$

2. Solve the discount factor model forward and take expectations, to find bond prices

$$P_t^{(N)} = E_t\left(\frac{\Lambda_{t+N}}{\Lambda_t}\right).$$

3. Alternatively, from the basic pricing equation $0 = E[d(\Lambda P)]$ we can find a differential equation that the price must follow,

$$\frac{\partial P}{\partial r}\mu_r + \frac{1}{2}\frac{\partial^2 P}{\partial r^2}\sigma_r^2 - \frac{\partial P}{\partial N} - rP = \frac{\partial P}{\partial r}\sigma_r\sigma_\Lambda.$$

You can solve this back from $P_N^{(0)} = 1$.

I contrast the discount factor approach to the market price of risk and arbitrage pricing approaches.

Term structure models are usually more convenient in continuous time. As always, I specify a discount factor process and then find bond prices. A wide and popular class of term structure models are based on a discount factor process of the form

$$\frac{d\Lambda}{\Lambda} = -r\,dt - \sigma'_\Lambda(\cdot)\,dz,$$

$$dr = \mu_r(\cdot)\,dt + \sigma'_r(\cdot)\,dz. \tag{19.10}$$

This specification is analogous to a discrete-time model of the form

$$m_{t+1} = x_t + \sigma\varepsilon_{t+1},$$

$$x_{t+1} = \rho x_t + \varepsilon_{t+1}.$$

This is a convenient representation rather than a generalized autoregressive process, since the state variable x carries the mean discount factor information.

The r variable starts out as a state variable for the drift of the discount factor. However, you can see quickly that it will become the short-rate process since $E_t(d\Lambda/\Lambda) = -r_t^j\,dt$. The dots $(\cdot)$ remind you that these terms can be functions of state variables whose evolution must also be modeled. We can also write $\sigma_{\Lambda t}, \mu_{rt}, \sigma_{rt}$ to remind ourselves that these quantities vary over time.

Term structure models differ in the specification of the functional forms for $\mu_r, \sigma_r, \sigma_\Lambda$. We will study three famous examples, the Vasicek model, the Cox–Ingersoll–Ross model, and the general affine specification. The first two are

$$\text{Vasicek:} \qquad \frac{d\Lambda}{\Lambda} = -r\,dt - \sigma_\Lambda\,dz,$$
$$dr = \phi(\bar{r} - r)\,dt + \sigma_r\,dz. \tag{19.11}$$

$$\text{CIR:} \qquad \frac{d\Lambda}{\Lambda} = -r\,dt - \sigma_\Lambda\sqrt{\Lambda}\,dz,$$
$$dr = \phi(\bar{r} - r)\,dt + \sigma_r\sqrt{r}\,dz. \tag{19.12}$$

The Vasicek model is quite similar to the AR(1) we studied in the last section. The CIR model adds the square root terms in the volatility. This specification captures the fact that higher interest rates seem to be more volatile. In the other direction, it keeps the level of the interest rate from falling below zero. (We need $\sigma_r \le 2\phi\bar{r}$ to guarantee that the square root process does not get stuck at zero.)

Having specified a discount factor process, it is a simple matter to find bond prices. Once again,

$$P_t^{(N)} = E_t\left(\frac{\Lambda_{t+N}}{\Lambda_t}\right).$$

We can solve the discount factor forward and take the expectation. We can also use the instantaneous pricing condition $0 = E(d(\Lambda P))$ to find a partial differential equation for prices, and solve that backward.

Both methods naturally adapt to pricing term structure derivatives— call options on bonds, interest rate floors or caps, "swaptions" that give you the right to enter a swap, and so forth. We simply put any payoff x^C that depends on interest rates or interest rate state variables inside the expectation

$$P_t^{(N)} = E_t \int_{s=t}^{\infty} \frac{\Lambda_s}{\Lambda_t} x^C(s) \, ds.$$

Alternatively, the price of such options will also be a function of the state variables that drive the term structure, so we can solve the bond pricing differential equation backwards using the option payoff rather than one as the boundary condition.

Expectation Approach

As with the Black–Scholes option pricing model, we can solve the discount factor forward, and then take the expectation. We can write the solution[2] to (19.10) as

$$\frac{\Lambda_T}{\Lambda_0} = e^{-\int_{s=0}^{T} \left(r_s + \frac{1}{2}\sigma_{\Lambda s}^2\right) ds - \int_{s=0}^{T} \sigma_{\Lambda s} \, dz_s}$$

and thus,

$$P_0^{(T)} = E_0 \left(e^{-\int_{s=0}^{T} \left(r_s + \frac{1}{2}\sigma_{\Lambda s}^2\right) ds - \int_{s=0}^{T} \sigma_{\Lambda s} \, dz} \right). \tag{19.13}$$

For example, in a riskless economy $\sigma_\Lambda = 0$, we obtain the continuous-time present-value formula,

$$P_0^{(T)} = e^{-\int_{s=0}^{T} r_s \, ds}.$$

With a constant interest rate r,

$$P_0^{(T)} = e^{-rT}.$$

In more interesting situations, solving the Λ equation forward and taking the expectation analytically is not so easy. Conceptually and numer-

---

[2]If this is mysterious, write first

$$d \ln \Lambda = \frac{d\Lambda}{\Lambda} - \frac{1}{2}\frac{d\Lambda^2}{\Lambda^2} = -\left(r + \frac{1}{2}\sigma_\Lambda^2\right) dt - \sigma_\Lambda \, dz$$

and then integrate both sides from zero to T.

ically, it is easy, of course. Just simulate the system (19.10) forward a few thousand times, and take the average.

Differential Equation Approach

Recall the basic pricing equation for a security with price S and no dividends is

$$E_t\left(\frac{dS}{S}\right) - r\, dt = -E_t\left(\frac{dS}{S}\frac{d\Lambda}{\Lambda}\right). \tag{19.14}$$

The left-hand side is the expected excess return. As we guessed an option price $C(S, t)$ and used (19.14) to derive a differential equation for the call option price, so we will guess a bond price $P(N, t)$ and use this equation to derive a differential equation for the bond price.

If we specified bonds by their maturity *date* T, $P(t, T)$, we could apply (19.14) directly. However, it is nicer to look for a bond pricing function $P(N, t)$ that fixes the *maturity* rather than the *date*. Equation (19.2) gives the holding period return for this case, which adds an extra term to correct for the fact that you sell younger bonds than you buy,

$$\text{return } = \frac{dP(N, t)}{P} - \frac{1}{P}\frac{\partial P(N, t)}{\partial N}\, dt.$$

Thus, the fundamental pricing equation, applied to the price of bonds of given *maturity* $P(N, t)$, is

$$E_t\left(\frac{dP}{P}\right) - \left(\frac{1}{P}\frac{\partial P(N, t)}{\partial N} + r\right) dt = -E_t\left(\frac{dP}{P}\frac{d\Lambda}{\Lambda}\right). \tag{19.15}$$

Now, we are ready to find a differential equation for the bond price, just as we did for the option price to derive the Black–Scholes formula. Guess that all the time dependence comes through the state variable r, so $P(N, r)$. Using Ito's lemma,

$$dP = \left(\frac{\partial P}{\partial r}\mu_r + \frac{1}{2}\frac{\partial^2 P}{\partial r^2}\sigma_r^2\right) dt + \frac{\partial P}{\partial r}\sigma_r\, dz.$$

Plugging in to (19.15) and canceling dt, we obtain the fundamental differential equation for bonds,

$$\frac{\partial P}{\partial r}\mu_r + \frac{1}{2}\frac{\partial P}{\partial r^2}\sigma_r^2 - \frac{\partial P}{\partial N} - rP = \frac{\partial P}{\partial r}\sigma_r\sigma_\Lambda. \tag{19.16}$$

All you have to do is specify the functions $\mu_r(\cdot)$, $\sigma_r(\cdot)$, $\sigma_\Lambda(\cdot)$ and solve the differential equation.

Market Price of Risk and Risk-Neutral Dynamic Approaches

The bond pricing differential equation (19.16) is conventionally derived without discount factors.

One conventional approach is to write the short-rate process $dr = \mu_r(\cdot)\, dt + \sigma_r(\cdot)\, dz$, and then specify that any asset whose payoffs have shocks $\sigma_r\, dz$ must offer a Sharpe ratio of $\lambda(\cdot)$. We would then write

$$\frac{\partial P}{\partial r}\mu_r + \frac{1}{2}\frac{\partial^2 P}{\partial r^2}\sigma_r^2 - \frac{\partial P}{\partial N} - rP = \frac{\partial P}{\partial r}\sigma_r\lambda.$$

With $\lambda = \sigma_\Lambda$, this is just (19.16) of course. (If the discount factor and shock are imperfectly correlated, then $\lambda = \sigma_\Lambda\rho$.) Different authors use the words "market price of risk" in different ways. Cox, Ingersoll, and Ross (1985, p. 398) warn against modeling the right-hand side as $\partial P/\partial r\psi(\cdot)$ directly; this specification could lead to a positive expected return when $\sigma_r = 0$ and hence an infinite Sharpe ratio or arbitrage opportunity. By generating expected returns as the covariance of payoff shocks and discount factor shocks, we naturally avoid this mistake and other subtle ways of introducing arbitrage opportunities without realizing that you have done so.

A second conventional approach is to use an alternative process for the interest rate and discount factor,

$$\frac{d\Lambda}{\Lambda} = -r\, dt,$$

$$dr = (\mu_r - \sigma_r\lambda)\, dt + \sigma_r\, dz. \tag{19.17}$$

If we use this alternative process, we obtain

$$\frac{\partial P}{\partial r}(\mu_r - \sigma_r\lambda) + \frac{1}{2}\frac{\partial P}{\partial r^2}\sigma_r^2 - \frac{\partial P}{\partial N} - rP = 0,$$

which is of course the same thing. This is the "risk-neutral probability" approach, since the drift term in (19.17) is not the true drift that you would estimate in the data, and since the discount factor is nonstochastic. Since (19.17) gives the same prices, we can find and represent the bond price via the integral

$$P_t^{(N)} = E_t^*\left[e^{-\int_{s=0}^{T} r_s\, ds}\right],$$

where E^* represents expectation with respect to the risk-neutral process defined in (19.17) rather than the true probabilities defined by the process (19.10).

When we derive the model from a discount factor, the single discount factor carries two pieces of information. The drift or conditional mean of the discount factor gives the short rate of interest, while the covariance of the discount factor shocks with asset payoff shocks generates expected returns or "market prices of risk." I find it useful to write the discount factor model to keep the term structure connected with the rest of asset pricing, and to remind myself where "market prices of risk" come from, and reasonable values for their magnitude. Of course, this beauty is in the eye of the beholder, as the result is the same no matter which method you follow.

The fact that there are fewer factors than bonds means that once you have as many bond prices as you have factors, you can derive all the others by "no-arbitrage" arguments and make this look like option pricing. Some derivations of term structure models follow this approach, setting up arbitrage portfolios.

Solving the Bond Price Differential Equation

Now we have to solve the partial differential equation (19.16) subject to the boundary condition $P(N = 0, r) = 1$. Solving this equation is straightforward conceptually and numerically. Express (19.16) as

$$\frac{\partial P}{\partial N} = \frac{\partial P}{\partial r}\left(\mu_r - \sigma_r\sigma_\Lambda\right) + \frac{1}{2}\frac{\partial^2 P}{\partial r^2}\sigma_r^2 - rP.$$

We can start at $N = 0$ on a grid of r, and $P(0, r) = 1$. For fixed N, we can work to one step larger N by evaluating the derivatives on the right-hand side. The first step is

$$P(\Delta N, r) = \frac{\partial P}{\partial N}\Delta N = -r\Delta N.$$

At the second step, $\partial P/\partial r = \Delta N$, $\partial^2 P/\partial r^2 = 0$, so

$$P(2\Delta N, r) = \Delta N^2(\mu_r - \sigma_r\sigma_\Lambda) - r^2\Delta N^2.$$

Now the derivatives of μ_r and σ_r with respect to r will start to enter, and we let the computer take it from here. Analytic solutions only exist in special cases, which we study next.

19.5 Three Linear Term Structure Models

> I solve the Vasicek, the Cox, Ingersoll, and Ross, and the Affine model. Each model gives a *linear* function for log bond prices and yields, for example,
>
> $$\ln P(N, r) = A(N) - B(N)r.$$

As we have seen, term structure models are easy in principle and numerically: specify a discount factor process and find its conditional expectation or solve the bond pricing partial differential equation back from maturity. In practice, the computations are hard. I present next three famous special cases of term structure models—specifications for the discount factor process—that allow analytical or quickly calculable solutions.

Analytical or close-to-analytical solutions are still important, because we have not yet found good techniques for reverse-engineering the term structure. We know how to start with a discount factor process and find bond prices. We do not know how to start with the characteristics of bond prices that we want to model and construct an appropriate discount factor process. Thus, in evaluating term structure models, we will have to do lots of the "forward" calculations—from assumed discount factor model to bond prices—and it is important that we should be able to do them quickly.

Vasicek Model via PDE

The Vasicek (1977) model is a special case that allows a fairly easy analytic solution. The method is the same as the more complex analytic solution in the CIR and affine classes, but the algebra is easier, so this is a good place to start.

The Vasicek discount factor process is

$$\frac{d\Lambda}{\Lambda} = -r \, dt - \sigma_\Lambda \, dz,$$

$$dr = \phi(\bar{r} - r) \, dt + \sigma_r \, dz.$$

Using this process in the basic bond differential equation (19.16), we obtain

$$\frac{\partial P}{\partial r}\phi(\bar{r} - r) + \frac{1}{2}\frac{\partial^2 P}{dr^2}\sigma_r^2 - \frac{\partial P}{\partial N} - rP = \frac{\partial P}{\partial r}\sigma_r\sigma_\Lambda. \tag{19.18}$$

I will solve this equation with the usual unsatisfying nonconstructive technique—guess the functional form of the answer and show it is right.

I guess that log yields and hence log prices are a linear function of the short rate,

$$P(N, r) = e^{A(N)-B(N)r}. \tag{19.19}$$

I take the partial derivatives required in (19.18) and see if I can find $A(N)$ and $B(N)$ to make (19.18) work. The result is a set of *ordinary* differential equations for $A(N)$ and $B(N)$, and these are of a particularly simple form that can be solved by integration. I solve them, subject to the boundary condition imposed by $P(0, r) = 1$. The result is

$$B(N) = \frac{1}{\phi}(1 - e^{-\phi N}), \tag{19.20}$$

$$A(N) = \left(\frac{1}{2}\frac{\sigma_r^2}{\phi^2} + \frac{\sigma_r \sigma_\Lambda}{\phi} - \bar{r}\right)(N - B(N)) - \frac{\sigma_r^2}{4\phi}B(N)^2. \tag{19.21}$$

The exponential form of (19.19) means that log prices and log yields are linear functions of the interest rate,

$$p(N, r) = A(N) - B(N)r,$$

$$y(N, r) = -\frac{A(N)}{N} + \frac{B(N)}{N}r.$$

Solving the PDE: Details
The boundary condition $P(0, r) = 1$ will be satisfied if

$$A(0) - B(0)r = 0.$$

Since this must hold for every r, we will need

$$A(0) = 0, \qquad B(0) = 0.$$

Given the guess (19.19), the derivatives that appear in (19.18) are

$$\frac{1}{P}\frac{\partial P_r}{\partial r} = -B(N),$$

$$\frac{1}{P}\frac{\partial^2 P}{\partial r^2} = B(N)^2,$$

$$\frac{1}{P}\frac{\partial P}{\partial N} = A'(N) - B'(N)r.$$

Substituting these derivatives in (19.18),

$$-B(N)\phi(\bar{r} - r) + \frac{1}{2}B(N)^2\sigma_r^2 - A'(N) + B'(N)r - r = -B(N)\sigma_r \sigma_\Lambda.$$

This equation has to hold for every r, so the terms multiplying r and the constant terms must separately be zero:

$$A'(N) = \frac{1}{2} B(N)^2 \sigma_r^2 - \left(\phi \bar{r} - \sigma_r \sigma_\Lambda\right) B(N),$$

$$B'(N) = 1 - B(N)\phi.$$

$$\text{(19.22)}$$

We can solve this pair of ordinary differential equations by simple integration. The second one is

$$\frac{dB}{dN} = 1 - \phi B,$$

$$\int \frac{dB}{1 - \phi B} = dN,$$

$$-\frac{1}{\phi} \ln(1 - \phi B) = N,$$

and hence

$$B(N) = \frac{1}{\phi} \left(1 - e^{-\phi N}\right). \qquad \text{(19.23)}$$

Note $B(0) = 0$ so we did not need a constant in the integration.

We solve the first equation in (19.22) by simply integrating it, and choosing the constant to set $A(0) = 0$. Here we go:

$$A'(N) = \frac{1}{2} B(N)^2 \sigma_r^2 - (\phi \bar{r} - \sigma_r \sigma_\Lambda) B(N),$$

$$A(N) = \frac{\sigma_r^2}{2} \int B(N)^2 dN - (\phi \bar{r} - \sigma_r \sigma_\Lambda) \int B(N) dN + C,$$

$$A(N) = \frac{\sigma_r^2}{2\phi^2} \int \left(1 - 2e^{-\phi N} + e^{-2\phi N}\right) dN - \left(\bar{r} - \frac{\sigma_r \sigma_\Lambda}{\phi}\right) \int \left(1 - e^{-\phi N}\right) dN + C,$$

$$A(N) = \frac{\sigma_r^2}{2\phi^2} \left(N + \frac{2e^{-\phi N}}{\phi} - \frac{e^{-2\phi N}}{2\phi}\right) - \left(\bar{r} - \frac{\sigma_r \sigma_\Lambda}{\phi}\right)\left(N + \frac{e^{-\phi N}}{\phi}\right) + C.$$

We pick the constant of integration to give $A(0) = 0$. You can do this explicitly, or figure out directly that the result is achieved by subtracting one from the $e^{-\phi N}$ terms,

$$A(N) = \frac{\sigma_r^2}{2\phi^2} \left(N + \frac{2\left(e^{-\phi N} - 1\right)}{\phi} - \frac{\left(e^{-2\phi N} - 1\right)}{2\phi}\right)$$

$$- \left(\bar{r} - \frac{\sigma_r \sigma_\Lambda \rho}{\phi}\right)\left(N + \frac{\left(e^{-\phi N} - 1\right)}{\phi}\right).$$

Now, we just have to make it pretty. I am aiming for the form given in (19.21). Note

$$B(N)^2 = \frac{1}{\phi^2}\left(1 - 2e^{-\phi N} + e^{-2\phi N}\right),$$

$$\phi B(N)^2 = 2\frac{1 - e^{-\phi N}}{\phi} + \frac{e^{-2\phi N} - 1}{\phi},$$

$$\phi B(N)^2 - 2B(N) = \frac{e^{-2\phi N} - 1}{\phi}.$$

Then

$$A(N) = \frac{\sigma_r^2}{2\phi^2}\left(N - 2B(N) - \frac{\phi}{2}B(N)^2 + B(N)\right) - \left(\bar{r} - \frac{\sigma_r\sigma_\Lambda}{\phi}\right)(N - B(N)),$$

$$A(N) = -\frac{\sigma_r^2}{4\phi}B(N)^2 - \left(\bar{r} - \frac{\sigma_r\sigma_\Lambda}{\phi} - \frac{\sigma_r^2}{2\phi^2}\right)(N - B(N)).$$

We are done.

Vasicek Model by Expectation

What if we solve the discount rate forward and take an expectation instead? The Vasicek model is simple enough that we can follow this approach as well, and get the same analytic solution. The same methods work for the other models, but the algebra gets steadily worse.

The model is

$$\frac{d\Lambda}{\Lambda} = -r\,dt - \sigma_\Lambda\,dz, \tag{19.24}$$

$$dr = \phi(\bar{r} - r)\,dt + \sigma_r\,dz. \tag{19.25}$$

The bond price is

$$P_0^{(N)} = E_0\left(\frac{\Lambda_N}{\Lambda_0}\right). \tag{19.26}$$

I use 0 and N rather than t and $t + N$ to save a little bit on notation.

To find the expectation in (19.26), we have to solve the system (19.24)–(19.25) forward. The steps are simple, though the algebra is a bit daunting. First, we solve r forward. Then, we solve Λ forward. ln Λ_t turns out to be conditionally normal, so the expectation in (19.26) is the expectation of a lognormal. Collecting terms that depend on r_0 as the $B(N)$ term, and the constant term as the $A(N)$ term, we find the same solution as (19.20)–(19.21).

The interest rate is just an AR(1). By analogy with a discrete-time AR(1), you can guess that its solution is

$$r_t = \int_{s=0}^{t} e^{-\phi(t-s)} \sigma_r \, dz_s + e^{-\phi t} r_0 + (1 - e^{-\phi t})\bar{r}. \qquad (19.27)$$

To derive this solution, define $\tilde{r}$ by

$$\tilde{r}_t = e^{\phi t}(r_t - \bar{r}).$$

Then,

$$d\tilde{r}_t = \phi \tilde{r}_t \, dt + e^{\phi t} \, dr_t,$$
$$d\tilde{r}_t = \phi \tilde{r}_t \, dt + e^{\phi t} \phi(\bar{r} - r) \, dt + e^{\phi t} \sigma_r \, dz_t,$$
$$d\tilde{r}_t = \phi \tilde{r}_t \, dt - e^{\phi t} \phi e^{-\phi t} \tilde{r}_t \, dt + e^{\phi t} \sigma_r \, dz_t,$$
$$d\tilde{r}_t = e^{\phi t} \sigma_r \, dz_t.$$

This equation is easy to solve,

$$\tilde{r}_t - \tilde{r}_0 = \sigma_r \int_{s=0}^{t} e^{\phi s} \, dz_s,$$

$$e^{\phi t}(r_t - \bar{r}) - (r_0 - \bar{r}) = \sigma_r \int_{s=0}^{t} e^{\phi s} \, dz_s,$$

$$r_t - \bar{r} = e^{-\phi t}(r_0 - \bar{r}) + \sigma_r \int_{s=0}^{t} e^{-\phi(t-s)} \, dz_s.$$

And we have (19.27).

Now, we solve the discount factor process forward. It is not pretty, but it is straightforward:

$$d \ln \Lambda_t = \frac{d\Lambda}{\Lambda} - \frac{1}{2} \frac{d\Lambda^2}{\Lambda^2} = -\left(r_t + \frac{1}{2}\sigma_\Lambda^2\right) dt - \sigma_\Lambda \, dz_t,$$

$$\ln \Lambda_t - \ln \Lambda_0 = -\int_{s=0}^{t} \left(r_s + \frac{1}{2}\sigma_\Lambda^2\right) ds - \sigma_\Lambda \int_{s=0}^{t} dz_s.$$

Plugging in the interest rate solution (19.27),

$$\ln \Lambda_t - \ln \Lambda_0 = -\int_{s=0}^{t} \left[\left(\int_{u=0}^{s} e^{-\phi(s-u)} \sigma_r \, dz_u \right) \right.$$

$$\left. + e^{-\phi s}(r_0 - \bar{r}) + \bar{r} + \frac{1}{2}\sigma_\Lambda^2 \right] ds - \sigma_\Lambda \int_{s=0}^{t} dz_s.$$

Interchanging the order of the first integral, evaluating the easy ds integrals, and rearranging,

$$= -\sigma_\Lambda \int_{s=0}^{t} dz_s - \sigma_r \int_{u=0}^{t} \left[\int_{s=u}^{t} e^{-\phi(s-u)} \, ds \right] dz_u$$
$$- \left[\left(\bar{r} + \frac{1}{2}\sigma_\Lambda^2 \right) t + (r_0 - \bar{r}) \int_{s=0}^{t} e^{-\phi s} \, ds \right],$$

and simplifying,

$$= - \int_{u=0}^{t} \left[\sigma_\Lambda + \frac{\sigma_r}{\phi}\left(1 - e^{-\phi(t-u)} \right) \right] dz_u$$
$$- \left(\bar{r} + \frac{1}{2}\sigma_\Lambda^2 \right) t - (r_0 - \bar{r}) \frac{1 - e^{-\phi t}}{\phi}. \tag{19.28}$$

The first integral includes a deterministic function of time u times dz_u. This gives rise to a normally distributed random variable—it is just a weighted sum of independent normals dz_u:

$$\int_{u=0}^{t} f(u) \, dz_u \sim N\left(0, \int_{u=0}^{t} f^2(u) \, du \right).$$

Thus, $\ln \Lambda_t - \ln \Lambda_0$ is normally distributed with mean given by the second set of terms in (19.28) and variance

$$\text{var}_0(\ln \Lambda_t - \ln \Lambda_0)$$
$$= \int_{u=0}^{t} \left[\sigma_\Lambda + \frac{\sigma_r}{\phi}\left(1 - e^{-\phi(t-u)} \right) \right]^2 du \tag{19.29}$$
$$= \int_{u=0}^{t} \left[\left(\sigma_\Lambda + \frac{\sigma_r}{\phi} \right)^2 - 2\frac{\sigma_r}{\phi}\left(\sigma_\Lambda + \frac{\sigma_r}{\phi} \right) e^{-\phi(t-u)} + \frac{\sigma_r^2}{\phi^2} e^{-2\phi(t-u)} \right] du$$
$$= \left(\sigma_\Lambda + \frac{\sigma_r}{\phi} \right)^2 t - 2\frac{\sigma_r}{\phi^2}\left(\sigma_\Lambda + \frac{\sigma_r}{\phi} \right)(1 - e^{-\phi t}) + \frac{\sigma_r^2}{2\phi^3}(1 - e^{-2\phi t}).$$

Since we have the distribution of Λ_N we are ready to take the expectation:

$$\ln P(N, 0) = \ln E_0 \left(e^{\ln \Lambda_N - \ln \Lambda_0} \right) = E_0 \left(\ln \Lambda_N - \ln \Lambda_0 \right)$$
$$+ \frac{1}{2}\sigma_0^2 \left(\ln \Lambda_N - \ln \Lambda_0 \right).$$

Plugging in the mean from (19.28) and the variance from (19.29),

$$\ln P_0^{(N)} = -\left[\left(\bar{r} + \frac{1}{2}\sigma_\Lambda^2\right)N + (r_0 - \bar{r})\frac{1 - e^{-\phi N}}{\phi}\right] \tag{19.30}$$

$$+ \frac{1}{2}\left(\frac{\sigma_r}{\phi} + \sigma_\Lambda\right)^2 N - \frac{\sigma_r}{\phi^2}\left(\frac{\sigma_r}{\phi} + \sigma_\Lambda\right)(1 - e^{-\phi N})$$

$$+ \frac{\sigma_r^2}{4\phi^3}(1 - e^{-2\phi N}) \tag{19.31}$$

All that remains is to make it pretty. To compare it with our previous result, we want to express it in the form $\ln P(N, r_0) = A(N) - B(N)r_0$. The coefficient on r_0 (19.30) is

$$B(N) = \frac{1 - e^{-\phi N}}{\phi}, \tag{19.32}$$

the same expression we derived from the partial differential equation.
    To simplify the constant term, recall that (19.32) implies

$$\frac{1 - e^{-2\phi N}}{\phi} = -\phi B(N)^2 + 2B(N).$$

Thus, the constant term (the terms that do not multiply r_0) in (19.30) is

$$A(N) = -\left[\left(\bar{r} + \frac{1}{2}\sigma_\Lambda^2\right)N - \bar{r}\frac{1 - e^{-\phi N}}{\phi}\right] + \frac{1}{2}\left(\frac{\sigma_r}{\phi} + \sigma_\Lambda\right)^2 N$$

$$- \frac{\sigma_r}{\phi^2}\left(\frac{\sigma_r}{\phi} + \sigma_\Lambda\right)(1 - e^{-\phi N}) + \frac{\sigma_r^2}{4\phi^3}(1 - e^{-2\phi N})$$

$$= -\left[\left(\bar{r} + \frac{1}{2}\sigma_\Lambda^2\right)N - \bar{r}B(N)\right] + \frac{1}{2}\left(\frac{\sigma_r}{\phi} + \sigma_\Lambda\right)^2 N$$

$$- \frac{\sigma_r}{\phi}\left(\frac{\sigma_r}{\phi} + \sigma_\Lambda\right)B(N) - \frac{\sigma_r^2}{4\phi^2}(\phi B(N)^2 - 2B(N))$$

$$= \left(\frac{1}{2}\frac{\sigma_r^2}{\phi^2} + \sigma_\Lambda\frac{\sigma_r}{\phi} - \bar{r}\right)(N - B(N)) - \frac{\sigma_r^2}{4\phi^2}\phi B(N)^2.$$

Again, this is the same expression we derived from the partial differential equation.

This integration is usually expressed under the risk-neutral measure. If we write the risk-neutral process

$$\frac{d\Lambda}{\Lambda} = -r\,dt,$$

$$dr = \left[\phi(\bar{r} - r) - \sigma_r\sigma_\Lambda\right]dt + \sigma_r\,dz.$$

Then the bond price is

$$P_0^{(N)} = E e^{-\int_{s=0}^{N} r_s\,ds}.$$

The result is the same, of course.

Cox–Ingersoll–Ross Model

For the Cox–Ingersoll–Ross (1985) model

$$\frac{d\Lambda}{\Lambda} = -r\,dt - \sigma_\Lambda\sqrt{r}\,dz,$$

$$dr = \phi(\bar{r} - r)\,dt + \sigma_r\sqrt{r}\,dz,$$

our differential equation (19.16) becomes

$$\frac{\partial P}{\partial r}\phi(\bar{r} - r) + \frac{1}{2}\frac{\partial^2 P}{\partial r^2}\sigma_r^2 r - \frac{\partial P}{\partial N} - rP = \frac{\partial P}{\partial r}\sigma_r\sigma_\Lambda r. \qquad (19.33)$$

Guess again that log prices are a linear function of the short rate,

$$P(N, r) = e^{A(N) - B(N)r}. \qquad (19.34)$$

Substituting the derivatives of (19.34) into (19.33),

$$-B(N)\phi(\bar{r} - r) + \frac{1}{2}B(N)^2\sigma_r^2 r - A'(N) + B'(N)r - r = -B(N)\sigma_r\sigma_\Lambda r.$$

Again, the coefficients on the constant and on the terms in r must separately be zero,

$$B'(N) = 1 - \frac{1}{2}\sigma_r^2 B(N)^2 - (\sigma_r\sigma_\Lambda + \phi)B(N),$$

$$A'(N) = -B(N)\phi\bar{r}. \qquad (19.35)$$

The ordinary differential equations (19.35) are quite similar to the Vasicek case, (19.22). However, now the variance terms multiply an r, so the $B(N)$ differential equation has the extra $B(N)^2$ term. We can still solve both differential equations, though the algebra is a little bit more complicated. The result is

$$B(N) = \frac{2(1 - e^{\gamma N})}{(\gamma + \phi + \sigma_r \sigma_\Lambda)(e^{\gamma N} - 1) + 2\gamma},$$

$$A(N) = \frac{\phi \bar{r}}{\sigma_r^2} \left(2 \ln \left(\frac{2\gamma}{\psi(e^{\gamma N} - 1) + 2\gamma} \right) + \psi N \right),$$

where

$$\gamma = \sqrt{(\phi + \sigma_r \sigma_\Lambda)^2 + 2\sigma_r^2},$$

$$\psi = \phi + \sigma_\Lambda \sigma_r + \gamma.$$

The CIR model can also be solved by expectation. In fact, this is how Cox, Ingersoll, and Ross (1985) actually solve it—their marginal value of wealth J_W is the same thing as the discount factor. However, where the interest rate in the Vasicek model was a simple conditional normal, the interest rate now has a noncentral χ^2 distribution, so taking the integral is a little messier.

Multifactor Affine Models

The Vasicek and CIR models are special cases of the *affine* class of term structure models (Duffie and Kan [1996], Dai and Singleton [1999]). These models allow multiple factors, meaning all bond yields are not just a function of the short rate. Affine models maintain the convenient form that log bond prices are linear functions of the state variables. This means that we can take K bond yields themselves as the state variables, and the yields will reveal anything of interest in the hidden state variables. The short rate and its volatility will be forecast by lagged short rates but also by lagged long rates or interest rate spreads. My presentation and notation are similar to Dai and Singleton's, but as usual I add the discount factor explicitly.

Here is the affine model setup:

$$dy = \phi(\bar{y} - y) \, dt + \Sigma \, dw, \tag{19.36}$$

$$r = \delta_0 + \delta' y, \tag{19.37}$$

$$\frac{d\Lambda}{\Lambda} = -r \, dt - b'_\Lambda \, dw, \tag{19.38}$$

$$dw_i = \sqrt{\alpha_i + \beta'_i y} \, dz_i, \qquad E(dz_i \, dz_j) = 0. \tag{19.39}$$

Equation (19.36) describes the evolution of the state variables. In the end, yields will be linear functions of the state variables, so we can take the state variables to be yields; thus I use the letter y. y denotes a K-dimensional vector of state variables. ϕ is now a $K \times K$ matrix, $\bar{y}$ is a K-dimensional vector, Σ is a $K \times K$ matrix. Equation (19.37) describes the mean of the discount factor or short rate as a linear function of the state variables. Equation (19.38) is the discount factor. b_Λ is a K-dimensional vector that describes how the discount factor responds to the K shocks. The more Λ responds to a shock, the higher the market price of risk of that shock. Equation (19.39) describes the shocks dw. The functional form nests the CIR square root type models if $\alpha_i = 0$ and the Vasicek type Gaussian process if $\beta_i = 0$. You cannot pick α_i and β_i arbitrarily, as you have to make sure that $\alpha_i + \beta_i' y > 0$ for all values of y that the process can attain. Duffie and Kan (1996) and Dai and Singleton characterize this "admissibility" criterion.

We find bond prices in the affine setup following exactly the same steps as for the Vasicek and CIR models. Again, we guess that prices are linear functions of the state variables y:

$$P(N, y) = e^{A(N) - B(N)'y}.$$

We apply Ito's lemma to this guess, and substitute in the basic bond pricing equation (19.15). We obtain ordinary differential equations that $A(N)$ and $B(N)$ must satisfy,

$$\frac{\partial B(N)}{\partial N} = -\phi' B(N) - \sum_i \left(B(N)_i b_{\Lambda i} + \frac{1}{2} \left[\Sigma' B(N) \right]_i^2 \right) \beta_i + \delta, \quad (19.40)$$

$$\frac{\partial A(N)}{\partial N} = \sum_i \left(B(N)_i b_{\Lambda i} + \frac{1}{2} \left[\Sigma' B(N) \right]_i^2 \right) \alpha_i - B(N)' \phi \bar{y} - \delta_0. \quad (19.41)$$

I use the notation $[x]_i$ to denote the ith element of a vector x. As with the CIR and Vasicek models, these are ordinary differential equations that can be solved by integration starting with $A(0) = 0$, $B(0) = 0$. While they do not always have analytical solutions, they are quick to solve numerically—much quicker than solving a partial differential equation.

Derivation

To derive (19.41) and (19.40), we start with the basic bond pricing equation (19.15), which I repeat here,

$$E_t \left(\frac{dP}{P} \right) - \left(\frac{1}{P} \frac{\partial P}{\partial N} + r \right) dt = -E_t \left(\frac{dP}{P} \frac{d\Lambda}{\Lambda} \right). \quad (19.42)$$

We need dP/P. Using Ito's lemma,

$$\frac{dP}{P} = \frac{1}{P} \frac{\partial P'}{\partial y} dy + \frac{1}{2} \frac{1}{P} dy' \frac{\partial^2 P}{\partial y \partial y'} dy.$$

The derivatives are

$$\frac{1}{P}\frac{\partial P}{\partial y} = -B(N),$$

$$\frac{1}{P}\frac{\partial^2 P}{\partial y\,\partial y'} = B(N)B'(N),$$

$$\frac{1}{P}\frac{\partial P}{\partial N} = \frac{\partial A(N)}{\partial N} - \frac{\partial B(N)}{\partial N}' y.$$

Thus, the first term in (19.42) is

$$E_t\left(\frac{dP}{P}\right) = -B(N)'\phi(\bar{y}-y)\,dt + \frac{1}{2}E_t(dw'\Sigma'B(N)B'(N)\Sigma\,dw).$$

$E_t(dw_i\,dw_j) = 0$, which allows us to simplify the last term. If $w_1 w_2 = 0$, then,

$$(w'bb'w) = \begin{bmatrix} w_1 & w_2 \end{bmatrix}\begin{bmatrix} b_1 b_1 & b_1 b_2 \\ b_2 b_1 & b_2 b_2 \end{bmatrix}\begin{bmatrix} w_1 \\ w_2 \end{bmatrix} = b_1^2 w_1^2 + b_2^2 w_2^2 = \sum b_i^2 w_i^2.$$

Applying the same algebra to our case,

$$E_t\left(dw'\Sigma'B(N)B'(N)\Sigma\,dw\right) = \sum_i \left[\Sigma'B(N)\right]_i^2 dw_i^2$$

$$= \sum_i \left[\Sigma'B(N)\right]_i^2\left(\alpha_i + \beta_i'y\right)dt.$$

I use the notation $[x]_i$ to denote the ith element of the K-dimensional vector x. In sum, we have

$$E_t\left(\frac{dP}{P}\right) = -B(N)'\phi(\bar{y}-y)\,dt + \frac{1}{2}\sum_i \left[\Sigma'B(N)\right]_i^2\left(\alpha_i + \beta_i'y\right)dt. \quad (19.43)$$

The right-hand side term in (19.42) is

$$-E_t\left(\frac{dP\,d\Lambda}{P\,\Lambda}\right) = -B(N)'\,dw\,dw'b_\Lambda.$$

$dw\,dw'$ is a diagonal matrix with elements $(\alpha_i + \beta_i'y)$. Thus,

$$-E_t\left(\frac{dP\,d\Lambda}{P\,\Lambda}\right) = -\sum_i B(N)_i b_{\Lambda i}\left(\alpha_i + \beta_i'y\right). \quad (19.44)$$

Now, substituting (19.43) and (19.44) in (19.42), along with the easier $\partial P \partial N$ central term, we get

$$- B(N)'\phi(\bar{y} - y) + \frac{1}{2}\sum_i [\Sigma'B(N)]^2_i(\alpha_i + \beta'_i y)$$

$$- \left(\frac{\partial A(N)}{\partial N} - \frac{\partial B(N)}{\partial N}' y + \delta_0 + \delta'y\right) = -\sum_i B(N)_i b_{\Lambda i}(\alpha_i + \beta'_i y).$$

Once again, the terms on the constant and each y_i must separately be zero. The constant term:

$$-B(N)'\phi\bar{y} + \frac{1}{2}\sum_i [\Sigma'B(N)]^2_i\alpha_i - \frac{\partial A(N)}{\partial N} - \delta_0 = -\sum_i B(N)_i b_{\Lambda i}\alpha_i,$$

$$\frac{\partial A(N)}{\partial N} = \sum_i \left(B(N)_i b_{\Lambda i} + \frac{1}{2}[\Sigma'B(N)]^2_i\right)\alpha_i - B(N)'\phi\bar{y} - \delta_0.$$

The terms multiplying y:

$$B(N)'\phi y + \frac{1}{2}\sum_i [\Sigma'B(N)]^2_i\beta'_i y + \frac{\partial B(N)}{\partial N}' y - \delta'y = -\sum_i B(N)_i b_{\Lambda i}\beta'_i y.$$

Taking the transpose and solving,

$$\frac{\partial B(N)}{\partial N} = -\phi'B(N) - \sum_i \left(B(N)_i b_{\Lambda i} + \frac{1}{2}[\Sigma'B(N)]^2_i\right)\beta_i + \delta.$$

19.6 Bibliography and Comments

The choice of discrete versus continuous time is really one of convenience. Campbell, Lo, and MacKinlay (1997) give a discrete-time treatment, showing that bond prices are linear functions of the state variables even in a discrete-time two-parameter square root model. Backus, Foresi and Telmer (1998) is a good survey of bond pricing models in discrete time.

Models also do not have to be affine. Constantinides (1992) is a nice discrete-time model; its discount factor is driven by the squared value of AR(1) state variables. It gives closed-form solutions for bond prices. The bond prices are not linear functions of the state variables, but it is the existence of closed forms rather than linearity of the bond price function that makes affine models so attractive. Constantinides' model allows for both signs of the term premium, as we seem to see in the data.

So far most of the term structure literature has emphasized the risk-neutral probabilities, rarely making any reference to the separation between drifts and market prices of risk. This is not a serious shortcoming for option pricing uses, for which modeling the volatilities is much more important than modeling the drifts. It is also not a serious shortcoming when the model is used to draw smooth yield curves across maturities. However, it makes the models unsuitable for bond portfolio analysis and other uses. Many models imply high and time-varying market prices of risk or conditional Sharpe ratios. Recently, Backus, Foresi, Mozumdar and Wu (1997), Duffee (1999), Duarte (2000) and Dai and Singleton (2000) have started the important task of specifying term structure models that fit the empirical facts about expected returns in term structure models. In particular, they try to fit the Fama–Bliss (1986) and Campbell and Shiller (1991) regressions that relate expected returns to the slope of the term structure (see Chapter 2), while maintaining the tractability of affine models.

Term structure models used in finance amount to regressions of interest rates on lagged interest rates. Macroeconomists also run regressions of interest rates on a wide variety of variables, including lagged interest rates, but also lagged inflation, output, unemployment, exchange rates, and so forth. They often interpret these equations as the Federal Reserve's policy-making rule for setting short rates as a function of macroeconomic conditions. This interpretation is particularly clear in the Taylor rule literature (Taylor 1999) and monetary VAR literature; see Christiano, Eichenbaum, and Evans (1999) and Cochrane (1994) for surveys. Someone, it would seem, is missing important right-hand variables.

The criticism of finance models is stinging when we use the short rate as the only state variable. Multifactor models are more subtle. If any variable forecasts future interest rates, then it becomes a state variable, and it should be revealed by bond yields. Thus, bond yields should completely drive out any other macroeconomic state variables as interest rate forecasters. They do not, which is an interesting observation.

In addition, there is an extensive literature that studies yields from a purely statistical point of view, Gallant and Tauchen (1997) for example, and a literature that studies high-frequency behavior in the federal funds market, for example Hamilton (1996).

Obviously, these three literatures need to become integrated. Balduzzi, Bertola, and Foresi (1996) consider a model based on the federal funds target, and Piazzesi (2000) integrated a careful specification of high-frequency moves in the federal funds rate into a term structure model.

The models studied here are all based on diffusions with rather slow-moving state variables. These models generate one-day-ahead densities that are almost exactly normal. In fact, as Das and Foresi (1994) and Johannes (2000) point out, one-day-ahead densities have much fatter tails than normal distributions predict. This behavior could be modeled by fast-moving state variables. However, it is more natural to think of this behavior as generated by a jump process, and Johannes nicely fits a combined jump-diffusion for yields. This specification can change pricing and hedging characteristics of term structure models significantly.

All of the term structure models in this chapter describe many bond yields as a function of a few state variables. This is a reasonable approximation to the data. Almost all of the variance of yields can be described in terms of a few factors, typically a "level", "slope", and "hump" factor. Knez, Litterman, and Scheinkman (1994) make the point with a formal maximum-likelihood factor analysis, but you can see the point with a simple eigenvalue decomposition of log yields. See Table 19.1.

Not only is the variance of yields well described by a factor model, but the information in current yields about future yields—the expected changes in yields and the conditional volatility of yields—is well captured by one level and a few spreads as well.

It is a good approximation, but it is an approximation. Actual bond prices do not exactly follow any smooth yield curve, and the covariance matrix of actual bond yields does not have an exact K-factor structure— the remaining eigenvalues are not zero. Hence you cannot estimate a term structure model directly by maximum likelihood; you either have to estimate the models by GMM, forcing the estimate to ignore the stochastic singularity, or you have to add distasteful measurement errors.

As always, the importance of an approximation depends on how you use the model. If you take the model literally, a bond whose price deviates

Table 19.1

σ	Maturity					
	1	2	3	4	5	
6.36	0.45	0.45	0.45	0.44	0.44	"Level"
0.61	−0.75	−0.21	0.12	0.36	0.50	"Slope"
0.10	0.47	−0.62	−0.41	0.11	0.46	"Hump"
0.08	0.10	−0.49	0.39	0.55	−0.55	
0.07	0.07	−0.36	0.68	−0.60	0.21	

Eigenvalue decomposition of the covariance matrix of zero-coupon bond yields, 1952–1997. The first column gives the square root of the eigenvalues. The columns marked 1–5 give the eigenvectors corresponding to 1–5 year zero-coupon bond yields. I decomposed the covariance matrix as $\Sigma = Q \Lambda Q'$; σ^2 gives the diagonal entries in Λ and the rest of the table gives the entries of Q. With this decomposition, we can say that bond yields are generated by $y = Q \Lambda^{1/2} \varepsilon$, $E(\varepsilon \varepsilon') = I$, thus Q give "loadings" on the shocks ε.

by one basis point is an arbitrage opportunity. In fact, it is at best a good Sharpe ratio, but a K-factor model will not tell you how good—it will not quantify the risk involved in using the model for trading purposes. Hedging strategies calculated from K-factor models may be sensitive to small deviations as well.

One solution has been to pick different parameters at each point in time (Ho and Lee [1986]). This approach is useful for derivative pricing, but is obviously not a satisfactory solution. Models in which the whole yield curve is a state variable, Kennedy (1994), Santa Clara and Sornette (1999), are another interesting response to the problem, and potentially provide a realistic description of the data.

The market price of interest rate risk reflects the market price of real interest rate changes and the market price of inflation—or whatever real factors are correlated with inflation and explain investors' fear of it. The relative contributions of inflation and real rates in interest rate changes are very important for the nature of the risks that bondholders face. For example, if real rates are constant and nominal rates change on inflation news, then short-term bonds are the safest real long-term investment. If inflation is constant and nominal rates change on real rate news, then long-term bonds are the safest long-term investment. The data seem to suggest a change in regime between the 1970s and 1990s: in the 1970s, most interest rate changes were due to inflation, while the opposite seems true now. Despite all these provocative thoughts, though, little empirical work has been done that usefully separates interest rate risk premia into real and inflation premium components. Buraschi and Jiltsov (1999) is one recent effort in this direction, but a lot more remains to be done.

Problems—Chapter 19

1. Complete the proof that each of the three statements of the expectations hypothesis implies the other. Is this also true if we add a constant risk premium? Are the risk premia in each of the three statements of the yield curve of the same sign?

2. Under the expectations hypothesis, if long-term yields are higher than short-term yields, does this mean that future *long*-term rates should go up, down, or stay the same? (Hint: a plot of the expected log bond prices over time will really help here.)

3. Start by assuming risk neutrality, $E(HPR_{t+1}^{(N)}) = Y_t^{(1)}$ for all maturities N. Try to derive the other representations of the expectations hypothesis. Now you see why we specify that the expected log returns are equal.

4. Look at (19.13) and show that adding orthogonal dw to the discount factor has no effect on bond pricing formulas.

5. Look at (19.13) and show that $P = e^{-rT}$ if interest rates are constant, i.e., if $d\Lambda/\Lambda = -r\,dt + \sigma_\Lambda\,dz$.

6. Show that if interest rates follow a Gaussian AR(1) process

$$dr = \phi(\bar{r} - r)\,dt + \sigma\,dz$$

and the market price of interest rate risk is zero,

$$\frac{d\Lambda}{\Lambda} = -r\,dt,$$

then the expectation hypothesis with constant risk premia holds.

7. Show that a flat yield curve that shifts up and down is impossible. Start with (19.2). If yields follow $y(N, t) = y(t)$; $dy(t) = \mu(y)dt + \sigma(y)dz$ find holding period returns on N-year zeros. Show that the Sharpe ratio increases to infinity as N grows.

PART IV
Empirical Survey

This part surveys some of the empirical issues that are changing our theoretical understanding of the nature of risk and risk premia.

This part draws heavily on two previous review articles, Cochrane (1998) and (1999a) and on Cochrane and Hansen (1992). Fama's (1970) and (1991) efficient market reviews are classic and detailed reviews of much of the underlying empirical literature, focusing on cross-sectional questions. Campbell (1999, 2000) and Kocheralkota (1996) are good surveys of the equity premium literature.

20

Expected Returns in the Time Series and Cross Section

THE FIRST REVOLUTION in finance started the modern field. Peaking in the early 1970s, this revolution established the CAPM, random walk, efficient markets, portfolio-based view of the world. The pillars of this view are:

1. The CAPM is a good measure of risk and thus a good explanation why some stocks, portfolios, strategies, or funds (assets, generically) earn higher average returns than others.

2. Returns are unpredictable. In particular,

   (a) Stock returns are close to unpredictable. Prices are close to random walks; expected returns do not vary greatly through time. "Technical analysis" that tries to divine future returns from past price and volume data is nearly useless. Any apparent predictability is either a statistical artifact which will quickly vanish out of sample, or cannot be exploited after transactions costs. The near unpredictability of stock returns is simply stated, but its implications are many and subtle. (Malkiel [1990] is a classic and easily readable introduction.) It also remains widely ignored, and therefore is the source of lots of wasted trading activity.

   (b) Bond returns are nearly unpredictable. This is the expectations model of the term structure. If long-term bond yields are higher than short-term yields—if the yield curve is upward sloping—this does not mean that expected long-term bond returns are any higher than those on short-term bonds. Rather, it means that short-term interest rates are expected to rise in the future, so you expect to earn about the same amount on short-term or long-term bonds at any horizon.

   (c) Foreign exchange bets are not predictable. If a country has higher interest rates than are available in the United States for bonds of a similar risk class, its exchange rate is expected to depreciate. After

387

you convert your investment back to dollars, you expect to make the same amount of money holding foreign or domestic bonds.

(d) Stock market volatility does not change much through time. Not only are returns close to unpredictable, they are nearly identically distributed as well.

3. Professional managers do not reliably outperform simple indices and passive portfolios once one corrects for risk (beta). While some do better than the market in any given year, some do worse, and the outcomes look very much like good and bad luck. Managers who do well in one year are not more likely to do better than average the next year. The average actively managed fund does about 1% *worse* than the market index. The more actively a fund trades, the lower returns to investors.

Together, these views reflected a guiding principle that asset markets are, to a good approximation, *informationally efficient* (Fama 1970, 1991). This statement means that market prices already contain most information about fundamental value. Informational efficiency in turn derives from *competition*. The business of discovering information about the value of traded assets is extremely competitive, so there are no easy quick profits to be made, as there are not in every other well-established and competitive industry. The only way to earn large returns is by taking on additional risk.

These statements are not doctrinaire beliefs. Rather, they summarize the findings of a quarter-century of extensive and careful empirical work. However, every single one of them has now been extensively revised by a new generation of empirical research. Now, it seems that:

1. There are assets, portfolios, funds, and strategies whose average returns cannot be explained by their market betas. Multifactor models dominate the empirical description, performance attribution, and explanation of average returns.

2. Returns are predictable. In particular,

   (a) Variables including the dividend/price ratio and term premium can in fact predict substantial amounts of stock return variation. This phenomenon occurs over business cycle and longer horizons. Daily, weekly, and monthly stock returns are still close to unpredictable, and "technical" systems for predicting such movements are still close to useless after transactions costs.

   (b) Bond returns are predictable. Though the expectations model works well in the long run, a steeply upward sloping yield curve means that expected returns on long-term bonds are higher than on short-term bonds for the next year.

   (c) Foreign exchange returns are predictable. If you buy bonds in a country whose interest rates are unusually higher than those in the

United States, you expect a greater return, even after converting back to dollars.

(d) Stock market volatility does in fact change through time. Conditional second moments vary through time as well as first moments. Means and variances do not seem to move in lockstep, so conditional Sharpe ratios vary through time.

3. Some funds seem to outperform simple indices, even after controlling for risk through market betas. Fund returns are also slightly predictable: past winning funds seem to do better in the future, and past losing funds seem to do worse than average in the future. For a while, this seemed to indicate that there is some persistent skill in active management. However, we now see that multifactor performance attribution models explain most fund persistence: funds earn persistent returns by following fairly mechanical "styles," not by persistent skill at stock selection (Carhart [1997]).

Again, these views summarize a large body of empirical work. The strength and interpretation of many results are hotly debated.

This new view of the facts need not overturn the view that markets are reasonably competitive and therefore reasonably efficient. It does substantially enlarge our view of what activities provide rewards for holding risks, and it challenges our economic understanding of those risk premia. As of the early 1970s, asset pricing theory anticipated the possibility and even probability that expected returns should vary over time and that covariances past market betas would be important for understanding cross-sectional variation in expected returns. What took another 15 to 20 years was to see how important these long-anticipated theoretical possibilities are in the data.

20.1 Time-Series Predictability

I start by looking at patterns in expected returns over time in large market indices, and then look at patterns in expected returns across stocks.

Long-Horizon Stock Return Regressions.

Dividend/price ratios forecast excess returns on stocks. Regression coefficients and R^2 rise with the forecast horizon. This is a result of the fact that the forecasting variable is persistent.

The left-hand regression in Table 20.1 gives a simple example of market return predictability, updating Fama and French (1988). "Low" prices

Table 20.1. *OLS regressions of percent excess returns (value weighted*
NYSE − treasury bill rate) and real dividend growth on the percent VW
dividend/price ratio

Horizon k	$R_{t \to t+k} = a + b(D_t/P_t)$			$D_{t+k}/D_t = a + b(D_t/P_t)$		
(years)	b	$\sigma(b)$	R^2	b	$\sigma(b)$	R^2
1	5.3	(2.0)	0.15	2.0	(1.1)	0.06
2	10	(3.1)	0.23	2.5	(2.1)	0.06
3	15	(4.0)	0.37	2.4	(2.1)	0.06
5	33	(5.8)	0.60	4.7	(2.4)	0.12

$R_{t \to t+k}$ indicates the k-year return. Standard errors in parentheses use GMM to correct for
heteroskedasticity and serial correlation. Sample 1947–1996.

relative to dividends forecast higher subsequent returns. The one-year
horizon 0.17 R^2 is not particularly remarkable. However, at longer and
longer horizons larger and larger fractions of return variation are forecastable. At a five-year horizon 60% of the variation in stock returns is
forecastable ahead of time from the price/divided ratio.

One can object to dividends as the divisor for prices. However, ratios
formed with just about any sensible divisor work about as well, including
earnings, book value, and moving averages of past prices.

Many other variables forecast excess returns, including the term
spread between long- and short-term bonds, the default spread, the T-bill
rate (Fama and French [1989]), and the earnings/dividend ratio (Lamont
[1998]). Macro variables forecast stock returns as well, including the
investment/capital ratio (Cochrane [1991]) and the consumption/wealth
ratio (Lettau and Ludvigson [2000]).

Most of these variables are correlated with each other and correlated
with or forecast business cycles. This fact suggests a natural explanation,
emphasized by Fama and French (1999): Expected returns vary over business cycles; it takes a higher risk premium to get people to hold stocks
at the bottom of a recession. When expected returns go up, prices go
down. We see the low prices, followed by the higher returns expected and
required by the market. (Regressions do not have to have causes on the
right and effects on the left. You run regressions with the variable orthogonal to the error on the right, and that is the case here since the error is a
forecasting error. This is like a regression of actual weather on a weather
forecast.)

Table 20.2, adapted from Lettau and Ludvigson (2000), compares several of these variables. At a one-year horizon, both the consumption/

Table 20.2. *Long-horizon return forecasts*

Horizon (years)	cay	d − p	d − e	rrel	R^2
1	6.7				0.18
1		0.14	0.08		0.04
1				−4.5	0.10
1	5.4	0.07	−0.05	−3.8	0.23
6	12.4				0.16
6		0.95	0.68		0.39
6				−5.10	0.03
6	5.9	0.89	0.65	1.36	0.42

The return variable is log excess returns on the S&P composite index. *cay* is
Lettau and Ludvigson's consumption to wealth ratio. *d − p* is the log dividend
yield and *e − p* is the log earnings yield. *rrel* is a detrended short-term interest
rate. Sample 1952:4–1998:3.
Source: Lettau and Ludvigson (2000, Table 5).

wealth ratio and the detrended T-bill rate forecast returns, with R^2 of
0.18 and 0.10, respectively. At the one-year horizon, these variables are
more important than the dividend/price and dividend/earnings ratios,
and their presence cuts the dividend ratio coefficients in half. However,
the d/p and d/e ratios are slower moving than the T-bill rate and con-
sumption/wealth ratio. They track decade-to-decade movements as well as
business cycle movements. This means that their importance builds with
horizon. By six years, the bulk of the return forecastability again comes
from the dividend ratios, and it is their turn to cut down the cay and
T-bill regression coefficients. The cay and d/e variables have not been
that affected by the late 1990s, while this time period has substantially cut
down our estimate of dividend yield forecastability.

I emphasize that *excess* returns are forecastable. We have to understand this as time-variation in the reward for risk, not time-varying interest
rates. One naturally slips in to nonrisk explanations for price variation; for
example that the current stock market boom is due to life-cycle savings of
the baby boomers. A factor like this does not reference *risk*; it predicts
that interest rates should move just as much as stock returns.

Persistent d/p; Long Horizons Are Not A Separate Phenomenon
The results at different horizons are not separate facts, but reflections of
a single underlying phenomenon. If daily returns are very slightly predictable by a slow-moving variable, that predictability adds up over long
horizons. For example, you can predict that the temperature in Chicago
will rise about 1/3 degree per day in the springtime. This forecast explains

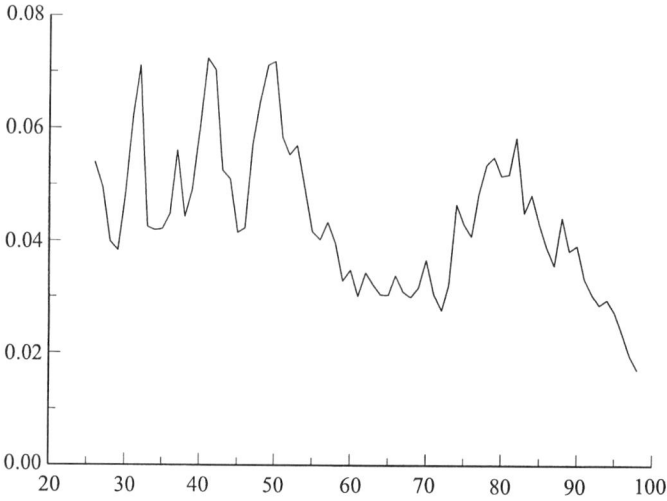

Figure 20.1. *Dividend/price ratio of value-weighted NYSE.*

very little of the day-to-day variation in temperature, but tracks almost all of the rise in temperature from January to July. Thus, the R^2 rises with horizon.

Thus, a central fact driving the predictability of returns is that the dividend/price ratio is very persistent. Figure 20.1 plots the d/p ratio and you can see directly that it is extremely slow-moving. Below, I estimate an AR(1) coefficient around 0.9 in annual data.

To see more precisely how the results at various horizons are linked, and how they result from the persistence of the d/p ratio, suppose that we forecast returns with a forecasting variable x, according to

$$r_{t+1} = ax_t + \varepsilon_{t+1}, \tag{20.1}$$

$$x_{t+1} = \rho x_t + \delta_{t+1}. \tag{20.2}$$

(Obviously, you de-mean the variables or put constants in the regressions.) Small values of b and R^2 in (20.1) and a large coefficient ρ in (20.2) imply mathematically that the long-horizon regression has a large regression coefficient b and large R^2. To see this, write

$$r_{t+1} + r_{t+2} = a(1+\rho)x_t + a\delta_{t+1} + \varepsilon_{t+1} + \varepsilon_{t+2},$$

$$r_{t+1} + r_{t+2} + r_{t+3} = a(1+\rho+\rho^2)x_t + a\rho\delta_{t+1} + a\delta_{t+2} + \varepsilon_{t+1} + \varepsilon_{t+2} + \varepsilon_{t+3}.$$

You can see that with ρ near one, the coefficients increase with horizon, almost linearly at first and then at a declining rate. The R^2 are a little messier to work out, but also rise with horizon.

The numerator in the long-horizon regression coefficient is

$$E[(r_{t+1} + r_{t+2} + \cdots + r_{t+k})x_t], \qquad (20.3)$$

where the symbols represent deviations from their means. With stationary r and x, $E(r_{t+j}x_t) = E(r_{t+1}x_{t-j})$, so this is the same moment as

$$E[r_{t+1}(x_t + x_{t-1} + x_{t-2} + \cdots)], \qquad (20.4)$$

the numerator of a regression coefficient of one-year returns on many lags of price/dividend ratios. Of course, if you run a multiple regression of returns on lags of p/d, you quickly find that most lags past the first do not help the forecast power. (That statement would be exact in the AR(1) example.)

This observation shows once again that one-year and multiyear forecastability are two sides of the same coin. It also suggests that on a purely *statistical* basis, there will not be a huge difference between one-year return forecasts and multiyear return forecasts (correcting the latter for the serial correlation of the error term due to overlap). Hodrick (1991) comes to this conclusion in a careful Monte Carlo experiment, comparing moments of the form (20.3), (20.4), and $E(r_{t+1}x_t)$. The direct or implied multiyear regressions are thus mostly useful for illustrating the dramatic *economic* implications of forecastability, rather than as clever statistical tools that enhance power and allow us to distinguish previously foggy hypotheses.

The slow movement of the price/dividend ratio means that on a purely statistical basis, return forecastability is an open question. What we really know (see Figure 20.1) is that low prices relative to dividends and earnings in the 1950s preceded the boom market of the early 1960s; that the high price/dividend ratios of the mid-1960s preceded the poor returns of the 1970s; that the low price ratios of the mid-1970s preceded the current boom. We really have three postwar data points: a once-per-generation change in expected returns. In addition, the last half of the 1990s has seen a historically unprecedented rise in stock prices and price/dividend ratios (or any other ratio). This rise has cut the postwar return forecasting regression coefficient in half. On the other hand, another crash or even just a decade of poor returns will restore the regression. Data back to the 1600s show the same pattern, but we are often uncomfortable making inferences from centuries-old data.

Volatility

Price/dividend ratios can only move at all if they forecast future returns, if they forecast future dividend growth, or if there is a bubble—if the price/dividend ratio is nonstationary and is expected to grow explosively. In the data, most variation in price/dividend ratios results from varying expected returns. "Excess volatility"—relative to constant discount rate present-value models—is thus exactly the same phenomenon as forecastable long-horizon returns.

I also derive the very useful price/dividend and return linearizations. Ignoring constants (means),

$$p_t - d_t = E_t \sum_{j=1}^{\infty} \rho^{j-1}(\Delta d_{t+j} - r_{t+j}),$$

$$r_t - E_{t-1}r_t = (E_t - E_{t-1})\left[\sum_{j=0}^{\infty} \rho^j \Delta d_{t+j} - \sum_{j=1}^{\infty} \rho^j r_{t+j}\right],$$

$$r_{t+1} = \Delta d_{t+1} - \rho(d_{t+1} - p_{t+1}) + (d_t - p_t).$$

The volatility test literature starting with Shiller (1981) and LeRoy and Porter (1981) (see Cochrane [1991] for a review) started out trying to make a completely different point. *Predictability* seems like a sideshow. The stunning fact about the stock market is its extraordinary *volatility*. On a typical day, the value of the U.S. capital stock changes by a full percentage point, and days of 2 or 3 percentage point changes are not uncommon. In a typical year it changes by 16 percentage points, and 30 percentage point changes are not uncommon. Worse, most of that volatility seems not to be accompanied by any important news about future returns and discount rates. Thirty percent of the capital stock of the United States vanished in a year and nobody noticed? Surely, this observation shows directly that markets are "not efficient"—that prices do not correspond to the value of capital—without worrying about predictability?

It turns out, however, that "excess volatility" is *exactly* the same thing as return predictability. Any story you tell about prices that are "too high" or "too low" necessarily implies that subsequent returns will be too low or too high as prices rebound to their correct levels.

When prices are high relative to dividends (or earnings, cashflow, book value, or some other divisor), one of three things must be true: (1) Investors expect dividends to rise in the future. (2) Investors expect returns to be low in the future. Future cashflows are discounted at a lower than usual rate, leading to higher prices. (3) Investors expect prices to rise forever, giving an adequate return even if there is no growth in dividends.

This statement is not a theory, it is an identity: If the price/dividend ratio is high, either dividends must rise, prices must decline, or the price/dividend ratio must grow explosively. The open question is, which option holds for our stock market? Are prices high now because investors expect future earnings, dividends, etc. to rise, because they expect low returns in the future, or because they expect prices to go on rising forever?

Historically, we find that *virtually all variation in price/dividend ratios has reflected varying expected excess returns.*

Exact Present-Value Identity
To document this statement, we need to relate current prices to future dividends and returns. Start with the identity

$$1 = R_{t+1}^{-1} R_{t+1} = R_{t+1}^{-1} \frac{P_{t+1} + D_{t+1}}{P_t} \tag{20.5}$$

and hence

$$\frac{P_t}{D_t} = R_{t+1}^{-1} \left(1 + \frac{P_{t+1}}{D_{t+1}}\right) \frac{D_{t+1}}{D_t}.$$

We can iterate this identity forward and take conditional expectations to obtain the identity

$$\frac{P_t}{D_t} = E_t \sum_{j=1}^{\infty} \left(\prod_{k=1}^{j} R_{t+k}^{-1} \Delta D_{t+k}\right), \tag{20.6}$$

where $\Delta D_t \equiv D_t/D_{t-1}$. (We could iterate (20.5) forward to

$$P_t = \sum_{j=1}^{\infty} \left(\prod_{k=1}^{j} R_{t+k}^{-1}\right) D_{t+j},$$

but prices are not stationary, so we cannot find the variance of prices from a time-series average. Much of the early volatility test controversy centered on stationarity problems. Equation (20.6) also requires a limiting condition that the price/dividend ratio cannot explode faster than returns, $\lim_{j \to \infty} E_t \left(\prod_{k=1}^{j} R_{t+k}^{-1}\right) P_{t+j}/D_{t+j}$. I come back to this condition below.)

Equation (20.6) shows that high prices must, mechanically, come from high future dividend growth or low future returns.

Approximate Identity
The nonlinearity of (20.6) makes it hard to handle, and means that we cannot use simple time-series tools. You can linearize (20.6) directly with a Taylor expansion. (Cochrane [1991] takes this approach.) Campbell and

Shiller (1988) approximate the one-period return identity before iterating, which is algebraically simpler. Start again from the obvious,

$$1 = R_{t+1}^{-1} R_{t+1} = R_{t+1}^{-1} \frac{P_{t+1} + D_{t+1}}{P_t}.$$

Multiplying both sides by P_t/D_t and massaging the result,

$$\frac{P_t}{D_t} = R_{t+1}^{-1} \left(1 + \frac{P_{t+1}}{D_{t+1}} \right) \frac{D_{t+1}}{D_t}.$$

Taking logs, and with lowercase letters denoting logs of uppercase letters,

$$p_t - d_t = -r_{t+1} + \Delta d_{t+1} + \ln\left(1 + e^{p_{t+1} - d_{t+1}}\right).$$

Taking a Taylor expansion of the last term about a point $P/D = e^{p-d}$,

$$p_t - d_t = -r_{t+1} + \Delta d_{t+1} + \ln\left(1 + \frac{P}{D}\right)$$

$$+ \frac{P/D}{1 + P/D} [p_{t+1} - d_{t+1} - (p - d)]$$

$$= -r_{t+1} + \Delta d_{t+1} + k + \rho(p_{t+1} - d_{t+1}). \tag{20.7}$$

Since the average dividend yield is about 4% and average price/dividend ratio is about 25, ρ is a number very near one. I will use $\rho = 0.96$ for calculations,

$$\rho = \frac{P/D}{1 + P/D} = \frac{1}{1 + D/P} \approx 1 - D/P = 0.96.$$

Without the constant k, the equation can also apply to deviations from means or any other point.

Now, iterating forward is easy, and results in the approximate identity

$$p_t - d_t = \text{const.} + \sum_{j=1}^{\infty} \rho^{j-1} (\Delta d_{t+j} - r_{t+j}). \tag{20.8}$$

(Again, we need a condition that $p_t - d_t$ does not explode faster than ρ^{-t}, $\lim_{j \to \infty} \rho^j (p_{t+j} - d_{t+j}) = 0$. I return to this condition below.)

Since (20.8) holds *ex post*, we can take conditional expectations and relate price/dividend ratios to *ex ante* dividend growth and return forecasts,

$$p_t - d_t = \text{const.} + E_t \sum_{j=1}^{\infty} \rho^{j-1} (\Delta d_{t+j} - r_{t+j}). \tag{20.9}$$

Now it is really easy to see that a high price/dividend ratio *must* be followed by high dividend growth Δd, or low returns r. Which is it?

Decomposing The Variance of Price/Dividend Ratios
To address this issue, equation (20.8) implies

$$\mathrm{var}(p_t - d_t) = \mathrm{cov}\left(p_t - d_t, \sum_{j=1}^{\infty} \rho^{j-1}\Delta d_{t+j}\right)$$

$$- \mathrm{cov}\left(p_t - d_t, \sum_{j=1}^{\infty} \rho^{j-1} r_{t+j}\right). \qquad (20.10)$$

In words, price/dividend ratios can *only* vary if they forecast changing dividend growth or if they forecast changing returns. (To derive (20.10) from (20.8), multiply both sides by $(p_t - d_t) - E(p_t - d_t)$ and take expectations.) Notice that both terms on the right-hand side of (20.10) are the numerators of exponentially weighted long-run regression coefficients.

This is a powerful equation. At first glance, it would seem a reasonable approximation that returns are unforecastable (the "random walk" hypothesis) and that dividend growth is not forecastable either. But if this were the case, the price/dividend ratio would have to be a *constant*. Thus the fact that the price/dividend ratio varies *at all* means that either dividend growth or returns must be forecastable—that the world is not i.i.d.

At a simple level, Table 20.1 includes regressions of long-horizon dividend growth on dividend/price ratios to match the return regressions. The coefficients in the dividend growth case are much smaller, typically one standard error from zero, and the R^2 are tiny. Worse, the *signs* are wrong. To the extent that a high price/dividend ratio forecasts any change in dividends, it seems to forecast a small *decline* in dividends!

Having seen equation (20.10), one is hungry for estimates. Table 20.3 presents some, taken from Cochrane (1991b). As one might suspect from Table 20.1, Table 20.3 shows that in the past *almost all variation in price/dividend ratios is due to changing return forecasts.*

The elements of the decomposition in (20.10) do not have to be between 0 and 100%. For example, −34, 138 occurs because high prices seem to forecast lower real dividend growth (though this number is not statistically significant). Therefore they must and do forecast really low returns, and returns must account for more than 100% of price/dividend variation.

This observation solidifies one's belief in price/dividend ratio forecasts of returns. Yes, the statistical evidence that price/dividend ratios forecast returns is weak, and many return forecasting variables have been

Table 20.3.   *Variance decomposition of value-weighted NYSE price/dividend ratio*

	Dividends	Returns
Real	−34	138
Std. error	10	32
Nominal	30	85
Std. error	41	19

Table entries are the percent of the variance of the price/dividend ratio attributable to dividend and return forecasts, $100 \times \mathrm{cov}(p_t - d_t, \sum_{j=1}^{15} \rho^{j-1} \Delta d_{t+j}) / \mathrm{var}(p_t - d_t)$ and similarly for returns.

tried and discarded, so selection bias is a big worry in forecasting regressions. But the price/dividend ratio (or price/earning, market book, etc.) has a special status since it must forecast something. To believe that the price/dividend ratio is stationary and varies, but does not forecast returns, you have to believe that the price/dividend ratio does forecast dividends. Given this choice and Table 20.1, it seems a much firmer conclusion that it forecasts returns.

It is nonetheless an uncomfortable fact that almost all variation in price/dividend ratios is due to variation in expected excess returns. How nice it would be if high prices reflected expectations of higher future cashflows. Alas, that seems not to be the case. If not, it would be nice if high prices reflected lower interest rates. Again, that seems not to be the case. High prices reflect low risk premia, lower expected *excess* returns.

Campbell's Return Decomposition
Campbell (1991) provides a similar decomposition for unexpected returns,

$$r_t - E_{t-1} r_t = (E_t - E_{t-1}) \left[\sum_{j=0}^{\infty} \rho^j \Delta d_{t+j} - \sum_{j=1}^{\infty} \rho^j r_{t+j} \right]. \qquad (20.11)$$

A positive shock to returns must come from a positive shock to forecast dividend growth, or from a negative shock to forecast returns.

Since a positive shock to time-t dividends is directly paid as a return (the first sum starts at $j = 0$), Campbell finds some fraction of return variation is due to current dividends. However, once again, the bulk of index return variation comes from shocks to future returns, i.e., discount rates.

To derive (20.11), start with the approximate identity (20.8), and move it back one period,

$$p_{t-1} - d_{t-1} = \text{const.} + \sum_{j=0}^{\infty} \rho^j (\Delta d_{t+j} - r_{t+j}).$$

Now take innovations of both sides,

$$0 = (E_t - E_{t-1}) \sum_{j=0}^{\infty} \rho^j (\Delta d_{t+j} - r_{t+j}).$$

Pulling r_t over to the left-hand side, you obtain (20.11). (Problem 3 at the end of the chapter guides you through an alternative and more constructive derivation.)

Cross Section
So far, we have concentrated on the index. One can apply the same analysis to firms. What causes the variation in price/dividend ratios, or, better book/market ratios (since dividends can be zero) across firms, or over time for a given firm? Vuolteenaho (2000) applies the same sort of analysis to individual stock data. He finds that as much as half of the variation in individual firm book/market ratios reflects expectations of future cashflows. Much of the expected cashflow variation is idiosyncratic, while the expected return variation is common, which is why variation in the index book/market ratio, like variation in the index dividend/price ratio, is almost all due to varying expected excess returns.

Bubbles
In deriving the exact and linearized present-value identities, I assumed an extra condition that the price/dividend ratio does not explode. Without that condition, and taking expectations of both sides, the exact identity reads

$$\frac{P_t}{D_t} = E_t \sum_{j=1}^{\infty} \left(\prod_{k=1}^{j} R_{t+k}^{-1} \Delta D_{t+k} \right) + \lim_{j \to \infty} E_t \left(\prod_{k=1}^{j} R_{t+k}^{-1} \right) \frac{P_{t+j}}{D_{t+j}}, \qquad (20.12)$$

and the linearized identity reads

$$p_t - d_t = \text{const.} + E_t \sum_{j=1}^{\infty} \rho^{j-1} (\Delta d_{t+j} - r_{t+j})$$

$$+ E_t \lim_{j \to \infty} \rho^j (p_{t+j} - d_{t+j}). \qquad (20.13)$$

As you can see, the limits in the right-hand sides of (20.12) and (20.13) are zero if the price/dividend ratio is stationary, or even bounded.

For these terms not to be zero, the price/dividend ratio must be expected to grow explosively, and faster than R or ρ^{-1}. Especially in the linearized form (20.13) you can see that stationary r, Δd *implies* stationary $p - d$ if the last term is zero, and $p - d$ is not stationary if the last term is not zero. Thus, you might want to rule out these terms just based on the view that price/dividend ratios do not and are not expected to explode in this way. You can also invoke economic theory to rule them out. The last terms must be zero in an equilibrium of infinitely lived agents or altruistically linked generations. If wealth explodes, optimizing long-lived agents will consume more. Technically, this limiting condition is a first-order condition for optimality just like the period-to-period first-order condition. The presence of the last term also presents an arbitrage opportunity in complete markets, as you can short a security whose price contains the last term, buy the dividends separately, and eat the difference right away.

On the other hand, there are economic theories that permit the limiting terms—overlapping generations models, and they capture the interesting possibility of "rational bubbles" that many observers think they see in markets, and that have sparked a huge literature and a lot of controversy.

An investor holds a security with a rational bubble not for any dividends, but on the expectation that someone else will pay even more for that security in the future. This does seem to capture the psychology of some investors from the (alleged, see Garber [2000]) tulip bubble of 17th century Holland to the dot-com bubble of the millennial United States—why else would anyone buy Cisco Systems at a price/earnings ratio of 217 and market capitalization 10 times that of General Motors in early 2000?

A "rational bubble" imposes a little discipline on this centuries-old description, however, by insisting that the person who is expected to buy the security in the future also makes the same calculation. He must expect the price to rise even further. Continuing recursively, the price in a rational bubble must be expected to rise forever. A Ponzi scheme, in which everyone knows the game will end at some time, cannot rationally get off the ground.

The *expectation* that prices will grow at more than a required rate of return forever does not mean that sample paths do so. For example, consider the bubble process

$$
P_{t+1} = \begin{cases} \gamma R P_t, & \text{prob} = \frac{P_t R - 1}{\gamma P_t R - 1}, \\ 1, & \text{prob} = \frac{P_t R}{\gamma P_t R - 1}. \end{cases}
$$

Figure 20.2 plots a realization of this process with $\gamma = 1.2$. This process yields an expected return R, and the dashed line graphs this expectation as of the first date. Its price is positive though it never pays dividends. It repeatedly grows with a high return γR for a while and then bursts back

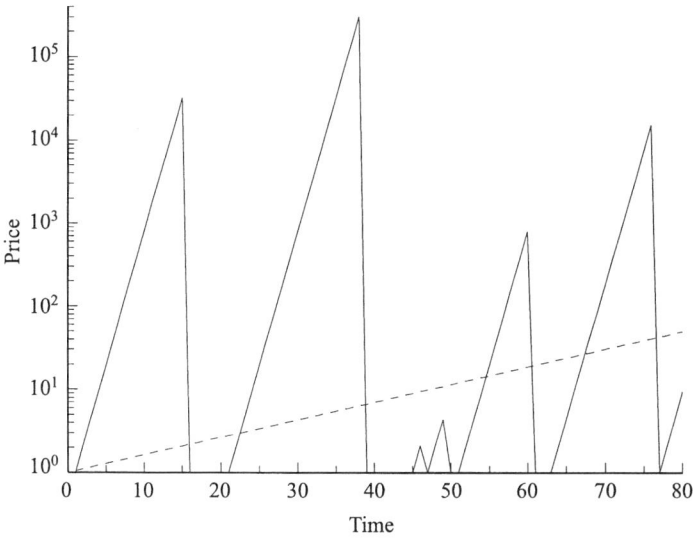

Figure 20.2. *Sample path from a simple bubble process. The solid line gives a price realization. The dashed line gives the expected value of prices as of time zero, i.e., $p_0 R^t$.*

to one. The *expected* price always grows, though almost all sample paths do not do so.

Infinity is a long time. It is really hard to believe that prices will rise *forever*. The solar system will end at some point; any look at the geological and evolutionary history of the earth suggests that our species will be around a lot sooner than that. Thus, the infinity in the bubble must really be a parable for "a really long time." But then the "rational" part of the bubble pops—it must hinge on the expectation that someone will be around to hold the bag; to buy a security without the expectation of dividends or further price increases. (The forever part of usual present-value formulas is not similarly worrying because 99.99% of the value comes from the first few hundred years of dividends.)

Empirically, bubbles do not appear to be the reason for historical price/dividend ratio variation. First, price/dividend ratios do seem stationary. (Craine [1993] runs a unit root test with this conclusion.) Even if statistical tests are not decisive, as is expected for a slow-moving series or a series such as that plotted in Figure 20.2, it is hard to believe that price/dividend ratios can explode rather than revert back to their four-century average level of about 20 to 25. Second, Table 20.3 shows that return and dividend forecastability terms add up to 100% of the variance of price/dividend ratios. In a bubble, we would expect price variation not matched by any variation in expected returns or dividends, as is the case in Figure 20.2.

I close with a warning: The word "bubble" is widely used to mean very different things. Some people seem to mean any large movement in prices. Others mean large movements in prices that do correspond to low or perhaps negative expected excess returns (I think this is what Shiller [2000] has in mind), i.e., any price movement not explained by a present-value model *with constant expected returns.*

A Simple Model for Digesting Predictability

> To unite the various predictability and return observations, I construct a simple VAR representation for returns, price growth, dividend growth, dividend/price ratio. I start only with a slow-moving expected return and unforecastable dividends.
>
> This specification implies that d/p ratios reveal expected returns.
>
> This specification implies return forecastability. To believe in a lower predictability of returns, you must either believe that dividend growth really is predictable, or that the d/p ratio is really much more persistent than it appears to be.
>
> This specification shows that small but persistent changes in expected returns add up to large price changes.

We have isolated two important features of the long-horizon forecast phenomenon: dividend/price ratios are highly persistent, and dividend growth is essentially unforecastable. Starting with these two facts, a simple VAR representation can tie together many of the predictability and volatility phenomena.

Start by specifying a slow-moving state variable x_t that drives expected returns, and unforecastable dividend growth,

$$x_t = bx_{t-1} + \delta_t, \tag{20.14}$$

$$r_{t+1} = x_t + \varepsilon_{rt+1}, \tag{20.15}$$

$$\Delta d_{t+1} = \varepsilon_{dt+1}. \tag{20.16}$$

All variables are de-meaned logs. (The term structure models of Chapter 19 were of this form.)

From this specification, using the linearized present-value identity and return, we can *derive* a VAR representation for prices, returns, dividends, and the dividend/price ratio,

$$(d_{t+1} - p_{t+1}) = b(d_t - p_t) + \frac{\delta_{t+1}}{1 - \rho b}, \tag{20.17}$$

$$r_{t+1} = (1 - \rho b)(d_t - p_t) + \left(\varepsilon_{dt+1} - \frac{\rho}{1 - \rho b}\delta_{t+1}\right), \tag{20.18}$$

$$\Delta p_{t+1} = (1 - b)(d_t - p_t) + \left(\varepsilon_{dt+1} - \frac{1}{1 - \rho b}\delta_{t+1}\right), \tag{20.19}$$

$$\Delta d_{t+1} = \varepsilon_{dt+1}. \tag{20.20}$$

I derive each of these equations, I look at data to come up with parameter values, and then I use this system to digest predictability.

Dividend/price ratio: Using the approximate present-value identity (20.9), we can find the dividend/price ratio

$$d_t - p_t = E_t \sum_{j=1}^{\infty} \rho^{j-1}(E_t r_{t+1} - E_t d_{t+j}) = \frac{x_t}{1 - \rho b}. \tag{20.21}$$

Equation (20.17) follows. Equation (20.21) makes precise my comment that the dividend/price ratio reveals expected returns x_t. Obviously, the feature that the dividend/price ratio is exactly proportional to the expected return x_t does not generalize. If dividend growth is also forecastable, then the dividend/price ratio is a combination of dividend growth and return forecasts. Actual return forecasting exercises can often benefit from cleaning up the dividend/price ratio to focus on the implied return forecast.

Returns: Since we know where the dividend/price ratio and dividends are going, we can figure out where returns are going. Use the return linearization (this is equivalent to (20.7))

$$R_{t+1} = \left(1 + \frac{P_{t+1}}{D_{t+1}}\right)\frac{D_{t+1}}{D_t} \Big/ \frac{P_t}{D_t},$$

$$r_{t+1} = \rho(p_{t+1} - d_{t+1}) + (d_{t+1} - d_t) - (p_t - d_t). \tag{20.22}$$

Now, plug in from (20.17) and (20.16) to get (20.18).

Prices: Write

$$p_{t+1} - p_t = -(d_{t+1} - p_{t+1}) + (d_t - p_t) + (d_{t+1} - d_t). \tag{20.23}$$

Then, plugging in from (20.17) and (20.16), we get (20.19).

Parameters

We can back out parameters from the reduced form return – d/p VAR. (Any two equations carry all the information of this system.) Table 20.4 presents some estimates.

I report both the more intuitive coefficients of returns on the actual d/p ratio, denoted $a, D/P$ and the coefficients on the log d/p ratio, denoted a, which is a more useful specification for our transformations. The two line up; a coefficient of 5 on D_t/P_t implies a coefficient of $5 \times D/P \approx 0.25$ on $(D_t/P_t)/(D/P)$.

You can see that the parameters depend somewhat on the sample. In particular, the dramatic returns of the late 1990s, despite low dividend yields, cut the postwar return forecast coefficients in half and the overall sample estimate by about one third. That dramatic decline in the d/p ratio also induces a very high apparent persistence in the d/p ratio, rising to a 0.97 estimate in the 48–98 sample. (Faced with an apparent trend in the data, an autoregression estimates a root near unity.)

With these estimates in mind, given the considerations outlined below, I make calculations using parameters

$$b = 0.9,$$

$$\rho = 0.96,$$

$$\sigma(\varepsilon_r) = 15, \qquad\qquad (20.24)$$

$$\sigma(\varepsilon_{dp}) = 12.5,$$

$$\rho(\varepsilon_r, \varepsilon_{dp}) = -0.7.$$

Table 20.4. *Estimates of log excess return and log dividend/price ratio regressions, using annual CRSP data*

Sample	a	$a, D/P$	b	$\sigma(\varepsilon_r)$	$\sigma(\varepsilon_{dp})$	$\rho(\varepsilon_r, \varepsilon_{dp})$
27–98	0.16	4.7	0.92	19.2	15.2	−0.72
48–98	0.14	4.0	0.97	15.0	12.6	−0.71
27–92	0.28	6.7	0.82	19.0	15.0	−0.69
48–92	0.27	6.2	0.87	14.5	12.4	−0.67

r is the difference between the log value-weighted return and the log treasury bill rate. The estimates are of the system

$$r_{t+1} = a(d_t - p_t) + \varepsilon_{rt+1},$$
$$d_{t+1} - p_{t+1} = b(d_t - p_t) + \varepsilon_{dp, t+1},$$

and

$$r_{t+1} = (a, D/P)\frac{D_t}{P_t} + \varepsilon_{t+1}.$$

From these parameters, we can find the underlying parameters of (20.14)–(20.16). I comment on each one below as it becomes useful. From (20.17)

$$\sigma(\delta) = \sigma(\varepsilon_{dp})(1 - \rho b) = 1.7. \tag{20.25}$$

From (20.18),

$$\sigma(\varepsilon_d) = \sigma(\varepsilon_r + \rho\varepsilon_{dp})$$

$$= \sqrt{\sigma^2(\varepsilon_r) + \rho^2\sigma^2(\varepsilon_{dp}) + 2\rho\sigma(\varepsilon_r, \varepsilon_{dp})} = 10.82,$$

$$\sigma(\varepsilon_d, \varepsilon_{dp}) = \sigma(\varepsilon_r, \varepsilon_{dp}) + \rho\sigma^2(\varepsilon_{dp}),$$

and hence

$$\rho(\varepsilon_d, \varepsilon_{dp}) = \frac{\rho(\varepsilon_r\varepsilon_{dp})\sigma(\varepsilon_r) + \rho\sigma(\varepsilon_{dp})}{\sigma(\varepsilon_d)} = 0.139. \tag{20.26}$$

Now we are ready to use (20.17)–(20.20) in order to integrate predictability issues.

The Size of the Return Forecasting Coefficient.
Does the magnitude of the estimated return predictability make sense? Given the statistical uncertainties, do other facts guide us to higher or lower predictability?

The coefficient of the one-year excess return on the dividend/price ratio in Table 20.1 is about 5, and the estimates in Table 20.4 vary from 4 to 6 depending on the sample. These values are surprisingly large. For example, a naive investor might think that dividend yields move one-for-one with returns; if they pay more dividends, you get more money. This logic implies a coefficient of 1. Before predictability, we would have explained that high dividend yield means that prices are low now in anticipation of lower future dividends, leaving the expected return unchanged. This logic implies a coefficient of 0. Now we recognize the possibility of time-varying expected returns, but does it make sense that expected returns move even more than dividend yields?

Return forecastability follows from the fact that dividends are not forecastable, and that the dividend/price ratio is highly but not completely persistent. We see this in the calculated coefficients of prices and returns on the dividend price ratio in (20.18) and (20.19). We derived

$$r_{t+1} = (1 - \rho b)(d_t - p_t) + \varepsilon_{rt+1},$$

$$\Delta p_{t+1} = (1 - b)(d_t - p_t) + \varepsilon_{pt+1}.$$

To transform units to regressions on D/P, multiply by 25, e.g.,

$$r_{t+1} = \frac{1 - \rho b}{D/P} \frac{D_t}{P_t} + \varepsilon_{rt+1}.$$

Suppose the d/p ratio were not persistent at all, $b = 0$. Then both return and price growth coefficients should be 1 in logs or about 25 in levels! If the D/P ratio is one percentage point above its average, we must forecast enough of a rise in prices to restore the D/P ratio to its average in one year. The average D/P ratio is about 4%, though, so prices and hence returns must rise by 25% to change the D/P ratio by one percentage point. $d(D/P) = -D/P \, d(P)/P$.

Suppose instead that the d/p ratio were completely persistent, i.e., a random walk with $b = 1$. Then the return coefficient is $1 - \rho = 0.04$, and about 1.0 in levels, while the price coefficient is 0. If the d/p ratio is one percent above average and expected to stay there, and dividends are not forecastable, then prices must not be forecast to change either. The return is one percentage point higher, because you get the higher dividends as well. Thus, the naive investor who expects dividend yield to move one for one with expected returns not only implicitly assumes that dividends are not forecastable—which turns out to be true—but also that the d/p ratio will stay put forever.

A persistence parameter $b = 0.90$ implies price and return regression coefficients of

$$
\begin{aligned}
1 - b &= 0.10, \\
1 - \rho b &= 1 - 0.96 \times 0.90 = 0.14
\end{aligned}
\tag{20.27}
$$

or about 2.5 and 3.4 on D/P. If the dividend yield is one percentage point high, and is expected to be 0.9 percentage points high one year from now, then prices must be expected to increase by $P/D \times 0.1 = 2.5$ percentage points in the next year. The return gets the additional dividend as well as the expected price change. This, fundamentally, is how unforecastable dividend growth together with persistent D/P imply that expected returns move more than one for one with the dividend yield.

Now, we can turn to the central question: how much return forecastability should we believe? The calculations of equation (20.27) are a little below most of the estimates in Table 20.1 and Table 20.4, which suggest coefficients on D/P of 4–6. In the sample, a high price seems to forecast *lower* dividend growth. This is the wrong sign, which is hard to believe. To believe in this much return forecastability without such perverse dividend growth forecastability, we have to lower the persistence coefficient.

For example, a persistence coefficient $b = 0.8$ implies a return coefficient $(1 - \rho b) = (1 - 0.96 \times 0.8) = 0.23$ or $0.23 \times 25 = 5.75$ on D/P. However, given the slow movement of D/P seen in Figure 20.1 and the fact that autoregression estimates are downward biased, it is hard to believe that D/P ratios really do revert that much more quickly. It seems more sensible to believe $b = 0.9$ and hence that return predictability is in fact something like 0.14, or roughly 3.4 on D/P. This value is equal to the estimate in the 48–98 sample, though distinctly lower than in some earlier samples.

Going in the other direction, statistical uncertainty, the recent runup in stocks despite low dividend yields, and the dramatic portfolio implications of time-varying returns for investors whose risks or risk aversion do not change over time all lead one to consider even lower return predictability. As we see from these calculations though, there are only two ways to make sense of lower predictability. You have to believe that high prices really do forecast higher dividend growth, or you have to believe that dividend price ratios are substantially more persistent than $b = 0.9$.

Much more persistent d/p is a tough road to follow, since D/P ratios already move very slowly. They basically change sign once a generation; high in the 50's, low in the 60's, high in the mid-70's, and decreasing ever since (see Figure 20.1.) Can this be a sample of unusually *fast* D/P movement? As a quantitative example, suppose the D/P ratio had an AR(1) coefficient of 0.96 in annual data. This means a half life of $\ln 0.5 / \ln 0.96 = 17$ years. In this case, the price coefficient would be

$$\frac{1 - b}{D/P} = \frac{1 - 0.96}{0.04} = 1$$

and the return coefficient would be

$$\frac{1 - \rho b}{D/P} = \frac{1 - 0.96^2}{0.04} \approx 2$$

A one percentage point higher d/p ratio means that prices must rise 1 percentage point next year, so returns must be about 2 percentage points higher. A two for one movement of expected returns with the dividend yield thus seems about the lower bound for return predictability.

The only other option is to believe that dividend growth really is forecastable. "New economy" advocates believe that *this* time, prices really are rising on advance news of dividend growth, even though prices have not forecast dividend growth in the past. This would be wonderful if it were true. However, you have to face the fact that every variation of the market D/P in the past was *not* followed by unusual dividend growth. You have to believe that our data were generated from a very unlucky sample.

Persistence, Price Volatility, and Expected Returns

From the dividend/price ratio equation (20.17) we can find the volatility of the dividend/price ratio and relate it to the volatility and persistence of expected returns:

$$\sigma(d_t - p_t) = \frac{1}{1 - \rho b}\sigma(x_t).$$

With $b = 0.9$, $1/(1 - \rho b) = 1/(1 - 0.96 \times 0.9) = 7.4$. Thus, the persistence of expected returns means that a small expected return variation translates into a large price variation. A one percentage point change in expected returns with persistence $b = 0.9$ corresponds to a 7.4% increase in price.

The Gordon growth model is a classic and even simpler way to see this point. With constant dividend growth g and return r, the present-value identity becomes

$$P = \frac{D}{r - g}.$$

A price/dividend ratio of 25 means $r - g = 0.04$. Then, a one percentage point permanent change in expected return translates into a 25 percentage point change in price! This is an overstatement, since expected returns are not this persistent, but it allows you clearly to see the point.

This point also shows that small market imperfections in expected returns can translate into substantial market imperfections in prices, if those expected return changes are persistent. We know markets cannot be perfectly efficient (Grossman and Stiglitz [1980]). If they were perfectly efficient, there would be no traders around to make them efficient. Especially where short sales or arbitrage are constrained by market frictions, *prices* of similar assets can be substantially different, while the *expected returns* of those assets are almost the same. For example the "closed-end fund" puzzle (Thompson [1978]) noted that baskets of securities sold for substantial price discounts relative to the sum of the individual securities. Even if we concede this as an anomaly,[1] it is a small difference in expected returns. The price differentials persist for a long time. You cannot short the closed-end funds to buy the securities and keep that short position on for years.

---

[1]Interestingly, recently introduced exchange-traded funds, which are passive closed end funds, trade at net asset value almost exactly. This fact suggests that the closed-end fund puzzle had more to do with entrenched active management than investor psychology.

Mean Reversion

> I introduce long-horizon return regressions and variance ratios. I show that they are related: each one picks up a string of small negative return autocorrelations. I show though that the direct evidence for mean-reversion and Sharpe ratios that rise with horizon is weak.

Long-Run Regressions and Variance Ratios

The first important evidence of long-run forecastability in the stock market did not come from regressions of returns on d/p ratios, but rather from clever ways of looking at the long-run univariate properties of returns. Fama and French (1988a) ran regressions of long-horizon returns on past long-horizon returns,

$$r_{t \to t+k} = a + b_k r_{t-k \to t} + \varepsilon_{t+k}, \tag{20.28}$$

basically updating classic autocorrelation tests from the 1960s to long-horizon data. They found negative and significant b coefficients: a string of good past returns forecasts bad future returns.

Poterba and Summers (1988) considered a related "variance ratio" statistic. If stock returns are i.i.d., then the variance of long-horizon returns should grow with the horizon,

$$\mathrm{var}(r_{t \to t+k}) = \mathrm{var}(r_{t+1} + r_{t+2} + \cdots + r_{t+k}) = k \, \mathrm{var}(r_{t+1}). \tag{20.29}$$

They computed the variance ratio statistic

$$v_k = \frac{1}{k} \frac{\mathrm{var}(r_{t \to t+k})}{\mathrm{var}(r_{t+1})}.$$

They found variance ratios below one. Stocks, it would seem, really are safer for "long-run investors" who can "afford to wait out the ups and downs of the market," common Wall Street advice, long maligned by academics.

These two statistics are closely related, and reveal the same basic fact: stock returns have a string of small negative autocorrelations. To see this relation, write the variance ratio statistic

$$v_k = \frac{1}{k} \frac{\mathrm{var}\left(\sum_{j=1}^{k} r_{t+j}\right)}{\mathrm{var}(r_{t+1})} = \sum_{j=-k}^{k} \frac{|k-j|}{k} \rho_j = 1 + 2 \sum_{j=1}^{k} \frac{|k-j|}{k} \rho_j, \tag{20.30}$$

and write the regression coefficient in (20.28),

$$b_k = \frac{1}{\text{var}(r_{t \to t+k})} \text{cov}\left(\sum_{j=1}^{k} r_{t+j}, \sum_{j=1}^{k} r_{t-j+1}\right)$$

$$= \frac{k \, \text{var}(r_{t+1})}{\text{var}(r_{t \to t+k})} \sum_{j=-k}^{k} \frac{|k-j|}{k} \rho_{k+j} = \frac{1}{v_k} \sum_{j=-k}^{k} \frac{|k-j|}{k} \rho_{k+j}.$$

Both statistics are based on tent-shaped sums of autocorrelations, as illustrated by Figure 20.3. If there are many small negative autocorrelations which bring returns back slowly after a shock, these autocorrelations might be individually insignificant. Their sum might be economically and statistically significant, however, and these two statistics will reveal that fact by focusing on the sum of autocorrelations. The long-horizon regression weights emphasize the middle of the autocorrelation function, so a k-year horizon long-horizon regression is comparable to a somewhat longer variance ratio.

Impulse-Response Function and Mean-Reversion
We think of many negative higher order autocorrelations as "bringing prices back after a shock," so it is natural to characterize mean-reversion via the impulse-response function of prices to a shock directly. If, after a shock, prices are expected to trend upward, we have "momentum." If, after a shock, prices are expected to come back a bit, we have "mean-reversion."

To think about this characterization more precisely, start by writing returns as a moving average of their own shocks. From a regression of

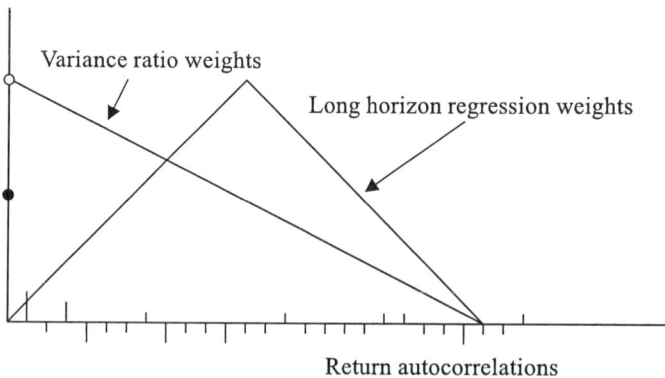

Figure 20.3. *Long-horizon regression and variance ratio weights on autocorrelations.*

returns on past returns

$$a(L)r_t = \varepsilon_t \tag{20.31}$$

you can find the θ_j in the representation

$$r_t = \sum_{j=0}^{\infty} \theta_j \varepsilon_{t-j} = \theta(L)\varepsilon_t = a(L)^{-1}\varepsilon_t.$$

(Most simply, just simulate [20.31] forward.) The θ_j are the moving average representation or impulse-response function—they tell you what happens to all future expected returns following a shock. Let p_t represent the cumulative returns, or the log value of a dollar invested, $p_t - p_{t-1} = r_t$. Then, the partial sum $\sum_{j=1}^{k} \theta_j$ tells you the effect on invested wealth p_{t+k} of a univariate shock ε_t. The sum $\sum_{j=1}^{\infty} \theta_j = \theta(1)$ measures the long-run effect of a shock. I normalize the scale of the moving average representation with $\theta_0 = 1$.

A natural measure of mean-reversion, then, is whether the long-run effect of a shock is greater or less than its instantaneous effect—whether $\theta(1)$ is greater than, equal to, or less than one.

This measure is also closely related to autocorrelations, long-horizon regressions, and variance ratios, by

$$\lim_{k \to \infty} v_k = 1 + 2\sum_{j=1}^{\infty} \rho_j = \frac{\theta(1)^2}{\sum_{j=0}^{\infty} \theta_j^2}. \tag{20.32}$$

If returns are i.i.d., the variance ratio is one at all horizons; all autocorrelations are zero, and all θ past the first are zero so $\theta(1) = 1$, $\sum \theta_j^2 = 1$. A long string of small negative autocorrelations means a variance ratio less than one, and means $\sum_{j=0}^{\infty} \theta_j < 1$ so the long-run effect on price is lower than the impact effect—that is "mean-reversion."

The right-hand equality of (20.32) follows by just taking the $k \to \infty$ in (20.30). For the second equality, you can recognize in both expressions the spectral density of r at frequency zero. The $\sum \theta_j^2$ term enters because the variance ratio is scaled by the variance of the series, and the long-run response is scaled by the impact response, or equivalently by the variance of the shock to the series. It is possible in extreme cases for the variance ratio to be below one, but $\theta(1) > 1$ and vice versa.

Numbers
Table 20.5 presents long-horizon return regressions and an estimate of the variance of long-horizon returns. The long-horizon regressions do show some interesting mean reversion, especially in the 3–5 year range. However, that turns around at year 7 and disappears by year 10. The variance

Table 20.5.   *Mean-reversion using logs, 1926–1996*

| | Horizon k (years) | | | | | |
	1	2	3	5	7	10
$\sigma(r_k)/\sqrt{k}$	19.8	20.6	19.7	18.2	16.5	16.3
β_k	0.08	−0.15	−0.22	−0.04	0.24	0.08
Sharpe/$\sqrt{k}$	0.31	0.30	0.30	0.31	0.36	0.39

r denotes the difference between the log value-weighted NYSE return and the log treasury bill return. $\sigma(r_k) = \sigma(r_{t \to t+k})$ is the variance of long-horizon returns. β_k is the long-horizon regression coefficient in $r_{t \to t+k} = \alpha + \beta_k r_{t-k \to t} + \varepsilon_{t+k}$. The Sharpe ratio is $E(r_{t \to t+k})/\sigma(r_{t \to t+k})$.

ratios do show some long-horizon stabilization. At year 10, the variance ratio is $(16.3/19.8)^2 = 0.68$.

The last row of Table 20.5 calculates Sharpe ratios, to evaluate whether stocks really are safer in the long run. The mean log return grows linearly with horizon whether returns are autocorrelated or not—$E(r_1 + r_2) = 2E(r)$. If the variance also grows linearly with the horizon, as it does for nonautocorrelated returns, then the Sharpe ratio grows with the square root of the horizon. If the variance grows more slowly than the horizon, then the Sharpe ratio grows faster than the square root of the horizon. This is the fundamental question for whether stocks are (unconditionally) "safer for the long run." Table 20.5 includes the long-horizon Sharpe ratios, and you can see that they do increase.

You would not be to blame if you thought that the evidence of Table 20.5 was rather weak, especially compared with the dramatic dividend/price regressions. It is, and it is for this reason that most current evidence for predictability focuses on other variables such as the d/p ratio.

In addition, Table 20.6 shows that the change from log returns to levels of returns, while having a small effect on long-horizon regressions,

Table 20.6.   *Mean-reversion using gross returns, 1926–1996*

| | Horizon k (years) | | | | | |
	1	2	3	5	7	10
$\sigma(r_k)/\sqrt{k}$	20.6	22.3	22.5	24.9	28.9	39.5
β_k	0.02	−0.21	−0.22	−0.03	0.22	−0.63
Sharpe/$\sqrt{k}$	0.41	0.41	0.41	0.40	0.40	0.38

r denotes the difference between the gross (not log) long-horizon value-weighted NYSE return and the gross treasury bill return.

Table 20.7. *Mean-reversion in postwar data*

1947–1996 logs	Horizon k (years)					
	1	2	3	5	7	10
$\sigma(r_k)/\sqrt{k}$	15.6	14.9	13.0	13.9	15.0	15.6
β_k	−0.10	−0.29*	0.30*	0.30	0.17	−0.18
Sharpe/$\sqrt{k}$	0.44	0.46	0.51	0.46	0.41	0.36
1947–1996 levels	1	2	3	5	7	10
$\sigma(r_k)/\sqrt{k}$	17.1	17.9	16.8	21.9	29.3	39.8
β_k	−0.13	−0.33*	0.30	0.25	0.13	−0.25
Sharpe/$\sqrt{k}$	0.50	0.51	0.55	0.48	0.41	0.37

destroys any evidence for higher Sharpe ratios at long horizons. Table 20.7 shows the same results in the postwar period. Some of the negative long-horizon regression coefficients are negative and significant, but there are just as large positive coefficients, and no clear pattern. The variance ratios are flat or even rising with horizons, and the Sharpe ratios are flat or even declining with horizon.

In sum, the direct evidence for mean-reversion in index returns seems quite weak. I consider next whether indirect evidence, values of these statistics implied by other estimation techniques, still indicate mean-reversion. (The mean-reversion of individual stock returns as examined by Fama and French (1988a) is somewhat stronger, and results in the stronger cross-sectional "reversal" effect described in Section 20.2.)

Mean-Reversion and Forecastability

> I reconcile large forecastability from d/p ratios with a small mean-reversion. I calculate the univariate return process implied by the simple VAR, and find that it displays little mean-reversion.
>
> I show that if dividend shocks are uncorrelated with expected return shocks, there must be some mean-reversion. If we rule out the small positive correlation between dividend and expected return shocks in our sample, we get a slightly higher estimate of univariate mean-reversion.
>
> I tie the strong negative correlation between return and d/p shocks to an essentially zero correlation between expected return and dividend growth shocks.

How is it possible that variables such as the dividend/price ratio forecast returns strongly, but there seems to be little evidence for mean-reversion in stock returns? To answer this question, we have to connect the d/p regressions and the mean-reversion statistics.

Forecastability from variables such as the dividend/price ratios is related to, but does not necessarily imply, mean-reversion. (Campbell [1991] emphasizes this point.) Mean-reversion, is about the *univariate* properties of the return series, forecasts of r_{t+j} based on $\{r_t, r_{t-1}, r_{t-2}, \ldots\}$. Predictability is about the *multivariate* properties, forecasts of r_{t+j} based on $\{x_t, x_{t-1}, x_{t-2}, \ldots\}$ as well as $\{r_t, r_{t-1}, r_{t-2}, \ldots\}$. Variables $\{x_{t-j}\}$ can forecast r_{t+1}, while $\{r_{t-j}\}$ fail to forecast r_{t+1}. As a simple example, suppose that returns are i.i.d., but you get to see tomorrow's newspaper. You forecast returns very well with $x_t = r_{t+1}$, but lagged returns do not forecast returns at all.

To examine the relationship between d/p forecasts and mean-reversion, continue with the VAR representation built up from a slowly moving expected return and unforecastable dividend growth, (20.14)–(20.20). We want to find the *univariate* return process implied by this VAR: what would happen if you took infinite data from the system and ran a regression of returns on lagged returns? The answer, derived below, is of the form

$$r_t = \frac{1 - \gamma L}{1 - bL} \nu_t. \tag{20.33}$$

This is just the kind of process that can display slow mean-reversion or momentum. The moving average representation is

$$r_t = \nu_t - (\gamma - b)\nu_{t-1} - b(\gamma - b)\nu_{t-2}$$
$$- b^2(\gamma - b)\nu_{t-3} - b^3(\gamma - b)\nu_{t-4} - \cdots . \tag{20.34}$$

Thus, if $\gamma > b$, a positive return shock sets off a long string of small negative returns, which cumulatively bring the value back towards where it started. If $\gamma < b$, a positive shock sets off a string of small positive returns, which add "momentum" to the original increase in value.

Now, what value of γ does our VAR predict? Is there a sensible structure of the VAR that generates substantial predictability but little mean-reversion? The general formula, derived below, is that γ solves

$$\frac{1 + \gamma^2}{\gamma} = \frac{(1 + b^2)\sigma^2(\varepsilon_d) + (1 + \rho^2)\sigma^2(\varepsilon_{dp}) - 2(\rho + b)\sigma(\varepsilon_d, \varepsilon_{dp})}{b\sigma^2(\varepsilon_d) + \rho\sigma^2(\varepsilon_{dp}) - (\rho + b)\sigma(\varepsilon_d, \varepsilon_{dp})} = 2q, \tag{20.35}$$

and hence,

$$\gamma = q - \sqrt{q^2 - 1}.$$

Case 1: No Predictability
If returns are not predictable in this system—if $\sigma(\delta) = 0$ so $\sigma(\varepsilon_{dp}) = 0$, then (20.35) specializes to

$$\frac{1+\gamma^2}{\gamma} = \frac{1+b^2}{b}.$$

$\gamma = b$, so returns in (20.33) are not autocorrelated. Sensibly enough, no predictability implies no mean-reversion.

Case 2: Constant Dividend Growth
Next, suppose that dividend growth is constant; $\sigma(\varepsilon_d) = 0$ and variation in expected returns is the *only* reason that ex-post returns vary at all. In this case, (20.35) specializes quickly to

$$\frac{1+\gamma^2}{\gamma} = \frac{1+\rho^2}{\rho},$$

and thus $\gamma = \rho$.

These parameters imply a substantial amount of mean-reversion. $(\gamma - b)$ in (20.34) is then $0.96 - 0.90 = 0.06$, so that each year j after a shock returns come back by $6 \times b^j$ percent of the original shock. The cumulative impact is that value ends up at $(1-\gamma)/(1-b) = (1-0.96)/(1-0.9) = 0.4$ or only 40% of the original shock.

Case 3: Dividend Growth Uncorrelated With Expected Return Shocks
Pure variation in expected returns is of course not realistic. Dividends do vary. If we add dividend growth uncorrelated with expected return shocks $\sigma(\varepsilon_{dp}, \varepsilon_d) = 0$, (20.35) specializes to

$$\frac{1+\gamma^2}{\gamma} = \frac{1+b^2}{b} \frac{b\sigma^2(\varepsilon_d)}{b\sigma^2(\varepsilon_d) + \rho\sigma^2(\varepsilon_{dp})}$$
$$+\frac{1+\rho^2}{\rho} \frac{\rho\sigma^2(\varepsilon_{dp})}{b\sigma^9(\varepsilon_d) + \rho\sigma^2(\varepsilon_{dp})} = 2q. \qquad (20.36)$$

In this case, $b < \gamma < \rho$. There will be some mean reversion in returns—this model cannot generate $\gamma \le b$. However, the mean-reversion in returns will be lower than with no dividend growth, because dividend growth obscures the information in ex post returns about time-varying expected returns. How much lower depends on the parameters.

Using the parameters (20.24), I find that (20.36) implies

$$\gamma = q - \sqrt{q^2 - 1} = 0.928.$$

Our baseline VAR with no correlation between dividend growth and expected return shocks thus generates a univariate return process that is slightly on the mean-reversion edge of uncorrelated. The long-run response to a shock is

$$\frac{1-\gamma}{1-b} = \frac{1-0.928}{1-0.9} = 0.72.$$

This is a lot less mean-reversion than 0.4, but still somewhat more mean-reversion than we see in direct estimates such as Tables 20.5–20.7.

This case is an important baseline worth stressing. *If expected returns are positively correlated, realized returns are negatively autocorrelated.* If (unchanged) expected dividends are discounted at a higher rate, today's price falls. You can see this most easily by just looking at the return or its linearization, (20.22),

$$r_{t+1} = \Delta d_{t+1} - \rho(d_{t+1} - p_{t+1}) + (d_t - p_t). \tag{20.37}$$

The $d - p$ ratio is proportional to expected returns. Thus, the second term on the right hand side implies that a positive shock to expected returns, uncorrelated with dividend growth, lowers actual returns. A little more deeply, look at the return innovation identity (20.11),

$$r_t - E_{t-1}r_t = (E_t - E_{t-1})\left[\sum_{j=0}^{\infty} \rho^j \Delta d_{t+j} - \sum_{j=1}^{\infty} \rho^j r_{t+j}\right]. \tag{20.38}$$

If expected returns $(E_t - E_{t-1})\sum_{j=1}^{\infty}\rho^j r_{t+j}$ *increase*, with no concurrent news about current or future dividends, then $r_t - E_{t-1}r_t$ *decreases*.

This is the point to remark on a curious feature of the return-dividend/price VAR: the negative correlation between ex post return shocks and dividend/price ratio shocks. All the estimates were around -0.7. At first glance such a strong correlation between VAR residuals seems strange. At second glance, it is expected. From (20.37) you can see that a positive innovation to the dividend price ratio will correspond to a negative return innovation, unless a striking dividend correlation gets in the way. More deeply, you can see the point in (20.38). Quantitatively, from (20.18), the return shock is related to the dividend growth shock and the expected return shock by

$$\varepsilon_r = \varepsilon_d - \frac{\rho}{1-\rho b}\delta = \varepsilon_d - \rho\varepsilon_{dp}.$$

Thus, a zero correlation between the underlying dividend growth and expected return shocks, $\rho(\varepsilon_d, \delta) = 0$, implies a negative covariance between return shocks and expected return shocks,

$$\sigma(\varepsilon_r, \delta) = -\frac{\rho}{1 - \rho b}\sigma^2(\delta).$$

The correlation is a perfect -1 if there are no dividend growth shocks. At the parameters $\sigma(\varepsilon_{dp}) = 12.5$, $\sigma(\varepsilon_r) = 15$, we obtain

$$\rho(\varepsilon_r, \delta) = \rho(\varepsilon_r, \varepsilon_{dp}) = -\frac{\rho}{1 - \rho b}\frac{\sigma(\delta)}{\sigma(\varepsilon)}$$

$$= -\rho\frac{\sigma(\varepsilon_{dp})}{\sigma(\varepsilon)} = -0.96 \times \frac{12.5}{15} = -0.8.$$

The slight 0.1 positive correlation between dividend growth and expected return shocks in (20.26) results (or, actually, results from) a slightly lower -0.7 specification for the correlation of return and d/p shocks.

The strong negative correlation between return shocks and expected return shocks, expected from a low correlation between dividend growth shocks and expected return shocks, is crucial to the finding that returns are not particularly correlated despite predictability. Consider what would happen if the correlation $\rho(\varepsilon_r, \varepsilon_{dp}) = \rho(\varepsilon_r, \delta)$ were zero. The expected return x_t is slow moving. If it is high now, it has been high for a while, and there has likely been a series of good past returns. But it also will remain high for a while, leading to a period of high future returns. This is "momentum," positive return autocorrelation, the opposite of mean-reversion.

Case 4: Dividend Growth Shocks Positively Correlated With Expected Return Shocks
As we have seen, the VAR with no correlation between expected return and dividend growth shocks cannot deliver uncorrelated returns or positive "momentum" correlation patterns. At best, volatile dividend growth can obscure an underlying negative correlation pattern. However, looking at (20.37) or (20.38), you can see that adding dividend growth shocks positively correlated with expected return shocks could give us uncorrelated or positively correlated returns.

The estimates in Table 20.4 and (20.24) implied a slight positive correlation of dividend growth and expected return shocks, $\rho_{\varepsilon_d\delta} = 0.14$ in (20.26). If we use that estimate in (20.35), we recover an estimate

$$\gamma = 0.923, \qquad \frac{1 - \gamma}{1 - b} = 0.77.$$

This γ is quite close to $b = 0.9$, and the small mean-reversion is more closely consistent with the direct estimates in Tables 20.5–20.7.

Recall that point estimates as in Table 20.1 showed that a high d/p ratio forecast slightly higher dividends—the wrong sign. This point estimate means that shocks to the d/p ratio and expected returns are positively correlated with shocks to expected dividend growth. If you generalize the VAR to allow such shocks, along with a richer specification allowing additional lags and variables, you find that VARs give point estimates with slight but very small mean-reversion. (See Cochrane [1994] for a plot.) The estimated univariate process has slight mean-reversion, with an impulse response ending up at about 0.8 of its starting value, and no different from the direct estimate.

Can we generate unforecastable returns in this system? To do so, we have to increase further the correlation between expected return shocks and dividend growth. Equating (20.35) to $(1 + b^2)/b$ and solving for $\rho(\varepsilon_d, \varepsilon_{dp})$, we obtain

$$\rho(\varepsilon_d, \varepsilon_{dp}) = \frac{(1 - \rho b)(\rho - b)}{(1 - b)^2(\rho + b)} \frac{\sigma(\varepsilon_{dp})}{\sigma(\varepsilon_d)} = 0.51.$$

This is possible, but not likely. Any positive correlation between dividend growth and expected return shocks strikes me as suspect. If anything, I would expect that since expected returns rise in "bad times" when risk or risk aversion increases, we should see a positive shock to expected returns associated with a *negative* shock to current or future dividend growth. Similarly, if we are going to allow dividend/price ratios to forecast dividend growth, a high dividend/price ratio should forecast lower dividends.

Tying together all these thoughts, I think it is reasonable to impose zero dividend forecastability and zero correlation between dividend growth and expected return shocks. This specification means that returns are really less forecastable than they seem in some samples. As we have seen, $b = 0.9$ and no dividend forecastability means that the coefficient of return on D/P is really about 3.4 rather than 5 or 6. This specification means that expected returns really account for 100% rather than 130% of the price/dividend variance. However, it also means that univariate mean reversion is slightly stronger than it seems in our sample.

This section started with the possibility that the implied mean-reversion from a multivariate system could be a lot larger than that revealed by direct estimates. Instead, we end up by reconciling strong predictability and slight mean-reversion.

How to Find the Univariate Return Representation
This section ties up one technical loose end – how to derive equation (20.33). To find the implied univariate representation, we have to start

with the VAR and find a representation

$$r_{t+1} = a(L)v_t \tag{20.39}$$

in which the $a(L)$ is invertible. The Wold decomposition theorem tells us that there is a unique moving invertible moving average representation in which the v_t are the one-step-ahead forecast error shocks, i.e., the errors in a regression model $a(L)r_{t+1} = v_{t+1}$. Thus, if you find any invertible moving average representation, you know you have the right one. We cannot do this by simply manipulating the systems starting with (20.14), because they are expressed in terms of multivariate shocks, errors in regressions that include x.

There are three fundamental representations of a time series: its Wold moving average representation, its autocorrelation function, and its spectral density. To find the univariate representation (20.39), you either calculate the autocorrelations $E(r_t r_{t-j})$ from (20.14) and then try to recognize what process has that autocorrelation pattern, or you calculate the spectral density and try to recognize what process has that spectral density.

In our simple setup, we can write the return-d/p VAR (20.17)–(20.18) as

$$r_{t+1} = (1 - \rho b)(d_t - p_t) + (\varepsilon_{dt+1} - \rho \varepsilon_{dpt+1}),$$

$$(d_{t+1} - p_t) = b(d_t - p_t) + \varepsilon_{dpt+1}.$$

Then, write returns as

$$r_{t+1} = \frac{(1 - \rho b)}{1 - bL} \varepsilon_{dpt} + (\varepsilon_{dt+1} - \rho \varepsilon_{dpt+1}),$$

$$(1 - bL)r_{t+1} = (1 - \rho b)\varepsilon_{dpt} + (\varepsilon_{dt+1} - \rho \varepsilon_{dpt+1}) - b(\varepsilon_{dt} - \rho \varepsilon_{dpt}),$$

and hence,

$$(1 - bL)r_{t+1} = (\varepsilon_{dt+1} - \rho \varepsilon_{dpt+1}) + (\varepsilon_{dpt} - b\varepsilon_{dt}). \tag{20.40}$$

Here, you can see that r_t must follow an ARMA(1,1) with one root equal to b and the other root to be determined. Define $y_t = (1 - bL)r_t$, and thus $y_t = (1 - \gamma L)v_t$. Then the autocovariances of y from (20.40) are

$$E(y_{t+1}^2) = (1 + b^2)\sigma^2(\varepsilon_d) + (1 + \rho^2)\sigma^2(\varepsilon_{dp}) - 2(\rho + b)\sigma(\varepsilon_d, \varepsilon_{dp}),$$

$$E(y_{t+1}y_t) = -b\sigma^2(\varepsilon_d) - \rho\sigma^2(\varepsilon_{dp}) - (\rho + b)\sigma(\varepsilon_d, \varepsilon_{dp}),$$

while $y_t = (1 - \gamma L)v_t$ implies

$$E(y_{t+1}^2) = (1 + \gamma^2)\sigma_v^2,$$

$$E(y_{t+1}y_t) = -\gamma\sigma_v^2.$$

Hence, we can find γ from the condition

$$\frac{1 + \gamma^2}{\gamma} = \frac{(1 + b^2)\sigma^2(\varepsilon_d) + (1 + \rho^2)\sigma^2(\varepsilon_{dp}) - 2(\rho + b)\sigma(\varepsilon_d, \varepsilon_{dp})}{b\sigma^2(\varepsilon_d) + \rho\sigma^2(\varepsilon_{dp}) - (\rho + b)\sigma(\varepsilon_d, \varepsilon_{dp})} = 2q.$$

The solution (the root less than one) is

$$\gamma = q - \sqrt{q^2 - 1}.$$

For more general processes, such as computations from an estimated VAR, it is better to approach the problem via the spectral density. This approach allows you to construct the univariate representation directly without relying on cleverness. If you write $y_t = [r_t \ x_t]'$, the VAR is $y_t = A(L)\eta_t$. Then spectral density of returns $S_r(z)$ is given by the top left element of $S_y(z) = A(z)E(\eta\eta')A(z^{-1})'$ with $z = e^{-i\omega}$. Like the auto-correlation, the spectral density is the same object whether it comes from the univariate or multivariate representation. You can find the autocorre-lations by (numerically) inverse-Fourier transforming the spectral density of returns. To find the univariate, invertible moving average represen-tation from the spectral density, you have to factor the spectral density $S_{rr}(z) = a(z)a(z^{-1})$, where $a(z)$ is a polynomial with roots outside the unit circle, $a(z) = (1 - \gamma_1 z)(1 - \gamma_2 z) \cdots \gamma_i < 1$. Then, since $a(L)$ is invertible, $r_t = a(L)\varepsilon_t$, $\sigma_\varepsilon^2 = 1$ is the univariate representation of the return process.

The autocorrelations and spectral densities are directly revealing: a string of small negative autocorrelations or a dip in the spectral density near frequency zero correspond to mean-reversion; positive autocorrela-tions or a spectral density higher at frequency zero than elsewhere corre-sponds to momentum.

Multivariate Mean-Reversion

I calculate the responses to multivariate rather than univariate shocks. In a multivariate system you can isolate expected return shocks and divi-dend growth shocks. The price response to expected return shocks is *entirely* stationary.

We are left with a troubling set of facts: high price/dividend ratios strongly forecast low returns, yet high past returns do not seem to forecast low subsequent returns. Surely, there must be some sense in which "high prices" forecast lower subsequent returns?

The resolution must involve dividends (or earnings, book value, or a similar divisor for prices). A price rise with no change in dividends results in lower subsequent returns. A price rise that comes with a dividend rise does not result in lower subsequent returns. A high return combines dividend news and price/dividend news, and so obscures the lower expected return message. In a more time-series language, instead of looking at the response to a univariate return shock, a return that was unanticipated based on lagged returns, let us look at the responses to multivariate shocks, a return that was unanticipated based on lagged returns and dividends.

This is easy to do in our simple VAR. We can simulate (20.17)–(20.20) forward and trace the responses to a dividend growth shock and an expected return (d/p ratio) shock. Figures 20.4 and 20.5 present the results of this calculation. (Cochrane [1994] presents a corresponding calculation using an unrestricted VAR, and the results are very similar.)

Start with Figure 20.4. The negative expected return shock raises prices and the p-d ratio immediately. We can identify such a shock in the data as a return shock with no contemporaneous movement in dividends. The p-d ratio then reverts to its mean. Dividends are not forecastable, so they show no immediate or eventual response to the expected return shock. Prices show a long and *complete* reversion back to the level of dividends. This shock looks a lot like a negative yield shock to bonds: such a shock raises prices now so that bonds end up at the same maturity value despite a smaller expected return.

The cumulative return "mean-reverts" even more than prices. For given prices, dividends are now smaller (smaller d-p) so returns deviate from their mean by more than price growth. The cumulative return ends up *below* its previously expected value. Compare this value response to the univariate value response, which we calculated above, and ends up at about 0.8 of its initial response.

The dividend shock shown in Figure 20.5 raises prices and cumulative returns immediately and proportionally to dividends, so the price/dividend ratio does not change. Expected returns or the discount rate, reflected in any slope of the value line, do not change. If the world were i.i d., this is the only kind of shock we would see, and dividend/price ratios would always be constant.

Figures 20.4 and 20.5 plot the responses to "typical," one-standard-deviation shocks. Thus you can see that actual returns are typically about half dividend shocks and half expected return shocks. That is why returns alone are a poor indicator of expected returns.

In sum, at last we can see some rather dramatic "mean-reversion." Good past returns by themselves are not a reliable signal of lower subsequent returns, because they contain substantial dividend growth noise. Good returns that do not include good dividends isolate an expected

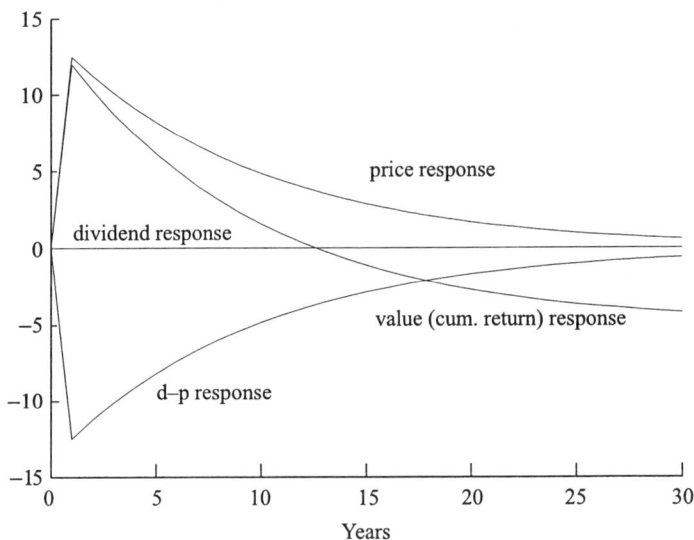

Figure 20.4. *Responses to a one-standard-deviation (1.7%) negative expected return shock in the simple VAR.*

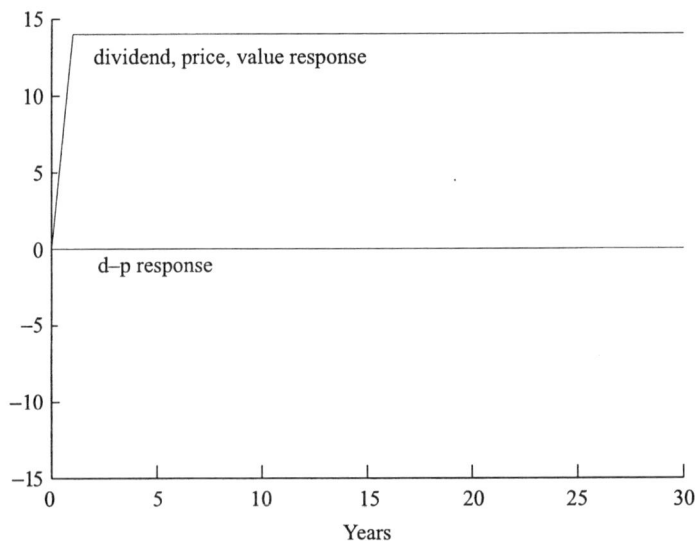

Figure 20.5. *Responses to a one-standard-deviation (14%) dividend growth shock in the simple VAR.*

return shock. This does signal low subsequent returns. It sets off a *completely* transitory variation in prices.

Cointegration and Short- vs. Long-Run Volatility

> If $d - p$, Δp, and Δd are stationary, then the long-run variance of Δd and Δp must be the same, long-run movements in d and p must be perfectly correlated, and d and p must end up in the same place after any shock. Thus, the patterns of predictability, volatility, and univariate, and multivariate mean-reversion really all just stem from these facts, the persistence of $d - p$ and the near-unforecastability of Δd.

You might think that the facts about predictability depend on the exact structure of the VAR, including parameter estimates. In fact, most of what we have learned about predictability and mean-reversion comes down to a few facts: the dividend/price ratio, returns, and dividend growth are all stationary; dividend growth is not (or is at best weakly) forecastable, and dividend growth varies less than returns.

These facts imply that the dividend and price responses to each shock are eventually equal in Figures 20.4 and 20.5. If $d - p$, Δp, and Δd are stationary, then d and p must end up in the same place following a shock. The responses of a stationary variable $(d-p)$ must die out. If dividends are not forecastable, then it must be the case that prices do all the adjustment following a price shock that does not affect dividends.

Stationary $d - p$, Δp, and Δd also implies that the variance of long-horizon Δp must equal the variance of long-horizon Δd:

$$\lim_{k \to \infty} \frac{1}{k} \text{var}(p_{t+k} - p_t) = \lim_{k \to \infty} \frac{1}{k} \text{var}(d_{t+k} - d_t), \qquad (20.41)$$

and the correlation of long-run price and dividend growth must approach one. These facts follow from the fact that the variance ratio of a stationary variable must approach zero, and $d - p$ is stationary. Intuitively, long-run price growth cannot be more volatile than long-run dividend growth, or the long-run $p - d$ ratio would not be stationary.

Now, if dividend growth is not forecastable, its long-run volatility is the same as its short-run volatility—its variance ratio is one. Short-run price growth is more volatile than short-run dividend growth, so we conclude that prices must be mean-reverting; their variance ratio must be below one.

Quantitatively, this observation supports the magnitude of univariate mean-reversion that we have found so far. Dividend growth has a short run, and thus long-run, standard deviation of about 10% per year, while returns and prices have a standard deviation of about 15% per year. Thus, prices must have a long-run variance ratio of about $(2/3)^2$, or a long-run response to univariate shocks of $2/3$.

The work of Lettau and Ludvigson (2000) suggests that we may get much more dramatic implications by including consumption data. The ratio of stock market values to consumption should also be stationary; if wealth were to explode people would surely consume more and vice versa. The ratio of dividends to aggregate consumption should also be stationary. Consumption growth seems independent at all horizons, and consumption growth is very stable, with roughly 1% annual standard deviation. For example, Lettau and Ludvigson (2000) find that none of the variables that forecast returns in Table 20.2—including $d - p$ and a consumption to wealth ratio—forecast consumption growth at any horizon.

These facts suggest that aggregate dividends *are* forecastable, by the consumption/dividend ratio, and strongly so—the long-run volatility of aggregate dividend growth must be the 1% volatility of consumption growth, not the 10% short-run volatility of dividend growth.

These facts also suggest that almost all of the 15% or more variation in annual stock market wealth must be transitory—the long-run volatility of stock market value must be no more than the 1% consumption growth volatility!

However, total market value is not the same thing as price, price is not the same thing as cumulated return, and aggregate dividends are not the same thing as the dividend concept we have used so far (dividends paid to a dollar investment with dividends consumed), or dividends paid to a dollar investment with dividends reinvested. Lettau and Ludvigson show that the consumption/wealth ratio does forecast returns, but no one has yet worked out the mean-reversion implications of this fact.

My statements about the implications of stationary $d - p, \Delta d, \Delta p, r$ are developed in detail in Cochrane (1994). They are special cases of the representation theorems for *cointegrated* variables developed by Engel and Granger (1987). A regression of a difference like Δp on a ratio like $p - d$ is called the *error-correction* representation of a cointegrated system. Error-correction regressions have subtly and dramatically changed almost all empirical work in finance and macroeconomics. The vast majority of the successful return forecasting regressions in this section, both time-series and cross-section, are error-correction regressions of one sort or another. Corporate finance is being redone with regressions of growth rates on ratios, as is macroeconomic forecasting. For example, the consumption/GDP ratio is a powerful forecaster of GDP growth.

Bonds

> The expectations model of the term structure works well on average
> and for horizons of four years or greater. At the one-year horizon, however,
> a forward rate one percentage point higher than the spot rate seems entirely
> to indicate a one percentage point higher expected excess return rather
> than a one percentage point rise in future interest rates.

The venerable expectations model of the term structure specifies that
long-term bond yields are equal to the average of expected future short-
term bond yields. As with the CAPM and random walk, the expectations
model was the workhorse of empirical finance for a generation. And as
with those other views, a new round of research has significantly modified
the traditional view.

Table 20.8 calculates the average return on bonds of different maturities. The expectations hypothesis seems to do pretty well. Average holding
period returns do not seem very different across bond maturities, despite
the increasing standard deviation of bond returns as maturity rises. The
small increase in returns for long-term bonds, equivalent to a slight average upward slope in the yield curve, is usually excused as a small "liquidity
premium." In fact, the curious pattern in Table 20.8 is that bonds do *not*
share the high Sharpe ratios of stocks. Whatever factors account for the
volatility of bond returns, they seem to have very small risk prices.

Table 20.8 is again a tip of an iceberg of an illustrious career for
the expectations hypothesis. Especially in times of great inflation and
exchange rate instability, the expectations hypothesis does a very good
first-order job.

Table 20.8. *Average continuously compounded* (log)
one-year holding period returns on zero-coupon bonds of
varying maturity

Maturity N	Avg. Return $E(\mathrm{hpr}_{t+1}^{(N)})$	Std. error	Std. dev. $\sigma(\mathrm{hpr}_{t+1}^{(N)})$
1	5.83	0.42	2.83
2	6.15	0.54	3.65
3	6.40	0.69	4.66
4	6.40	0.85	5.71
5	6.36	0.98	6.58

Annual data from CRSP 1953–1997.

However, one can ask a more subtle question. Perhaps there are *times* when long-term bonds can be forecast to do better, and other times when short-term bonds are expected to do better. If the times even out, the unconditional averages in Table 20.8 will show no pattern. Equivalently, we might want to check whether a forward rate that is *unusually high* forecasts an unusual *increase* in spot rates.

Table 20.9 gets at these issues, updating Fama and Bliss' (1986) classic regression tests. (Campbell and Shiller [1991] and Campbell [1995] make the same point with regressions of yield changes on yield spreads.) The left-hand panel presents a regression of the change in yields on the forward-spot spread. The expectations hypothesis predicts a coefficient of 1.0, since the forward rate should equal the expected future spot rate. At a one-year horizon we see instead coefficients near zero and a negative adjusted R^2. Forward rates one year out seem to have no predictive power whatsoever for changes in the spot rate one year from now. On the other hand, by four years out, we see coefficients within one standard error of 1.0. Thus, the expectations hypothesis seems to do poorly at short (1 year) horizons, but much better at longer horizons and on average (Table 20.8).

If the yield expression of the expectations hypothesis does not work at one-year horizons, then the expected return expression of the expectations hypothesis must not hold either—one must be able to forecast one-year bond returns. To check this fact, the right-hand panel of Table 20.9 runs regressions of the one-year excess return on long-term bonds on the forward-spot spread. Here, the expectations hypothesis predicts a coefficient of zero: no signal (including the forward-spot spread) should be able to tell you that this is a particularly good time for long bonds versus short bonds. As you can see, the coefficients in the right-hand panel of

Table 20.9. *Forecasts based on forward-spot spread*

| | Change in yields | | | | | Holding period returns | | | | |
| | $y_{t+N}^{(1)} - y_t^{(1)}$ $= a + b(f_t^{(N \to N+1)} - y_t^{(1)}) + \varepsilon_{t+N}$ | | | | | $\text{hpr}_{t+1}^{(N+1)} - y_t^{(1)}$ $= a + b(f_t^{(N \to N+1)} - y_t^{(1)}) + \varepsilon_{t+1}$ | | | | |
N	a	$\sigma(a)$	b	$\sigma(b)$	$\overline{R}^2$	a	$\sigma(a)$	b	$\sigma(b)$	$\overline{R}^2$
1	0.1	0.3	−0.10	0.36	−0.02	−0.1	0.3	1.10	0.36	0.16
2	−0.01	0.4	0.37	0.33	0.005	−0.5	0.5	1.46	0.44	0.19
3	−0.04	0.5	0.41	0.33	0.013	−0.4	0.8	1.30	0.54	0.10
4	−0.3	0.5	0.77	0.31	0.11	−0.5	1.0	1.31	0.63	0.07

OLS regressions 1953–1997 annual data. Yields and returns in annual percentages. The left-hand panel runs the change in the one-year yield on the forward-spot spread. The right-hand panel runs the one-period excess return on the forward-spot spread.

Table 20.9 are all about 1.0. A high forward rate does not indicate that interest rates will be higher one year from now; it seems entirely to indicate that you will earn that much more holding long-term bonds. (The coefficients in yield and return regressions are linked. For example in the first row $1.10 + (-0.10) = 1.0$, and this holds as an identity. Fama and Bliss call them "complementary regressions.")

Figures 20.6 and 20.7 provide a pictorial version of the results in Table 20.9. Suppose that the yield curve is upward sloping as in the top panel. What does this mean? A naive investor might think this pattern indicates that long-term bonds give a higher return than short-term bonds. The expectations hypothesis denies this conclusion. If the expectations hypothesis were true, the forward rates plotted against maturity in the top panel would translate one-for-one to the forecast of future spot rates in the bottom panel, as plotted in the line marked "Expectations model." Rises in future short rates should lower bond prices, cutting off the one-period advantage of long-term bonds. The rising short rates would directly raise the multiyear advantage of short-term bonds.

We can calculate the actual forecast of future spot rates from the estimates in the left-hand panel of Table 20.9, and these are given by the line marked "Estimates" in Figure 20.7. The essence of the phenomenon is sluggish adjustment of the short rates. The short rates do eventually rise to meet the forward rate forecasts, but not as quickly as the forward rates predict that they should.

As dividend growth should be forecastable so that returns are not forecastable, short-term yields *should* be forecastable so that returns are *not* forecastable. In fact, yield changes are almost unforecastable at a one-year horizon, so, mechanically, bond returns are. We see this directly in the first row of the left-hand panel of Table 20.9 for the one-period yield. It is an implication of the right-hand panel as well. If

$$\text{hpr}_{t+1}^{(N+1)} - y_t^{(1)} = 0 + 1(f_t^{(N \to N+1)} - y_t^{(1)}) + \varepsilon_{t+1}, \qquad (20.42)$$

then, writing out the definition of holding period return and forward rate,

$$p_{t+1}^{(N)} - p_t^{(N+1)} + p_t^{(1)} = 0 + 1(p_t^{(N)} - p_t^{(N+1)} + p_t^{(1)}) + \varepsilon_{t+1},$$

$$p_{t+1}^{(N)} = 0 + 1(p_t^{(N)}) + \varepsilon_{t+1}, \qquad (20.43)$$

$$y_{t+1}^{(N)} = 0 + 1(y_t^{(N)}) - \varepsilon_{t+1}/N$$

A coefficient of 1.0 in (20.42) is equivalent to yields or bond prices that follow random walks: yield changes that are completely unpredictable.

Of course yields are stationary and not totally unpredictable. However, they move slowly. Thus, yield changes are very unpredictable at short

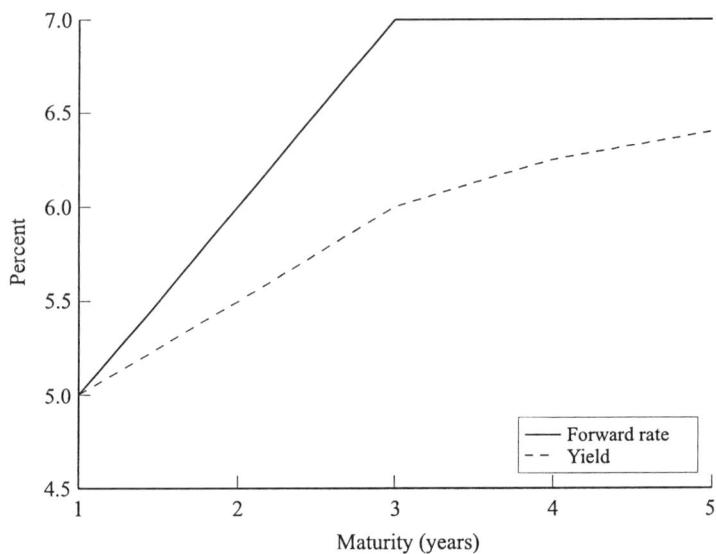

Figure 20.6.   *If the current yield curve is as plotted here. . . .*

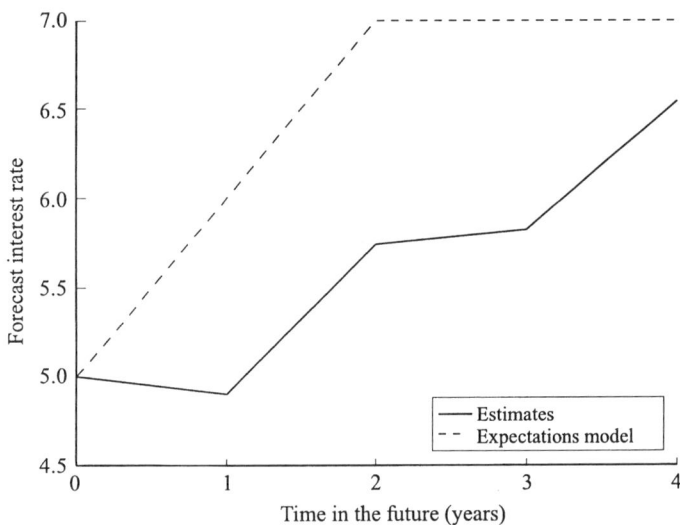

Figure 20.7.   *. . . this is the forecast of future one-year interest rates. The dashed line gives the forecast from the expectations hypothesis. The solid line is constructed from the estimates in Table 20.8*

horizons but much more predictable at long horizons. That is why the coefficients in the right-hand panel of Table 20.9 build with horizon. If we did holding period return regressions at longer horizons, they would gradually approach the expectations hypothesis result.

The roughly 1.0 coefficients in the right-hand panel of Table 20.9 mean that a one percentage point increase in forward rate translates into a one percentage point increase in expected return. It seems that old fallacy of confusing bond yields with their expected returns also contains a grain of truth, at least for the first year. However, the one-for-one variation of expected returns with forward rates does not imply a one-for-one variation of expected returns with yield spreads. Forward rates are related to the slope of the yield curve,

$$
\begin{aligned}
f_t^{(N \to N+1)} - y_t^{(1)} &= p_t^{(N)} - p_t^{(N+1)} - y_t^{(1)} \\
&= -N y_t^{(N)} + (N+1) y_t^{(N+1)} - y_t^{(1)} \\
&= N\left(y_t^{(N+1)} - y_t^{(N)} \right) + \left(y_t^{(N+1)} - y_t^{(1)} \right).
\end{aligned}
$$

Thus, the forward-spot spread varies more than the yield spread, so regression coefficients of holding period yields on yield spreads give coefficients greater than one. Expected returns move *more* than one-for-one with yield spreads. Campbell (1995) reports coefficients of excess returns on yield spreads that rise from one at a two-month horizon to 5 at a five-year horizon.

The facts are analogous to the dividend/price regression. There, dividends should be forecastable so that returns are not forecastable. But dividends were essentially unforecastable and the dividend yield was persistent. These facts implied that a one percentage point change in dividend yield implied a 3–5 percentage point change in expected excess returns.

Of course, there is risk: the R^2 are all about 0.1–0.2, about the same values as the R^2 from the dividend/price regression at a one-year horizon, so this strategy will often go wrong. Still, 0.1–0.2 is not zero, so the strategy does pay off more often than not, in violation of the expectations hypothesis. Furthermore, the forward-spot spread is a slow-moving variable, typically reversing sign once per business cycle. Thus, the R^2 build with horizon as with the D/P regression, peaking in the 30% range (Fama and French [1989]).

The fact that the regressions in Table 20.9 run the *change* in yield and the excess *return* on the forward-spot *spread* is very important. The overall level of interest rates moves up and down a great deal but slowly over time. Thus, if you run $y_{t+j}^{(N)} = a + b f_t^{(N+1)} + \varepsilon_{t+N}$, you will get a coefficient b almost exactly equal to 1.0 and a stupendous R^2, seemingly a stunning validation of the expectations hypothesis. If you run a regression of tomorrow's temperature on today's temperature, the regression coefficient will be near 1.0 with a huge R^2 as well, since the temperature varies a lot over the year. But today's temperature is not a useful temperature forecast. To measure a temperature forecast we want to know if the forecast can predict the *change* in temperature. Is (forecast – today's temperature) a good measure of (tomorrow's temperature – today's temperature)? Table 20.9 runs this regression.

The decomposition in (20.43) warns us of one of several econometric traps in this kind of regression. Notice that two of the three right-hand variables are the same. Thus any measurement error in $p_t^{(N+1)}$ and $p_t^{(1)}$ will induce a spurious common movement in left- and right-hand variables. In addition, since the variables are a triple difference, the difference may eliminate a common signal and isolate measurement error or noise. There are pure measurement errors in the bond data, and we seldom observe pure discount bonds of the exactly desired maturity. In addition, various liquidity and microstructure effects can influence the yields of particular bonds in ways that are not exploitable for typical investors.

As an example of what this sort of "measurement error" can do, suppose all bond yields are 5%, but there is one "error" in the two-period bond price at time 1: rather than being -10 it is -15. Table 20.10 tracks the effects of this error. It implies a blip of the one-year forward rate in year one, and then a blip in the return from holding this bond from year one to year two. The price and forward rate "error" automatically turns into a subsequent return when the "error" is corrected. If the price is real, of course, this is just the kind of event we want the regression to tell us about—the forward rate did not correspond to a change in future spot rate, so there was a large return; it was a price that was "out of line" and if you could trade on it, you should. But the regression will also pounce on measurement error in prices and indicate spuriously forecastable returns.

Foreign Exchange

> The expectations model works well on average. However, a foreign interest rate one percentage point higher than its usual differential with the U.S. rate (equivalently, a one percentage point higher forward-spot spread) seems to indicate even more than one percentage point expected excess return; a further appreciation of the foreign currency.

Suppose interest rates are higher in Germany than in the United States. Does this mean that one can earn more money by investing in German bonds? There are several reasons that the answer might be no.

Table 20.10. *Numerical example of the effect of measurement error in yields on yield regressions*

t	0	1	2	3
$p_t^{(1)}$	-5	-5	-5	-5
$p_t^{(2)}$	-10	-15	-10	-10
$p_t^{(3)}$	-15	-15	-15	-15
$y_t^{(i)}, i \neq 2$	5	5	5	5
$y_t^{(2)}$	5	7.5	5	5
$f_t^{(1 \to 2)}$	5	10	5	5
$f_t^{(1 \to 2)} - y_t^{(1)}$	0	5	0	0
$\mathrm{hpr}_t^{(2 \to 1)} - y_t^{(1)}$	0	0	5	0

First, of course, is default risk. While not a big problem for German government bonds, Russia and other governments have defaulted on bonds in the past and may do so again. Second, and more important, is the risk of devaluation. If German interest rates are 10%, U.S. interest rates are 5%, but the Euro falls 5% relative to the dollar during the year, you make no more money holding the German bonds despite their attractive interest rate. Since lots of investors are making this calculation, it is natural to conclude that an interest rate differential across countries on bonds of similar credit risk should reveal an expectation of currency devaluation. The logic is exactly the same as the "expectations hypothesis" in the term structure. Initially attractive yield or interest rate differentials should be met by an offsetting event so that you make no more money on average in one country or another, or in one maturity versus another. As with bonds, the expectations hypothesis is slightly different from pure risk neutrality since the expectation of the log is not the log of the expectation. Again, the size of the phenomena we study usually swamps this distinction.

As with the expectations hypothesis in the term structure, the expected depreciation view ruled for many years, and still constitutes an important first-order understanding of interest rate differentials and exchange rates. For example, interest rates in east Asian currencies were very high on the eve of the currency collapses of 1997, and many banks were making tidy sums borrowing at 5% in dollars to lend at 20% in local currencies. This situation should lead one to suspect that traders expect a 15% devaluation, or a small chance of a larger devaluation. That is, in this case, exactly what happened. Many observers and policy analysts who ought to know better often attribute high nominal interest rates in troubled countries to "tight monetary policy" that is "strangling the economy" to "defend the currency." In fact, one's first-order guess should be that such high nominal rates reflect a large probability of devaluation—loose monetary and fiscal policy—and that they correspond to much lower real rates.

Still, does a 5% interest rate differential correspond to an exactly 5% expected depreciation, or does some of it still represent a high expected return from holding debt in that country's currency? Furthermore, while expected depreciation is clearly a large part of the story for high interest rates in countries that have constant high inflation or that may suffer spectacular depreciation of a pegged exchange rate, how does the story work for, say, the United States versus Germany, where inflation rates diverge little, yet exchange rates fluctuate a surprisingly large amount?

Table 20.11 presents the facts, as summarized by Hodrick (2000) and Engel (1996). The first row of Table 20.11 presents the average appreciation of the dollar against the indicated currency over the sample period. The dollar fell against DM, yen, and Swiss Franc, but appreciated against the pound. The second row gives the average interest rate differential— the amount by which the foreign interest rate exceeds the U.S. interest rate. According to the expectations hypothesis, these two numbers should be equal—interest rates should be higher in countries whose currencies depreciate against the dollar.

The second row shows roughly the right pattern. Countries with steady long-term inflation have steadily higher interest rates, and steady depreciation. The numbers in the first and second rows are not exactly the same, but exchange rates are notoriously volatile so these averages are not well measured. Hodrick shows that the difference between the first and second rows is not statistically different from zero. This fact is exactly analogous to the fact of Table 20.8 that the expectations hypothesis works well "on average" for U.S. bonds and is the tip of an iceberg of empirical successes for the expectations hypothesis as applied to currencies.

As in the case of bonds, however, we can also ask whether times of *temporarily* higher or lower interest rate differentials correspond to times of above and below average depreciation as they should. The third and fifth rows of Table 20.11 address this question, updating Hansen and Hodrick's (1980) and Fama's (1984) regression tests. The number here should be +1.0 in each case—an extra percentage point interest differential should correspond to one extra percentage point expected depreciation. As you can see, we have exactly the opposite pattern: a higher than usual interest rate abroad seems to lead, if anything, to further *ap*preciation. It seems that the old fallacy of confusing interest rate differentials across countries with expected returns, forgetting about depreciation, also contains a grain of truth. This is the "forward discount puzzle," and takes its place along-

Table 20.11.

	DM	£	¥	SF
Mean appreciation	−1.8	3.6	−5.0	−3.0
Mean interest differential	−3.9	2.1	−3.7	−5.9
b, 1975–1989	−3.1	−2.0	−2.1	−2.6
R^2	.026	.033	.034	.033
b, 1976–1996	−0.7	−1.8	−2.4	−1.3

The first row gives the average appreciation of the dollar against the indicated currency, in percent per year. The second row gives the average interest differential—foreign interest rate less domestic interest rate, measured as the forward premium—the 30-day forward rate less the spot exchange rate. The third through fifth rows give the coefficients and R^2 in a regression of exchange rate changes on the interest differential = forward premium,

$$s_{t+1} - s_t = a + b(f_t - s_t) + \varepsilon_{t+1} = a + b(r_t^f - r_t^d) + \varepsilon_{t+1},$$

where s = log spot exchange rate, f = forward rate, r^f = foreign interest rate, r^d = domestic interest rate.
Source: Hodrick (1999) and Engel (1996).

side the forecastability of stock and bond returns. Of course it has produced a similar avalanche of academic work dissecting whether it is really there and if so, why. Hodrick (1987), Engel (1996), and Lewis (1995) provide surveys.

The R^2 shown in Table 20.11 are quite low. However, like D/P, the interest differential is a slow-moving forecasting variable, so the return forecast R^2 build with horizon. Bekaert and Hodrick (1992) report that the R^2 rise to the 30–40% range at six-month horizons and then decline again. Still, taking advantage of this predictability, like the bond strategies described above, is quite risky.

The puzzle does *not* say that one earns more by holding bonds from countries with higher interest rates than others. Average inflation, depreciation, and interest rate differentials line up as they should. If you just buy bonds with high interest rates, you end up with debt from Turkey and Brazil, whose currencies inflate and depreciate steadily. The puzzle *does* say that one earns more by holding bonds from countries whose interest rates are *higher than usual* relative to U.S. interest rates.

However, the fact that the "usual" rate of depreciation and "usual" interest differential varies through time, if they are well-defined concepts at all, may diminish if not eliminate the out-of-sample performance of trading rules based on these regressions.

The foreign exchange regressions offer a particularly clear-cut case in which "Peso problems" can skew forecasting regressions. Lewis (1995) credits Milton Friedman for coining the term to explain why Mexican interest rates were persistently higher than U.S. interest rates in the early 1970s even though the currency had been pegged for more than a decade. A small probability of a huge devaluation each period can correspond to a substantial interest differential. You will see long stretches of data in which the expectations hypothesis seems not to be satisfied, because the collapse does not occur in sample. The Peso subsequently collapsed, giving substantial weight to this view. Since then, "Peso problems" have become a generic term for the effects of small probabilities of large events on empirical work. Rietz (1988) offered a Peso problem explanation for the equity premium that investors are afraid of another great depression which has not happened in sample. Selling out-of-the-money put options and earthquake insurance in Los Angeles are similar strategies whose average returns in a sample will be severely affected by rare events that may not be seen in surprisingly long samples.

20.2 The Cross Section: CAPM and Multifactor Models

Having studied how average returns change over time, now we study how average returns change across different stocks or portfolios.

The CAPM

> For a generation, portfolios with high average returns also had high betas. I illustrate with the size-based portfolios.

The first tests of the CAPM such as Lintner (1965) were not a great success. If you plot or regress the average returns versus betas of individual stocks, you find a lot of dispersion, and the slope of the line is much too flat—it does not go through any plausible risk-free rate.

Miller and Scholes (1972) diagnosed the problem. Betas are measured with error, and measurement error in right-hand variables biases down regression coefficients. Fama and MacBeth (1973) and Black, Jensen, and Scholes (1972) addressed the problem by grouping stocks into portfolios. Portfolio betas are better measured because the portfolio has lower residual variance. Also, individual stock betas vary over time as the size, leverage, and risks of the business change. Portfolio betas may be more stable over time, and hence easier to measure accurately.

There is a second reason for portfolios. Individual stock returns are so volatile that you cannot reject the hypothesis that all average returns are the same. $\sigma/\sqrt{T}$ is big when $\sigma = 40\text{–}80\%$. By grouping stocks into portfolios based on some characteristic (other than firm name) related to average returns, you reduce the portfolio variance and thus make it possible to see average return deferences. Finally, I think much of the attachment to portfolios comes from a desire to more closely mimic what actual investors would do rather than simply form a statistical test.

Fama and MacBeth and Black, Jensen, and Scholes formed their portfolios on betas. They found individual stock betas, formed stocks into portfolios based on their betas, and then estimated the portfolio's beta in the following period. More recently, size, book/market, industry, and many other characteristics have been used to form portfolios.

Ever since, the business of testing asset pricing models has been conducted in a simple loop:

1. Find a characteristic that you think is associated with average returns. Sort stocks into portfolios based on the characteristic, and check that there is a difference in average returns between portfolios. Worry here about measurement, survival bias, fishing bias, and all the other things that can ruin a pretty picture out of sample.
2. Compute betas for the portfolios, and check whether the average return spread is accounted for by the spread in betas.
3. If not, you have an anomaly. Consider multiple betas.

This is the traditional procedure, but econometrics textbooks urge you not to group data in this way. They urge you to use the characteristic as an instrument for the poorly measured right-hand variable instead. It is an interesting and unexplored idea whether this instrumental variables approach could fruitfully bring us back to the examination of individual securities rather than portfolios.

The CAPM proved stunningly successful in empirical work. Time after time, every strategy or characteristic that seemed to give high average returns turned out to also have high betas. Strategies that one might have thought gave high average returns (such as holding very volatile stocks) turned out not to have high average returns when they did not have high betas.

To give some sense of that empirical work, Figure 20.8 presents a typical evaluation of the Capital Asset Pricing Model. (Chapter 15 presented some of the methodological issues surrounding this evaluation; here I focus on the facts.) I examine 10 portfolios of NYSE stocks sorted by size (total market capitalization), along with a portfolio of corporate bonds and long-term government bonds. As the spread along the vertical axis shows, there is a sizeable spread in average returns between large stocks

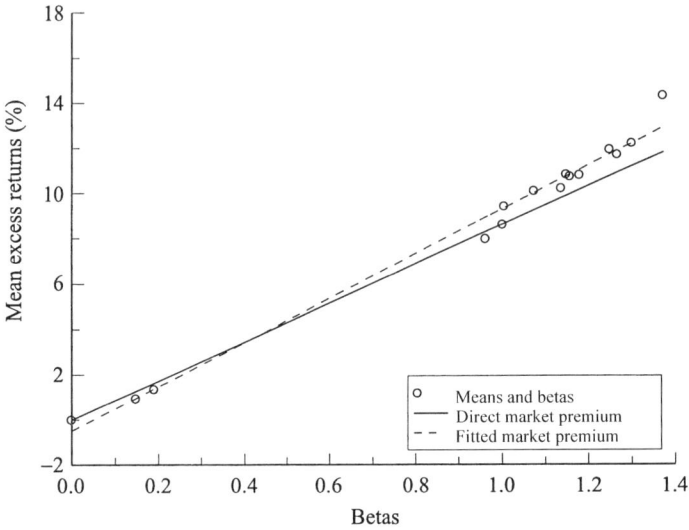

Figure 20.8.   The CAPM. Average returns vs. betas on the NYSE value-weighted portfolio for 10 size-sorted stock portfolios, government bonds, and corporate bonds, 1947–1996. The solid line draws the CAPM prediction by fitting the market proxy and treasury bill rates exactly (a time-series test). The dashed line draws the CAPM prediction by fitting an OLS cross-sectional regression to the displayed data points. The small-firm portfolios are at the top right. The points far down and to the left are the government bond and treasury bill returns.

(lower average return) and small stocks (higher average return), and also a large spread between stocks and bonds. The figure plots these average returns against market betas. You can see how the CAPM prediction fits: portfolios with higher average returns have higher betas. In particular, notice that the long-term and corporate bonds have mean returns in line with their low betas, despite their standard deviations nearly as high as those of stocks. Comparing this graph with the similar Figure 2.4 of the consumption-based model, the CAPM fits very well.

In fact, Figure 20.8 captures one of the first significant *failures* of the CAPM. The smallest firms (the far right portfolio) seem to earn an average return a few percent too high given their betas. This is the celebrated "small-firm effect" (Banz [1981]). Would that all failed economic theories worked so well! It is also atypical in that the estimated market line through the stock portfolios is steeper than predicted, while measurement error in betas usually means that the estimated market line is too flat.

Fama–French 3 Factors

> Book market sorted portfolios show a large variation in average returns that is unrelated to market betas. The Fama and French three-factor model successfully explains the average returns of the 25 size and book market sorted portfolios with a three-factor model, consisting of the market, a small minus big (SMB) portfolio, and a high minus low (HML) portfolio.

In retrospect, it is surprising that the CAPM worked so well for so long. The assumptions on which it is built are very stylized and simplified. Asset pricing theory recognized at least since Merton (1971a,b) the theoretical possibility, indeed probability, that we should need factors, state variables, or sources of priced risk beyond movements in the market portfolio in order to explain why some average returns are higher than others.

The Fama–French model is one of the most popular multifactor models that now dominate empirical research. Fama and French (1993) presents the model; Fama and French (1996) gives an excellent summary, and also shows how the three-factor model performs in evaluating expected return puzzles beyond the size and value effects that motivated it.

"Value" stocks have market values that are small relative to the accountant's book value. (Book values essentially track past investment expenditures. Book value is a better divisor for individual-firm price than are dividends or earnings, which can be negative.) This category of stocks has given large average returns. "Growth" stocks are the opposite of value and have had low average returns. Since low prices relative to dividends, earnings, or book value forecast *times* when the market return will be high, it is natural to suppose that these same signals forecast categories of stocks that will do well; the "value effect" is the cross-sectional analogy to price-ratio predictability in the time series.

High average returns are consistent with the CAPM, if these categories of stocks have high sensitivities to the market, high betas. However, small and especially value stocks seem to have abnormally high returns even after accounting for market beta. Conversely, "growth" stocks seem to do systematically worse than their CAPM betas suggest. Figure 20.9 shows this value-size puzzle. It is just like Figure 20.8, except that the stocks are sorted into portfolios based on size and book/market ratio[2] rather than size alone. As you can see, the highest portfolios have *three* times the average excess return of the lowest portfolios, and this variation has nothing at all to do with market betas.

Figures 20.10 and 20.11 dig a little deeper to diagnose the problem, by connecting portfolios that have different size within the same

[2]I thank Gene Fama for providing me with these data.

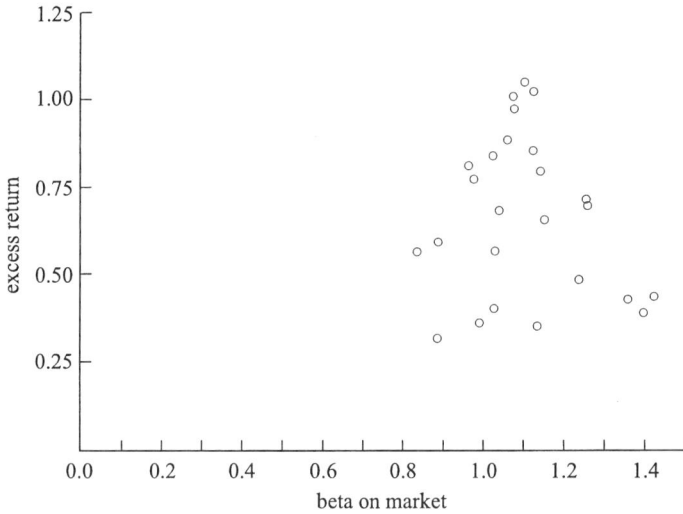

Figure 20.9. *Average returns vs. market beta for 25 stock portfolios sorted on the basis of size and book/market ratio.*

book/market category, and different book/market within size category. As you can see, variation in size produces a variation in average returns that is positively related to variation in market betas, as we had in Figure 20.9. Variation in book/market ratio produces a variation in average return that is *negatively* related to market beta. Because of this value effect, the CAPM is a disaster when confronted with these portfolios. (Since the size effect disappeared in 1980, it is likely that almost the whole story can be told with book/market effects alone.)

To explain these patterns in average returns, Fama and French advocate a multifactor model with the market return, the return of small less big stocks (SMB) and the return of high book/market minus low book/market stocks (HML) as three factors. They show that variation in average returns of the 25 size and book/market portfolios can be explained by varying loadings (betas) on the latter two factors. (All their portfolios have betas close to one on the market portfolio. Thus, market beta explains the average return difference between stocks and bonds, but not across categories of stocks.)

Figures 20.12 and 20.13 illustrate Fama and French's results. The vertical axis is still the average return of the 25 size and book/market portfolios. Now, the horizontal axis is the predicted values from the

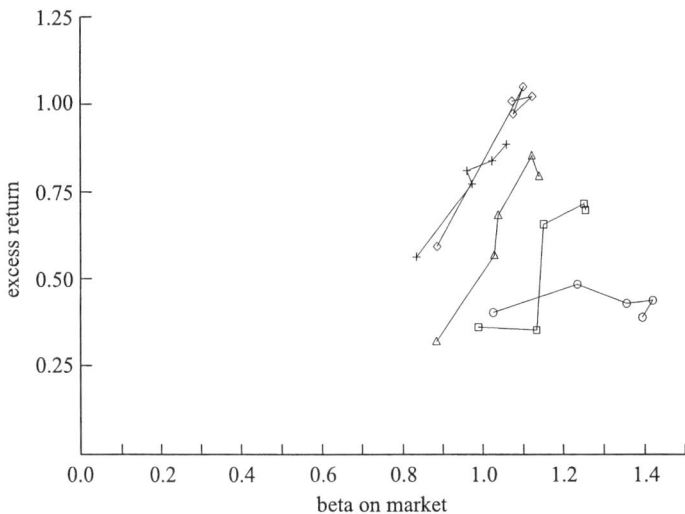

Figure 20.10. *Average excess returns vs. market beta. Lines connect portfolios with different size category within book market categories.*

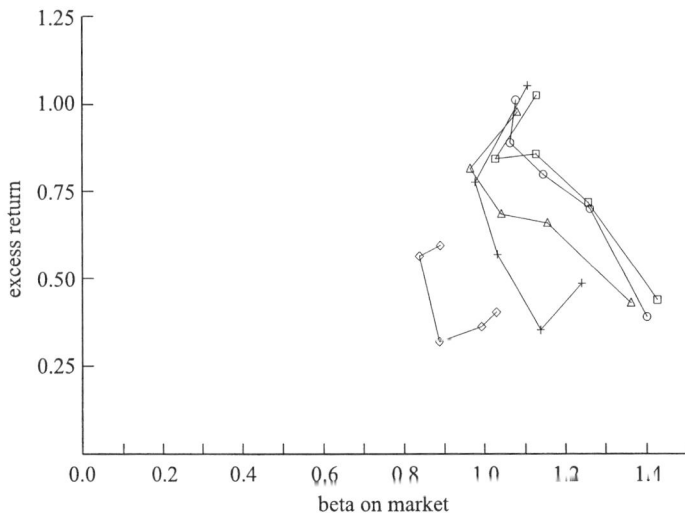

Figure 20.11. *Average excess returns vs. market beta. Lines connect portfolios with different book market categories within size categories.*

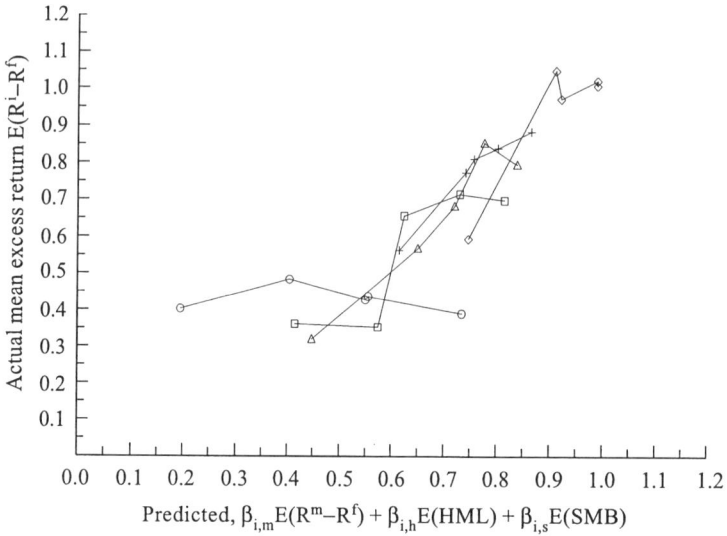

Figure 20.12.   *Average excess return vs. prediction of the Fama–French three-factor model. Lines connect portfolios of different size categories within book/market category.*

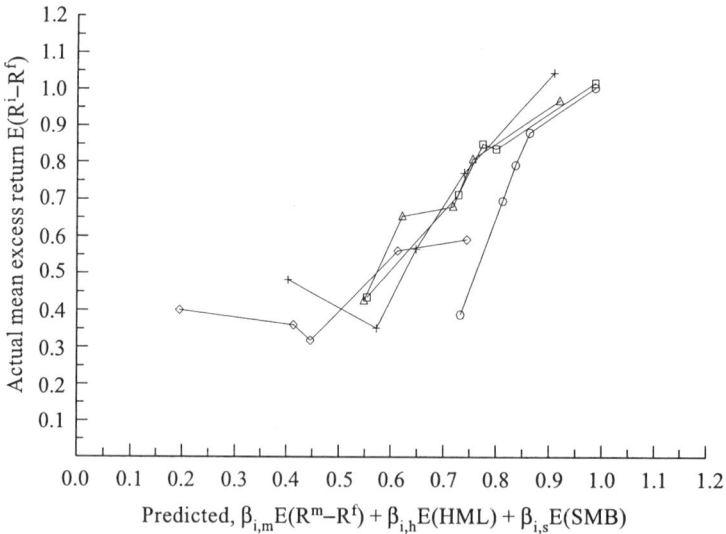

Figure 20.13.   *Average excess return vs. prediction of the Fama–French three-factor model. Lines connect portfolios of different book market category within the same size category.*

Fama–French three-factor model. The points should all lie on a 45° line if the model is correct. The points lie much closer to this prediction than they do in Figures 20.10 and 20.11. The worst fit is for the growth stocks (lowest line, Figure 20.12), for which there is little variation in average return despite large variation in size beta as one moves from small to large firms.

What are the Size and Value Factors?

What are the macroeconomic risks for which the Fama–French factors are proxies or mimicking portfolios? There are hints of some sort of "distress" or "recession" factor at work.

A central part of the Fama–French model is the fact that these three pricing factors also explain a large part of the ex post variation in the 25 portfolios—the R^2 in time-series regressions are very high. In this sense, one can regard it as an APT rather than a macroeconomic factor model.

The Fama–French model is not a tautology, despite the fact that factors and test portfolios are based on the same set of characteristics.

We would like to understand the real, macroeconomic, aggregate, nondiversifiable risk that is proxied by the returns of the HML and SMB portfolios. Why are investors so concerned about holding stocks that do badly at the times that the HML (value less growth) and SMB (small-cap less large-cap) portfolios do badly, even though the market does not fall?

Fama and French (1995) note that the typical "value" firm has a price that has been driven down from a long string of bad news, and is now in or near financial distress. Stocks bought on the verge of bankruptcy have come back more often than not, which generates the high average returns of this strategy. This observation suggests a natural interpretation of the value premium: If a credit crunch, liquidity crunch, flight to quality, or similar financial event comes along, stocks in financial distress will do *very* badly, and this is just the sort of time at which one particularly does not want to hear that one's stocks have become worthless! (One cannot count the "distress" of the individual firm as a "risk factor." Such distress is idiosyncratic and can be diversified away. Only aggregate events that average investors care about can result in a risk premium.) Unfortunately, empirical support for this theory is weak, since the HML portfolio does not covary strongly with other measures of aggregate financial distress. Still, it is a possible and not totally tested interpretation, since we have so few events of actual systematic financial stress in recent history.

Heaton and Lucas' (1997) results add to this story for the value effect. They note that the typical stockholder is the proprietor of a small, privately held business. Such an investor's income is of course particularly sensitive to the kinds of financial events that cause distress among small firms and distressed value firms. Such an investor would therefore demand a substantial premium to hold value stocks, and might hold growth stocks despite a low premium.

Lettau and Ludvigson (2000) (also discussed in the next section) document that HML has a *time-varying* beta on both the market return and on consumption. Thus, though there is very little unconditional correlation between HML and recession measures, Lettau and Ludvigson document that HML is sensitive to bad news *in bad times.*

Liew and Vassalou (1999) is an example of current attempts to link value and small-firm returns to macroeconomic events. They find that in many countries counterparts to HML and SMB contain information above and beyond that in the market return for forecasting GDP growth. For example, they report a regression

$$GDP_{t \to t+1} = a + 0.065\ MKT_{t-1 \to t} + 0.058\ HML_{t-1 \to t} + \varepsilon_{t+1}.$$

$GDP_{t \to t+1}$ denotes the next year's GDP growth and MKT, HML denote the previous year's return on the market index and HML portfolio. Thus, a 10% HML return reflects a 1/2 percentage point rise in the GDP forecast.

On the other hand, one can ignore Fama and French's motivation and regard the model as an arbitrage pricing theory. If the returns of the 25 size and book/market portfolios could be perfectly replicated by the returns of the three-factor portfolios—if the R^2 in the time-series regressions were 100%—then the multifactor model would have to hold exactly, in order to preclude arbitrage opportunities. In fact the R^2 of Fama and French's time-series regressions are all in the 90–95% range, so extremely high Sharpe ratios for the residuals would have to be invoked for the model *not* to fit well. Equivalently, given the average returns and the failure of the CAPM to explain those returns, there would be near-arbitrage opportunities if value and small stocks did not move together in the way described by the Fama–French model.

One way to assess whether the three factors proxy for real macroeconomic risks is by checking whether the multifactor model prices additional portfolios, and especially portfolios that do *not* have high R^2 values. Fama and French (1996) extend their analysis in this direction: They find that the SMB and HML portfolios comfortably explain strategies based on alternative price multiples (P/E, B/M), strategies based on five-year sales growth (this is especially interesting since it is the only strategy that does not form portfolios based on price variables), and the tendency of five-year returns to reverse. All of these strategies are not explained by CAPM betas. However, they all also produce portfolios with high R^2 values in a time-series regression on the HML and SMB portfolios! This is good and bad news. It might mean that the model is a good APT: that the size and book/market characteristics describe the major sources of priced variation in all stocks. On the other hand, it might mean that these extra sorts just have not identified other sources of priced variation in stock returns. (Fama and French also find that HML and SMB do not explain "momentum," despite large R^2 values. More on momentum later.)

One's first reaction may be that explaining portfolios sorted on the basis of size and book/market by factors sorted on the same basis is a tautology. This is not the case. For example, suppose that average returns were higher for stocks whose ticker symbols start later in the alphabet. (Maybe investors search for stocks alphabetically, so the later stocks are "overlooked.") This need not trouble us if Z stocks happened to have higher betas. If not—if letter of the alphabet were a CAPM anomaly like book/market—however, it would not necessarily follow that letter-based stock portfolios *move together*. Adding A–L and M–Z portfolios to the right-hand side of a regression of the 26 A,B,C, etc. portfolios on the market portfolio need not (and probably does not) increase the R^2 at all. The size and book/market premia are hard to measure, and seem to have declined substantially in recent years. But even if they decline back to CAPM values, Fama and French will still have found a surprisingly large source of common movement in stock returns.

More to the point, in testing a model, it is exactly the right thing to do to sort stocks into portfolios based on characteristics related to expected returns. When Black, Jensen, and Scholes and Fama and MacBeth first tested the CAPM, they sorted stocks into portfolios based on betas, because betas are a good characteristic for sorting stocks into portfolios that have a spread in average returns. If your portfolios have no spread in average returns—if you just choose 25 random portfolios, then there will be nothing for the asset pricing model to test.

In fact, despite the popularity of the Fama–French 25, there is really no fundamental reason to sort portfolios based on two-way or larger sorts of individual characteristics. You should use all the characteristics at hand that (believably!) indicate high or low average returns and simply sort stocks according to a one-dimensional measure of expected returns.

The argument over the status of size and book/market factors continues, but the important point is that it does so. Faced with the spectacular failure of the CAPM documented in Figures 20.9 and 20.11 one might have thought that any hope for a rational asset pricing theory was over. Now we are back where we were, examining small anomalies and arguing over refinements and interpretations of the theory. That is quite an accomplishment!

Macroeconomic Factors

> Labor income, industrial production, news variables, and conditional asset pricing models have also all had some successes as multifactor models.

I have focused on the size and value factors since they provide the most empirically successful multifactor model to date, and have therefore attracted much attention.

Several authors have used macroeconomic variables as factors in order to examine directly the story that stock performance during bad macroeconomic times determines average returns. Jagannathan and Wang (1996) and Reyfman (1997) use labor income; Chen, Roll, and Ross (1986) use industrial production and inflation among other variables. Cochrane (1996) uses investment growth. All these authors find that average returns line up against betas calculated using these macroeconomic indicators. The factors are theoretically easier to motivate, but none explains the value and size portfolios as well as the (theoretically less solid, so far) size and value factors.

Lettau and Ludvigson (2000) specify a macroeconomic model that does just as well as the Fama–French factors in explaining the 25 Fama–French portfolios. Their plots of actual average returns versus model predictions show a relation as strong as those of Figures 20.12 and 20.13. Their model is

$$m_{t+1} = a + b(\text{caw}_t)\Delta c_{t+1},$$

where caw is a measure of the consumption-wealth ratio. This is a "scaled factor model" of the sort advocated in Chapter 8. You can think of it as capturing a time-varying risk aversion.

Though Merton's (1971a,b) theory says that variables which predict market returns should show up as factors which explain cross-sectional variation in average returns, surprisingly few papers have actually tried to see whether this is true, now that we do have variables that we think forecast the market return. Campbell (1996) and Ferson and Harvey (1999) are among the few exceptions.

Momentum and Reversal

Sorting stocks based on past performance, you find that a portfolio that buys long-term losers and sells long-term winners does better than the opposite—individual stock long-term returns mean-revert. This "reversal" effect makes sense given return predictability and mean-reversion, and is explained by the Fama–French three-factor model. However, a portfolio that buys short-term winners and sells short-term losers also does well—"momentum." This effect is a puzzle.

Since a string of good returns gives a high price, it is not surprising that stocks that do well for a long time (and hence build up a high price) subsequently do poorly, and stocks that do poorly for a long time (and hence dwindle down to a low price, market value, or market/book ratio) subsequently do well. Table 20.12, taken from Fama and French (1996), reveals that this is in fact the case. (As usual, this table is the tip of an iceberg of research on these effects, starting with DeBont and Thaler [1985] and Jagadeesh and Titman [1993].)

Reversal

Here is the "reversal" strategy. Each month, allocate all stocks to 10 portfolios based on performance in year -5 to year -1. Then, buy the best-performing portfolio and short the worst-performing portfolio. The first row of Table 20.12 shows that this strategy earns a hefty -0.74% monthly return[3]. Past long-term losers come back and past winners do badly. This is a cross-sectional counterpart to the mean-reversion that we studied in Section 1.4. Fama and French (1998a) already found substantial mean-reversion—negative long-horizon return autocorrelations—in disaggregated stock portfolios, so one would expect this phenomenon.

Spreads in average returns should correspond to spreads in betas. Fama and French verify that these portfolio returns are explained by their three-factor model. Past losers have a high HML beta; they move together with value stocks, and so inherit the value stock premium.

Momentum

The second row of Table 20.12 tracks the average monthly return from a "momentum" strategy. Each month, allocate all stocks to 10 portfolios

---

[3]Fama and French do not provide direct measures of standard deviations for these portfolios. One can infer, however, from the betas, R^2 values, and standard deviation of market and factor portfolios that the standard deviations are roughly 1–2 times that of the market return, so that Sharpe ratios of these strategies are comparable to that of the market return.

Table 20.12.   Average monthly returns from reversal and
momentum strategies

Strategy	Period	Portfolio Formation Months	Average Return, 10-1 (Monthly %)
Reversal	6307-9312	60-13	−0.74
Momentum	6307-9312	12-2	+1.31
Reversal	3101-6302	60-13	−1.61
Momentum	3101-6302	12-2	+0.38

Each month, allocate all NYSE firms on CRSP to 10 portfolios based on
their performance during the "portfolio formation months" interval. For
example, 60–13 forms portfolios based on returns from 5 years ago to
1 year, 1 month ago. Then buy the best-performing decile portfolio and
short the worst-performing decile portfolio.
Source: Fama and French (1996, Table VI).

based on performance in the last *year*. Now, quite surprisingly, the winners continue to win, and the losers continue to lose, so that buying the winners and shorting the losers generates a positive 1.31% monthly return.

At every moment there is a most-studied anomaly, and momentum is that anomaly as I write. It is not explained by the Fama–French three-factor model. The past losers have low prices and tend to move with value stocks. Hence the model predicts they should have *high* average returns, not *low* average returns. Momentum stocks move together, as do value and small stocks, so a "momentum factor" works to "explain" momentum portfolio returns. This is so obviously ad hoc (i.e., an APT factor that will only explain returns of portfolios organized on the same characteristic as the factor) that nobody wants to add it as a risk factor.

A momentum factor is more palatable as a performance attribution factor. If we run fund returns on factors including momentum, we may be able to say that a fund did well by following a mechanical momentum strategy rather than by stock-picking ability, leaving aside why a momentum strategy should work. Carhart (1997) uses it in this way.

Momentum is really a new way of looking at an old phenomenon, the small apparent predictability of monthly individual stock returns. A tiny regression R^2 for forecasting monthly returns of 0.0025 (1/4%) is more than adequate to generate the momentum results of Table 20.12. The key is the large standard deviation of individual stock returns, typically 40% or more at an annual basis. The average return of the best performing decile of a normal distribution is 1.76 standard deviations above the mean,[4] so the winning momentum portfolio typically went up about 80% in the previous year, and the typical losing portfolio went down about 60% per year. Only a small amount of continuation will give a 1% monthly return when multiplied by such large past returns. To be precise, the monthly individual stock standard deviation is about $40\%/\sqrt{12} \approx 12\%$. If the R^2 is 0.0025, the standard deviation of the predictable part of returns is $\sqrt{0.0025} \times 12\% = 0.6\%$. Hence, the decile predicted to perform best will earn $1.76 \times 0.6\% \approx 1\%$ above the mean. Since the strategy buys the winners and shorts the losers, an R^2 of 0.0025 implies that one should earn a 2% monthly return by the momentum strategy—more even than the 1.3% shown in Table 20.12. Lewellen (2000) offers a related explanation for momentum coming from small *cross*-correlations of returns.

We have known at least since Fama (1965) that monthly and higher-frequency stock returns have slight, statistically significant predictability with R^2 in the 0.01 range. However, such small though statistically significant high-frequency predictability, especially in small stock returns, has also since the 1960s always failed to yield exploitable profits after one accounts for transactions costs, thin trading, high short-sale costs, and other microstructure issues. Hence, one naturally worries whether momentum is really exploitable after transactions costs.

Momentum does require frequent trading. The portfolios in Table 20.12 are reformed every month. Annual winners and losers will not change that often, but the winning and losing portfolios must still be turned over at least once per year. Carhart (1996) calculates transactions costs and concludes that momentum is not exploitable after those costs are taken into account. Moskowitz and Grinblatt (1999) note that most of the apparent gains come from short positions in small, illiquid stocks, positions that also have high transactions costs. They also find that a large part of momentum profits come from short positions taken November, anticipating tax-loss selling in December. This sounds a lot more like a small microstructure glitch rather than a central parable for risk and return in asset markets.

Table 20.12 already shows that the momentum effect essentially disappears in the earlier data sample, while reversal is even stronger in that sample. Ahn, Boudoukh, Richardson, and Whitelaw (1999) show that

---

[4]We are looking for

$$F(r|r \geq M) = \frac{\int_x^\infty rf(r)\,dr}{\int_x^\infty f(r)\,dr},$$

where x is defined as the top 10th cutoff,

$$\int_x^\infty f(r)\,dr = \frac{1}{10}.$$

With a normal distribution, $x = 1.2816\sigma$ and $E(r|r \geq x) = 1.755\sigma$.

apparent momentum in international index returns is missing from the futures markets, also suggesting a microstructure explanation.

Of course, it is possible that a small positive autocorrelation is there and related to some risk. However, it is hard to generate real positive autocorrelation in realized returns. As we saw in Section 20.2, a slow and persistent variation in *expected* returns most naturally generates negative autocorrelation in *realized* returns. News that expected returns are higher means future dividends are discounted at a higher rate, so today's price and return declines. The only way to overturn this prediction is to suppose that expected return shocks are positively correlated with shocks to current or expected future dividend growth. A convincing story for such correlation has not yet been constructed. On the other hand, the required positive correlation is very small and not very persistent.

20.3 Summary and Interpretation

While the list of new facts appears long, similar patterns show up in every case. Prices reveal slow-moving market expectations of subsequent excess returns, because potential offsetting events seem sluggish or absent. The patterns suggest that there are substantial expected return premia for taking on risks of recession and financial stress unrelated to the market return.

Magnifying Glasses
The effects are not completely new. We knew since the 1960s that high-frequency returns are slightly predictable, with R^2 of 0.01 to 0.1 in daily to monthly returns. These effects were dismissed because there did not seem to be much that one could do about them. A 51/49 bet is not very attractive, especially if there is any transactions cost. Also, the increased Sharpe ratio one can obtain by exploiting predictability is directly related to the forecast R^2, so tiny R^2, even if exploitable, did not seem like an important phenomenon.

Many of the new facts amount to clever magnifying glasses, ways of making small facts economically interesting. For forecasting market returns, we now realize that R^2 rise with horizon when the forecasting variables are slow-moving. Hence small R^2 at high frequency can mean really substantial R^2, in the 30–50% range, at longer horizons. Equivalently, we realize that small expected return variation can add up to striking price variation if the expected return variation is persistent. For momentum and reversal effects, the ability to sort stocks and funds into momentum-based portfolios means that small predictability times portfolios with huge past returns gives important subsequent returns.

Dogs that Did Not Bark

In each case, an apparent difference in yield should give rise to an offsetting movement, but seems not to do so. Something *should* be predictable so that returns are *not* predictable, and it is not.

The d/p forecasts of the market return were driven by the fact that dividends *should* be predictable, so that returns are not. Instead, dividend growth seems nearly unpredictable. As we saw, this fact and the speed of the d/p mean-reversion imply the observed magnitude of return predictability.

The term structure forecasts of bond returns were driven by the fact that bond yields *should* be predictable, so that returns are not. Instead, yields seem nearly unpredictable at the one-year horizon. This fact means that the forward rate moves one for one with expected returns, and that a one percentage point increase in yield spread signals as much as a 5 percentage point increase in expected return.

Exchange rates should be forecastable so that foreign exchange returns are not. Instead, a one percentage point increase in interest rate abroad seems to signal a greater than one percentage point increase in expected return.

Prices Reveal Expected Returns

If expected returns rise, prices are driven down, since future dividends or other cash flows are discounted at a higher rate. A "low" price, then, can *reveal* a market expectation of a high expected or required return.

Most of our results come from this effect. Low price/dividend, price/earnings, price/book values signal times when the market as a whole will have high average returns. Low market value (price times shares) relative to book value signals securities or portfolios that earn high average returns. The "small-firm" effect derives from low prices—other measures of size such as number of employees or book value alone have no predictive power for returns (Berk [1997]). The "5 year reversal" effect derives from the fact that five years of poor returns lead to a low price. A high long-term bond yield means that the price of long-term bonds is "low," and this seems to signal a time of good long-term bonds returns. A high foreign interest rate means a low price on foreign bonds, and this seems to indicate good returns on the foreign bonds.

The most natural interpretation of all these effects is that the expected or required return—the risk premium—on individual securities as well as the market as a whole varies slowly over time. Thus we can track market expectations of returns by watching price/dividend, price/earnings, or book/market ratios.

Macroeconomic Risks

The price-based patterns in time-series and cross-sectional expected returns suggest a premium for holding risks related to recession and economy-wide financial distress. All of the forecasting variables are connected to macroeconomic activity (Fama and French [1989]). The dividend/price ratio is highly correlated with the default spread and rises in bad times. The term spread forecasts bond and stock returns, and is also one of the best recession forecasters. It rises steeply at the bottoms of recessions, and is inverted at the top of a boom. Thus, return forecasts are high at the bottom of business cycles and low at the top of booms. "Value" and "small-cap" stocks are typically distressed. Formal quantitative and empirically successful economic models of the recession and distress premia are still in their infancy (I think Campbell and Cochrane [1999] is a good start), but the story is at least plausible, and the effects have been expected by theorists for a generation.

To make this point come to life, think concretely about what you have to do to take advantage of the value or predictability strategies. You have to buy stocks or long-term bonds at the bottom, when stock prices are low after a long and depressing bear market; in the bottom of a recession or financial panic; a time when long-term bond prices and corporate bond prices are unusually low. This is a time when few people have the guts (the risk-tolerance) or the wallet to buy risky stocks or risky long-term bonds. Looking across stocks rather than over time, you have to invest in "value" companies, dogs by any standards. These are companies with years of poor past returns, years of poor sales, companies on the edge of bankruptcy, far off of any list of popular stocks to buy. Then, you have to sell stocks and long-term bonds in good times, when stock prices are high relative to dividends, earnings, and other multiples, when the yield curve is flat or inverted so that long-term bond prices are high. You have to sell the popular "growth" stocks with good past returns, good sales, and earnings growth.

I am going on a bit here to counter the widespread impression, best crystallized by Shiller (2000) that high price/earnings ratios must signal "irrational exuberance." Perhaps, but is it just a coincidence that this exuberance comes at the top of an unprecedented economic expansion, a time when the average investor is surely feeling less risk averse than ever, and willing to hold stocks despite historically low risk premia? I do not know the answer, but the rational explanation is surely not totally impossible! Is it just a coincidence that we are finding premia just where a generation of theorists said we ought to—in recessions, credit crunches, bad labor markets, investment opportunity set variables, and so forth?

This line of explanation for the foreign exchange puzzle is still a bit farther off, though there are recent attempts to make economic sense of the puzzle. (See Engel's [1996] survey; Atkeson, Alvarez, and Kehoe [1999] is a recent example.) At a verbal level, the strategy leads you to invest in countries with high interest rates. High interest rates are often a sign of monetary instability or other economic trouble, and thus may mean that the investments may be more exposed to the risks of global financial stress or a global recession than are investments in the bonds of countries with low interest rates, who are typically enjoying better times.

Overall, the new view of finance amounts to a profound change. We have to get used to the fact that most returns and price variation come from variation in *risk premia*, not variation in expected cash flows, interest rates, etc. Most interesting variation in priced risk comes from nonmarket factors. These are easy to say, but profoundly change our view of the world.

Doubts

Momentum is, so far, unlike all the other results. The underlying phenomenon is a small predictability of high-frequency returns. However, the price-based phenomena make this predictability important by noting that, with a slow-moving forecasting variable, the R^2 build over horizon. Momentum is based on a fast-moving forecast variable—the last year's return. Therefore the R^2 decline with horizon. Instead, momentum makes the tiny autocorrelation of high-frequency returns significant by forming portfolios of extreme winners and losers, so a small continuation of huge past returns gives a large current return. All the other results are easily digestible as a slow, business-cycle-related time-varying expected return. This specification gives negative autocorrelation (unless we add a distasteful positive correlation of expected return and dividend shocks) and so does not explain momentum. Momentum returns have also not yet been linked to business cycles or financial distress in even the informal way that I suggested for the price-based strategies. Thus, it still lacks much of a plausible economic interpretation. To me, this adds weight to the view that it is not there, it is not exploitable, or it represents a small illiquidity (tax-loss selling of small illiquid stocks) that will be quickly remedied once a few traders understand it. In the entire history of finance there has always been an anomaly-du-jour, and momentum is it right now. We will have to wait to see how it is resolved.

Many of the anomalous risk premia seem to be declining over time. The small-firm effect completely disappeared in 1980; you can date this as the publication of the first small-firm effect papers or the founding of small firm mutual funds that made diversified portfolios of small stocks available to average investors. To emphasize this point, Figure 20.14 plots size portfolio average returns versus beta in the period since 1979. You can see that not only has the small-firm *premium* disappeared, the size-related variation in beta and expected return has disappeared.

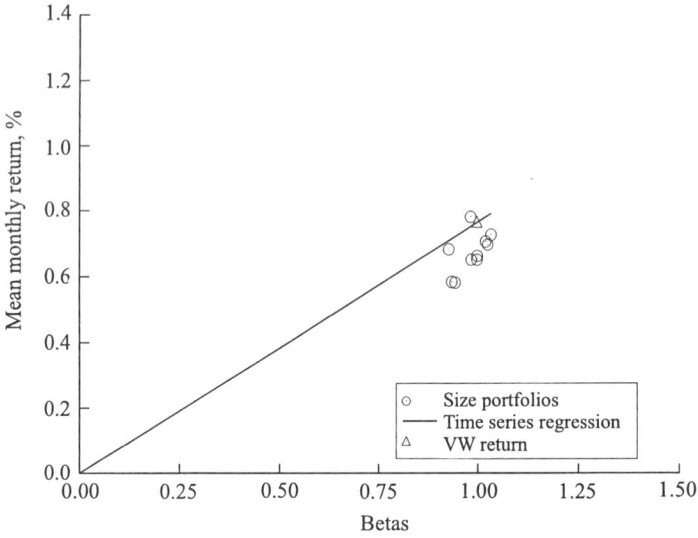

Figure 20.14. *Average returns vs. market betas. CRSP size portfolios less treasury bill rate, monthly data 1979–1998.*

The value premium has been cut roughly in half in the 1990s, and 1990 is roughly the date of widespread popularization of the value effect, though $\sigma/\sqrt{T}$ leaves a lot of room for error here. As you saw in Table 20.4, the last five years of high market returns have cut the estimated return predictability from the dividend/price ratio in *half*.

These facts suggest an uncomfortable implication: that at least some of the premium the new strategies yielded in the past was due to the fact that they were simply overlooked, they were artifacts of data-dredging, or they survived only until funds were created that allow many investors to hold diversified portfolios that exploit them.

Since they are hard to measure, one is tempted to put less emphasis on these average returns. However, they are crucial to our interpretation of the facts. The CAPM is perfectly consistent with the fact that there are additional sources of common variation. For example, it was long understood that stocks in the same industry move together; the fact that value or small stocks also move together need not cause a ripple. The surprise is that investors seem to earn an average return premium for holding these additional sources of common movement, whereas the CAPM predicts that (given beta) such common movements should have no effect on a portfolio's average returns.

Problems—Chapter 20

1. Does equation (20.11) condition down to information sets coarser than those observed by agents? Or must we assume that whatever VAR is used by the econometrician contains all information seen by agents?

2. Show that the two regressions in Table 20.9 are complementary—that the coefficients add up to one, mechanically, in sample.

3. Derive the return innovation decomposition (20.11), directly. Write the return

$$r_t = \Delta d_t + \rho \left(p_t - d_t \right) - (p_{t-1} - d_{t-1}).$$

Apply $E_t - E_{t-1}$ to both sides,

$$r_t - E_{t-1} r_t = (E_t - E_{t-1}) \Delta d_t + \rho (E_t - E_{t-1})(p_t - d_t). \qquad (20.44)$$

Use the price/dividend identity and iterate forward to obtain (20.11).

4. Find the univariate representation and mean-reversion statistics for *prices* implied by the simple VAR and the three dividend examples.

5. Find the univariate return representation from a general return forecasting VAR,

$$r_{t+1} = a x_t + \varepsilon_{rt+1},$$

$$x_{t+1} = b x_t + \varepsilon_{xt+1}.$$

Find the correlation between return and x shocks necessary to generate uncorrelated returns.

6. Show that stationary $x_t - y_t$, Δx_t, Δy_t imply that x_t and y_t must have the same variance ratio and that long-run differences must become perfectly correlated. Start by showing that the long-run variance $\lim_{k \to \infty} \mathrm{var}(x_{t+k} - x_t)/k$ for any stationary variable must be zero. Apply that fact to $x_t - y_t$.

7. Compute the long-horizon regression coefficients and R^2 in the VAR (20.14)–(20.20). Show that the R^2 do indeed rise with horizon. Do coefficients and R^2 rise forever, or do they turn around at some point?

21

Equity Premium Puzzle and Consumption-Based Models

THE ORIGINAL SPECIFICATION of the consumption-based model was not a great success, as we saw in Chapter 2. Still, it is in some sense the only model we have. The central task of financial economics is to figure out what are the real risks that drive asset prices and expected returns. Something like the consumption-based model—investors' first-order conditions for savings and portfolio choice—has to be the starting point.

Rather than dream up models, test them, and reject them, financial economists since the work of Mehra and Prescott (1986) and Hansen and Jagannathan (1991) have been able to work backwards to some extent, characterizing the properties that discount factors must have in order to explain asset return data. Among other things, we learned that the discount factor had to be extremely volatile, while not too conditionally volatile; the risk-free rate or conditional mean had to be pretty steady. This knowledge is now leading to a much more successful set of variations on the consumption-based model.

21.1 Equity Premium Puzzles

The Basic Equity Premium/Risk-Free Rate Puzzle

The postwar U.S. market Sharpe ratio is about 0.5—an 8% return and 16% standard deviation. The basic Hansen–Jagannathan bound

$$\frac{E(R^e)}{\sigma(R^e)} \le \frac{\sigma(m)}{E(m)} \approx \gamma\sigma(\Delta c)$$

implies $\sigma(m) \ge 50\%$ on an annual basis, requiring huge risk aversion or consumption growth volatility.

The average risk-free rate is about 1%, so $E(m) \approx 0.99$. High risk aversion with power utility implies a very high risk-free rate, or requires a negative subjective discount factor.

Interest rates are quite stable over time and across countries, so $E_t(m)$ varies little. High risk aversion with power utility implies that interest rates are very volatile.

In Chapter 1, we derived the basic Hansen–Jagannathan (1991) bounds. These are characterizations of the discount factors that price a given set of asset returns. Manipulating $0 = E(mR^e)$, we found

$$\frac{\sigma(m)}{E(m)} \ge \frac{|E(R^e)|}{\sigma(R^e)}. \tag{21.1}$$

In continuous time, or as an approximation in discrete time, we found that time-separable utility implies

$$\gamma\sigma(\Delta c) \ge \frac{|E(R^e)|}{\sigma(R^e)}, \tag{21.2}$$

where $\gamma = -cu''/u'$ is the local curvature of the utility function, and risk aversion coefficient for the power case.

Equity Premium Puzzle

The postwar mean value-weighted NYSE is about 8% per year over the T-bill rate, with a standard deviation of about 16%. Thus, the market Sharpe ratio $E(R^e)/\sigma(R^e)$ is about 0.5 for an annual investment horizon. If there were a constant risk-free rate,

$$E(m) = 1/R^f$$

would nail down $E(m)$. The T-bill rate is not very risky, so $E(m)$ is not far from the inverse of the mean T-bill rate, or about $E(m) \approx 0.99$. Thus, these basic facts about the mean and variance of stocks and bonds imply

$\sigma(m) > 0.5$. The volatility of the discount factor must be about 50% of its level in annual data!

Per capita consumption growth has standard deviation about 1% per year. With log utility, that implies $\sigma(m) = 0.01 = 1\%$ which is off by a factor of 50. To match the equity premium we need $\gamma > 50$, which seems a huge level of risk aversion. Equivalently, a log utility investor with consumption growth of 1% and facing a 0.5 Sharpe ratio should be investing dramatically more in the stock market, borrowing to do so. He should invest so much that his wealth and hence consumption growth *does* vary by 50% each year.

Correlation Puzzle
The bound takes the extreme possibility that consumption and stock returns are perfectly correlated. They are not, in the data. Correlations are hard to measure, since they are sensitive to data definition, timing, time-aggregation, and so forth. Still, the correlation of annual stock returns and nondurable plus services consumption growth in postwar U.S. data is no more than about 0.2. If we use this information as well—if we characterize the mean and standard deviation of all discount factors that have correlation less than 0.2 with the market return, the calculation becomes

$$\frac{\sigma(m)}{E(m)} \geq \frac{1}{|\rho_{m,R^e}|} \frac{|E(R^e)|}{\sigma(R^e)} = \frac{1}{0.2} 0.5 = 2.5$$

with $\sigma(m) \approx \gamma\sigma(\Delta c)$; we now need a risk aversion coefficient of *250*!

Here is a classier way to state the correlation puzzle. Remember that $\text{proj}(m|\underline{X})$ should price assets just as well as m itself. Now, $m = \text{proj}(m|\underline{X}) + \varepsilon$ and $\sigma^2(m) = \sigma^2(\text{proj}(m|\underline{X})) + \sigma^2(\varepsilon)$. Some of the early resolutions of the equity premium puzzle ended up adding noise uncorrelated with asset payoffs to the discount factor. This modification increased discount factor volatility and satisfied the bound. But as you can see, adding ε increases $\sigma^2(m)$ with no effect whatsoever on the model's ability to price assets. As you add ε, the correlation between m and asset returns declines. A bound with correlation, or equivalently comparing $\sigma^2(\text{proj}(m|\underline{X}))$ rather than $\sigma^2(m)$ to the bound, avoids this trap.

Average Interest Rates and Subjective Discount Factors
It has been traditional to use risk aversion numbers of 1 to 5 or so, but perhaps this is tradition, not fact. What is wrong with $\gamma = 50$ to 250?

The most basic piece of evidence for low γ comes from the relation between consumption growth and interest rates:

$$R_t^f = E_t(m_{t+1}) = E_t\left[\beta\left(\frac{C_{t+1}}{C_t}\right)^{-\gamma}\right]$$

or, in continuous time,

$$r_t^f = \delta + \gamma E_t(\Delta c). \tag{21.3}$$

We can take unconditional expectations to compare these equations with average interest rates and consumption growth.

Average real interest rates are also about 1%. Thus, $\gamma = 50$ to 250 with a typical δ such as $\delta = 0.01$ implies a very high risk-free rate, of 50–250%. To get a reasonable interest rate we have to use a subjective discount factor $\delta = -0.5$ to -2.5, or -50% to -250%. That is not impossible—present values can converge with negative discount rates (Kocherlakota [1990])—but it does not seem reasonable. People prefer earlier utility.

Interest Rate Variation and the Conditional Mean of the Discount Factor
Again, however, maybe we are being too doctrinaire. What evidence is there against $\gamma = 50$–250 with corresponding $\delta = -0.5$ to -2.5?

Real interest rates are not only low on average, they are also relatively stable over time and across countries. $\gamma = 50$ in equation (21.3) means that a country or a boom time with consumption growth 1 percentage point higher than normal must have real interest rates 50 percentage points higher than normal, and consumption 1 percentage point lower than normal should be accompanied by real interest rates of 50 percentage points lower than normal—you pay them 48% to keep your money. We do not see anything like this.

$\gamma = 50$ to 250 in a time-separable utility function implies that consumers are essentially unwilling to substitute (expected) consumption over time, so huge interest rate variation must force them to make the small variations in consumption growth that we do see. This level of aversion to *intertemporal substitution* is too large. For example, think about what interest rate you need to convince someone to skip a vacation. Take a family with $50,000 per year consumption, which spends $2,500 (5%) on an annual vacation. If interest rates are good enough, though, the family can be persuaded to skip this year's vacation and go on a much more lavish vacation next year. The required interest rate is ($52,500/$47,500)$^\gamma - 1$. For $\gamma = 250$, that is an interest rate of 3×10^{11}! For $\gamma = 50$, we still need an interest rate of 14,800%. I think most of us would give in and defer the vacation for somewhat lower interest rates! A reasonable willingness to substitute intertemporally is central to most macroeconomic models that try to capture the dynamics of output, investment, consumption, etc.

As always, we can express the observation as a desired characteristic of the discount factor. Though m_{t+1} must vary a lot, its conditional mean $E_t(m_{t+1}) = 1/R_t^f$ must not vary much. You can get variance in two ways—variance in the conditional mean and variance in the unexpected component; $\mathrm{var}(x) = \mathrm{var}[E_t(x)] + \mathrm{var}[x - E_t(x)]$. The fact that interest rates are stable means that almost all of the 50% or more unconditional discount factor variance must come from the second term.

The power functional form is really not an issue. To get past the equity premium and these related puzzles, we will have to introduce other arguments to the marginal utility function—some nonseparability. One important key will be to introduce some nonseparability that distinguishes intertemporal substitution from risk aversion.

Variations

> Just raising the interest rate will not help, as all-stock portfolios have high Sharpe ratios too.
>
> Uninsured individual risk is not an obvious solution. Individual consumption is not volatile enough to satisfy the bounds, and is less correlated with stock returns than aggregate consumption.
>
> The average return in postwar data may overstate the true expected return; a target of 3–4% is not unreasonable.

Is the Interest Rate "Too Low"?
A large literature has tried to explain the equity premium puzzle by introducing frictions that make treasury bills "money-like" and so argues that the short-term interest rate is artificially low. (Aiyagari and Gertler [1991] is an example). However, high historical Sharpe ratios are pervasive in financial markets. Portfolios long small stocks and short big stocks, or long value (high book/market) and short growth stocks, give Sharpe ratios of 0.5 or more as well.

Individual Shocks
Maybe we should abandon the representative agent assumption. Individual income shocks are not perfectly insured, so individual income and consumption is much more volatile than aggregate consumption. Furthermore, through most of the sample, only a small portion of the population held any stocks at all.

This line of argument faces a steep uphill battle. The basic pricing equation applies to *each* investor. Individual income growth may be more volatile than the aggregate, but it is not credible that any individual's consumption growth varies by *50–250% per year!* Keep in mind, this is non durable and services consumption and the flow of services from durables, not durables purchases.

Furthermore, individual consumption growth is likely to be less correlated with stock returns than is aggregate consumption growth, and the more volatile it is, the less correlated. As a simple example, write individual consumption growth equal to aggregate consumption growth plus an idiosyncratic shock, uncorrelated with economywide variables,

$$\Delta c_t^i = \Delta c_t^a + \varepsilon_t^i.$$

Hence,

$$\text{cov}(\Delta c_t^i, r_t) = \text{cov}(\Delta c_t^a + \varepsilon_t^i, r_t) = \text{cov}(\Delta c_t^a, r_t).$$

As we add more idiosyncratic variation, the correlation of consumption with any aggregate such as stock returns declines in exact proportion. Following correlation puzzle logic, the asset pricing implications are completely unaffected.

Luck and a Lower Target
One nagging doubt is that a large part of the U.S. postwar average stock return may represent good luck rather than ex ante expected return.

First of all, the standard deviation of stock returns is so high that standard errors are surprisingly large. Using the standard formula $\sigma/\sqrt{T}$, the standard error of average stock returns in 50 years of data is about $16/\sqrt{50} \approx 2.3$. This fact means that a two-standard-error confidence interval for the expected return extends from about 3% to about 13%!

This is a pervasive, simple, but surprisingly underappreciated problem in empirical asset pricing. In 20 years of data, $16/\sqrt{20} = 3.6$ so we can barely say that an 8% average return is above zero. Five-year performance averages of something like a stock return are close to meaningless on a statistical basis, since $16/\sqrt{5} = 7.2$. (This is one reason that many funds are held to tracking error limits relative to a benchmark. You may be able to measure performance relative to a benchmark, even if your return and the benchmark are both very volatile. If $\sigma(R^i - R^m)$ is small, then $\sigma(R^i - R^m)/\sqrt{T}$ can be small, even if $\sigma(R^i)$ and $\sigma(R^m)$ are large.)

However, large standard errors can argue that the equity premium is really higher than the postwar return. Several other arguments suggest a bias—that a substantial part of the 8% average excess return of the last 50 years was good luck, and that the true equity premium is more like 3–4%.

Brown, Goetzmann, and Ross (1995) suggest that the U.S. data suffer from selection bias. One of the reasons that I write this book in the United States, and that the data has been collected from the United States, is precisely because U.S. stock returns and growth have been so good for the last 50–100 years.

One way to address this question is to look at other samples. Average returns were a lot lower in the United States before WWII. In Shiller's (1989) annual data from 1871–1940, the S&P500 average excess return was only 4.1%. However, Campbell (1999, table 1) looks across countries for which we have stock market data from 1970–1995, and finds the average equity premium practically the same as that for the United States in that period. The other countries averaged a 4.6% excess return while the United States had a 4.4% average excess return in that period.

On the other hand, Campbell's countries are Canada, Japan, Australia, and Western Europe. These probably shared a lot of the U.S. "good luck" in the postwar period. There are lots of countries for which we do not have data, and usually because returns were very low in those countries. As Brown, Goetzmann, and Ross (1995) put it, "Looking back over the history of the London or the New York stock markets can be extraordinarily comforting to an investor—equities appear to have provided a substantial premium over bonds, and markets appear to have recovered nicely after huge crashes. . . . Less comforting is the past history of other major markets: Russia, China, Germany and Japan. Each of these markets has had one or more major interruptions *that prevent their inclusion in long term studies*" [my emphasis].

Think of the things that did not happen in the last 50 years. We had no banking panics, and no depressions; no civil wars, no constitutional crises; we did not lose the Cold War, no missiles were fired over Berlin, Cuba, Korea, or Vietnam. If any of these things had happened, we might well have seen a calamitous decline in stock values, and I would not be writing about the equity premium puzzle.

A view that stocks are subject to occasional and highly non-normal crashes—world wars, great depressions, etc.—makes sampling uncertainty even larger, and means that the average return from any sample that does not include a crash will be larger than the actual average return—the Peso Problem again (Reitz [1988]).

Fama and French (2000) notice that the price/dividend ratio is low at the beginning of the sample and high at the end. Much of that is luck— the dividend yield is stationary in the very long run, with slow-moving variation through good and bad times. We can understand their alternative calculation most easily using the return linearization,

$$r_{t+1} = \Delta d_{t+1} + (d_t - p_t) - \rho(d_{t+1} - p_{t+1}).$$

Then, imposing the view that the dividend/price ratio is stationary, we can estimate the average return as

$$E(r_{t+1}) = E(\Delta d_{t+1}) + (1 - \rho)E(d_t - p_t).$$

The right-hand expression gives an estimate of the unconditional average return on stocks equal to 3.4%. This differs from the sample average return of 9%, because the d/p ratio declined dramatically in the postwar sample.

Here is the fundamental issue: Was it clear to people in 1947 (or 1871, or whenever one starts the sample) and throughout the period that the average return on stocks would be 8% greater than that of bonds, subject only to the 16% year-to-year variation? Given that knowledge, would investors have changed their portfolios, or would they have stayed pat, patiently explaining that these average returns are earned in exchange for risk that they are not prepared to take? If people expected these mean returns, then we face a tremendous challenge of explaining why people did not buy more stocks. This is the basic assumption and challenge of the equity premium puzzle. But phrased this way, the answer is not so clear. I do not think it *was* obvious in 1947 that the United States would not slip back into depression, or another world war, but would instead experience a half century of economic growth and stock returns never before seen in human history. Eight percent seems like an extremely—maybe even irrationally—exuberant expectation for stock returns as of 1947, or 1871. (You can ask the same question, by the way, about value effects, market timing, or other puzzles we try to explain. Only if you can reasonably believe that people understood the average returns and shied away because of the risks does it make sense to explain the puzzles by risk rather than luck. Only in that case will the return premia continue!)

This consideration mitigates, but cannot totally solve, the equity premium puzzle. Even a 3% equity premium is tough to understand with 1% consumption volatility. If the premium is 3%, the Sharpe ratio is $3/16 \approx 0.2$, so we still need risk aversion of 20, and 100 if we include correlation. Twenty to 100 is a lot better than 50–250, but is still quite a challenge.

Predictability and the Equity Premium

> The Sharpe ratio varies over time. This means that discount factor volatility must vary over time. Since consumption volatility does not seem to vary over time, this suggests that risk aversion must vary over time—a conditional equity premium puzzle.
>
> Conventional portfolio calculations suggest that people are not terribly risk averse. These calculations implicitly assume that consumption moves proportionally to wealth, and inherits the large wealth volatility.
>
> If stock returns mean-revert, $E(R^e)/\sigma(R^e)$ and hence $\sigma(m)/E(m)$ rises faster than the square root of the horizon. Consumption growth is roughly i.i.d., so $\sigma(\Delta c)$ rises about with the square root of horizon. Thus, mean-reversion means that the equity premium puzzle is even worse for long-horizon investors and long-horizon returns.

We have traced the implications of the unconditional Sharpe ratio, and of low and relatively constant interest rates. The predictability of stock returns also has important implications for discount factors.

Heteroskedasticity in the Discount Factor–Conditional Equity Premium Puzzle
The Hansen–Jagannathan bound applies conditionally of course,

$$\frac{E_t(R^e_{t+1})}{\sigma_t(R^e_{t+1})} = -\frac{1}{\rho_t(R^e_{t+1}, m_{t+1})}\frac{\sigma_t(m_{t+1})}{E_t(m_{t+1})}.$$

Mean returns are predictable, and the standard deviation of returns varies over time. So far, however, the two moments are forecasted by different sets of variables and at different horizons—d/p, term premium, etc. forecast the mean at long horizons; past squared returns and implied volatility forecast the variance at shorter horizons—and these variables move at different times. Hence, it seems that the conditional Sharpe ratio on the left-hand side moves over time. (Glosten, Jagannathan, and Runkle [1993], French, Schwert, and Stambaugh [1987], and Yan [2000] find some co-movements in conditional mean and variance, but do not find that *all* movement in one moment is matched by movement in the other.)

On the right-hand side, the conditional mean discount factor equals the risk-free rate and so must be relatively stable over time. Time-varying conditional correlations are a possibility, but hard to interpret. Thus, the predictability of returns strongly suggests that the discount factor must be conditionally heteroskedastic—$\sigma_t(m_{t+1})$ must vary through time. Certainly the discount factors on the volatility bound, or the mimicking portfolios for discount factors must have time-varying volatility, since both of them have $\rho = 1$.

In the standard time-separable model, $\sigma_t(m_{t+1}) = \gamma_t \sigma_t(\Delta c_{t+1})$. Thus, we need either time-varying consumption risk or time-varying curvature; loosely speaking, a time-varying risk aversion. The data do not show much evidence of conditional heteroskedasticity in consumption growth, leading one to favor a time-varying curvature. However, this is a case in which high curvature helps: if γ is sufficiently high, a small and perhaps statistically hard-to-measure amount of consumption heteroskedasticity can generate a lot of discount factor heteroskedasticity. (Kandel and Stambaugh [1990] follow this approach to explain predictability.)

CAPM, Portfolios, and Consumption
The equity premium puzzle is centrally about the smoothness of consumption. This is why it was not noticed as a major puzzle in the early development of financial theory. In turn, the smoothness of consumption is centrally related to the predictability of returns.

In standard portfolio analyses, there is no puzzle that people with normal levels of risk aversion do not want to hold far more stocks. From the usual first-order condition and with $\Lambda = V_W(W)$, we can also write the

Hansen–Jagannathan bound in terms of wealth, analogously to (21.2),

$$\frac{|E(r) - r^f|}{\sigma(r)} \leq \frac{-WV_{WW}}{V_W}\sigma(\Delta w). \tag{21.4}$$

The quantity $-WW_{WW}/V_W$ is in fact the measure of risk aversion corresponding to most survey and introspection evidence, since it represents aversion to bets on wealth rather than to bets on consumption.

For an investor who holds the market, $\sigma(\Delta w)$ is the standard deviation of the stock return, about 16%. With a market Sharpe ratio of 0.5, we find the lower bound on risk aversion,

$$\frac{-WV_{WW}}{V_W} = \frac{0.5}{0.16} \approx 3.$$

Furthermore, the correlation between wealth and the stock market is one in this calculation, so no correlation puzzle crops up to raise the required risk aversion. This is the heart of the oft-cited Friend and Blume (1975) calculation of risk aversion, one source of the idea that 3–5 is about the right level of risk aversion rather than 50 or 250.

The Achilles heel is the hidden simplifying assumption that returns are independent over time, and the investor has no other source of income, so no variables other than wealth show up in its marginal value V_W. In such an i.i.d. world, consumption moves one-for-one with wealth, and $\sigma(\Delta c) = \sigma(\Delta w)$. If your wealth doubles and nothing else has changed, you double consumption. This calculation thus hides a consumption-based "model," and the model has the drastically counterfactual implication that consumption growth has a 16% standard deviation!

All this calculation has done is say that "in a model in which consumption has a 16% volatility like stock returns, we do not need high risk aversion to explain the equity premium." Hence the central point—the equity premium is about *consumption* smoothness. Just looking at wealth and portfolios, you do not notice anything unusual.

In the same way, retreating to the CAPM or factor models does not solve the puzzle either. The CAPM is a specialization of the consumption-based model, not an alternative to it, and thus hides an equity premium puzzle. Most implementations of the CAPM take the market premium as given, ignoring the link to consumption in the model's derivation, and estimate the market premium as a free parameter. The equity premium puzzle asks whether the market premium itself makes any sense.

The Long-Run Equity Premium Puzzle

The fact that annual consumption is much smoother than wealth is an important piece of information. In the long run, consumption must move one-for-one with wealth, so consumption and wealth volatility must be the same. Therefore, we know that the world is very far from i.i.d., so predictability will be an important issue in understanding risk premia.

Predictability can imply mean-reversion and Sharpe ratios that rise faster than the square root of horizon. Thus,

$$\frac{E\left(R^e_{t \to t+k}\right)}{\sigma\left(R^e_{t \to t+k}\right)} \leq \frac{\sigma\left(m_{t \to t+k}\right)}{E\left(m_{t \to t+k}\right)} \approx \gamma \sigma\left(\Delta c_{t \to t+k}\right).$$

If stocks do mean-revert, then discount factor volatility must increase faster than the square root of the horizon. Consumption growth is close to i.i.d., so the volatility of consumption growth only increases with the square root of horizon. Thus mean-reversion implies that the equity premium puzzle is even worse at long investment horizons.

21.2 New Models

We want to end up with a model that explains a high market Sharpe ratio, and the high level and volatility of stock returns, with low and relatively constant interest rates, roughly i.i.d. consumption growth with small volatility, and that explains the predictability of excess returns—the fact that high prices today correspond to low excess returns in the future. Eventually, we would like the model to explain the predictability of bond and foreign exchange returns as well, the time-varying volatility of stock returns and the cross-sectional variation of expected returns, and it would be nice if in addition to fitting all of the facts, people in the models did not display unusually high aversion to wealth bets.

I start with a general outline of the features shared by most models that address these puzzles. Then, I focus on two models, the Campbell–Cochrane (1999) habit persistence model and the Constantinides and Duffie (1996) model with uninsured idiosyncratic risks. The mechanisms we uncover in these models apply to a large class. The Campbell–Cochrane model is a representative from the literature that attacks the equity premium by modifying the representative agent's preferences. The Constantinides and Duffie model is a representative of the literature that attacks the equity premium by modeling uninsured idiosyncratic risks, market frictions, and limited participation.

Outlines of New Models

Additional state variables are the natural route to solving the empirical puzzles. Investors must not be particularly scared of the wealth or consumption effects of holding stocks, but of the fact that stocks do badly at particular times, or in particular states of nature. Broadly speaking, most solutions introduce something like a "recession" state variable. This fact makes stocks different, and more feared, than pure wealth bets, whose risk is unrelated to the state of the economy.

In the ICAPM view, we get models of this sort by specifying things so there is an additional recession state variable z in the value function $V(W, z)$. Then, expected returns are

$$E(r) - r^f = \frac{-WV_{WW}}{V_W} \operatorname{cov}(\Delta W, r) + \frac{zV_{Wz}}{V_W} \operatorname{cov}(z, r). \tag{21.5}$$

In a utility framework, we add other arguments to the utility function $u(C, z)$, so

$$E(r) - r^f = \frac{-Cu_{CC}}{u_C} \operatorname{cov}(\Delta C, r) + \frac{zu_{Cz}}{u_C} \operatorname{cov}(z, r). \tag{21.6}$$

The extra utility function arguments must enter *nonseparably*. If $u(C, z) = f(C) + g(z)$, then $u_{Cz} = 0$. All utility function modifications are of this sort—they add extra goods like leisure, nonseparability over time in the form of habit persistence, or nonseparability across states of nature so that consumption if it rains affects marginal utility if it shines.

The lesson of the equity premium literature is that the second term must account for essentially all of the market premium. Since the cross-sectional work surveyed in Chapter 20 seemed to point to something like a recession factor as the primary determinant of cross-sectional variation in expected returns, and since the time-series work pointed to a recession-related time-varying risk premium, a gratifying unity seems close at hand—and a fundamental revision of the CAPM-i.i.d. view of the source of risk prices.

The predictability of returns suggests a natural source of state variables. Unfortunately, the sign is wrong. The fact that stocks go *up* when their expected subsequent returns are *low* means that stocks, like bonds, are good hedges for shocks to their own opportunity sets. Therefore, adding the effects of predictability typically lowers expected returns. (The "typically" in this sentence is important. The sign of this effect—the sign of zV_{Wz}—does depend on the utility function and environment. For example, there is no risk premium for log utility.)

Thus, we need an additional state variable, and one strong enough to not only explain the equity premium, given that the first terms in (21.5) and (21.6) are not up to the job, but one stronger still to overcome the effects of predictability. Recessions are times of low prices and high expected returns. We want a model in which recessions are bad times, so that investors fear bad stock returns in recessions. But high expected returns are good times for a pure Merton investor. Thus, the other state variable(s) that describe a recession—high risk aversion, low labor income, high labor income uncertainty, liquidity, etc.—must overcome the "good times" of high expected returns and indicate that times really are bad after all.

Habits

A natural explanation for the predictability of returns from price/dividend ratios is that people get less risk averse as consumption and wealth increase in a boom, and more risk averse as consumption and wealth decrease in a recession. We cannot tie risk aversion to the *level* of consumption and wealth, since that increases over time while equity premia have not declined. Thus, to pursue this idea, we must specify a model in which risk aversion depends on the level of consumption or wealth relative to some "trend" or the recent past.

Following this idea, Campbell and Cochrane (1999) specify that people slowly develop habits for higher or lower consumption. Thus, the "habits" form the "trend" in consumption. The idea is not implausible. Anyone who has had a large pizza dinner or smoked a cigarette knows that what you consumed yesterday can have an impact on how you feel about more consumption today. Might a similar mechanism apply for consumption in general and at a longer time horizon? Perhaps we get used to an accustomed standard of living, so a fall in consumption hurts after a few years of good times, even though the same level of consumption might have seemed very pleasant if it arrived after years of bad times. This thought can at least explain the perception that recessions are awful events, even though a recession year may be just the second or third best year in human history rather than the absolute best. Law, custom, and social insurance also insure against falls in consumption as much as low levels of consumption.

We specify an external, or "keep up with the Joneses" form of habit formation, following Abel (1990). In the model, this is primarily a technical convenience, and we argue that it does not make much difference to the results for aggregate consumption and asset prices. (See problem 2.) It does seem to capture much interesting behavior, however. Many investors seem more concerned about staying ahead of their colleagues that they are in absolute performance. They demand low "tracking error" of their investments, meaning that they give up average return opportunities (such as value) to make sure that their investments do not fall behind as the market rises. We also argue that this specification may be crucial to reconcile strong habits in the aggregate with microeconomic data. Given a windfall, most people spend it quickly. This behavior is consistent with an internal habit, but if each person's habit were driven by his own consumption, consumption would ramp up slowly following a windfall.

The Model
We model an endowment economy with i.i.d. consumption growth:

$$\Delta c_{t+1} = g + v_{t+1}, \qquad v_{t+1} \sim \text{i.i.d. } \mathcal{N}(0, \sigma^2).$$

We replace the utility function $u(C)$ with $u(C - X)$, where X denotes the level of habits:

$$E \sum_{t=0}^{\infty} \delta^t \frac{(C_t - X_t)^{1-\gamma} - 1}{1 - \gamma}.$$

Habits should move slowly in response to consumption, something like

$$x_t \approx \lambda \sum_{j=0}^{\infty} \phi^j c_{t-j} \tag{21.7}$$

or, equivalently,

$$x_t = \phi x_{t-1} + \lambda c_t. \tag{21.8}$$

(Small letters denote the logs of large letters throughout this section; $c_t = \ln C_t$, etc.)

Rather than letting habit itself follow an AR(1), we let the "surplus consumption ratio" of consumption to habit follow an AR(1):

$$S_t = \frac{C_t - X_t}{C_t},$$

$$s_{t+1} = (1 - \phi)\bar{s} + \phi s_t + \lambda(s_t)(c_{t+1} - c_t - g). \tag{21.9}$$

Since s contains c and x, this equation also specifies how x responds to c, and it is locally the same as (21.7). We also allow consumption to affect habit differently in different states by specifying a square root type process rather than a simple AR(1),

$$\lambda(s_t) = \frac{1}{S}\sqrt{1 - 2(s_t - \bar{s})} - 1, \tag{21.10}$$

$$\bar{S} = \sigma \sqrt{\frac{\gamma}{1 - \phi}}. \tag{21.11}$$

The extra complication of (21.9) rather than (21.7) means consumption is always above habit, since $S = e^s > 0$. Other habit models in endowment economies can give consumption below habit which leads to infinite or imaginary marginal utility.

S_t becomes the single *state variable* in this economy. Time-varying expected returns, price/dividend ratios, etc. are all functions of this state variable.

Marginal utility is

$$u_c(C_t, X_t) = (C_t - X_t)^{-\gamma} = S_t^{-\gamma} C_t^{-\gamma}.$$

The model assumes an *external* habit—each individual's habit is determined by everyone else's consumption. This simplification, allows us to ignore terms by which current consumption affect future habits.

With marginal utility, we now have a discount factor:

$$M_{t+1} \equiv \delta \frac{u_c(C_{t+1}, X_{t+1})}{u_c(C_t, X_t)} = \delta \left(\frac{S_{t+1}}{S_t} \frac{C_{t+1}}{C_t} \right)^{-\gamma}.$$

Since we have a stochastic process for S and C, and each is lognormal, we can evaluate the conditional mean of the discount factor to evaluate the risk-free rate,

$$r_t^f = -\ln E_t(M_{t+1}) = -\ln(\delta) + \gamma g - \frac{1}{2}\gamma(1 - \phi). \tag{21.12}$$

We gave up on analytic solutions and evaluated the price/dividend ratio as a function of the state variable by iteration on a grid:

$$\frac{P_t}{C_t}(s_t) = E_t \left[M_{t+1} \frac{C_{t+1}}{C_t} \left(1 + \frac{P_{t+1}}{C_{t+1}}(s_{t+1}) \right) \right].$$

With price/dividend ratios, we can calculate returns, expected returns, etc.

Equity Premium and Predictability

We choose parameters, simulate 100,000 artificial data points, and report standard statistics and tests in artificial data. The parameters $g = 1.89$, $\sigma = 1.50$, $r^f = 0.94$ match their values in postwar data. The parameter $\phi = 0.87$ matches the autocorrelation of the price/dividend ratio and the choice $\gamma = 2.00$ matches the postwar Sharpe ratio. $\delta = 0.89$, $\overline{S} = 0.57$ follow from the model.

Table 21.1. *Means and standard deviations of simulated and historical data*

Statistic	Consumption claim	Dividend claim	Postwar data
$E(R - R)^*/\sigma(R - R)^*$	0.50		0.50
$E(r - r^f)$	6.64	6.52	6.69
$\sigma(r - r^f)$	15.2	20.0	15.7
$\exp[E(p - d)]$	18.3	18.7	24.7
$\sigma(p - d)$	0.27	0.29	0.26

The model is simulated at a monthly frequency; statistics are calculated from artificial time-averaged data at an annual frequency. Asterisks (*) denote statistics that model parameters were chosen to replicate. All returns are annual percentages.

Table 21.1 presents means and standard deviations predicted by the model. The model replicates the postwar Sharpe ratio, with a constant 0.94% risk-free rate and a reasonable subjective discount factor $\delta < 1$. Of course, we picked the parameters to do this, but given the equity premium discussion it is already an achievement that we are able to pick any parameters to hit these moments.

Some models can replicate the Sharpe ratio, but do not replicate the level of expected returns and return volatility. $E = 1\%$ and $\sigma = 2\%$ will give an 0.5 Sharpe ratio. This model predicts the right levels as well. The model also gets the level of the price/dividend ratio about right.

Table 21.2 shows how the artificial data match the predictability of returns from price/dividend ratios. The paper goes on, and shows how the model matches the volatility test result that almost all return variation is due to variation in expected excess returns, the "leverage effect" of higher volatility after a big price decline, and several related phenomena.

Table 21.2. *Long-horizon return regressions*

Horizon (Years)	Consumption claim		Postwar data	
	$10 \times$ coef.	R^2	$10 \times$ coef.	R^2
1	−2.0	0.13	−2.6	0.18
2	−3.7	0.23	−4.3	0.27
3	−5.1	0.32	−5.4	0.37
5	−7.5	0.46	−9.0	0.55
7	−9.4	0.55	−12.1	0.65

How Does It Work?

How does this model get around all the equity premium – risk-free rate difficulties described above, and explain predictability as well?

When a consumer has a habit, local curvature depends on how far consumption is above the habit, as well as the power γ,

$$\eta_t \equiv \frac{-C_t\,u_{cc}(C_t - X_t)}{u_c(C_t - X_t)} = \frac{\gamma}{S_t}.$$

As consumption falls toward habit, people become much less willing to tolerate further falls in consumption; they become very risk averse. Thus a low power coefficient γ can still mean a high, and time-varying curvature. Recall our fundamental equation for the Sharpe ratio,

$$\frac{E_t(r) - r_t^f}{\sigma_t(r)} = \eta_t \sigma_t(\Delta c)\mathrm{corr}_t(\Delta c, r).$$

High curvature η_t means that the model can explain the equity premium, and curvature η_t that varies over time as consumption rises in booms and falls toward habit in recessions means that the model can explain a time-varying and countercyclical (high in recessions, low in booms) Sharpe ratio, despite constant consumption volatility $\sigma_t(\Delta c)$ and correlation $\mathrm{corr}_t(\Delta c, r)$.

So far so good, but did we not just learn that raising curvature implies high and time-varying interest rates? This model gets around interest rate problems with *precautionary saving*. Suppose we are in a bad time, in which consumption is low relative to habit. People want to borrow against future, higher, consumption, and this force should drive up interest rates. (In fact, many habit models have very volatile interest rates.) However, people are also much more risk averse when consumption is low. This consideration induces them to *save* more, in order to build up assets against the event that tomorrow might be even worse. This "precautionary" desire to save drives down interest rates. Our $\lambda(s)$ specification makes these two forces exactly offset, leading to constant real rates.

The precautionary saving motive also makes the model more plausibly consistent with variation in consumption growth across time and countries. Adding (21.11) to (21.12), we can write

$$r^f = \rho + \gamma g - \frac{1}{2}\left(\frac{\gamma}{S}\right)^2 \sigma^2.$$

The *power* coefficient $\gamma = 2$ controls the relation between consumption growth and interest rates, while the *curvature* coefficient γ/S_t controls the risk premium. Thus this habit model allows high "risk aversion" with low "aversion to intertemporal substitution," and it *is* consistent with the consumption and interest rate data.

As advertised, this model explains the equity premium and predictability by fundamentally changing the story for why consumers are afraid of holding stocks. The k-period stochastic discount factor is

$$M_{t \to t+k} = \delta^k \left(\frac{S_{t+k}}{S_t} \frac{C_{t+k}}{C_t} \right)^{-\gamma}.$$

Covariances with S shocks now drive average returns as well as covariances with C shocks. $S = (C - X)/C$ is a recession indicator—it is low after several quarters of consumption declines and high in booms.

While $(C_{t+k}/C_t)^{-\gamma}$ and $(S_{t+k}/S_t)^{-\gamma}$ enter symmetrically in the formula, the volatility of $(C_{t+k}/C_t)^{-\gamma}$ with $\gamma = 2$ is so low that it accounts for essentially no risk premia. Therefore, it must be true, and it is, that variation in $(S_{t+k}/S_t)^{-\gamma}$ is much larger, and accounts for nearly all risk premia. In the Merton language of (21.5) and (21.6), variation across assets in expected returns is driven by variation across assets in covariances with *recessions* far more than by variation across assets in covariances with consumption growth.

At short horizons, shocks to S_{t+1} and C_{t+1} move together, so the distinction between a recession state variable and consumption risk is minor; one can regard S as an amplification mechanism for consumption risks in marginal utility. $dS/\partial C \approx 50$, so this amplification generates the required volatility of the discount factor.

At long horizons, however, S_{t+k} becomes less and less conditionally correlated with C_{t+k}. S_{t+k} depends on C_{t+k} relative to its recent past, but the overall level of consumption may be high or low. Therefore, *investors fear stocks because they do badly in occasional serious recessions*, times of recent belt-tightening. These risks are at the long run *unrelated* to the risks of long-run average consumption growth.

As another way to digest how this model works, we can substitute in the s process from (21.9) and write the marginal rate of substitution as

$$M_{t+1} = \delta \left(\frac{S_{t+1}}{S_t} \frac{C_{t+1}}{C_t} \right)^{-\gamma},$$

$$\ln M_{t+1} = \ln \delta - \gamma \left(s_{t+1} - s_t \right) - \gamma (c_{t+1} - c_t)$$
$$= \left\{ \ln \delta - \gamma (1 - \phi) \bar{s} \right\} + \left\{ \gamma (1 - \phi) s_t + \gamma g \lambda (s_t) \right\}$$
$$- \gamma \left[\lambda(s_t) + 1 \right] (c_{t+1} - c_t)$$
$$= a + b(s_t) + d(s_t)(c_{t+1} - c_t).$$

Up to the question of logs versus levels, this is a "scaled factor model" of the form we studied in Chapter 8. It still is a consumption-based model, but the sensitivity of the discount factor to consumption changes over time.

The long-run equity premium is even more of a puzzle. Most recession state variables, such as GDP growth, labor, and instruments for time-varying expected returns ("shifts in the investment opportunity set"), are stationary. Hence, the standard deviation of their growth rates eventually stops growing with horizon. At a long enough horizon, the standard deviation of the discount factor is dominated by the standard deviation of the consumption growth term, and we return to the equity premium puzzle at a long enough run.

Since this model produces predictability of the right sign, it produces a long-run equity premium puzzle. How it manages this feat with a stationary state variable S_t is subtle (and we did not notice it until the penultimate draft!). The answer is that while S_t is stationary, $S_t^{-\gamma}$ is not. S_t has a fat tail approaching zero so the conditional variance of $S_{t+k}^{-\gamma}$ grows without bound.

While the distinction between stationary S and nonstationary $S^{-\gamma}$ seems initially minor, it is in fact central. *Any* model that wishes to explain the equity premium at long and short runs by means of an additional, stationary state variable must find some similar transformation so that the volatility of the stochastic discount factor remains high at long horizons.

This model does have high risk aversion. The utility curvature and value function curvature are both high. Many authors require that a "solution" of the equity premium puzzle display low risk aversion. This is a laudable goal, and no current model has attained it. No current model generates the equity premium with a low and relatively constant interest rate, low risk aversion, and the right pattern of predictability—high prices forecast low returns, not high returns, and consumption is roughly a random walk. Constantinides (1990) and Boldrin, Christiano, and Fisher (1997) are habit models with a large equity premium and low risk aversion, but they do not get the pattern of predictability right. Boldrin, Christiano, and Fisher have highly variable interest rates to keep consumption from being predictable. Constantinides (1990) has a constant interest rate, but consumption growth that is serially correlated, so consumption rises to meet i.i.d. wealth growth. The long-run equity premium is solved with counterfactually high long-run consumption volatility.

Heterogeneous Agents and Idiosyncratic Risks

A long, increasing, and important literature in the equity premium attacks the problem with relatively standard preferences, but instead adds uninsured idiosyncratic risk. As with the preference literature, this literature is interesting beyond the equity premium. We are learning a lot about who holds stocks and why, what risks they face. We are challenged to think of new assets and creative ways of using existing assets to share risks better.

Constantinides and Duffie (1996) provide a very clever and simple model in which idiosyncratic risk can be tailored to generate *any* pattern of aggregate consumption and asset prices. It can generate the equity premium, predictability, relatively constant interest rates, smooth and unpredictable aggregate consumption growth, and so forth. Furthermore, it requires *no* transactions costs, borrowing constraints, or other frictions, and the individual consumers can have *any* nonzero value of risk aversion. Of course, we still have to evaluate whether the idiosyncratic risk process we construct to explain asset pricing phenomena are reasonable and consistent with microeconomic data.

A Simple Version of the Model

I start with a very simplified version of the Constantinides–Duffie model. Each consumer i has power utility,

$$U = E \sum_t e^{-\delta t} C_{it}^{1-\gamma}.$$

Individual consumption growth C_{it+1} is determined by an independent, idiosyncratic normal $(0,1)$ shock η_{it},

$$\ln \left(\frac{C_{it+1}}{C_{i,t}} \right) = \eta_{it+1} y_{t+1} - \frac{1}{2} y_{t+1}^2, \tag{21.13}$$

where y_{t+1} is, by construction since it multiplies the shock η_{it}, the cross-sectional standard deviation of consumption growth. y_{t+1} is dated $t+1$ since it is the cross-sectional standard deviation *given* aggregates at $t+1$. The aggregates are determined first, and then the shocks η_{it+1} are handed out.

Now, y_{t+1} is specified so that people suffer a *high* cross-sectional variance of consumption growth on dates of a *low* market return R_{t+1},

$$y_{t+1} = \sigma \left[\ln \left(\frac{C_{it+1}}{C_{it}} \right) \middle| R_{t+1} \right] = \sqrt{\frac{2}{\gamma(\gamma+1)}} \sqrt{\delta - \ln R_{t+1}}. \tag{21.14}$$

Given this structure, the individual is exactly happy to consume $\{C_{it}\}$ without further trading in the stock. (We can call C_{it} income I_{it}, and prove the optimal decision rule is to consume income $C_{it} = I_{it}$.) His first-order condition for an optimal consumption-portfolio decision

$$1 = E_t \left[e^{-\delta} \left(\frac{C_{it+1}}{C_{it}} \right)^{-\gamma} R_{t+1} \right]$$

holds, exactly.

To prove this assertion, just substitute in for C_{it+1}/C_{it} and take the expectation:

$$1 = E_t \exp\left[-\delta - \gamma\eta_{it+1}y_{t+1} + \frac{1}{2}\gamma y_{t+1}^2 + \ln R_{t+1}\right].$$

Since η is independent of everything else, we can use $E[f(\eta y)] = E[E(f(\eta y|y)]$. Now, with η normal $(0,1)$,

$$E\left(\exp\left[-\gamma\eta_{it+1}y_{t+1}\right] \mid y_{t+1}\right) = \exp\left[\frac{1}{2}\gamma^2 y_{t+1}^2\right].$$

Therefore, we have

$$1 = E_t \exp\left[-\delta + \frac{1}{2}\gamma^2 y_{t+1}^2 + \frac{1}{2}\gamma y_{t+1}^2 + \ln R_{t+1}\right].$$

Substituting in from (21.14),

$$1 = E_t \exp\left[-\delta + \frac{1}{2}\gamma(\gamma+1)\left(\frac{2}{\gamma(\gamma+1)}\right)(\delta - \ln R_{t+1}) + \ln R_{t+1}\right]$$

$$= 1!$$

The General Model

In the general model, Constantinides and Duffie define

$$y_{t+1} = \sqrt{\frac{2}{\gamma(\gamma+1)}}\sqrt{\ln m_{t+1} + \delta + \gamma\ln\frac{C_{t+1}}{C_t}}, \qquad (21.15)$$

where C_t denotes aggregate consumption and m_t is a strictly positive discount factor that prices all assets under consideration,

$$p_t = E_t[m_{t+1}x_{t+1}] \qquad \text{for all } x_{t+1} \in \underline{X}. \qquad (21.16)$$

By starting with a discount factor that can price a large collection of assets, where I used the discount factor R_{t+1}^{-1} to price the single return R_{t+1} in (21.14), idiosyncratic risk can be constructed to price exactly a large collection of assets. We can exactly match the Sharpe ratio, return forecastability, and other features of the data.

Then, they let

$$\ln\left(\frac{v_{it+1}}{v_{it}}\right) = \eta_{it+1}y_{t+1} - \frac{1}{2}y_{t+1}^2,$$

$$C_{it+1} = v_{it+1}C_{t+1}.$$

y_{t+1} is still the conditional standard deviation of consumption growth, given aggregates—returns and aggregate consumption. This variation allows uncertainty in aggregate consumption. We can tailor the idiosyncratic risk to and consumption-interest rate facts as well.

Following exactly the same argument as before, we can now show that

$$1 = E_t\left[e^{-\delta}\left(\frac{C_{it+1}}{C_{it}}\right)^{-\gamma}R_{t+1}\right]$$

for all the assets priced by m.

A Technical Assumption

Astute readers will notice the possibility that the square root term in (21.14) and (21.15) might be negative. Constantinides and Duffie rule out this possibility by assuming that the discount factor m satisfies

$$\ln m_{t+1} \geq \delta + \gamma \ln \frac{C_{t+1}}{C_t} \qquad (21.17)$$

in every state of nature, so that the square root term is positive.

We can sometimes construct such discount factors by picking parameters a, b in $m_{t+1} = \max[a+b'x_{t+1}, e^{\delta}(C_{t+1}/C_t)^{\gamma}]$ to satisfy (21.16). However, neither this construction nor a discount factor satisfying (21.17) is guaranteed to exist for any set of assets. The restriction (21.17) is a tighter form of the familiar restriction that $m_{t+1} \geq 0$ that is equivalent to the absence of arbitrage in the assets under consideration. Ledoit and Bernardo (1997) show that the restriction $m > a$ is equivalent to restrictions on the maximum gain/loss ratio available from the set of assets under consideration. Thus, the theorem really does not apply to *any* set of arbitrage-free payoffs.

The example $m = 1/R$ is a positive discount factor that prices a single asset return $1 = E(R^{-1}R)$, but does not necessarily satisfy restriction (21.17). For high R, we can have very negative $\ln 1/R$. This example only works if the distribution of R is limited to $R \leq e^{\delta}$.

How the Model Works

As the Campbell–Cochrane model is blatantly (and proudly) reverse-engineered to surmount (and here, to illustrate) the known pitfalls of representative consumer models, the Constantinides–Duffie model is reverse-engineered to surmount the known pitfalls of idiosyncratic risk models.

Idiosyncratic risk stories face two severe challenges, as explained in Section 21.1. First, the basic pricing equation applies to each individual. If we are to have low risk aversion and power utility, the required huge volatility of consumption is implausible for any individual. Second, if you add idiosyncratic risk uncorrelated with asset returns, it has no effect on pricing implications. Constantinides and Duffie's central contribution is very cleverly to solve the second problem.

In idiosyncratic risk models, we cannot specify individual consumption directly as we do in representative agent endowment economies, and go straight to finding prices. The endowment economy structure says that *aggregate* consumption is fixed, and prices have to adjust so that consumers are happy consuming the given aggregate consumption stream. However, individuals can always trade consumption with each other. The whole point of assets is that one individual can sell another some consumption, in exchange for the promise of some consumption in return in the next period. We have to give individuals idiosyncratic *income* shocks, and then either check that they do not want to trade away the idiosyncratic shock, or find the equilibrium consumption after they do so.

Early idiosyncratic risk papers found quickly how clever the consumers could be in getting rid of the idiosyncratic risks by trading the existing set of assets. Telmer (1993) and Lucas (1994) found that if you give people transitory but uninsured income shocks, they respond by borrowing and lending or by building up a stock of savings. As in the classic permanent income model, consumption then only responds by the interest rate times the change in permanent income, and at low enough interest rates, not at all. "Self-insurance through storage" removes the extra income volatility and we are back to smooth individual consumption and an equity premium puzzle.

Constantinides and Duffie get around this problem by making the idiosyncratic shocks *permanent*. The normal η_{it} shocks determine consumption *growth*. In an evaluation in microeconomic data, this makes us look for sources of permanent shocks.

This, at a deeper level, is why idiosyncratic consumption shocks have to be uncorrelated with the market. We can give individuals idiosyncratic income shocks that are correlated with the market. Say, agent A gets more income when the market is high, and agent B gets more income when it is low. But then A will short the market, B will go long, and they will trade away any component of the shock that is correlated with the returns on available assets. I argued in Section 21.1 that this effect made idiosyncratic shocks unlikely candidates to explain the equity premium puzzle. Shocks uncorrelated with asset returns have no effect on asset pricing, and shocks correlated with asset returns are quickly traded away.

The only way out is to exploit the nonlinearity of marginal utility. We can give people *income* shocks that are uncorrelated with returns, so they cannot be traded away. Then we have a nonlinear marginal utility function turn these shocks into *marginal utility* shocks that are correlated with asset returns, and hence can affect pricing implications. This is why

Constantinides and Duffie specify that the *variance* of idiosyncratic risk rises when the market declines. If marginal utility were linear, an increase in variance would have no effect on the average level of marginal utility. Therefore, Constantinides and Duffie specify power utility, and the interaction of nonlinear marginal utility and changing conditional variance produces an equity premium.

As a simple calculation that shows the basic idea, start with individuals i with power utility so

$$0 = E\left[\left(\frac{C_{t+1}^i}{C_t^i}\right)^{-\gamma} R_{t+1}^e\right].$$

Now aggregate across people by summing over i, with $E_N = \frac{1}{N}\sum_{i=1}^N$,

$$0 = E\left[E_N\left(\left(\frac{C_{t+1}^i}{C_t^i}\right)^{-\gamma}\right)R_{t+1}^e\right].$$

If the cross-sectional variation of consumption growth is lognormally distributed,

$$0 = E\left[\left(e^{-\gamma E_N \Delta c_{t+1}^i + \frac{\gamma^2}{2}\sigma_N^2 \Delta c_{t+1}^i}\right)R_{t+1}^e\right].$$

As you see, the economy displays more risk aversion than would a "representative agent" with aggregate consumption $\Delta c_{t+1}^a = E_N \Delta c_{it+1}$. That risk aversion can also vary over time if σ_N varies over time, and this variation can generate risk premia.

Microeconomic Evaluation and Risk Aversion

Like the Campbell–Cochrane model, this could be either a new view of stock market (and macroeconomic) risk, or just a clever existence proof for a heretofore troubling class of models. The first question is whether the microeconomic picture painted by this model is correct, or even plausible. Is idiosyncratic risk large enough? Does idiosyncratic risk really rise when the market falls, and enough to account for the equity premium? Are there enough permanent idiosyncratic shocks? Do people really shy away from stocks because stock returns are low at times of high labor market risk?

This model does not change the first puzzle. To get power utility consumers to shun stocks, they still must have tremendously volatile consumption growth or high risk aversion. The point of this model is to show how consumers can get stuck with high consumption volatility in equilibrium, already a difficult task.

More seriously than volatility itself, consumption growth variance also represents the amount by which the distribution of individual consumption and income spreads out over time, since the shocks must be permanent and independent across people. The 50% or larger consumption growth volatility that we require to reconcile the Sharpe ratio with risk aversion of one means that the distribution of consumption (and income) must also spread out by 50% per year. The distribution of consumption does spread out, but not this much.

For example, Deaton and Paxson (1994) report that the cross-sectional variance of log consumption within an age cohort rises from about 0.2 at age 20 to 0.6 at age 60. This estimate means that the cross-sectional standard deviation of consumption rises from $\sqrt{0.2} = .45$ or 45% at age 20 to $\sqrt{0.6} = .77$ or 77% at age 60. (77% means that an individual one standard deviation better off than the mean consumes 77% more than the mean consumer.) We are back to about 1% per year.

Finally, and most crucially, the cross-sectional uncertainty about individual income must not only be large, it must be higher when the market is lower. This risk factor is after all the central element of Constantinides and Duffie's explanation for the market premium. Figure 21.1 shows how the cross-sectional standard deviation of consumption growth varies with the market return and risk aversion in my simple version of Constantinides and Duffie's model. If we insist on low ($\gamma = 1$ to 2) risk aversion, the cross-sectional standard deviation of consumption growth must be extremely sensitive to the level of the market return. Looking at the $\gamma = 2$ line, for example, is it plausible that a year with 5% market return would show a 10% cross-sectional variation in consumption growth, while a mild 5% decline in the market is associated with a 25% cross-sectional variation?

All of these empirical problems are avoided if we allow high risk aversion rather than a large risk to drive the equity premium. The $\gamma = 25$ line in Figure 21.1 looks possible; a $\gamma = 50$ line would look even better. With high risk aversion, we do not need to specify highly volatile individual consumption growth, spreading out of the income distribution, or dramatic sensitivity of the cross-sectional variance to the market return.

As in any model, a high equity premium must come from a large *risk*, or from large *risk aversion*. Labor market risk correlated with the stock market does not seem large enough to account for the equity premium without high risk aversion.

The larger set of asset pricing facts has not yet been studied in this model. It is clearly able to generate return predictability, but that requires a pattern of variation in idiosyncratic risk that remains to be characterized and evaluated. It can generate cross-sectional patterns such as value premia if value stocks decline at times of higher cross-sectional volatility; that too remains to be studied.

Summary

In the end, the Constantinides–Duffie model and the Campbell–Cochrane model are quite similar in spirit. First, both models make a similar, fundamental change in the description of stock market risk. Consumers do not

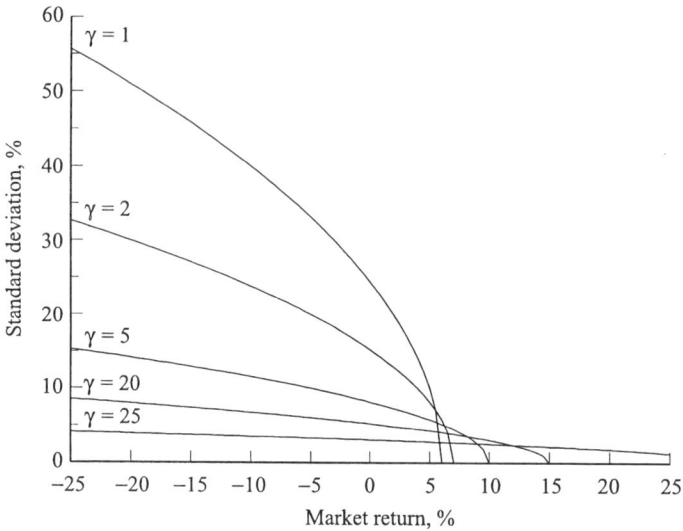

Figure 21.1. *Cross-sectional standard deviation of individual consumption growth as a function of the market return in the simple version of the Constantinides-Duffie model. The plot is the variable* $y_t = \sqrt{\frac{2}{\gamma(\gamma+1)}} \sqrt{\ln \frac{1}{R_t} + \delta + \gamma \ln \frac{C_t}{C_{t-1}}}$. *Parameter values are* $\rho = 0.05$, $\ln C_t/C_{t-1} = 0.01$.

fear much the loss of wealth of a bad market return per se. They fear that loss of wealth because it tends to come in recessions, in one case defined as times of heightened idiosyncratic labor market risk, and in the other case defined as a fall of consumption relative to its recent past. This recession state variable or risk factor drives most variation in expected returns.

Second, both models require high risk aversion. While Constantinides and Duffie's proof shows that one can dream up a labor income process to rationalize the equity premium for any risk aversion coefficient, we see that even vaguely plausible characterizations of actual labor income uncertainty require high risk aversion to explain the historical equity premium.

Third, both models provide long-sought demonstrations that it is possible to rationalize the equity premium in their respective class of models. This existence proof is particularly stunning in Constantinides and Duffie's case. Many authors (myself included) had come to the conclusion that the effort to generate an equity premium from idiosyncratic risk was hopeless because any idiosyncratic risk that would affect asset prices would be traded away.

21.3 Bibliography

Shiller (1982) made the first calculation that showed either a large risk aversion coefficient or counterfactually large consumption variability was required to explain means and variances of asset returns. Mehra and Prescott (1985) labeled this fact the "equity premium puzzle." However, they described these puzzles in the context of a two-state Markov model for consumption growth, identifying a stock as a claim to consumption and a risk-free bond. Weil (1989) emphasized the interaction between equity premium and risk-free rate puzzles. Hansen and Jagannathan (1991) sparked the kind of calculations I report here in a simplified manner. Cochrane and Hansen (1992) derived many of the extra discount factor moment restrictions I surveyed here, calculating bounds in each case. Luttmer (1996, 1999) tackled the important extension to transactions costs.

Kocherlakota (1996) is a nice summary of equity premium facts and models. Much of the material in this chapter is adapted from a survey in Cochrane (1997). Campbell (1999) and (2000) are two excellent recent surveys. Ferson (1995) is a nice survey of consumption-based model variations as well as some of the beta pricing models discussed in the last chapter.

The Campbell–Cochrane model I presented here is a tip of an iceberg of habit research, including prominent contributions by Constantinides (1990), Ferson and Constantinides (1991), Heaton (1995), and Abel (1990).

Models can be *nonseparable across goods* as well. Leisure is the most natural extra variable to add to a utility function. It is not clear a priori whether more leisure enhances the marginal utility of consumption (why bother buying a boat if you are at the office all day and cannot use it) or vice versa (if you have to work all day, it is more important to come home to a really nice big TV). However, we can let the data speak on this matter. Explicit versions of this approach have not been very successful to date (Eichenbaum, Hansen, and Singleton [1989]). On the other hand, recent research has found that adding labor income as an extra ad hoc "factor" can be useful in explaining the cross section of average stock returns, especially if it is scaled by a conditioning variable (Jagannathan and Wang [1996], Reyfman [1997], Lettau and Ludvigson [2000]).

The non-*state* separable utility functions following Epstein and Zin (1989) are a major omission of this presentation. The expectation E in the standard utility function sums over states of nature, e.g.,

$$U = \text{prob(rain)} \times u(C \text{ if it rains}) + \text{prob(shine)} \times u(C \text{ if it shines}).$$

"Separability" means one adds across states, so the marginal utility of consumption in one state is unaffected by what happens in another state. But perhaps the marginal utility of a little more consumption in the sunny state of the world is affected by the level of consumption in the rainy state of the world. Epstein and Zin (1989), and Hansen, Sargent, and Tallarini (1997) propose recursive utility functions of the form

$$U_t = C_t^{1-\gamma} + \beta f[E_t f^{-1}(U_{t+1})].$$

If $f(x) = x$, this expression reduces to power utility. These utility functions are not state separable. As with habits, these utility functions distinguish risk aversion from intertemporal substitution—one coefficient can be set to capture the consumption-interest rate facts, and a completely separate coefficient can be set to capture the equity premium. So far, this style of model as in Epstein and Zin (1989), Weil (1989), Kandel and Stambaugh (1991), and Campbell (1996) does not generate time-varying risk aversion, but that modification should not be too difficult, and could lead to a model that works very much like the habit model I surveyed here.

Habit persistence is the opposite of durability. If you buy a durable good yesterday, that lowers your marginal utility of an additional purchase today, while buying a habit-forming good raises your marginal utility of an additional purchase today. Thus the durability of goods should introduce a non–time-separability of the form $u(c_t + \theta x_t)$, $x_t = f(c_{t-1}, c_{t-2}, \dots)$ rather than the habit persistence form $u(c_t - \theta x_t)$. Since goods are durable, and we have a lot of data on durables purchases, it would be good to include both durability and habit persistence in our models. (In fact, even "nondurables" data contain items like clothing; the truly nondurable purchases are such a small fraction of total consumption that we rely on very little data.)

One must be careful with the time horizon in such a specification. At a sufficiently small time horizon, all goods are durable. A pizza eaten at noon lowers marginal utility of more pizza at 12:05. Thus, our common continuous-time, time-separable assumption really cannot be taken literally. Hindy and Huang (1992) argue that consumption should be "locally substitutable" in continuous-time models. Heaton (1993) found that at monthly horizons, consumption growth displays the negative autocorrelation suggestive of durability with constant interest rates, while at longer horizons consumption is nearly unforecastable after accounting for time aggregation.

There is also a production first-order condition that must be solved, relating asset prices to marginal rates of transformation. The standard here is the q theory of investment, which is based on an adjustment cost. If the stock market is really high, you issue stock and make new investments. The trouble with this view is that $f'(K)$ declines very slowly, so the observed price volatility implies huge investment volatility. The q theory adds adjustment costs to damp the investment volatility. The q theory has had as much trouble fitting the data as the consumption-based model.

Cochrane (1991d) reports one success when you transform the data to returns—high stock *returns* are associated with high investment *growth*. The more recent investment literature has focused on specifying the adjustment cost problem with asymmetries and irreversibilities, for example, Abel and Eberly (1996) but has not yet been applied to asset pricing puzzles.

There is an important literature that puts new utility functions together with production functions, to construct complete explicit economic models that replicate the asset pricing facts. Such efforts should also at least preserve if not enhance our ability to understand the broad range of dynamic microeconomic, macroeconomic, international, and growth facts that the standard models were constructed around. Jermann (1998) tried putting habit-persistence consumers in a model with a standard technology $Y = \theta f(K, L)$ from real business cycle models. The easy opportunities for intertemporal transformation provided by that technology meant that the consumers used it to smooth consumption dramatically, destroying the prediction of a high equity premium. To generate the equity premium, Jermann added an adjustment cost technology, as the production-side literature had found necessary. This modification resulted in a high equity premium, but also large variation in risk-free rates.

Boldrin, Christiano, and Fisher (1997) also added habit-persistence preferences to real business cycle models with frictions in the allocation of resources to two sectors. They generate about $1/2$ the historical Sharpe ratio. They find some quantity dynamics are improved over the standard model. However, they still predict highly volatile interest rates and persistent consumption growth.

To avoid the implications of highly volatile interest rates, I suspect we will need representations of technology that allow easy transformation across time but not across states of nature, analogous to the need for easy intertemporal substitution but high risk aversion in preferences. Alternatively, the Campbell–Cochrane model above already produces the equity premium with constant interest rates, which can be interpreted as a linear production function $f(K)$. Models with this kind of precautionary savings motive may not be as severely affected by the presence of inter *temporal* transformation opportunities in production.

Tallarini (1999) uses non–state-separable preferences similar to those of Epstein and Zin in a general equilibrium model with production. He shows a beautiful observational equivalence result: A model with standard preferences and a model with non–state-separable preferences can predict the same path of *quantity* variables (output, investment, consumption, etc.) but differ dramatically on *asset prices*. This result offers one explanation of how the real business cycle and growth literature could go on for 25 years examining quantity data in detail and miss all the modifications to preferences that we seem to need to explain asset pricing data. It also means that asset price information is crucial to identifying preferences and calculating welfare costs of policy experiments. Finally, it offers hope that adding the deep modifications necessary to explain asset pricing phenomena will not demolish the success of standard models at describing the movements of quantities.

The Constantinides and Duffie model has roots in a calculation by Mankiw (1986) that idiosyncratic risk could make the representative consumer seem more risk averse than the individuals. Work on evaluating the mechanisms in this model in microeconomic data is starting. Heaton and Lucas (1996) calibrate idiosyncratic risk from the PSID, but their model explains at best 1/2 of the sample average stock return, and less still if they allow a net supply of bonds with which people can smooth transitory shocks. More direct tests of these features in microeconomic consumption data are underway, for example Brav, Constantinides and Geczy (1999), Storesletten, Telmer, and Yaron (1999) and Vissing-Jorgenson (1999).

Kandel and Stambaugh (1986) present a model in which a small amount of time-varying consumption volatility and a high risk aversion coefficient generate the large time-varying discount factor volatility we need to generate returns predictability.

Aiyagari and Gertler (1991), though aimed at the point that the equity premium might be explained by a "too low" riskless rate, nonetheless was an important paper in specifying and solving models with uninsured individual risks and transactions costs to keep people from trading them away.

Problems—Chapter 21

1. Suppose habit accumulation is linear, and there is a constant risk-free rate or linear technology equal to the discount rate, $R^f = 1/\delta$. The consumer's problem is then

$$\max \sum_{t=0}^{\infty} \delta^t \frac{(C_t - X_t)^{1-\gamma}}{1-\gamma} \quad s.t. \sum_t \delta^t C_t = \sum_t \delta^t e_t + W_0, \quad X_t = \theta \sum_{j=1}^{\infty} \phi^j C_{t-j},$$

where e_t is a stochastic endowment. In an internal habit specification, the consumer considers all the effects that current consumption has on future utility through X_{t+j}. In an external habit specification, the consumer ignores such terms. Show that the two specifications give *identical* asset pricing predictions in this simple model, by showing that internal habit marginal utility is proportional to external habit marginal utility, state by state.

2. Suppose a consumer has quadratic utility with a constant interest rate equal to the subjective discount rate, but a habit or durable consumption good, so that utility is

$$u(c_t - \theta c_{t-1}) = -\frac{1}{2}(c^* - c_t + \theta c_{t-1}).$$

Show that external habit persistence $\theta > 0$ implies positive serial correlation in consumption changes. Show that the same solution holds for internal habits, or durability. Show that durability leads to negative serial correlation in consumption changes.

3. Many models predict too much variation in the conditional mean discount factor, or too much interest rate variation. This problem guides you through a simple example. Introduce a simple form of external habit formation,

$$u = (C_t - \theta C_{t-1})^{1-\gamma},$$

and suppose consumption growth C_{t+1}/C_t is i.i.d. Show that interest rates still vary despite i.i.d. consumption growth.

4. We showed that if m satisfies the Hansen–Jagannathan bound, then $\mathrm{proj}(m|X)$ should also do so. Hansen and Jagannathan also compute bounds with positivity, solutions to

$$\min \sigma(m) \ s.t. \ p = E(mx), \qquad m \geq 0, \quad E(m) = \mu.$$

Does $\mathrm{proj}(m|X)$ also lie in the same bound?

5. One most often compares consumption-based models to Hansen–Jagannathan bounds. Can you compare the CAPM discount factor $m = a - bR^{em}$ to the bound? To the bound with positivity?

PART V
Appendix

Appendix
Continuous Time

THIS APPENDIX is a brief introduction to the mechanics of continuous-time stochastic processes; i.e., how to use dz and dt. I presume the reader is familiar with discrete-time ARMA models, i.e., models of the sort $x_t = \rho x_{t-1} + \varepsilon_t$. I draw analogies of continuous-time constructs to those models.

The formal mathematics of continuous-time processes are a bit imposing. For example, the basic random walk z_t is not time-differentiable, so one needs to rethink the definition of an integral and differential to write obvious things like $z_t = \int_{s=0}^{t} dz_s$. Also, since z_t is a random variable, one has to specify not only the usual measure-theoretic foundations of random variables, but their evolution over a continuous-time index. However, with a few basic, intuitive rules like $dz^2 = dt$, you can *use* continuous-time processes quite quickly, and that is the aim of this chapter.

A.1 Brownian Motion

z_t, dz_t are defined by $z_{t+\Delta} - z_t \sim \mathcal{N}(0, \Delta)$.

Diffusion models are a standard way to represent random variables in continuous time. The ideas are analogous to discrete-time stochastic processes. We start with a simple shock series, ε_t in discrete time and dz_t in continuous time. Then we build up more complex models by building on this foundation.

The basic building block is a *Brownian motion*, which is the natural generalization of a random walk in discrete time. For a random walk

$$z_t - z_{t-1} = \varepsilon_t,$$

the variance scales with time; $\text{var}(z_{t+2} - z_t) = 2\,\text{var}(z_{t+1} - z_t)$. Thus, define a Brownian motion as a process z_t for which

$$z_{t+\Delta} - z_t \sim \mathcal{N}(0, \Delta). \tag{A.1}$$

We have added the normal distribution to the usual definition of a random walk. As $E(\varepsilon_t \varepsilon_{t-1}) = 0$ in discrete time, increments to z for nonoverlapping intervals are also independent. I use the notation z_t to denote z as a function of time, in conformity with discrete-time formulas; many people prefer to use the standard representation of a function $z(t)$.

It is natural to want to look at very small time intervals. We use the notation dz_t to represent $z_{t+\Delta} - z_t$ for arbitrarily small time intervals Δ, and we sometimes drop the subscript when it is obvious we are talking about time t. Conversely, the level of z_t is the sum of its small differences, so we can write the *stochastic integral*

$$z_t - z_0 = \int_{s=0}^{t} dz_s.$$

The variance of a random walk scales with time, so the standard deviation scales with the square root of time. The standard deviation is the "typical size" of a movement in a normally distributed random variable, so the "typical size" of $z_{t+\Delta} - z_t$ in time interval Δ is $\sqrt{\Delta}$. This fact means that $(z_{t+\Delta} - z_t)/\Delta$ has typical size $1/\sqrt{\Delta}$, so though the sample path of z_t *is continuous, z_t is not differentiable*.

For this reason, it is important to be a little careful with notation. dz, dz_t, or $dz(t)$ mean $z_{t+\Delta} - z_t$ for arbitrarily small Δ. We are used to thinking about dz as the derivative of a function, but since a Brownian motion is not a differentiable function of time, $dz = (dz(t)/dt)\,dt$ makes no sense.

From (A.1), it is clear that

$$E_t(dz_t) = 0.$$

Again, the notation is initially confusing—how can you take an expectation at t of a random variable dated t? Keep in mind, however, that $dz_t = z_{t+\Delta} - z_t$ is the forward difference. The variance is the same as the second moment, so we write it as

$$E_t\left(dz_t^2\right) = dt.$$

It turns out that not only is the *variance* of dz_t equal to dt, but

$$dz_t^2 = dt$$

for every sample path of z_t. z^2 is a differentiable function of time, though z itself is not. We can see this with the same sort of argument I used for z_t itself. If $x \sim \mathcal{N}(0, \sigma^2)$, then var $(x^2) = 2\sigma^4$. Thus,

$$\text{var}[(z_{t+\Delta} - z_t)^2] = 2\Delta^4.$$

The mean of $(z_{t+\Delta} - z_t)^2$ is Δ, while the standard deviation of $(z_{t+\Delta} - z_t)^2$ is $\sqrt{2}\Delta^2$. As Δ shrinks, the ratio of standard deviation to mean shrinks to zero; i.e., the series becomes deterministic.

A.2 Diffusion Model

I form more complicated time-series processes by adding drift and diffusion terms,

$$dx_t = \mu(\cdot)\, dt + \sigma(\cdot)\, dz_t.$$

I introduce some common examples,

$$\text{Random walk with drift: } dx_t = \mu\, dt + \sigma\, dz_t,$$

$$\text{AR(1): } dx_t = -\phi(x - \mu)\, dt + \sigma\, dz_t,$$

$$\text{Square root process: } dx_t = -\phi(x - \mu)\, dt + \sigma\sqrt{x_t}\, dz_t,$$

$$\text{Price process: } \frac{dp_t}{p_t} = \mu\, dt + \sigma\, dz_t.$$

You can simulate a diffusion process by approximating it for a small time interval,

$$x_{t+\Delta} - x_t = \mu(\cdot)\Delta t + \sigma(\cdot)\sqrt{\Delta t}\, \varepsilon_{t+\Delta}, \qquad \varepsilon_{t+\Delta} \sim \mathcal{N}(0, 1).$$

As we add up serially uncorrelated shocks ε_t to form discrete-time ARMA models, we build on the shocks dz_t to form *diffusion models*. I proceed by example, introducing some popular examples in turn.

Random walk with drift. In discrete time, we model a random walk with drift as

$$x_t = \mu + x_{t-1} + \varepsilon_t.$$

The obvious continuous-time analogue is

$$dx_t = \mu\, dt + \sigma\, dz_t.$$

Integrating both sides from 0 to t, we can find the implications of this process for discrete horizons,

$$x_t = x_0 + \mu t + \sigma(z_t - z_0)$$

or

$$x_t = x_0 + \mu t + \varepsilon_t, \qquad \varepsilon_t \sim \mathcal{N}(0, \sigma^2 t).$$

This is a random walk with drift.

AR(1). The simplest discrete-time process is an AR(1),

$$x_t = (1 - \rho)\mu + \rho x_{t-1} + \varepsilon_t$$

or

$$x_t - x_{t-1} = -(1 - \rho)(x_{t-1} - \mu) + \varepsilon_t.$$

The continuous-time analogue is

$$dx_t = -\phi(x_t - \mu)\, dt + \sigma\, dz_t.$$

This is known as the *Ohrnstein–Uhlenbeck* process. The mean or drift is

$$E_t(dx_t) = -\phi(x_t - \mu)\, dt.$$

This force pulls x back to its steady-state value μ, but the shocks $\sigma\, dz_t$ move it around.

Square root process. Like its discrete-time counterpart, the continuous-time AR(1) ranges over the whole real numbers. It would be nice to have a process that was always positive, so it could capture a price or an interest rate. An extension of the continuous-time AR(1) is a workhorse of such applications,

$$dx_t = -\phi(x_t - \mu)\, dt + \sigma\sqrt{x_t}\, dz_t.$$

Now, volatility also varies over time,

$$E_t(dx_t^2) = \sigma^2 x_t\, dt;$$

as x approaches zero, the volatility declines. At $x = 0$, the volatility is entirely turned off, so x drifts up towards μ.

This is a nice example because it is decidedly *nonlinear*. Its discrete-time analogue

$$x_t = (1 - \rho)\mu + \rho x_{t-1} + \sqrt{x_t}\varepsilon_t$$

is not a standard ARMA model, so standard linear time-series tools would fail us. We could not, for example, give a pretty equation for the distribution of x_{t+s} for finite s. It turns out that we can do this in continuous time. Thus, one advantage of continuous-time formulations is that they give rise to a toolkit of interesting nonlinear time-series models for which we have closed-form solutions.

Price processes. A modification of the random walk with drift is the most common model for prices. We want the *return* or *proportional* increase in price to be uncorrelated over time. The most natural way to do this is to specify

$$dp_t = p_t \mu \, dt + p_t \sigma \, dz_t,$$

or more simply,

$$\frac{dp_t}{p_t} = \mu \, dt + \sigma \, dz_t.$$

Diffusion models more generally. A general picture should emerge. We form more complex models of stochastic time series by changing the local mean and variance of the underlying Brownian motion:

$$dx_t = \mu(x_t) \, dt + \sigma(x_t) \, dz_t.$$

More generally, we can allow the drift μ and diffusion to be a function of other variables and of time explicitly. We often write

$$dx_t = \mu(\cdot) \, dt + \sigma(\cdot) \, dz_t$$

to remind us of such possible dependence. There is nothing mysterious about this class of processes; they are just like easily understandable discrete-time processes

$$x_{t+\Delta} - x_t = \mu(\cdot)\Delta t + \sigma(\cdot)\sqrt{\Delta t}\, \varepsilon_{t+\Delta}, \qquad \varepsilon_{t+\Delta} \sim \mathcal{N}(0, 1). \tag{A.2}$$

In fact, when analytical methods fail us, we can figure out how diffusion models work by simulating the discretized version (A.2) for a fine time interval Δ.

The local mean of a diffusion model is

$$F_t(dx_t) = \mu(\cdot) \, dt$$

and the local variance is

$$dx_t^2 = E_t(dx_t^2) = \sigma^2(\cdot) \, dt.$$

Variance is equal to second moment because means scale linearly with time interval Δ, so mean squared scales with Δ^2, while the second moment scales with Δ.

Stochastic integrals. For many purposes, simply understanding the differential representation of a process is sufficient. However, we often want to understand the random variable x_t at longer horizons. For example, we might want to know the distribution of x_{t+s} given information at time t.

Conceptually, what we want to do is to think of a diffusion model as a *stochastic differential equation* and solve it forward through time to obtain the finite-time random variable x_{t+s}. Putting some arguments in for μ and σ for concreteness, we can think of evaluating the integral

$$ x_t - x_0 = \int_0^t dx_s = \int_0^t \mu(x_s, s, \dots) \, ds + \int_0^t \sigma(x_s, s, \dots) \, dz_s. $$

We have already seen how $z_t = z_0 + \int_0^t dz_s$ generates the random variable $z_t \sim \mathcal{N}(0, t)$, so you can see how expressions like this one generate random variables x_t. The objective of solving a stochastic differential equation is thus to find the *distribution* of x at some future date, or at least some characterizations of that distribution such as conditional mean, variance, etc. Some authors dislike the differential characterization and always write processes in terms of stochastic integrals.

A.3 Ito's Lemma

Do second-order Taylor expansions; keep only dz, dt, and $dz^2 = dt$ terms:

$$ dy = f'(x) \, dx + \frac{1}{2} f''(x) \, dx^2, $$

$$ dy = \left(f'(x)\mu_x + \frac{1}{2} f''(x)\sigma_x^2 \right) dt + f'(x)\sigma_x \, dz. $$

You often have a diffusion representation for one variable, say

$$ dx_t = \mu_x(\cdot) \, dt + \sigma_x(\cdot) \, dz_t. $$

Then you define a new variable in terms of the old one,

$$ y_t = f(x_t). \tag{A.3} $$

Naturally, you want a diffusion representation for y_t. Ito's lemma tells you how to get it. It says,

Use a *second-order* Taylor expansion, and think of dz as $\sqrt{dt}$; thus as $\Delta t \to 0$, keep terms dz, dt, and $dz^2 = dt$, but terms $dt \times dz$, dt^2, and higher go to zero.

Applying these rules to (A.3), start with the second order expansion

$$dy = \frac{df(x)}{dx} dx + \frac{1}{2} \frac{d^2 f(x)}{dx^2} dx^2.$$

Expanding the second term,

$$dx^2 = [\mu_x \, dt + \sigma_x \, dz]^2 = \mu_x^2 \, dt^2 + \sigma_x^2 \, dz^2 + 2\mu_x \sigma_x \, dt \, dz.$$

Now apply the rule $dt^2 = 0$, $dz^2 = dt$, and $dt \, dz = 0$. Thus,

$$dx^2 = \sigma_x^2 \, dt.$$

Substituting for dx and dx^2,

$$dy = \frac{df(x)}{dx} (\mu_x \, dt + \sigma_x \, dz) + \frac{1}{2} \frac{d^2 f(x)}{dx^2} \sigma_x^2 \, dt$$

$$= \left(\frac{df(x)}{dx} \mu_x + \frac{1}{2} \frac{d^2 f(x)}{dx^2} \sigma_x^2 \right) dt + \frac{df(x)}{dx} \sigma_x \, dz.$$

Thus, *Ito's lemma*:

$$dy = \left(\frac{df(x)}{dx} \mu_x(\cdot) + \frac{1}{2} \frac{d^2 f(x)}{dx^2} \sigma_x^2(\cdot) \right) dt + \frac{df(x)}{dx} \sigma_x(\cdot) \, dz.$$

The surprise here is the second term in the drift. Intuitively, this term captures a "Jensen's inequality" effect. If a is a mean zero random variable and $b = f(a)$ with $f''(a) > 0$, then the mean of b is higher than the mean of a. The more variance of a, and the more concave the function, the higher the mean of b.

A.4 Problems—Appendix

1. If
$$\frac{dp}{p} = \mu \, dt + \sigma \, dz$$
find the diffusion followed by the log price,

$$y = \ln(p).$$

2. Find the diffusion followed by xy.

3. Suppose $y = f(x, t)$. Find the diffusion representation for y. (Follow the obvious multivariate extension of Ito's lemma.)

4. Suppose $y = f(x, w)$, with both x, w diffusions. Find the diffusion representation for y. Denote the correlation between dz_x and dz_w by ρ.

References

Abel, Andrew B., 1988, "Stock Prices under Time-Varying Dividend Risk: An Exact Solution in an Infinite-Horizon General Equilibrium Model," *Journal of Monetary Economics* 22, 375–393.

———, 1990, "Asset Prices Under Habit Formation and Catching Up With the Jones," *American Economic Review* 80, 38–42.

———, 1994, "Exact Solutions for Expected Rates of Return under Markov Regime Switching: Implications for the Equity Premium Puzzle," *Journal of Money, Credit, and Banking* 26, 345–361.

———, 1999, "Risk Premia and Term Premia in General Equilibrium," *Journal of Monetary Economics* 43, 3–33.

Abel, Andrew B., and Janice C. Eberly, 1996, "Optimal Investment with Costly Reversibility," *Review of Economic Studies* 63, 581–593.

———, 1999, "The Effects of Irreversibility and Uncertainty on Capital Accumulation," *Journal of Monetary Economics* 44, 339–377.

Aiyagari, S. Rao, and Mark Gertler, 1991, "Asset Returns with Transactions Costs and Uninsured Individual Risk: A Stage III Exercise," *Journal of Monetary Economics* 27, 309–331.

Andrews, Donald W. K., 1991, "Heteroskedasticity and Autocorrelation Consistent Covariance Matrix Estimation," *Econometrica* 59, 817–858.

Atkeson, Andrew, Fernando Alvarez, and Patrick Kehoe, 1999, "Volatile Exchange Rates and the Forward Premium Anomaly: A Segmented Asset Market View," working paper, University of Chicago.

Bachelier, L., 1964, "Theory of Speculation," in P. Cootner (ed.), *The Random Character of Stock Prices*, MIT Press, Cambridge, MA.

Backus, David, Silverio Foresi, A. Mozumdar and L. Wu, 1997, "Predictable Changes in Yields and Forward Rates," Manuscript, New York University.

Backus, David, Silverio Foresi and Chris Telmer, 1998, "Discrete-Time Models of Bond Pricing," NBER working paper 6736.

Balduzzi, Pierluigi, Giuseppe Bertola, and Silverio Foresi, 1996, "A Model of Target Changes and the Term Structure of Interest Rates," *Journal of Monetary Economics* 39, 223–249.

Banz, Rolf W., 1981, "The Relationship Between Return and Market Value of Common Stocks," *Journal of Financial Economics* 9, 3–18.

Barsky, Robert, and Bradford J. DeLong, 1993, "Why Does the Stock Market Fluctuate?," *Quarterly Journal of Economics* 108, 291–311.

Bekaert, Geert, and Robert J. Hodrick, 1992, "Characterizing Predictable Components in Excess Returns on Equity and Foreign Exchange Markets," *Journal of Finance* 47, 467–509.

Becker, Connie, Wayne E. Ferson, Michael Schill, and David Myers, 1999, "Conditional Market Timing with Benchmark Investors," *Journal of Financial Economics* 52, 119–148.

Berk, Jonathan, 1997, "Does Size Really Matter?," *Financial Analysts Journal*, September/October 1997, 12–18.

Bernardo, Antonio, and Olivier Ledoit, 1999, "Gain Loss and Asset Pricing," *Journal of Political Economy* 108, 144–172.

Black, Fischer, Michael Jensen, and Myron Scholes, 1972, "The Capital Asset Pricing Model: Some Empirical Tests," in Michael Jensen (ed.), *Studies in the Theory of Capital Markets*, Praeger, New York.

Black, Fischer, and Myron Scholes, 1973, "The Valuation of Options and Corporate Liabilities," *Journal of Political Economy* 81, 637–654.

Bollerslev, Tim, R. Chou, and K. Kroner, 1992, "ARCH Modeling in Finance: A Review of Theory and Empirical Evidence," *Journal of Econometrics* 52, 5–59.

Boudoukh, Jacob, and Matthew Richardson, 1994, "The Statistics of Long-Horizon Regressions Revisited," *Mathematical Finance* 4, 103–119.

Boudoukh, Jacob, Matthew Richardson, Robert Stanton, and Robert Whitelaw, 1998, "The Stochastic Behavior of Interest Rates: Implications from a Nonlinear, Continuous-time, Multifactor Model," manuscript, University of California at Berkeley.

Brav, Alon, George Constantinides, and Christopher Geczy, 1999, "Asset Pricing with Heterogeneous Consumers and Limited Participation: Empirical Evidence," manuscript, Duke University.

Breeden, Douglas T., 1979, "An Intertemporal Asset Pricing Model with Stochastic Consumption and Investment Opportunities," *Journal of Financial Economics* 7, 265–296.

Breeden, Douglas T., Michael R. Gibbons, and Robert H. Litzenberger, 1989, "Empirical Tests of the Consumption-Oriented CAPM," *Journal of Finance* 44, 231–262.

Brown, Stephen, William Goetzmann, and Stephen A. Ross, 1995, "Survival," *Journal of Finance* 50, 853–873.

Buraschi, Andrea, and Alexei Jiltsov, 1999, "How Large is the Inflation Risk Premium in the U.S. Nominal Term Structure," manuscript, London Business School.

Burnside, Craig, Martin Eichenbaum, and Sergio Rebelo, 1993, "Labor Hoarding and the Business Cycle," *Journal of Political Economy* 101, 245–373.

Campbell, John Y., 1991, "A Variance Decomposition for Stock Returns," *Economic Journal* 101, 157–179.

———, 1995, "Some Lessons from the Yield Curve," *Journal of Economic Perspectives* 9, 129–152.

———, 1996, "Understanding Risk and Return," *Journal of Political Economy* 104, 298–345.

———, 1999, "Asset Prices, Consumption, and the Business Cycle," in John B. Taylor and Michael Woodford (eds.), *Handbook of Macroeconomics*, North-Holland, Amsterdam.

———, 2000, "Asset Pricing at the Millennium," *Journal of Finance*, August.

Campbell, John Y., and John H. Cochrane, 1999, "By Force of Habit: A Consumption-Based Explanation of Aggregate Stock Market Behavior," *Journal of Political Economy* 107, 205–251.

Campbell, John Y., Andrew W. Lo, and A. Craig MacKinlay, 1997, *The Econometrics of Financial Markets*, Princeton University Press, Princeton, NJ.

Campbell, John Y., and Robert J. Shiller, 1988a, "The Dividend-Price Ratio and Expectations of Future Dividends and Discount Factors," *Review of Financial Studies* 1, 195–227.

———, 1988b, "Stock Prices, Earnings, and Expected Dividends," *Journal of Finance* 43, 661–676.

———, 1991, "Yield Spreads and Interest Rates: A Bird's Eye View," *Review of Economic Studies* 58, 495–514.

Carhart, Mark M., 1997, "On Persistence in Mutual Fund Performance," *Journal of Finance* 52, 57–82.

Chamberlain, Gary, and Michael Rothschild, 1983, "Arbitrage, Factor Structure, and Mean-Variance Analysis on Large Asset Markets," *Econometrica* 51, 1281–1304.

Chen, Nai-Fu, Richard Roll, and Stephen A. Ross, 1986, "Economic Forces and the Stock Market," *Journal of Business* 59, 383–403.

Christiano, Lawrence, Martin Eichenbaum, and Charles Evans, 1999, "Monetary Policy Shocks: What Have We Learned and to What End?," in John Taylor (ed.), *Handbook of Monetary Economics*, forthcoming.

Cochrane, John H., 1988, "How Big is the Random Walk in GNP?," *Journal of Political Economy* 96, 893–920.

———, 1991a, "Explaining the Variance of Price-Dividend Ratios," 5, 243–280.

———, 1991b, "A Simple Test of Consumption Insurance," *Journal of Political Economy* 99, 957–976.

———, 1991c, "Volatility Tests and Efficient Markets: A Review Essay," *Journal of Monetary Economics* 27, 463–485.

———, 1991d, "Production-Based Asset Pricing and the Link Between Stock Returns and Economic Fluctuations," *Journal of Finance* 46, 207–234.

———, 1994, "Permanent and Transitory Components of GNP and Stock Prices," *Quarterly Journal of Economics* 109, 241–266.

———, 1994, "Shocks," *Carnegie-Rochester Conference Series on Public Policy* 41, 295–364.

———, 1996, "A Cross-Sectional Test of an Investment-Based Asset Pricing Model," *Journal of Political Economy* 104, 572–621.

———, 1997, "Where is the Market Going? Uncertain Facts and Novel Theories," *Economic Perspectives Federal Reserve Bank of Chicago* 21, 6.

———, 1999a, "New Facts in Finance," *Economic Perspectives Federal Reserve Bank of Chicago* 23, 36–58.

———, 1999b, "Portfolio Advice for a Multifactor World," *Economic Perspectives Federal Reserve Bank of Chicago* 23, 59–78.

———, 2000, "A Resurrection of the Stochastic Discount Factor/GMM Methodology," manuscript, University of Chicago.

Cochrane, John H., and Lars Peter Hansen, 1992, "Asset Pricing Explorations for Macroeconomics," in Olivier Blanchard and Stanley Fisher (eds.), *1992 NBER Macroeconomics Annual*, 115–165.

Cochrane, John H., and Jesús Saá-Requejo, 2000, "Beyond Arbitrage: Good Deal Asset Price Bounds in Incomplete Markets," *Journal of Political Economy* 108, 79–119.

Cochrane, John H., and Argia M. Sbordone, 1988, "Multivariate Estimates of the Permanent Components in GNP and Stock Prices," *Journal of Economic Dynamics and Control* 12, 255–296.

Constantinides, George M., 1989, "Theory of Valuation: Overview and Recent Developments," in Sudipto Bhattacharya and George M. Constantinides (eds.), *Theory of Valuation*, Rowman & Littlefield, Totwa NJ.

———, 1990, "Habit Formation: A Resolution of the Equity Premium Puzzle," *Journal of Political Economy* 98, 519–543.

———, 1992, "A Theory of the Nominal Term Structure of Interest Rates," *Review of Financial Studies* 5, 531–52.

———, 1998, "Transactions Costs and the Volatility Implied by Option Prices," manuscript, Graduate School of Business, University of Chicago.

Constantinides, George M., and Darrell Duffie, 1996, "Asset Pricing with Heterogeneous Consumers," *Journal of Political Economy* 104, 219–240.

Constantinides, George M., and Thaleia Zariphopoulou, 1997, "Bounds on Option Prices in an Intertemporal Setting with Proportional Transaction Costs and Multiple Securities," manuscript, Graduate School of Business, University of Chicago.

Cox, John C., and Chi-fu Huang, 1989, "Optimal Consumption and Portfolio Policies when Asset Prices Follow a Diffusion Process," *Journal of Economic Theory* 39, 33–83.

Cox, John C., Jonathan E. Ingersoll, and Stephen A. Ross, 1985, "A Theory of the Term Structure of Interest Rates," *Econometrica* 53, 385–408.

Cox, John C., Stephen A. Ross, and Mark Rubinstein, 1979, "Option Pricing: A Simplified Approach," *Journal of Financial Economics* 7, 229–263.

Cox, John C., and Mark Rubinstein, 1985, *Options Markets*, Prentice-Hall, Englewood Cliffs, NJ.

Dai, Qiang, and Kenneth J. Singleton, 1999, "Specification Analysis of Affine Term Structure Models," *Journal of Finance*, forthcoming.

Dai, Qiang, and Kenneth J. Singleton, 2000, "Expectation Puzzles, Time-varying Risk Premia, and Dynamic Models of the Term Structure," Manuscript, Stanford University.

Das, Sanjiv, and Silverio Foresi, 1996, "Exact Solutions for Bond and Option Prices with Systematic Jump Risk," *Review of Derivatives Research* 1, 7–24.

Daniel, Kent, David Hirshleifer, and Avanidhar Subrahmanyam, 1998, "Investor Psychology and Security Market Under- and Overreactions," *Journal of Finance* 53, 1839–1885.

Debreu, Gerard, 1959, *The Theory of Value*, Wiley and Sons, New York.

DeBondt, Werner F. M., and Richard H. Thaler, 1985, "Does the Stock Market Overreact?," *Journal of Finance* 40, 793–805.

Dixit, Avinash, and R. Pindyck, 1994, *Investment Under Uncertainty*, Princeton University Press, Princeton, NJ.

Duarte, Jefferson, 2000, "The Relevance of the Price of Risk in Affine Term-Structure models," manuscript, University of Chicago.

Duffee, Gregory, 1999, "Forecasting Future Interest Rates: Are Affine Models Failures?," manuscript, University of California at Berkeley.

Duffie, J. Darrel, and Rui Kan, 1996, "A Yield Factor Model of the Term Structure of Interest Rates," *Mathematical Finance* 6, 379–406.

Dybvig, Philip H., and Jonathan E. Ingersoll Jr., 1982, "Mean-Variance Theory in Complete Markets," *Journal of Business* 55, 233–51.

Dybvig, P., and Stephen Ross, 1985, "Yes, the APT is Testable," *Journal of Finance* 40, 1173–1188.

Dybvig, P., J. Ingersoll Jr., and Stephen Ross, 1996, "Long Forward and Zero-Coupon Rates Can Never Fall," *Journal of Business*, 69, 1–25.

Eichenbaum, Martin, Lars Peter Hansen, and Kenneth Singleton, 1988, "A Time-Series Analysis of Representative Agent Models of Consumption and Leisure Choice under Uncertainty," *Quarterly Journal of Economics* 103, 51–78.

Engel, Charles, 1996, "The Forward Discount Anomaly and the Risk Premium: A Survey of Recent Evidence," *Journal of Empirical Finance* 3, 123–192.

Engle, Robert F., and Clive W. J. Granger, 1987, "Cointegration and Error Correction: Representation, Estimation, and Testing," *Econometrica* 55, 251–276.

Epstein, Larry G., and Stanley E. Zin, 1989, "Substitution, Risk Aversion and the Temporal Behavior of Asset Returns," *Journal of Political Economy* 99, 263–286.

Fama, Eugene F., 1965, "The Behavior of Stock Market Prices, *Journal of Business* 38, 34–105.

———, 1970, "Efficient Capital Markets: A Review of Theory and Empirical Work," *Journal of Finance* 25, 383–417.

———, 1984, "Forward and Spot Exchange Rates," *Journal of Monetary Economics* 14, 319–338.

———, 1991, "Efficient Markets II," *Journal of Finance* 46, 1575–1618.

Fama, Eugene F., and Robert R. Bliss, 1987, "The information in Long-Maturity Forward Rates," *American Economic Review,* 77, 680–692.

Fama, Eugene F., and Kenneth R. French, 1988a, "Permanent and Temporary Components of Stock Prices," *Journal of Political Economy* 96, 246–273.

———, 1988b, "Dividend Yields and Expected Stock Returns," *Journal of Financial Economics* 22, 3–27.

———, 1989, "Business Conditions and Expected Returns on Stocks and Bonds," *Journal of Financial Economics* 25, 23–49.

———, 1993, "Common Risk Factors in the Returns on Stocks and Bonds," *Journal of Financial Economics* 33, 3–56.

———, 1996, "Multifactor Explanations of Asset-Pricing Anomalies," *Journal of Finance* 47, 426–465.

———, 1997a, "Size and Book-to-Market Factors in Earnings and Returns," *Journal of Finance* 50, 131–155.

———, 1997b, "Industry Costs of Equity," *Journal of Financial Economics* 43, 153–193.

———, 2000, "The Equity Premium," working paper, University of Chicago.

Fama, Eugene F., and James D. MacBeth, 1973, "Risk Return and Equilibrium: Empirical Tests," *Journal of Financial Political Economy* 71, 607–636.

Ferson, Wayne E., 1995, "Theory and Empirical Testing of Asset Pricing Models," in R. A. Jarrow, V. Maksimovic, and W. T. Ziemba (eds.), *Handbooks in OR & MS, Volume 9, Finance,* Elsevier Science B.V., Amsterdam.

Ferson, Wayne E., and George Constantinides, 1991, "Habit Persistence and Durability in Aggregate Consumption: Empirical Tests," *Journal of Financial Economics* 29, 199–240.

Ferson, Wayne E., and Stephen R. Foerster, 1994, "Finite Sample Properties of the Generalized Method of Moments in Tests of Conditional Asset Pricing Models," *Journal of Financial Economics* 36, 29–55.

Ferson, Wayne E., and Campbell R. Harvey, 1999, "Conditioning Variables and Cross-section of Stock Returns," *Journal of Finance* 54, 1325–1360.

French, Kenneth, G. William Schwert, and Robert F. Stambaugh, 1987, "Expected Stock Returns and Volatility," *Journal of Financial Economics* 19, 3–30.

Friedman, Milton, 1953, "The Methodology of Positive Economics," in *Essays in Positive Economics*, University of Chicago Press, Chicago, IL.

Friend, I., and M. Blume, 1975, "The Demand for Risky Assets," *American Economic Review* 65, 900–922.

Fuhrer, Jeffrey C., George R. Moore, and Scott D. Schuh, 1995, "Estimating the Linear-Quadratic Inventory Model: Maximum Likelihood versus Generalized Method of Moments," *Journal of Monetary Economics* 35, 115–157.

Gallant, A. Ronald, Lars Peter Hansen, and George Tauchen, 1990, "Using Conditional Moments of Asset Payoffs to Infer the Volatility of Intertemporal Marginal Rates of Substitution," *Journal of Econometrics* 45, 141–179.

Gallant, A. Ronald, and George Tauchen, 1997, "Estimation of Continuous-Time Models for Stock Returns and Interest Rates," *Macroeconomic Dynamics* 1, 135–168.

Garber, Peter M., 2000, *Famous First Bubbles*, Cambridge MA: MIT Press.

Gibbons, Michael, Stephen A. Ross, and Jay Shanken, 1989, "A Test of the Efficiency of a Given Portfolio," *Econometrica* 57, 1121–1152.

Glosten, Lawrence, Ravi Jagannathan, and David Runkle, 1993, "On the Relation Between the Expected Value and the Volatility of the Nominal Excess Return on Stocks," *Journal of Finance* 48, 1779–1801.

Grinblatt, Mark and Sheridan Titman, 1985, "Factor Pricing in a Finite Economy," *Journal of Financial Economics* 12, 497–507.

Grossman, Sanford J., and Robert J. Shiller, 1981, "The Determinants of the Variability of Stock Market Prices," *American Economic Review* 71, 222–227.

Grossman, Sanford J., and Joseph E. Stiglitz, 1980, "On the Impossibility of Informationally Efficient Markets,"*American Economic Review* 70, 393–408.

Hamilton, James, 1994, *Time Series Analysis,* Princeton University Press, Princeton, NJ.

———, 1996, "The Daily Market for Federal Funds," *Journal of Political Economy* 104, 26–56.

Hansen, Lars Peter, 1982, "Large Sample Properties of Generalized Method of Moments Estimators," *Econometrica* 50, 1029–1054.

———, 1987, "Calculating Asset Prices in Three Example Economies," in T.F. Bewley (ed.), *Advances in Econometrics, Fifth World Congress*, Cambridge University Press.

Hansen, Lars Peter, John Heaton, and Erzo Luttmer, 1995, "Econometric Evaluation of Asset Pricing Models," *The Review of Financial Studies* 8, 237–274.

Hansen, Lars Peter, John Heaton, and Amir Yaron, 1996, " Finite-Sample Properties of Some Alternative GMM Estimators," *Journal of Business and Economic Statistics* 4, 262–280.

Hansen, Lars Peter, and Robert J. Hodrick, 1980, "Forward Exchange Rates as Optimal Predictors of Future Spot Rates: An Econometric Analysis," *Journal of Political Economy* 88, 829–853.

Hansen, Lars Peter, and Ravi Jagannathan, 1991, "Implications of Security Market Data for Models of Dynamic Economies," *Journal of Political Economy* 99, 225–262.

———, 1997, "Assessing Specification Errors in Stochastic Discount Factor Models," *Journal of Finance* 52, 557–590.

Hansen, Lars Peter, and Scott F. Richard, 1987, "The Role of Conditioning Information in Deducing Testable Restrictions Implied by Dynamic Asset Pricing Models," *Econometrica* 55, 587–614.

Hansen, Lars Peter, and Kenneth J. Singleton, 1982, "Generalized Instrumental Variables Estimation of Nonlinear Rational Expectations Models," *Econometrica* 50, 1269–1288.

———, 1984, "Errata," *Econometrica* 52, 267–268.

———, 1983, "Stochastic Consumption, Risk Aversion, and the Temporal Behavior of Asset Returns," *Journal of Political Economy* 91, 249–268.

Harrison, J. Michael, and David M. Kreps, 1979, "Martingales and Arbitrage in Multiperiod Securities Markets," *Journal of Economic Theory* 20, 381–408.

Hayek, Friedrich A., 1945, "The Use of Knowledge in Society," *American Economic Review* 35, 519–530.

He, Hua, and Neil Pearson, 1992, "Consumption and Portfolio Policies with Incomplete Markets: The Infinite Dimensional Case," *Journal of Economic Theory* 54, 259–305.

Heaton, John C., 1993, "The Interaction Between Time-Nonseparable Preferences and Time Aggregation," *Econometrica* 61, 353–385.

———, 1995, "An Empirical Investigation of Asset Pricing with Temporally Dependent Preference Specifications," *Econometrica* 63, 681–717.

Heaton, John, and Deborah Lucas, 1996, "Evaluating the Effects of Incomplete Markets on Risk-Sharing and Asset Pricing," *Journal of Political Economy* 103, 94–117.

———, 1997, "Market Frictions, Saving Behavior and Portfolio Choice," *Macroeconomic Dynamics* 1, 76–101.

———, 1997, "Portfolio Choice and Asset Prices: The Importance of Entrepreneurial Risk," manuscript, Northwestern University.

Hendricks, Darryl, Jayendu Patel, and Richard Zeckhauser, 1993, "Hot Hands in Mutual Funds: Short-Term Persistence of Performance," *Journal of Finance* 48, 93–130.

Hindy, Ayman, and Chi-fu Huang, 1992, "Intertemporal Preferences for Uncertain Consumption: A Continuous-Time Approach," *Econometrica* 60, 781–801.

Ho, Thomas S. Y., and Sang-bin Ho Lee, 1986, "Term Structure Movements and Pricing Interest Rate Contingent Claims," *Journal of Finance* 41, 1011–1029.

Hodrick, Robert, 1987, *The Empirical Evidence on the Efficiency of Forward and Futures Foreign Exchange Markets*, Harwood Academic Publishers, Chur, Switzerland.

———, 1992, "Dividend Yields and Expected Stock Returns: Alternative Procedures for Inference and Measurement," *Review of Financial Studies* 5, 357–386.

———, 2000, *International Financial Management*, forthcoming, Prentice-Hall, Englewood Cliffs, NJ.

Hsieh, David, and William Fung, 1999, "Hedge Fund Risk Management," working paper, Duke University.

Jacquier, Eric, Nicholas Polson, and Peter Rossi, 1994, "Bayesian Analysis of Stochastic Volatility Models," *Journal of Business and Economic Statistics* 12, 371–418.

Jagannathan, Ravi, and Zhenyu Wang, 1996, "The Conditional CAPM and the Cross-Section of Expected Returns," *Journal of Finance* 51, 3–53.

———, 2000, "Efficiency of the Stochastic Discount Factor Method for Estimating Risk Premiums," manuscript, Northwestern University.

Jegadeesh, Narasimham, and Sheridan Titman, 1993, "Returns to Buying Winners and Selling Losers: Implications for Stock Market Efficiency," *Journal of Finance* 48, 65–91.

Jensen, Michael C., 1969, "The Pricing of Capital Assets and Evaluation of Investment Portfolios," *Journal of Business* 42, 167–247.

Jermann, Urban, 1998, "Asset Pricing in Production Economies," *Journal of Monetary Economics* 4, 257–275.

Johannes, Michael, 2000, "Jumps to Interest Rates: A Nonparametric Approach," manuscript, University of Chicago.

Jorion, Philippe, and William Goetzmann, 1999, "Global Stock Markets in the Twentieth Century," *Journal of Finance* 54, 953–980.

Kandel, Shmuel, and Robert F. Stambaugh, 1990, "Expectations and Volatility of Consumption and Asset Returns," *Review of Financial Studies* 3, 207–232.

———, 1991, "Asset Returns and Intertemporal Preferences," *Journal of Monetary Economics* 27, 39–71

———, 1995, "Portfolio Inefficiency and the Cross-Section of Expected Returns," *Journal of Finance* 50, 157–184.

Kennedy, Peter, 1994, "The Term Structure of Interest Rates as a Gaussian Random Field," *Mathematical Finance* 4, 247–258.

Keim, Donald, and Robert F. Stambaugh, 1986, "Predicting Returns in Stock and Bond Markets," *Journal of Financial Economics* 17, 357–390.

Kleidon, Allan, 1986, "Variance Bounds Tests and Stock Price Valuation Models," *Journal of Political Economy* 94, 953–1001.

Kocherlakota, Narayana R., 1990, "On the 'Discount' Factor in Growth Economies," *Journal of Monetary Economics* 25, 43–47.

———, 1996, "The Equity Premium: It's Still a Puzzle," *Journal of Economic Literature* 34, 42–71.

Kothari, S. P., Jay Shanken, and Richard G. Sloan, 1995, "Another Look at the Cross-Section of Expected Stock Returns, *Journal of Finance* 50, 185–224.

Knez, Peter, Robert Litterman, and José Scheinkman, 1994, "Explorations into Factors Explaining Money Market Returns," *Journal of Finance* 49, 1861–1882.

Knez, Peter J., and Mark J. Ready, 1997, "On the Robustness of Size and Book-to-Market in Cross-Sectional Regressions," *Journal of Finance* 52, 1355–1382.

Kuhn, Thomas, 1970, *The Structure of Scientific Revolutions* (2nd ed.), University of Chicago Press, Chicago, IL.

Kydland, Finn, and Edward C. Prescott, 1982, "Time to Build and Aggregate Fluctuations," *Econometrica* 50, 1345–1370.

Lakonishok, Josef, Andrei Shleifer, and Robert W. Vishny, 1992, "The Structure and Performance of the Money Management Industry," *Brookings Papers on Economic Activity: Microeconomics 1992*, 339–391.

Lamont, Owen, 1998, "Earnings and Expected Returns," *Journal of Finance* 53, 1563–1587.

Ledoit, Olivier, 1995, "Essays on Risk and Return in the Stock Market," Ph.D. dissertation, Massachusetts Institute of Technology.

Ledoit, Olivier, and Antonio Bernardo, 1999, "Gain, Loss and Asset Pricing," *Journal of Political Economy* 108, 144–172.

Leland, Hayne E., 1985, "Option Pricing and Replication with Transactions Costs," *Journal of Finance* 40, 1283–1301.

LeRoy, Stephen F., 1973, Risk Aversion and the Martingale Property of Stock Prices, *International Economic Review* 14, 436-446.

LeRoy, Stephen, and Richard Porter, 1981, "The Present Value Relation: Tests Based on Variance Bounds," *Econometrica* 49, 555–557.

Lettau, Martin, and Sydney Ludvigson, 1999, "Resurrecting the (C)CAPM: A Cross-Sectional Test When Risk Premia are Time-Varying," *Journal of Political Economy*, forthcoming.

———, 2000, "Consumption, Aggregate Wealth and Expected Stock Returns," manuscript, Federal Reserve Bank of New York.

Levy, Haim, 1985, "Upper and Lower Bounds of Put and Call Option Value: Stochastic Dominance Approach," *Journal of Finance* 40, 1197–1217.

Lewis, Karen K., 1995, "Puzzles in International Financial Markets," in G. Grossman and K. Rogoff (eds.), *Handbook of International Economics, Volume III*, Elsevier Science B.V, Amsterdam, 1913–1971.

Liew, Jimmy, and Maria Vassalou, 1999, "Can Book-to-Market, Size and Momentum be Risk Factors that Predict Economic Growth?," working paper, Columbia University.

Lintner, John, 1965a, "The Valuation of Risky Assets and the Selection of Risky Investment in Stock Portfolios and Capital Budgets," *Review of Economics and Statistics* 47, 13–37.

———, 1965b, "Security Prices, Risk and Maximal Gains from Diversification," *Journal of Finance* 20.

Longstaff, Francis, 2000, "Arbitrage and the Expectations Hypothesis," *Journal of Finance* 55, 989–994.

Lucas, Robert E., Jr., 1978, "Asset Prices in an Exchange Economy," *Econometrica* 46, 1429–1446.

———, 1987, *Models of Business Cycles*, Blackwell, London and New York.

———, 1988, "Money Demand in the United States: A Quantitative Review," *Carnegie-Rochester Conference Series on Public Policy* 29, 137–167.

Luttmer, Erzo G. J., 1996, "Asset Pricing in Economies with Frictions," *Econometrica* 64, 1439–1467.

Luttmer, Erzo G. J., 1999, "What Level of Fixed Costs Can Reconcile Consumption and Stock Returns?," *Journal of Political Economy* 107, 969–997.

Mace, Barbara, 1991, "Full Insurance in the Presence of Aggregate Uncertainty," *Journal of Political Economy* 99.

———, 1991, "Full Insurance in the Presence of Aggregate Uncertainty," *Journal of Political Economy* 99, 928–956.

MacKinlay, A. Craig, 1995, "Multifactor Models Do Not Explain Deviations from the CAPM," *Journal of Financial Economics* 38, 3–28.

Malkiel, Burton, 1990, *A Random Walk Down Wall Street*, Norton, New York.

Mankiw, N. Gregory, 1986, "The Equity Premium and the Concentration of Aggregate Shocks," *Journal of Financial Economics* 17, 211–219.

Mankiw, N. Gregory, and Stephen Zeldes, 1991, "The Consumption of Stockholders and Non-Stockholders," *Journal of Financial Economics* 29, 97–112.

Markowitz, Harry, 1952, "Portfolio Selection," *Journal of Finance* 7, 77–99.

McCloskey, Donald N., 1983, "The Rhetoric of Economics," *Journal of Economic Literature* 21, 481–517.

McCloskey, Deirdre N., 1998, *The Rhetoric of Economics* (2nd ed.), University of Wisconsin Press, Madison and London.

Mehra, Rajnish, and Edward Prescott, 1985, "The Equity Premium Puzzle," *Journal of Monetary Economics* 15, 145–161.

Merton, Robert C., 1969, "Lifetime Portfolio Selection Under Uncertainty: The Continuous Time Case," *Review of Economics and Statistics* 51, 247–257.

, 1971a, "Optimum Consumption and Portfolio Rules in a Continuous Time Model," *Journal of Economic Theory* 3, 373–413.

———, 1973a, "An Intertemporal Capital Asset Pricing Model," *Econometrica* 41, 867–887.

———, 1973, "The Theory of Rational Option Pricing," *Bell Journal of Economics and Management Science* 4, 141–183.

Miller, Merton, and Myron Scholes, 1972, "Rate of Return in Relation to Risk: A Reexamination of Some Recent Findings," in Michael C. Jensen (ed.), *Studies in the Theory of Capital Markets*, Praeger, New York.

Moskowitz, Tobias, and Mark Grinblatt, 1998, "Do Industries Explain Momentum?" CRSP Working Paper 480, University of Chicago.

———, 1999, "Tax Loss Selling and Return Autocorrelation: New Evidence," working paper, University of Chicago.

Newey, Whitney K., and Kenneth D. West, 1987a, "Hypothesis Testing with Efficient Method of Moments," *International Economic Review* 28, 777–787.

———, 1987b, "A Simple, Positive Semi-definite, Heteroskedasticity and Autocorrelation Consistent Covariance Matrix," *Econometrica* 55, 703–708.

Ogaki, Masao, 1992, "Generalized Method of Moments: Econometric Applications," in G. Maddala, C. Rao, and H. Vinod (eds.), *Handbook of Statistics, Volume 11: Econometrics*, North-Holland, Amsterdam.

Piazzesi, Monika, 1999, "An Econometric Model of the Yield Curve With Macroeconomic Jump Effects," manuscript, Stanford University.

Popper, Karl, 1959, *The Logic of Scientific Discovery*, Harper, New York.

Poterba, James, and Lawrence H. Summers, 1988, "Mean Reversion in Stock Returns: Evidence and Implications," *Journal of Financial Economics* 22, 27–60.

Reyfman, Alexander, 1997, "Labor Market Risk and Expected Asset Returns," Ph.D. Thesis, University of Chicago.

Rietz, Tom, 1988, The Equity Risk Premium: A Solution? *Journal of Monetary Economics* 21, 117–132.

Ritchken, Peter H., 1985, "On Option Pricing Bounds," *Journal of Finance* 40, 1219–1233.

Roll, Richard, 1977, "A Critique of the Asset Pricing Theory's Tests: Part I," *Journal of Financial Economics* 4, 129–176.

———, 1984, "Orange Juice and Weather," *The American Economic Review* 74, 861–880.

Roll, Richard, and Stephen A. Ross, 1995, "On the Cross-sectional Relation between Expected Returns and Betas," *Journal of Finance* 49, 101–121.

Ross, Stephen A., 1976a, "The Arbitrage Theory of Capital Asset Pricing," *Journal of Economic Theory* 13, 341–360.

———, 1976b, "Options and Efficiency," *Quarterly Journal of Economics* 90, 75–89.

———, 1976c, "Risk, Return and Arbitrage," in I. Friend and J. Bicksler (eds.), *Risk and Return in Finance, Volume 1* Ballinger, Cambridge, 189–218.

Rubinstein, Mark, 1976, "The Valuation of Uncertain Income Streams and the Price of Options," *Bell Journal of Economics*, 7, 407–425.

Samuelson, Paul A., 1965, "Proof that Properly Anticipated Prices Fluctuate Randomly," *Industrial Management Review* 6, 41–49.

———, 1969, "Lifetime Portfolio Selection by Dynamic Stochastic Programming," *Review of Economics and Statistics* 51, 239–246.

Santa Clara, Pedro, and Didier Sornette, 1999, "The Dynamics of the Forward Interest Rate Curve with Stochastic String Shocks," *Review of Financial Studies*, forthcoming.

Sargent, Thomas J., 1993, *Bounded Rationality in Macroeconomics*, Oxford University Press, Oxford.

————, 1989, "Two Models of Measurements and the Investment Accelerator," *Journal of Political Economy* 97, 251–287.

Schwert, William, 1990, "Stock Market Volatility," *Financial Analysts Journal* May–June, 23–44.

Shanken, Jay, 1982, "The Arbitrage Pricing Theory: Is It Testable?" *Journal of Finance* 37, 1129–1140.

Shanken, Jay, 1985, "The Arbitrage Pricing Theory: Is It Testable?" *Journal of Finance*, 40, 1189–1196.

————, 1987, Multivariate Proxies and Asset Pricing Relations: Living with the Roll Critique," *Journal of Financial Economics* 18, 91–110.

————, 1992a, "The Current State of the Arbitrage Pricing Theory," *Journal of Finance* 47 1569–1574.

————, 1992b, "On the Estimation of Beta Pricing Models," *Review of Financial Studies* 5, 1–34.

Sharpe, William, 1964, "Capital Asset Prices: A Theory of Market Equilibrium Under Conditions of Risk," *Journal of Finance* 19, 425–442.

Shiller, Robert J., 1981, "Do Stock Prices Move Too Much to be Justified by Subsequent Changes in Dividends?," *American Economic Review* 71, 421–436.

————, 1982, "Consumption, Asset Markets, and Macroeconomic Fluctuations," *Carnegie Rochester Conference Series on Public Policy* 17, 203–238.

————, 1989, *Market Volatility*, MIT Press, Cambridge MA.

Stambaugh, Robert F., 1982, "On the Exclusion of Assets from Tests of the Two-Parameter Model: A Sensitivity Analysis," *Journal of Financial Economics* 10, 237–268.

————, 1988, "The Information in Forward Rates: Implications for Models of the Term Structure," *Journal of Financial Economics* 10, 235–268.

Storesletten, Kjetil, Christopher Telmer, and Amir Yaron, 1999, "Asset Pricing with Idiosyncratic Risk and Overlapping Generations," manuscript, Carnegie Mellon University.

Sundaresan, Suresh M., 1989, "Intertemporally Dependent Preferences and the Volatility of Consumption and Wealth," *Review of Financial Studies* 2, 73–88.

Tallarini, Thomas, 1999, "Risk-Sensitive Real Business Cycles," manuscript, Carnegie Mellon University.

Taylor, John B. (ed.), 1999, *Monetary Policy Rules*, University of Chicago Press, Chicago, IL.

Thompson, Rex, 1978, "The Information Content of Discounts and Premiums on Closed-End Fund Shares," *Journal of Financial Economics* 6, 151–186.

Tobin, James, 1958, "Liquidity Preference as a Behavior Towards Risk," *Review of Economic Studies* 25, 68–85.

Vasicek, Oldrich, 1977, "An Equilibrium Characterization of the Term Structure," *Journal of Financial Economics* 5, 177–188.

Vassalou, Maria, 1999, "The Fama-French Factors as Proxies for Fundamental Economic Risks," working paper, Columbia University.

Vissing-Jorgenson, Annette, 1999, "Limited Stock Market Participation and the Equity Premium Puzzle," Manuscript, University of Chicago.

Vuoltennaho, Tuomo, 1999, "What Drives Firm-Level Stock Returns?" working paper, University of Chicago.

Weil, Philippe, 1989, "The Equity Premium Puzzle and the Risk-Free Rate Puzzle," *Journal of Monetary Economics* 24, 401–421.

Wheatley, Simon, 1988a, "Some Tests of the Consumption-Based Asset Pricing Model," *Journal of Monetary Economics* 22, 193–218.

————, 1988b, "Some Tests of International Equity Integration," *Journal of Financial Economics* 21, 177–212.

White, Halbert, 1980, "A Heteroskedasticity-Consistent Covariance Matrix Estimator and a Direct Test for Heteroskedasticity," *Econometrica* 48, 817–838.

Yan, Shu, 2000, Ph.D. dissertation, University of California at Los Angeles.

Author Index

511

Subject Index

absolute pricing, xiv, 184
absolute risk aversion, 33, 154–155
admissibility criterion, 375
affine models, 298–299, 374–377
American options, 311, 316
APT. *See* Arbitrage Pricing Theory
arbitrage, 47, 71, 170–180, 345
  complete markets and, 71
  definition of, 69
  discount factors and, 63, 179,
    182, 476
  edges of, 325–346
  equilibrium and, 74
  Fama–French model, 441
  ICAPM and, 180–183
  idiosyncratic components, 174
  irrationality and, 128
  law of one price and, 77, 178–179,
    181
  near-arbitrage pricing, 47
  no arbitrage restriction, 63, 69–71,
    182, 318, 355, 476
  option pricing and, 130, 182,
    325–346
  pricing equation, 130
  rational model, 128
  volatility and, 181
  See also specific concepts, models
Arbitrage Pricing Theory (APT)
  basic ideas of, 47, 173–174
  CAPM and, 173–174
  controversy over, 181
  discount factor volatility and, 344
  factor structure in, 175–179
  Fama–French model and, 430, 442

ICAPM and, 173, 183–185
  law of one price and, 178–179, 182
  limits of, 181
  momentum and, 445
  relative pricing and, 184
  Ross bounds, 344
  Sharpe ratios and, 181–182
asset pricing theory, principles of, 1–8,
  37–50
asymptotic distribution theory, 220, 267
autoregression models
  diffusion and, 491
  discrete-time models, 358, 377, 492
  dividend/price ratio and, 392, 407
  downweighting and, 222
  habit and, 468
  heteroskedasticity and, 223
  income and, 297
  maximum likelihood and, 268, 296
  mean-reversion and, 415–417
  momentum and, 417, 447
  null hypothesis and, 225
  parametric models and, 223
  shocks and, 409, 415–416
  spectral densities and, 420
  square root process, 492
  term structure models and, 355–357,
    370
  time-series models and, 296
  Vasicek model and, 361
aversion. *See* Risk aversion

baby boomers, 391
bankruptcy, 441
Bartlett estimate, 221

515